THE
BATTLE
OF
JUTLAND

NAVIES AND MEN

THE
BATTLE
OF
JUTLAND

HOLLOWAY H. FROST

ARNO PRESS
A New York Times Company
New York • 1980

Editorial Supervision: Erin Foley

Reprint Edition 1980 by Arno Press Inc.

Copyright © 1936, 1964 in the United States of America
by the United States Naval Institute

Reprinted by permission of Naval Institute Press

NAVIES AND MEN
ISBN for complete set: 0-405-13030-9
See last pages of this volume for titles.

Manufactured in the United States of America

Library of Congress Cataloging in Publication Data

Frost, Holloway Halstead, 1889-1935.
  The Battle of Jutland.

  (Navies and men)
  Reprint of the 1970? ed. published by U. S. Naval
Institute, Annapolis.
  Bibliography.: p.
  Includes index.
  1. Jutland, Battle of, 1916. I. Title. II. Se-
ries.
[D582.J8F67 1980]   940.4'56   79-6108
ISBN 0-405-13037-6

THE BATTLE OF JUTLAND

HOLLOWAY HALSTEAD FROST
1889–1935

This portrait was made in 1925, when the author was a
Lieutenant Commander.

THE
BATTLE
OF
JUTLAND

BY

HOLLOWAY H. FROST
COMMANDER, UNITED STATES NAVY

UNITED STATES NAVAL INSTITUTE,
ANNAPOLIS, MARYLAND

HOLLOWAY HALSTEAD FROST

A Brief Transcript of His Service Record

1906   Appointed Midshipman in the U. S. Navy from the Fifth
        Congressional District, Brooklyn, New York.

1910   Graduated from U. S. Naval Academy as Passed Midship-
        man and ordered to the U.S.S. *Michigan* for duty.

1912   Commissioned Ensign in the U. S. Navy.

1914   Ordered to the U.S.S. *Ozark* for submarine duty.

1915   Commissioned Lieutenant (junior grade) in the U. S.
        Navy.

1916   Detached submarine duty and ordered to course at Naval
        War College, Newport, Rhode Island.

1917   Officer in charge Navy Recruiting Station, Little Rock,
        Arkansas.

        Ordered as aid on staff of Commander, Squadron One,
        Patrol Force, U. S. Atlantic Fleet.

        Temporarily appointed Lieutenant in the U. S. Navy.

1918   Commissioned Lieutenant in the U. S. Navy.

        Temporarily appointed Lieutenant Commander in the
        U. S. Navy.

        Ordered to duty on staff of Commander, American Patrol
        Detachment, U. S. Atlantic Fleet.

1919–20 Duty in Naval Operations, Navy Department, Washing-
        ton, D.C.

1921   Ordered to command U.S.S. *Breck*.

1922   Commissioned Lieutenant Commander in the U. S. Navy.

        Detached Commander of *Breck* and to duty as Assistant
        Chief of Staff, Commander Naval Forces Operating in
        European waters.

        Aid on staff, Commander in Chief, Asiatic Fleet.

1923–24 Detached staff duty and to duty in command of U.S.S.
        John D. Ford.

1925–26 Duty in Planning Division, Bureau of Navigation, Navy
        Department, Washington, D.C.

1927   Ordered to sea in command of U.S.S. *Toucey*.

1927   Temporary additional duty as naval member of American delegation to the conference for limitation of naval armaments, Geneva, Switzerland.

1928   Commanding U.S.S. *Toucey*.

1929   Under instruction at Army War College, Washington, D.C.

Commissioned Commander in the U. S. Navy.

1930–31   Member of faculty, Army War College, Washington, D.C.

1932   Ordered to the U.S.S. *California* as navigator.

1933   Ordered as Fleet Operations Officer on staff of Commander in Chief, U. S. Fleet.

1934   Duty on staff of Commandant of the Command and General Staff School, Fort Leavenworth, Kansas.

1935   Died at Research Hospital, Kansas City, Missouri, as a result of meningitis following mastoidectomy.

Special Attainments:

Qualified for command of submarines.
Designated as naval aviator.
Completed Naval War College senior course.
Completed Army War College course.

Special Decoration:

Navy Cross, with following citation:

For distinguished service in the line of his profession as Aid to Commander, American Patrol Detachment, Atlantic Fleet, and particularly in the development of the tactics of surface vessels and aircraft in combined operations against submarines.

Foreword

I KNOW of no one better fitted to write on the subject of this book than the late Commander Frost. Endowed as he was with a brilliant and analytical mind, he began at the outset of his naval career to be a student of military and naval history. It was only natural that accounts of the Battle of Jutland chronicling as they do the events of the greatest naval battle in modern times should at once have commanded his attention. This book represents the result of his studies of the famous battle covering a period of about eighteen years and reveals him as a naval historian of the highest order. Having known Commander Frost as well as I did, I feel that his descriptions, maps, opinions, and stated conclusions are all based not only upon the very highest authority obtainable but are the result of a critical analysis only possible to a man of his high professional attainments.

DAVID FOOTE SELLERS
Rear Admiral, United States Navy

United States Naval Academy
February 1, 1936

Prefatory Note

THIS BOOK is the product of eighteen years' work, commencing shortly after the Battle of Jutland. It represents the fine scholarship of a historian qualified by talent and temperament in judicial appraisal and analysis, and the first-hand experience acquired on the bridge of the flagship of a modern fleet.

In 1916, the then Lieutenant (junior grade) Holloway Halstead Frost became the youngest officer ever ordered to the United States Naval War College. This appointment doubtless was in part the result of prize-winning articles and other distinguished papers he had contributed to the United States Naval Institute PROCEEDINGS since his graduation from the Academy in 1910, written while Frost was performing the usual varied duties of a young officer in ships of all types.

A fellow student at the War College was Rear Admiral Edwin A. Anderson, one of the heroes of the Cienfuegos wirecutting exploit of 1898, wearer of the Congressional Medal of Honor, and an officer with an altogether outstanding career. There developed between the elder and the younger of these two men a deep mutual regard and affection which endured until Admiral Anderson's death. When, during the World War, and shortly after graduating from the War College, the Admiral was placed in command of the American Patrol Detachment of the United States Atlantic Fleet, he procured Frost's appointment to his staff as Senior Aid and Operations Officer. Some years later, when Admiral Anderson became, first, Commander of the United States Naval Forces in European waters, and then Commander in Chief of the Asiatic Fleet, he once more called upon Frost to serve under him in a similar capacity.

Frost's last and most important service afloat was as Operations Officer on the staff of Admiral David Foote Sellers, then the Commander in Chief of the United States Fleet, under whom the Fleet held the most elaborate and war-like maneuvers that it ever had conducted up to that time.

Between and after those two tours of staff duty, Frost spent several years in destroyer command, in other important sea duty, in the Planning Division of the Bureau of Navigation, and on the Faculty of the Army War College.

At the time of his death in January, 1935, at the age of forty-five, Commander Frost represented the Navy at the Army Staff and Command School at Fort Leavenworth.

Throughout all of these years, ashore and afloat, despite the heavy obligations of his various duties and his many inter-mediate writings—*We Build a Navy,* a history of the early United States Navy; *On a Destroyer's Bridge,* a technical work which not only is used in the United States Navy but also has been translated into foreign languages for use in other navies; a brochure on "Old Ironsides," of which over 100,000 copies have been sold for the benefit of the Navy Relief Society; and many articles on naval subjects—Frost continued his intensive study of the Battle of Jutland which he had begun at the Naval War College. His first description, necessarily based on the rela-tively meager and unreliable data then available, was published in the United States Naval Institute PROCEEDINGS in 1919 and copies were sent to the leading authorities in both participating Fleets, from some of whom, including Admiral Scheer, Admiral Hipper, and Lieutenant Commander von Hase, interesting and helpful comments were received. In later years, Frost went to Europe as one of the naval experts at the Geneva Conference of 1927 and on vacation trips to England and Germany. In va-rious parts of the world he met many of the officers who had served at Jutland.

Every time new authentic material served further to dissipate the fogs and mists that had obscured the study of the Battle of Jutland, Frost checked it against his previous sketches and nar-ratives. When the official lifting of the censorship veils at Berlin and London made it evident that there probably were available substantially all of the data that ever would be procurable, he commenced his final sketches and the final redraft of his description, constituting this volume. Altogether, he had made over a dozen series of sketches. Fortunately, he completed the sketches and substantially completed the text before his illness and untimely death in January, 1935.

From Commander Frost's notes, it is evident that, were he here to write his own acknowledgment for assistance rendered in the preparation of this book, he would express gratitude to Rear Admiral Otto Groos of the German Navy, a veteran of the battle, who generously told the author to take unlimited guidance from the former's battle charts. Frost found the tracks of the German ships as shown on the Groos charts exceedingly helpful.

The author also would extend deep thanks to Mr. G. J. Hazard, of the staff of the United States Naval War College, for assistance in connection with the drafting of the sketches. In a letter to a third party, Frost once expressed the opinion that Mr. Hazard was the ablest draftsman of naval sketches in the world.

This acknowledgment would not be complete without an expression of appreciation for the painstaking and careful check-up of the manuscript and its preparation for publication by Captain Oscar Smith, United States Navy, who during the author's last cruise served as Operations Officer on the staff of Commander Cruisers, United States Fleet, and who, while himself a close student of the Battle of Jutland with very pronounced opinions of his own, has carefully avoided any alteration of Commander Frost's views as expressed or indicated in the text; and to Commander A. B. Anderson, United States Navy, who guided this book during the difficult and important period of transition from a manuscript into the present bound volume.

EDWIN A. FALK

New York City
February 1, 1936

Publisher's Preface

WHEN *The Battle of Jutland* was first published in 1936, the battleship was queen of the seas and memories of the classic engagement between two battle lines was still fresh. Destroyers attacking the battle line hid from battleships behind their own smoke screens—radar was unknown—and charged in for short range torpedo attacks because long range guided missiles were equally unknown. Yet such tactics were rarely seen in World War II, and rapid technological advances since then have made "crossing the T" nearly as archaic an expression as "repel boarders."

No more do destroyers charge through swirling smoke toward a hostile battle line; indeed, the battle line itself is long gone. Aside from the pleasure of it then, for what professional reason would an officer study the Battle of Jutland—a large, indecisive action fought in the mists of the North Sea more than half a century ago?

One reason is that some of the problems facing the Germans and British in World War I were much the same as those faced by navies today. Any field or fleet commander can appreciate the frustration caused by "... the futile attempts of the Admiralty to direct tactical operations from a distance." This problem continues today, but in 1916 it was a new and untested tactical consideration.

German communications security was bad; British intelligence was good and knew how to take advantage of that German failing, so the British always knew when the Germans intended to go to sea and were ready to meet them. Many who fought in more recent wars know that this situation can as easily happen now as it did in 1916.

There were the interesting situations and attitudes of the commanders: the German leader, Scheer, who commanded a force too expensive and too powerful to remain unused but too weak to succeed in any important way, and his rival, Jellicoe, a man who, through his determination not to risk defeat, insured that victory was unattainable.

Always important to both the officer and the interested civilian, are the actions of brave men in battle: Admiral Beatty, with one third of his force blown up before his eyes, turning two points closer to the enemy; Admiral Scheer, returning to the fray against a far more powerful foe to rescue the doomed *Wiesbaden*; Captain Wolfgang Zenker of the *Von der Tann* keeping his crippled ship in the line so the fire directed at his compatriots would be lessened by each shell fired at him; the wounded Commander Loftus Jones of the *Shark*, with but a single gun left, fighting until finally his ship dipped beneath the waves.

While he was writing this book, Commander Frost was Operations Officer of the U.S. Fleet, a force much like those fleets whose last great battle took place at Jutland. He had spent eighteen years in collecting material for this book, much of it by interviewing participants whose observations and memories might otherwise have been lost forever.

In order to make these lessons of the past once more available for those scholars, historians, and officers who may bring them to bear on in the future, the U.S. Naval Institute is pleased to issue once again *The Battle of Jutland*.

CONTENTS

Contents

LIST OF ILLUSTRATIONS

CHAPTER I

THE COURSE OF THE WAR DURING 1914

To PRESENT the proper setting for the great drama of Jutland, it is essential that we should give a brief account of the World War until May, 1916. Also we must describe in some detail the naval operations of 1916 which led inevitably to a meeting of the British and German Fleets. Then, and only then, can we realize the tremendous responsibilities that rested on the shoulders of Jellicoe and Scheer and appreciate fully the enormous stakes that could have been won by a decisive victory at sea. Then, and only then, can we judge justly the opposing commanders in chief and their subordinate commanders.

When the German leaders perfected their plans for a short and decisive war, it was upon their incomparable Army that their confident hopes of success were based. In accordance with the long-calculated plans of their General Staff, the main blow was to fall with overwhelming power and impetus upon France. On the Eastern Front the Germans counted heavily upon the comparative slowness of the Russian mobilization and a strong Austrian offensive in the Galician sector. A covering force was to delay the advance of the Russians into East Prussia until the decision in France had been gained. The German Navy was to serve, in like manner, as a covering force on the North Sea and Baltic Fronts, while the small, but efficient, Austrian Navy performed similar duties in the Adriatic.

On the other hand, the overwhelming superiority of the allied navies was to be used to gain the control of the North Sea, the Mediterranean, and the oceans. While the command of these vital water areas was being thus secured, the allied armies were to crush the Central Powers with three simultaneous offensives. Undeterred by the probability of a German offensive on the Western Front, the aggressive French Army, soon to be supported by the small, but highly trained, British Expeditionary

Force, was to launch a powerful, headlong offensive into Alsace-Lorraine. Russia planned to use the bulk of her enormous forces first to stem the Austrian advance from Galicia and then to overwhelm the hostile armies. In addition to this major effort, in loyal response to insistent French demands, the Russians had agreed to invade East Prussia with two powerful armies. This was done in such haste that their supply trains could not be made available (Fig. 1–c).

This offensive, carried through with a loyal self-sacrifice beyond all praise, ended in the last days of August in the annihilation of one of the Russian armies at Tannenberg. However, this ill-fated offensive had well served its primary purpose of drawing large units of German troops from the Western Front before a decision had been reached in that most important theater.

After great, and well-nigh decisive, successes along the French frontier and in Belgium (Fig. 1–b), over-confidence and careless leadership brought the seemingly irresistible German tide to a standstill along the Marne. Thence Joffre's spirited counter-offensive (Fig. 1–h) early in September drove the Germans back to the line of the Aisne. But here they, in turn, recovered themselves, resolutely consolidated their positions and commenced extending their front toward the sea. Desperately fought but indecisive battles followed in rapid succession. Position warfare gradually came into being.

Meanwhile a confused series of great battles had been fought between the Austrians and Russians in Galicia. The original Austrian plans for this campaign had been seriously hindered by their operations on the Serbian Front. Instead of leaving a small covering force to dispute the passage of the Danube by the Serbians, the Austrians had withdrawn many divisions from their Galician armies for an ill-timed and large-scale offensive into Serbia (Fig. 1–d). This gained some initial successes by the latter part of August. At the same time the inferior Austrian armies in Galicia were experiencing a series of severe defeats and were retreating on a wide front before an energetic Russian advance (Fig. 1–e). By mid-September the Austrian resistance was definitely broken. By the end of the month the Russians had overrun nearly all Galicia. In the south they were fighting their way through the Carpathian passes toward the plains of Hungary. In the west they were nearing the key point of Cracow. A numerous Austrian army, surrounded in the fortress of Przemysl, was on the point of surrender.

The only ray of hope for the Central Powers came from stouthearted old Hindenburg. After annihilating the army of Samsonof at Tannenberg, he had turned on Rennenkampf early in September, driving him out of East Prussia in complete rout. It was evident that Hindenburg in some manner must take the pressure off the Austrians until they could stabilize their front. Early in October, therefore, he cleverly shifted the bulk of his re-enforced army southward from East Prussia into Silesia. Then, linking up with the left of the Austrian line, he advanced boldly in a northeasterly direction against the line of the Vistula (Fig. 1–J). At first the Germans advanced rapidly and the Austrians relieved Przemysl; but their offensive was spent against the strongly posted superior Russian armies along the Vistula. In the latter part of October, therefore, the Austro-Germans commenced a difficult retreat, closely followed by the Russians.

Hindenburg, in a bold attempt to regain the initiative, launched a detachment under Mackensen along the Vistula against the right flank and rear of the Russians. Taking the enemy completely by surprise, Mackensen won great initial successes (Fig. 1–N). Soon, however, he found himself virtually surrounded by greatly superior numbers. The battle developed into a confused series of desperately fought actions on reversed fronts. The results, in general, were favorable to the Germans. After prolonged fighting the front became stabilized a short distance to the west of Warsaw. During this fighting, it had been necessary for the Germans to give ground again in East Prussia. The Austrians finally slowed down the advance of the Russians in the Carpathians. At the end of the year we find that the Russians on the northern flank held part of East Prussia; in the center the Germans held a large area of Poland; and on the southern flank the Russians had practically all of Galicia.

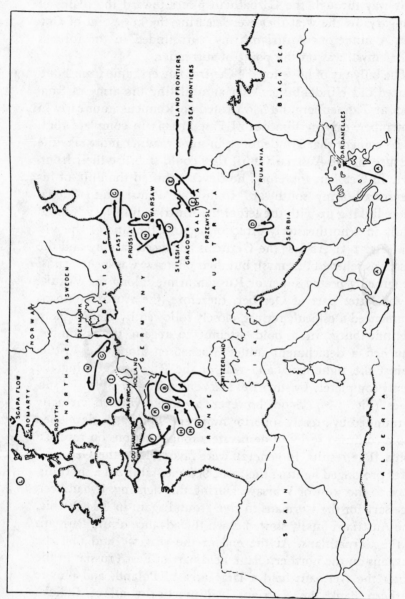

Fig. 1. Operations in Europe during 1914.

Przemysl was undergoing a second siege and the food supplies for its large garrison were rapidly failing. The Austrian army in Serbia had recrossed the Danube with heavy losses (Fig. 1–D).

Just as Hindenburg was commencing his advance against the Vistula in early October, General Falkenhayn, who had relieved Moltke as chief of the General Staff, attacked Antwerp. The Belgian capital, though heavily fortified and strongly garrisoned by the main body of the Belgian Army, offered little resistance. The Belgian Army, after its fall, was pursued to the French border, where its divisions, with British and French support, prolonged the allied line to the sea, fortunately in front of the highly important French channel ports. In an attempt to follow up and exploit this success, Falkenhayn launched a large-scale offensive with newly mobilized reserve corps with the channel ports as his objectives (Fig. 1–K). This was the first of the attempts to break through an organized position, which later became so familiar on the Western Front. It followed a course which became typical of such battles. At the cost of heavy casualties extending over a month, a short advance over a wide front was accomplished. When the results were weighed, it was seen that they were favorable to the defenders. But all the armies were now worn out and their ammunition was practically exhausted. Mid-November saw the end of major operations along the Western Front.

If the end of 1914 saw the establishment of stabilized warfare on all the land fronts, the same could not be said of the war at sea. For several centuries the British battle squadrons had been disposed in a far-flung array that encircled the globe and, with the assistance of numerous well-placed naval bases, had commanded virtually every ocean and sea. But the building of the efficient German Navy had profoundly altered this traditional disposition. The mission of the German Navy, as stated in the Navy Bill, was rather a curious one: "Germany must have a fleet of such strength that even for the mightiest naval power a war with her would involve such risks as to jeopardize its own supremacy."

Great Britain had reacted to this powerful threat by withdrawing her battle squadrons from distant seas and massing her strength in home waters. The Germans maintained their entire naval strength at home, except for cruisers operating on detached duty to show the flag.

In the North Sea the Germans had available 13 first-line battleships and 3 battle cruisers—16 first-line capital ships. The British had 20 first-line battleships and 4 battle cruisers—24 first-line capital ships. At Queenstown, Ireland, a fifth battle cruiser was immediately available. The British were immensely superior in second-line battleships and in armored and light cruisers. They were considerably superior in destroyers, submarines, and patrol craft. Thus their superiority in fighting strength could be estimated as about 3 to 2.

In addition to this superiority in ships, the British had a great advantage in the 12-year enlistment as against the 3-year compulsory service of the German Navy. They had a further advantage in the fact that practically their entire Fleet had been mobilized since July 15 for a review. Prince Louis of Battenburg and Winston Churchill, with far-sighted and bold initiative, had not demobilized the Fleet when the review was completed on July 26. Thus, the British had over two weeks' advantage over the Germans in their naval mobilization.

Furthermore, the German Navy acted under an immense geographical disadvantage. Virtually, all the over-seas routes to Germany led into the North Sea directly past the British naval bases. Therefore, the closing of these over-seas routes was a simple matter for the British. On the other hand, the British over-sea trade could, if necessary, reach England through ports on her western and southern coasts. These British routes could be reached by the German Fleet only if it passed close to British naval bases and allowed its line of retreat to be blocked by a concentrated and very superior British Fleet. Therefore, to cover their own trade routes or to attack those of the British, the German Fleet, greatly inferior in fighting strength, would have to maintain itself at a great distance from its own bases, in hostile waters, and with its line of retreat occupied by hostile forces. On the other hand, the British could secure their own trade routes against attack in force and cut almost all the German routes by fighting in their own waters when, where, and how they pleased. Thus the difficulties of the Germans in taking the offensive were almost insuperable.

The British Grand Fleet was concentrated in Scapa Flow. Its backbone consisted of the 24 first-line battleships and battle cruisers, plus 8 second-line battleships. Admiral Sir John Jellicoe was commander in chief. The Channel Fleet was based on Portsmouth. Its principal strength consisted of 17 second-line battleships. Vice Admiral Sir Cecil Burney commanded. Other forces covered the British coast at Dover, Harwich, and in the Humber.

The German High Seas Fleet was based in the Jade and in the mouths of the Elbe and Weser Rivers. Its backbone consisted of 16 first-line battleships and battle cruisers and 8 second-line battleships. Admiral von Ingenohl was commander in chief.

Von Ingenohl feared that the British, according to Nelsonian tradition, would attack the German coast. The British feared a similar attack. Each Navy took elaborate steps to resist the attacks which neither had the slightest idea of making. Thus, the war commenced with each fleet guarding its own waters. It was a curious page of naval history. This defensive attitude, however, resulted to the advantage of the British for, as we have seen, the geographical position permitted them to secure their own trade routes and cut most of those of the enemy. On August 7, the British Expeditionary Force, less two divisions kept at home for defensive purposes, commenced its crossing to France (Fig. 1–F). By August 17, the entire force, 150,000 strong, had landed. Thenceforth, its divisions acted on the left flank of the French Army during the Marne campaign.

In the Baltic, on the other hand, the Germans had all the advantage. Here Prince Heinrich exercised a separate command. He had only a few second-line battleships, cruisers, and light craft, but the Kiel Canal would permit re-enforcements from the High Seas Fleet to reach him quickly. The Russians, therefore, did not seriously contest the command of the Baltic. While all at first was quiet along the North Sea and Baltic Fronts, let

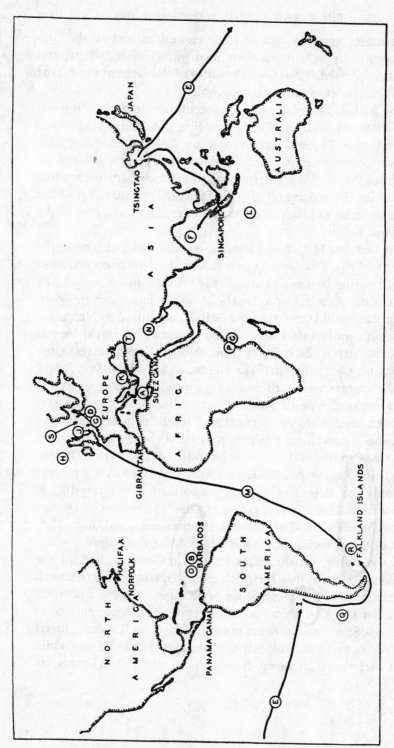

Fig. 2. Extended operations during 1914.

us see what had happened to the forces in the Mediterranean.

When the war began the Germans had 10 cruisers on detached duty. In the Mediterranean were the battle cruiser
Goeben and the light cruiser *Breslau,* under command of Rear
Admiral Souchon. At Malta was the British Mediterranean
Fleet: 3 battle cruisers, 4 cruisers, 4 light cruisers, and attached
destroyers. At Toulon was a strong French Fleet, having available 8 first-line battleships, 9 second-line battleships, with attached cruisers and destroyers. While the French were convoy-
ing their troops from Algeria to France, the British attempted
to run down the two German cruisers. Souchon was given a free
hand by the German Naval Staff. He slipped through the British
cordon and escaped into the neutral waters of the Dardanelles
(Fig. 1–A). The Turks had already been exasperated by the
seizure by the British of two of their battleships under construction. Now, they took the two German ships, with their
German crews intact, into their own service. This most unusual
action clearly indicated the intention of the Turks to assume
a benevolent attitude toward Germany. The British, hard
pressed elsewhere, withdrew 1 battle cruiser, 1 cruiser, and
4 light cruisers from the Mediterranean. The remainder were
used to watch the Dardanelles and to patrol the Red Sea.
The French Fleet based on Malta to hold the Austrians in the
Adriatic. The latter, greatly outnumbered, were constrained to
remain on the defensive. The defection of Italy from the Triple
Alliance greatly eased the situation for the Allies.

After the British Expeditionary Force had crossed to France,
the British Admiralty authorized a sweep into Helgoland Bight.
Commodore Keyes' submarines had determined that the German capital ships normally remained in their protected anchorages, and that the Helgoland Bight was patrolled by light cruisers
and destroyers. It was hoped that a surprise attack in great
strength at dawn would result in the interception of some of
these light forces while returning to their base. A powerful
force was concentrated for the operation: 5 battle cruisers under
Beatty; 6 light cruisers under Goodenough; 2 light cruisers and

35 destroyers of the Harwich Force under Tyrwhitt; and 2 destroyers and 8 submarines under Keyes. The attack was carried through on August 28 (Figs. 1–G and 2–D). Three German light cruisers and 1 destroyer were sunk. Taken completely by surprise, all the Germans could do was to fight to the finish with unsurpassed heroism.

Meanwhile the German cruisers had commenced operations on the high seas. Graf von Spee, with the cruisers *Scharnhorst* and *Gneisenau,* had proceeded from his base at Tsingtao on his long and eventful cruise across the Pacific (Fig. 2–E). He detached the light cruiser *Emden* to create a diversion by attacking trade in the Indian Ocean and ordered the auxiliary cruisers *Prinz Eitel Friedrich* and *Kronprinz Wilhelm* to proceed independently across the Pacific. To counter-balance these detachments, he called in the light cruisers *Leipzig* and *Nürnberg* from American waters. Another light cruiser, *Dresden,* left the West Indies to join him. The *Karlsruhe* commenced her highly effective cruise against trade in the Atlantic (Fig. 2–B). And, finally, the *Königsberg,* after sinking the British cruiser *Pegasus* in a surprise attack at Zanzibar (Fig. 2–C), withdrew into German East Africa to assist von Lettow-Vorbeck in his remarkable defense of that isolated colony.

The first use made by the British of their strong China and Australian Squadrons was to occupy undefended German territories in the Pacific and to escort their troop convoys. On September 10, the *Emden* commenced her reign of terror against British trade in the Indian Ocean (Fig. 2–F). Her successes were facilitated by the necessity for the British to use most of their cruisers to escort the convoys of Australian troops toward Egypt. When Japan entered the war on August 23, her powerful Fleet was used to occupy the defenseless Caroline and Marshall Islands and to assist the Japanese Army in a leisurely siege of Tsingtao. The British contributed a second-line battleship to this task, apparently for political effect. It was evident that the Japanese were more interested in the permanent possession of valuable territories than in the destruction of von Spee's squadron.

For these various reasons no attempt was made for a long time to follow von Spee across the Pacific, although he advertised his intentions by the bombardment of British Samoa. Thence, he proceeded via Easter Island toward Chili. The *Leipzig* and *Nürnberg* joined him. In consequence of the failure of the China and Australian Squadrons to follow von Spee and the diversion of the Japanese Navy toward other objectives, the British had to organize a new force to meet him in American waters. The ravages of the *Karlsruhe* in the Atlantic had attracted so many British cruisers to that area, that there remained for Rear Admiral Cradock who was ordered against the Germans only an ill-assorted squadron of 1 fast light cruiser, 2 medium-speed cruisers, and 1 slow second-line battleship. Not wishing to tie himself down to the latter which could never hope to bring the faster German vessels to action, Cradock pushed up the west coast of Chili with his 3 cruisers and an auxiliary cruiser of little fighting value. On paper, these ships were very nearly the equal of the German squadron, but the *Scharnhorst* and *Gneisenau* were both crack gunnery ships, while the *Monmouth* and *Good Hope* had been recently mobilized with reservists and, as Corbett admits, "had not done their gunnery." So, when on November 1 the two squadrons came into action, the result was a decisive victory for von Spee. Gallant Cradock, fighting to the end, went down in the *Good Hope*. The *Monmouth,* terribly damaged in the action, was sunk during the night by a torpedo from the *Nürnberg,* after heroically declining to surrender. The German ships were virtually unhit.

Already British trade in the Atlantic and Indian Oceans had suffered heavily from the operations of the *Karlsruhe* and *Emden*. Von Spee with four fine ships had gained at least temporary control of a wide area in the Southern Pacific—in much the same way as had our Commodore Porter a century before. The prestige of the Royal Navy was at stake. It was evident that re-enforcements must be sent from home waters to meet this threatening situation abroad; but affairs at home had also taken rather a dangerous turn. On September 22, Lieutenant

Commander von Weddigen, in the little submarine $U-9$* had performed his immortal feat of sinking three British cruisers in rapid succession (Figs. 1–I and 2–G). Fear of submarine attack had caused the withdrawal of the Grand Fleet to Irish waters until the elaborate defenses of Scapa Flow could be completed; but Jellicoe had left one danger only to expose himself to another. Late in October the German auxiliary cruiser *Berlin* had laid a mine field north of Ireland. On the twenty-seventh one of these mines had sunk the powerful first-line battleship *Audacious* (Figs. 1–L and 2–H). Insistent, but futile, denials by the British that this fine ship had sunk so easily only demonstrated the seriousness of the disaster. Three days later Russia declared war on Turkey, as the result of a bombardment of Odessa by the *Goeben* and *Breslau*. This provided new responsibilities for the British Admiralty. Then, on November 3 German cruisers had the temerity to bombard the English port of Yarmouth (Figs. 1–M and 2–J).

As their submarines failed to discover strong British forces in the North Sea, the Germans had become more venturesome. The Kaiser, in supreme command, exercised through the chief of Naval Staff strategic direction over the High Seas Fleet. While in itself this might not have been so bad, the missions given the commander in chief were unfortunately most vague and indefinite. Thus, poor von Ingenohl had been given neither a free hand nor a clearly phrased mission. However, despite this very embarrassing situation, he had prepared for an attack against the English coast. Arriving off Yarmouth early in the morning, Vice Admiral Hipper, with the scouting forces, surprised the patrol craft of the Harwich Force and conducted a brief bombardment of Yarmouth. Then, turning back at high speed, he joined the main body of the High Seas Fleet which had occupied a position in support. As the Grand Fleet was just assem-

* NOTE.—The Germans used both letters and numbers in the names of their destroyers and submarines. To help the reader readily to distinguish between the two classes of ships, the names of submarines are written with a hyphen between the letter and the number (thus $U-9$) and the names of destroyers are written without the hyphen (thus $V67$).

bling from the Irish coast at Scapa, it could not intercept the Germans during their return to their bases.

The British Admiralty had three problems: (1) to secure the command of the North Sea and prevent the recurrence of raids against the English coast; (2) to commence a blockade of Turkish waters; and (3) to destroy von Spee's squadron.

The situation in the North Sea was met by basing all the first-line capital ships at Scapa, while three squadrons of second-line battleships were placed at Rosyth, Sheerness, and Dover, respectively. This formidable array of battle squadrons, with the assistance of the Harwich Force and the Dover Patrol, was to execute the newly formulated plan to frustrate the long-expected, but entirely imaginary, German invasion of England.

How this immense naval concentration was to be used against the High Seas Fleet was laid down in Jellicoe's famous letter of October 30. This momentous, even fateful, document will be described in detail later. At this time it will suffice to say that Jellicoe's general plan was as follows: (1) to fight a fleet action only in the northern part of the North Sea, close to British and distant from German, bases; (2) to avoid closing in upon the High Seas Fleet in battle for fear of under-water damage by mines and torpedoes that might disable half the British battle fleet "before the guns opened fire"; (3) to receive the support of all the forces not attached to the Grand Fleet as soon as action was imminent. On November 7 the Admiralty approved the first two provisions and promised to comply with the request contained in the third. How so aggressive a leader as Churchill consented to such a defensive attitude in complete variance with the Nelsonian tradition is a mystery that has never been explained.

Off the Dardanelles was a British force of 2 battle cruisers, 2 light cruisers, 12 destroyers, and 3 submarines, supported by 2 French second-line battleships. On November 2, in an endeavor to dissuade the Turks from war against Great Britain and France, this force conducted a heavy bombardment of the Turkish forts (Fig. 2–K). On this occasion, unfortunately, Nelson's

opinion that a force of British battleships was the best nego-
tiator in Europe, was not verified. So a few days later Great
Britain reluctantly had to declare war on Turkey. On November 22 a British joint force occupied Basra near the head of the
Persian Gulf in Mesopotamia (Fig. 2–N). This force, which
operated under the Viceroy of India, was gradually increased for
a forward movement up the Tigris toward the historic city of
Bagdad. This movement was made largely for the political effect
it would have on the many millions of Moslems in the British
Empire. In December Enver Pasha's army in Armenia was
virtually annihilated by the Russians (Fig. 2–T).

Immediately after the news of Cradock's defeat reached England on November 4, Rear Admiral Stoddart, commanding the
South Atlantic Squadron, was directed to concentrate his cruisers at Montevideo. Vice Admiral Sturdee was assigned to the
command of a detachment of two battle cruisers of the Grand
Fleet and ordered to proceed to the Falkland Islands, where the
British had a valuable naval base, as soon as they could be fitted
for this extended duty (Fig. 2–M). The battle cruiser *Princess
Royal* was sent to Halifax to meet von Spee should he take advantage of the newly opened Panama Canal to enter the Carib-
bean. In the Pacific the battle cruiser *Australia,* supported by
Japanese cruisers, was directed to sweep down the western coast
of the American continent from California. All these movements
were made with great secrecy.

In the face of this triple concentration, of which he was entirely ignorant, von Spee decided to round Cape Horn to attack
the Falkland Islands (Fig. 2–Q). The joining of the *Dresden* gave
him five cruisers. Unfortunately, the German admiral decided
to attack early on December 8, when Sturdee had arrived in
port just the night before. The British squadron, in overwhelming strength, had a full period of daylight in which to run down
the German cruisers. The latter fought to the finish with extraordinary heroism. Only the *Dresden* escaped (Fig. 2–R).

Already the *Emden,* on November 9, had ended her dramatic
cruise after a grimly fought action with the Australian cruiser
Sydney (Fig. 2–L). The *Karlsruhe,* after having captured many

merchant vessels, was herself destroyed by the accidental explosion of her own magazine, just as she was about to attack the British base at Barbados (Fig. 2–o). The *Königsberg* was blockaded in German East Africa (Fig. 2–p). Only the *Dresden* and the 2 auxiliary cruisers were still at large on the high seas.

After these most opportune British successes, their four detached battle cruisers and many cruisers and light cruisers on foreign stations were called home to re-enforce the Grand Fleet. But before any of these strong re-enforcements could arrive a momentous event had occurred—the German sortie of December 16 (Figs. 1–n and 2–s). With the addition of the *Derfflinger*, the Germans had four battle cruisers in the North Sea. Temporarily, the British were reduced to an equal number of vessels of that type. Hipper, commanding the scouting forces, was directed to bombard Scarborough and Hartlepool with his battle cruisers, while a light cruiser laid a mine field. He was then to retire toward a rendezvous with the main body, which was composed of three battle squadrons and attached light forces. Von Ingenohl hoped by this scheme to draw inferior British forces into contact with his main body.

His plan came near to success. The British counter-measures were most inadequate. In the south the 5th Battle Squadron and the Harwich Force were watching the approaches to the coast. In the center Vice Admiral Beatty was on guard. His squadron of four battle cruisers was to be supported by the 2d Battle Squadron—six fine battleships. In the north the remainder of the Grand Fleet was operating from its base in the Scapa-Cromarty area.

The weather was rough and the visibility low—favorable to the Germans. But von Ingenohl, hearing that British destroyers were ahead, felt bound by his orders to turn back after reaching the rendezvous appointed for the scouting forces, a procedure which drew from Grand Admiral von Tirpitz bitter comments. This over-anxiety to follow the letter of imperial orders, written without the slightest knowledge of the existing situation, not only ended all hope of winning a decisive success over the scattered British squadrons, but exposed Hipper to being attacked by superior numbers. However, fortune this day was singularly impartial. A series of lucky incidents allowed Hipper to avoid action with the superior British forces disposed directly across his line of retreat.

After this day of lost opportunities, the Admiralty asked Jellicoe to bring the Grand Fleet south to Rosyth. When he declined to do so, the Battle Cruiser Fleet, under Beatty, was based there. While still technically a part of the Grand Fleet, in reality the status of this fleet became very similar to that of the Harwich Force, which was directly under the control of the Admiralty. The Kaiser likewise increased still more his control over the High Seas Fleet. He directed that no further sorties should be conducted by the main body without his approval in advance. This prohibited the High Seas Fleet from winning any decisive success. Only the scouting forces could now be used for offensive operations. As the return of the British battle cruisers from foreign stations had restored their superiority in that type, any operations of the German scouting forces—unsupported by their main body—would be attended with great risk. Of this, January was to give a most conclusive proof.

CHAPTER II

THE CAMPAIGNS OF 1915

THE CAMPAIGN of 1915 commenced on the sea. While, as already noted, von Ingenohl was prevented from using the main body of the High Seas Fleet without express permission of the Kaiser, he had been given a rather free hand with the battle cruisers and their attached light forces. Hipper had but four vessels of that type as against six for Beatty and time would still further increase this disparity. Also, the Battle Cruiser Fleet had been moved south to Rosyth for the specific purpose of countering German raids.

In this situation it was decided to relax the state of readiness for action of the High Seas Fleet to afford more opportunity for both training and repair. One battle squadron was sent into the Baltic for training, while a number of other vessels were permitted to disable their engines for repairs. On January 24, however, there was unexpected fine weather. This induced von Ingenohl to authorize a sweep of the scouting forces over the Dogger Bank. The orders to Vice Admiral Hipper, sent unnecessarily by radio, were quickly deciphered by the British Intelligence Service. With this invaluable information at its disposal, the Admiralty ordered Beatty and Tyrwhitt to rendezvous in a fixed position off the Dogger Bank to trap the German scouting forces. These forces were to be supported by a battle squadron, while the entire Grand Fleet would hurry down in readiness for any eventuality.

Thus, the cards were stacked against Hipper. Only one thing saved him. This was the great mistake of the Admiralty in ordering the British forces to take up a fixed position at daylight, rather than giving Beatty all the available information and directing him merely to intercept and destroy the enemy. As it happened, Hipper was able to locate the immensely superior British forces before they could get astride his line of retreat

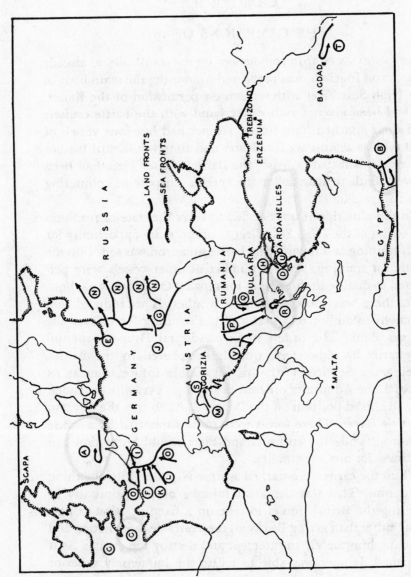

FIG. 3. Operations during 1915.

(Fig. 3–A). However, his situation was still sufficiently dangerous. His principal strength consisted of three battle cruisers, to
which had been attached the large cruiser *Blücher*. While her
8.2-inch guns would be useless against the British battle cruisers,
five in number, her weak armor could easily be penetrated by
their heavy shells. And, worst of all, her slow speed of 24 knots
forced upon Hipper the very embarrassing choice between
abandoning a large ship to certain destruction or allowing the
British to overtake his inferior force of battle cruisers at the
rate of several knots.

In the running fight that ensued, the *Blücher's* speed was
reduced by a lucky hit and Hipper reluctantly abandoned her
to the superior British forces. The *Seydlitz* was hit only three
times, but one shell ignited the powder in both her after turrets,
killing all their crews. Immense clouds of smoke poured from
the after part of the ship and the gunnery officer expected every
second that her magazines would explode. With magnificent
courage, seldom equaled in all naval history, this brave officer
ordered rapid fire with his three remaining turrets in order to
get out every shot possible before his own ship blew up. For a
time 3-shot salvos were fired at the incredibly short interval of
10 seconds. This terrible incident taught the Germans the necessity of taking every precaution against powder fires in turrets,
and particularly to prevent their reaching the magazines. The
British did not learn this lesson until the Battle of Jutland, and
then only at the cost of three battle cruisers.

The *Lion*, Beatty's flagship, was hit no less than twelve times
by the rapid and accurate German fire. She was put completely
out of action and fell out of column. The *Tiger*, second ship in
column, was also very heavily hit. In the confusion caused by
the *Lion's* erratic movements, the pursuit of the scouting forces
was very prematurely abandoned.

Because he had failed to provide support for the scouting
forces, von Ingenohl was relieved as commander in chief. Von
Pohl, who had been acting as chief of the Naval Staff, took his
place. It was decided that the High Seas Fleet should take a still
more defensive attitude, for now the Germans had decided to

launch their first submarine offensive. This, in accordance with public announcement, commenced on February 18. The waters about the British Isles were proclaimed to be a barred zone in which merchant vessels could be sunk without warning (Fig. 3–c). Submarines were not available in sufficient numbers to win a decisive result. While large numbers of vessels were sunk, the British counter-balanced this material gain by using their deadly propaganda to stir up neutral opinion against the Germans. The sinking of the *Lusitania* with heavy loss of life brought about a situation very unfavorable to the Germans. The net gain for the Germans was, therefore, very small. It would have been better to have followed the wise advice of von Tirpitz: To wait until there were enough submarines available to make the result decisive regardless of the possible action of neutral nations. As it was, the Germans had shown the Allies one of their trump cards. The latter were given an opportunity to develop naval counter-measures and to mobilize neutral opinion against the Germans.

The inactivity of the High Seas Fleet and the re-enforcement of the Grand Fleet by numerous new vessels permitted the British to detach a large number of their second-line battleships, supported by strong light forces, for a naval attack on the Dardanelles. This was launched primarily as the result of a request by Russia. It was thought that a threat against the Turkish capital would relieve the pressure against the Russian armies on the Armenian Front. It was also designed as a counter-blow for the venturesome and gallant attacks that the Turks had made on the Suez Canal without result on February 2 (Fig. 3–B).

The Dardanelles offensive commenced with initial successes in mid-February (Fig. 3–D), just as the German submarines were striking their first blows and a great battle in East Prussia was commencing.

The Germans had, in fact, learned one lesson from the Flanders offensive of 1914. It had convinced them that a large-scale offensive on the Western Front was entirely impracticable at that time. They planned, therefore, to reduce their forces in that area to those necessary for holding the line. This would permit them to mass their strategic reserve against Russia, where the longer front and their superiority in heavy artillery gave an offensive more chances of success. As a prelude to the main attacks, Hindenburg commenced in mid-February a powerful offensive against the Russian army holding the Masurian Lakes line in East Prussia. The Russian forces were well-nigh annihilated and some of the reserves of Grand Duke Nicholas, the Russian commander in chief, had to be used to re-establish the front (Fig. 3–E).

While Hindenburg was waiting for the weather to improve for further operations and a new army under von Mackensen was being organized about Cracow, the British took the offensive in France and at the Dardanelles. As March began, the British Army in France, now re-enforced to about half a million men, tried its strength in the Battle of Neuve Chapelle (Fig. 3–F). A costly check demonstrated that they were not yet ready for large-scale offensive operations.

On March 18 the naval attack on the Dardanelles came to an abrupt end with the complete and decisive repulse of the allied fleets with heavy losses. Despite the fact that powerful spring offensives were being prepared for the Western Front, the Allies decided to storm the Gallipoli Peninsula. For this purpose, British and French Expeditionary Forces were combined under the command of the gallant and accomplished Ian Hamilton. On April 25 his brave troops gained a few precarious footholds ashore at the cost of very heavy losses. Efficient and resolute Liman von Sanders, Turkish commander in chief, prevented the British from extending their gains (Fig. 3–H). Desperately fought battles cost each army heavy losses without any decisive result.

Meanwhile the last of the German cruisers on the high seas were being accounted for. In March the *Dresden* was sunk in neutral waters of Chili and the auxiliary cruiser *Prinz Eitel Friedrich* was interned in Norfolk. In April the *Kronprinz Wilhelm* ended her cruise in the same port. And finally the *Königsberg* was securely blockaded in German East Africa, although it was not until July that British monitors, using seaplane spotting, could finally put her out of action with long-range gunfire. Even then, her fine crew proved an important re-enforcement to Lettow-Vorbeck and participated with honor in one of the most brilliant military defenses recorded by history.

In April the Germans made local attacks on the northern flank of the Western Front to forestall the hostile spring offensives that they knew to be impending. These operations met with such success that on May 1 the British were compelled to move back closer to Ypres (Fig. 3–I).

On the same day Mackensen launched his tremendous offensive against the poorly fortified Russian Front in western Galicia (Fig. 3–J). Since the surrender of Przemysl on March 22 (Fig. 3–G), the Russians had been fighting their way through the snow-bound passes toward the plains of Hungary. Their supplies and munitions had run very low; so Mackensen's drum fire blasted a great gap in their defenses. The German infantry penetrated over a wide front and compelled an extensive retirement with huge losses of men and material.

The allied armies on the Western Front reacted quickly and strongly to this German success. In the second week of May, the British attacked at Festubert (Fig. 3–K), while Foch commenced a prolonged fight for Lens (Fig. 3–L). The British repulse was instant and complete. The French offensive developed into a month-long battle of attrition in which negligible gains of ground were made at the cost of tremendous losses. It was one of the worst defeats experienced by the French on the Western Front.

Curiously enough, it was in the midst of these numerous allied disasters that Italy entered the war late in May. The Austrians used covering forces to hold her armies in check along the mountainous frontier, feeding in re-enforcements as necessary to keep the front stabilized (Fig. 3–M).

The failure of the allied offensives on the Western Front permitted the Germans to exploit Mackensen's success. After his armies had recaptured most of Galicia, they were turned northward early in July against Warsaw (Fig. 3–N). Von Gallwitz, advancing southward from East Prussia, broke through the

Russian lines north of Warsaw. Early in August the Polish capital and the line of the Vistula had to be abandoned. The Germans moved forward along the entire Eastern Front (Fig. 3–N), taking immense numbers of prisoners and guns. Finally, in September the German drives spent their force, but only after the Russian Army and people had been dealt shattering blows from which they never recovered.

Meanwhile, August had seen the repulse of a new landing which large British re-enforcements had made on the Gallipoli Peninsula. The untrained British divisions had proved unequal to their task, although wonderful opportunities had been presented for an energetic advance and forceful offensive action.

By the last week in September, the Allies were ready at last for the aggressive campaign that the Russians had been so long demanding. A triple offensive was launched at Vimy, Loos, and in the Champagne (Fig. 3–O). The German armies had been reduced to a minimum to allow the great offensive in the East to be pressed. In consequence, their troops, very inferior to the allied concentrations at the point of contact and having few reserves, were very hard pressed. Still, with the assistance of some re-enforcements that were en route from the Eastern Front, they were able to hold up the desperate thrusts of the French and British. As usual the attackers could claim the gain of some ground and prisoners at the cost of far heavier losses. The attacks were, in fact, really costly defeats for the British and French.

The German submarine campaign continued to fall short of the expectations of its fervent advocates. The extension of the campaign to the Mediterranean considerably increased the sinkings of allied shipping. However, the political situation went from bad to worse. The diplomatic controversy with the United States over the sinking of the *Lusitania* was aggravated by the sinking of the *Arabic* on August 19. This made the situation so tense that on September 1 the German government felt compelled to announce that merchant vessels would no longer be sunk without warning. Under such conditions the submarines could never hope to exert decisive pressure on the Allies. Nevertheless, the sinkings of merchant vessels, particularly in the

Mediterranean, greatly increased the difficulties of the British Navy. The increasing effectiveness of the German submarines, even under their restrictions, is shown by the constantly mounting losses of allied shipping during 1915:

1st quarter	320,477 gross tons
2d quarter	380,419 gross tons
3d quarter	529,481 gross tons
4th quarter	494,373 gross tons

The High Seas Fleet made five cruises into the North Sea during 1915. These served to preserve the state of training of the Fleet, but were not extended far enough to make probable any contact with the Grand Fleet.

Seeing that the Allies had been definitely stopped in the west and finding it impracticable to advance further from their railheads in the east, the strategic reserves of the Central Powers were used to form an army under Mackensen to attack Serbia. While these forces were being assembled, Bulgaria was persuaded to join the side of the Central Powers. Mackensen commenced his advance from the north and west into Serbia early in October (Fig. 3–P). A week later Bulgaria declared war and attacked Serbia from the eastward (Fig. 3–Q). The Allies in haste landed an ill-assorted army in Salonika, thus deliberately violating the neutrality of Greece (Fig. 3–R). This force failed to come to the relief of the Serbians until they had been overwhelmed by the Germans and Bulgarians, who completed their occupation of Serbia during November. The Serbian Army was virtually annihilated. Its disorganized survivors escaped through Albania. The French and British forces were compelled to withdraw within the defenses of Salonika. There the Serbian Army joined them when reconstituted. As the year ended the Austro-Germans were preparing to launch a joint attack on Montenegro. This was completely successful during the early weeks of January (Fig. 3–v).

Meanwhile, the Italians, slowly mobilizing their full strength, had gradually increased their pressure on Austria. They had even won some minor successes. However, the termination of the Russian campaign and the conquest of Serbia allowed Austria to increase her defensive forces on the Italian Front. The Italian drive came to a stop (Fig. 3-s). Gorizia, on the Isonzo, the much-heralded objective of the Italians, was not gained.

The allied cause had fared no better on Turkish soil. During the fall impetuous General Townshend had commenced an ambitious and aggressive campaign against Bagdad. Winning a splendid series of successes, he advanced rapidly up the Tigris to exploit them to the full. Unfortunately, just before he could reach Bagdad, a strongly re-enforced Turkish army disputed his further advance. A desperately fought battle failed to drive the Turks from the field; so Townshend reluctantly ordered a retreat toward Kut-el-Amara (Fig. 3-T). There he was soon besieged by a strong Turkish army under command of the famous Field Marshal von der Goltz.

In December and January the British evacuated the Gallipoli Peninsula. Though most skillfully conducted without loss, this retirement conceded the failure of another bitterly fought campaign (Fig. 3-U). Thus the year 1915 ended with the tide of war running strongly for the Central Powers. New victories seemed to be imminent, and in fact they were.

CHAPTER III

THE EARLY CAMPAIGNS OF 1916

THE GREAT successes of the Central Powers in 1915 gave them the strategic reserves necessary for the renewal of their offensive in 1916. In general, their plan was as follows:

Turkey—to defend the Armenian Front and take the offensive in Mesopotamia.

Bulgaria—to hold the Salonika Front.

Austria—to hold the Eastern Front against Russia and the Isonzo Front against Italy, while launching a powerful offensive against the latter power through the Trentino.

Germany—to hold the Eastern Front against Russia, while attacking the French on the Western Front and using the High Seas Fleet offensively against the British.

While the Central Powers were staking their hopes for a decision on these four offensives, the Allies were contemplating offensive operations against Turkey only. While the British were making every effort to relieve Kut-el-Amara, the Russians were to break through the Armenian Front to seize Erzerum and Trebizond. In Europe the British Army was to be brought to its full strength, while the Russian forces were to be reconstituted. Then, finally, in July or August, there was to be a grand concerted offensive by British, French, Italians, and Russians.

The campaign opened well for the Central Powers, except for the Caucasus Front. There in mid-February the Russian troops, under the effective leadership of Grand Duke Nicholas, captured Erzerum (Fig. 4–A). However, this allied success was over-shadowed by the prolonged and costly failures of the British to bring urgently needed relief to Townshend in Kut-el-Amara (Fig. 4–C). Then on February 21 came the sensational success of the Army Group of the Crown Prince at Verdun (Fig. 4–C). In order to relieve this pressure, which was designed by Falkenhayn to "bleed the French armies white," the Russians, now under the supreme command of the Czar, commenced gigantic, but premature, offensives on the northern sectors of the Eastern Front. These were repulsed with such enormous losses that over half the Russian forces were immobilized for the rest of the year. The immense losses of these ill-advised attacks contributed greatly to the Russian debacle.

The Russians, who were greatly in need of munitions, asked the British Admiralty to launch a naval offensive into the Baltic. The British replied, with justice, that they could not do so as long as the High Seas Fleet remained intact. They agreed, however, to take more active measures to bring the Germans to battle.

Meanwhile a series of energetic sorties by the High Seas Fleet, to be described in more detail later, were concentrating British attention on the North Sea. On April 25 the High Seas Fleet made a bold cruise far from its bases. Cruisers bombarded the English coast for the first time since 1914 (Fig. 4–E). The auxiliary cruiser *Moewe* completed a highly successful cruise on the high seas, sinking 15 allied ships. These German successes, while of little actual effect, were a shock to British public opinion and not without their effect upon neutral thought. It was becoming evident that the British Navy no longer was being commanded in accordance with the old Nelsonian tradition.

Against these successes of the Central Powers, the Allies could claim only the capture of Trebizond on the Black Sea (Fig. 4–F). But even this item of good publicity was far outweighed by the stunning tidings that Townshend had surrendered at Kut-el-Amara (Fig. 4–G). This disaster made an impression far out of proportion to the comparatively small number of the British garrison, because it was virtually a confession of failure by the British. This incident, following so closely upon the evacuation of Gallipoli, was expected to have far-reaching results among the Moslem population of the East. Fears that they would unite in a holy war against the British were aroused.

Finally, on May 2, came the startling news of an Austrian penetration of the Italian Front in the Trentino (Fig. 4–H).

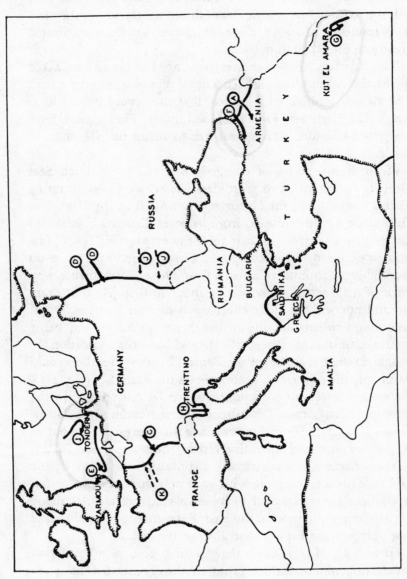

FIG. 4. Early operations during 1916.

Meanwhile the Germans continued their converging attack against Verdun, inflicting on the French considerably heavier losses than they were themselves receiving. Falkenhayn's policy of bleeding France white was meeting with success.

In order to relieve the terrific pressure upon Verdun, the date set for the combined British and French offensive on the Somme was advanced. But even with all haste, it could not be launched until July. Therefore, Brusiloff agreed to commence early in June, in loyal support of the allied plans, the offensive on the southern sector of the Russian Front that had been originally set for July. Whether this premature attack would be more effective than the disastrous Russian offensives of March and April was highly doubtful.

Meanwhile, the British, with all their astuteness, had lost a remarkable diplomatic opportunity. In a momentous conference at London on February 14, clever Lloyd George had obtained from our roving ambassador-at-large, Colonel House, a definite promise for America to join the war on the side of the Allies if Germany failed to agree with the British peace proposals. As it was known that Germany would accept no such terms, House had virtually committed the United States to intervene actively in the war; but, unfortunately for the Allies, it seems that House had exceeded somewhat his instructions. President Wilson added, as Lloyd George says, "one fatal word," which broke up this most promising intrigue.

Well might the commander in chief of the Grand Fleet have said, as Sir John Jervis had remarked at an equally critical moment over a century before, "A victory is very essential to England at this moment." For it was at this crisis of the war that there occurred the long-awaited contact of the opposing fleets in the North Sea.

We have noted the failure of the German submarine campaign to gain a decision in 1915. Due to forceful protests of the United States, the Germans had been compelled to abandon their system of attacking merchant vessels without warning. Still, by legitimate warfare and by mining operations, they had been able to accomplish results of considerable, if not of decisive, importance. Their campaign in the Mediterranean continued to be particularly effective.

General von Falkenhayn, to support his projected Verdun attack, had demanded that unrestricted submarine warfare be reopened early in 1916. The chief of Naval Staff enthusiastically supported this project. He even went so far as to promise that the submarines would force Great Britain to sue for peace in six months. The German Chancellor, Bethmann-Hollweg, vetoed the entire proposal. The familiar argument between soldiers, sailors, and statesmen continued.

While these interminable discussions were proceeding, a momentous event occurred. Admiral von Pohl, in the last stages of a mortal illness, resigned his command on January 18. Reinhard Scheer, though only a vice admiral, was appointed commander in chief of the High Seas Fleet. In 1914, Scheer had commanded the old second-line battleships of Squadron II; thence, he had been promoted to Squadron III, composed of 8 of the latest ships. Thus, he had worked up through the Fleet. For chief of staff he selected the careful and methodical Captain von Trotha. For operations officer he chose the brilliant, high-spirited, and venturesome Captain von Levetzow, then in command of the battle cruiser *Moltke*.

On February 1, Scheer attended a conference in Berlin which discussed the naval situation. The decisions were:

(1) To commence submarine warfare without restriction on March 1.

(2) To reduce the naval force in the Baltic so as to re-enforce the High Seas Fleet.

(3) To initiate a more aggressive campaign with the High Seas Fleet.

The fleet offensive could take the following forms: mining operations, airship attacks, destroyer and cruiser raids, bombardments of the English coast, and advances with the entire Fleet.

As regards the operations of the entire Fleet, it was perfectly evident that the Germans could not, with an inferiority of about 4 to 7 (not counting in the Harwich Force, Dover Patrol, or the

3d Battle Squadron), risk a stand-up finish fight with the entire Grand Fleet. "The ratio of strength," wrote Scheer, "prevents us from seeking a battle to a decision with the concentrated British Fleet. Our leadership must prevent this fight to a decision from being forced upon us."

However, if a finish fight offered little prospect of success, the High Seas Fleet, if operated aggressively, still had some chances of winning lesser successes that might contribute to the prosecution of the war as a whole. It might:

(1) Surprise and defeat British detachments.

(2) Inflict losses on the enemy by drawing them through submarine or, possibly, mine traps.

(3) Create moral effects by bombardments of the English coast.

(4) At least prevent the Grand Fleet from re-enforcing the anti-submarine forces.

To accomplish such results without receiving heavy losses was evidently a most difficult task for Scheer to accomplish. Being inferior in both strength and speed, his own detachments were more liable to be brought to action by superior forces than were the British. He stood to lose more than he could gain by submarine and mine traps, for every time the High Seas Fleet left port and returned to its anchorages, it had to accept these dangers in their worst form, not to mention the danger from these weapons that must be incurred whenever he attempted a bombardment of British ports. Furthermore, the probability of defeat or at least heavy losses was likely to create in Germany far more unfavorable moral effects than he could hope to create in England by the bombardment of a few unimportant coastal towns. It is true that he could hope for a time to create a diversion in favor of his submarines in their attack on merchant ships, but the risking of his Fleet for such a temporary advantage was liable to cost him dearly.

Possibly, Scheer counted on two factors, which might seem to favor his success. First, he had the initiative. This advantage, however, was almost entirely lost because of the remarkable efficiency of the British Intelligence Service in giving advance warning of German movements. The carelessness of the Germans in the unnecessary use of radio and their failure to change their codes and to use proper ciphers contributed greatly to the British success in this respect. Second, the German airships were available for scouting. These craft, unfortunately, again and again proved to have little, if any, practical value. The weather almost always prevented their effective use. When it permitted them to go to sea, the reports of British forces sighted were frequently not only valueless, but positively misleading. Thus, these two possible advantages really were non-existent.

While Scheer's decision to use the High Seas Fleet as a whole for offensive operations involved risks out of all proportion to the results he might reasonably hope to gain, we nevertheless heartily approve his bold resolve. Such a splendid organization as the Imperial Navy could not remain idle forever without even an attempt to win success. For reasons of morale alone it was necessary that these fine men and ships should enter the fight and get to grips with the enemy before inactivity ruined both.

As the first movement in the campaign, Scheer sent out the light cruiser *Rostock* with Flotillas II, VI, and IX on February 10 to conduct a raid in the vicinity of the Dogger Bank. This force in a surprise encounter sank the sloop *Arabis*.

Immediately upon the return of this striking force, Scheer received authority for his submarines to attack without warning all merchant vessels mounting guns. When he protested vigorously against this half-measure, he was informed that it was a preliminary step to unrestricted warfare. The only question still in doubt was the date upon which it might begin.

On February 23, the Kaiser visited the Fleet and publicly approved Scheer's plan for offensive operations. This definitely ended the old system of command that permitted no offensive movements without advance approval of the Kaiser. "I was invested with authority," Scheer wrote, "that gave me liberty of action to an extent I myself had defined." However, the date for beginning unrestricted submarine warfare still remained in doubt. Scheer accepted the situation and sent out two submarines to see what they could accomplish under the new order. This imposed an almost insuperable difficulty on their captains, because it was generally impossible for the submarine to determine whether a target ship mounted guns during her submerged approach from ahead. In the meantime Scheer resolved to commence operations with the High Seas Fleet.

While these changes were occurring in the method of operation of the High Seas Fleet, a similar movement was making progress across the North Sea. There the able Captain von Schoultz, Russian liaison officer in the Grand Fleet, had proposed, in accordance with instructions from his government, that the Grand Fleet should attempt to penetrate the Baltic, thus opening a route by which the Russians could receive much-needed munitions of all kinds. Lord Balfour, First Lord of the Admiralty, replied that nothing could be attempted along this line until the High Seas Fleet was defeated. It was resolved, however, that the Grand Fleet should make renewed efforts to accomplish this purpose. Thus, we see that each Fleet commenced a series of offensive movements that continued during the months of March, April, and May. These provide the basis for a very interesting comparison.

Scheer commenced the campaign with a sortie of the High Seas Fleet on March 5-6. The main body, consisting of Battle Squadrons I and III, screened by light cruisers and destroyers, took station off the Dutch coast near Terschelling Island. The scouting forces, consisting of battle cruisers, light cruisers, and destroyers, proceeded to the southward between Yarmouth and the Dutch coast. An interesting feature of this enterprise was the assignment of an airship to act with the scouting forces, while three more covered the northern flank of the Fleet and incidentally dropped some bombs on British towns. Twelve of the Flanders submarines watched the English coast, ready to attack any British vessels that might be drawn from their bases.

The British had only the Harwich Force within striking distance of the German concentration. So the Admiralty recalled all patrol craft and ordered Tyrwhitt to make a limited and

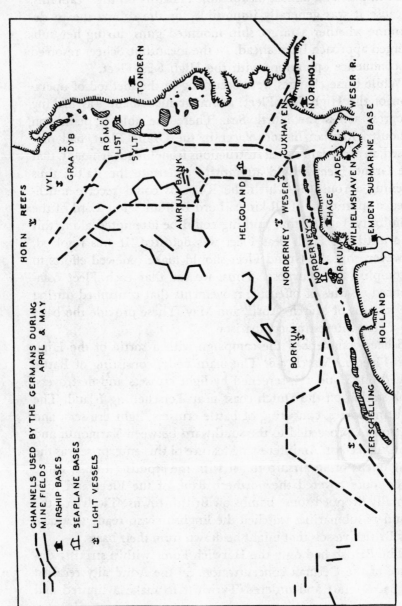

SKETCH I. Approaches to the German bases.

cautious reconnaissance. The 3d Battle Squadron, consisting of second-line battleships, had just sailed from Rosyth toward the center of the North Sea. The remainder of the Grand Fleet was directed to proceed to the vicinity of the "Long Forties" (Latitude 57-20; Longitude 00-00) to make a sweep to the southward. By such a movement Jellicoe, of course, could not hope to intercept the Germans; in fact, he does not even mention in his book the fact that the High Seas Fleet was at sea.

No contacts between surface craft occurred. However, several submarines were sighted by the German battleships. This brought home one of the grave disadvantages under which the High Seas Fleet was forced to operate. The configuration of the Dutch and Danish coasts limited the Germans to a sector of only 90° through which they must pass when leaving or returning to their bases. This sector (Sketch I) was thickly planted with both German and British mines. Three channels through these mine fields were all the German mine sweepers could keep reasonably clear of mines. As the location of these channels was known with considerable accuracy by the British, their submarines could maintain constant patrols in the limited areas off the outer ends of the swept channels. This gave them excellent opportunities for making contact with the German capital ships whenever they put to sea and was particularly the case when the Germans used the single channel extending to the westward toward Terschelling.

On March 18 the two submarines sent out to try their luck with the new attack orders reported having gained only unimportant successes. On the same day the sad news of the resignation of Grand Admiral von Tirpitz arrived. It seems that on the sixth there had been a show-down between Bethmann-Hollweg and the naval and military leaders. A compromise was reached. It was decided to sink British ships, except passenger ships, in the war zone, but to delay general, unrestricted submarine warfare. This was a most unsatisfactory arrangement, for it was impossible for anyone, much less a submarine captain, to say what was a passenger ship and what was not. But von Tirpitz had not even been invited to attend this crucial conference. He resigned his important post, which the Kaiser hastened to fill. It was one of the great tragedies of the war for Germany that its most able admiral, imbued with correct appreciation of Germany's rôle on the seas, should not at the beginning of the war have been placed in supreme command of the German Navy. His return to civil life, just when he was most useful to his country, was nothing less than a disaster.

The resignation of such a strong supporter of unrestricted submarine warfare indicated definitely that Bethmann-Hollweg had won his fight to have it indefinitely postponed. As it was impossible to accomplish anything of decisive importance with submarines under the present orders, Scheer decided to conduct an offensive campaign with the High Seas Fleet regardless of the grave dangers such action must inevitably entail.

But before there was time to commence operations the British struck. The frequent raids by German airships had rather exasperated them. It was decided to attack with seaplanes the airship hangars thought to be at Hoyer, but actually at Tondern, behind the island of Sylt. Five seaplanes, equipped with bombs, were to be lowered onto the open sea by the seaplane carrier *Vindex*. This ship was to be protected by the Harwich Force and the Battle Cruiser Fleet. The Grand Fleet would not be at sea, except as above stated.

The air attack was launched at dawn on March 25 (Fig. 4–1). Three of the five planes were lost. The only result was the discovery that the hangars were at Tondern, not Hoyer. In searching for the lost planes in the vicinity of the island of Römö, British destroyers sank two German trawlers. In turn, German seaplanes from the station at List on the island of Sylt attacked the destroyers. Though the bombs missed, the destroyer *Laverock* rammed the *Medusa*, reducing her speed to 8 knots. Other seaplanes from Helgoland also bombed British destroyers without result. All during the day Tyrwhitt towed his damaged destroyer, while Beatty moved in to support him against the expected German sortie.

Fortunately for the British, the situation was not realized by Scheer. Although the British had sent many radio messages, which they expected the Germans to read or decipher, Scheer did not learn that the very opportunity to strike inferior detachments he most desired was present. In consequence, he sent out only some cruisers and destroyers. One of the latter was sunk by a mine.

As the weather had become very bad by early evening, Tyrwhitt reluctantly gave the order to sink the *Medusa*. Soon afterward two German destroyers of an old type made contact with three vessels of the 5th Light Cruiser Squadron. Both forces, of course, were proceeding without lights, but the German vessels disclosed their presence by flames from their stacks, a disadvantage of the old coal-burning boats when running at high speed. The *Cleopatra* rammed and sank a German destroyer, but was herself rammed by another ship in her column, the *Undaunted*. The latter's bows were stove in and her speed reduced to 6 knots. As the Battle Cruiser Fleet was 50 miles away, Tyrwhitt was in a most critical situation. However, Scheer did not know of the *Undaunted's* injuries. So, with the rising sea, he recalled his forces. By 11:00 P.M. the Admiralty obtained this invaluable information and furnished it to Tyrwhitt. It also informed him that the German cruisers were coming out again the next morning.

Early on the twenty-sixth the entire High Seas Fleet put to sea for a sweep against the British forces. Being correctly informed of this movement, the Admiralty ordered Tyrwhitt to retire on Beatty and instructed Jellicoe to bring the Battle Fleet to a supporting position east of the "Long Forties." Beatty advanced through mountainous seas to join Tyrwhitt and cover the *Undaunted*. For a time it seemed that the High Seas Fleet must gain touch with Tyrwhitt and Beatty off Horn Reefs. "An action now seemed inevitable," Corbett admits, "and it must begin long before our battle fleet could appear." Very, very fortunately for the British, Scheer did not know that the *Undaunted* was damaged and that he had a wonderful opportunity to strike an inferior force. As the weather was extremely bad and the sea very rough, he gave the order to return to port. Had the German deciphering unit at Neumünster been able to give Scheer one-tenth the information that the British had of his movements, the Germans might well have gained a brilliant success.

This operation probably had some influence on the Battle of Jutland. As such it merits some comment. The first striking point is that the Admiralty, by issuing repeated orders to Tyrwhitt and Beatty, exercised general tactical control over forces far distant, with little knowledge of the actual tactical situation. Jellicoe, the nominal superior of Beatty, issued no orders during the operation. The second point is that the possible bombing of an aircraft hangar was a very unimportant result for which to risk the overwhelming of such important British forces. The Battle Fleet should have been within close supporting distance from the beginning of the operation. Then it could both protect the advanced British forces and bring to action the High Seas Fleet should it be lured out to sea. It was fortunate for the British that this enterprise did not end in disaster. The third point of interest was the almost incredible carelessness of the Germans in breaking radio silence much earlier than necessary and in using such insecure ciphers that the British had indispensable information of their intentions long in advance. Early in the war one of the German naval code books had been obtained by the Russians from the wreck of the light cruiser *Magdeburg*. Apparently, in all this time no new code book had been issued. However, had secure ciphers, changed at frequent intervals, been used even in conjunction with the old code book, the British could have obtained their information of the enemy only after a long delay. The British also had a marked advantage in the possession of numerous radio direction-finder stations. These could take bearings of every ship making radio transmissions. A number of these stations spread along the long line of the English coast were able to obtain simultaneous bearings of the same transmission and fix with a considerable degree of accuracy its position. So far as can be determined, the Germans did not at that time have direction finders. Even if they had, their short coast line would not have permitted them in most cases to fix accurately the positions of British ships, because of the small angle between the bearings obtained by the various stations.

As the operations just described were taking place off Horn Reefs, an event occurred in the English Channel that had momentous consequence. With the lifting of some of the restrictions against submarine operations, the effectiveness of the campaign had increased progressively since the beginning of the year. According to Lloyd George, the British shipping losses in gross tons during this period were as follows: January, 62,288; February, 75,860; March, 99,090.

In April the figure was rapidly mounting much higher; but with the Germans attacking all ships, except passenger ships, without warning, the catastrophe was bound to come sooner or later. On the afternoon of March 24, the *UB-29* of the Flanders U-Flotilla had torpedoed the British channel steamer *Sussex* without warning. Not only were American citizens on board, but two Spaniards were killed. The German chancellor handled the situation in a manner that showed singular lack of diplomatic skill. At first he claimed that the damage was caused by a mine. Then, it was admitted that a submarine was at fault. Next, it was alleged that her captain thought the *Sussex* was a transport. Finally, it was claimed that she had been taken for a new mine layer. The President of the United States, exasperated by these conflicting excuses, had a forceful note sent to the German government. This gave Germany the choice between abandonment of submarine warfare and severance of diplomatic relations. This virtual ultimatum arrived in Berlin on April 20. A conference was hastily called. Falkenhayn and Holtzendorff, chief of the Naval Staff, were against the slightest concession, but the Kaiser sided with Bethmann-Hollweg. Holtzendorff directed Scheer to conduct the submarine campaign in strict accordance with international law. Scheer, therefore, as we have seen, recalled the submarines on April 25. This was a death blow to the submarine campaign, which had been attaining such effectiveness. During April, despite the fact that all submarines were recalled on the twenty-fifth, the gross tonnage of British shipping lost reached the imposing total of 141,193.

When Scheer issued this order he was at sea with the High Seas Fleet in an operation of great importance. This we must now describe in detail.

CHAPTER IV

PRELIMINARIES TO THE SORTIE OF APRIL 25

UNTIL THE middle of April, the High Seas Fleet had conducted its operations skillfully, with the exception of its careless use of radio, but without having made any important contacts with the enemy. The operations of the Grand Fleet had been equally ineffective. But at this time both commanders commenced a series of large-scale operations that was certain to culminate sooner or later in a contact between the fleets. This was just missed in the very interesting operations which culminated in the sortie of April 25.

The German General Staff had decided to assist the Irish revolution planned for Easter Sunday, April 24. The Naval Staff accordingly was directed to arrange for landing Sir Roger Casement on the Irish coast with 10 German machine guns and 20,000 Russian rifles. This undertaking, so far as the Navy was concerned, was planned and executed in a most skillful manner. The merchant vessel *Libau* was manned by a carefully selected crew under the able command of Lieutenant Spindler. She was disguised as the Norwegian ship *Aud* and loaded with her arms and ammunition. The *Libau* sailed on April 10 from Warnemünde in the Baltic, passed out through the Skagerrak, and evaded the British blockading squadrons patrolling between Scotland and Norway. On the fifteenth the *U–19* left Helgoland with the unfortunate Sir Roger Casement and two other Irish leaders on board. She was to meet the *Libau* off Tralee, Ireland.

Scheer's last sortie had led him well into the southern part of the North Sea. He planned a demonstration against the English coast itself and decided to make this sortie coincide with the outbreak of the Irish revolution.

Meanwhile, the British had been working on three plans. In order to allow the Russians to re-lay their mine fields after the ice had broken up, the Grand Fleet had planned a demonstration in the Kattegat for April 21. At Dover Admiral Bacon was planning to lay an extensive barrage of mines and submarine nets off the Belgian coast on the twenty-fourth. Jellicoe was preparing for a second attack on the airship base at Tondern for May 4.

The German Intelligence Service had gained certain information of the British preparations that led Scheer to believe Tondern would be attacked about the middle of April. On the thirteenth, therefore, he had commenced making his defensive dispositions. The outpost lines were re-enforced until they reached a strength of four destroyer flotillas. The remainder of the Fleet, except the *Hamburg*, flagship of the leader of submarines, was assembled in readiness in the outer anchorages. No hostile attack having been made by the nineteenth, Scheer ordered the greater part of his battleships and cruisers to return to the inner anchorages to fuel in preparation for the sortie against the English coast.

On the twentieth a British cruiser force proceeded toward the Kattegat to operate against trade, to attack naval vessels encountered, and to engage hostile forces that might be drawn out from their North Sea bases. Three submarines were stationed in the exits from the Baltic.

During the twentieth German seaplanes making their routine search of the Helgoland Bight reported no contacts. The lookouts on the island of Baltrum reported a British submarine. Half Flotilla I, the auxiliary mine-sweeping flotilla, and all available seaplanes hunted for it without success. In the evening Flotilla IX advanced from List in a northwesterly direction toward Horn Reefs.

At dawn on the twenty-first Scouting Group IV, composed of 4 light cruisers, took station south of Amrum Bank. Two battle cruisers were in close support. During the day neither destroyers, cruisers, nor seaplanes reported any enemy vessels. At 3:00 P.M., however, the radio station at Neumünster reported that, according to a deciphered British dispatch, a British detachment, including battleships and cruisers, had proceeded out of the Firth of Forth during the evening of the twentieth. It had passed May Island, off the entrance of the Firth, on course ESE (100°).* This message apparently referred to the cruiser force bound for the Kattegat, but the course reported would have taken it toward Horn Reefs.

Scheer assumed that the British were now commencing the long-awaited attack against Tondern, particularly as the weather was favorable. He decided to concentrate the High Seas Fleet south of Horn Reefs. Accordingly, about 8:00 P.M. Scouting Groups I and II, with two fast flotillas, proceeded toward Horn Reefs to search that vicinity (Fig. 5–A). At 10:00 P.M. the main body followed (Fig. 5–B). The *U–20* and *U–32* left the Ems to take station at the western entrance to the Helgoland Bight (Fig. 5–C). A large number of radio messages were sent in order to initiate these movements. With proper arrangements this should have been unnecessary.

The British Admiralty knew that the High Seas Fleet had been in readiness for an operation for the last week. Late on the twenty-first it was determined from intercepted dispatches that the Germans were putting to sea. The purpose of their sortie, however, could not be determined. The Kattegat demonstration was promptly canceled and the Admiralty ordered out the entire Grand Fleet. The Battle Fleet was to be in position 100 miles east of Aberdeen early on the twenty-second, with the Battle Cruiser Fleet advanced from it 40 miles toward the German bases. The 3d Battle Squadron and 3d Cruiser Squadron were to take station so they could easily re-enforce the Battle Fleet in case of necessity. The Grand Fleet put to sea with its usual promptness (Fig. 5–D). The Germans were in entire ignorance of its movements.

Meanwhile, the scouting forces had been advancing toward Horn Reefs to cover Tondern. Toward midnight the light cruiser *Graudenz*, flagship of Scouting Group II, ran on a mine 15 miles southwest of Amrum Bank light vessel (Fig. 5–E). After the admiral had shifted his flag to the *Pillau*, the damaged ship returned to port. It was now evident that the swept channel

* NOTE.—In all references to courses and bearings, the degrees in parentheses represent the true courses and bearings.

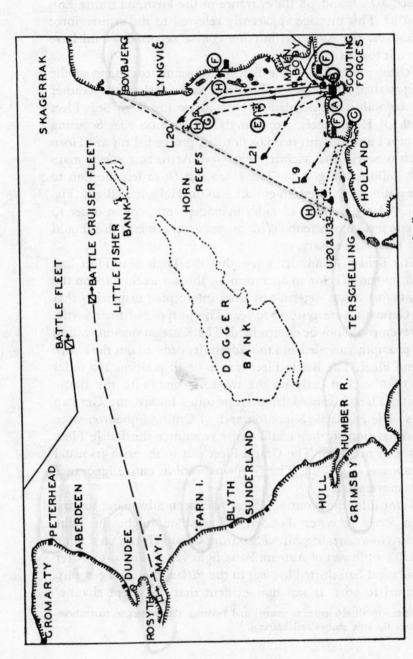

Fig. 5. Operations from noon, April 21, to noon, April 22.

west of Amrum Bank was unsafe; so the scouting forces turned back to the southward, rounded the light vessel, and proceeded northward a second time in the swept channel that ran to the eastward of the bank.

At 2:30 A.M. of the twenty-second the *L20**, *L21*, and *L9* took the air from Tondern, Nordholz, and Hage, respectively, to commence scouting the approaches to the Helgoland Bight at daylight (Fig. 5–F). At 4:25 Scouting Groups I and II each sighted, or believed they sighted, submarines to the southward of Vyl light vessel (Fig. 5–G). By this time the airships had reported that there were no enemy forces inside a line from Terschelling to Bovbjerg (Fig. 5). Had the British force that left Rosyth on the evening of the twentieth been proceeding toward Tondern its advance would have been detected by this time. A further advance of the High Seas Fleet therefore appeared unnecessary and would only expose the ships to submarine attack without any commensurate advantage. At 4:40 all ships, including the two submarines, were ordered back to the outer roads (Fig. 5–H). While returning, the *Frankfurt* reported being attacked by a submarine. About 6:00, the airships, as frequently happened, were recalled because of unfavorable weather.

During the morning of the twenty-second the Admiralty informed Jellicoe that the German battle cruisers had gone beyond Horn Reefs and the battleships as far as Lister Deep, but that now all were returning to their bases. The efficiency of the British Intelligence Service was thereby again proved, but such remarkable success in learning the movements of the enemy were made possible only by the incredible carelessness of the Germans in their use of the radio. The failure of the German Navy to take the most elementary precautions is the more remarkable in that Hindenburg had been enabled to win his crushing victory at Tannenberg only because of similar carelessness on the part of the Russian generals. In view of the changed situation, the Admiralty suggested that Jellicoe send a light cruiser force into the Skagerrak and keep the remainder of the Grand Fleet within supporting distance.

* NOTE.—The names of all German airships were made up of the letter "L" and a number (thus *L20*).

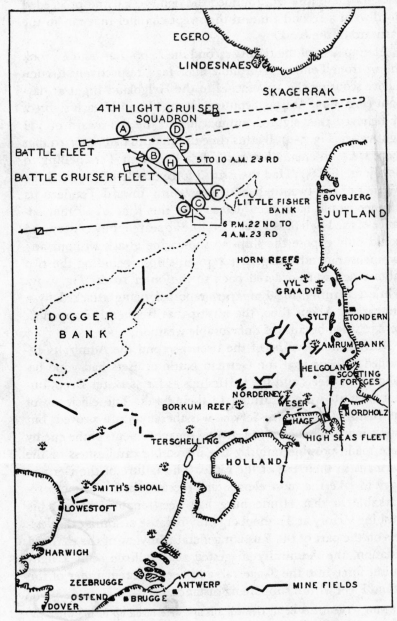

FIG. 6. Operations from noon, April 22, to noon, April 23.

In accordance with this suggestion, which was little less than an order, Jellicoe at 2:30 P.M. ordered the 4th Light Cruiser Squadron with three destroyers to proceed into the Skagerrak (Fig. 6–A). It was to arrive off The Skaw (Cape Skagen), the northern point of Denmark, at daylight on the twenty-third and then sweep to the westward. In the hope that this demonstration would draw out the High Seas Fleet, Jellicoe decided to assume a position of readiness in the vicinity of Horn Reefs early on the twenty-third. He ordered the Battle Cruiser Fleet to proceed directly toward Horn Reefs, and he continued to the eastward with the Battle Fleet to assume a supporting position (Fig. 6–B).

At 3:00 P.M. of the twenty-second Beatty ran into decreasing visibility. Soon he encountered a dense fog. At 6:00 P.M. the battle cruiser Australia and New Zealand collided (Fig. 6–C). Both ships were badly damaged. As they started back toward Rosyth, Beatty kept cruising back and forth in a position about 75 miles northwest (302°) from Horn Reefs, with the intention of closing the light vessel at daylight.

Shortly before dark, about 8:00 P.M., the Battle Fleet, preceded by its cruiser squadrons, steered 149° for Horn Reefs (Fig. 6–D). At 10:00 P.M. dense fog was encountered. Somewhat later the battleship Neptune collided with a merchant vessel. As the night wore on Jellicoe decided that it would be unwise to approach the Danish coast in such bad weather; so at 4:30 A.M. the Battle Fleet, then to the westward of Little Fisher Bank, turned to the northward. Although special signals had been arranged for a reversal of the Fleet's course by squadrons in succession from the rear, the destroyers Garland, Ambuscade, and Ardent staged a triple collision. The Ardent had to be towed home stern first. It can be imagined that the British commander in chief was none too well pleased with the numerous collisions that had marked the night's work. Making due allowance for the difficulty of operating a large fleet in fog, collisions were far too frequent. This comment is offered with an intimate knowledge of the operations of our own fleet in fog and low visibility.

Jellicoe had been seriously considering another advance

toward Horn Reefs on the twenty-fourth. However, the low fuel capacity of his destroyers made this plan difficult of execution. Finally, hearing that all was quiet in the Helgoland Bight, he decided not to attempt a further advance. This was a most fortunate decision for Scheer, for had Jellicoe remained in the vicinity of Horn Reefs for another day, he could easily have cut the line of retreat of the High Seas Fleet off Terschelling with a priceless opportunity to annihilate it.

The Battle Cruiser Fleet must have been authorized to return to port soon after 4:30 A.M. of the twenty-third (Fig. 6–G), because it arrived at Rosyth at 8:30 P.M. the same day. To do this 18 knots must have been averaged, even if the start were made promptly at 4:30 A.M. The Battle Fleet remained cruising to the westward of Little Fisher Bank to cover the return of the disabled destroyers. It probably commenced its return at about 10:00 A.M. (Fig. 6–H). It arrived at Scapa at 6:00 A.M. of the twenty-fourth.

About April 17 Admiral Bayly, commanding at Queenstown, Ireland, had been warned that an Irish revolution would break out about Easter and that the Germans would endeavor to land arms. This was another proof of the uncanny efficiency of the British Intelligence Service. Bayly had stationed his armed trawlers on patrol stations off the coast. Also, on the twentieth he had received as a temporary re-enforcement from the Grand Fleet the light cruiser *Gloucester* and 4 destroyers.

Meanwhile, on April 12 the *Libau* had passed out of the North Sea between Scotland and Norway. Keeping well to the northward, she had reached the vicinity of Iceland on the seventeenth. Then Lieutenant Spindler headed southward for the Irish coast. Promptly at 4:00 P.M. of the twentieth he reached Tralee Bight, the appointed rendezvous with the *U–19*. The submarine actually arrived during the night, but could not find the *Libau,* probably as neither vessel dared to show lights. Casement and his two companions were landed from the *U–19.* However, he conducted himself so carelessly that he was soon captured; and, what was worse, Spindler was unable to make contact with the Irish to deliver his equipment. Possibly the British agents had much to do with this failure.

The next morning, the twenty-first, the *Libau* was boarded at 5:00 A.M. by the captain and six men of an armed trawler. Spindler played his part so well as to gain the complete confidence of the British officer, who said that he was searching for a German steamer with munitions for the Irish. However, the news of Casement's discovery aroused the suspicions of the British. The auxiliary cruiser *Bluebell* appeared and directed the *Libau* to proceed with her to Queenstown. En route six more patrol craft and a destroyer detachment joined the escort. The British did not attempt to board and kept at a good distance, apparently fearing concealed torpedo tubes.

Spindler now saw that he was caught. Escape was impossible, as was likewise any effective resistance. It remained only to prevent his munitions from falling into the hands of the enemy. Quietly shifting his crew into naval uniform, he boldly hoisted the German man-of-war flag on the *Libau* and blew up his ship, which in 4 minutes had disappeared. He and his crew were rescued by the British.

Spindler's handling of the *Libau* on this hazardous adventure was most creditable. So much cannot be said for the other arrangements. Better contact with the Irish should have been provided for. Also, Casement or other Irish agents should have proceeded in the *Libau*, for the purpose of getting in touch with the revolutionists ashore. To expect that two vessels, proceeding without lights, could effect a rendezvous at night close off an enemy's coast was too much. However, when all is said, there was never much chance that the *Libau's* mission could succeed. Secret undertakings that have to be co-ordinated far in advance and from a great distance have rarely succeeded.

By a most unusual coincidence three important events occurred on Easter Sunday, April 24. The Irish with some 12,000 men under arms seized Dublin. Admiral Bacon with the Dover Patrol, supported by part of the Harwich Force, laid a great barrage of mines and nets off the Flanders coast, while Commodore Tyrwhitt had the remainder of his force at sea for a practice cruise. Scheer commenced his demonstration against Lowestoft and Yarmouth on the English coast, assisted by the Airship Detachment and the Flanders U-Flotilla.

Let us describe first the interesting developments along the Belgian coast. At 4:00 P.M. of the twenty-third 4 large mine layers left Sheerness (Fig. 7–A). They were escorted by 8 Harwich destroyers, of which the *Laforey* was the flag boat. About the same time six divisions of drifters and 6 mine-laying trawlers left Dover Fig. (7–B). They were escorted by 4 more Harwich destroyers and supported by 2 monitors of the Dover Patrol. At 4:00 A.M. of the twenty-fourth these various forces were off the Belgian coast (Fig. 7–C). There they were joined by the remainder of the Dover Patrol. By 7:30 A.M. the mine layers had completed a double row of mines about 15 miles long generally parallel to the coast. They commenced their return in company with the *Laforey's* detachment. Meanwhile, the drifters had completed laying a barrage of 13 miles of mined anchored nets and remained to watch them, supported by detachments of the Dover Patrol.

The purpose, of course, of these operations was to prevent the exit of the German submarines from their bases at Ostend and Zeebrugge. The effectiveness of the barrage was, as it happened, soon to be given its first test and on a scale little expected by Bacon. Admiral Schröder had been directed by the Naval Staff to send out all his available submarines to assist in Scheer's demonstration against Lowestoft. Accordingly, Commander Bartenbach, the efficient commander of the Flanders U-Flotilla had directed that 7 UC-boats should lay mine fields off Harwich and the Thames. Four UB-boats were to form a submarine line 17 miles long at right angles to the coast at Southwold. Two others were to take station south of the old German mine fields running past Smith's Knoll light vessel to assist the scouting forces in avoiding this hazard.

It was probably late in the evening of the twenty-third that the 6 UB-boats left Zeebrugge. Five of them were clear before the arrival of the British forces the next morning, but *UB–13* apparently was lost in the newly laid barrage, as she failed to return (Fig. 7–D). The UC-boats, of which only 5 were available, left port early on the twenty-fourth. In consequence, they ran directly into the barrage. Only the *UC–6* was able to break through. The *UC–5* ran down her battery and returned to port. The *UC–1* ran directly into the mined nets. After several explosions, she broke clear and was able to return to port. The *UC–7*, after unsuccessful attempts to pierce the barrage, lay on the bottom until dark. The *UC–10* became entangled in a net and was attacked by patrol craft with depth charges. Finally, at 8:35 P.M. she came to the surface. However, when she ran into another net, her captain decided to return to port. Thus, Bacon's barrage had quickly proved its effectiveness. One submarine had been destroyed and 4 others forced to return to port after many narrow escapes.

Meanwhile, great activity was seen along the Belgian coast. An English seaplane dropped two bombs near the Zeebrugge lock gate. In return, 6 German seaplanes had bombed British vessels. No hits resulted from these attacks, as the art of bombing and the design of bomb sights were then in a very elementary stage.

About 11:00 A.M. German seaplane 503 directed a distant-controlled motor boat loaded with explosives, toward a British monitor. Unfortunately, when 4 miles from its target, the motor stopped and the seaplane had to explode this novel form of surface-running torpedo. A German seaplane was shot down by a British fighting plane. At 12:40 P.M. Tirpitz Battery, four 11-inch guns, straddled the monitor *General Wolfe* at 32,000 yards with four salvos without hitting (Fig. 8–A).

At 3:00 P.M. 3 destroyers of the German Z-Flotilla (*V67**, *V68*, and *V47*) engaged 4 British destroyers of the M-class (Fig. 8–F). Coming under the fire of a monitor, the German boats were forced back toward the support of their coast defense

---

* NOTE.—The Germans used both letters and numbers in the names of their destroyers and submarines. To help the reader readily to distinguish between the two classes of ships, the names of destroyers are written without the hyphen (thus *V67*) and the names of submarines are written with a hyphen between the letter and the number (thus *U-9*).

batteries. When the British destroyers followed in hot pursuit, all 4 of them were hit at 16,000 yards by the remarkably accurate fire of the shore batteries. The *Melpomene* was brought to a stop with a shell in her engine-room. Another destroyer was put out of action.

Mines also took their toll of the allied forces. The British drifter *Clover Bank* was sunk and the French destroyer *Obusier* severely damaged by these weapons. The mines causing the damage apparently were planted by the Allies (Fig. 8–G). Thus nearly every form of coastal warfare and every naval weapon had been used in the numerous combats that resulted from Bacon's offensive.

While these operations were taking place off the Irish and Belgian coasts, the High Seas Fleet had been preparing to leave its bases early on the twenty-fourth. Suddenly, at 3:38 A.M. the seaplane station at List reported that a plane of unknown nationality had landed by the Hoyer lock gate near the Tondern airship hangars. The British radio calls used during the previous attack on March 25 were reported, probably erroneously, to have been heard. At daylight, seaplanes commenced scouting from List (Fig. 7–E). However, at 5:15 A.M. army headquarters at Hamburg reported that only propeller noises had been heard during a fog over Hoyer. Scheer then ordered the patrol forces to scout northwestward from Amrum Bank. The rest of the fleet was directed to assemble in the outer roads ready to proceed on short notice. At 6:40 A.M. "false alarm" was broadcast, the patrol forces were recalled, and preparations were made to commence the attack on Lowestoft. Commander Strasser, chief of the Naval Airship Detachment, reported that he was sending 7 or 8 airships to bomb English towns during the night. Due to the sickness of Vice Admiral Hipper, Rear Admiral Boedicker assumed command of the scouting forces, flying his flag from the *Seydlitz*. All was ready for the execution of Scheer's ambitious plan. He was commencing it under the most favorable conditions. The weather was good and the Grand Fleet had just arrived in its distant bases, where the vessels were now engaged in refueling.

CHAPTER V

THE OPERATION OF APRIL 25

AT 9:55 A.M. of the twenty-fourth the scouting forces, consisting of Scouting Groups I and II and attached destroyer flotillas, left the outer Jade Roads (Fig. 7–F). Forty minutes later Scheer received the first news of Bacon's offensive against the Belgian coast. By 12:40 P.M. the main body had left port to follow the scouting forces (Fig. 8–B). It consisted of Battle Squadrons I, II, and III; Scouting Group IV; and attached destroyer flotillas. At 1:00 P.M. Boedicker, when off Norderney Island, turned to the northward to avoid being sighted by observers on the Dutch Islands in the very clear weather (Fig. 8–C). He was confronted with the usual option of difficulties that war presents to responsible commanders. The location of neutral territory so close to the German naval bases was one of the geographical disadvantages against which the Germans had to contend. However, to avoid the observers who he knew would report his movements, Boedicker had to leave the main swept channel that led past Terschelling. This exposed him to the hazards of mines. At first the scouting forces were escorted by seaplanes. At 2:35 the airship *L7* which had left Tondern at 10:40 A.M. joined. The use of this airship for escort duty was advantageous in that it provided an excellent opportunity for sighting submarines on the surface or running with periscope out. On the other hand, the submarine could see the airship for long distances. Suspecting that she was escorting a force of surface vessels, submarine captains might be attracted towards her and thus make contact with the battle cruisers.

After proceeding 40 miles to the northward, the scouting forces turned to course WNW. (279°). Almost immediately the *Seydlitz* at 2:48 ran on a mine (Fig. 8–E). The explosion tore in her side a hole 90 square meters in area. Unfortunately, the damage was abreast the torpedo room, a large compartment

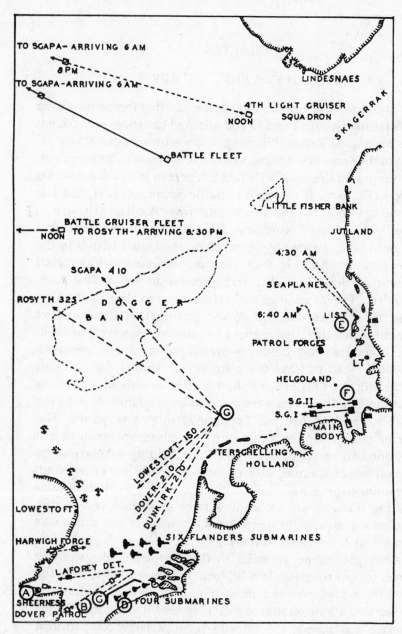

TO SCAPA–ARRIVING 6 AM

8 PM

TO SCAPA–ARRIVING 6 AM

NOON

4TH LIGHT CRUISER SQUADRON

BATTLE FLEET

LINDESNAES

SKAGERRAK

LITTLE FISHER BANK

JUTLAND

BATTLE CRUISER FLEET
TO ROSYTH–ARRIVING 8:30 PM

NOON

SCAPA 410

ROSYTH 325

D O G G E R
B A N K

4:30 AM

SEAPLANES

6:40 AM

LIST

E

PATROL FORCES

L 7

HELGOLAND

S.G. II

S.G. I

F

MAIN
BODY

G

TERSCHELLING
HOLLAND

LOWESTOFT–150

DOVER–210

DUNKIRK–2TO

LOWESTOFT

HARWICH FORCE

SIX FLANDERS SUBMARINES

LAFOREY DET.

A

SHEERNESS
DOVER PATROL

B

C

D

FOUR SUBMARINES

FIG. 7. Operations from noon, April 23, to noon, April 24.

which is one of the weak spots in the defensive strength of battleships and battle cruisers with torpedo armament. The scouting forces had run into a field of 850 mines laid by the British
ships *Princess Margaret* and *Angora* in November, 1915. The
other 4 battle cruisers turned back quickly to the southward, but
the *Seydlitz* believed it safer to keep on to the westward, particularly as two submarines were reported, possibly erroneously,
astern. Scouting Group II and the *L7* remained with the *Seydlitz* which continued to fly Boedicker's flag. The placing of his
flagship out of action in so sudden a manner must have been
disconcerting and inconvenient for the commander of the scouting forces, upon whose skill and resolute judgment the result
of the operation so largely depended. This was the more unfortunate in that Boedicker was only temporarily in command.

Meanwhile, at about noon the airships had left their hangars
for the attack on the English coast: the *L11, L13,* and *L18* from
Hage; the *L14, L17,* and *L21* from Nordholz; and the *L20* and
L23 from Tondern. Soon the *L14* was forced to return because
of motor trouble.

Towards 4:00 P.M. the 4 remaining battle cruisers, which
were returning toward Norderney on a southerly course, met the
main body proceeding to the westward (Fig. 8–I). They took
station ahead of the main body on a westerly course. Proceeding
at high speed, they gradually left the battleships astern. Because
of the mining of the *Seydlitz,* Scheer decided that the northerly
route was impracticable. He accepted the risk of being sighted
and reported from the Dutch Islands in the unusually clear
weather.

At 6:00 P.M. the *Seydlitz* was stopped and Boedicker with his
staff embarked in the *V28.* Heading for the position of Scouting
Group I, he hoisted his flag in the *Lützow* at 7:30 P.M. (Fig.
8–K). Scouting Group II had joined the battle cruisers about
half an hour earlier. Meanwhile, the *Seydlitz,* at 6:07 having discharged the flag officer, steered to the southward (Fig. 8–J). At
7:30 the *L7* headed for Hage (Fig. 8–L), where she landed at
11:40 P.M. At 8:52 P.M. the *Seydlitz* headed eastward for the Ems
under the escort of two destroyers. She had lost 11 men and

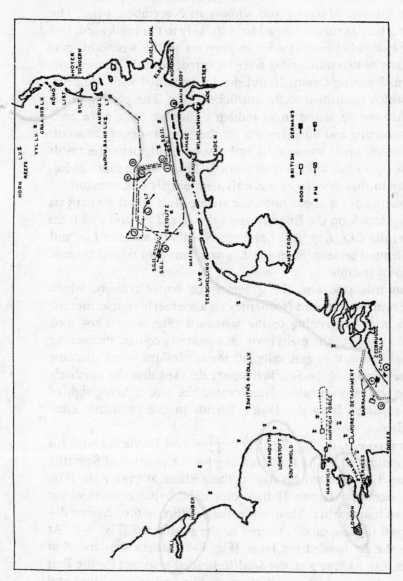

Fig. 8. Operations from noon to 8:00 P.M., April 24.

taken on board 1,400 tons of water. Extensive repairs would be necessary before she could again proceed to sea.

At 9:00 P.M. the scouting forces went on a southwesterly course at 21 knots (Fig. 9). Scouting Group I was screened ahead and on each beam by three groups, each consisting of 2 light cruisers and 4 destroyers. At 8:30 P.M. Scheer was informed that the British had recalled all patrol vessels. This was a clear indication that his advance toward the English coast was known to the enemy. He also received for the first time the news that British light cruisers had been seen off the Norwegian coast on the twenty-third. At midnight the main body changed course to the southwestward (Fig. 9) and followed the track of the scouting forces at 14 knots. Six light cruisers of Scouting Group IV and 34 destroyers were screening the 3 battle squadrons.

As Scheer could well guess, the British Intelligence Service had long since determined the fact that the High Seas Fleet was advancing toward the English coast. It had functioned with its usual efficiency. Perhaps, it might be said that its achievements during this operation were finer than any thus far. Of this the reader may judge. As early as 3:50 P.M. The Admiralty informed Jellicoe that Dublin was held by the Irish insurgents, that the High Seas Fleet seemed to be coming out, and that a demonstration against the east coast was possible. The Harwich Force was recalled from its practice cruise and the Grand Fleet was placed on 2 hours' notice. At 5:00 P.M. Beatty reported that the battle cruisers could leave on 2 hours' notice as directed. Jellicoe stated that he could not reach this condition of readiness until 7:00 P.M. He added that a strong southerly wind was blowing. This would slow down the speed of his fleet if ordered toward Terschelling.

At 6:00 P.M. Jellicoe received news, probably from deciphered German dispatches and direction-finder bearings, that Scouting Group I at 3:00 had been 40 miles west (257°) of Helgoland, steering northwest (302°). This information was remarkably correct. The only error was about 15 minutes in the time. It will be remembered that the *Seydlitz* had been mined at 2:48 and that the other battle cruisers had then proceeded to the southward. According to Corbett, Jellicoe ordered the Battle

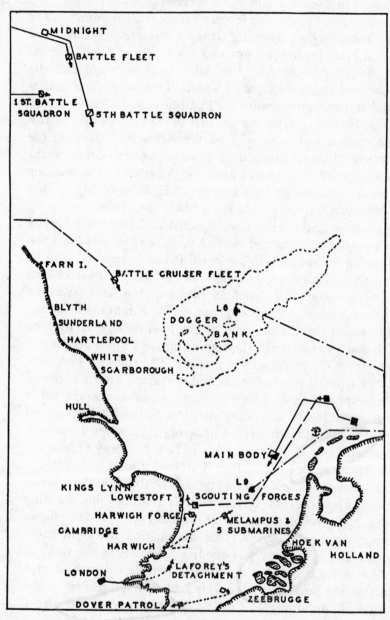

FIG. 9. Operations from 8:00 P.M., April 24, to 4:00 A.M., April 25.

Fleet to raise steam for full speed "upon receipt of word that the High Seas Fleet was moving." He directed the Battle Cruiser Fleet "to proceed at once" on a southeasterly course. The 5th Battle Squadron was directed to join the Battle Cruiser Fleet. Beatty was warned not to engage superior forces until the Battle Fleet was within supporting distance. The 3d Battle Squadron and 3d Cruiser Squadron, then based at Rosyth, were to take station off Farn Island to cover the Tyne. While the wording of Corbett's account is most indefinite, it may be inferred that these orders were issued shortly after 6:00 P.M.

At 7:50 P.M. the Admiralty, apparently not cognizant of Jellicoe's orders, ordered the Grand Fleet to proceed to sea to intercept the enemy. Meanwhile, it had already recalled the auxiliary patrols; ordered the local defense destroyer flotillas and the submarines to be in readiness; and directed the coastal aircraft to search to seaward at daybreak, attacking enemy forces encountered.

At 8:10 P.M. Jellicoe received a report that the *Seydlitz* had been mined. The other battle cruisers were said to be 50 miles northwest (302°) from Borkum. This was their actual position at 7:30. Finally, Battle Squadron III, which the other two battle squadrons seemed to be accompanying, was said to be proceeding along the Dutch islands toward a position 35 miles north (347°) of Terschelling, whence it was to steer southwest (212°). As Scheer actually went southwest (212°) from that exact position at midnight, it will be seen that the British leaders had the most unusual advantage of four hours' advance information of the enemy's intentions. This remarkable work of the British Intelligence Service, assisted evidently by carelessness on the part of the Germans, placed Scheer under a great disadvantage. It was indeed most fortunate that he was commencing his offensive at the most favorable time, when the Grand Fleet was fueling. Had it been at sea or even ready to leave its bases immediately, his daring offensive might have resulted disastrously.

A glance at the configuration of the North Sea is essential to a clear understanding of the advance toward Lowestoft. Let us, for example, take the point through which the German scouting forces passed on the way to their attack—35 miles bearing 000° from Terschelling Island (Fig. 7–G). From this point the distance to Lowestoft by a safe route through the mine fields was 150 miles. If we double this and add 25 miles steaming for the conduct of the bombardment, we have 325 miles of steaming that Boedicker would have to accomplish before he could regain point G. As it happened the distance from this point to Rosyth was also 325 miles. Therefore, unless Boedicker could get well to the westward of G before Beatty left Rosyth, a contact between these opposing forces was probable. To the best of Scheer's knowledge, Beatty had 10 battle cruisers, 15 light cruisers and destroyers. Boedicker had only 4 battle cruisers, 6 light cruisers and destroyers. It was evident that Scheer could not permit Beatty to attack Boedicker unless the latter was closely supported by the main body. This risk could be avoided by keeping the main body southwest of Terschelling and scouting to the northwestward to obtain information of the approach of the Battle Cruiser Fleet. By this means there was also some chance of luring Beatty into contact with the German main body, especially in low visibility.

If the Battle Fleet were in Scapa when the scouting forces passed G, there was little to fear from it, for it would have to steam 410 miles while the faster German units were going 325 miles. However, if the Battle Fleet had been at sea at the time within about 275 miles of G, there was a strong probability that the scouting forces could be intercepted during their return past Terschelling. This meant that Scheer would have to fight to the finish a greatly superior enemy posted directly on his line of retreat. To show the danger of such a contingency, it is only necessary to suppose that Scheer had commenced his operation on the twenty-third rather than the twenty-fourth, when the Grand Fleet was cruising near the Little Fisher Bank, only 165 miles from G. It could easily have intercepted the scouting forces. In supporting them, Scheer would have exposed his entire fleet to the danger of annihilation.

However, let us cease speculation and return to the actual situation on the evening of the twenty-fourth. When the British heard of Scheer's intended movements, they feared not only a bombardment of Lowestoft, but also attacks on shipping in the Downs, raids on the cross-channel routes, blocking operations against Dunkirk, and even landing attacks on the French coast. Instead of being concerned over such possibilities, the British should have welcomed them with delight. The distance from G to Dover and Dunkirk is no less than 210 miles. When this is doubled and 25 miles added for the accomplishment of the German mission, the total miles of steaming to regain G would be 445. When this is compared with the distance of 410 miles to Scapa, it will be seen that an operation so far afield would have imposed enormous risks of interception by the entire Grand Fleet. Assuming that the Battle Fleet were in Scapa when the Germans passed G, it could intercept them by steaming at 19 knots, as compared with a speed of 21 knots for the German scouting forces. Furthermore, there was a grave risk that some of the German vessels might be mined or torpedoed with consequent loss of speed. It must be concluded that the attack on Lowestoft was a sufficiently daring operation for Vice Admiral Scheer. A raid farther to the southward would have been foolhardy. As no decisive results could be expected from the actual attack on the coast or shipping, Lowestoft served Scheer's purpose best. The British should not have feared but rather welcomed a more extended advance.

In view of the unusual opportunity afforded to attack the High Seas Fleet and the probably decisive results of such an encounter, it appears that the Grand Fleet did not act with its usual promptness on this occasion. Beatty did not leave Rosyth until 10:45 P.M., or about 4 hours after the probable time of receipt of his orders. The 5th Battle Squadron left Scapa quite promptly at 9:00 P.M. The 1st Battle Squadron and the 7th Cruiser Squadron left Cromarty about 10:30. The remainder of the Battle Fleet did not proceed from Scapa until about 11:00, or 5 hours after Jellicoe had made his decision. Probably, there was some good reason for this delay.

The Admiralty drew up a detailed plan of operations for the forces immediately available for meeting the High Seas Fleet. This was as follows (Fig. 10):

(1) Six large submarines and a destroyer of the Harwich Submarine Flotilla were to take station midway between Southwold and Hoek van Holland. The Harwich submarines were commanded by Captain Waistell in the *Maidstone*. Corbett calls these boats the "Yarmouth submarines," although showing that they were based on Harwich.

(2) Commodore Tyrwhitt, with the 5th Light Cruiser Squadron, was to take station 20 miles NNE. (9°) from the submarines and endeavor to lead the Germans into their line.

(3) All Harwich Force destroyers, including those at the Nore, were to rendezvous with the submarines at daylight and *await instructions*.

(4) Six additional submarines of the Harwich Flotilla were to take station within gun range of Yarmouth.

The absolute futility of such orders will soon be amply demonstrated. Let it suffice at this time to make these points:

(1) It was highly inadvisable for a command ashore and distant from the theater of operations to issue detailed instructions concerning the tactical operation of forces afloat.

(2) The idea of massing a large destroyer force with the British submarines at daylight and in an area in which it was known that German submarines would operate shows a singular lack of tactical knowledge. Such concentrations were most liable to result in mistaking friend for foe. An order to "await instructions" is the one worst method of exercising command.

At 11:40 P.M. the Admiralty determined that the German scouting forces were steering for Yarmouth, followed at an interval of about 50 miles by their main body. The destroyer *Melamphus*, with the *E–55*, *E–29*, *E–26*, *E–22*, and *D–4*, had left Harwich just 30 minutes before (Fig. 10–A). Their assigned station was changed to one 33 miles more to the northward. Bacon was ordered to withdraw all his forces from the Belgian coast. His seaplanes were to fly up the coast to attack the enemy.

These orders meant that the newly laid barrage was to be left without any protection. This, in our opinion, was entirely unnecessary, as there was little possibility that the Germans would proceed that far from their bases. In any event it was premature.

At 10:10 P.M. seven German airships commenced crossing the English coast. They were frequently picked up by searchlights and brought under anti-aircraft gunfire. The *L13* was hit in the forward gondola by a high-explosive shell. A strong southwesterly wind prevented any of the airships from reaching London. Fog, rain, and thick layers of clouds made it so difficult to locate suitable targets that only a few ships could launch all their bombs. The *L13* reported bombing Norwich and a battery at Winterton. The *L16* bombed Cambridge and Norwich. The *L17* claimed to have made an effective bombing attack, probably on Lincoln. The *L20* attacked ships off Harwich. The other airships dropped only a few bombs. Corbett states that little damage was done by this bombing attack. It is true that the actual material effects probably were very slight. The Germans counted more on their moral effects and the cessation of work in the munition plants necessitated by the extinguishment of all lights during the attack.

Meanwhile, three other airships were to scout for the Fleet. The *L6* left Nordholz at 11:15 P.M. to commence scouting from a position 100 miles northwest (302°) from Terschelling Island. Another ship was to join the main body. The third was to scout to the southward. However, one of the airships, the *L7*, which had escorted the *Seydlitz* the day before, was unable to leave Hage until 2:30 A.M. Therefore, the *L9*, which had proceeded from Hage at 8:35 P.M., was ordered to take station between the scouting forces and the main body.

About 11:00 P.M. the *UB-18* and *UB-29* of the Flanders U-Flotilla reached their stations off the German mine fields (Fig. 10). They displayed the signal lights prearranged to warn the scouting forces out of this danger area. The *UB-6* and *UB-10* were on their appointed line off Southwold, but through error the *UB-12* took station off Lowestoft.

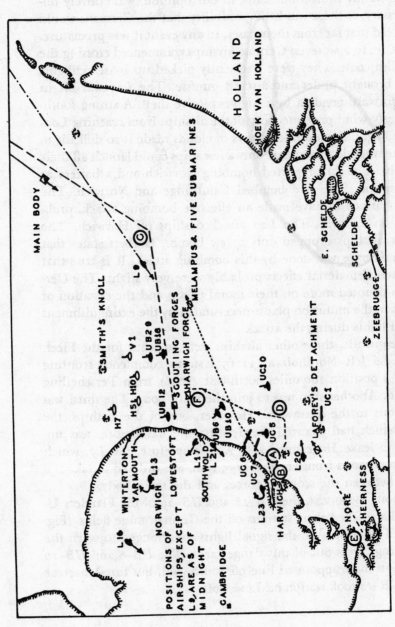

FIG. 10. Operations of the English coast from 8:00 P.M., April 24, to 4:00 A.M., April 25.

Now let us see how the British units executed the orders of the Admiralty. Of the six submarines directed to take station off Yarmouth, only the *H-5* ever reached its correct station within gun range of that port. Three others, *H-7, H-10,* and *V-1,* were from 12 to 20 miles off the port due to faulty interpretation of their orders. The two others did not arrive in time. Thus, in this respect, the orders of the Admiralty had failed almost completely to accomplish their purpose.

About 12:30 A.M. Commodore Tyrwhitt left Harwich (Fig. 10–B) with the following forces:

5th Light Cruiser Squadron—*Conquest, Cleopatra,* and *Penelope.*

Flotilla leader *Lightfoot* and 7 destroyers.

Flotilla leader *Nimrod* and 9 destroyers.

Before leaving port, the commodore had received the Admiralty's orders, together with the position and course of the German scouting forces. It was obvious that the enemy would pass the position assigned to the submarines long before the latter could reach it. In view of this neglect of the Admiralty to take cognizance of elementary considerations of time and space, it would obviously be futile for Tyrwhitt to try to take a station north of the submarines with the 5th Light Cruiser Squadron. Evidently he also considered that it would be useless for the destroyers in company with him to rendezvous with the submarines at daybreak. Thus, very properly, he decided entirely to disregard the orders issued by the Admiralty. He determined to take station off Lowestoft with both light cruisers and destroyers. At about 1:53 A.M. he headed in that direction with a flotilla on either beam (Fig. 10–D).

The two divisions of L-class destroyers of the Harwich Force, which under the leadership of the *Laforey* had escorted the mine layers of the Dover Patrol back to the Nore, could not again get to sea until 2:00 A.M. (Fig. 10–E). Therefore, they could not keep their rendezvous with the submarines. Thus, every single part of the Admiralty's combination had completely failed. One rarely finds in history such a futile and ill-advised

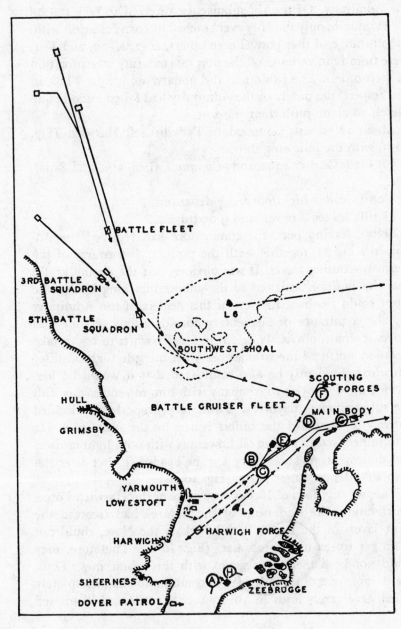

FIG. 11. Operations from 4:00 A.M. to noon, April 25.

attempt to exercise tactical command. By all means Tyrwhitt should have been given all the information at the disposition of the Admiralty and complete charge over the operations of all British forces in the vicinity.

While the British were making these dispositions to resist the German attack, the scouting forces were continuing at high speed toward their objective. At 1:30 A.M. the scouting forces had changed course directly for Lowestoft (Fig. 10–C). At 3:15 the *UB–18,* in position off the southern end of the mine fields, sighted the black smoke clouds of the battle cruisers to the eastward. In the moonlight to the northward loomed the silvery shape of the *L21,* in which the brilliant Commander Strasser was flying.

At 3:50 Commodore Tyrwhitt sighted the German forces to the northward just as the first dawn was breaking (Fig. 10–F). He immediately changed course to the northwestward. At 4:03 he counter-marched to the southward in a well-conceived attempt to draw the Germans after him (Fig. 12–A). As his ships were changing course they were made out by the *Rostock* and *Elbing* about two points forward of their port beam. These light cruisers, with four destroyers, were guarding the southern flank of Scouting Group I. The British light cruisers were at first thought to be the *Frankfurt* and *Wiesbaden,* which were stationed ahead of the German battle cruisers. As soon as Commodore Michelsen in the *Rostock* made out the strange ships to be British, he reported the fact to Rear Admiral Boedicker in the *Lützow.* The *Frankfurt* sank an armed trawler with gunfire.

At 4:07 the *Lützow,* leading the *Derfflinger, Moltke,* and *Von der Tann* and having arrived off Lowestoft, turned to the northward (Fig. 12–B). At 4:11 fire was opened at the town at ranges from 11,000 to 14,000 yards. After 6 minutes of rather heavy firing, the bombardment ended and the ships kept on to the northward toward Yarmouth. The shore batteries of Lowestoft had been silenced and about 200 houses had been destroyed.

At 4:24 the battle cruisers opened fire on Yarmouth (Fig. 12–G). However, the visibility was so poor that only the *Derf-*

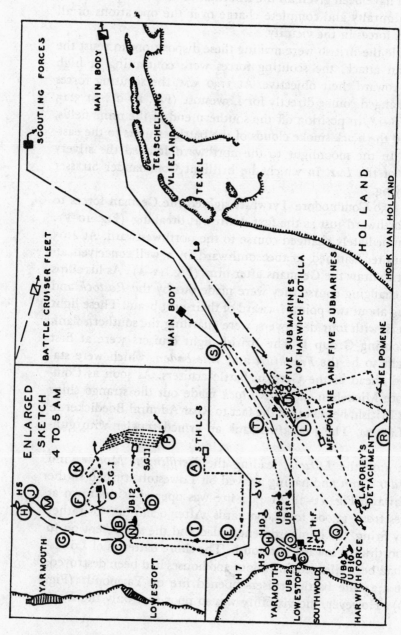

FIG. 12. Operations off the English coast from 4:00 A.M. to noon, April 25.

flinger continued after the first salvo. She fired only 14 rounds in 4 minutes. Even these had to be controlled with compass bearings. Meanwhile, the *Lützow* had sunk a second armed trawler with a 6-inch salvo. About 4:30 she led a counter-march to the southward (Fig. 12–H). Her turn was made just in time to avoid the *H–5* which was approaching to attack. Two other submarines were sighted by their own seaplanes. The latter, as Corbett admits, "knew nothing of the Yarmouth submarines and attacked them with bombs." This failure to co-ordinate the operations of the submarines and aircraft must be laid directly upon the Admiralty. Three other British seaplanes attacked the battle cruisers, but were driven off by gunfire (Fig. 12–J). Corbett admits that "their gallant efforts had no success." This is not surprising when we consider the crude bomb sights then available.

In the meantime the *Rostock* and *Elbing* had turned to the northward (Fig. 12–D) at 4:12 to follow the battle cruisers. In doing so they had lost contact with the British light cruisers. When the Germans disappeared, Tyrwhitt at 4:21 turned again to the northward (Fig. 12–E). This was certain to result in another contact with his far superior enemy, but Tyrwhitt in seeking it proved himself a proper commander of light forces. At 4:23 the *Rostock* turned southward (Fig. 12–F). At 4:30 she was again sighted by Tyrwhitt, who opened fire at long range (Fig. 12–I). His salvos fell short and the Germans reversed course in the hope of leading him under the fire of their battle cruisers. At 4:37 the two leading German light cruisers, now re-enforced by the remaining four, turned back to the southeastward (Fig. 12–K). They were now under the close support of their battle cruisers. At this critical moment, 4:42, the *Lützow* uselessly fired eight 12-inch rounds at Great Yarmouth lighthouse.

Tyrwhitt probably either saw or heard this firing, for about 4:47 he went ships left about (Fig. 12–N) in order to escape from a most dangerous situation. After the turn had been completed, he found that the six light cruisers of Scouting Group II were slightly abaft his port beam on a parallel southerly course. Slightly on his port quarter were the four battle cruisers of Scouting Group I distant between 13,000 and 15,000 yards. They were steering a slightly diverging course. Both these German units were firing rapidly and accurately on his three light cruisers. He was indeed in a bad spot.

Curiously enough, the situation which had existed in the Helgoland Bight action was now almost exactly repeated, but with the rôles reversed. Again 3 light cruisers were under the guns of a powerful battle cruiser squadron. Boedicker had a priceless opportunity to revenge the German light cruisers *Mainz, Köln,* and *Ariadne,* which had fought so gallantly on August 28, 1914. However, he failed to grasp it. The light cruisers of Scouting Group II, which later shot so effectively at Jutland, did not converge on their enemy quickly enough and their fire could not be effective at such long range. The fire of the battle cruisers was extremely accurate but, as they were steering a slightly diverging course instead of following directly in the track of the enemy, their gun range gradually increased. One 12-inch salvo landed squarely on the *Conquest.* It killed and wounded 40 and reduced her speed to 20 knots. Destroyers promptly covered her with a smoke screen and thus concealed her loss of speed from the enemy. One hit on the destroyer *Laertes* injured a boiler and wounded 5 men.

During the pursuit, several reports of submarines and torpedo tracks were received by the commander scouting forces. Two more seaplanes were driven off. Therefore, at 4:56 Boedicker prematurely broke off the pursuit and headed eastward (Fig. 12–O) toward his main body, which then was distant some 70 miles. Two minutes later Scouting Group II followed him (Fig. 12–P).

It is our opinion that Boedicker missed a splendid opportunity to win a marked success. To have annihilated a squadron of three light cruisers and possibly some destroyers was certainly more important from the viewpoints of both actual results and propaganda value than knocking down some houses ashore. Furthermore, to eliminate such a leader as Tyrwhitt was in itself no mean success, for, with the possible exception of Commodore Goodenough, he was the best leader of light forces on duty in the North Seas. However, there is much to be said for Boedicker. He had to bear in mind the constant danger of being intercepted by superior forces off Terschelling. Also, there was the ever-present danger from mines and submarines, which might reduce the speed of one of his battle cruisers at any instant. Furthermore, the very conception of the German "hit and run" tactics served to prevent them from waiting long enough to gain any decided success. Finally, it was not wise to expend too much ammunition on light cruisers when he might have to engage capital ships later. Perhaps, it was too much to expect that a commander suddenly given a higher and merely temporary command should accept the risks so necessary to gain a striking success; but it is only by accepting such risks that a naval commander may win greatness for himself and victory for his country. Remember what Nelson said: "Something must be left to chance; nothing is sure in a sea fight beyond all others."

In all, Scouting Group I had expended 198 rounds with their main, 330 with their secondary, and 37 with their secondary batteries against aircraft.

The *UB–6, UB–10,* and *UB–12* had observed the various actions off Lowestoft but, having been forced to submerge by the British seaplanes, their slow speed had prevented them from reaching positions for effective torpedo fire.

At 4:38 the *L9,* having reached its position between the scouting forces and the main body, was attacked by two British seaplanes. The airship turned before the wind to the northeastward and commenced to zigzag. One of the planes did not follow her. The first attack of the other was repulsed by machine-gun fire from the upper platform. In a second attack, however, the plane dropped five bombs from a position above the airship. Fortunately for the Germans, all missed. During the fight, the British seaplane had sighted the screen of the main body, but apparently did not make out the battle squadrons. Her pilot had done well. Bombing is the best method even today for attacking rigid airships.

When the distance to the returning scouting forces had been

reduced to 50 miles, Scheer at 5:20 reversed the course of the main body by squadrons. He steered at 15 knots (Fig. 11–B) for the prearranged position off Terschelling. Scouting Group IV, under the second leader of destroyers in the *Regensburg*, scouted toward the northwestward to cover the northern flank. This was a very essential procedure to locate British forces that might be approaching from Rosyth and Scapa. The *L9* also was ordered to scout to the northwestward, but as usual could not obey her orders, as Strasser had felt compelled to recall all airships due to southeast winds. These winds had carried the *L6* far to the northward of her assigned station. At 3:20 A.M. she had headed southward to rectify her station; but at 4:05 she also had been forced to turn back toward Tondern by the general recall. The recall of these two airships lost for us some interesting war experience. Had they continued scouting, the airships might well have located the Battle Cruiser Fleet, for which Scheer might have attempted to lay a trap off Terschelling.

It was not until about 5:45, two hours late, that the *Melampus* and her 5 submarines arrived in the vicinity of their prescribed stations. The submarine flotilla commander, Captain Waistell, in order to maintain a more direct control over his boats, had joined Tyrwhitt in the *Lurcher*, accompanied by another destroyer. He directed that the submarine line be extended as far north as 53°-15'. The use of destroyers as flag boats of submarine flotillas and as radio relay ships was an excellent feature of the British organization and greatly facilitated command by permitting the rapid transmission of orders to the submarines, a very difficult task, especially when they were submerged. In this case the orders apparently were received promptly by the submarines, but the Germans were able to evade the northernmost submarine, the *E–55*, by about 4 miles. At 5:40 Tyrwhitt, after having made emergency repairs to the *Conquest*, proceeded northeastward at 22 knots to regain contact. His 3 light cruisers were in line abreast at 3 miles distance (Fig. 12–Q). At 5:55 the *Laforey's* detachment also headed to the northeastward, but from a position about 25 miles south of Tyrwhitt (Fig. 12–R). At 7:10 the *Melampus* joined the *Laforey*.

While the British were making these new dispositions, the *UB–18* and *UB–29* left their appointed stations off the mine fields and proceeded southeastward. The *UB–29* was commanded by the efficient Lieutenant Pustkuchen. Having been forced to submerge by the British seaplanes, this boat at 6:00 saw the battle cruisers pass on their return journey. An hour later it sighted a British submarine and avoided her by submerging. As Tyrwhitt passed she was sighted by the *Cleopatra*. At 8:25 the submarine, again proceeding on the surface, sighted the *Laforey's* detachment heading directly for her and once more submerged.

At 8:30 Tyrwhitt sighted the smoke of the German battle cruisers but 15 minutes later he was recalled by the Admiralty (Figs. 11–c and 12–s). Unless the Admiralty had given up all hope of inflicting losses on the Germans, this recall was decidedly premature. If it had any hope of accomplishing anything with the Battle Cruiser Fleet or the submarines which probably were stationed off Terschelling, it was of primary importance that some force should maintain contact with and track the German battle cruisers. If the Admiralty had given up all hope of doing anything, to be consistent it should have recalled the Grand Fleet also. During his return Tyrwhitt again made contact with the active *UB–29*. This time her hunting was more successful. At 9:25 a skillfully directed torpedo blew away the *Penelope's* rudder and reduced her speed to 20 knots (Fig. 12–t).

During the forenoon the *UB–18*, commanded by Lieutenant Otto Steinbrinck, was also enjoying herself. At 5:45 she had seen 2 German light cruisers and 4 destroyers pass to the northward. Soon thereafter she sighted the *Melampus* and 2 British submarines with their radio masts rigged. Her attack on 1 submarine was unsuccessful. At 8:00 A.M. 9 destroyers passed to the northward. Three more submarines were seen assembling near a destroyer, probably the *Lurcher*. At 10:20 Steinbrinck was nearly rammed by the *E–26*, but escaped by a deep dive. About an hour later he commenced stalking the *E–22*. At 11:40 he sank her with a torpedo fired at about 400 yards (Fig. 12–u). Although hostile submarines were in sight, Steinbrinck saved two British seamen. After sinking a fishing cutter, this expertly handled submarine returned to port.

During the return of the scouting forces, the destroyer *G41* sank the British trawler *King Stephen* and took prisoner her crew of 13. It was this vessel that, contrary to all the customs of honorable warfare on the sea, had deliberately allowed the crew of the wrecked airship *L19* to drown without any attempt at rescue. This behavior had now brought its just reward. Five neutral steamers were boarded and sent into Cuxhaven with prize crews.

At 6:30 A.M. the deciphering station at Bruges, Belgium, had reported the reception of British radio messages directing their forces to return from the Belgian coast and for the destroyers of the Dover Patrol to refuel and assemble off Dunkirk. As the Harwich Force had not again been sighted, Scheer believed that there was no further hope of inflicting any losses on the enemy; so at 9:20 A.M. he directed the High Seas Fleet to return to port. This may have been influenced by two submarine attacks on Battle Squadron II off Terschelling (Fig. 11–D). It might appear that this retirement of the main body placed the scouting forces in danger of being intercepted by Beatty, but presumably Scouting Group IV had covered enough distance to the northwestward to show that no such danger existed. It would have been well for the German historians to have covered this important point more specifically.

Boedicker, in order to avoid the submarines that had attacked the main body off Terschelling, set his course at 9:30 for a position 40 miles northward of that island (Fig. 11–E). This change of direction increased the possibility of a contact with the Battle Cruiser Fleet. Evidently this must have been given consideration by Boedicker when he made his decision. To secure his line of retreat he should have used his light forces to scout to the northward to give warning of the approach of hostile forces. It is not stated whether or not this essential precaution was taken. In any event, as we shall soon see, the scouting forces arrived to the northward of Terschelling somewhat before the Battle Cruiser Fleet. Thence, at 11:45 they changed course to the eastward and about 12:00 noon again to the southeast to skirt the Belgian coast (Fig. 11–F). The main body which was about 45 miles ahead was again attacked by a submarine at noon (Fig. 11–G). The British make no mention of these submarine attacks. They may have been some of the frequent false alarms.

During the morning the Grand Fleet had been steaming in a southeasterly direction in an attempt to cut off the retreat of the Germans. At 4:06 a report was received from Tyrwhitt that he had sighted battle cruisers and light cruisers off the coast. As he had not sighted the Germans until 3:50, this was very prompt work on his part. It also shows the efficiency of the British communications. Jellicoe ordered full speed for the entire Grand Fleet. At 4:20 the Admiralty informed the Fleet that Lowestoft was being bombarded. At 5:40 the Aldeburgh radio station stated that the German battle cruisers were steaming to the eastward. These messages gave Jellicoe and Beatty an accurate picture of the situation.

At 8:07 A.M. Beatty rounded the southern edge of the southwest shoal off the Dogger Bank and headed somewhat to the northward of Terschelling. Had he set his course at 12:47 A.M. toward Terschelling across that part of the Dogger Bank that shows a minimum depth of 12 fathoms, he could have saved 12 miles. However, such a course probably was considered unsafe because of mine fields and wrecks. It is noted on Corbett's chart that Beatty's speed from 2:48 to 3:35 was 22.2 knots; from 3:35 to 8:07, 22.5 knots; and from 8:07 to 12:30 P.M., 19.6 knots. This reduction of speed lost 12 miles. The delay of two hours in leaving Rosyth was equivalent to a loss of 45 miles. Thus, the total delay of the Battle Cruiser Fleet could be counted as 57 or, possibly, 69 miles.

At 12:30 P.M. Beatty reversed course and returned to port. He had missed Boedicker by only 45 miles. Thus, it appears that by more prompt action Beatty could have made contact with Boedicker. However, in this case Scouting Group IV might have discovered his advance and in all probability Scheer would have been able to come to the support of his scouting forces. He might even have been able to lure Beatty under the guns of his Battle Squadrons, if the British Light Cruiser Squadrons were poorly handled. In fact, any success by either side was contingent upon faulty handling of the hostile light cruisers, the duty of which it was to prevent surprise by superior forces.

The retirement of the British forces from the Belgian coast left the newly laid barrage at the mercy of the Germans. Their torpedo boats on the twenty-fifth were able to destroy part of it and to sink an armed trawler that had not received the order to withdraw (Fig. 11–H).

The material losses in this interesting operation were not important. The mining of the *Seydlitz* constituted the principal loss for the Germans. It was over a month before her hull was properly repaired. This indirectly delayed considerably the German sortie that resulted in the Battle of Jutland. The Germans also lost 1 submarine and 1 seaplane, while an airship was hit and slightly damaged by a high-explosive shell. The British lost 1 submarine, had 2 light cruisers severely damaged, 5 destroyers damaged, and 5 patrol craft sunk. The French had 1 destroyer damaged. The moral effects were quite considerable. These will soon be described.

The notable errors were the futile attempts of the Admiralty to direct tactical operations from a distance and the carelessness of the Germans in sending radio messages without the use of proper ciphers. This last observation does not detract from the work of the British Intelligence Service, which was little short of miraculous. The British commanders not only had accurate knowledge of the positions and courses of the German forces at frequent intervals, but also knew Scheer's intentions many hours in advance. This to a great extent transferred the initiative from the Germans to the British.

The operations demonstrated in a striking way the complete inability of the German airships to accomplish anything either by scouting or bombing.

Submarines also played a disappointing rôle when it is considered how many were massed in a small area. The unusually high speed of the surface craft doubtless increased the difficulty of their attacks.

While the use of seaplanes for bombing naval vessels was a complete failure, the art was then in its infancy. In fact, this was the first case, so far as known, where aircraft actually bombed capital ships under way at high speed.

Due to improvements in submarines and aircraft, a bombardment such as that of Lowestoft by capital ships would today be attended by risks out of all proportion to the direct material results that might be gained.

The effects of the operation of April 25 were considerable in both Germany and England. The ability of the High Seas Fleet to carry through with fair success an operation of such considerable danger naturally encouraged the Germans. In England, as Corbett says, "the impunity with which the enemy had insulted our east coast after his long inactivity came with something of a shock to public opinion." Lord Balfour even felt it necessary to issue a "reassuring pronouncement" to the mayors of Lowestoft and Yarmouth. He openly promised a redistribution of naval forces that would make another raid, as Corbett says, "highly dangerous to the enemy." The issuance of such a statement was highly questionable from both naval and political viewpoints. It magnified the effect of the German blow in allied and neutral nations and served to encourage the Germans. Also, it gave the enemy information which would be of value in his future operations. Furthermore, if the Germans should now repeat their success, Balfour's idle threats would place him in an insecure political position. He had, as it were, asked for a vote of confidence on a matter of very secondary importance. Would it have not been far better to have openly said "C'est la guerre," and then made secret and adequate dispositions to intercept the Germans the next time they came out? Finally, should he not have pointedly informed the British commander in chief that his old letter of October 30, 1914, no longer had the approval of the Admiralty?

Curiously enough, the one good point made by Jellicoe in this letter no longer met with the approval of the Admiralty, although Jellicoe was not so informed. The commander in chief had asked that when battle was imminent, the Harwich Force should re-enforce his fleet. The bombardment of Lowestoft apparently convinced the Admiralty that this was no longer desirable, for it declined to allow Tyrwhitt to carry out the agreement while Jutland was being fought. This tying down of the Harwich Force to local defense was an important effect of the operation of April 25.

The distribution of the British naval forces advertised by Balfour was of very doubtful value. Various plans had been discussed for several months. In general the Admiralty and Beatty favored the movement of a part of the Grand Fleet to the southward. Jellicoe resisted this argument with all his power. We have seen the same disagreement in 1914, when Beatty's forces were moved south to Rosyth and made virtually an independent command. The new proposals would increase Beatty's forces at the expense of those under Jellicoe's direct command. In view of the contrast between the characteristics of the two principal officers afloat, it is possible that personalities played their parts in these discussions.

The first point at issue was the transfer of the 3d Battle Squadron of second-line battleships and the 3d Cruiser Squadron of armored cruisers from Rosyth to the Thames. Jellicoe seems to have consented readily to this proposal which, in fact, was not of primary importance. These squadrons arrived at their new stations on May 2. Their senior officer, Vice Admiral Bradford, was formally detached from the Grand Fleet and placed directly under the orders of the Admiralty. It was further agreed that the 3d Battle Squadron should be re-enforced by the *Dreadnought*. This would, as Corbett says, make them "quite able to deal with the German battle cruisers at their present strength." It was believed that there were only four German battle cruisers available.

To improve further the defensive position along the east coast, it was agreed that the submarine flotilla then at Rosyth should be moved south to Yarmouth. This, except for two boats, was done. There were already other flotillas at Dover, Harwich, and Blyth. At the latter base was the newly formed 11th Flotilla of the Grand Fleet.

Now that a part of the forces based at Rosyth had been moved southward, the Admiralty proposed that the fast 5th Battle Squadron be moved there from Scapa. This squadron was composed of 5 splendid new battleships, the most powerful in the Grand Fleet. The attitude of Jellicoe and Beatty upon this proposal to transfer such a force from one to the other was not difficult to forecast. "This solution," as Corbett naïvely writes, "was warmly recommended by Admiral Beatty, but the commander in chief saw serious objections." Yes, quite naturally!

The arguments advanced by Beatty were, to say the least, quite ingenuous. After having agreed very readily that 1 very old first-line and 6 very inferior second-line battleships (equal perhaps to 3 battle cruisers) "were quite able to deal with the German battle cruisers at their present strength," it was claimed that, because of 2 new ships, the *Lützow* and *Hindenburg*, the 10 British battle cruisers would require "some corresponding re-enforcement." Some comments on this line of reasoning are in order. First, it was perfectly futile to effect a naval redistribution based partly on the present enemy strength and partly on his strength at some future date, using whichever figure fitted best to each distinct argument. Second, it is difficult to believe that the highly efficient British Intelligence Service really thought the *Hindenburg* was ready for service. In any event both the *Lützow* and *Hindenburg* would be as much a menace to Bradford as to Beatty. Thus we see that the argument narrowed down to the fact that Bradford, with the equivalent of 3 or 4 battle cruisers, could better meet a force, variously estimated as from 4 to 6 battle cruisers, than could Beatty with 10 battle cruisers, supported by numerous light cruisers and destroyers.

It is no wonder that Jellicoe saw "serious objections" to such a line of reasoning. Furthermore, he argued with justice that the 5 powerful 25-knot battleships formed his advanced wing and that his tactical plans for a fleet action counted heavily upon their being present and in proper station. After properly resisting this proposal to greatly magnify the force of his principal subordinate, with whom he did not see eye to eye on tactical

questions, Jellicoe submitted an alternate proposal. He would
bring the entire Grand Fleet south to Rosyth and the Humber
as soon as those bases could be properly protected. Thus, he
would retain direct control over his own battleships and also
bring the Battle Cruiser Fleet much more closely under his
command. This would permit the operation of the Grand Fleet
as a single well-co-ordinated force. It was decidedly the thing to
do.

CHAPTER VI

THE OPERATION OF MAY 4

DURING A brief intermission in these interminable discussions, the Grand Fleet carried out a well-planned operation. This, while generally similar to the previous air attack on Tondern, was superior to it in every respect. While the initial step in the plan was again to be a seaplane attack on the airship hangars at Tondern, this had for its primary purpose the luring of the High Seas Fleet into a carefully prepared trap. Thus, the Fleet's mission was far superior in conception to the mere bombing of the airship hangars, which before had proved so futile. The glaring defects of the previous plan had been avoided. In the first place, the entire Grand Fleet was to support the attacking forces. And, what is even more important, Jellicoe was now to exercise full tactical command. On this occasion, the Admiralty apparently agreed to limit its activities to furnishing information to Jellicoe. This duty it performed with uncanny effective-ness.

The British plan is of much interest. The Germans (Sketch I) had three usual exits from their bases. Two of them ran parallel to the northward along the Schleswig and Danish coasts past Sylt and Horn Reefs light vessel. One of the northerly channels ran close to the coast to the eastward of Helgoland and Amrum Bank. The other ran to the westward. These parallel routes from the strategic viewpoint and for the purpose of the British plan could be considered as one, particularly as they ended in practically the same area off Horn Reefs. The third swept channel ran westward along the Dutch coast past Borkum and Terschelling. On this occasion, as the Tondern hangars were to be attacked, it was expected that the Germans would emerge from their northerly channels. Therefore, the light mine layer *Abdiel,* a fast vessel of the destroyer type attached to the Grand Fleet, was to lay a mine field across the northern channels south of Vyl light vessel. To the westward of Vyl light vessel 3 submarines would be on watch, 3 more would be off Horn Reefs. In this area would be the Battle Cruiser Fleet. Slightly to the northward, the Battle Fleet would be in immediate support. In case the Germans, for some unexpected reason, should come out through the western channel they would run into another mine field to be laid by the mine layer *Princess Margaret*. They would also encounter 3 submarines on station off Terschelling.

Once these preliminary dispositions had been made, the striking force was to appear off Sylt early on May 4. This force, led by Commodore Alexander-Sinclair, would consist of the 1st Light Cruiser Squadron (4 vessels), the 1st Flotilla (16 destroyers), and the seaplane carriers *Engadine* and *Vindex* carrying 9 seaplanes. The latter would then attempt to bomb the airship hangars at Tondern.

As the Grand Fleet was about to commence the execution of this well-drawn plan of operations, 8 German airships left Hage, Nordholz, and Tondern for a bombing raid against the English and Scottish coast towns. During the evening of May 2, six of them bombed the English ports from Whitby to Blyth. Two more, the *L14* and *L20*, went as far north as Edinburgh during the night. News of this air attack found the units of the Grand Fleet proceeding toward their assigned stations. The Battle Cruiser Fleet had avoided being sighted by the *UB–21* on patrol off Rosyth, though Lieutenant Commander Hashagen was one of the best German submarine commanders. As it was a well-known custom of the Germans to send detachments of the High Seas Fleet to sea to cover the return of their airships, there was some apprehension that this might result in Alexander-Sinclair being attacked by superior forces off Horn Reefs.

On this occasion there was ample reason for the High Seas Fleet to cover the return of their airships, for they encountered strong winds, accompanied by clouds and snowstorms. These very unfavorable conditions had so delayed the attacks of the airships that, when the ships started for home, their fuel supply had become dangerously low. In addition, ice which formed on the propellers had been thrown into the gas cells of the *L11*, *L14*, and *L21*. So much hydrogen escaped that only the speed of the motors kept the ships in the air. When head winds were encountered on the return trip, it was seen by Commander Strasser that they would have difficulty in getting home. He ordered the injured craft to head for Hage and asked that the Fleet send vessels to their assistance.

At 2:20 A.M. of the third Vice Admiral Schmidt, commanding Battle Squadron I, ordered the light cruisers *Regensburg*, *Pillau*, and *Elbing* to proceed toward the opening in the mine field at Norderney with Flotilla I and Half Flotillas X and XVII. At 4:25 the *L21*, which had two cells leaking, reported herself 70 miles northwest (302°) of Terschelling. She asked that destroyers might come to her assistance (Fig. 13–A). Flotillas were ordered toward her reported position and all forces available were quickly made ready for sea. However, Scheer now found himself much embarrassed by the fact that Scouting Group IV, Flotilla VI, and Half Flotilla IX, as well as five ships of Battle Squadron III, were in the Baltic. These units would be badly missed if a sortie to save the airships should bring on a fleet action.

Meanwhile, bad news had arrived also from the northward. At 4:50 A.M. the *L20* had been about 165 miles WSW. (234°) from Lindesnaes (The Naze), Norway. At 6:00 she learned from a fishing steamer that she was then about 135 miles west (257°) from the same point (Fig. 13–B). This indicated that she was being swept rapidly to the northward. So at 6:40 she reported that probably it would be impracticable for her to reach a German port. Nevertheless, her captain said that he would endeavor to reach the Danish coast at Hanstholm and proceed along it to the southward in the hope that he might get to Tondern.

At 7:00 the *L11*, with cells leaking from ice splinters, was 165 miles west (257°) of Bovbjerg (Fig. 13–D). By this time all the other airships were making good progress on their homeward journey. The first, the *L16*, had already landed at Hage at 6:50 (Fig. 13–C). At 8:50 the *L13* also secured at that base. At

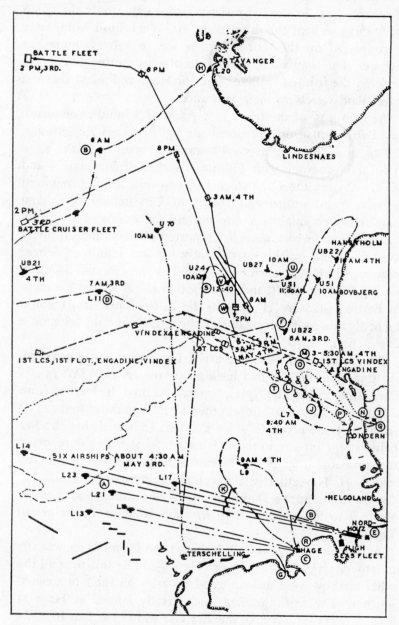

FIG. 13. Operations from 4:00 A.M., May 3, to 2:00 P.M., May 4.

7:15 the *L17* arrived at Nordholz (Fig. 13–E), followed at 8:40 by the *L21*, the ship that had asked for assistance. The *L23* and *L14* also were close at hand and beyond danger. As a result of this information, Vice Admiral Schmidt recalled all the forces proceeding toward the westward and ordered a fast flotilla toward Horn Reefs. Two submarines, which had been operating in patrol areas off Horn Reefs (Fig. 13–F), were directed to assist the *L20*. They proceeded toward the vicinity of Hanstholm in the hope of gaining contact with her there. This, as will later be seen, was very fortunate for the British.

Meanwhile, the British Intelligence Service had been working with its customary efficiency. It had reported promptly to the Grand Fleet that groups of German battle cruisers and light cruisers were coming out. It also fixed, possibly by radio direction finders, the position of the *L20*. Jellicoe ordered the 4th Light Cruiser Squadron to search for her. However, the airship had already sighted the Norwegian coast at 8:00. Three hours later she passed Stavanger (Fig. 13–H). There was now fuel for four hours only. The wind was still contrary. About noon Lieutenant Commander Stabbert reluctantly brought his ship down into the water at Gande Fiord. It was completely wrecked. The crew was interned.

Meanwhile, at 10:40 the *L23* had secured at Nordholz and at noon the *L14* reached safely the same base. At about 1:30 the seventh airship, the *L11*, was sighted at Tondern. Twenty minutes later she landed (Fig. 13–I). All surface craft were now ordered to return to their bases. This message was quickly deciphered in London and passed on to the Grand Fleet. There it raised hopes for the success of the morrow's undertakings. Incidentally, although they did not know it, there was, as we have hinted, another reason for the British to be happy. The *UB–22* and *U–51*, instead of being on the normal patrol areas off Horn Reefs where the Grand Fleet was about to operate were far to the northward along the Danish coast, returning from Hanstholm, whither they had proceeded to assist the *L20*. This is a vivid example of the part played in war by pure unadulterated luck.

The British plan was executed on schedule. By 1:30 A.M. of the fourth both the *Abdiel* (Fig. 13–J) and *Princess Margaret* (Fig. 13–K) had completed their mine fields without incident. Shortly after 3:00 A.M. Alexander-Sinclair arrived close off the Danish coast just north of Horn Reefs. The 6 submarines had reached their assigned positions off the Horn Reefs and Vyl light vessels (Fig. 13–L). However, 2 of them collided under water in the darkness—not an auspicious beginning for the enterprise. The Battle Cruiser Fleet and the Battle Fleet were in their positions by 5:00.

Meanwhile, the 2 seaplane carriers, *Engadine* and *Vindex,* had lowered their 9 planes on to the sea. Although conditions were quite favorable, 7 of the planes smashed their propellers in trying to take off through the swells. Of the 2 that finally got into the air, 1 ran into the destroyer *Goshawk's* aerial and was destroyed. The 1 remaining plane started off to bomb the Tondern airship hangars (Fig. 13–M). She never reached her objective, but the Germans saw her cross the coast in the vicinity of Tondern (Fig. 13–N).

News of the unknown plane was broadcast by the Germans, but the expected attack on the hangars failed to materialize. Flights of the List seaplanes (Fig. 13–P) and Tondern airplanes likewise failed to detect enemy forces. So the *L7* left Tondern (Fig. 13–Q) and the *L9* proceeded from Hage (Fig. 13–R) to scout toward the northward and westward. The *L9* cruised until within 60 miles of Horn Reefs without sighting anything. She returned to Hage at noon. At 9:40 the *L7* reported that she was 25 miles to the southwestward of Vyl light vessel, heading toward Horn Reefs. That was the last news received from her that day. Shortly after making her report she ran into the *Galatea* and *Phaeton* of the 1st Light Cruiser Squadron. After the British seaplane had returned to her carrier at about 5:30, this squadron had proceeded to take station on the western end of Beatty's cruiser screen, reaching their posts about 7:30 (Fig. 13–O). When the two light cruisers sighted the airship, they headed in her direction and fired a few rounds at long range. By a lucky or unlucky. depending upon the viewpoint, chance one of these projectiles hit the fuel tank and the airship took a vertical dive into the sea (Fig. 13–T). The *E–31* surfaced and took prisoner the seven survivors of this disaster. So quickly had the airship been destroyed that there had been no time to make a radio report of her contact. Curiously enough, on this occasion the British wanted to have their presence reported, so as to lure out the Germans. So their lucky shot in this way was unfortunate for them. The failure of the two airships to report strong British forces within 60 miles of their hangars was another demonstration of the many limitations of airship operation.

While both seaplanes and airships had failed to gain intelligence of the Grand Fleet, the chance encounter of a submarine at last resulted in its presence being reported to Vice Admiral Scheer. On May 3 the *U–24* and *U–70* had left Emden (Fig. 13–G). One was to take station on the line between Peterhead and Egero and the other between Fair Island and Marsten. By mere chance the courses of both submarines carried them close to the Grand Fleet. At 9:30 A.M. the *U–24* sighted two cruisers of the *Minotaur* class and a destroyer (Fig. 13–S). At 10:10 Lieutenant Commander Schneider submerged and commenced an approach on the cruisers. However, a casualty, as usual, caused the attack to be abandoned. At 10:55 Schneider came to the surface and sent a radio report of his contact. At 11:16 this news was being read by Scheer—an excellent bit of communication work. Lieutenant Commander Wünsche of the *U–70* took in Schneider's message, but continued on his course to the northwestward, away from the reported contact. By doing so he failed, in our opinion, to display the bold initiative so essential to submarine captains.

The report of the *U–24*, together with information received from German agents, induced Scheer to believe that a fleet operation against Helgoland Bight was possible. Unfortunately, the strong southwesterly wind prevented the airships from scouting as far to the northward as the position of the *U–24's* contact. The recent disasters to these craft had demonstrated that great caution was necessary in their handling. However, there were five submarines in the North Sea, the *UB–21, UB–22, UB–27,*

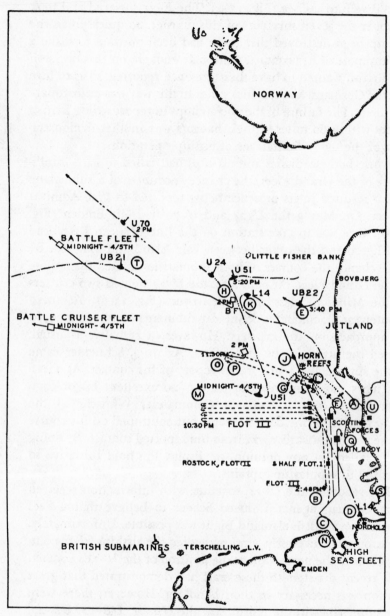

FIG. 14. Operations from 2:00 P.M., May 4, to 5:00 A.M., May 5.

U–24, and *U–70.* All were ordered to scout in the reported direction of the enemy. Little reliance could be placed on their effectiveness, as it was very difficult for them to receive radio messages. The forces in the Baltic (five ships of Battle Squadron III, Scouting Group IV, Flotilla VI, and Half Flotilla IX) were ordered to proceed immediately via the Kaiser Wilhelm Canal to the North Sea.

By this time as it was too late to attempt any sortie with the concentrated forces of the Fleet during daylight of the third, Scheer decided to leave during the late evening. At daylight next morning the Fleet would be beyond the mine fields ready to attack any enemy forces in the vicinity. Meanwhile, First Leader of Destroyers, Commodore Michelsen, in the *Rostock,* was ordered to proceed northward with the flotillas then on outpost duties, making a night search and attack toward the probable position of the British forces. At dawn he was to rejoin the High Seas Fleet south of Horn Reefs light vessel. At 2:00 P.M. a seaplane left List to scout toward Horn Reefs (Fig. 14–A). She sighted nothing.

Of the five submarines at sea, only the *U–24* accomplished anything of importance. At 12:40 P.M. Schneider saw in the distance the thick masts of ten warships moving to the southward (Fig. 13–V). At 1:10 he reported this important information by radio. At 2:48 Commander Hollmann left Helgoland with Flotilla III (Fig. 14–B). At the same time Commodore Michelsen left the Jade with five boats of Flotilla II and Half Flotilla I (Fig. 14–c). It was, in fact, the British Battle Fleet that Schneider had seen. During the forenoon, Jellicoe had been maneuvering on northerly and southerly courses over a rather wide area. This not only reduced the chance of successful submarine attack, but also rendered probable erroneous contact reports should his ships be sighted by submarines and aircraft. Thus, we see Schneider reporting a southerly course for the Battle Fleet at 1:10 P.M. When the British took a westerly course at 2:00 P.M., the Germans were entirely deceived. As will be seen later, all their blows were in the air.

Meanwhile, at 11:30 A.M. the *U–51* had received her orders to proceed toward the *U–24's* contact with the British cruisers and had proceeded in that direction (Fig. 13–U). At 3:36 P.M. the *UB–22* also received her orders (Fig. 14–E). At 5:20 P.M. the *U–51* encountered the *U–24* and received the latest information (Fig. 14–H); but the German submarines were too late. At 2:00 Jellicoe had ordered a retirement toward his bases (Fig. 13–W). This decision, under the circumstances, was a curious one. The British plan was to draw the High Seas Fleet into a trap. Why then did not Jellicoe wait long enough for the Germans to come out? He continually stresses the fact that the German sorties were liable to find the Grand Fleet only partly ready to come out for a counter-blow. He did not seem to realize that when he arrived off the German bases, he might also find them unprepared. It must have been known that the Germans made a practice of sending units into the Baltic for training purposes. It would seem that, if his plan were really to draw the Germans into a trap, he should give them enough time to take the bait. Also, the bait he offered was not very tempting. The Germans advertised their presence in English waters by bombarding the coast. Jellicoe attacked with a single seaplane, which did not even reach its objective. In view of the futility of the previous seaplane raid, it is suggested that he should have taken more aggressive measures to provoke the Germans into coming out. A bombardment of the seaplane station at List by light cruisers would seem to have been practicable. At any rate, the very premature withdrawal of the Grand Fleet lost Jellicoe a splendid opportunity to bring on a fleet action under favorable conditions.

While the German flotillas were standing out, aircraft were scouting to the northward. As previously mentioned, the seaplane that left List at 2:00 saw nothing. She seems to have circled Horn Reefs light vessel about 2:30. At 3:20 the *L14*, which only the day before had returned to Nordholz from her English cruise, ascended and stood northward (Fig. 14–D). At 4:00 List seaplane 560 took off for a search toward Horn Reefs (Fig. 14–F). At 5:00 she attacked with bombs a submarine lying between the Horn Reefs and Vyl light vessels (Fig. 14–G). At 6:23 the *L14* reached Horn Reefs light vessel and reported that she had sighted nothing (Fig. 14–J). At 7:20 she said that nothing had been seen as far as 30 miles south of Little Fisher Bank (Fig. 14–K). The submarines also had reported nothing in that area. As it was apparent that the British forces had left the area in which the U–24 had reported them, it seemed useless to Michelsen to launch a night destroyer attack in that direction. The U–24 had said that the British vessels had disappeared to the southward. So Michelsen decided to launch his attack on the assumption that they had continued on that course. So at 6:00 P.M. Flotilla III composed of new, fast boats commenced its night search to the westward in four groups (Fig. 14–1). Speed was about 16 knots. At 8:00 P.M. the commodore launched his remaining flotillas in a northwesterly direction (Fig. 14–L). These destroyers were in two groups, about 10 miles apart. In one group were five boats of Flotilla II; in the other an equal number of Half Flotilla I. Midway between the two groups was the Rostock, followed by the V190. All the German destroyers passed close to, or even through, the field of mines laid by the Abdiel the previous night. The mines were probably planted too deep below the surface to hit the light-draft destroyers. Also, the latter passed through the area in which the British submarines were operating. However, in case of a contact during darkness, all the chances were on the side of the destroyers.

The destroyer search was without event of importance. At 10:30 P.M. Flotilla III reversed its course (Fig. 14–M). Ten minutes later the High Seas Fleet left the Jade (Fig. 14–N). Although it was still far short of its full strength, Scheer had decided to proceed out to the northward. In advance was Scouting Group II with Half Flotilla XVIII. Then followed Scouting Group I with Half Flotilla X. In the rear came the main body (Battle Squadron I, Battle Squadron II, three ships of Battle Squadron III, and Flotilla VII). Scheer, therefore, still lacked five battleships of Battle Squadron III, four of which were still in the canal; Scouting Group IV; and three destroyer flotillas.

As the High Seas Fleet was passing Weser light vessel, Michelsen at 11:30 P.M. reversed the course of Flotilla II and Half

Flotilla I (Fig. 14–O). Twenty minutes later the *Rostock* sighted a submarine about 300 yards away (Fig. 14–P). At first there was much doubt as to her identity, because the German destroyers were in the patrol area of the *UB–22*. However, searchlights soon illuminated the submarine's conning tower. There in large black letters was *"E–31."* Rapid fire was promptly opened. One shell struck the conning tower squarely and the Germans credited themselves with a British submarine. However, the shell failed to explode and the *E–31* made port safely. Thus, by a remarkable train of events did a failure of German munitions save the lives of the seven German survivors of the *L7*. As it was now evident that the British forces had gone home, Scheer at 2:30 A.M. turned back the main body (Fig. 14–Q). Half an hour later Hipper reversed the course of the scouting forces. The four ships of Battle Squadron III that were still in the canal returned to Kiel (Fig. 14–S).

Only the *U–70* and *UB–21* were near the tracks of the returning British forces. At dawn on the fifth, the *U–70* made out 4 destroyers steering westward. The *UB–21* spoke a neutral sailing ship. She stated that during the fourth there had been 200 British vessels in the vicinity of Little Fisher Bank (Fig. 14–T). As the submarines radio was out of order, it was impossible to send home this important information. At 4:20 A.M. the *L14* landed in Tondern (Fig. 14–U).

Thus ended an operation that had very interesting possibilities. The British plan, in general, was good. However, it would have been well to have taken more positive means to advertise their presence. Also, the British should have withdrawn sufficiently during the night to avoid destroyer attack against their capital ships and then have reappeared off Horn Reefs early on the fifth. Such a decision might well have resulted in an action with the High Seas Fleet with many of its ships missing.

CHAPTER VII

THE PRELUDE TO JUTLAND

ON MAY 12 Jellicoe and Beatty met the First Sea Lord in a conference at Rosyth. It was decided that Rosyth should be made ready for two battle squadrons before the winter and the Humber ready for one. No definite conclusion, however, was reached on Jellicoe's proposal to bring the Grand Fleet to those bases. Beatty again raised the point of bringing down the 5th Battle Squadron. Jellicoe, as before, vigorously opposed the proposal. He finally consented to allowing the 5th Battle Squadron to come to Rosyth "occasionally." Beatty then reminded him that the 3d Battle Cruiser Squadron was about to proceed to Scapa for training. Jellicoe agreed to replace it with the 5th Battle Squadron. Soon after the conference the 3d Battle Cruiser Squadron went to Scapa (Fig. 15–A). Then the 5th Battle Squadron went to Rosyth (Fig 15–B).

This basic decision to allow the 5th Battle Squadron to alternate between Rosyth and Scapa had the usual bad effects of a compromise. It was of utmost importance that such an important unit should be permanently under the orders of one commander. This was particularly important in view of the marked divergence in the tactical ideas of Beatty and Jellicoe. This last-minute change had some unfortunate effects. Beatty had no time to work this powerful unit into his own organization, while Jellicoe was deprived of one of the elements of the Battle Fleet, upon which he greatly depended. On the other hand, the presence of the 5th Battle Squadron on some occasions would be very valuable to Beatty. During the battle the operations of the 3d Battle Cruiser Squadron stationed with the Battle Fleet proved very fortunate, but this was largely a matter of chance. On the other hand, the 5th Battle Squadron very narrowly and by rare good luck escaped being overwhelmed by the German main body; but this grave danger could have been avoided by

reasonably good management. On the question of assigning the
5th Battle Squadron permanently to Beatty, there was much to
be said both pro and con. But to alternate it between two commanders was an unsatisfactory arrangement. It is an interesting
fact that much of the post-Jutland controversy between Beatty
and Jellicoe centers about the operations of the 5th Battle
Squadron.

A second cause of embarrassment to Jellicoe at this time was
the reorganization of his destroyer flotillas that was gradually
becoming effective. Commodore Hawksley, in the light cruiser
Castor, had just been placed in command of the flotillas. It
seems, however, that no effective steps had yet been taken to
co-ordinate the action of the various flotillas. We will find, in
our description of the action, that Hawksley made practically
no attempt to exercise tactical command, except over his own
flotilla. The failure of the British to organize their destroyers
in two groups, as was done in the High Seas Fleet, prevented
them from being used to best effect in battle.

The Germans had been encouraged by the results of the
Lowestoft raid. For a time Scheer had hopes that the order of
April 24 concerning submarine operations would be rescinded;
but on May 4 the German Chancellor had made public a note
to the United States definitely renouncing the campaign against
merchant vessels, except so far as it could be conducted under
the existing provisions of international law. Scheer saw that the
Fleet was the only offensive weapon ready to his hand. Therefore, he resolved on an undertaking even more dangerous than
the attack on Lowestoft, namely, the bombardment of Sunderland, a port only a short distance south of Rosyth. He believed
that in this operation he would have two advantages that he had
not previously enjoyed: (1) Lord Balfour's announcement indicated a dispersal of the British naval forces; (2) the end of the
submarine campaign would permit him to use the numerous
submarine flotillas with the High Seas Fleet. They could be
placed on patrol stations off the British bases to observe and
attack British forces leaving or entering them. Both these de-

velopments would facilitate his plans for falling upon inferior British detachments.

Scheer's general plan for the Sunderland operation was much like Jellicoe's dispositions for the Tondern attack. Submarines were to lay mines off the English bases and to report the exit of British forces from them. Airships were to observe the English coast and scout on the flanks of the High Seas Fleet. The scout-ing forces would bombard Sunderland early in the morning. The main body would be in a supporting position in the center of the North Sea, 50 miles eastward of Flamborough Head. When the British forces emerged from the Thames, Harwich, the Humber, Rosyth, Cromarty, and Scapa, submarines and airships would report their movements. The High Seas Fleet would then surprise and annihilate inferior detachments. It was an excellent plan if the submarines and airships could per-form effectively their assigned tasks.

The great danger was that the Grand Fleet might evade the submarines placed in advance off their bases and might actually be in the North Sea when the attack on Sunderland took place. In such a case the line of retreat of the scouting forces would be cut and disaster was probable. The presence of the Grand Fleet in the North Sea when the German plan was executed might result from intelligence of the departure of the High Seas Fleet or be merely the chance coincidence of a simultaneous British offensive. To prevent the British from knowing of the departure of the High Seas Fleet, measures were devised to de-ceive the enemy; but to cover the possibility of a chance en-counter of the two fleets (as actually happened on May 31) it was considered essential that the flanks of the High Seas Fleet be screened by airships.

Before the operation could be initiated it was necessary to repair the extensive damage to the *Seydlitz*, caused by her mine hit on April 24. It also was necessary to effect many engineering repairs. On the last trip there had been no less than seven engineering casualties to the vessels of Battle Squadron III. Rear Admiral Behncke with four ships of Battle Squadron III

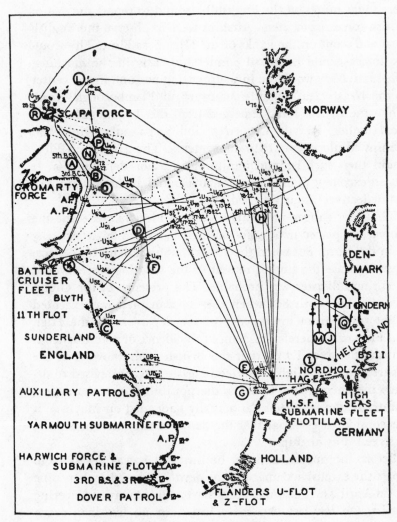

FIG. 15. Operations from May 12 to 30.

was exercising in the Baltic. It was therefore decided that the plan should be executed on May 17. All ships were to be ready on that date.

On the ninth Behncke returned to the North Sea bases, but several of his ships had condenser casualties. The operation thus had to be delayed until the twenty-third. Battle Squadron II, the *Rostock*, the *Lützow*, and Flotillas III and IX went into the Baltic for training.

On May 13 the large mine layer, *U–74*, sailed to lay a field of 22 mines in the approaches to Rosyth. On the same day Captain Bauer, Leader of Submarines, recommended that the ten submarines then ready should proceed into the center of the North Sea on a preliminary reconnaissance. On the twenty-third these boats were to be on station off the British bases in readiness for the Sunderland offensive. In order to prepare the submarines for their part in the operation, it is suggested that it would have been preferable to send them direct to their stations off the British bases on the twenty-first, utilizing the time until that date for training exercises in home waters. These submarines had been used almost exclusively in attacks on merchant vessels. Training in observing, attacking, and reporting large forces of heavy ships, screened by light cruisers and destroyers, would have been invaluable.

On the seventeenth and eighteenth the German submarines put to sea. They were the *U–52, U–24, U–70, U–32, U–66, U–47, U–43, U–44, U–63,* and *U–51.* Each was to occupy a quadrangle about 15 by 100 nautical miles, extending generally in a north and south line (Fig. 15). It had been planned for the *U–46* to make a reconnaissance off Sunderland, but a last-minute machinery derangement prevented her from sailing; so the *U–47,* which already was at sea, was directed to perform that duty. The *U–46* was directed, upon completion of her repairs, to take station off Terschelling.

On the twentieth the *UB–27* left Emden to penetrate into the Firth of Forth. On the night of the twenty-first the *U–47* reconnoitered Sunderland (Fig. 15–c). On the twenty-third she reported the results by pre-arranged code groups (Fig. 15–F). On the twenty-second, the *UB–21* and *UB–22* proceeded from Emden to take station off the Humber, while the *U–46* and *U–67* commenced a patrol off Terschelling. On the same day the 9 boats that had been patrolling in the North Sea proceeded to take their appointed stations off the British bases: 2 off Scapa and 7 off Rosyth. One of the latter, the *U–52*, broke one of her periscopes on a submarine net (Fig. 15–D). The *U–47*, en route from Sunderland, assumed a position off Kinnaird Head. Thus, by the twenty-third no less than 15 of the High Seas Fleet submarines were on their patrol stations (Fig. 15).

These submarine operations did not remain long unknown to the British. As early as the sixteenth and seventeenth there had been indications of the departure of nine boats, "an incident sufficiently unusual in itself to arouse attention." On the eighteenth Jellicoe was informed that "an exceptionally large force of enemy submarines was now operating in the North Sea." By the twenty-second it was known that at least eight submarines were out. However, this was taken to indicate a resumption of submarine warfare rather than a large-scale offensive by the Fleet. The belief that Battle Squadron III was still in the Baltic argued against any probability of the latter.

However, on the twenty-second the German detachments in the Baltic passed through the Kaiser Wilhelm Canal into the North Sea. The battle cruiser *Seydlitz* reported that her repairs had been completed, but a flooding test showed that important structural defects still existed. Her date of readiness was postponed until the twenty-eighth. As Scheer felt that he must have this important vessel, the Sunderland offensive was also postponed.

The submarines off the English coast were continually being attacked by the patrol forces and accomplished nothing of moment. Frequently, they were sighted and reported. There were many opportunities for them to attack light forces, but all their attempts were ineffective. The detailed account of their operations by Groos reveals clearly the limitations of submarine operations in those days against naval vessels. We can relate only a bare outline of their adventures.

At 3:00 A.M. of the twenty-third the *U–67* reported 20 destroyers 40 miles northwestward of Terschelling. This report cannot be connected with any British operation. On the same day the *U–72* sailed from Emden to lay a mine field in Moray Firth. On the twenty-fourth she sighted, in a position about 120 miles west of Hanstholm, what were thought to be 3 light cruisers and 2 submarines (Fig. 15–H). These actually were the 4th Light Cruiser Squadron and attached destroyers making a sweep from Rosyth toward the Norwegian coast. Also, on the twenty-fourth the *U–46* reported being attacked by 2 British submarines off Terschelling (Fig. 15–G).

On the twenty-fourth Helgoland seaplanes 562 and 483 sighted a British submarine and the Danish steamer *June* to the northwestward of their base (Fig. 15–I). During the evening Flotilla VI made a night search for the steamer, but without result (Fig. 15–J). The next night a similar night search was made by Flotilla IX (Fig. 15–M).

Meanwhile, on the twenty-fifth the *U–75* sailed to lay a mine field off Scapa. On the same day the *U–72*, en route to Moray Firth, sighted two light cruisers on a westerly course (Fig. 15–L). They were probably a detachment of the 4th Light Cruiser Squadron. Also on the twenty-fifth the *UB–27* attempted to penetrate into the Firth of Forth. She found that the anti-submarine measures taken by the British were very effective. One of her engine shafts was jammed by a floating net (Fig. 15–K). After a long series of thrilling adventures, the submarine started for home on the twenty-seventh, having accomplished nothing of moment.

On the twenty-sixth the *U–72* developed a bad oil leak when about 100 miles east of Moray Firth (Fig. 15–N). As this would permit the submarine to be trailed by patrol craft when submerged, she turned back the next day without having laid her mines. On the twenty-ninth she arrived in Lister Deep (Fig. 15–Q).

On the twenty-seventh the *U–74*, detailed to lay mines in the Firth of Forth, was destroyed by 4 armed trawlers, Unit 42 of the Peterhead Patrol, in a position 25 miles southeast of

Peterhead (Fig. 15–O). Also on this day the destroyer leader
Broke and 12 destroyers came out of Scapa to operate against
the *U–43* and *U–44* (Fig. 15–P). The third of the large mine-
laying submarines had better fortune than her sister-ships. On
the night of the twenty-eighth the *U–75* laid 22 mines just to
the westward of Scapa. It was a mine of this field that later sank
the cruiser *Hampshire,* with Lord Kitchener on board.

On the twenty-eighth the *Seydlitz* was reported ready, but her
accession was counter-balanced by a condenser casualty to the
new battleship *König Albert,* which rendered her unavailable
for operation. The weather for some time had been unfavorable
for the airship scouting upon which Scheer relied so heavily.
Predictions for the future gave no better promise. On the evening of June 1 the submarines were to leave their patrol stations.
If this opportunity were lost a wait of several weeks would be
necessary before another operation could be attempted. Also,
the postponement would have a bad moral effect upon his personnel. Scheer was determined to carry through an offensive
operation. He judged that the Sunderland plan could not be
executed unless airships were available to cover his flanks and
prevent the Grand Fleet from gaining a position on his line of
retreat. He, therefore, prepared an alternate plan for an advance
toward the Skagerrak. He thought this would "considerably
reduce the chances of the Fleet becoming involved in battle
unwillingly." The Fleet would not approach so closely the
British bases. Also, as the Germans thought, the Danish coast
"would furnish a certain protection against surprise from that
quarter." While this may be so, it also, in our opinion, presented a barrier against which the High Seas Fleet could be
driven and trapped by superior forces—a very grave disadvantage.

On May 30, early in the morning, the weather still was unfavorable for airship scouting. Scheer then reluctantly abandoned the long-planned Sunderland operation and approved the
alternate plan for the Skagerrak offensive. Strangely enough,
Jellicoe had been planning an operation to lure Scheer toward
the Skagerrak. These plans required that a strong cruiser force,

supported by a battle squadron, penetrate far into the Kattegat as a bait. The remainder of the Grand Fleet would then be in readiness to trap the oncoming Germans near Horn Reefs. The *Abdiel* was to extend the mine field she had laid on May 4. Three Harwich submarines were to proceed off Vyl light vessel to lie on the bottom until June 1, when they were to emerge and commence operations. Two Blyth submarines were to take station east of the Dogger Bank, where they were to patrol until June 3. While these plans were being prepared in detail, based upon information obtained by submarine reconnaissance in the Kattegat, fresh intelligence from Germany arrived on the twenty-eighth. This made it "clear that some considerable movement was on foot." On the thirtieth the situation quickly developed into the movements which led to the Battle of Jutland. Before we proceed further let us record the forces stationed in the North Sea on May 30; then let us analyze the situation which confronted the British and German commanders.

It will be of interest to list the total strengths of the British and German forces at the end of May. This list includes all serviceable vessels assigned to the respective commanders, whether ready for sea, temporarily under repair, or otherwise not immediately available.

BRITISH FORCES

Battle Fleet (Jellicoe) at Scapa and Cromarty: 26 battleships, 3 battle cruisers, 10 cruisers, 11 light cruisers, 5 destroyer leaders, 53 destroyers, 1 mine layer, and 1 seaplane carrier.

Battle Cruiser Fleet (Beatty) at Rosyth: 5 battleships, 7 battle cruisers, 15 light cruisers, 38 destroyers, 2 submarines, and 2 seaplane carriers.

Eleventh Submarine Flotilla at Blyth: 2 destroyers and a number of submarines.

Harwich Force (Tyrwhitt) at Harwich: 5 light cruisers, 2 destroyer leaders, and 27 destroyers.

Dover Patrol (Bacon) at Dover: 1 light cruiser, 1 destroyer leader, 25 destroyers, and a number of submarines.

Thames Forces (Bradford) in the Thames: 1 battleship, 7 battleships second-line, and 3 cruisers.

Harwich Submarine Flotilla at Harwich: 2 destroyers and a number of submarines.

Coastal Patrol, Sherries to Beachy Head: 35 destroyers.

GERMAN FORCES

High Seas Fleet (Scheer) in the Elbe, Jade, and Ems: 18 battleships, 5 battle cruisers, 7 battleships second-line, 14 light cruisers, 76 destroyers, 31 submarines, and 10 airships.

Flander Forces (Schröder): 3 destroyers and 14 submarines.

A comparison of the numbers of ships by types follows:

Type	No. available		No. at Jutland	
	British	German	British	German
Battleships	32	18	28	16
Battle cruisers	10	5	9	5
Battleships, second-line	7	7	0	6
Armored cruisers	13	0	8	0
Light cruisers	32	14	26	11
Destroyer leaders	8	0	5	0
Destroyers	182	79	73	61
Mine layers	1	1	1	0
Seaplane carriers	3	0	1	0
Airships	0	10	0	0
Submarines	*	45	0	0
Total			151	99

* Note: The British had about as many submarines as the Germans.

As will be seen by an examination of the above tables, the Royal Navy had greatly increased its margin of material superiority over the Imperial German Navy. This, as it happened, was accurately measured by a comparison of first-line capital ships in home waters, or 42 to 23. These figures include the *Royal Sovereign* and *Bayern,* newly commissioned battleships not quite ready to accompany their respective fleets to sea.

In destroyers, the British superiority was about the same as in capital ships. If it be objected that some of the British destroyers were not attached to the Grand Fleet, the answer is that they were in the North Sea and could have been attached to the

Grand Fleet if so desired. All these British destroyers were at least the equal of the smaller German destroyers that accompanied the High Seas Fleet to sea.

In cruisers and light cruisers the superiority of the British was simply overwhelming. In submarines the forces were probably about equal. Only in airships did the Germans have an advantage, but their airships were of little or no value to them. The second-line battleships were of practically no value as compared with first-line ships. Had the British so desired, they could have maintained an immense superiority of second-line battleships in the North Sea.

Furthermore, the ships actually available do not tell the whole story of British, or allied, superiority. The Germans had only 1 battleship and 1 battle cruiser nearing completion. The British had 2 battleships, 2 battle cruisers, and 3 large cruisers of the *Furious* class, each mounting four 15-inch guns. Taking into consideration the weak defensive strength of these cruisers, the British had a superiority in ships nearing completion of nearly 3 to 1. Finally, the British Allies, excluding Russia, had no less than 12 first-line capital ships as against 4 for the Allies of Germany. If second-line battleships be considered as a final reserve, we find that the Allies had an immense superiority over the Central Powers. This superiority was not only in numbers, but also in quality and size of ships, the British and French having a number of ships similar to the *Lord Nelson* that were much more powerful than the best German second-line ships. The Russians also had powerful forces in both the Baltic and Black Seas. While their fleets were considerably handicapped in these theaters by the geographical situation, still they were able to keep occupied considerable German and Turkish forces. The Russian Baltic Fleet would provide a strong re-enforcement for any British force penetrating into the Baltic.

Thus, we have a picture of overwhelming British superiority in naval force. Without exaggeration, we can estimate their material superiority as 2 to 1; even more if we take into consideration the forces of France, Italy, and Russia as compared with those of Austria and Turkey.

In addition, we must remember that the geographical situation greatly favored the British. We have shown that the British Navy by remaining in its own waters could, except for the Baltic, shut off all German sea communications and protect their own —the primary object of naval warfare. The Germans, on the other hand, could shut off some of the British communications and protect some of their own only by taking their Fleet around the British Isles and maintaining it permanently in the Atlantic Ocean. This would require the establishment of one or more German naval bases in the British Isles, preferably Ireland. While doing so, it would be necessary for them to leave sufficient forces in the North Sea and Baltic to control those key areas. To have any chance to accomplish such an almost impracticable task it would be necessary for the Germans to have a superiority in naval forces of at least 2 to 1, whereas the reverse was actually the case.

The virtual annihilation of the Grand Fleet was the only way the Germans could gain such a superiority. The destruction of a British detachment or the winning of an indecisive victory over the Grand Fleet would be only the first step of many toward the accomplishment of Scheer's mission. While such an initial success would encourage the Germans, it would render the future operations of the British more cautious. It would probably result in the re-enforcement of the Grand Fleet by a number of French battleships. Thus, the further prosecution of the German naval campaign would be even more difficult for them after their first success. And remember also that they, and not the British, had to force the campaign to a decision. Thus, they could not choose the conditions under which the battle would be fought, but would have to engage when the British were willing. As the British blockade was constantly becoming more effective and its cumulative effects more decisive, time was on the side of the British so far as the naval campaign in the North Sea was concerned.

It will be noted that the situation that confronted Scheer was very similar to that which confronted the German military leaders in their 1918 offensive in France, except that Scheer had far less chance of success than Hindenburg and Ludendorff. In each case it was improbable that one decisive success could win the campaign. A long series of victories, without a single defeat, was necessary for ultimate success, with each victory becoming more difficult to win.

Finally, the very configuration of the North Sea, as has been stated, was highly unfavorable to the Germans. They had to launch their sorties from a single point through a 90-degree sector. This (Sketch I) was largely blocked by mine fields and could be watched easily by British submarines. This not only permitted the British an early opportunity to gain information of the movements of the High Seas Fleet, but also subjected the latter to grave danger from submarines and mines before it could even reach the high seas. Furthermore, it had a very limited sector through which it could retreat, which permitted the enemy, in any given situation, to determine almost the exact track along which the Germans would retreat. There was always present the danger that this line of retreat would be occupied by the enemy in greatly superior strength and the High Seas Fleet hemmed in against a neutral coast. In returning to port, the Fleet had to run a second time the gauntlet of mines and submarines, while damaged vessels were greatly restricted by shoals due to their increased draft. On the other hand, the German submarines and mine craft were unable to operate effectively off the British bases, while it was practically impossible for them to cut all the lines of retreat of an inferior detachment, due to the many bases in which it could seek refuge.

In still another respect the geographical situation favored the British. As their bases were far distant from any neutral territory and on an island, it was difficult, if not impracticable, for German secret agents to gain any advance information of their operations. On the other hand, the proximity of Danish and Dutch territory facilitated the operations of the British agents near the German bases. Also, the fact that German swept channels led close to neutral territory gave British agents an opportunity to gain direct information of their sorties. On some occasions the High Seas Fleet passed within plain sight of the

Dutch islands, on which the British undoubtedly had agents

In only one respect were the British at a disadvantage. The anchorage area in Rosyth or any one of the southern bases was too small for the entire Grand Fleet. This resulted in a separation of the Fleet into two main detachments, a condition that not only had strategic disadvantages, but also interfered with the training of the entire Grand Fleet as a single fighting force. The tactical training of a fleet can reach its highest efficiency only when there is every-day contact between the commander in chief and his flag officers. As will be demonstrated later, the British had no unified system of tactical command. To a great degree, the British had two fleets that operated, even thought, independently.

Also, it should be noted that the very distant position of the Battle Fleet, normally divided between Scapa and Cromarty, made it difficult to bring it into contact with the enemy in the southern part of the North Sea.

With such extremely slight chances of success, one may ask why Scheer should have initiated his daring, even reckless, campaign. First, we must remember that the swift-running current of German success was now slowing up. The Verdun offensive had become another long battle of attrition, in which the French losses did not greatly exceed the German. As skillfully as this battle was being fought by the Germans, it was becoming evident that their reserves were almost exhausted. Von Falkenhayn's original idea of the battle had been changed by the inexorable course of events. Verdun had become a symbol to both the French and Germans. Who held the battered city at the end of the battle would be psychologically the victor; and there was little chance that by this changed standard of measurement the Germans could win. True, the Austrian Trentino offensive was making some progress, but it was seen that no great success could be expected on that front. On the Eastern Front preparations for a Russian offensive in the Galician sector were apparent. Rumania, with a million potentially hostile troops, was assuming a more and more threatening attitude. It evidently was time for the Germans to throw in their last reserves, at sea as well as ashore.

Second, we have the desire of Scheer to make some use of the High Seas Fleet. Thus far nothing but the control of the Baltic and the defense of the North Sea coast had been accomplished by that costly organization. It was high time that something be done to justify the existence of a force that had cost so much in money and energy and upon which the nation had built such high hopes. As for Scheer himself, it was natural that, having been given a free hand by the Kaiser, he should wish to justify the confidence thus expressed in his ability.

Third, there was some chance of defeating a British detachment or of fighting an indecisive battle with the Grand Fleet. The favorable moral effect of such an encounter could be exploited at home and abroad, even though it might have no material effect upon the campaign for the command of the sea. This moral effect was, in itself, a goal worth striving for.

Fourth, it was necessary to demonstrate once and for all whether the High Seas Fleet had any real chance of breaking British command of the sea in order that the Kaiser should be convinced of the necessity for authorizing a resumption of the submarine campaign, upon which all naval effort could then be concentrated. That this idea may have been in Scheer's mind is indicated by his report of the approaching battle. In this, as will be seen, the German admiral, while claiming a victory, said that the High Seas Fleet could not hope for eventual success. This, he argued, was possible only by means of unrestricted submarine warfare.

As against these reasons for a naval offensive there was the very strong probability that the High Seas Fleet would lose by mines, submarines, and minor actions more than it could gain. There was also the virtual certainty that, if the campaign were continued long enough, the German Fleet would be trapped and destroyed by the Grand Fleet, provided always that the latter was commanded by a man who would force the fight to a finish. Scheer fully realized these dangers. He doubtless believed that he could reduce these ever-present hazards by planning carefully his operations, leaving port in secrecy, limiting his objectives, and using submarines and airships to give him warning of the approach of the enemy. It is probable that he relied greatly upon the cautious, Fabian character of the British commander in chief, if it should be necessary for him to extricate the High Seas Fleet from a desperate situation.

Now let us analyze the situation from the viewpoint of Admiral Jellicoe. We have seen that by a maintenance of the *status quo* he was accomplishing satisfactorily, if not perfectly, all the missions of the Grand Fleet, except (1) gaining the control of the Baltic with all its evident and important advantages; (2) furnishing a more effective protection to British trade against the attacks of German submarines and cruisers, the operations of which gave promise of considerable danger to British command of the sea; and (3) gaining moral effects by the spectacular Nelsonian victory that the world had come to expect from the British Navy.

If Jellicoe limited his task to the maintenance of the *status quo,* his position was almost impregnable and his chances of ultimate success as certain as they could be in war. This was the course he had adopted in his famous letter of October 30, 1914. He still, after 18 months of war, studiously and deliberately adhered to his original conception. It will be remembered that this contained three main provisions: (1) to fight only in the northern half of the North Sea or near the English bases; (2) not to pursue a retiring enemy, except in such a wide detour as would make pursuit ineffective; and (3) to receive the prompt support of all forces not attached to the Grand Fleet when he reported that a fleet action was imminent. These proposals had been expressly approved by the Admiralty and nothing had been done to alter the Admiralty's action. It is true that the British had good reason to be pleased with the naval situation; but there still remained important objectives to be won.

First, there was a practical object of outstanding importance: the naval command of the Baltic. This inevitably would result from a decisive victory over the High Seas Fleet. British command of the Baltic would have important effects in three ways. (1) It would establish direct contact between Russia and Great Britain, thus permitting the supply of the former's armies from outside sources. The vital importance of a closer entente with Russia is demonstrated by the mission on which Lord Kitchener was about to depart. It is one of the underlying ideas running through Lloyd George's memoirs. (2) It would cut the all-important trade routes between Germany and the Scandinavian countries, with the loss of the Swedish iron ore so necessary to the German munitions industry. (3) It would compel the Germans to draw upon their fast-diminishing reserves to defend their long and vulnerable coastal frontiers. It requires no argument to demonstrate the importance of gaining command of the Baltic.

Second, the annihilation of the High Seas Fleet with its remarkably efficient personnel would have greatly crippled the German Navy in the war against trade that every navy initiates when it becomes evident that it can no longer challenge the hostile fleet to a decisive fight to the finish. The British had seen the French turn to cruiser warfare after their defeat at Trafalgar. They were certainly well conversant with the effectiveness of our cruisers and privateers in the War of 1812. They had watched with ill-concealed delight the Confederate attack against our trade, which forced our merchant shipping to seek the protection of a neutral flag. They had recently seen the great successes of the *Emden, Karlsruhe,* and *Moewe.* The menace of the submarine certainly must have been recognized, even if its full potential power was not realized. Only with the trained personnel of the Fleet could the Germans carry through a large-scale warfare against trade.

Third, there were the tremendous moral effects of a great British naval victory, confirming again that superiority of British sea power which many had begun to doubt. Coming at such a critical time, when the tide of success seemed about to turn, the effects of such a victory would have been shattering to the morale of the German people and inspiring to those of the allied nations. On neutrals also its results would have been profound.

To gain these three important results of a successful fleet action, we believe the British were perfectly justified, with their immense superiority in both material strength and geographical position, in accepting every reasonable risk. But such was not Jellicoe's intention. "A third consideration," he wrote, "that was present in my mind was the necessity for *not leaving anything to chance in a fleet action, because our Fleet was the one and only factor that was vital to the existence of the Empire,* as indeed to the allied cause." To make certain that his intentions would not be misunderstood, Jellicoe wrote the greater part of this very clear and specific sentence in italics.

This sentence written by Jellicoe calls to mind the traditional sentence of Nelson: "Something must be left to chance; nothing is certain in a sea fight beyond all others." Jellicoe must have had this sentence in mind when he defends boldly his abrupt divergence from the British traditional system of naval warfare. He alleges two grounds for his rather remarkable action: (1) that in the old wars the naval situation was never so dangerous as in the World War; (2) that the introduction of new weapons had altered all conceptions of naval tactics.

As to the first point, it would be interesting to compare the almost impregnable position of England in 1916 with that which existed in 1588. It was then that Sir Francis Drake wrote a memorandum, "To maintain my opinion that I have thought it meeter to go for the coast of Spain." Thomas Fenner supported his opinion: "There never happened the like opportunity to beat down the Spanish pride, if it be effectually followed." Lord Howard acted in full accordance with this bold advice and was prevented only by continuous head winds from entering the base of the Spanish Armada and engaging it at anchor. Sir Julian Corbett writes:

Than that final swoop for Spain at the eleventh hour no more brilliant or daring movement was ever executed by a great naval commander. . . . The risks were great, but they were calculated to a hair's breadth. To sail with an unvictualed fleet and stake its existence on being able to replenish stores from the holds of a powerful enemy, to leave England uncovered when actually threatened by invasion, savors perhaps of rashness. But it was not so. It was a great conception heroically undertaken.

It was at the end of a week of desperate fighting that Howard said: "Though our powder and shot were well-nigh spent, we put on a brag countenance and gave them chase, as though we had wanted nothing."

On August 16, 1805, Admiral Cornwallis had off Brest a total force of 46 units, counting a three-decker as 2 units. In Brest was Ganteaume with 24 units. At Ferrol was Villeneuve with 30 units. Napoleon was at Boulogne with the army of invasion, waiting for Villeneuve to effect a junction with Ganteaume.

Cornwallis issued the following order to Calder, one of his subordinates:

The French and Spanish squadrons from the West Indies having arrived at Ferrol, you are hereby required and directed to proceed off that port immediately with the ships named in the margin [23 units]. You are to endeavor, as soon as possible, to get information of the enemy's force and situation, and use your utmost exertion to prevent their sailing or to intercept them should they attempt it.

Here in a situation of the utmost danger, Cornwallis had repeated the plan of Howard and Drake of going for the enemy. Calder, arriving off Ferrol, found that the enemy had sailed. Making a correct decision of remarkable boldness, Calder sailed on to Cadiz on his own responsibility and there found Villeneuve. Had Villeneuve evaded Calder and sailed into the Channel, as was easily possible, Cornwallis would have had only 23 units against 54 French and Spanish units. That shows the boldness with which the British fleets were handled in 1805 when England single-handed faced the great Napoleon.

Having already recited in detail accounts of the campaigns of 1588 and 1805, we do not hesitate to express the definite opinion that on both of those historic occasions, when England was threatened not only by superior naval concentrations but also by overwhelming military forces led by the greatest generals of the time, she was in a far more dangerous situation than in 1916. Furthermore, we believe that (1) the fleets of Howard and Cornwallis were even more vital to her existence than that of Jellicoe; (2) they had far less naval forces at their disposal (relative to those of the enemy) than had Jellicoe; (3) they had far less military forces to protect England should the fleet fail; (4) they had far less advantages of position; and (5) there was less chance of receiving assistance from an ally. We invite those readers of a historical turn of mind to verify these statements for themselves.

Jellicoe's claim that the introduction of new weapons had profoundly modified all tactical conceptions merits consideration. In his letter of October 30, 1914, Jellicoe refers principally to the dangers of mines and submarines. In fact, he makes the startling statement that:

It is quite within the bounds of possibility that half of our Battle Fleet might be disabled by under-water attack before the guns opened fire at all, if a false move is made, and I feel that I must constantly bear in mind the great probability of such attack and be prepared tactically to prevent its success.

Notice the very positive tone of the admiral's language. At the time of this letter Jellicoe expressed confidence in his ability to repel the torpedo attacks of German destroyers but, as the war progressed, this threat became ever present in his mind. Together with the danger of mines and submarines, it made, in his opinion, the difficulty of forcing action on a retiring enemy "to a certain extent insuperable."

Actually, in May, 1916, the threat of mines and submarines was imaginary. It could have been well known that no mine layers accompanied the High Seas Fleet on its sorties. There was, of course, the possibility that cruisers and destroyers might carry floating mines; but this could only have been done by sacrificing the armament in other respects and rendering the ships very vulnerable to gunfire. Furthermore, a mine field would be both easy to detect and to avoid. It was necessary only to avoid following in the tracks of German light forces suspected of laying mines, a notoriously inefficient weapon in a fleet action. The fact that the Germans had laid no mines in the Dogger Bank action, which had afforded a perfect opportunity for such tactics, should have dissipated Jellicoe's original fears on this subject. It is not unreasonable to state, therefore, that the Grand Fleet ran no appreciable risks from mines in a fleet action. It is believed that the Germans never laid mines in action during the entire war.

As regards submarines, it should have been evident that the problem of their co-ordination with the Fleet in battle was, and still is, a very difficult one. It was well known that the Germans had employed all their submarines on independent duty throughout the entire war until April 24, 1916. It could properly have been concluded that one month was an insufficient time for training the submarines to act in immediate tactical touch with the Fleet. In fact, their present possibilities in this regard are still very problematical. German submarines, of course, might be encountered in the North Sea and by chance might happen to be present during a fleet action. This latter possibility was much reduced by the fact that large numbers of submarines were known to be operating off the English coast. At any rate, as has already been demonstrated, the Germans ran far greater risks from submarine attack than did the British.

Torpedo fire from destroyers did present a real danger to the Grand Fleet. Between 1912 and 1916 we had studied this interesting problem in great detail. During that period four detailed analyses were written by this author and published. We had a high idea of the value of torpedo fire by destroyers in a fleet action. It certainly imposed a handicap on the commander of a pursuing fleet. It compelled him to act with prudence, particularly at the beginning of an action and until the tactics of the enemy and their effectiveness could be determined. But, just as certainly, we did not think that the torpedo eliminated all possibility of offensive action. It was the privilege of this author to present the Battle of Jutland on the game board to the Naval War College classes in the fall of 1916 in substantially its correct form. It resembled one of our own tactical games and, except for Scheer's famous battle turns, caused no surprise.

The use of destroyer smoke screens to disengage a battle line and permit its orderly retirement also imposed a handicap on a pursuing enemy. The Germans had used this method successfully at the Dogger Bank action.

Jellicoe's tactical decision not to pursue a retiring enemy, except by a wide detour, followed directly from his strategical decision not to leave anything to chance in a fleet action. His attitude was consistent throughout his entire period of command in the Grand Fleet. In our opinion, his strategical decision was contrary to the very fundamentals of warfare. The idea that any leader in war, business, politics, or finance can accomplish great results without leaving something to chance is disproved by forty centuries of history. It was an error of the greatest consequence. It is almost past belief that a naval service founded on the traditions of Drake, Howard, Blake, Hawke, Rodney, Jervis, Nelson, and Cornwallis could have accepted such an erroneous doctrine. In the days of sailing ships, the difficulties of forcing a sea fight to a decision were just as great as in 1916. Nevertheless, those old fellows had found ways of coming to grips with their enemies and winning decisive victories but not, it is true, without leaving something to chance.

In particular, so supercautious and Fabian an attitude on the part of one who enjoyed such a great numerical superiority and such enormous advantages of geographical position cannot be condoned. Nelson had never hesitated to engage with equal or slightly inferior forces, but he wanted numbers to annihilate his enemy. Jellicoe had the numbers for which Nelson longed. It is perfectly true that the British commander would have run some risk in trying to bring on a finish fight. However, in our opinion, such risk could have been kept within moderate limits. At any time the British could have disengaged themselves from a dangerous situation by means of the same methods they attributed to the Germans. In fact, we consider that the reasonable risks of torpedo hits to which the Grand Fleet might have been exposed would have been counter-balanced by one grave disadvantage always inherent to a retiring fleet, the necessity for abandoning ships whose speed had been reduced. This caused the loss of the *Blücher* at Dogger Bank. At Jutland it was soon to cause the loss of the *Lützow, Wiesbaden, Elbing,* and *Rostock* and nearly cause the abandonment of the *Seydlitz, Derfflinger,* and *Markgraf.*

It is also fair to point out that another fear of Admiral Jellicoe proved to be entirely unfounded. In his book he emphasizes again and again the point that the Germans, by selecting the time of their offensive, could come out in full fighting strength, while the British would be caught with a number of their ships unavailable. It will be interesting to compare the normal composition of the High Seas Fleet, as recently listed, with the ships shown in Appendix I that actually participated in the operation. It will be noted that the Germans had the following ships entirely missing from the operation: 2 battleships, the *König Albert* and *Bayern;* 1 battleship second-line, the *Preussen;* 3 light cruisers, the *Graudenz, Stralsund,* and *Berlin;* 1 mine layer, the *Brummer;* and 15 destroyers. As will be seen later, no German submarines nor airships took part in the battle as distinct from the operation or played any important part in the latter.

As against this list of German ships missing, the British were temporarily without the services of 4 battleships, the *Royal Sovereign, Emperor of India, Queen Elizabeth,* and *Dreadnought;* 1 battle cruiser, the *Australia;* 2 cruisers, the *Achilles* and *Donegal;* and 19 destroyers. As 8 Harwich Force destroyers were in the Fleet temporarily, this reduced the number of destroyers missing to 11. The light cruiser *Canterbury* of the Harwich Force was present in the action.

Thus, it will be seen that the proportion of total German strength actually used in the battle was about the same as a similar proportion of the British. Jellicoe's fear of a superior German destroyer force certainly did not materialize. Instead of the 88 boats he thought they had used at Jutland even as late as 1919, we find that they had only 61. Against this number the British had 78, including 6 destroyer leaders. The Germans, it is true, had 10 destroyers of Flotilla II that were about the size of the British leaders, but they also had a number of very small destroyers. Thus, the total numbers represented fairly accurately the relative strengths of the two Fleets in the destroyer arm.

From the above analysis of the situation on May 30, it is our conclusion that the British commander in chief should have been prepared to run reasonable risks in an earnest endeavor to gain the great advantages that a decisive victory over the High Seas Fleet would have won for the allied cause. Specifically, he should have been prepared to follow a retiring enemy, with reasonable precautions against the torpedo fire of large units of German destroyers, until he had received some appreciable losses. And certainly, he should have been prepared to take advantage of any favors of fortune or mistakes of the enemy in a bold and aggressive manner. While caution might possibly have been the watchword in the initial contact, Jellicoe should certainly have watched eagerly for the first opportunity to strike an overwhelming and decisive blow. In particular, he should have tried to gain a position on the German line of retreat, thus throwing the Germans away from their bases should they use the retiring tactics that Jellicoe feared.

Having now the strategical and tactical background for the battle and being conversant with the situation as it existed on May 30, let us return to our narrative of the greatest naval battle of modern times.

JOHN RUSHWORTH JELLICOE

As Admiral, he was Commander in Chief of Grand Fleet at Jutland, at the age of fifty-six. First Sea Lord and Chief of Naval Staff, 1916–17; Admiral of the Fleet, 1919; Governor General of New Zealand, 1920–24; retired, 1924. Viscount Jellicoe of Scapa, 1918; Viscount Brocas of Southampton, 1925; First Earl Jellicoe, 1925. Died November 20, 1935, and buried in St. Paul's Cathedral.

REINHARD KARL FRIEDRICH HEINRICH SCHEER

As Vice Admiral, he was Commander in Chief of High Seas Fleet at Jutland, at the age of fifty-two. Admiral, June 5, 1916; Chief of Admiralty Staff, August-November, 1918; retired, January, 1919. Died November 26, 1928.

CHAPTER VIII

THE OPERATION COMMENCES

WE HAVE NOTED that early on the thirtieth Scheer decided to substitute for the long-planned Sunderland operation an advance toward the Skagerrak. At 9:48 A.M. he sent a general message to the Fleet that the concentration in the outer Jade Roads must be completed by 7:00 P.M. At 10:00 A.M. the ships in the Jade commenced the execution of this order (Fig. 16–A). At 10:37 the mine sweepers and seaplanes were ordered by Vice Admiral Hipper to search for submarines along the channel that passed west of Helgoland and Amrum Bank in a northwesterly direction. At 11:31 Mine-Sweeper Group I was directed to sweep this channel (Fig. 16–C). These various orders were sent by radio, an unnecessary procedure.

The British had evidently intercepted some or all of the German messages. Corbett states that during the forenoon there were indications that the High Seas Fleet was assembling in the Jade Roads. At noon the Admiralty warned Jellicoe that the German Fleet might go to sea early the next morning. He was told that there were 16 German submarines at sea. Vice Admiral Bacon was directed to return to Tyrwhitt the 8 Harwich Force destroyers temporarily on duty with the Dover Patrol. The Belgian coast patrol was ordered back to port (Fig. 16–B). Also the rear admiral, East Coast, who had headquarters at Grimsby, was directed to recall his mine sweepers (Fig. 16–D). Bradford was instructed to have the 3d Battle Squadron and the 3d Cruiser Squadron in the Swin ready to proceed next morning on short notice.

Only a few minutes after these messages had been dispatched by land wire, the sloop *Gentian,* in a position about 22 miles 80° from Pentland Skerries, radioed that at 12:30 P.M. a torpedo, evidently fired by a submarine, had missed her (Fig. 16–E).

At 12:37 the Admiralty ordered the Harwich Submarine

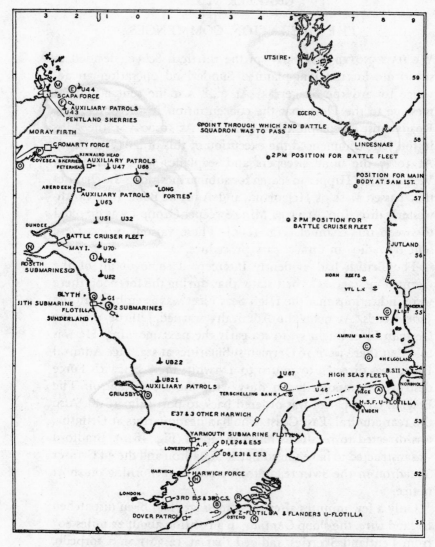

FIG. 16. Movements from 8:00 A.M. to midnight, May 30. Positions of submarines are approximate only.

Flotilla to prepare for sea on short notice. At 2:37 P.M. Tyrwhitt reported to Beatty that he had 5 light cruisers and 15 destroyers ready for service; these did not include the 8 boats ordered to return from Dover.

It was the *U–43*, Lieutenant Commander Jürst, that had fired her torpedo at the *Gentian* at a range of about 2,500 yards. This unlucky advertisement of his position resulted in a concentration of the British patrol forces against the *U–43* and her comrade to the southward, the *U–44*, Lieutenant Commander Wagenführ. A division of destroyers of the 12th Flotilla (probably the *Marksman, Mischief, Narwhal,* and *Mary Rose*) were ordered out in support. Both German submarines were driven down during the night. This prevented their observation of the eastern exit from Scapa while the Battle Fleet was proceeding into the North Sea. The torpedo at the *Gentian* had proved most unfortunate. However, the submarine commander did not know that the operation was to commence that night and we cannot blame him for striking at the patrol craft that were his particular enemies.

At 3:40 Vice Admiral Scheer sent a cryptic radio message to the High Seas Fleet and the Flanders Forces. It was simply: "31 Gg 2490." This was the code group indicating that the operation order for the advance into the Skagerrak would be executed on the thirty-first.

It was shortly after 5:00 P.M. when the Admiralty learned that a seemingly important radio message had been broadcast to the entire High Seas Fleet. This evidently was the code group sent out by Scheer. This failure to observe the essentials of radio security might well have cost the Germans dearly, for at 5:15 the Admiralty ordered Jellicoe and Beatty to raise steam.

At 5:35 came a report from the trawler *Dunpedril*, via the destroyer *Owl*, that at 3:45 P.M. she had sighted a submarine about 14 miles 120° from Pentland Skerries (Fig. 16–F). This was the *U–44*.

Finally, at 5:50 P.M. there was flashed to Jellicoe the Admiralty's laconic message: "You should concentrate to eastward of Long Forties ready for eventualities." Immediately the preparatory signals to leave Scapa and Cromarty were flown by Jellicoe and Jerram. Only 5 minutes later Beatty ordered his fleet to raise steam for 22 knots. Patrolling light cruisers and the *Marksman's* detachment were recalled to join their respective commands. The battleship *Royal Oak* was instructed to return to the anchorage. Both the Admiralty and the Grand Fleet had acted with almost incredible promptness and alacrity.

While the Grand Fleet was to concentrate far at sea, it was decided at 5:55 that the Harwich Force and Bradford's detachment would "not be sent out until more is known." Apparently the Admiralty sensed the possibility of another raid on Yarmouth and did not desire that the forces in southern waters should be surprised by superior numbers. However, it might be inquired whether these forces would be of any real utility if they must remain safely in their bases until the exact dispositions of the enemy were known. It could not be expected that the Germans would always be so polite as to inform their opponents of their intentions. At 6:20 the Admiralty directed that the Harwich Force should be ready to sail at daylight of the thirty-first, if required. By the time this message was received 7 destroyers had returned to Harwich from Dover (Fig. 16–H). Tyrwhitt reported that he had ready for sea 5 light cruisers, 2 destroyer leaders, and 21 destroyers. These included, however, 8 destroyers that he had been ordered to send to the Swin to screen the 3d Battle Squadron.

The decision to hold the Harwich Force in port was, in our opinion, a grave error. It should have been sent to occupy a position in readiness off Terschelling. The Germans might have, in general, two plans of operation. The first was a movement into the northern part of the North Sea. In this case the Harwich Force off Terschelling would have been well located to gain the line of retreat of the High Seas Fleet to deliver night torpedo attacks. Should the Germans be proceeding on another raid against Yarmouth, Tyrwhitt would be perfectly located to detect their advance and probably would have an opportunity to make night torpedo attacks before the bombardment took place. In any case. Tyrwhitt would be able to re-enforce the Grand Fleet on short notice, as agreed upon between Jellicoe and the Admiralty. The high speed of his force would prevent its being brought under the fire of superior German forces if destroyer groups were disposed in the direction of the enemy to give warning of their approach.

Scheer's original plan for the Skagerrak operation had been, in general, as follows:

(1) Vice Admiral Hipper, with the scouting forces (Scouting Groups I and II; the *Regensburg*; and Flotillas II, VI, and IX) would leave Jade Roads at daylight (3:00 A.M.) May 31. He would proceed northward beyond visibility range of the Danish coast and show himself off the Norwegian coast before dark (9:00 P.M.) the same day.

(2) Vice Admiral Scheer, with the main body (Battle Squadrons I and III; Scouting Group IV; the *Rostock*, the *Hamburg*; and Flotillas I, III, V, and VII) would follow the scouting forces at a considerable interval, so as to arrive in a supporting position 45 miles to the southward of Lindesnaes at 5:00 A.M., June 1.

(3) The submarines of the High Seas Fleet were to attack British forces leaving Scapa, Cromarty, Rosyth, and the Humber, reporting their strength and movements.

(4) The submarines of the Flanders U-Flotilla were to perform similar duties off Harwich, the Thames, and Dover.

(5) Airships, if weather permitted, would proceed on radial courses from their bases and search as far as practicable over the North Sea.

(6) Battle Squadron II, assisted by seaplanes from Helgoland and List, and by the *U–53, U–22, U–19*, and *U–64*, was to guard the approaches to the German bases.

At the last minute, 5:41 P.M., Scheer altered this plan in two important particulars. It had been based largely on effective airship scouting, which it was hoped would be more practicable off the near-by Danish coast than along the distant shores of England. However, the admiral now decided that airship scouting might be impracticable even toward the Skagerrak. It would be necessary in this case for the main body to follow the scouting forces more closely. Accordingly, it was directed to leave the

Jade Roads at 4:30 A.M., or 1½ hours after Hipper. Even then the greater speed of the scouting forces would gradually open out a considerable interval from the main body as the Fleet proceeded northward. This was a wise change in the original plan.

The second, on the other hand, was of very doubtful expediency. The admiral decided that Battle Squadron II should accompany the main body of the Fleet. The fighting strength of these distinctly second-line battleships was very slight. Their main battery consisted of only four 11-inch guns. Their defensive strength was even less. Their thin armor could not hope to resist the heavy British shells, some as large as 15-inch. A single hit by a mine or torpedo was liable to send them to the bottom or, at the least, to reduce greatly their speed; but the greatest defect of the second-line battleships was their low speed. They could steam only at 18 knots, as compared with the usual 21-knot speed of first-line battleships.

An inferior force which may owe its safety to what Jellicoe called retiring tactics, certainly should not be hampered by the presence of ships having a considerably inferior speed. Here was Scheer forcing himself, in all probability, to a choice between abandoning six large ships to their fate or reducing the speed of his battle line by 3 knots in order to give them support. His decision is all the more remarkable in view of the Dogger Bank action. It would seem that the dramatic destruction of the slow cruiser *Blücher* would have demonstrated clearly the folly of attaching slow-steaming, weakly armed vessels of greatly inferior defensive strength to a battle line of modern first-line battleships. Scheer admits that his decision was influenced largely by the pleadings of Rear Admiral Mauve and his desire to preserve the high morale of Battle Squadron II, which he himself had commanded. While the moral factor is certainly of great importance, we believe that it was given undue weight in this case. If Scheer had been compelled to abandon several of these slow ships, the moral effect might almost have broken the spirit of the Fleet. Of even greater importance was the fact that Scheer by his own act greatly reduced what Jellicoe called the "insuperable" difficulty of pressing a close pursuit of the High Seas Fleet. Here was the first of the "breaks" that fortune insisted on giving an admiral determined to leave nothing to chance.

Evidently, the Germans realized, or at least suspected, that their radio messages were giving valuable information to their enemy. Partly to remedy this situation, it was directed that the guardship anchored at Entrance III should take over the radio guard for the fleet flagship. She also took over and used the radio call then in use by the commander in chief in the *Friedrich der Grosse*. The latter would observe radio silence until contacts with the enemy were reported. All messages addressed to Scheer would be receipted for by the guardship and broadcast to the flagship, which would not answer or receipt for them by radio. If the British should use their radio direction finders to fix the position of the ship using the commander in chief's call, they would find that she was still in the Jade Roads and infer from this that the High Seas Fleet was still in port. That wise precaution served the Germans well. Up to that time the British naval commanders had received remarkably accurate information of both the actual and projected movements of the High Seas Fleet. Henceforth they would cease to enjoy this advantage until the Fleets came into contact.

At 8:00 P.M., May 30, the *U-46*, stationed off Terschelling light vessel, reported that she had been having a busy time. No less than six times she had made contact with enemy submarines (Fig. 16-J). Once she had been a target for torpedo fire; another time for gunfire. She returned to Emden to effect repairs on her periscope. This, as will be seen later, gave her a marvelous chance to torpedo a British battleship.

The *Arcona*, the old cruiser that acted as a submarine tender at Emden, and the Naval Radio at Bruges (Fig. 16-K) commenced broadcasting to all submarines: "Prepare for enemy forces standing out on May 31 and June 1." This informed the submarines that the High Seas Fleet would be at sea on those days, but did not tell that the advance into the Skagerrak had been substituted for the Sunderland offensive. The time at which this message was first broadcast is not stated, but it evidently was repeated at frequent intervals, for one submarine, the *U–66,* recorded its receipt at 1:00 A.M. of the thirty-first. Unfortunately, only four other Emden submarines received this warning message—the *U–67, UB–22, U–70,* and *U–32.*

The captain of the latter submarine, the celebrated Graf Spiegel von und zu Peckelsheim, estimated that the Battle Cruiser Fleet would put to sea during the dark period, then about 6 hours in duration. Therefore, he decided to take a position about 80 miles due east of Fair Island in order to make contact with the enemy at daylight the next morning, i.e., about 3:00 A.M., May 31. This was a wise estimate of the situation and, as we shall see, led to an interesting incident. Also the *U–66,* Lieutenant Commander von Bothmer, being severely harassed by British patrol craft, left her station and went somewhat to the northward, reporting her action by radio (Fig. 16–L).

It will be remembered that, in accordance with Jellicoe's plan for an operation in the Kattegat, three Harwich submarines were to occupy stations off Vyl light vessel from June 1 to 3. Early on May 30, these three submarines had been given their preliminary orders. At 6:44 P.M., the Admiralty ordered them to proceed immediately. At 7:00, with admirable promptness, the *E–55, E–26,* and *D–1* sailed for their assigned stations. The original order for these submarines, based on the Kattegat plan, was for them to remain on the bottom until June 2. In the haste, no change was made in the orders, though the submarines were now being sent out under entirely different conditions. This was a most unfortunate error. During the evening numerous reports of German submarines were received by the British commanders. The senior officer, mine sweepers, reported as late as 8:20 P.M. that he was harassing 2 German submarines with 12 sloops. The submarines were the *U–43* and *U–44.* They were forced under water and unable to rig their radio masts to receive the important warning message from the *Arcona* and Bruges.

At 7:30 P.M. Jellicoe gave his orders to Vice Admiral Jerram at Cromarty. He was directed to proceed with the 2d Battle Squadron and accompanying light forces through a position in Lat. 58–15, Long. 2–00 East. He was to join the forces sailing from Scapa at 2:00 P.M. of the thirty-first in Lat. 57–45, Long. 4–15 East.

At 7:37 Jellicoe sent the following order to Beatty:

Available vessels, Battle Cruiser Fleet, Fifth Battle Squadron, and t.b.d's, including Harwich t.b.d's, proceed to approximate position Lat. 56°–40′ N, Long. 5°–00′ E. Desire to economize t.b.d's fuel. Presume you will be there about 2:00 P.M. thirty-first. I shall be in about Lat. 57°–45′ N, Long. 4°–15′ E, by 2:00 P.M. unless delayed by fog. Third Battle Cruiser Squadron, *Chester*, and *Canterbury* will leave with me. I will send them on to your rendezvous. If no news by 2:00 P.M., stand toward me to get in visual touch. I will steer for Horn Reef from position in Lat. 57°–45′ N, Long. 4°–15′ E. Repeat back rendezvous. 1937.

Just an hour later Beatty acknowledged these orders and repeated back the rendezvous correctly. As both dispatches were by land wire, the Germans would have no reason to believe that the Grand Fleet was going to sea.

At 8:27 P.M. the commander, Harwich Submarine Flotilla, reported that three more of his submarines had sailed—the *D–6*, *E–31*, and *E–53*. These boats presumably took the usual patrol stations off Terschelling to relieve the four that were reported returning to Harwich at 9:43 A.M., May 31. According to Corbett, two Blyth submarines sailed to take station east of the Dogger Bank, as provided in Jellicoe's original plan for the Kattegat operation (Fig. 16–s). This statement is not confirmed by any official signal in the British record.

At 9:30 P.M. the Scapa Force commenced leaving port (Fig. 16–M). After passing the Skerries, course was set about 66° and speed of 17 knots was directed. As this was not the direct route to the rendezvous, it is possible that it was selected to avoid submarines reported to the eastward of the Skerries. By 10:30 the entire force was clear of the harbor, except for the seaplane carrier *Campania*. About 9:31 the *Iron Duke* received a report that the destroyer *Trident* on patrol off the entrance to Rosyth had been attacked by a submarine at 6:45 (Fig. 16–I).

It was the usual custom for the Scapa Force to use three routes after leaving the Skerries for the rest of the night, the entire force concentrating at daybreak; but on this occasion practically the entire force used Route A, passing through Lat. 58–47, Long. 2–37 W. Only the 4th Light Cruiser Squadron and the 3d Battle Cruiser Squadron used Route B, 2 miles to the southward.

At 10:15 P.M. Vice Admiral Jerram left Cromarty (Fig. 16–O). He headed on course 90° close along the coast directly for his 2:00 P.M. rendezvous. As he had a greater distance to make good, speed was set at 19 knots. To assist his navigation, Covesea light was lighted from 10:30 to 11:30 P.M. (Fig. 16–P) and Kinnaird light from 1:00 to 1:45 A.M. The arrangements for leaving port were made with such admirable thoroughness that a study of the British communication record will be well repaid. At 10:00 Jellicoe had made the usual signal:

Cease W/T communication except on sighting the enemy or replying to the admiral. W/T guards may use auxiliary in case of necessity.

Neither the *U–43* nor *U–44* gained any information of the sortie of the Scapa Force. Having been forced to submerge, they had not received the warning message. Being constantly hunted by patrol craft, they were unable to see anything of the passing squadrons; and it is doubtful whether they would have done so under any circumstances in their present positions. They were in too close for covering a sortie by night. They should have retired, if permitted by patrol craft, to positions about 80 miles off Scapa, as the *U–32* had done.

At 10:00 P.M. the Battle Cruiser Fleet commenced leaving Rosyth, followed 40 minutes later by the 5th Battle Squadron (Fig. 16–N). Only at 9:30 there had arrived the reports of the attack on the *Trident,* a destroyer attached to the 11th Submarine Flotilla, in a position about 39 miles, 120° from May Island (Fig. 16–I). Beatty, therefore, ordered all squadrons to pass north of May Island and to steer 66° at 18 knots for 20 miles. Course was then to be set direct to the 2:00 P.M. position assigned by Jellicoe.

At 10:30 P.M. Commodore Tyrwhitt was ordered to send eight destroyers to join the 3d Battle Squadron in the Swin. The remaining destroyers were to remain on an hour's notice after daylight. We have already commented adversely upon the holding of Tyrwhitt's splendid force in port. We repeat this criticism. The sending of eight good destroyers to protect a perfectly useless squadron of second-line battleships that practically did not leave their anchorage during the entire operation was inexcusable. It can be accounted for only by the paralyzing effect of the bombardment of Lowestoft upon the Lords of the Admiralty. Whatever happened they were going to prevent another bombardment at all costs. No comment upon such an attitude is necessary.

At 11:00 P.M. the submarine *G–1*, of the 11th Submarine Flotilla, returned to Blyth from a cruise (Fig. 16–Q). At 11:20 P.M. Jellicoe reported to the Admiralty, apparently by low-powered radio, that this flotilla was ready for sea. He asked the Admiralty to give it orders as the situation developed. This was a correct procedure, as Jellicoe could not now give orders to his submarines by radio without disclosing his position and giving the Germans an opportunity to decipher his instructions. It would have been better had he sent this message by land wire just before leaving port.

At midnight the *Lion* was approaching May Island. At the same time the *Iron Duke* was approaching Pentland Skerries. By that time all elements of the Grand Fleet were well at sea and proceeding at high speeds, while the High Seas Fleet still rode quietly at anchor in the Jade Roads. So great was the advantage the British received from the careless use of radio by their enemies. The submarines of the Flanders Flotilla were alone setting out to take station off the English coast in the vicinity of Harwich (Fig. 17–A).

It was at 12:40 A.M. that Scheer received the customary report via the guardship at Entrance III from the Naval Airship Base at Nordholz that unfavorable weather made airship scouting impracticable. Nevertheless, Scheer permitted the operation to commence as per plan. At 1:00 A.M. the scouting forces proceeded from the roads northward past Helgoland at 16 knots (Fig. 17–B). At 2:30 A.M. the main body followed at 14 knots (Fig.

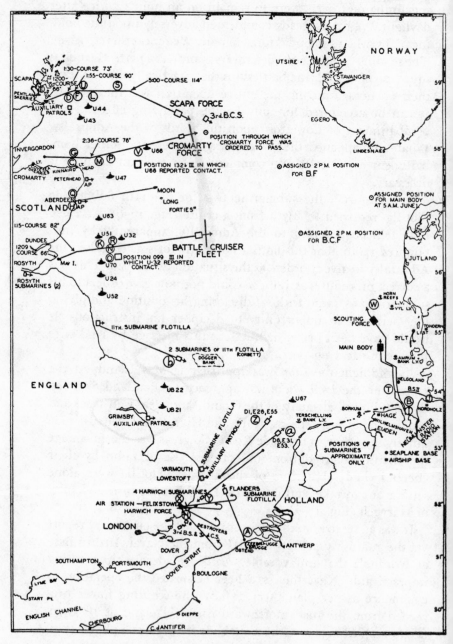

FIG. 17. The High Seas Fleet puts to sea. Midnight to 8:00 A.M., May 31, showing positions of all forces at the latter time.

17–I). At the same time Battle Squadron II proceeded from the Elbe to join the main body (Fig. 17–J). Soon after it became daylight, about 3:00 A.M., the seaplane stations at List and Helgoland reported that the weather was unsuited for the air scouting that had been ordered.

While the Germans were proceeding in this uneventful manner, the Grand Fleet was passing through the patrol areas of the German submarines. A few minutes after midnight, the *Iron Duke* had passed Pentland Skerries on course 66° at 17 knots. At 1:00, as has been related, Kinnaird Head light burned for 45 minutes to assist the navigation of the Cromarty Force (Fig. 17–C). At 1:22 Jellicoe sent an entirely unnecessary radio message to the Admiralty giving the rendezvous of the Battle Fleet and Battle Cruiser Fleet for 2:00 P.M. of the thirty-first. Some staff officer evidently had forgotten to send this dispatch by land wire before sailing. In fact, the order to Beatty should have been forwarded by land wire to the Admiralty for information. Even if sent by low-power radio, the message might have been picked up by a near-by German submarine and forwarded to the German cryptanalysis agency at Neumünster. A rendezvous for 12 hours in advance was most dangerous to put on the air.

At 1:30 A.M. the Scapa Force changed course to 73°. Its battle squadrons formed in four parallel columns at intervals of 1,600 yards (Fig. 17–D). At 1:45 the seaplane carrier *Campania* left Scapa to overtake the Battle Fleet (Fig. 17–E). At 1:55 the Scapa Force made a further change of course to 90°. About the same time the 2d Cruiser Squadron commenced forming a screen 10 miles ahead of the *Iron Duke* in cruising disposition LS1–10 (Fig. 17–F). The 2d Battle Squadron, proceeding from Cromarty, formed in two parallel columns at an interval of 1,200 yards. At 2:35 the Scapa Force commenced zigzagging. The speed of individual ships was 17 knots, while the fleet speed, the speed of advance along the fleet course, was 16 knots (Fig. 17–L). The destroyer flotillas formed anti-submarine screens about the battleship divisions at 4:00 A.M.

Beatty passed May Island at 12:05 A.M., speed 18 knots, course 66°. The light cruiser squadrons which had preceded the *Lion*

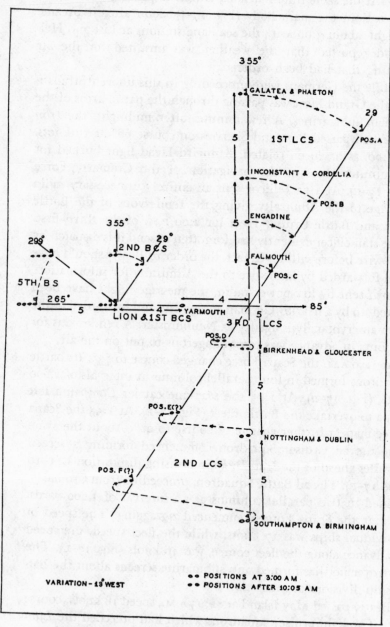

SKETCH II. Change of cruising disposition of Battle Cruiser
Fleet at 10:05 A.M., May 31, 1916.

took up cruising disposition LS6, 8 miles ahead of her. Despite the darkness, the destroyer flotillas formed anti-submarine screens about the capital ships, in contrast with the procedure in the Battle Fleet, where the screen was not formed until daylight. The *Lion,* as fleet guide, led the 1st Battle Cruiser Squadron. The 2d Battle Cruiser Squadron was 5 miles ahead. The 5th Battle Squadron was an equal distance astern. After running 20 miles from May Island, Beatty at 1:15 changed course to 82°. At 2:30 zigzagging commenced with a fleet speed of 18 knots (Fig. 17-K). About 3:00 the *Nottingham, Nicator,* and *Nomad,* which had been on "dark night patrol," joined the Fleet (Fig. 17-O). The 2d Battle Cruiser Squadron now took station 3 miles, bearing 352° from the *Lion.* The 5th Battle Squadron still remained 5 miles astern.

The Fleet was in this cruising disposition when the first contact was made with the enemy. Had the *U-32* been in her correct patrol station, she would have sighted the southern flank vessels of the British light cruiser screen. However, Graf Spiegel was actually 20 miles farther to the northward. So, instead, about 3.40 A.M. he sighted two light cruisers, which he believed to be the *Attentive* and *Adventure* (Fig. 17-R). Actually, they were the *Galatea,* flagship of the 3d Light Cruiser Squadron, and the *Phaeton* on the northern flank of the screen (Sketch II). The German captain, one of the most efficient of the submarine commanders, decided to fire two bow shots at the first cruiser and one stern shot at the second. It seemed that the operation was about to commence with a brilliant success for the Germans; but unfortunately, just after the first torpedo was fired at 3:50, the periscope jammed. It is a remarkable fact that practically no German submarine in the entire Jutland operation escaped some sort of a casualty just as she was firing torpedoes. One of the torpedoes broached while approaching the target. The *Galatea* was maneuvered rapidly and succeeded in avoiding both torpedoes, one passing ahead and the other astern. Not only was the *U-32* unable to fire her stern shot at the *Phaeton,* but she had to dive quickly to 50 feet to avoid being rammed. At 3:55 the *Galatea* signaled by searchlight to the *Lion,* "Have just been fired at by submarine." Upon receipt of this message, Beatty at 4:04 made a general flag signal to change course together 22° to the right, steadying on about 130°.

Soon after this, at 4:10, the U–32 came up to the 32-foot depth for another look around. Far in the distance to the southward were seen two battle cruisers surrounded by destroyers. They were the 2d Battle Cruiser Squadron and six boats of the 9th and 10th Flotillas. Graf Spiegel estimated that their course was southerly, as it was. It was impracticable to attack because of his low surface speed. So he surfaced, rigged his radio masts, and sent the following message: "2 battleships, 2 cruisers, and several destroyers on southerly course." He appended his estimated position in square 099 of the German confidential position chart.

Beatty's change of course had resulted in the sending of a most confusing message. This brings up an interesting point. Suppose the U–32 had not attacked the Galatea. Then her captain would probably have seen ten British capital ships on an easterly course. That would have been interesting and highly important news to Scheer. However, there was no definite reason to believe that British capital ships were following the light cruisers. In this case we believe that he was entirely right in trying to sink the two cruisers. The old adage about "a bird in the hand" applies perfectly to submarine operations. However, could he have guessed that the entire Battle Cruiser Fleet was present, it is possible that Graf Spiegel could have passed under the cruisers for an attack on the capital ships. It is unfortunate that he did not see the light cruisers in the screen next to the Galatea that were distant only 5 miles. That might have given him an idea that there was bigger game to be hunted.

It was not until 1:00 A.M. of the thirty-first that the U–66 received the warning message from Bruges. Lieutenant Commander von Bothmer had an interesting decision to make. Believing that the Sunderland offensive had commenced, he thought it highly improbable that the Battle Cruiser Fleet would emerge from Rosyth to the northeastward through the sector which he had been forced to leave. He thought it probable, however, that the Battle Fleet would leave Scapa and head toward

Horn Reefs to cut off the retreat of the High Seas Fleet. Therefore, he decided to take station on that track about 60 miles east
of Kinnaird Head. Actually, he was some 15 miles farther to the
northward and directly in the track of the 2d Battle Squadron
en route from Cromarty to join Jellicoe. At 2:36 Jerram had
changed course to 79° to head directly for the position through
which he had been ordered to pass. As previously stated, his
battleships were disposed in two parallel columns of four ships
each, 1,200 yards or 6 cables apart. Since 2:45 they had been
zigzagging with 18 knots speed of advance (Fig. 17-M). The
battleships were screened against submarine attack by part of
the 11th Flotilla, consisting of the leader *Kempenfelt* and nine
destroyers. One mile ahead was the attached light cruiser
Boadicea. Since 3:15 the four vessels of the 1st Cruiser Squadron
had been 10 miles ahead of the battleships, spread 5 miles apart
in accordance with LS1–10, i.e., Cruising Diagram No. 1 with
10 miles distance. Their order from north to south was *Warrior*,
Defence, *Duke of Edinburgh*, and *Black Prince*. The destroyer
Moon, which at 2:20 had arrived at Aberdeen to fuel (Fig. 17-H),
had proceeded at 3:18 (Fig. 17-Q) to join the 2d Battle Squadron
in its 2:00 P.M. rendezvous. The rapidity with which this
destroyer was fueled was an excellent example of British ad-
ministrative efficiency.

At 5:00 von Bothmer saw a large cruiser coming out of the
mist directly toward the *U–66* (Fig. 17-V). This was probably
the *Duke of Edinburgh* in her position about 10 miles ahead
of the battleship divisions. When sighted, the cruiser was distant
about 5,000 yards. The submarine submerged. Von Bothmer
advanced for a bow tube attack; but, unfortunately for him,
the unknown cruiser executed a zigzag and passed out of torpedo
range. Next a light cruiser was sighted, probably the *Boadicea*.
As the German captain was approaching for a shot at her, he
saw a line of eight battleships surrounded by destroyers. The
heaven-sent opportunity for which every submarine captain
hopes had arrived. Just as the *U–66* was about to fire at a range
of 300 yards a destroyer forced her to dive. By the time von
Bothmer could come up to periscope depth for another look,

the battleships had passed, and the opportunity had been lost.

The *U–66* came to the surface as soon as the enemy was clear. At 6:35 she got off a radio report as follows: "Eight enemy battleships, light cruisers, destroyers on northerly course in 132 Beta III." The square in which the *U–66* reported herself was 15 miles south of her actual position, an error of no importance. The generally excellent report of the *U–66* was made most misleading by the statement that the enemy was on a northerly course. In the first place, this was a very loose term. A submarine making such a prolonged contact with a large force should have been able to report its course more specifically than this. Actually, the *U–66* seems to have caught the 2d Battle Squadron on a zigzag two points ($22\frac{1}{2}°$) to the left of the base course, which was recorded in the signal log at 5:40, about the time the contact was made. As the base course at this time was 76°, the actual course steered would have been 54°. This evidently was considered to be a "northerly course" by von Bothmer. A submarine reporting the course of an enemy should endeavor to estimate it within 10° and should not be deceived by any zigzag or other temporary course steered to avoid the submarine. It must be remembered that this was the first time the German submarines had operated with the Fleet.

At 2:00 A.M. Tyrwhitt sent 8 destroyers to join the 3d Battle Squadron in the Swin. This detachment left him 5 light cruisers and 15 destroyers. In accordance with orders, the seaplane squadrons scattered along the English coast scouted far to seaward at daybreak. Nothing was sighted. At 4:50 Tyrwhitt, properly becoming impatient, sent the significant dispatch to the Admiralty: "No orders have been received for the Harwich Force yet." There are many ways in which a subordinate may intimate that all is not well without overstepping the bounds of discipline and courtesy. One of the easiest is to imply that there may have been a failure of the communication service, or that someone may have forgotten to send him his orders. This was just what Tyrwhitt had done. The Admiralty quickly read between the lines. A curt reply was sent: "Orders are to remain at one hour's notice." It evidently was hoped that this would restrain Tyrwhitt's desire to get out to sea and come within supporting distance of the Grand Fleet. We have already commented sufficiently for the present upon the Admiralty's highly improper handling of the Harwich Force.

Meanwhile, at 5:00 A.M. the Scapa Force had come to course 116°, which pointed it directly at the 2:00 P.M. rendezvous. The four battleship divisions were now at intervals of 1,600 yards (8 cables). Since 4:01 destroyers had been disposed in antisubmarine screens about the battleship divisions (Fig. 17–s). Three miles ahead of them were the five vessels of the 4th Light Cruiser Squadron, disposed abreast from left to right as follows: *Calliope, Constance, Comus, Royalist, Caroline.* Two miles farther ahead was the light cruiser *Active* in the position usually occupied by the 5th Battle Squadron. Five miles ahead of the *Active* was the cruiser screen, consisting of the *Minotaur, Shannon,* and *Cochrane.* The fourth ship, the *Hampshire,* had taken station midway between the *Minotaur* and *Active* as a linking ship. Each cruiser was screened by a destroyer: the *Hampshire* by the *Midge;* the *Minotaur* by the *Owl;* the *Shannon* by the *Hardy;* the *Cochrane* by the *Mischief.* Five miles ahead of the cruiser screen was the light cruiser *Chester* and an equal distance ahead of her the 3d Battle Cruiser Squadron. The *Canterbury,* another light cruiser, was somewhat ahead of the battle cruisers. The formation of the Scapa Force at this time was quite similar to that of the Battle Fleet (Sketch IV) for 2:00 P.M., except that the vessels comprising the Cromarty Force were not present.

The various cruiser squadrons were to keep within visual distance and to maintain position on the fleet guide, the *Iron Duke,* through linking ships. In the comparatively low visibility, there was great difficulty in keeping proper station. The communication record shows a long series of signals asking if a certain ship were in sight and for her bearing and distance. In particular, the 3d Battle Cruiser Squadron was almost entirely out of signal touch with the fleet guide and seems to have increased its distance from that vessel considerably above the 20 miles ordered. In fact, at 7:50 A.M., it seems that the distance was about 30 miles, as indicated by a signal from the *Chester* that the *Invincible* was about 18 miles from the *Minotaur*. As the cruiser screen was disposed to the northward of the fleet axis, the battle cruisers also seem to have got to the northward. In the early morning, the seaplane carrier *Campania* had reported an engineering casualty. At 4:37 she had been directed to return to Scapa (Fig. 17–U).

While the British forces were advancing to their appointed rendezvous, the High Seas Fleet had been passing through the swept channel west of Helgoland without incident. As the scouting forces were steaming at 16 knots, they had gained an interval of 24 miles by 2:30 A.M., when the main body got under way. As the latter force proceeded at 14 knots, this interval increased at the rate of 2 miles an hour. At 4:00 the main body was joined by Battle Squadron II from the Elbe (Fig. 17–T). An hour later the main body passed Helgoland on the starboard beam.

At 5:37 there arrived in the *Friedrich der Grosse*, via the *Arcona* and Entrance III, the *U–32's* contact report. About an hour later, at 6:40, came a report from the Radio Station at Neumünster: "Two large warships or groups with destroyers left Scapa Flow." Only 8 minutes later there came the contact report of the *U–66*. Thus Scheer had fairly accurate information of the three main forces of the Grand Fleet. However, he was much confused by the statement that the Cromarty Force was on a northerly course, while the Rosyth Force should be reported on a southerly course. For this reason he failed to deduce the probable intentions of the British. However, the information increased his hope of meeting an inferior British detachment. He saw no reason to change his dispositions or plans in any respect.

At 7:50 A.M. Scouting Group II and Flotillas II and VI formed a screen about Scouting Group I in the sector between north-west and northeast at a distance of 8 miles (Sketch VI and Fig. 17–W). The five light cruisers were each accompanied by from three to five destroyers. Apparently, by this time Hipper had cleared the swept channel and was entering the open sea. There being then no British submarines on watch off the Danish coast, the German advance was not detected. Thus the two fleets proceeded toward Little Fisher Bank, where fate had prescribed their famous rendezvous.

The detachments of British submarines were now well at sea. The *D–1*, *E–26*, and *E–55* were about to pass through the patrol area of the *U–67* off Terschelling (Fig. 17–z), en route to Vyl light vessel. The *D–6*, *E–31*, and *E–53* had nearly reached their stations off Terschelling (Fig 17–a). Two boats of the 11th Flotilla, if Corbett be correct, were nearing their positions east of the Dogger Bank (Fig. 17–b).

As the sun rose higher in the sky and the fleets got farther into the North Sea, the visibility improved. At 8:17 A.M. the light cruiser *Yarmouth*, 5 miles directly ahead of the *Lion*, hoisted a green flag indicating that a submarine had been sighted to starboard (Fig. 18–A). Five minutes later Beatty signaled a 90° change of course to the left to avoid the reported submarine. As nothing further developed, the base course was soon resumed. It is probable that this was one of the frequent false alarms. At 9:08 the destroyer *Turbulent*, in the screen of the 1st Battle Cruiser Squadron, reported having sighted another submarine (Fig. 18–c). These false reports of submarines were to continue throughout the day, at times with very disturbing effects. Apparently, the British went on the principle that it was better to make ten false reports than to fail to make one true report.

The 3d Battle Cruiser Squadron, having got about 10 miles ahead of its position, reversed course for ten minutes at 8:20. When the base course was resumed, the *Invincible* was about 23 miles from the *Iron Duke*. The fact that these battle cruisers were not a permanent part of the Battle Fleet probably accounts for their difficulty in keeping station. It was at 8:20 that the *Warrior*, the northernmost cruiser in the screen of the Cromarty Force, sighted the Scapa Force bearing 336° (Fig. 18–B). At 9:17 the 1st and 2d Cruiser Squadrons joined up and gradually rectified their stations in the screen 10 miles ahead of the *Iron Duke* (Fig. 18–D). Finally, at 11:22, Jerram brought the 2d Battle Squadron into station on the left of the 4th Battle Squadron (Fig. 18–G). He received from Jellicoe a signal: "Manoeuvre well executed." At noon the fleet guide, the *Iron Duke*, taking the

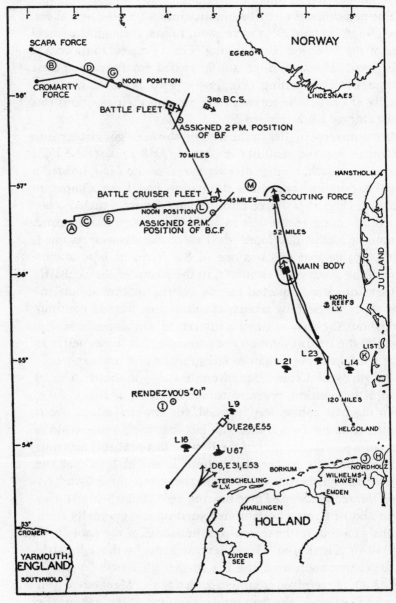

FIG. 18. The fleets approach, 8:00 A.M. to 2:15 P.M., May 31. Position of submarines approximate only.

mean of all ships' positions, established her position as Lat. 58–07, Long. 3–01.5 E. At that time the *Lion* bore 164°, distant 85 miles. Her position was Lat. 56–46, Long. 3–36.5 E. At noon the 3d Battle Cruiser Squadron was in Lat. 58–06, Long. 3–53 E. The *Invincible* bore practically 90° from the *Iron Duke*, distant 27½ miles. This checks closely with the distance of 23 miles between the *Chester* and *Iron Duke* reported at 12:05. The fact that the 3d Battle Cruiser Squadron was considerably to the left of the fleet axis and ahead of its station was not a matter of any special importance. It possibly resulted from the fact that the advance of the Battle Fleet had been slowed so that cruisers and destroyers could examine the large number of neutral ships sighted. This was necessary to prevent possible agents in German pay on neutral vessels from reporting by radio the position of the British forces. This might be done by sending apparently innocent messages. At noon the speed of advance of the Battle Fleet was only 14 knots.

At 10:05 Beatty had readjusted his formation so that it would be better disposed to meet an enemy approaching from the southeastward (Sketch II). He had shifted the line of bearing of his light cruiser screen from 355° to 29°. The center of the screen then bore 119° from the *Lion* (Fig. 18–E). At the same time he ordered the 2d Battle Cruiser Squadron to station itself in a position bearing 29° from the *Lion*, while the 5th Battle Squadron bore 299°.

Meanwhile, the situation had definitely cleared along the southern coast. At 8:05 the rear admiral, East Coast, at Grimsby, and the senior naval officer, Lowestoft, had been ordered to send their auxiliary patrols out 30 miles from the coast. At 8:45 the commander in chief, Nore, reported to the Admiralty that seaplanes scouting from Felixstowe, Isle of Grain, and West Gate had nothing to report (Fig. 17–X). At 10:12 the senior naval officer, Harwich, reported in detail four seaplane flights from Felixstowe that had reached on the average 60 miles from the coast. Furthermore, at 9:43, the commander of the Harwich Submarine Flotilla reported that four of his submarines were returning, presumably from off Terschelling, and that they had

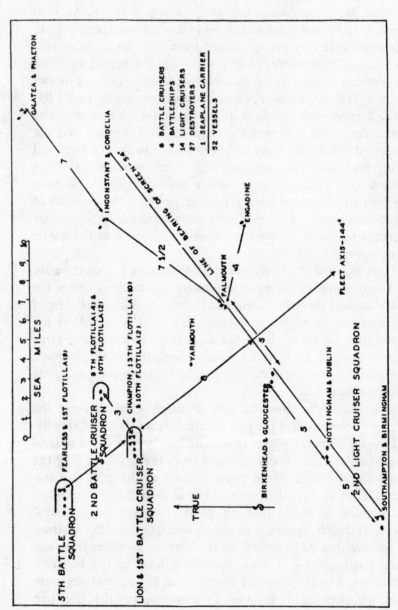

SEA MILES
0 1 2 3 4 5 6 7 8 9 10

5TH BATTLE SQUADRON

2ND BATTLE CRUISER SQUADRON

9TH FLOTILLA (4) & 10TH FLOTILLA (2)

FEARLESS 1ST FLOTILLA (9)

GALATEA & PHAETON

INCONSTANT & CORDELIA

CHAMPION, 13TH FLOTILLA (9) & 10TH FLOTILLA (2)

LION & 1ST BATTLE CRUISER SQUADRON

LINE OF BEARING OF SCREEN—N-S

ENGADINE

FALMOUTH

YARMOUTH

FLEET AXIS—144°

BIRKENHEAD & GLOUCESTER

NOTTINGHAM & DUBLIN

2ND LIGHT CRUISER SQUADRON

SOUTHAMPTON & BIRMINGHAM

TRUE

6 BATTLE CRUISERS
4 BATTLESHIPS
14 LIGHT CRUISERS
27 DESTROYERS
1 SEAPLANE CARRIER
52 VESSELS

SKETCH III. Battle Cruiser Fleet at 2:15 P.M., May 31, 1916.

nothing to report. These were evidently the boats that were to be relieved by the *D–6, E–31,* and *E–53.* That the latter must have been on their stations is shown by a radio message that the *U–67* sent at 10:50, reporting contacts with two enemy submarines. Nevertheless, despite the evident fact that there could be no attack on the southern coast until the next morning, the Harwich Force was not sent out. If the attack were made at that time, the Grand Fleet was perfectly disposed to cut the retreat of the High Seas Fleet. To facilitate this maneuver, it was highly desirable that the advance of the enemy toward Yarmouth be detected as soon as possible. This could be accomplished best by placing the Harwich Force off Terschelling so that contact could be made in the early evening.

At 10:20 the Admiralty ordered the Blyth Flotilla to send one destroyer and four submarines to rendezvous "01" in Lat. 54–30, Long. 4–00 E., to wait there 24 hours (Fig. 18–1). At noon the destroyer *Talisman* and the submarines *G–2, G–3, G–4,* and *G–5* sailed.

Meanwhile, the main body of the High Seas Fleet had passed through the swept channel and was now well at sea. Horn Reefs light vessel was passed 35 miles on the starboard beam. A condenser casualty compelled the *V186* to return to port. This reduced the German destroyers to 61.

As the weather had become somewhat better, the airships had been directed to commence scouting. At 11:25 the *L9* ascended from Nordholz (Fig. 18–H). In an hour's time the *L16, L21, L23,* and *L14* followed. It is interesting to note that two of the airships designated to scout could not leave their hangars due to cross winds. Their places had been taken by the *L21* and *L23,* which were in the revolving hangars at Nordholz. This costly apparatus thus proved its usefulness. Revolving hangars have now been superseded by mooring masts and better equipment to take the ships from their hangars. Nevertheless, under some conditions it will still be impracticable for airships to take the air. The five airships were to proceed radially to specified points and then to turn to the left, passing through the line of points in turn, thus protecting the westward flank of the High Seas Fleet. The

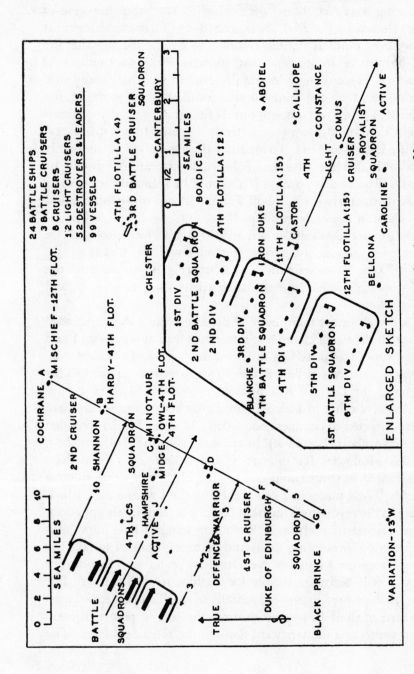

SKETCH IV AND SKETCH V. Battle Fleet and attached cruisers at 2:15 P.M., May 31.

assigned point for the *L23* was off the Norwegian coast and her course toward it would take her over the two Fleets.

Not to be outdone by the airships, the seaplane station at List sent up seaplane 559 (Fig. 18–κ), but it returned after an hour's flight because of the very low ceiling. The airships reported visibility of from $\frac{1}{2}$ to 4 miles. By 2:00 P.M., however, the *L21*, then about 60 miles northwest of Helgoland, reported a ceiling of 900 feet and a visibility of 6 miles. The operations of airships under such conditions were highly dangerous. They could be seen by ships before the ships could be seen by them. Therefore, if contact were made with enemy forces, the destruction of the airship was very possible. The British probably intercepted their numerous radio messages and might thereby have concluded that they were covering an offensive of the Fleet. However, there is nothing to show that the British gained any information in this way.

According to Corbett, the British direction-finder stations had taken bearings up to noon of the ship using the call of the German commander in chief. This, as we have seen, was the guard-ship of Entrance III (Fig. 18–J). Corbett further states that the Admiralty had informed Jellicoe of the position of the ship using this call. The communication record does not disclose any such dispatch. At any rate the British seem to have been quite convinced that the High Seas Fleet was still in port and that the hurried sortie of the Grand Fleet had been another futile blow in the air.

At 2:15 P.M. Jellicoe was in position Lat. 57–54, Long. 3–58 E. He was still distant about 15 miles from his appointed position for 2:00. However, this was not a matter of any importance. He had just been joined by the destroyer *Moon,* which had made a 20-knot run from Aberdeen.

Meanwhile, at 1:30 P.M., as nothing had been sighted, Beatty prepared to carry out his orders to proceed toward Jellicoe at 2:00. He swung the axis of his formation to the right (Fig. 18–L). The center of the screen was to bear 144° from the *Lion,* while the line of bearing of the screen was to be 54°. When the maneuver was completed, the 2d Battle Cruiser Squadron would

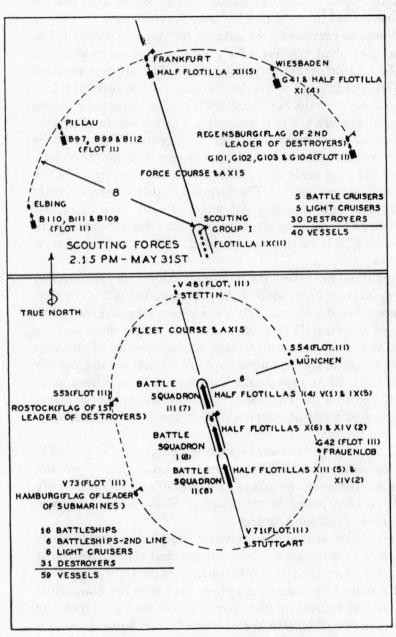

SKETCH VI. Main Body, 2:15 P.M., May 31.

bear from the *Lion* 54°, distant 3 miles, while the 5th Battle Squadron would bear 90° to the left, or 324°, distant 5 miles. The cruising disposition ordered was very similar to the actual disposition of the Battle Cruiser Fleet at 2:15 P.M. (Sketch III), except for the stations of the 1st Light Cruiser Squadron.

At 2:00 Beatty was about 10 miles to the northward of his assigned position for that hour. However, the movements of his light cruisers to effect the fleet disposition ordered at 1:30 had not been completed. An officer in tactical command does not like to order a change of course or a new maneuver before his fleet has completed the last one ordered, although in case of necessity this can be done. So it was not until 2:15 that Beatty executed his change of course to 357° to close the Battle Fleet.

When this change of course was executed, all units of the Battle Cruiser Fleet were in position except the 1st Light Cruiser Squadron. There was an important reason for this. About 2:07 several suspicious vessels had been sighted to the eastward (Fig. 18–M). At that time the *Galatea's* signal log reads: "Sighted enemy TBD's." However, this does not necessarily mean that the suspicious vessels were definitely recognized as destroyers at that time, for at 2:10 the *Galatea's* signal to Beatty read: "Two-funneled ship has stopped steamer bearing ESE. (100°). Am closing." Alexander-Sinclair's squadron, therefore, continued on to the southeastward to determine the identity of the suspicious vessels.

At 2:15 Beatty's flagship, the *Lion,* was in Lat. 56–50, Long. 4–54 E. She was 69½ miles distant from the *Iron Duke,* bearing 158° from that vessel. About 45 miles to the eastward of the *Lion* was the *Lützow,* flagship of the German scouting forces. About 52 miles to the southward of the *Lützow* was the *Friedrich der Grosse,* flagship of the German main body. The relative positions of these forces are shown in Fig. 18. The dispositions of the four principal forces are shown in Sketches III, IV, V, and VI.

About 2:00 P.M. the German light cruiser *Elbing* on the western flank of the screen of the Scouting Forces (Sketch VI) had sighted the Danish freighter *N. J. Fjord* to the westward (Fig.

18–M). Captain Madlung of the *Elbing* directed the commander of Half Flotilla IV, Commander Adolf Dithmar, to proceed with the large destroyers *B109* and *B110* to search the steamer. These vessels stopped the steamer which was blowing off steam when sighted by the *Galatea*. Such was the position at 2:15 P.M. At last the two Fleets had come into contact. The curtain rose slowly upon the greatest drama of modern naval warfare.

CHAPTER IX

THE FIRST CONTACTS
2:15 P.M. to 3:15 P.M.

In this chapter we describe the operations of the Battle Cruiser Fleet and the scouting groups during the first hour after contact was made between their light forces. Figure 19 shows the movements of the units of these opposing forces for this entire period. Figures 20–23, inclusive, are enlargements of Fig. 19, showing their movements for periods of 15 minutes. Figure 26 shows the movements of the entire British and German Fleets from 2:15 P.M. to 3:15 P.M., but need not be consulted at this time, as it is drawn to show the movements of Jellicoe, Scheer, and Hood, which do not directly concern us in this chapter. In Fig. 19 the positions numbered "1" are the actual positions of the British vessels making enemy information reports; those numbered "2" are the positions in which the vessels reported themselves at the time their reports were made. The difference between the two positions of a certain vessel indicates the error of her navigation. The Germans used a special chart for reporting positions in the North Sea. This was divided into small rectangles, 6 minutes of latitude and 10 or 12 minutes of longitude, about 6 miles square. These were indicated by a number of three digits, followed by a Greek letter and Roman numerals. The squares used by the Germans for reporting their contacts with the enemy are shown (Fig. 19) with their numbers.

It was at 2:15 P.M. that Beatty, as above stated, executed the signal for a simultaneous change of course of all station units to 357°. All ships executed the order promptly except the 1st Light Cruiser Squadron. These four vessels kept on to the eastward to close the strange vessels that had been sighted in that direction. At 2:18 the *Galatea* hoisted the general flag signal: "Enemy in sight." At the same time an even more electrifying signal was broadcast by radio: "Urgent. Two cruisers, probably

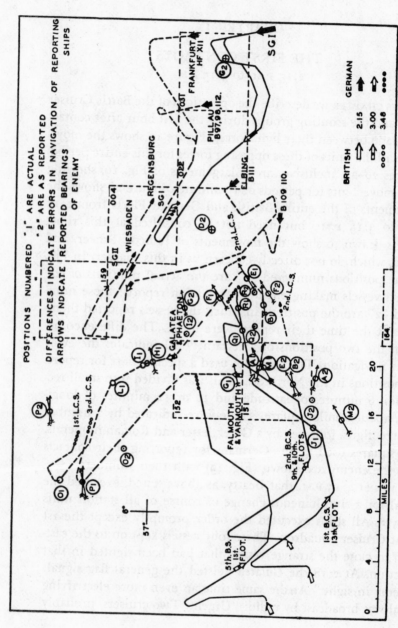

FIG. 19. Battle Cruiser Fleet and Scouting Forces, 2:15-3:48 P.M.

POSITIONS NUMBERED "1" ARE ACTUAL
"2" ARE AS REPORTED
DIFFERENCES INDICATE ERRORS IN NAVIGATION OF REPORTING
SHIPS
ARROWS INDICATE REPORTED BEARINGS
OF ENEMY

BRITISH
2.15
3.00
3.48

GERMAN

FRANZ HIPPER

As Vice Admiral, commanded Scouting Forces of High Seas Fleet at Jutland, at the age of fifty-two. Commander in Chief of High Seas Fleet, July-November, 1918; retired, December, 1918. Baron von Hipper and Commander Bavarian Military Order of Max Joseph, 1916. Died May 25, 1932.

DAVID BEATTY

As Vice Admiral, commanded Battle Cruiser Fleet at Jutland, at the age of forty-five. Commander in Chief of Grand Fleet, 1916–19; Admiral of the Fleet, 1919; First Sea Lord, 1919–27; retired, 1936. Viscount Borodale of Wexford, 1919; Earl of the North Sea and of Brooksby, 1919. Died March 11, 1936.

hostile, in sight bearing ESE. (100°), course unknown. My position Lat. 56–48, Long. 5–21" (Figs. 19–A and 20–A).

In four instances during this period, the *Galatea's* times of sending dispatches were 2 to 5 minutes after the time of their receipt by the *Iron Duke* and other vessels. In such cases, the time of receipt is used in this account. In the excitement of contact with the enemy, such discrepancies in time are to be expected. The times logged by the *Iron Duke* at a distance are probably more correct than those of the *Galatea* in contact with the enemy.

At 2:20 the seaplane carrier *Engadine* "sighted two enemy cruisers bearing east (77°)," but made no report (Fig. 20–C). It is interesting to note that both British vessels mistook the German destroyers for light cruisers. This was an easy mistake to make, particularly as the German destroyers were large boats of about 1,500 tons displacement.

The *Iron Duke* received the *Galatea's* contact report immediately—2:18 P.M. The *Lion* received the same dispatch at 2:20. It took Beatty just 5 minutes to decode the message and make his decision to head for Horn Reefs in order to cut off the retreat of the enemy. At 2:25 Beatty signaled his destroyers by flag hoist to "take up position as submarine screen when course is altered to SSE. (145°)." About 2:26 Commodore Alexander-Sinclair turned the *Galatea* and *Phaeton* to the northeastward toward the *B109* and *B110*. The *Galatea* added to her former message the statement that "cruisers are stopped." About 2:28 (Fig. 20–F) the British light cruisers opened fire on the German destroyers, which quickly ran out of range without receiving a hit. At that time the battleship *St. Vincent,* which had been specially detailed to listen for German radio, reported to Jellicoe that she had intercepted a high-power code message.

At 2:30 the *Galatea* sent in a second contact report: "One cruiser, probably hostile, bearing east (77°), steering SSE. (145°)." She was in position Fig. 19–B at that time. The *Galatea* also stated in a separate message that the two cruisers she had first reported were destroyers. At this time the *Inconstant* and *Cordelia* were paralleling the *Galatea* and *Phaeton,* but strange-

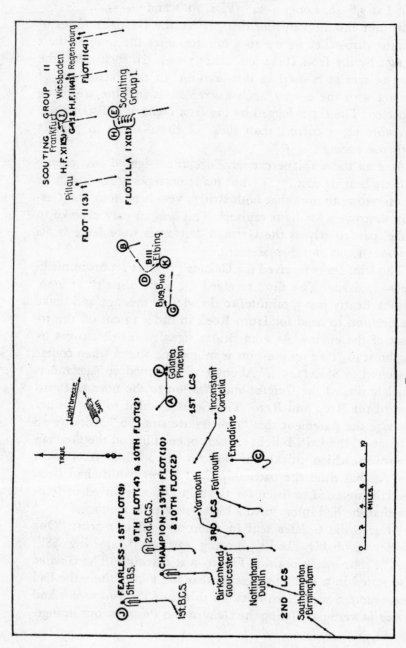

FIG. 20. 2:15-2:30 P.M.

ly enough did not close them. At 2:31 Rear Admiral Napier in the *Falmouth* reported to the *Lion* by searchlight that he was closing the *Galatea*. The remaining vessels of the 1st and 2d Light Cruiser Squadrons were also steering to the northeastward toward the point of contact.

It was not until 2:30 that the *Barham* (Fig. 20–J) acknowledged the *Lion's* flag signal to change course to SSE. (145°). At 2:32, therefore, Beatty hauled down his flags as the signal of execution for the change of course (Fig. 21–B). Speed was increased to 22 knots. Instead of executing this important change of course to the right to 145°, the 5th Battle Squadron turned together to the left 22° to a course of 335° (Fig. 21–C). This evidently was a routine zigzag. It had the effect, however, of sending the battleships in almost exactly the opposite direction from the battle cruisers. The assigned interval of 5 miles was opening out rapidly.

Now, let us turn to the German side of the picture. We have seen how the *B109* and *B110* had been sent by the *Elbing* to search the Danish steamer *N. J. Fjord*. While doing so, they had reported to the *Elbing* by searchlight the sighting of smoke. The *Elbing* also sighted this smoke at 2:18 (Fig. 20–B). She steamed rapidly toward the direction in which it was seen, followed by the *B111*. At 2:25 the *B109* reported by radio scattered enemy vessels in square 164 of the German position chart (Figs. 19 and 20–C). Two minutes later the *Elbing* broadcast the following: "Enemy armored cruiser in sight W. by N. (267°)." She was then in position Fig. 20–D. She also had magnified the size of the enemy, but reported only one of the two British light cruisers present. At 2:28 Captain Madlung saw salvos falling about the two German destroyers. As his ship was headed almost directly at the enemy, he altered course about 90° to the left, slightly opening the range. Apparently, Madlung still thought the *Galatea* an armored cruiser; or, possibly, by this time he had made out the *Phaeton*.

The *Elbing's* enemy information report brought immediate results. It was received at once by both Scheer and Hipper. The latter at 2:27 instantly turned Scouting Group I together to

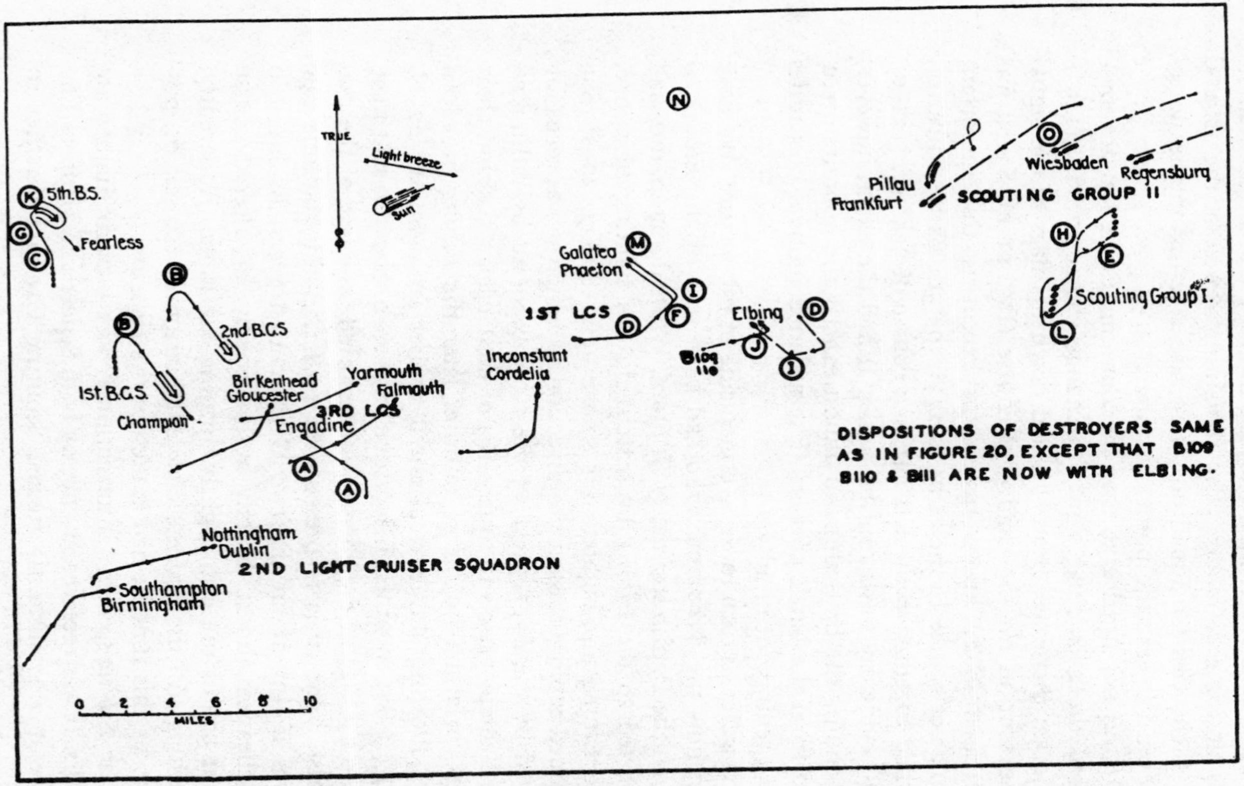

DISPOSITIONS OF DESTROYERS SAME
AS IN FIGURE 20, EXCEPT THAT B109
B110 & B111 ARE NOW WITH ELBING.

FIG. 21. 2:30-2:45 P.M., May 31.

WSW. (234°) or somewhat to the southward of the reported contact (Fig. 20–E). At the same time Hipper repeated to Scheer the reports of his light forces that the smoke of several enemy vessels had been sighted in square 164. This square was considerably to the southward of the actual position of the *Galatea* and *Phaeton* (Fig. 19). At 2:29 Hipper increased speed by visual signal to 18 knots (Fig. 20–H). His screen of light cruisers and destroyers conformed promptly to the movement of Scouting Group I without signal. The smart maneuvering of the scouting forces demonstrated that an alert and decided leader was at the helm and that he had a splendidly indoctrinated command. This was in marked contrast to the British forces, the strongest unit of which was proceeding away from the remainder of the Battle Cruiser Fleet.

At 2:30 the *Elbing* sent a searchlight message to both the *Frankfurt* and *Lützow* (Fig. 20–K). This was interpreted to mean that she had sighted 24 to 26 battleships, an early example of the many mistakes in communications that marked this action, but which to some degree must be expected in all naval operations. Rear Admiral Boedicker in the *Frankfurt* headed directly for the point of contact at full speed. He directed the *Wiesbaden* and *Regensburg* to close him (Fig. 20–I). The *Pillau* already was doing so. This commenced the concentration of Scouting Group II and the two destroyer flotillas in company. Hipper changed course 45° with his flagship and ordered the other battle cruisers to "follow the leader." This somewhat complicated maneuver was made in order to permit Hipper to retain the lead in the column which was being formed on a course of SSW. (189°). Both German commanders, undeterred by the *Elbing's* report of such overwhelming forces in the close vicinity, were determined to develop the situation, the primary mission of the scouting forces.

Meanwhile, the *Galatea* was still steering on a northeasterly course, closely followed by the *Phaeton*, when at 2:32, she came under the *Elbing's* accurate and closely spaced salvos at 14,000 yards. A minute later the *Elbing* also reported that she was under fire (Fig. 21–D). It is interesting to note that the *Elbing* could bring on the broadside four 5.9-inch guns, while the *Galatea* and *Phaeton* could each bring three 6-inch guns. The British light cruisers were rated 1 knot faster than the German ship.

At 2:32 Hipper increased speed to 21 knots (Fig. 21-E). Four minutes later he went full speed (Fig. 21-H). At the same time he reported to Scheer that he was on course SSW. (189°) in square 031. At 2:38 alert Commander Dithmar in the *B109* reported to Commodore Michelsen in the *Rostock* that the British recognition signal was "PL" (Fig. 21-J). At 2:43 Scouting Group I on visual signal turned to WSW. (234°) and slowed again to 18 knots (Fig. 21-L).

While the German salvos were falling about the *Galatea*, Commodore Alexander-Sinclair at 2:35 broadcast an important information report: "Have sighted large amount of smoke as though from a fleet bearing ENE. (54°). My position Lat. 56–50 N., Long. 5–19 E." (Figs. 19-E and 21-F). The *Galatea's* position as stated in this dispatch is shown in Fig. 19 at E2. Her actual position, as determined later, was at E1. Considering her actual position at the latter point and the bearing of 54° true in which Alexander-Sinclair reported the heavy smoke, it appears that Alexander-Sinclair actually saw the smoke of Scouting Group II and not that of the battle cruisers of Scouting Group I, which then bore about 90°. Nevertheless, the message created the correct impression that large forces were in sight contact. When it was received by Jellicoe, he ordered full speed for the Battle Fleet by flag signal. At the same time, the 5th Battle Squadron, which was still proceeding at high speed away from Beatty, was directed by Rear Admiral Evan-Thomas to increase the distance between ships from 600 yards to 800 yards (Fig. 21-G).

It was about 2:37, after five minutes of fire, that one of the *Elbing's* 5.9-inch shells hit the *Galatea* squarely under her bridge (Fig. 21-I). Fortunately for the British, this shell did not explode and consequently did little damage. Immediately after this hit, Alexander-Sinclair turned directly away from the *Elbing* to the northwestward. The Germans had drawn first blood. The *Elbing* promptly turned and followed in the track of the *Galatea* and *Phaeton*. The *B109* and *B110* rejoined her. Due to the superiority in speed of the British vessels, the range gradually increased. Firing became intermittent.

It was not until 2:37 that the *Barham* records the execution of the flag signal to turn to course SSE. (145°), 5 minutes after it was actually executed and the other large ships had turned. In addition, 3 minutes more elapsed until Evan-Thomas at 2:40 finally commenced the turn and increased speed to 22 knots (Fig. 21–K). This delay of 8 minutes increased the interval between the *Lion* and *Barham* from 5 to 10 miles. As this question has aroused much controversy, a brief analysis will be appropriate.

In the first place, as radio silence was essential, it is evident that the 5th Battle Squadron should have been kept within easy signal distance from the fleet flagship, the *Lion*. There seems to be no special reason why an interval of 3 miles should not have been as good as one of 5. The second question one might ask is: "Why were flag signals alone used for the change of course, when the flags after the turn would fly almost directly in line with the *Barham*, thus making them difficult to read?" Why, in fact, were they not supplemented with searchlight signals? We note that at this very time the *Falmouth* signaled the *Lion* by searchlight at over 8 miles distance. Finally, why did not Evan-Thomas turn with the battle cruisers, signal or no signal? At 2:23 the radio contact report of the *Galatea* had been received. We know that at 2:30 the *Barham* "received a signal indicating the course that the vice admiral intended to steer." It must have been seen that the *Lion* and the 1st Battle Cruiser Squadron actually changed to this course. Was anything more required for the 5th Battle Squadron to turn after the *Lion*, at least until the situation had been cleared up? We believe not. Already we see an instance of the disadvantage of changing the fleet task organization just prior to battle. Had Evan-Thomas served with Beatty for a long period, such a mistake would probably not have occurred. Already the Germans were demonstrating superiority in the tactical handling of their forces.

At 2:31 the British were able to establish the positions of a German light cruiser (Figs. 19–C and 21–O) and a destroyer (Figs. 19–D and 21–N) by their radio direction-finder stations along the English coast. The former probably was obtained from the *Frankfurt's* 2:30 dispatch and was thus somewhat in error. The latter probably was obtained from the *B109's* 2:32 dispatch and was also slightly in error. These positions were not sent out by the Admiralty until 3:10. They were received in the *Lion* at 3:29, or about one hour after the German vessels made the radio transmissions from which the positions were established. Therefore, while they provide an early example of this interesting and valuable method of obtaining intelligence of the enemy, they were in this case of no practical value.

At 2:38 Beatty ordered action stations just as tea was being served. At 2:45, Alexander-Sinclair signaled by searchlight to the *Lion:* "Enemy apparently turned north" (Fig. 21–M). This was entirely misleading, as only the *Elbing* and her destroyers were heading to the northward of west, while all the other German forces were heading to the southward of west. The use of the term "enemy" was most vague and improper. While this searchlight dispatch was being sent, Alexander-Sinclair was attempting to clarify the situation by a longer radio report (Figs. 19–F and 22–A). This read: "Urgent. My 1435. Smoke seems to be seven vessels besides destroyers and cruisers. They have turned north. My position Lat. 56°–52′ N., Long. 5°–33′ E." While this was addressed to Beatty, it was intercepted very properly by the *Iron Duke* at 2:51. While this dispatch clarified the meaning of the vague term "enemy," it still contained the error as to the course of the enemy. Evidently, the fact that the *Elbing* and her three destroyers were heading northwestward induced Alexander-Sinclair to infer that the other German vessels were doing the same. Incidentally, despite his positive statement about "seven vessels," all Alexander-Sinclair saw at this time were light cruisers and destroyers. The German battle cruisers were about 19 miles from him and it is practically certain that he could not have seen even their smoke. The report, nevertheless, by a curious freak of fortune, was substantially correct. Not only were there present a number of vessels larger than cruisers and destroyers, but soon the German battle cruisers would even turn to the northward in the most obliging manner to verify the report of an enemy who had never seen them. Certainly, history recounts few such favors of fortune. These interesting reports must have been highly encouraging to Beatty, for it looked as if he would have his long-awaited opportunity to cut off the retreat of a large German force. Knowing that the Germans could not have over five battle cruisers, it is not likely that Alexander-Sinclair's mention of "seven vessels" gave him much concern.

We must now give some account of the confusing operations of the British seaplane carrier *Engadine*. It will be noted in Sketch III and Fig. 20 that this vessel had been placed in advance of the light cruiser screen during the advance to the eastward. Perhaps her comparatively low speed and the necessity for not letting her drop too far in rear when stopping to lower planes to the water or to hoist them in was a reason for putting her out in advance of the Fleet. However, once the Fleet had turned to the northward, it appears difficult to find a reason for leaving such a slow and vulnerable vessel to act as a rear guard in the direction from which the enemy would probably appear. When the enemy did actually appear the exposed position of the *Engadine* naturally gave some concern to Rear Admiral Napier in the *Falmouth*. Accordingly, at 2:31 he directed the seaplane carrier to close the battle cruisers. At that time the signal was flying on the *Lion* for a change of course to SSE. (145)°. This, as will be remembered, was executed at 2:32. As the *Falmouth* was distant 8 miles from the *Lion,* it is doubtful whether Napier knew that this signal was flying. Had he known so, perhaps he would not have directed the *Engadine* to leave what was apparently her station for an easterly movement.

By 2:45 the *Engadine* was within signal distance of Beatty, about 5 miles directly ahead of the 2nd Battle Cruiser Squadron. Beatty accordingly directed her to send up seaplanes (Fig. 22–B) to scout NNE. (9°). There were no enemy ships in that direction. The *Elbing* bore about 75° and the other German

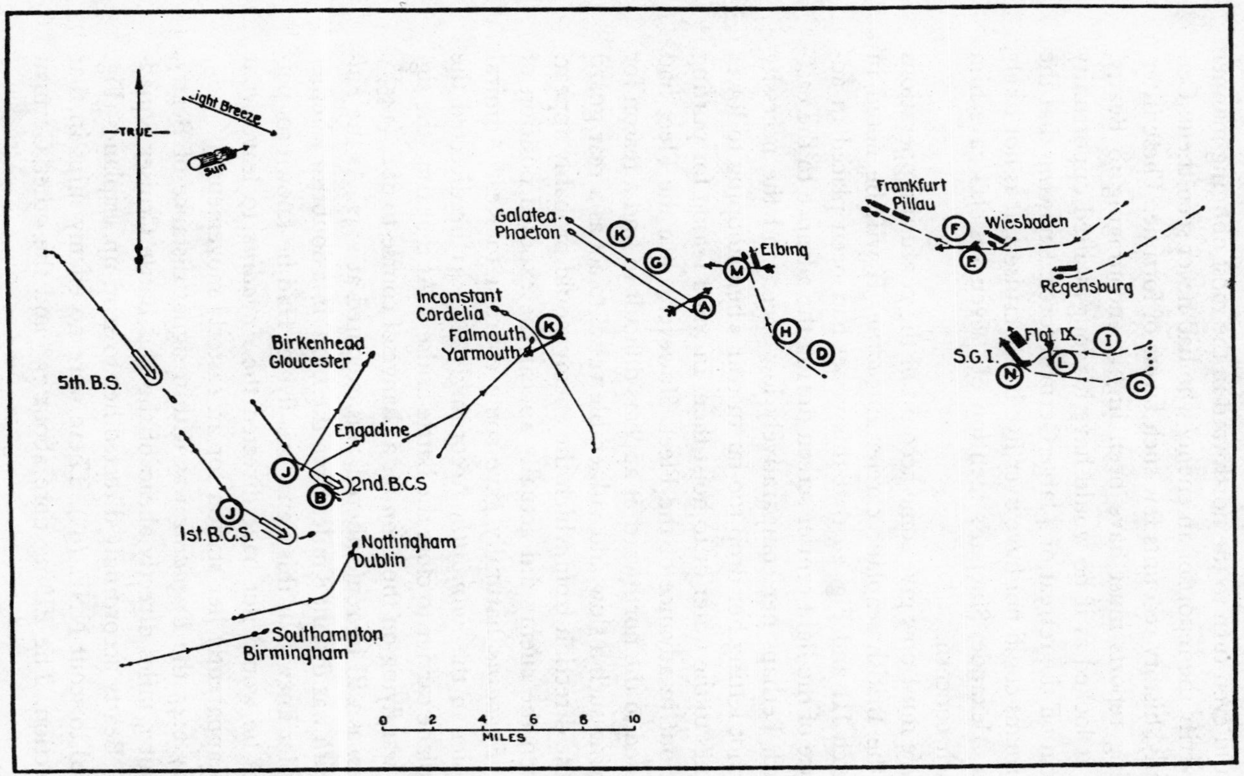

FIG. 22. 2:45–3:00 P.M.

units were farther to the right. The order to search on a bearing of 9° must have arisen from some misconstruction of the *Galatea's* reports. It is true that she had reported the Germans as bearing about 55°, much farther to the left than they actually were; but Beatty now had ordered the search to be made about 45° to the left of this bearing. Possibly this was to allow for an advance of the Germans while the *Engadine* was slowing down to hoist out her planes.

Also, at 2:45 Beatty ordered the commander of the 13th Flotilla, in the *Champion,* to send two destroyers to stand by the *Engadine.* If this were necessary now, it would seem that the destroyers should have accompanied the seaplane carrier during the entire cruise, so as to be in instant readiness. Such an assignment at the last minute cannot be carefully considered and is liable to become effective too late. Such proved to be the fact in this case. Instead of detaching for this duty the two Harwich destroyers of the 10th Flotilla, Captain Farie sent the *Moresby* and *Onslow* of his own, the 13th Flotilla. Thus, he lost a desirable opportunity to simplify the organization of his command. Possibly, there was some special reason why the two boats were assigned, but this has not been disclosed. As will be seen later, they did not arrive until after the *Engadine* had been stopped for some time and thus was in danger of being attacked by a submarine.

The *Engadine,* instead of heading to the northward and getting clear of the 2d Battle Cruiser Squadron so she could hoist out her planes, kept on to the northwestward, passing the *New Zealand* on the starboard hand on an opposite course. She then turned sharply under the stern of the *Indefatigable* to the northeastward. Her captain explained that the delay in hoisting out her seaplanes "was caused through the ship having to keep clear of the cruisers." In consequence, the opportunity to obtain timely information with her seaplanes was lost. It seems that the best position for the *Engadine* would have been slightly in rear of the 1st Battle Cruiser Squadron. There she could have quickly received her orders from Beatty and could have lowered her seaplanes without interference from any other vessels. The swells made by the battle cruisers would have subsided by the time she had stopped and lowered her first plane to the water. In this operation, the *Engadine,* though having no flying deck, was playing much the same rôle as are aircraft carriers of today. If she had been a small carrier, having among others a squadron of 18 scouting planes able to take the air in 3 minutes, it is quite evident that Beatty could have received a complete picture of the dispositions of the German scouting forces before 3:00 P.M.

But let us leave theories and return to facts. The *Elbing* and her three large destroyers had continued the pursuit of the *Galatea* and *Phaeton* to the northwestward, despite her inferiority in broadside fire of 6-inch guns of four to six. At 2:48 the *Elbing* opened an intermittent fire at long range (Fig. 22–D). At 2:51 she turned away somewhat to effect a junction with the *Frankfurt* (Fig. 22–H). Madlung evidently realized the futility of further pursuit of the British light cruisers and probably realized by this time that he was opposed to a greatly superior force. It was proper that he should rejoin his scouting group.

The correctness of the *Elbing's* signal reporting the presence of 24 to 26 battleships was meanwhile becoming more and more doubtful to Hipper. Certainly, if it were correct, the *Elbing* would not still be pursuing the enemy. So the vice admiral turned Scouting Group I to the right twice to keep headed for that light cruiser. The first turn was to west (257°) at 2:47 (Fig. 22–C). At that time speed also was increased to 21 knots. The second turn was to WNW. (279°) at 2:52 (Fig. 22–I). At 2:52 Hipper had reported to Scheer that he was in square 022.

Meanwhile, Rear Admiral Boedicker, in the *Frankfurt,* had entered the picture. At 2:50 he noted what were erroneously thought to be three torpedo tracks (Fig. 22–E). This was the first of many such mistakes made by vessels of both Fleets during the battle. Such was the psychological effect of submarine warfare that all hands seemed ready to call every suspicious piece of wreckage a periscope and every streak in the water a torpedo track. At the same time, 2:50 P.M., Boedicker specifically reported that four light, not armored, cruisers were in sight (Fig. 22-F). They were said to be steering NW. (302°) and located in square 047, which evidently was a mistake.

When Hipper received this news at 2:55, the situation became much clarified for him, especially as 4 minutes later the *Elbing* confirmed Boedicker's report of four enemy light cruisers (Fig. 22-M). At 2:55 Hipper also received a dispatch from Scheer that the main body at 2:45 was in square 065 (Fig. 26). Hipper at 2:59, immediately upon receipt of the *Elbing's* report or possibly while it was being transmitted, turned his battle cruisers to NNW. (324°), formed column and increased speed to 23 knots in order to follow Scouting Group II (Fig. 22-N). While doubtless it was cheering for Hipper to receive a message from his superior officer telling his exact position, the breaking of radio silence by the German main body must be condemned. It gave the English an opportunity to fix its position, information which would have been invaluable to Beatty. The latter, it should be noted, had not yet broken radio silence, a procedure which we heartily commend. In these days, when every ship has a direction finder, it is even more important for units that have not made direct contact with the enemy to maintain radio silence.

At this time Hipper's intention was merely to support Scouting Group II in its pursuit of the hostile light cruisers. Thus far he had no indication whatever that British capital ships were in the vicinity. He was playing into Beatty's hands. At 3:02 Flotilla IX concentrated for battle close on the *Lützow's* starboard beam (Fig. 23-C).

During this period, Beatty had enjoyed the great advantage of superior intelligence of the enemy. We have noted the various items of information furnished by Commodore Alexander-Sinclair. At 2:50 he sent a searchlight message to the *Lion*, apparently relayed through other ships, stating that he was under fire (Fig. 22-G). It is improbable that Beatty had received this information by the time he came left two points (Fig. 22-J) at 2:52 to SE. (122°). He evidently was still out of sight contact with the *Galatea* as late as 2:55, for at that time, Alexander-Sinclair asked the *Inconstant*: "Where are our battle cruisers?"

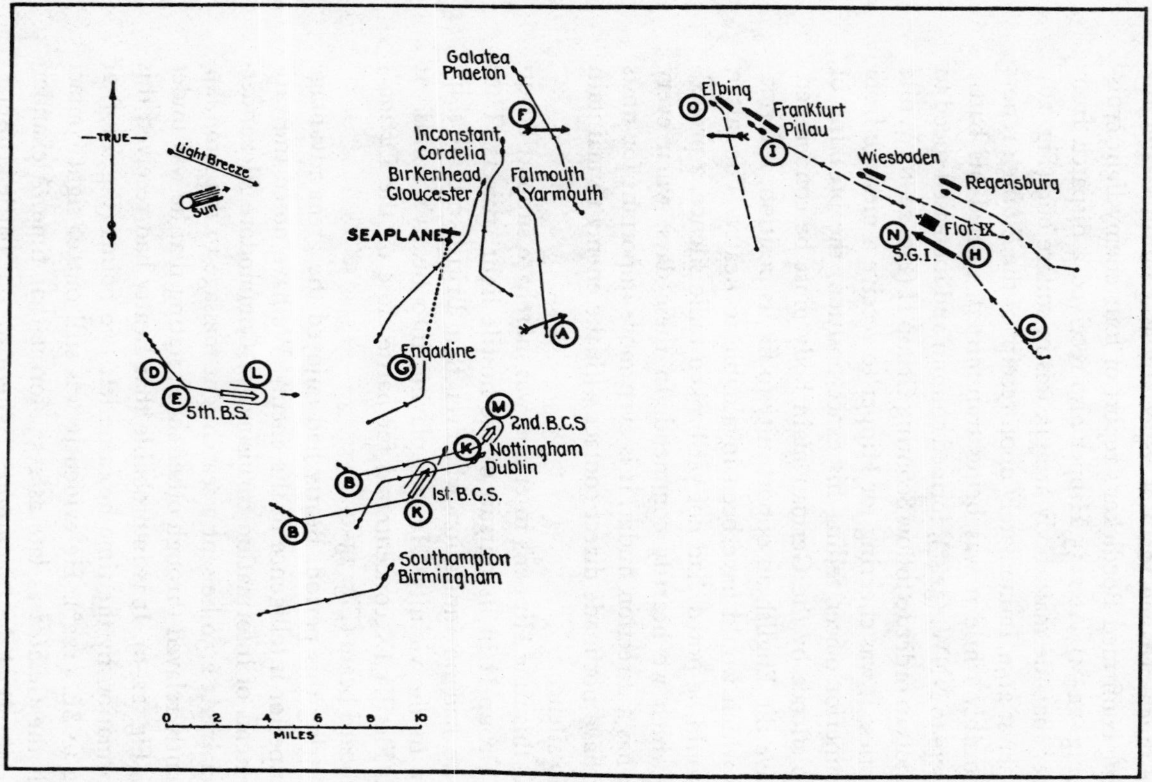

FIG. 23. 3:00–3:15 P.M.

The reply was prompt and accurate: "Bearing WSW. (234°), just hull down, apparently steering SE. (122°)." That signal (Fig. 22–K) encouraged Alexander-Sinclair in his plan to lead the German cruisers to the northwestward, while Beatty continued on an opposite course to cut off their retreat.

About 3:00 Beatty came to the conclusion that he had accomplished this purpose "and that it would be impossible for him to round the Horn Reefs without being brought to action." So the next minute he turned the 1st and 2d Battle Cruiser Squadrons to east (77°). As he was making this maneuver (Fig. 23–B), Evan-Thomas (Fig. 23–E) changed course to ESE. (100°). He had ordered 700 yards distance between the ships in his column at 3:03 (Fig. 23–D). Though still steaming only 22 knots, his converging course was decreasing his interval from the *Lion*.

It was at 3:00 that Rear Admiral Napier made his first contact report (Figs. 19–G and 23–A). He said that three enemy cruisers (evidently the *Elbing, Frankfurt,* and *Pillau*) were bearing east (77°) and steering north (347°). The bearing was correct, but only the *Elbing* was steering in the direction reported. At 3:07 Alexander-Sinclair (Figs. 19–I and 23–F) reported that the German cruisers were steering NW. (302°). Thus, for the first time Beatty had correct information of their course. Incidentally, Alexander-Sinclair had not further clarified those smoke clouds. Even in his official report he does not try to connect them with the German battle cruisers. He first mentions the latter when they opened fire on Beatty at 3:48 P.M.

At last the *Engadine* was to try her hand in gaining information of the enemy. At 3:00 she had stopped; 4 minutes later she hoisted out a seaplane. At 3:08 it took off to carry out Beatty's order of 2:45 (Fig. 23–G). Expertly piloted by the gallant and accomplished Flight Lieutenant F. J. Rutland, it disappeared to the NNE. (9°). Just 50 minutes had elapsed since the enemy had first been sighted. In addition to this long delay, the plane was proceeding in a direction poorly designed to clear up the situation. The course of the plane carried it toward the British light cruisers, not toward the German light cruisers or to their right to develop what lay in their rear. The handling of the seaplane carrier left much to be desired. For this deficiency Beatty is largely responsible.

At 3:10 Scouting Group I turned to NW. (302°) to take station in rear of Scouting Group II, which now was nearly concentrated (Fig. 23–H). Hipper reported to Scheer that the only British vessels in sight were four light cruisers. The *Elbing* had ceased fire on the *Galatea*, as the range was about 14,000 yards, too long for really effective shooting with her 5.9-inch guns. She was now nearing the *Frankfurt* and *Pillau*. At 3:12 the latter ships opened fire in great excess of zeal on the *Galatea* and *Phaeton*. The German official charts show a range at this time of 20,000 yards (Fig. 23–I). The range of the 5.9-inch guns of Scouting Group II was probably about the same as that of similar guns on the battle cruisers, about 16,000 yards. It is possible that this was approximately the actual range at this time and that the German charts are somewhat in error. Although the Germans made only one hit during all their shooting at the *Galatea* and *Phaeton*, they seem to have outranged the guns on those ships. This in turn seems to have convinced the British light cruiser commanders that they were helpless against the Germans. Thus it appears that a few ineffective salvos fired at enormous ranges, by moral effect alone practically drove the 1st and 3d Light Cruiser Squadrons out of the entire battle cruiser action. In our opinion, the stated motive of luring on the German light cruisers cannot explain away the complete failure of these two British squadrons. If such were the real intentions of their commanders, their plan could best be executed by remaining within long range of the German light cruisers to offer a better bait, being ready when the Germans turned back to concentrate all eight cruisers on them in a close and relentless pursuit.

At this time, 3:12, the *Elbing* reported that she could see six British light cruisers (Fig. 23–O). This was a message of much significance. The four vessels previously sighted might well have belonged to a single squadron making one of the customary

independent cruises through the North Sea; but the presence
of three groups of light cruisers disposed on a line of bearing
indicated that they might well be a screen for a force of battle
cruisers. Despite this indication, Boedicker continued to concentrate his group. This was a very questionable decision. It
looks very much as if his attention were being concentrated on
the bringing to action of a few light cruisers, to the neglect of
his more important mission of guarding the western flank of
Scouting Group I. Two interesting points present themselves.
(1) Why did six British cruisers withdraw before three German? Should not this fact have caused him to do some deep
thinking? (2) How was he to overtake an enemy of at least
equal speed 10 miles away and what could he do with such a
superior force once it was overtaken?

It appears to us that Boedicker had very little chance of gaining a local success over the British cruisers. On the other hand,
there was a distinct possibility that by concentrating his cruisers
and destroyers he would expose Scouting Group I to being cut
off by superior forces. It is suggested, therefore, that Boedicker
should have spread his cruisers to the westward and southwestward. Certainly the *Wiesbaden* and *Regensburg,* or at least a
few of the large destroyers of Flotilla II, should have been sent
in those directions to give warning of the approach of enemy
forces that would gravely threaten the German battle cruisers.

If Boedicker may be criticized for failing to screen Hipper's
western flank, it might be asked why Napier concentrated his
3d Light Cruiser Squadron on the 1st Light Cruiser Squadron?
He should have known that Alexander-Sinclair was in no danger
whatever from the German light cruisers and required no assistance from him. In fact, by concentrating on Alexander-Sinclair, he would defeat the former's project of drawing the German light cruisers to the northwestward. How could 8 British
cruisers expect to lure 3 or 4 German cruisers after them? Furthermore, Napier had two excellent courses of action open to
him. The first was to run to the eastward to cut off from their
bases the 3 German cruisers in sight, so that action could be

forced upon them—8 ships to 3. The second course of action was even more important: To proceed to the eastward in order to determine and report what were the smoke clouds reported by Alexander-Sinclair, so that this German force could be cut off by the British battle cruisers. It would appear, therefore, that Napier had every reason for proceeding to the eastward and none for going to the northward.

It is interesting to speculate on the subconscious reasoning of Boedicker and Napier. It seems that there is a natural tendency for cruisers on a scouting line or screen to concentrate toward the point of contact once the enemy is encountered. This is due to a number of reasons. First, there is the so-called principle of concentration, which is emphasized, perhaps far too much, by every naval and military authority. Second, there is the principle of self-preservation, which impels captains and flag officers to rally on stronger forces. Third, there is the natural desire, admirable in many ways, to come to the support of one's friends. A final reason is the desire of the cruiser commander to have his vessels close under his hand, where he can easily direct their movements.

These reasons are all excellent for battle, but they do not apply to scouting and screening, when the primary motive is to gain information of the enemy. This mission can be accomplished only by dispersion and often by independent effort. The 2d Light Cruiser Squadron, under the efficient and enterprising Commodore Goodenough, was operated correctly but, due to its station far to the southward, it was unable to gain a station to the eastward of its battle cruisers until much later.

It should be remembered that Napier had informed Beatty of his intention to support Alexander-Sinclair; and also that Beatty issued no orders to Napier although most of the time he was within visual signal distance. Thus, Beatty at the time apparently was satisfied with the operations of his light cruisers. Afterwards Beatty seems to have realized that his cruiser screen should have scouted to the eastward. In his official report he said:

After the first report of the enemy, the 1st and 3d Light Cruiser Squadrons changed their direction and without waiting for orders spread to the east, thereby forming a screen in advance of the Battle Cruiser Squadrons and the 5th Battle Squadron.

However, Beatty does not say that these two squadrons almost immediately left this advantageous position in the face of far inferior forces and concentrated far to the northward, keeping Beatty constantly informed of their intentions. We can hardly concur with the admiral's statement that "the work of the Light Cruiser Squadrons was excellent and of great value."

At 3:12 Beatty made a second unfortunate change of course. By this time he was confident that he had interposed between the German forces and their base. He thought these forces were "considerable and not merely an isolated unit of light cruisers." So at 3:12 Beatty turned his battle cruisers (Fig. 23–K) to NE. (32°). This headed them for the position of the *Elbing*, which vessel of course was well out of sight. Evidently, Beatty was operating against that "large amount of smoke as of a fleet" that Alexander-Sinclair had reported. But this smoke, as we have seen, was being made by light cruisers and destroyers, and not by German battle cruisers, which were far to the right, or eastward.

By this change of course toward the Germans, Beatty lost a remarkable opportunity to interpose not only his six battle cruisers but also his four battleships between the German battle cruisers and their bases. It is true that Alexander-Sinclair's mistake led him to believe that the German battle cruisers were farther to the westward than they actually were, a situation which could have been cleared up quickly had Napier steamed to the eastward. He should have made due allowance for this and made certain that he had cut the retreat of the Germans with not only his battle cruisers but also his battleships. As it turned out, Hipper voluntarily advanced to the fight when contact was made, but it is very questionable whether Beatty could have brought him to action had he desired to avoid it. It is certain that the 5th Battle Squadron was never brought across the German line of retreat, as might easily have been done.

At 3:14 Evan-Thomas turned the 5th Battle Squadron (Fig. 23–L) to east (77°). After this turn, he was distant from the *Lion* only 15,000 yards. By cutting corners, he had made up 5,000 yards of the interval he had inadvertently increased at 2:40. As he was converging on Beatty by 45°, this interval was still being rapidly decreased. He was quickly coming up into proper supporting distance of the battle cruisers.

CHAPTER X

APPROACH OF THE BATTLE CRUISERS
TO BATTLE
3:15 P.M. TO 3:48 P.M.

ACCORDING TO the British record of messages, the *New Zealand*
as early as 3:15 "sighted five enemy ships on starboard bow."
This evidently referred to the German battle cruisers. If so, it
was the first time they or their smoke had been sighted this
day by a British vessel. It is possible that the time mentioned
in the record is in error, as the *New Zealand's* report first mentions sighting the smoke of five ships at 3:24. However, if the
time were actually 3:15, then a prompt report by the *New Zealand* would have permitted Beatty to turn back to the eastward with excellent chances of interposing his entire Battle
Cruiser Fleet between the German scouting forces and their
base. It was not until much later that Beatty himself sighted
the German battle cruisers.

At 3:15 Beatty reported his position, course, and speed to
Jellicoe (Fig. 26-J). The course, as received in the *Iron Duke*,
was 5° in error, not a matter of any importance. Jellicoe in
turn furnished Beatty with his position, course, and speed at
3:15 (Fig. 26-K). The dispatch was sent 11 minutes later. This
was the first time that Beatty and Jellicoe had broken radio
silence. If the British knew that their codes and ciphers were
secure and they were also certain that the Germans could not
make effective use of the direction finders then established from
Borkum to Schleswig, which seems to have been the fact, this
exchange of information may be justified, as it was fairly important, though not essential, that each should have knowledge
of the other's position. Today such a procedure would be highly
disadvantageous.

Also, at 3:15 Scouting Group I increased speed to 25 knots
(Fig. 23-N). At the same time the *Elbing* reported scattered

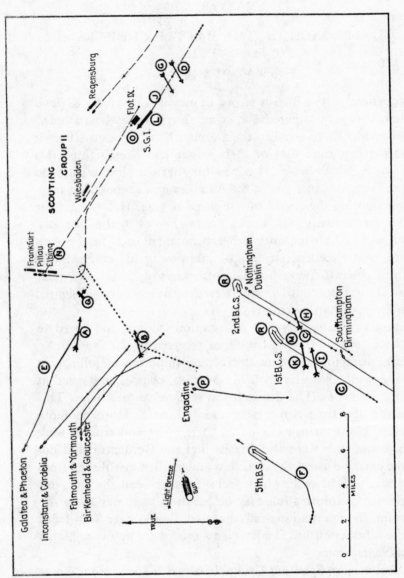

FIG. 24. 3:15-3:30 P.M.

enemy vessels (Fig. 23–O) steering NNW. (324°) in square 152 (Fig. 26).

Meanwhile, the British seaplane, piloted by Flight Lieutenant Rutland with Assistant Paymaster G. S. Trewin as observer, had been proceeding on course NNE. (9°). This, as will be remembered, was a very unfavorable one for sighting the enemy main forces. In addition, the ceiling was so low that the plane had to fly at 1,000 feet. The visibility varied from 1 to 4 miles. Fortunately, at 3:20, a brief break in the mist and clouds enabled the plane to sight three light cruisers and five destroyers distant about 8 miles (Fig. 24–B). The pilot closed in to get more definite information before making his report by radio.

While the visibility aloft was so unfavorable, it was excellent on the surface, as is frequently the case. At 3:20 the German battle cruisers actually sighted two columns of large ships at about 17 miles. These must have been the 1st and 2d Battle Cruiser Squadrons, which at that time increased speed to 24 knots (Fig. 24–C). Two minutes later the *Seydlitz* actually saw the tripod masts of the 2d Battle Cruiser Squadron projecting above the horizon (Fig. 24–G). At the same instant, 3:22, the *Nottingham* reported five columns of smoke bearing ENE. (54°). She was then in position Fig. 24–H. The next minute the *Princess Royal* (Fig. 24–I), having sighted the German battle cruisers, called Beatty's attention to them on bearing E. by N. (66°). Finally, at 3:25 Beatty himself sighted the enemy (Fig. 24–K). About this time, the admiral received a report from Alexander-Sinclair, timed at 3:15, that there was smoke bearing ESE. (100°), "apparently squadron astern of cruisers steering WNW. (279°)." This very possibly was the *Wiesbaden,* because Scouting Group I was then distant 19 miles from the *Galatea.* A few minutes later, at 3:29, Beatty received a dispatch from Alexander-Sinclair, timed at 3:20, that he was leading the enemy NW. (302°) and that they appeared to be following (Figs. 19–L and 24–E). It was also at this time that Beatty received the position, course, and speed of the Battle Fleet (Fig. 24–M).

As Beatty, at 3:25, was first sighting the enemy, Hipper had already been estimating the situation for several precious minutes. He had just slowed to 23 knots (Fig. 24-J). He could see clearly six capital ships on a northerly course. At 3:26 he altered course (Fig. 24-J) slightly away from them to NW. by N. (314°). Hipper decided to hold this course, which would soon place his column directly across the British line of advance, despite the fact that it would cause an action to be fought on a course away from his main body instead of towards it, as specified in Scheer's orders. At 3:29 he ordered fire distribution from the right (Fig. 24-0) and made ready to begin the action. This was a daring decision, which has our hearty admiration and approval. Hipper recalled Scouting Group II, informing it that strong enemy forces were in sight in square 151. At the same time, Hipper sent a radio message to all units informing them that the British main body of six vessels was in square 151 on course north (347°).

Meanwhile, at 3:21, Evan-Thomas had made an unfortunate decision. Though he was converging on the 1st Battle Cruiser Squadron at 45° and rapidly making up his lost distance, he now turned away to a parallel course (Fig. 24–F), steadying on NE. (32°). As he was proceeding at 23 knots, he just about maintained his distance of 7 miles. Had he maintained his converging course even until 3:30, he would have closed to 5½ miles. Why then did Evan-Thomas make his decision? Perhaps, it resulted from Beatty's general signal of 3:13 for a course of NE. (32°), although up to this time Evan-Thomas had very properly used his own judgment as to the course of his squadron. Again, he may have felt bound to regain his original position NNW. of Beatty. Neither of these reasons, however, should have outweighed his evident duty to close his commander for the purpose of giving him immediate support.

Still, on the other hand, it must be admitted that Beatty had done nothing whatever to state his intentions to his Fleet, so his subordinate commanders could act with intelligence. Until 3:30 he had issued only three instructions, other than prescribing courses and speeds:

(1) The *Champion* to send two destroyers to the *Engadine*, an arrangement that should have been made in advance.

(2) The *Engadine* to send a plane in the wrong direction.

(3) The 2d Light Cruiser Squadron at 3:00 to prepare to attack the van of the enemy, an obscure message impossible of execution, as this unit was the farthest in the British disposition from the enemy's van, i.e., Scouting Group II.

Beatty states that immediately upon the *Galatea's* first contact it was his plan to "place my force between the enemy and his base." Had he given Evan-Thomas only this precious sentence, it is hardly probable that Evan-Thomas would have gone NE. (32°) at 3:21, a movement which prevented this powerful squadron from ever getting "between the enemy and his base."

By 3:28 the British seaplane had penetrated to within 3,000 yards of the *Frankfurt, Pillau,* and *Elbing.* One minute later these three ships brought the plane under a heavy fire of shrapnel (Fig. 24–N). At that time Boedicker received Hipper's recall and counter-marched his three cruisers. At 3:30, evidently just before the turn began, the seaplane reported by radio that three cruisers and five destroyers were steering NW. (302°). This excellent work (Fig. 24–Q) was an indication of the usefulness of aircraft in scouting. Due to the delay in getting the plane in the air, this information was of no value. Also, the *Engadine* failed to send on the information by radio. Attempts to send the message by visual failed. It is evident that little or nothing had been done to insure the effective use of the *Engadine's* planes. The fact that such seaplane carriers were a new arm of the Fleet is some extenuation for this failure. At 3:30 the *Moresby* and *Onslow* joined the *Engadine* (Fig. 24–P) and accompanied her on course NNE. (9°). They had arrived about half an hour too late to protect the carrier while she was stopped to lower her plane.

At 3:30 Beatty ordered a change of course to east (77°). That move (Fig. 24–R) would tend to close the Germans and interpose between them and their bases if they continued on a westerly course. It was a last minute attempt by Beatty to remedy the errors he had made in abandoning his easterly course. The 5th Battle Squadron did not obey this general signal (whether general flag signals were considered binding on them is not defi-

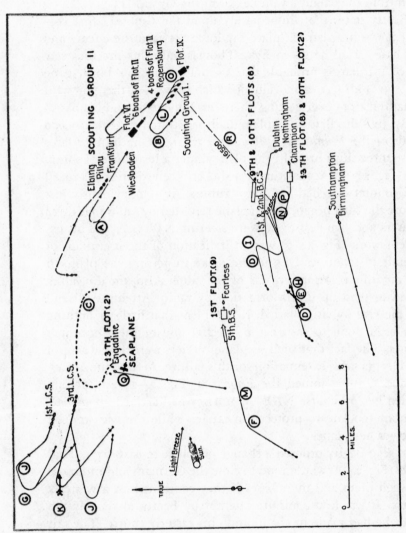

FIG. 25. 3:30–3:48 P.M.

nitely known) but continued to steer NE. (32°); thus this important unit rapidly opened the range on the *Lion*. It seems as if Evan-Thomas now considered that it was his primary mission to regain his originally assigned station NNW. (324°), 5 miles from the Fleet guide, the *Lion*.

By 3:32 the *Frankfurt, Pillau*, and *Elbing* had completed their counter-march to the southeastward and the *Wiesbaden* had commenced her turn (Fig. 25–A). It is interesting to note that the *Wiesbaden* considered it her primary duty to close the battle cruisers, and not to rejoin Scouting Group II. This was a correct decision and proved to be advantageous, for, as we shall see later, Scouting Group II was driven off by the fire of the 5th Battle Squadron, while the *Wiesbaden* continued her course toward Scouting Group I. Hipper's order had been very promptly executed by all the light cruisers. At 3:33 Boedicker reported a hostile plane in square 159. Four minutes later he reported scattered enemy forces in the same square.

It soon became evident that the British battle cruisers had changed course to the eastward at about 3:30. Hipper could tell that their bearing was drawing rapidly to his left. They would soon interpose between him and Scheer unless he quickly reversed the course of Scouting Group I. So, about 3:33 Hipper commenced a counter-march to the right (Fig. 25–B) to course SE. (122°). Speed was slowed to 18 knots to allow Scouting Group II to close. Hipper reported his position in square 004 (Fig. 26).

Groos says that the German battle cruisers sighted the 5th Battle Squadron about that time. This is substantiated also by the record of the *Seydlitz*. However, it is very probable that these ships were not sighted, or at least not definitely made out, by Vice Admiral Hipper. Although he twice reported the British battle cruisers to Scheer, the fact that he did not mention the battleships seems to prove conclusively that he did not know the battleships were present. He certainly would not have failed to report these ships had he seen them.

By 3:34 it had become obvious to Beatty that he was rapidly nearing firing range. He directed the 2d Battle Cruiser Squadron to take station astern of the 1st (Fig. 25–D). This disposition should have been taken at least 10 minutes before, preferably on the first indication that capital ships were present. At 3:36 Rear Admiral Pakenham promptly obeyed by counter-marching to the rear (Fig. 25–I). A minute later he ordered his six destroyers to take station ahead of the *Lion*.

Beatty now commenced to make other dispositions for deployment of the Battle Cruiser Fleet. He directed the 13th Flotilla, which had been screening the *Lion* and the 1st Battle Cruiser Squadron, to take station ahead (Fig. 25–D). The signals to both the destroyers and Pakenham were sent by flags. By the same method he informed all ships in sight (Fig. 25–E) that the enemy bore E. by N. (66°), and ordered an increase in speed to 24 knots (Fig. 25–H). This must have used his last signal halyards, demonstrating the disadvantage of delaying so long that many signals have to be sent simultaneously.

The *Lion's* searchlights also were busy. An unimportant message concerning the bearing of the *Galatea* was being sent to the *Falmouth* and a useless reply was received from that vessel. The flagship of the 1st Light Cruiser Squadron was still so far distant that she was not in sight from the *Lion's* bridge. In addition, a very important searchlight message was going to Evan-Thomas, directing him to steam on course east (77°) at 25 knots and telling him that the enemy was in sight (Fig. 25–F). We shall comment on this signal later.

Beatty's radio also was busy. It would seem that different members of his staff were writing the messages that were to go out by this method. Although a signal for 24 knots was flying, the senior officers of squadrons were informed by radio that the speed was 25 knots. Also, a report of the enemy in sight was being transmitted to Jellicoe (Fig. 25–E). This stated that five enemy battle cruisers and a large number of destroyers bore NE. (32°). The *Lion's* position was then appended (Figs. 19–Q and 26–Q). It will be noted that a flag signal then flying gave the bearing of the enemy as E. by N. (66°). Actually, the bearing was about midway between those contained in those reports. The course of the enemy was not included in the message.

It is true that Hipper was then just completing his counter-march and it would have been difficult to determine his course. However, that important information should have been furnished in a later message which could have been sent in plain language. This lack of vital information made it impracticable for Jellicoe to gain a correct idea of the actual situation.

Beatty's signal to Evan-Thomas to steam on course east (77°) at 25 knots merits our careful attention. The signal itself was sent most promptly by searchlight. Immediately, Evan-Thomas obeyed the order and proceeded on course east (77°). However, 24 knots was all he could make for the time being. At 3:40 he went 24½ knots. As the maximum speed of his individual ships was only 25 knots, a squadron speed only a half knot less was an excellent performance. Evan-Thomas had certainly executed Beatty's order promptly and completely; but this very fact proved most unfortunate for the British Navy on that busy day. It is hardly utilizing the talents of an officer of flag rank, commanding an independent squadron, to direct his course and speed. In fact, we contend that Beatty's signal was against every principle of effective leadership. He should have told Evan-Thomas of his intentions and given him general instructions. It would have been simple to have signaled his intention to deploy for decisive action on course SE. (122°) and to have directed the 5th Battle Squadron to support the battle cruisers. Similar instructions and information should have been sent to the other subordinate commanders.

Even if Beatty desired to handle Evan-Thomas as a corporal handles his squad on the drill ground, should he not have ordered a course of SE. (122°) instead of east (77°); or at least should he not have done so as soon as it was apparent that the Germans were heading to the southeastward? That fateful order to steam on course east was the last order Evan-Thomas was to receive from his superior for a long, long time—and the powerful battle squadron would never close on the battle cruisers as long as they went in that direction. Already, they were distant 8 miles. We believe that it is not too much to say that Beatty, after all his persistent arguments to receive the support of the 5th Battle

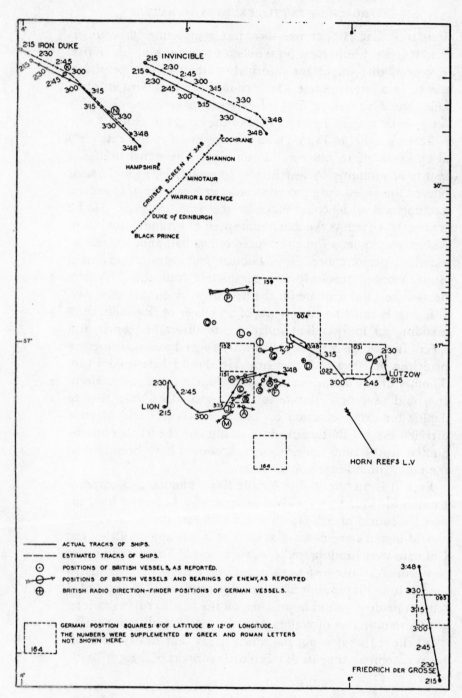

FIG. 26. Operations of the Grand and High Seas Fleets, 2:15-3:48 P.M.

Squadron, had made no provision to insure its effective use.

We must now return to those lost squadrons of Alexander-Sinclair and Napier. Those squadrons, when we last left them, had been fully 10 miles ahead of Scouting Group II, an entirely unnecessary distance, whether fighting the Germans or luring them on was the object in view. When the German light cruisers turned away at 3:30, the seaplane had promptly reported by radio to the *Engadine:* "Enemy's course is south" (Fig. 25–C). The carrier tried to relay this by visual signal to Evan-Thomas and Beatty, without the slightest luck. When we recollect the deluge of signals on the *Lion's* bridge at that time, 3:33, this is not surprising. Very unfortunately, the *Engadine* failed to broadcast that highly important message by radio. Possibly, there was no channel available to her for that purpose or it may have been contrary to some communication instructions. In any event, it was unfortunate that both Beatty and Jellicoe did not have that message, and it might have been more so if other vessels had not furnished the information.

It was not until 3:35 that Alexander-Sinclair and Napier finally realized that the German light cruisers had turned away from them. They then followed around (Fig. 25–J). When they had completed their counter-march, Alexander-Sinclair and Napier found themselves about 25,000 yards behind Scouting Group II. So, they missed the entire battle cruiser action. They had effectively lured themselves out of the fight.

In fairness to these two commanders, it must be stated that they sent in some good contact reports at that time. At 3:35 Alexander-Sinclair reported to Beatty by radio that the enemy light cruisers and destroyers had turned south (Fig. 25–C). He appended his own position (Figs. 19–o and 26–o). Jellicoe intercepted the message at 3:41, certainly with much interest. It will be noted that the course of the enemy as reported was considerably in error. This, however, was not a matter of primary importance. At 3:38 Napier sent a much better message, addressed to both Beatty and Jellicoe (Fig. 25–K). The report was quite complete and should have given Jellicoe a clear picture of the situation. Napier gave his own position (Figs. 19–P and 26–P).

He stated that the "enemy" bore E. by S. (88°). The distance was given as unknown. Therefore, it must have been great, possibly 10 to 15 miles. The enemy's course was correctly given as SE. (122°). His speed was stated as from 21 to 25 knots, also quite accurate. The only weak point of this message was the word "enemy." However, by good fortune, the very vagueness of the word probably was lucky in this case. Napier probably had seen only the light cruisers and destroyers. However, Jellicoe probably interpreted it to mean the German battle cruisers. As the contact report was correct for them as well as the light cruisers, Napier had conveyed, probably unwittingly, some correct information. At any rate he is to be commended for making an excellent report.

Beatty, seeing that the six destroyers of the 9th and 10th Flotillas were coming up on the port bow, ordered the 13th Flotilla to take station on the starboard beam. At 3:45 the 2d Battle Cruiser Squadron took station in rear of the 1st (Fig. 25–N). Pakenham had performed a difficult maneuver with skill and promptness. Beatty now, "to clear the smoke," ordered all six battle cruisers to turn together to ESE. (100°) and, at the same time, to take a line of bearing NW. (302°). Such a doubly complicated maneuver at such a critical instant was highly undesirable. It would have been preferable to have changed course in succession to SE. and then to have turned to the left two points together. At 3:46 Beatty directed the *Lion* and *Princess Royal* to concentrate their fire on the leading enemy ship (Fig. 25–P). While the British maneuvers were commencing at 3:45, Beatty reported to Jellicoe that the course of the enemy was S. 55° E. (112°) (Fig. 25–R). To this he appended his position (Figs. 19–R and 26–R), thus giving Jellicoe a complete picture of the situation.

While Beatty was issuing this large volume of orders and making his complicated last-minute maneuvers, Hipper had been making the few final arrangements necessary for bringing his forces effectively into action. At 3:39 he had ordered fire distribution from the left, ship against ship (Fig. 25–L)). Three minutes later he closed up his battle cruisers to 500 meters (about 550 yards) distance. At 3:45 he ordered (Fig. 25–o) the first *gefechtswendung* to course SSE. (145°). This was a battle turn to a designated course, in which the last ship commenced the turn first, the others doing so in rapid succession from the rear to the van. Hipper had always been much concerned over the fact that his main batteries of 11- and 12-inch guns were outranged by the 12- and 13.5-inch guns of the British battle cruisers. He feared that his enemy would open fire at ranges so great that he could not return it. It was his desire, therefore, to close to effective ranges as soon as possible. His turn sharply toward the British was with that object in view. Fortunately for him, the British were not in proper formation to take advantage of the longer ranges of their guns. In failing to do so, Beatty lost an important opportunity to get in the first hits. By 3:48 the range had decreased to 16,500 yards. As this was very satisfactory, Hipper opened fire (Fig. 25–R). Simultaneously, he sent Scheer a complete report (Fig. 27–A) of the situation:

Six enemy battle cruisers and light forces in 151 on course SE. (122°). Scouting Group I in 004, course SSE. (145°), 18 knots. Am engaged in battle with six battle cruisers. Report position of our main body.

This gave Scheer a splendid picture of the situation.

A detailed description of the opposing forces at 3:48 when fire was opened will be appropriate. The sudden reversal of course to the southeastward had caused a generally unfavorable disposition of their units. In particular, practically all the light forces were astern rather than ahead of the capital ships. On the German side, the five battle cruisers were perfectly disposed in a 2-point line of bearing. Every gun was bearing on the enemy. Their side armor made an oblique angle with the British line of fire, thus reducing the penetrative effect of the British shells. Their speed of only 18 knots, to allow Scouting Group II to catch up, allowed perfect position to be maintained.

On the other hand, the six British battle cruisers were in the midst of a complicated double maneuver. Their formation at this instant will never be exactly known, but it is probable that several ships at least could bring only their forward turrets to bear on the enemy. It is known that the British ships generally did not fire until a minute or more after the Germans fired their first salvos. The *New Zealand* was delayed about 3 minutes and the *Indefatigable* probably longer.

The 5th Battle Squadron bore from the *Lion* 293°, distant 8 miles. It was not so much the distance as the bearing that was unfavorable. It obviously was greatly to the advantage of the British to bring this squadron into action ahead rather than astern of the battle cruisers, for then it would be in a position to interpose between Beatty and Scheer. If Evan-Thomas had, under instruction from Beatty, steered a proper course at 3:20, it might have been at 3:48 just 3 miles in rear of the *Southampton*. A glance at Fig. 25 will show that this would have given Evan-Thomas a good opportunity to interpose between Hipper and Scheer with the most decisive results. Nevertheless, the situation of the 5th Battle Squadron was not without its advantages. As its presence still was unknown to Hipper, he was willing to engage the British battle cruisers despite their superiority of 6 to 5. This might well give Evan-Thomas a chance to enter the action at a critical stage. Also, in case of any disaster to the British battle cruisers, they could soon receive the powerful support of their battleships. So much for the dispositions of the opposing capital ships.

Of Scouting Group II, 3 ships were 7 miles in rear of Scouting Group I, while the fourth ship, the *Wiesbaden,* was about 5 miles behind. Nine destroyers of Flotilla VI and 6 of Flotilla II were 4 miles in rear of the *Lützow*. The *Regensburg* and 4 boats of Flotilla II were on the port beam of the *Von der Tann,* trying to take station ahead of the battle cruisers. Slightly ahead of the *Lützow* were the 11 destroyers of Flotilla IX. As Scouting Group I was proceeding at only 18 knots, all these light forces were slowly gaining more favorable stations toward the van.

In the Battle Cruiser Fleet, the 1st and 3d Light Cruiser Squadrons had completely lost themselves no less than 17 miles in rear of the *Lion*. They were even 12 miles distant from Scouting Group II. The 2d Light Cruiser Squadron was somewhat ahead of the battle cruisers, well disposed for an action on a southeasterly course. Fortunately for Beatty, it was commanded by Commodore Goodenough, by far the best commander of light forces in his fleet. The *Champion* and her destroyers (8 of the 13th Flotilla and 2 of the 10th) were about 2 miles ahead of the *Lion* well disposed for attack. However, the 6 boats of the 9th and 10th Flotillas that had been screening the 2d Battle Cruiser Squadron were in a very unfavorable position in the line of fire of the battle cruisers. As they had originally been well ahead of the *Lion,* there was no excuse for this faulty disposition. All of these light forces would have been greatly assisted by a simple signal from the *Lion* at 3:30 that the admiral intended to deploy to the southeastward. The *Fearless* and 9 boats of the 1st Flotilla were still in company with the 5th Battle Squadron and accordingly were out of the action. The *Onslow* and *Moresby* of the 13th Flotilla were 14 miles from the *Lion,* assisting the *Engadine* in picking up her plane which had just landed at 3:47 (Fig. 25–Q). The *Engadine* here drops out of the picture for several hours. As Beatty was proceeding at 25 knots, which was practically the maximum effective formation speed of his light cruisers and destroyers, there was little chance that his light forces would be able to improve their generally unfavorable positions.

To summarize the situation, it may be said that the dispositions of the light forces on both sides were generally unfavorable, but that the German capital ships were far better disposed for battle than those of the British.

A glance at Figs. 25 and 26 will show that Beatty's claim that he was "between the enemy and his base" was not correct as far as the German battle cruisers were concerned. In fact, the line of bearing between Hipper and Beatty was very nearly at right angles to the bearing of Horn Reefs light vessel. It is true that Beatty might have been able to cut the line of retreat of Scouting Group II. This fact might have, in some measure, induced Hipper to offer battle to his superior foe but, if so, it was certainly only a contributory cause. The facts demonstrate that Hipper was fighting of his own volition. He had prepared for a fight on the unfavorable northwesterly course, Then, after counter-marching, he had deliberately slowed to 18 knots as early as 3:40. Five minutes later he had headed sharply toward the enemy. Not only did he wish to fight, but he intended to do so at decisive ranges. Our hats are off to Hipper!

We must enlarge the scene of the Jutland drama and allow Jellicoe, Hood, and Scheer to play their secondary rôles during the period from 2:15 to 3:48 P.M.

At 2:15 the *Iron Duke* was distant 69½ miles, bearing about 336°, from the *Lion*. The Battle Fleet was proceeding on course SE. by E. (112°). It was zigzagging at speed sufficient to give a speed of advance, or fleet speed, of 14 knots. The *Invincible* bore from the *Iron Duke* 94° and was distant about 23 miles. Hood was, therefore, considerably to the left (northward) of the fleet axis. This was a matter of no special consequence. The *Invincible* was 64½ miles from the *Lion*. On the German side, the *Friedrich der Grosse* bore 170° from the *Lützow* and was distant about 59 miles. Jellicoe, Hood, and Scheer were therefore about three hours' steaming away from their advanced forces when the first contact was made.

The *Iron Duke*, as above stated, picked up the *Galatea's* first contact report promptly at 2:18 (Fig. 26–A). Radio communication was excellent in the Grand Fleet and Jellicoe received instantly all that Beatty's cruisers had to tell him. Their contact reports served their purpose quite well, except for the very inaccurate position of the reporting ships. The *Galatea's* reports were fantastic in this respect. As Jellicoe plotted her various positions (Fig. 26), he must have thought that she was steaming about in all directions. Her reported positions often were 8 miles south of her actual positions (Fig. 19). However, Jellicoe was still too far distant to make these comparatively minor inaccuracies of much importance at that time. At first he thought that only a German cruiser force was out. As this concerned Beatty, not the Battle Fleet, he kept on without changing base course or speed.

At 2:35 the Admiralty informed the commander in chief that the destroyer *Talisman*, with four submarines of the 11th (Blyth) Flotilla, was proceeding toward her rendezvous on the Dogger

Bank. At the same time, there came in Alexander-Sinclair's lucky report of a "large amount of smoke as though from a fleet" (Fig. 26–E). As we have seen, the *Galatea* had seen only Scouting Group II coming up to support the *Elbing;* but this information, correct in spite of its incorrectness, gave Jellicoe the first inkling that strong German forces were present. Immediately, he signaled for steam to be raised for full speed. At 2:43 speed was increased to 17 knots and zigzagging was ceased. As the *Galatea's* reported position bore about 150° from the *Iron Duke,* Jellicoe changed the line of bearing of his division guides two points to the right to NE. by E. (44°). This would bring his line more nearly at right angles to the bearing of the enemy, a condition which permits a rapid deployment against the enemy.

At 2:51 the *Iron Duke* intercepted a message from Alexander-Sinclair to Beatty stating that the smoke seemed to be seven vessels besides destroyers and cruisers (Fig. 26–F). Evidently the *Iron Duke* listened in on most of the fleet radio circuits. This was a most excellent and essential procedure by the fleet flagship. At 2:55 Jellicoe raised the speed to 18 knots and ordered steam to be raised for full speed "with all dispatch." At the same time, however, he kept in mind the ever-present necessity for conserving the fuel supply of his destroyers by ordering them to bank fires in all boilers not required for 21 knots, the maximum speed of his battleships.

At 3:00 the Battle Fleet changed course to SE. by S. (134°). This change brought the line of bearing of the division guides (44°) again at right angles to the fleet course. It is interesting to note that after this change of course the Battle Fleet was headed almost directly for Scouting Group I. At 3:00 the *Falmouth* reported three cruisers (Fig. 26–G). Her position, as reported, was far north of those given by the *Galatea,* though actually she was well to the southward. It is believed far preferable for both ships and aircraft to report the position of the enemy rather than that of their own ship.

All through this period, Jellicoe had very properly maintained radio silence. This, however, prevented him from telling Hood that he had changed course to the southward, as visual communication was very slow and uncertain. In consequence, Hood kept his detachment on his old course, which diverged two points from the new course of the Battle Fleet. The rear admiral had received the *Galatea's* first report at 2:23. Also, as *Indomitable* says, "many signals giving various positions of the enemy were received." However, Hood, like Jellicoe, thought there was nothing in these reports to give him any concern. So, he continued to advance on the old fleet course, about 115°, making great 4-point zigzags.

About 3:08 Jellicoe received the pleasing information from the *Galatea* (Fig 26–1) that the enemy were coming northwestwards, or directly towards him. The 1st and 2d Cruiser Squadrons, now disposed as a screen 10 miles ahead of the fleet guide, the *Iron Duke,* were ordered to increase this interval to 16 miles. However, as the fleet speed was now 18 knots, these cruisers, which could make only 21 knots, were able to gain interval but very slowly. In fact, as will be seen later, they were able to get little more than 10 miles ahead of the *Iron Duke*. This, however, made little difference.

Meanwhile, the British "directionals," called by us direction finders, had picked up some of the German radio messages. At 3:10 the Admiralty furnished Jellicoe with the positions of a German light cruiser (Fig. 26–c) and a destroyer (Fig. 26–d) at 2:31. As this information was 40 minutes late, it was of no value except as a check on the positions given by the *Galatea* and *Falmouth*. However, it clearly demonstrates how unfortunate it would have been for the Germans had they used radio before making contact with the British.

At 3:10 Hood sent a searchlight message to the *Chester* that he was changing course to ESE. (100°) and increasing speed to 22 knots. The Admiralty interpreted this as indicating that Hood was endeavoring to intercept the German cruisers that the *Galatea* had just reported steering NW. (302°). Only two minutes had elapsed since the *Galatea* had sent her signal and a change of course of one point away from the Germans would seem to have no particular significance. In fact, it is very doubtful whether this course was ever actually steered. Neither the *Indomitable, Inflexible,* nor *Canterbury* make any reference to it, while the increase of speed is mentioned. If this course, 100°, was ever steered, it must have been for only a few minutes, because otherwise it would be difficult to account for the later known position of the 3d Battle Cruiser Squadron. The *Chester* did not receive the signal until 3:26. By the time it was repeated via the *Minotaur,* the *Active,* and other ships to the *Iron Duke,* Hood had certainly changed his plans entirely. The sending of a signal, requiring so many relays, is of little value and is liable to be misleading rather than informative, particularly if its time group should be garbled in transmission.

Jellicoe continued his preparations to bring the Battle Fleet quickly to the scene of action and to prepare it for all eventualities. At 3:16 he made the interval between his division columns 2,000 yards. Upon deployment, this would make the distance between ships 500 yards. With a long battle line of 24 ships, it was highly desirable to concentrate the ships in the shortest possible distance, particularly as the German battle line contained fewer ships. Therefore, the comparatively short distance of 500 yards between ships was essential. With the greatly decreased number of capital ships today, it is not so necessary to make this distance so short and more room may be allowed for maneuvering. As will be seen later, the British battle line at one time greatly needed this maneuvering room.

At 3:18 Jellicoe ordered the extraordinary fleet speed of 19 knots. About three minutes later, the *Iron Duke* intercepted a radio report that Beatty had made to his squadron commanders at 3:15. This gave his position, course, and speed (Fig. 26–J). The position reported (Fig. 19–J2) was 3½ miles away from the *Lion's* actual position (Fig. 19–J1) and there was a 5° error in the course as reported. However, Jellicoe was still too far distant for these mistakes to have any practical disadvantage. It is just prior to the junction of two forces or contact with the enemy that these errors are so confusing. As will be seen from an examination of Fig. 26, Jellicoe's course was still very well selected to bring him promptly to the scene of action.

At 3:22 the situation looked so interesting that Jellicoe ordered his destroyers to raise steam for full speed. Five minutes later, the *Iron Duke* intercepted the *Galatea's* dispatch of 3:15 (Fig. 26–L). This stated that smoke bore ESE. (100°). This squadron, which actually was Scouting Group II, was said to be steering WNW. (279°). About the same time, a report came in from the *Nottingham,* timed as 3:22 (Fig. 26–M). This said the five columns of smoke bore ENE. (54°). This was a legitimate report of the German battle cruisers, distant about 15½ miles. The reported position was 8 miles to the southwestward of her actual position at the time of the report (Figs. 19–M2 and 19–M1).

At 3:29 the *Iron Duke* received Alexander-Sinclair's signal that he was leading the Germans to the northwestward (Fig. 26–L). This was good news for Jellicoe. It seemed that Beatty, Hood, and Jellicoe were converging from three sides on their foe, who was just now learning of Beatty's battle cruisers but who was still entirely ignorant of the presence of the 5th Battle Squadron and the forces of Jellicoe and Hood that were closing on him from the northward. Suppose Beatty had offered battle to Hipper on a northwesterly course in the hope of luring him still farther toward the Battle Fleet, while Evan-Thomas continued on the southeastward to cut his retreat via Horn Reefs. Certainly, Beatty did not utilize to the utmost his unique opportunity to cut the retreat of the inferior enemy forces. The failure of Scouting Group II to scout to the westward and to cover the flank of the scouting forces virtually gave them into the enemy's hands. Fortunately for Hipper, Beatty declined this gift.

We cannot avoid speculation as to what might have occurred in this interesting situation had each of the five separate forces possessed a modern aircraft carrier or even planes that could have been catapulted from battleships and cruisers. Certainly, the forces of both Hipper and Beatty would have been quickly reported in detail to the opposing commanders. If carriers had been present, their bombing squadrons would probably have attacked before this time. It is not probable, however, that the forces of Scheer, Jellicoe, and Hood would have been located by the enemy this early. At this time, the Germans were most urgently in need of their airships, but none were able to reach the scene, despite numerous radio reports.

About the time that Jellicoe received these last reports giving information of the enemy, there came in Beatty's message of 3:15 (Fig. 26–J). This gave his position quite accurately. Immediately at 3:26, Jellicoe gave Beatty his own position (Fig. 26–K). This was considerably in error, being 5½ miles west of his own dead reckoning position, as disclosed later by his 3:30 reference position. Jellicoe also furnished Beatty with his course and speed, as Beatty had done. These radio messages were the first sent by Beatty and Jellicoe. The disadvantages of breaking radio silence were well known to both British commanders, as they had profited greatly by similar procedure on the part of the Germans. They evidently considered that the time to use their radio had come and were the best judges of this difficult question. As it turned out, the Germans failed to profit by this breaking of radio silence on the part of their enemy.

At 3:31 Jellicoe ordered flag officers to inform their commands of the situation. This was an excellent idea from the viewpoint of morale, even though the messages contained many inaccuracies.

It was at 3:35 that Jellicoe informed the commodore of the flotillas, in the *Castor,* that "enemy cruisers and destroyers are being chased to the northward by our Battle Cruiser Force and should be in touch with our cruisers at 4:00 P.M." This message is of special interest in showing that Jellicoe had not yet definitely recognized the presence of battle cruisers in spite of many reports by the light cruisers of heavy smoke as of a fleet, seven columns of smoke, five columns of smoke, and other similar information.

Jellicoe's estimate of the situation was soon to be much changed. At 3:32 the *Iron Duke* intercepted a message from Beatty to his squadron commanders, stating that the course was east (77)° and the speed 25 knots. About 8 minutes later, there arrived Beatty's information report of 3:35 (Fig. 26–Q). This, as has already been related, reported five battle cruisers and a large number of destroyers bearing NE. (32°), but failed to give their speed and course. However, information on this point arrived in two signals from the *Galatea* and *Falmouth* between 3:41 and 3:44. The first said that the German light cruisers and destroyers had changed their course to south (167°). It gave the position of the *Galatea* (Fig. 26–o). The second said that the "enemy" was on course SE. (122°). This gave the position of the *Falmouth* (Fig. 26–p). As shown by Fig. 19, each of these positions was about 8 miles in error, but in different directions. Actually, as will be remembered, the German light cruisers had turned to the southeastward at 3:30 and the battle cruisers at 3:33.

At 3:45 Jellicoe issued a reference position of the fleet guide (Fig. 26–N). This was a very wise precaution, as it allowed all ships in visual touch to correct their positions in accordance with that of the flagship. Also, at 3:45 there came a report from Beatty (Fig. 26–R) that the course of "enemy," presumably the battle cruisers, was S. 55° E. (112°). At last Jellicoe had the full picture. At 3:48, when the guns began to shoot, he was 52½ miles from Beatty and steering almost for the German battle cruisers. All his arrangements had been admirable.

Meanwhile, Hood had continued on, probably steering about 115°, as reported by the *Indomitable*. At 3:20 the *Chester* received from the *Minotaur* the change of course and speed ordered by Jellicoe at about 3:00. This message probably reached Hood at about 3:30. It is assumed that between 3:41 and 3:44 he heard of the change of course of the Germans to the southeastward. Therefore, at 3:45 he changed the course of the 3d Battle Cruiser Squadron to S. 26° E. (141°). This course converged on Jellicoe's about 7°. As he kept on at only 22 knots as compared with 19 for Jellicoe, it would appear that his main object was to take proper station on the Battle Fleet and not to take independent action against the hostile cruisers. In fact, there was little, if any, action he could take against them. At 3:48 the *Invincible* bore 85° from the *Iron Duke*, distant 24½ miles (Fig. 26). Hood was, therefore, somewhat to the northward of his assigned station, but this was not of any special importance.

Now let us turn to the German side of the picture. Vice Admiral Scheer had expected to make effective use of the 11 ships of the High Seas Fleet Airship Detachment. Of this number only 5 had taken the air, as Commander Strasser had felt it necessary to reserve 6 for use the next day. None of the 5 airships in use was in the vicinity of the first contacts.

It was 2:28 when Scheer first received from the *B109* the report that scattered forces were in square 164. This position was about 12 miles to the southward of the actual position of the *Galatea* and *Phaeton*. All the squares mentioned in the German reports are shown in Figs. 19 and 26. At the time of this report, square 164 was about 52 miles distant from the *Friedrich der Grosse*, Scheer's flagship (Fig. 26). It was impossible to judge the situation, Groos says, from the first reports. Therefore, like Jellicoe, Scheer took no drastic action. His three battle squadrons were in a single long column, which probably had been used originally to facilitate the passage of the swept channel through the mine fields. The interval between the squadrons, as Scheer states, was 3,500 meters (about 3,825 yards). This appears to have been the distance between the last ship of the leading squadron to the first ship in the following squadron.

Immediately after the *B109's* report of scattered forces came a dispatch from the *Elbing* that told of a hostile armored cruiser. No position was given. At 2:36 Hipper reported his position correctly in square 031. This must have indicated to Scheer that the position of enemy forces reported by the *B109* was inaccurate. If it should be correct, it would have very serious possibilities, as the enemy force would have an opportunity to interpose between Hipper and Scheer. The *Frankfurt* at 2:55 reported correctly that it was not an armored cruiser that had been sighted, but instead four cruisers of the *Calliope* class. As a further complication, she gave the position of this force as 047 delta, which square cannot be discovered anywhere in the vicinity.

At 3:04 Scheer ordered Battle Squadrons III and I to close up, apparently to reduce the interval between squadrons to the normal interval between ships. Two minutes later he signaled for full speed, 15 knots, and "clear ship for action." At 3:15

he received Hipper's message stating that only four light cruisers had been sighted and giving the position of Scouting Group I in square 022. The *Elbing* sent in several reports of the enemy cruisers and fixed their position in square 152, steering NNW. (324°).

It was about 3:24 when Scheer heard that Scouting Group II was firing on the hostile cruisers. A few minutes later there came Hipper's report of 3:29, placing strong enemy forces in square 151. At the same time bad news arrived from the *L9*. While scouting far to the westward, her starboard propeller shaft had broken and she was returning to her hangar. Finally, at 3:35 there came a further report that six ships of the hostile main body were in sight on course north (347°). They were still in square 151. The *Frankfurt* now told of scattered forces in square 159. As this square was about 19 miles to the northeastward of 151, this report evidently referred to an entirely different force.

Scheer had already signaled for 700 meters (about 765 yards) distance between ships in the battle line. At 3:40 he went ahead at 17 knots, within 1 knot of the maximum speed of the old ships of the Battle Squadron II. At 3:48, when the action commenced, the *Lützow* and *Friedrich der Grosse* were 47 miles apart and steaming towards each other. At 3:49 Scheer received this last information in the form of a message from Hipper, timed at 3:32, that he was steaming SE. (122°) from square 004 at 21 knots. One hour must elapse before Scheer could come to the relief of his scouting forces. That was a long time for them to stand off the attack of evidently superior forces, but there was nothing Scheer could do but trust in the judgment and firm decision of Vice Admiral Hipper. Let us return to the fierce and dramatic sea fight, whose majestic cannon thunder was reverberating over the cold, gray waters of the North Sea. Let us see if these vikings of the twentieth century could equal those of the tenth!

CHAPTER XI

THE BATTLE CRUISER ACTION
3:48 P.M. to 4:30 P.M.

IT WAS AT 3:48 that Hipper executed the flag signal to open fire. Simultaneously, the five great ships loosed their salvos. The range to the enemy was 16,500 yards and decreasing at a very rapid rate. By the German signal for fire distribution, the five German vessels were to fire on the first five British vessels, leaving the last not under fire. The *Von der Tann*, however, selected the *Indefatigable* as her target. This left the *New Zealand* not under fire. In our Navy at that time, it was considered sound practice to keep all hostile ships under fire. We believed that, in order to accomplish this, a ship's fire should be divided against two targets. The forward turrets were used against one and the after turrets against the other. This evident strain on the fire control system was thought to be counter-balanced by the necessity for keeping all enemy ships under fire. It was considered that a ship not under fire could shoot much more effectively than one under the fire of even half the battery of an enemy ship. It is most significant that the Germans, whose fire control was then far more effective than ours, did not attempt this difficult task of dividing their fire. Neither, in fact, did the British. Undoubtedly, their decision was correct.

It was about 3:49 when the British ships, one by one, commenced returning the German fire (Fig. 27–B). However, it was not until 3:52 when the *New Zealand* opened fire (Fig. 27–E). The *Indefatigable* was probably as late, or even later. At 3:50 Beatty reported to Jellicoe that he was engaging the enemy and gave his position (Fig. 30–A). For a number of reasons, the accuracy of the British fire was poor. Unfortunately for the British, they cannot blame the much-maligned visibility for this failure. "The visibility at this time was good," says Beatty, "the sun behind us and the wind SE. Being between the enemy and

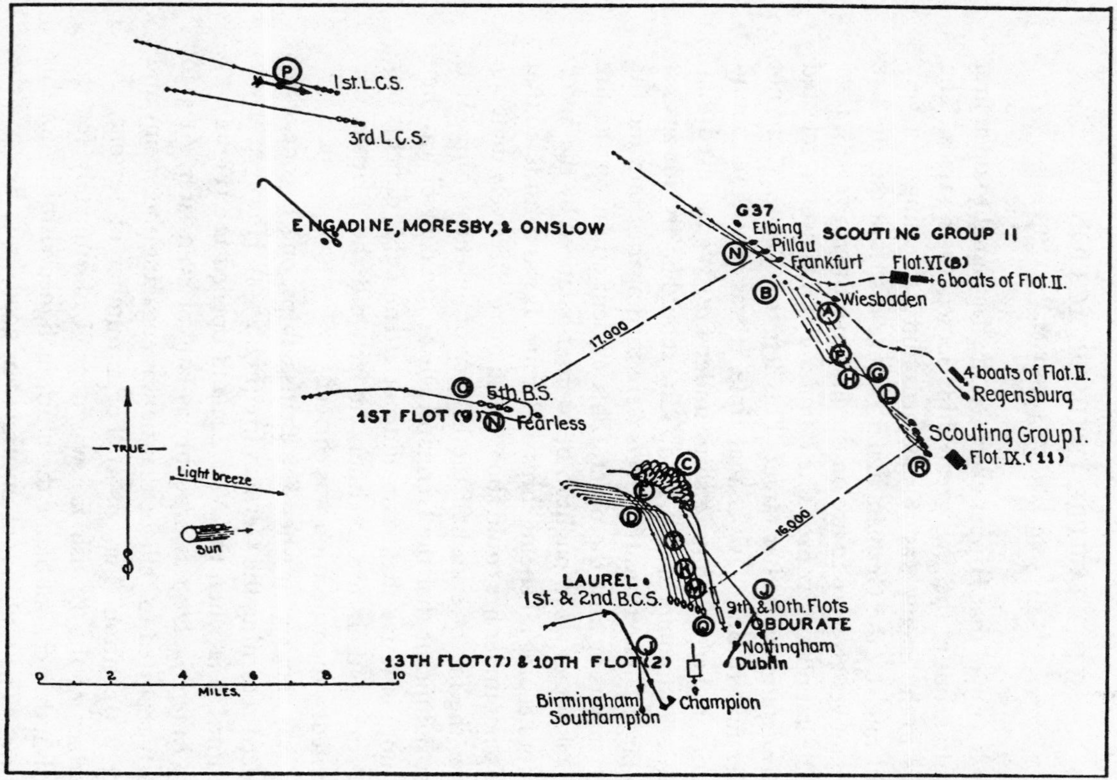

FIG. 27. 3:48-4:00 P.M.

his base, our situation was both tactically and strategically good."
What then were the reasons?

The British range finding was poor and combined with this
was an evident failure to realize that the two lines were converging at such a sharp angle. In consequence, nearly all the
British salvos fell far beyond their targets. In fact, the light
cruiser *Regensburg*, which was 2,000 yards beyond the battle
cruisers, was for some minutes in far more danger than the large
ships. One British vessel for fully 10 minutes continued to land
her salvos near this light cruiser. In addition to this, there were
several mistakes in the fire distribution. It was not until 3:46
that Beatty had made the flag signal for the *Lion* and *Princess
Royal* to concentrate on the leading enemy ship. Probably two,
and possibly three, other signals were flying from the *Lion's*
signal yards at the time. Apparently, this signal indicated that
the remaining four British ships should engage the four remaining German ships, ship for ship. However, both the *Queen Mary*
and *Tiger* must have missed the signal, for each pointed her guns
at one target too far to the rear (Sketch VII–A). This resulted
in a concentration of two ships against the *Moltke*, while for
10 minutes the *Derfflinger* was not under fire.

The British were firing under still another disadvantage.
Being to windward, the breeze blew the smoke from their stacks
and guns into the line of fire. Also, the six destroyers of the 9th
and 10th Flotillas were directly in the line of fire and their
smoke caused great inconvenience to the fire-control party. Had
these boats been warned of the intended deployment course
well in advance, it is probable that they could have gained a
position in the van before fire was opened. If they were now to
exceed the 25 knots at which the battle cruisers were steaming
in order to take station ahead, dense smoke screens were the
inevitable result. They should have been ordered out of the way
quickly.

The Germans also made their share of fire-control mistakes,
if the experience of Commander Georg von Hase, gunnery officer
of the battle cruiser *Derfflinger*, is to be taken as a fair example.
It was not until his sixth salvo, fired at 3:52, that he obtained

his first straddle. The various initial mistakes were soon corrected and the Germans proceeded to give an exhibition of marvelous shooting. Once they were straddling their targets, the very small spread of their salvos, which even today cannot be equaled, gave them numerous hits. As early as 3:51, the *Lion* was hit twice by the *Lützow* (Fig. 27–D). The next minute the *Tiger* was hit through the forecastle by the *Moltke* (Fig. 27–E). As injuries began to pile up on the British ships, Beatty at 3:52 turned quickly away from the enemy five points to S. by E. (157°) (Fig. 27–E).

Evan-Thomas had seen the battle cruisers open fire. As they turned away at 3:52, he changed the course of the 5th Battle Squadron to the right to about ESE. (100°). This course was diverging five points from Beatty's and obviously was increasing his distance from Beatty. On the other hand, by steering a course of about 135° to cut corners, he could have closed the battle cruisers and also the enemy. While possibly Evan-Thomas could have made this decision from his own observation, signals from Beatty giving his own course and the bearing of the enemy would have been helpful. It is probable that the flag signals for the change of course could not be seen from the *Barham's* bridge. This information could have been gained for the 5th Battle Squadron by the 1st and 3d Light Cruiser Squadrons had they not lost themselves to the northward. As it was, the only information Evan-Thomas had of the course and bearing of the enemy was as of 3:40, 12 minutes before. Furthermore, he might have been unwilling to depart too far from Beatty's specific order to steer east (77°).

To the eastward could be seen the dim shapes of ships. It was some time before they could be identified as German light cruisers. Directly in line with them were some of the screening destroyers of the 1st Flotilla, which had not yet been directed to concentrate for attack ahead of the battleships. So, at 3:56 Evan-Thomas directed them to get out of the way (Fig. 27–O). The light cruiser *Fearless*, in which the flotilla commander sailed, was ordered to take station in rear of the *Malaya*. This order is most difficult to understand, unless it was felt that the *Fearless'* low

R. Perkins, "Jane's Fighting Ships"

H.M.S. "LION"

The battle cruiser *Lion* flew the flag of Vice Admiral Beatty at the Battle of Jutland. As flagship of the Battle Cruiser Fleet, she left Rosyth for a rendezvous of the Grand Fleet in the North Sea. Beatty's force made contact with and engaged the Scouting Forces of the High Seas Fleet under command of Vice Admiral Hipper more than two hours before the general fleet engagement.

S.M.S. "LÜTZOW"

The battle cruiser *Lützow* was the flagship of Vice Admiral Hipper, Chief of Scouting Forces, at Jutland. This ship led the attack of the German battle cruisers on Beatty's battle cruiser squadrons which sank two of Beatty's ships, the *Queen Mary* and *Indefatigable* early in that action. The *Lützow* was so badly damaged in the Fleet action that Hipper was compelled to shift his flag to the *Moltke*. The *Lützow* was abandoned and sunk during the night while endeavoring to make her way back to the Jade. Her entire crew was taken off by German destroyers.

speed, 25.9 knots on full power trial, would prevent her from operating ahead of the battleships, which had nearly equal speed. In any event, we consider it undesirable to tie down the flagship of a destroyer commander to a definite position. As the boats of the 1st Flotilla had an excess of only 2 to 5 knots over the speed of the battleships they were screening, they should have been directed to take station ahead, long before fire was opened. This they could have accomplished by cutting corners, as this writer frequently did when in command of a destroyer able to make only about 28 knots.

Finally, about 3:58, the 5th Battle Squadron opened fire on the three cruisers of Scouting Group II at 17,000 yards (Fig. 27–N). After a few salvos, the Germans turned away sharply (Fig. 27–N). About 4:04 they commenced laying a smoke screen to cover their withdrawal (Fig. 28–E). The destroyer *G37*, which had fallen far behind Flotilla VI, assisted in laying the smoke. Thus was given an early example of the ease with which light cruisers, if handled with decision, could disengage themselves unhurt from the concentrated gunfire of capital ships. However, this detour of the ships of Scouting Group II greatly delayed their concentration on their battle cruisers and prevented them from gaining a position to support their destroyers in the van, the principal mission of light cruisers in action. In this respect the fire of the 5th Battle Squadron was of distinct value. Also, a little target practice in advance of the real fight probably had its advantages, if ammunition was carefully husbanded.

The action of the 1st and 3d Light Cruiser Squadrons could be neglected at this time if it were not for the fact that certain rather astounding signals are disclosed in the British record. Thus, at 3:50 we find Alexander-Sinclair asking Napier: "Am I right in trying to lead enemy?" As all German ships had for some time been running directly away from him at full speed, Napier apparently did not consider it necessary to answer this query. At 3:55 Alexander-Sinclair reported that the "enemy" bore ESE. (100°) and was steering in the same direction (Figs. 27–P and 30–B). The "enemy" he was reporting was only Scouting

Group II. However, Jellicoe would probably assume that Alexander-Sinclair had reference to the German battle cruisers. In this respect, his report was liable to be misleading. Such loose and vague expressions as "enemy" should carefully be omitted from contact codes such as the British evidently were using.

Meanwhile, at 3:55 Commodore Goodenough ordered the 2d Light Cruiser Squadron to form a protective screen ahead of the *Lion* (Fig. 27–J). This was an essential precaution to prevent Beatty from being surprised by the German main body which, it could be assumed, probably was to the southward. This was an entirely proper decision. It might even have been desirable to spread the light cruisers over a wider front and, in particular, to the southwestward.

By 3:54 the range between the opposing battle cruisers had decreased to 13,000 yards. Up to this time the German ships had been firing only their main batteries, one gun from each turret firing in each salvo. The secondary batteries of 5.9-inch guns were now in range. Accordingly, they also commenced firing. The *Seydlitz* aimed at the destroyers of the 9th and 10th Flotillas, which were in the line of fire. The other ships fired their secondary batteries at the same battle cruisers that were the targets for their main batteries. This was a most original use for the secondary batteries in a day action, as they are usually reserved for use against destroyers or possibly light cruisers, their guns' crews being kept behind armor until needed. While some of the British ships were hit by these small shells, there is no evidence that they caused any appreciable damage. On the other hand, the crews of the German secondary batteries were exposed to the fire of the British heavy guns and at times suffered somewhat heavily. Today, it probably would not be advantageous to use the secondary batteries against capital ships, except when fighting at close range as might be the case in low visibility or at night.

It will be remembered that Scouting Group I had been in a 2-point line of bearing since 3:45, when Hipper had turned sharply toward the enemy to run quickly through the range zone in which the British heavier guns had the advantage. At 3:54

the admiral directed the group (Fig. 27–G) to "follow the leader." The *Lützow* maintained her course of SSE. (145°) and the other vessels sheered in astern of her. While this maneuver interfered with their fire somewhat for a few minutes the use of column formation made station keeping easier and gave Hipper rather more control over the group. It clearly showed that he had no intention of turning away for the present, because, had he desired to do so, a simultaneous 2-point turn away would have brought his ships into column by a maneuver much simpler than the one employed.

At 3:55 the *Seydlitz* was hit by one of a salvo of 13.5-inch shells fired by the *Queen Mary* (Fig. 27–H). This hit did little damage, putting out of action an electrical switchboard. At the same time, two of the *Moltke's* 11-inch projectiles landed on the *Tiger* (Fig. 27–I) with considerable effect. One struck her "Q," or amidship, turret, while the other hit her "X," or after, turret. Both were put out of action for a considerable period. Thus, for the time the *Tiger's* fire was cut in half. The *Lion* also was hit by one of the *Lützow's* 12-inch, high-explosive shells. These had been made ready when it was thought that light cruisers would be their targets. When the battle cruisers had appeared, there had not been time to change. It was indeed fortunate for the *Lion* that the hits she received at this time were not made by armor-piercing shells.

Beatty now signaled to increase the rate of fire, using both flags and radio. By the latter system of communication, he informed the commander of the 13th Flotilla in the *Champion* that the "opportunity appears favorable for attacking." A minute later, at 3:56, he directed the 13th and 1st Flotillas by flags to "proceed at your utmost speed." Whether this order was ever received by the 1st Flotilla in the *Fearless* is very doubtful. However, it is interesting to note that just as Beatty was directing the 1st Flotilla to use its utmost speed in order to get into the fight, Evan-Thomas was directing its flagship, the *Fearless*, to take station astern of the 5th Battle Squadron.

At 3:56 the German fire was becoming highly effective. The *Moltke*, which had been shooting magnificently, landed one, and

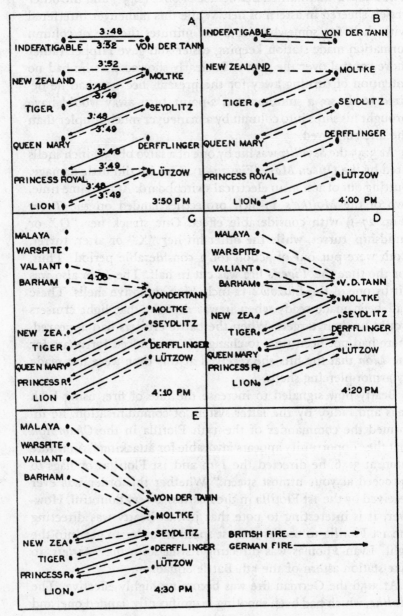

SKETCH VII. Fire distribution 3:50-4:30 P.M.

probably more, hits on the *Tiger* (Fig. 27–K). One shell that struck amidships did extensive damage. The explosion of its powder charge drove its base into the engine-room, where it just missed the main steam line. The engine-room instantly was filled with escaping steam from smaller lines that had been broken and with the poisonous fumes of burning powder; but the British engineers stuck to their posts with resolute courage and repaired the injuries without the slightest reduction of speed.

The *Derfflinger* now was really getting into the fight. Two of her 12-inch armor-piercing shells landed squarely on the *Princess Royal*. One damaged her "A," or forward, turret, while the other put her main control out of action for 20 minutes. In the face of these heavy losses, Beatty at 3:56 turned away one point (Fig. 27–K) to south (167°). This made a total of six points he had turned away since the fight began.

At 3:57 the British scored their second hit in 8 minutes of firing (Fig. 27–L). This did some serious damage to the *Seydlitz*. It was one of the *Queen Mary's* 13.5-inch shells that pierced the barbette of her "C," or amidship, turret. Its explosion ignited powder bags, whose heat and fumes killed practically the entire crew of the turret. However, the magazine was flooded before it could be reached by the flames. The Germans had given much thought to the protection of their magazines. That they surpassed the British in this respect was soon to be demonstrated in no uncertain fashion.

At 3:58 the *Derfflinger* hit the *Princess Royal* on "B" turret forward (Fig. 27–M) and about 2 minutes later sent two more shells through her foremast and funnel. The *Derfflinger's* fire, under the skillful direction of Commander von Hase, was now very effective. The *Tiger* was still under the *Moltke's* effective fire. As near as we can determine, she was hit about five times during the 7-minute period beginning at 3:58. These hits probably were through the funnel, into the secondary battery, against the side armor aft, into the flour store, and on "A" barbette, as related in *The Fighting at Jutland*. The seven or eight hits made in the first phase of the battle cruiser action by

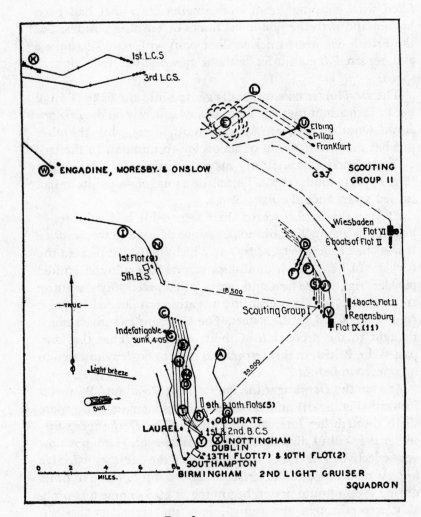

FIG. 28. 4:00-4:15 P.M.

the *Moltke* testify to the effectiveness of her gunnery department under Commander Schirmacher.

At 4:00 the main battery of the *Lützow*, ably directed by the
skillful Commander Paschen, scored its fourth hit on the *Lion*
with well-nigh decisive results. It penetrated "Q" turret amidships, killing all but Major Harvey and his sergeant of Marines
Harvey was horribly wounded and had but a few minutes to
live, but he devoted these precious moments to the performance of his duty. Sending the sergeant to the captain with news
of the disaster, the major himself gave the order to the handling-room crew to flood the magazines. As will be seen later,
it was to this heroic conduct that the safety of the British flagship was due. Harvey was awarded the Victoria Cross.

About 4:00 the *Lützow* was hit by the *Lion* and the *Derfflinger* by the *Princess Royal* (Fig. 27–R). By this time the range
had increased to about 16,000 yards, as a result of Beatty's
turns away. The secondary batteries of the German ships, which
were ranged only to 14,950 meters (about 16,350 yards), ceased
firing. The German distribution of main battery gunfire was
still the same as at 4:00 P.M. (Sketch VII–B). The British were
now fighting ship for ship, except that the *Tiger* and *New Zealand* were concentrating on the *Moltke*. However, neither of
these two British vessels had made a hit up to this time, as
compared with about 5 or 6 for the *Moltke*.

At 4:00 Hipper turned the battle cruisers away one point
together to SE. by E. (134°). As the range already was increasing
rapidly and as the Germans were enjoying such success, it is
difficult to see the reason for this movement. Groos says that
its purpose was to interfere with the fire control of the British,
but a turn toward the enemy would have served this purpose
just as well as a turn away. Furthermore, a change of course
of only one point would have little effect on the rate of change
of range. However, we are not disposed to be critical of a 1–
point change of course away from the enemy when such an
aggressive admiral as Hipper is concerned.

As the range now rapidly increased, the fire of the British
soon lost its effectiveness, while that of the German ships con-

tinued to be accurate. By 4:00 they had scored at least 12 hits against 4 for the British. In the next few minutes, their advantage was to mount rapidly and bring them a brilliant success. By chance the heaviest losses fell on the ships at the ends of the British column. The *Lion,* at the head of the line, continued to receive heavy punishment. At 4:03 she received one hit (Fig. 28–B). Although the range had already increased to 17,000 yards, Beatty turned his battle cruisers (Fig. 28–B) together three points more away from the enemy to SW. by S. (202°), a total of nine points (101°) he had turned away since the beginning of the battle. Groos claims that the *Lützow* hit the *Lion* no less than 6 times between 4:03 and 4:07, but this cannot be reconciled with the British claim that the latter was hit only 12 times with heavy shells. It is very possible, however, that the *Lion* was hit several times during this period. It must have been about this time that her main radio was wrecked, for at 4:05 she reported that fact to the *Princess Royal* (Fig. 28–H). This very serious casualty prevented Beatty from sending radio messages for several hours.

It was upon the rear of the British column that the heaviest German blows fell. By 4:03 the *Von der Tann* had fired no less than eleven 4-gun salvos at the *Indefatigable,* apparently without making a single hit. Strangely enough, the increase in range affected least of all this oldest of the German battle cruisers, for her 11-inch guns had been installed with a mounting that permitted an elevation of 20°, giving a maximum range of 20,500 meters (about 22,400 yards), the greatest range of all the German battle cruisers. At 4:04 at a range of about 17,500 yards, the *Von der Tann* landed a closely bunched salvo, 3 of the 4 shells hitting (Fig. 28–C). Simultaneously, Hipper gallantly turned his ships two points toward the British and formed column (Fig. 28–D) on course S. by E. (157°). Just as the *Von der Tann* was executing this signal, her second successive salvo landed abreast the forward turret of the *Indefatigable,* with terrible effect. Smoke had been pouring from her quarter-deck as a result of the first destructive salvo. Now, the ship sheered to the right with great smoke clouds rising from her forecastle.

Evidently, three 11-inch shells had pierced her thinly armored turret and barbette, protected by only 7 inches of steel. The explosion of these shells had ignited powder bags, which in turn sent great tongues of flame into the magazines. Flames and smoke burst from the ship's hull. A violent explosion sent debris higher than her mastheads. The *Indefatigable* had fought her last fight. Listing quickly to port, she capsized. This tragic drama had been enacted with startling suddenness. It was only 17 minutes after the fight started that the ship went down, at 4:05 (Fig. 28–G). Commander Mahrholz had fired fifty-two 11-inch armor-piercing shells to gain this astounding triumph. Just as the *Indefatigable* sank, a disaster probably not known to him for some minutes, Beatty turned two points toward the Germans to S. by W. (179°) (Fig. 28–H).

At 4:05 Hipper received the comforting news that at 4:00 his main body was in square 043 center on course NW. (302°) proceeding at 15 knots (Fig. 30). However, it was not only Hipper that received this important message. The British Admiralty picked it up, deciphered it, and had the translation in Jellicoe's hands at 5:00. The position reported to Jellicoe was exactly as Scheer had reported it to Hipper (Fig. 30–D). Incidentally, this position was one square to the north of Scheer's correct position as shown by the German official charts.

By about 4:07 the fire of both forces was decreasing and had become ineffective (Fig. 28–M). This was due to the fact that Beatty, fighter that he was, was now steering no less than seven points to the right of his original course. Hipper, on the other hand, was actually steering one point nearer the enemy than at 3:48, when the action began. With a gallantry worthy of those famous soldiers whose names his splendid ships so proudly bore, the German commander turned two points to the right to W. by S. (179°), parallel to the course of the enemy (Fig. 28–J). However, by the time this signal was executed, the range had increased to about 22,000 yards and all effective fire had ceased. At 4:10 Scouting Group I ceased firing (Fig. 28–P).

By this time the British battle cruisers received a powerful re-enforcement. Beatty's sharp retirement before Hipper and the latter's aggressive pressing of the fight had permitted Evan-Thomas to get into the fight sooner than otherwise might have been expected. There is no reason to believe that Beatty's retirement was designed to lure Hipper under the guns of this overwhelming force; but, by a rare stroke of fortune which this day certainly fought under the British ensign, Scouting Group I had been brought into an extremely dangerous situation. For the one hydra head that Hipper had cut off four had taken its place. Let us see how Evan-Thomas had brought his splendid squadron into the fight.

At 4:06 the 5th Battle Squadron had changed course to SE. by S. (134°). (Fig. 28–1). At 4:08 Evan-Thomas went two more points to the right (Fig. 28–N) to S by E (157°). It was just at that minute, as well as it can be determined by balancing the very contradictory evidence, that the *Barham* opened fire on the *Von der Tann* at about 19,000 yards (Fig. 28–N). The *Valiant* soon fired at the same target. The squadron went into the fight with great enthusiasm. Not being able to fire as early as the leading ships, the *Malaya's* crew cheered their salvos wildly. The fire of these splendid ships was excellent, when the long range and the uncertain visibility are considered. Moreover, since Hipper's turn at 4:07 toward the enemy, Evan-Thomas had been converging on his course by two points (22½°) and this caused the range to decrease rapidly. At 4:12 the *Von der Tann* was struck aft by one of the tremendous shells of the *Barham* (Fig. 28–S). This 1,950-pound bolt of hardened steel went far into the ship and did extensive damage. However, the well-trained damage-control party of the *Von der Tann* limited the amount of water that entered the ship to 600 tons. Now, Evan-Thomas for the first time hoisted a fire distribution signal. The *Barham* and *Valiant* shifted fire to the *Moltke*, while the *Warspite* and *Malaya* fired on the *Von der Tann*. Sensing the danger from the rear, Hipper increased speed to 23 knots. He commenced firing again on the British battle cruisers, ship for ship (Fig. 28–S). Even with this increase of speed, Scouting Group I was going about 1½ knots less than the 5th Battle Squadron.

As far back as 4:06 the *Moltke* had fired four torpedoes at the British battle cruisers (Fig. 28–F), Her position, far on the quarter of a fast-moving target, was most unfavorable for torpedo fire. As the torpedoes would have had to run at least 26,000 yards before reaching their target, it is evident that they had been wasted.

Before recounting the story of the second round of the battle cruiser action, we must tell something of the operations of the light forces. Let us start in the rear where little had been happening. At 4:07 Rear Admiral Napier (Fig. 28–K) had tried by searchlight to tell both Beatty and Evan-Thomas that the "enemy" was steering ENE. (54°). Fortunately, the message was not received by either of them. The "enemy" referred to evidently was Scouting Group II. We have commented already on the use of this confusing word. A commander receiving such a report would naturally believe that it referred to the most important enemy unit present. "Light forces" or "Scouting Group II" would have made Napier's meaning clear. As a matter of fact, neither Beatty nor Evan-Thomas had any interest in the course of the German light cruisers, particularly if it was away from the fight. Thus, Napier's message was both useless and confusing. By chance Scouting Group II actually changed course back again to the southeastward at 4:07, just when the signal under discussion was being sent. The three vessels of Scouting Group II that had been forced away by the fire of the 5th Battle Squadron had lost valuable time and distance. The *Wiesbaden,* which had kept on independently toward her battle cruisers, had avoided the fire of the British battleships and was now gaining rapidly on Hipper.

It was not until 4:12 that Boedicker reported the presence of the 5th Battle Squadron, after an unfortunate, if perhaps excusable, delay. He reported (Fig. 28–U) that the British "main body," consisting of five ships of the 2d Battle Squadron, was in square 151. The use of the German term *"Gros"* (main body) was rather confusing. The error in the name of the battle squadron was caused by the fact that the German lookouts could make out only one mast and two stacks on each ship. The light cruiser *Fearless* was mistaken for a fifth battleship, a mistake the British made later in the case of the *Regensburg*.

Far to the northward, the *Onslow* and *Moresby*, released from their duty with the *Engadine*, were steaming at their best speed to close the 5th Battle Squadron (Fig. 28–w). Their gallant captains would be sadly missed in the destroyer action that was about to begin.

Let us describe the movements of the British light forces in the van. In spreading to form a screen ahead of the battle cruisers, the *Nottingham* had taken station nearest the enemy. At 4:02 she fired for a time at long range on Flotilla IX in the German van (Fig. 28–A). There is no record of any hits.

As soon as Beatty gained a temporary respite from the German gunfire, at about 4:09, he ordered the 13th Flotilla to attack (Fig. 28–o). As the *Lion's* radio had been put out of action, this message had to be relayed through the *Princess Royal*. Captain Farie in the *Champion* did not receive it until an hour later.

Beatty now could see that the 5th Battle Squadron was entering the action. It was time for him to re-engage. As evidence of his preparations to do so, we have his signal to the destroyers at 4:11 to clear the range (Fig. 28–R). During all the action, the Harwich destroyers on the engaged side of the battle cruisers had been interfering with their gunnery. The *Laurel*, unable to make the speed, had moved over to the starboard beam of the *New Zealand*. The *Morris* and *Moorsom* had finally been able to get abreast the *Lion*, having the advantage of about 34 knots' speed. With them was the *Obdurate* of about the same speed, which had still been unable to rejoin the 13th Flotilla. The *Lydiard, Landrail,* and *Liberty,* having only 29 knots' speed, were still directly in the line of fire. Beatty had thought that they would be some protection against submarine attack, but at last he saw that he was paying a heavy price for a very doubtful advantage. At his order, they now fell back and about 4:16 took station in rear of the *New Zealand*. Curiously enough, none of these destroyers had made any effective attempt to save the survivors of the *Indefatigable*, though the German destroyers were able to save two of her crew nearly 2 hours after the battle cruiser had been destroyed.

At 4:12, just as Hipper had reopened fire, Beatty turned the battle cruisers three points toward the enemy to SSE. (145°). This maneuver converged the two columns at an angle of three points (34°). In consequence, the range decreased rapidly and soon the fire of both sides became effective. It was evident that the second round, due to the intervention of the 5th Battle Squadron, would be even more dangerous to the Germans than the first. It should be distinctly remembered that the British battleships were firing at the range at which the *Von der Tann* with her 11-inch guns sank the *Indefatigable*. Therefore, their 15-inch guns were really within moderate range of their targets and they were firing under target-practice conditions. If Hipper was bold to engage 6 battle cruisers at 3:48, how shall we characterize his fighting 5 battle cruisers and 4 battleships at 4:12? That he should escape from this death trap with very slight losses after sinking another great British battle cruiser is almost incredible. But we anticipate the narrative of a masterpiece of naval leadership, one that merits the word "Nelsonian."

Beatty describes the fight that occurred as "of a very fierce and resolute character." At 4:14 the *Lion* landed a salvo on the *Lützow* (Fig. 28–v). A minute later the *Lützow* retaliated (Fig. 28–y) with two hits in the *Lion's* mess deck, which caused heavy personnel losses and set the ship on fire. Smoke so enveloped her that the *Derfflinger*, thinking that she had left the line, changed target to the *Queen Mary* in the belief that she was firing at the second ship in column. There was similar confusion in the British fire distribution, for the light cruiser *Regensburg*, which had now gained her station at the head of the German line, was frequently counted as a battle cruiser. It was apparently for this reason that the *Tiger* shifted fire from the *Moltke* to the *Seydlitz* somewhat after 4:20. The *Queen Mary's* target at this time is disputed. Von Hase very positively states that she was firing at the *Derfflinger*, but Groos states that she was using the *Seydlitz* as a target. Probably, she was firing at the *Seydlitz* until about 4:20 and then shifted to the *Derfflinger*.

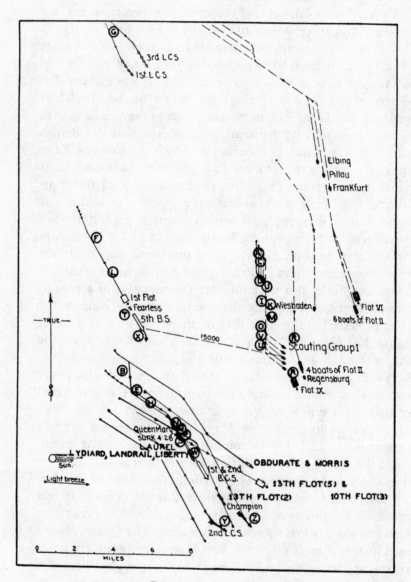

FIG. 29. 4:15-4:30 P.M.

Sketch VII gives the fire distribution at 10-minute intervals during the battle cruiser action as closely as we can determine it. It is not pretended that it is correct in all respects, because the data are both incomplete and conflicting.

Despite the fact that she was under the concentrated fire of the *Derfflinger* and *Seydlitz*, the *Queen Mary* scored a hit on the latter at 4:17, putting out of action a 5.9-inch gun (Fig. 29–C). About the same time, the *Derfflinger* hit the *Queen Mary* in her broadside battery (Fig. 29–E). At 4:18 Scouting Group I sheered into column in rear of the *Lützow* (Fig. 29–D).

Meanwhile, at 4:14 Hipper had ordered his destroyers to attack (Fig. 28–V). Possibly, he desired to relieve the pressure on the battle cruisers. Perhaps, seeing the British destroyers gaining a position to attack, he wished to forestall their attack by an advance of his own boats. At 4:15 Goodenough ordered the *Nottingham* to support the British destroyers (Fig. 28–X).

As the battle raged between the battle cruisers and the opposing destroyers raced ahead for their attacking positions, the fire of the 5th Battle Squadron became more and more effective. The *Barham* and *Valiant* were firing on the *Moltke*. At 4:16 one of them landed a shell on one of the 5.9-inch broadside guns (Fig. 29–A). At 4:18 Evan-Thomas ordered distance of 600 yards between ships (Fig. 29–F). The *Warspite* and *Malaya* were now combining with the *New Zealand* in a triple concentration against the little *Von der Tann*. Resolute Captain Zenker this day handled his ship with a gallantry and skill unsurpassed by the heroes of antiquity. At 4:20 the barbette of his forward turret was pierced by a 15-inch shell and the turret put out of action (Fig. 29–J). Three minutes later another great shell did the same for his after turret (Fig. 29–K). In reply, the German ship at the same time hit the *Barham* squarely (Fig. 29–L), but her 11–inch shell was ineffective against the heavy armor of the great battleship. Zenker now shifted fire to the *New Zealand* and hit her at 4:26, without appreciable damage (Fig. 29–Q). A small piece of armor knocked out of "X" turret was the only result. A gunnery casualty then put the *Von der Tann's*

No. 2 turret out of action, reducing her effective main armament to two guns.

The *Moltke* and the *Tiger* had been fighting a fierce duel. About 4:25 (Fig 29–Q) and 4:26 (Fig. 29–P), the *Tiger* seems to have received unimportant hits. She retaliated by landing two 13.5-inch shells on the *Moltke* at 4:27 (Fig. 29–v). As these last hits were being made, Scouting Group I, as will be described in detail later, turned away together to SE. (122°). This greatly eased the situation. Also, the *Moltke* and *Von der Tann* zigzagged right and left to throw out the fire control of their powerful antagonists, distant now only about 14,000 yards.

The Germans had an effective reply to this heavy pressure against the rear of their column. Here was a real opportunity for an attack of their destroyers against the 5th Battle Squadron. They could compel that squadron, by a resolute attack from a very favorable position, either to sheer off or run the risk of being torpedoed. At the very least, the destroyers could have concealed their battle cruisers with smoke screens. Flotilla VI and 6 boats of Flotilla II were available for this duty, or rather should have been. Instead of closing in on Scouting Group I, these destroyers had made a wide detour to the eastward. So, at the critical moment, they were 4 miles away when, by steering a proper course between 4:00 and 4:15 they could have been close under the lee of the *Von der Tann*. In that case it would have been simple for Hipper to order them to attack the 5th Battle Squadron. In any case, as soon as they saw the British battleships open fire, they should have proceeded to lay a smoke screen in the line of fire. The six B-boats of Flotilla II, 1,760 tons and 36 knots, were very well suited for that duty. Their commander lost a splendid opportunity to be of great service to the rear battle cruisers at a critical moment.

While the *Moltke* and *Von der Tann* were fighting against such heavy odds, their comrades in the van were winning the greatest success of the day, for there the *Seydlitz* and *Derfflinger* were continuing their deadly concentration on the *Queen Mary*. About 4:20, according to the brave little midshipman who was the senior survivor of *Queen Mary's* disaster, a shell struck

"Q" turret, located amidships, and put one of its guns out of action (Fig. 29–H). Shortly thereafter the *Queen Mary* hit the *Derfflinger* twice. The first hit occurred at about 4:20 (Fig. 29–I) and the second at about 4:23 (Fig. 29–M). These times are estimated only, but von Hase says that his ship was hit twice by the *Queen Mary* shortly after the latter sank!

At 4:24 three 12-inch shells of a salvo fired by the *Derfflinger* hit the *Queen Mary* at or near "Q" turret (Fig. 29–N). Two minutes later two more shells hit near the same place (Fig. 29–s). A terrific explosion occurred and the ship turned slowly over to port. The crews of "Q" and "X" turrets gained the deck. Some of them climbed down the starboard side and reached the water. The stern of the ship rose high out of the water, with the propellers still turning. It seemed as if this dying giant were using her last energies to keep in the fight.

Doubtless the arrows on her engine-room telegraphs still pointed to the sectors marked: "Full Speed—Ahead."

So rapidly did this disaster overtake the *Queen Mary* that it required quick decision and skillful handling for the ships following closely astern at 25 knots to avoid crashing into her. The *Tiger* was able to sheer out to port sufficiently to clear the wreck. Just as the *New Zealand* was passing her to starboard, a second explosion occurred. The ship sank under a great pall of black smoke, which rose to the height of several hundred feet. This was clearly seen by the Germans and proved very heartening to them in their perilous situation.

How many hits the stricken ship received can never be determined with accuracy. Von Hase, who had a clear, if distant, view of his target and who was concentrating all his attention on the observation of his salvos, claims no less than eight hits in three successive salvos. Our total of five is a very conservative estimate. As the *Queen Mary* probably had received previously three hits, this gives her a total of eight for the entire action. Her 9-inch armor had not been able to resist the *Derfflinger's* 12-inch shells, as the *Indefatigable's* 7-inch barbettes and turrets and 6-inch side armor had previously been unable to resist the *Von der Tann's* 11-inch projectiles. Perhaps, the concentrated effect of three shells hitting closely together at the same time was what really sank the British battle cruisers. These two triumphs for the Germans amply proved the correctness of von Tirpitz' theory of giving priority to defensive strength rather than offensive power; but it also proved the correctness of Farragut's saying that the best defense is a well-directed fire of your own guns. There can be no question that, at least so far as the battle cruisers were concerned, the German gunnery was far superior to that of the British. Brilliant as was Hipper's leadership, his success was due fundamentally to the thorough preparations made over a long course of years for this brief fight. Twenty-five years of exhaustive, systematic, and progressive gunnery training here showed their inevitable results. Admiral von Schröder, in command of the Flanders Naval Corps at the time of Jutland, in long past years had said to one of his subordinates: "If twenty-four hours isn't a long enough day for you, try using the night as well." All the hard work typified by that expressive remark was paying its dividends on this battle field, winning glory for those so fortunate as to have the opportunity to fight the German ships and satisfaction for those who had contributed only the drudgery of peace-time preparation.

While to the victor goes the praise, to the vanquished goes our admiration, for in this terrible disaster the crew of the *Queen Mary* behaved as British seamen always have when face to face with seemingly inevitable death. The survivors were so few that we know only a few incidents of heroism, which unknown heroes doubtless multiplied many fold. The handling-room of "X" turret was evacuated only when the rising water compelled the turret officer to give the word to leave the turret. The last man who appeared from below was Petty Officer Stares. When asked why he had not come up before, this simple seaman replied: "There was no order to leave the turret." Let this be the epitaph of the *Queen Mary* and her brave crew as they lie together beneath the North Sea waves.

Now, that Hipper had achieved this striking success against the British center, a threat was impending against his van, in addition to the one against his rear. His situation had not been improved by his necessity to reduce speed at 4:25 (Fig. 29–0). This probably brought down Scouting Group I to about 20 knots, perhaps less, for the British destroyers had gained a position almost directly ahead of the German battle cruisers, a perfect station for a torpedo attack.

We have seen that Beatty, way back at 4:09, had ordered the commander of the 13th Flotilla, in the *Champion,* to attack with torpedoes (Fig. 28–0). But as the *Lion's* radio had just been put out of action, this message had to be sent via the *Princess Royal.* The *Champion's* log shows that this important message was not received until 5:16. However, there is a possibility that this message did get through in some form, for Captain Farie records that at 4:15 "the whole flotilla was ordered to attack." It is an interesting point whether this torpedo attack should have been made at all. On the one hand, it might be argued that the British destroyers would drive the German battle cruisers away from a greatly superior British concentration. On the other hand, it might be claimed that the destroyer attack was designed to cut off the retirement of the Germans to the southward and to envelop the southern flank, while the battleships were turning the northern flank, this double envelopment forcing the enemy against the Danish coast. If the German main body were not in the vicinity, the second line of reasoning was excellent. If the main body were near at hand, the first was correct. As Scheer actually was close at hand, the destroyer attack had an unfortunate effect for the British in driving Hipper from a position in which they should have begged him to remain. However, this hindsight reasoning implies no criticism of Beatty, as he had no means of knowing the position of Scheer's forces. It is stated only to show that a torpedo attack is not necessarily always advisable.

Since 4:15 the British destroyers had been steaming out ahead of their battle cruisers to gain an attacking position. Unfortunately, in doing this they had become so scattered that all organization was lost and it became a case of every captain for himself. There were several reasons for this condition. First, we find that Captain Farie, after ordering his flotilla to attack, made no attempt to lead or direct it. Perhaps, his speed of 29 knots interfered with his leadership, but we find that he did not even use the *Champion's* fine battery of four center-line, 6-inch guns to support the destroyers. Second, the light cruisers *Nottingham* and *Dublin* had been ordered by Goodenough to support the destroyer attack. At 4:21 the *Nottingham* "barged" (to use the expression of a destroyer officer) at high speed directly through the flotilla, causing immense confusion. The order of the flotilla was then as follows: *Nestor, Nomad, Nicator, Narborough, Pelican, Petard, Turbulent, Nerissa,* and *Termagant.* The *Obdurate* had fallen well to the rear, while the *Moresby* and *Onslow* had been back with the *Engadine.* The *Nottingham* came through between the *Pelican* and *Petard.* The four rear destroyers, with what remarks of disgust we can imagine, had to turn off sharply or stop to avoid being rammed. The *Petard* and *Turbulent* in one group and the *Nerissa* and *Termagant* in another proceeded at full speed in an attempt to make up the distance they had lost. The *Narborough* and *Pelican* were far to the right, away from the enemy, how and why, the Admiralty admits, is "doubtful." The *Obdurate,* on the *Lion's* engaged bow, was coming on as fast as she could. Somewhat ahead of her, the *Morris* of the 10th Flotilla and therefore not included in the attack order, was hurrying on. The *Moorsom,* also of the 10th Flotilla, with excellent handling had made her way well towards the van of the 13th Flotilla. In lead of all went the splendid *Nestor.* On her bridge was Commander the Honorable Edward B. S. Bingham, so soon to write "V.C." after his name. At his side was Lieutenant M. J. Bethell, soon to win an equal, if sadder, honor: "Killed in action." Next came the *Nomad,* then the *Nicator.* When the *Nomad* fell back somewhat due to engineering trouble, the *Nicator* came past her into second place. The *Moorsom* followed closely.

As the British destroyers advanced in such irregular array, Flotilla IX, eleven strong, advanced in compact order to meet them. Far back at 4:14 (a few minutes count as years in the compressed activity of this fight) Hipper had issued the order to attack (Fig. 28–v). At 4:26 Commodore Heinrich, second leader of Destroyers in the *Regensburg* (Fig. 29–R), sent a brief and expressive signal: "IX Flotilla *Ran!*" Perhaps, one might translate that last untranslatable word as: "Go for them!" Commander Goehle, in the *V28*, quickly signaled: "*Torpedoboote zum Angriff*" (torpedo boats to the attack). This also was at 4:26—so prompt was alert Goehle. In fact, it is said that he hoisted his signal even before he saw that of Heinrich. It is for such quickness of decision that the German destroyer commanders had been trained these last 25 years. Incidentally, the Germans called their destroyers "torpedo boats," a much more correct term. It reflected the German idea that this type had as its primary mission the firing of torpedoes. The British, on the other hand, seem to have given more consideration to their gun armament. They used the full title: "Torpedo-boat destroyer," or often more simply "T.B.D.".

But now Hipper, despite his last great success, saw that the time had come when he must disengage. No longer could he fight such a superior force. His luck could not hold forever. So, at 4:27 he hoisted the flag signal for a "*Gefechtswendung auf SO*" (battle turn to SE.) (122°). As this turn was being executed at 4:28, the Germans got in their Parthian shots, hitting the *Princess Royal* three times (Fig. 29–w). These hits are credited to the *Derfflinger*, but perhaps they were made by the *Lützow*. The *Von der Tann* in the rear zigzagged in order to reduce the effectiveness of enemy gunfire. This may be the time that Chief Stoker Zenne of the *Wiesbaden* thought that her rudder had jammed.

Just as the Germans had turned away, Beatty narrowly escaped a disaster greater than the loss of the *Indefatigable* and *Queen Mary*. We have mentioned how Major Harvey, V.C., with his last remaining energy ordered that the magazines of the *Lion's* "Q" turret should be flooded. Some time after that was done, about 4:27 as an estimate, a terrible casualty occurred in the turret. All were dead in the gunhouse, except possibly Harvey, who was terribly wounded and unable to move. One or both of the guns were loaded and elevated in firing position. This permitted a powder bag to fall from the gun and catch fire, possibly from some debris that had been burning since the explosion of the German shell. The flames roared down into the handling-room and killed all the personnel there; but, the magazine having been flooded, no explosion such as had destroyed the other battle cruisers took place. An officer of the destroyer *Nicator* gives this graphic description:

Suddenly a large burst of flame shot up from her, and for one ghastly moment we thought that she had gone the way of the *Queen Mary* and *Indefatigable*. However, as soon as the smoke cleared away, we saw the *Lion's* remaining turrets fire together, and every one on board us burst into a cheer.

At 4:27, just as the Germans were turning away, Evan-Thomas ordered the 1st Flotilla to take station ahead (Fig. 29–T). At 4:30 he turned the 5th Battle Squadron two points away from the enemy, steadying on S. by W. (179°), a maneuver which must have had the hearty approval of Vice Admiral Hipper. As a result of the turns of both Germans and British away from each other, the range rapidly increased and the effectiveness of British fire soon ceased. After having executed the change of course to S. by W. (179°). Evan-Thomas hoisted a signal for the 5th Battle Squadron to turn four points toward the Germans. Unfortunately, this signal was soon canceled. One would like to know the story behind the simple facts of the British signal record.

Meanwhile, Napier and Alexander-Sinclair, with their 8 light cruisers closely concentrated, were following the 3 cruisers of Scouting Group II. At 4:30 Napier sent the following to Alexander-Sinclair: "It seems that they are going through Horn Reefs and not to Skagerrak." To this Alexander-Sinclair sent the grave reply: "Yes, I think so. If all light cruisers got together, I think we could deal with Northern Squadron." So far as we can see, 8 light cruisers had got together. These had a total of thirty-one 6-inch and 5.5-inch guns on the broadside. The 3 German cruisers had a broadside of thirteen 5.9-inch guns. Yes, it might be that they could be dealt with. There would be a chance soon.

It was at 4:30 that the first contacts occurred between the forces of Beatty and Scheer; but before we tell of them it will be necessary to see what Jellicoe, Hood, and Scheer had been doing during the period between 3:48 and 4:30 P.M. (Fig. 30).

It was at 3:55 when Jellicoe first heard from Beatty that he was engaging the enemy. The position of the *Lion* as reported by Beatty (Fig. 30–A) was fairly correct, only about 4½ miles to the southwestward of her actual position. Immediately upon the receipt of this dispatch, Jellicoe ordered a fleet speed of 20 knots. It speaks well for British seamanship and engineering that 24 battleships, some having a maximum of 21 knots, were able to maintain their stations so accurately at this extraordinarily high fleet speed.

At 3:59 a final contact report arrived from the *Galatea*, timed at 3:55 (Fig. 30–B). This time her position was quite accurately reported. In reporting the bearing of the "enemy," Alexander-Sinclair doubtless had in mind the German light cruisers. However, by good chance, the battle cruisers were in practically the same direction. So, in fact, his signal indicated quite accurately the position of the latter. The reported course of the "enemy," ESE. (100°) differed by four points from the actual course of the German battle cruisers, which was SSE. (145°). We have already commented upon this report.

At 4:00 Hood increased speed to 24 knots. Two minutes later he changed course 4° toward Jellicoe, steering SSE. (145°). At 4:04 Jellicoe ordered Hood to "proceed immediately to support the Battle Cruiser Force." For Hood's information, he forwarded the 3:50 position of the *Lion*. Beatty had not stated his course at that time, but had estimated that of the enemy as S. 55° E. (112°), a mistake of 33°. Jellicoe evidently assumed that Beatty was steering a course parallel to that of the enemy, as he had estimated it. Thus, he gave Hood S. 55° E. (112°) as Beatty's course. This dispatch broke Jellicoe's admirable radio silence for the second time. This shows the importance he attached to Hood's orders. The German radio direction-finder stations, established from Borkum to the Schleswig coast, appear to have made no use of this message to establish the position of

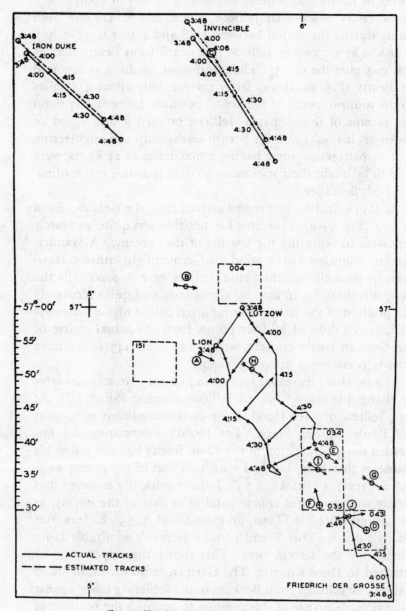

FIG. 30. Tracks of flagships, 3:48-4:48 P.M.

the Battle Fleet. Also, the three German airships that were scouting northward failed to locate any of the British forces.

At 4:06 Hood sent a radio dispatch to Jellicoe stating his position (Fig. 30–c). This was about 4 miles to the northward of his actual position. He gave his course as SSE. (145°) and his speed as 25 knots. He had not felt it necessary to alter course as a result of Jellicoe's order; as according to his information, he was already converging three points (34°) on Beatty, his decision was entirely correct. This dispatch was the first time that Hood had broken radio silence. The Germans also failed to make use of this opportunity to gain valuable intelligence of the enemy.

At 4:15 Jellicoe was somewhat concerned as to the whereabouts of the 5th Battle Squadron. Very properly, Evan-Thomas had not broken radio silence. Neither had the messages of other commanders or ships, mentioned this squadron. Therefore, Jellicoe broke radio silence a third time to inquire if Evan-Thomas were in contact with Beatty. At 4:30 came the laconic, but very satisfactory, reply: "Yes. I am engaging enemy." Now certainly must all be well.

As we have already related, Hipper, just as firing commenced at 3:48, had sent in an excellent report of the situation to Scheer. He stated that he was engaged with six battle cruisers. No mention was made of the four battleships, which had been sighted by some of the battle cruisers, but evidently not by Hipper. The course of Scouting Group I was stated as SSE. (145°), while that of the enemy was given as SE. (122°). Speed was given as 18 knots. This fact and the convergence of course between the opposing forces showed Scheer that Hipper was deliberately going in for a close-range fight with the enemy. Hipper gave his position in 004 (Fig. 30), but to indicate the location of the enemy he still used 151, as he had already done 19 minutes before. As the centers of squares 004 and 151 were distant 17½ miles and as the battle cruisers could not be fighting at any such enormous range, it must have been obvious to Scheer that one of these squares, probably 151, must be in error. Almost certainly, the enemy must be one square farther to the eastward. At the end of his message, Hipper asked for Scheer's position.

Scheer received this dispatch promptly at 3:54. One may well imagine the calm discussions on the *Friedrich der Grosse's* flag bridge between the simple and cool-as-ice admiral, the sure and methodical chief of staff, Captain von Trotha, and the eager, brilliant, high–spirited operations officer, Captain von Levetzow. Here was a splendid combination to handle a fleet under difficult conditions. As Hipper's message showed a confidence to meet the situation, Scheer decided that it was not necessary for him to bring immediate assistance to the scouting forces. Therefore, instead of heading directly for Scouting Group I, he decided to steer NW. (302°). This course led toward the left portion of square 151. As he could be sure that Beatty would be in the right portion of that square or even farther to the eastward, this change of course by the main body might bring the British to some degree between two fires. At the same time it would bring assistance to Hipper, if this should prove necessary, almost as quickly as a course directly toward him. At that time, it was unknown to Scheer, and almost certainly even to Hipper, that the 5th Battle Squadron had been attached to the Battle Cruiser Force. Much has been said, even by us, of the disadvantage that this last-minute change in organization brought to the British. Nothing has been said of the surprise that it effected against Scheer and Hipper.

Therefore, at 4:05 Scheer changed course to NW. (302°). Four minutes later he broke radio silence for the first time by giving Hipper this important information. He gave his position, as of 4:00, in square 043, probably one too far to the northward. It is not known whether Scheer's message was sent in plain language, coded, or coded and ciphered. Our guess is that it was sent in code without being ciphered. If ciphered, the cipher had already been broken by the British. At any rate, the British Admiralty learned the exact contents of Scheer's message very quickly. It placed the main body exactly in the center of 043 (Fig. 30–D). Perhaps, it was their direction finders that gave this remarkable result. More probably, they decoded the message with the copy of the German code taken from the wreck of the light cruiser *Magdeburg* and got the position from the German confidential position chart, a copy of which they also probably had. However. this excellent intelligence work failed to gain any practical results, because it was not until 5:00 P.M. that the information was transmitted to the Grand Fleet.

As the minutes flew by, Scheer came to an important decision. Confident in Hipper's ability to look out for himself, he decided to steer west (257°) for a time and then come back to north (347°), so as to catch the Battle Cruiser Fleet between two fires. Already at 4:11 he had closed up his battleships to the fighting distance of 500 meters (about 550 yards). At 4:18 he turned the main body to course west (257°), about at right angles to the bearing of the enemy. Apparently, the battleship division guides made this change simultaneously. At 4:20 the destroyers of the main body were ordered to leave their stations in the anti-submarine screen and to concentrate by flotillas.

No sooner had these signals been executed than a message arrived from Boedicker that entirely changed the situation as viewed by Scheer. Boedicker stated that a new British force had arrived in the familiar square 151. This was said to consist of five ships of the 2d Battle Squadron. They were steering SE. (122°). Two things were obvious. No longer was it possible to catch a British force so immensely superior to the Scouting Forces between them and the main body. What was more important, Scouting Group I was evidently in a highly dangerous situation; for if one of the battle cruisers should be damaged and reduced in speed, she must inevitably be destroyed by the British battleships. It was the old lesson that the loss of the *Blücher,* gallantly fighting to the end with marvelous courage, had so strongly impressed on the Germans. Therefore, at 4:25, Scheer again headed north (347°) and went ahead full speed. There was not even any time, so Scheer judged, to form an approach disposition with divisions abreast, so as to bring a maximum surprise fire on the enemy when he should be sighted.

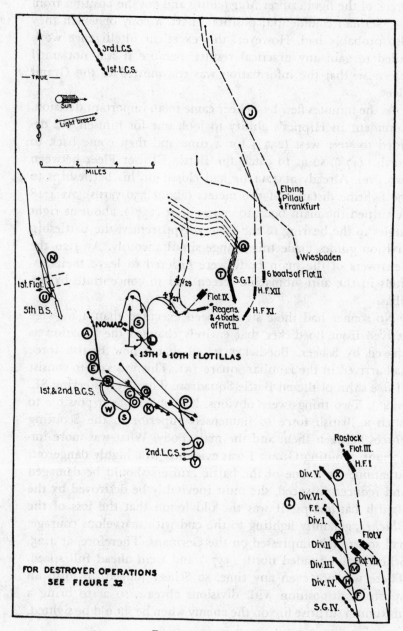

FIG. 31. 4:30-4:48 P.M.

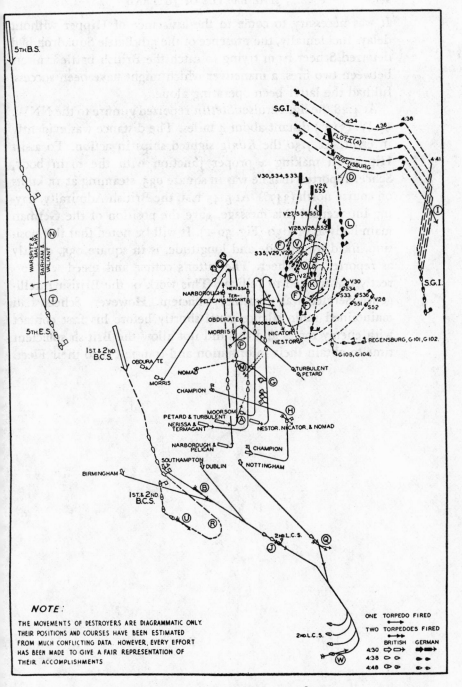

FIG. 32. Destroyer operations, 4:30-4:48 P.M.

It was necessary to come to the assistance of Hipper without delay. Incidentally, the presence of the 5th Battle Squadron had deterred Scheer from trying to catch the British battle cruisers between two fires, a maneuver which might have been successful had the latter been operating alone.

At 4:28 the light cruiser *Stettin* reported gunfire to the NNW. ½ W. (319°) distant about 4 miles. The distance was evidently in error. At 4:30 the *König* sighted ships in action. To assist Hipper in making a proper junction with the main body, Scheer reported that he was in square 035, steaming at 15 knots on course north (347°). At 5:45 P.M. the British Admiralty, having intercepted this message, gave the position of the German main body as of 4:30 (Fig. 30–F). It will be noted that this position, fixed by latitude and longitude, is in square 035, exactly as reported by Scheer. The latter's course and speed was correctly transmitted to Jellicoe. This work of the British Intelligence Service was amazingly efficient. However, Scheer had maintained radio silence until shortly before his first contact with enemy forces and this did not allow the British sufficient time to obtain their information and transmit it to their Fleet.

CHAPTER XII

SCHEER ENTERS THE FIGHT
4:30 P.M. to 5:10 P.M.

As THE FIRE of the battle cruisers and battleships rapidly decreased in efficiency, the destroyers engaged in an epic combat between the lines. It was the nearest approach to those ancient single-handed combats of the Homeric heroes that had been seen for many a century. Perhaps, the very name of Bingham's flag boat, *Nestor*, brought back memories of those far-off days.

Soon after 4:30 P.M. the *Nestor's* bow swung quickly to a northerly course. She was followed by the majority of the boats in rear. The *Obdurate* and *Morris*, far astern, cut corners (Fig. 32) by heading in gallantly towards Scouting Group I. The German destroyers of Flotilla IX came on in a compact formation of four subdivisions. At 4:32 the *Petard* fired a torpedo at them, set to run for a depth of 6 feet (Fig. 32-A). Gunfire was opened at 10,000 yards, but the range decreased very rapidly and soon the starboard batteries of the hostile flotillas were firing at ranges from 3,000 to 1,000 yards. A British officer of the *Moorsom* describes the fight as a "glorious sort of disorganized mêlée, in which the destroyers of both sides were dashing about at 30 knots in all directions, causing more anxiety to their friends than to their foes." Though somewhat of an exaggeration, this statement gives a graphic picture of the fight.

In this destroyer fight, the British destroyers had an advantage in the superiority of their gun armaments. The Germans believed that the true mission of their *"torpedoboote"* was to fire torpedoes at capital ships; therefore the boats of Flotilla IX carried six 50-centimeter (19.7-inch) torpedo tubes and only three 88-millimeter (3.4-inch) guns on the center line. Four of the torpedo tubes were carried on the center line in pairs. The other two were single tubes, one on each broadside forward. This arrangement would permit five torpedoes to be fired in a single salvo. Most of the British boats engaged in this fight carried three 4-inch guns on the center line and four 21-inch torpedo tubes in pairs on the center line.

However, the *Regensburg* and four boats of Flotilla II soon entered the fight (Fig. 32–L). This gave the Germans an advantage in gunfire. The *Regensburg* had a broadside of six 4.1-inch guns, while each of the destroyers which were of the very large 1,660-ton type had a broadside of four 4.1-inch guns. On the British side, the *Nottingham* fired her five 6-inch salvos at long range. The *Champion*, on the other hand, held aloof, as did the *Narborough* and *Pelican*. No explanation is given for the action of the *Champion*. In fact, Captain Farie omits from his official report all mention of her movements during the destroyer action. The *Narborough* and *Pelican* allege that other British destroyers were in the way, an excuse which, in our opinion, is no excuse at all. For these reasons, as the attack progressed, the British actually became inferior in gunfire.

Early in the fight, at about 4:34, the *V27* was brought to a stop by two hits in her engine-room that cut the main steam lines (Fig. 32–c). About a minute later the *Petard's* torpedo hit the *V29* (Fig. 32–E), causing very serious injuries. This torpedo, by the way, was aimed at the first boat of the German flotilla and hit the seventh. It was very bad luck for the German destroyers to receive a hit from the one torpedo fired by the British at that time. The *Nomad* was hit repeatedly by gunfire until at 4:35 a shell, probably fired by the *S51*, wrecked her engine-room (Fig. 32–G). About 4:38 two torpedoes, fired probably by the *S52*, passed directly under the crippled destroyer (Fig. 32–M). Evidently, these torpedoes, intended to be directed against deep-draft vessels, had been set to run at a depth of about 15 feet, while the *Nomad* drew only about 10 feet.

About 4:35 Flotilla IX fired 10 torpedoes, including the 2 that passed under *Nomad*, at the 1st and 2d Battle Cruiser Squadrons (Fig. 32–F). Four of these torpedoes came from the injured *V29* and obviously had to be fired from that position, if they were to be used at all. The firing of the other 6 torpedoes at such a target offered very few chances of hitting. When it is known that

they were fired from a position about 11,000 yards on the quarter
of a formation steaming at a speed practically equal to that of
the torpedoes, no further comment is required. It must have
been for this reason that the remaining 10 destroyers fired only
6 torpedoes when they could have fired 50. Torpedo fire at the
battle cruisers at that time offered the only real prospect of success. Had Goehle known at 4:35 that the main body was approaching, he might well have estimated that Beatty would
counter-march. A heavy torpedo salvo fired into the area into
which the counter-march would probably be made had some
chance of making hits. If hits could only be made, there was a
strong probability that the battle cruisers thus damaged might
be overtaken and destroyed by the German battleships.

While the destroyers were engaging in this mêlée between the
lines, momentous information arrived from the 2d Light Cruiser
Squadron, which was spread about 3 miles ahead of the *Lion*.
As early as 4:30 Goodenough, in the *Southampton* (Figs. 29–Y
and 30–E), had broadcast by radio the report that a cruiser bore
SE. (122°) and was steering NE. (32°). This enemy vessel was also
sighted and reported by the *Nottingham* and *Birmingham*. At
4:30 the former (Fig. 29–Z) signaled to Goodenough by semaphore: "Two cruisers SSE. (145°)." Two minutes later the *Bir-
mingham* reported by semaphore: "One 4-funneled cruiser"
(Fig. 31–B). Finally, at 4:33 Goodenough told Beatty by searchlight (Figs. 31–C and 32–B) "Battleships SE." (122°). This was an
admirably laconic signal when seconds were of vital importance.
As a final precaution, Goodenough at 4:35 challenged the *Stettin*
(Fig. 31–G). Receiving no reply, he formed the 2d Light Cruiser
Squadron in column and prepared to scout tactically. The
Stettin evidently mistook the British light cruisers for Scouting
Group II, for at 4:36 she reported that unit bearing 321° (Fig.
31–I). The next minute, Boedicker, who was not at all in the
direction reported, but far to the northward out of sight of the
Stettin, reported that the battle cruisers were four in number
(Fig. 31–J). This message was not received by Scheer until 5:10
and the full significance was probably never realized. It was not

until late at night that Scheer knew that two British battle cruisers had been destroyed in this early action.

Despite the increasing range caused by the turn away of Scouting Group I, their shells continued to find the British battle cruisers, though the actual damage done was comparatively slight. At 4:32 the *Princess Royal* was hit by the *Derfflinger* (Fig. 31–A). At 4:34 the *Tiger* used her secondary battery against a destroyer (Fig. 31–D). The *Seydlitz* retaliated by hitting her three times (Fig. 31–E). The time at which these hits were made is doubtful, but to bring the total to that shown in the sketch contained in *The Fighting at Jutland*, best evidence indicates that they were made about this time.

At 4:34 Hipper turned still farther away from Beatty and Evan-Thomas to ESE. (100°) and the *Lützow* fired a torpedo at the *Tiger* which had practically no chance of hitting (Fig. 32–D). Two minutes later he turned two more points to east (77°). Meanwhile, at 4:35 Scheer had ordered his destroyer flotillas to take station to starboard (Fig. 31–F) and the next minute he signaled: "Increase speed" (Fig. 31–H). The moment for which he had waited so long had arrived.

At 4:38 both Goodenough and Farie made detailed contact reports of the German main body. Goodenough (Figs. 30–G, 31–K, and 32–J) reported the course of the enemy to be north (347°), which was exactly correct. Farie, however, (Figs. 30–H, 31–L, and 32–H) said that the enemy was on course ENE. (54°). This was in error by six points (68°). Immediately upon receiving these reports, Beatty, with the instinct of a man who rode straight after the hounds, headed directly for the reported battleships. He evidently wanted, very properly, to confirm the reports with his own eyes. He had not long to wait, for at 4:40 he sighted the battleships and immediately counter-marched (Figs. 31–O and 32–R). Just as the *Lion* commenced her turn, she was hit twice by the *Lützow*, causing bad fires and damage to her sick bay. At the same time, the *Seydlitz* landed several salvos on the *Tiger*, hitting her twice in the sick bay and sending several more shells through her funnels and forecastle. This, according to the accurate sketch in *The Fighting at Jutland* brought her total hits to 15. None of these last hits, however, caused any important damage.

As soon as Beatty steadied on a northerly course at 4:43, the vice admiral recalled his destroyers (Fig. 31–s). As the *Lion* still could use only flag signals, the order had little effect on the attacking boats, for now gallant Bingham was in the thick of the fight. Here was the opportunity that British destroyer commanders, as well as German, had waited long to seize. We know not if Bingham, intent on torpedoing German battle cruisers and battleships, saw the *Lion's* flags; but we suspect that he was not looking to the rear at such a time as this. Also, we suspect that had he seen those signals, he might have echoed an exclamation that had come from the lips of Nelson himself: "Leave off action. Now damn me if I do." Other destroyer captains, as we shall duly relate, were imbued with the same sentiment.

To complete our picture we must return to Scouting Group I. At 4:38 Hipper sighted with unconcealed delight the German battleships which were just increasing speed to 17 knots. He had now completely disengaged himself from the 5th Battle Squadron; so he swung his battle-scarred ships right to SSE. (145°). It was only two minutes later, at 4:40, that Evan-Thomas turned two points away from the enemy by subdivisions, apparently to avoid the threat of torpedo fire by Flotilla IX (Figs. 31–N and 32–N). A minute later, at 4:41, Hipper turned Scouting Group I together four points toward the British, steadying on SSW. (189°) (Figs. 31–Q and 32–I). At 4:42 Scheer, to approach the dimly visible enemy battle cruisers, turned the main body toward them two points (Fig. 31–R) to NNW. (324°).

The turn of Scouting Group I toward the British destroyers placed the *Nestor* and *Nicator* on its bow in a very favorable position for torpedo fire. These destroyers had four center-line torpedo tubes mounted in pairs. The *Nestor* fired two of hers. The *Nicator* was able to get out only one. The second stuck in the tube, possibly having been fired on the up-roll (Fig. 32–s). This was about 4:42. The *Petard* had fired a torpedo at Scouting Group I two minutes before from a good position about 1 mile farther away (Fig. 32–P). As Flotilla IX was now withdrawing, Bingham saw that the time was propitious for a close-range torpedo attack against the German battle cruisers. So, about 4:43 the *Nestor* was swung sharply to the southeastward to make the most gallant destroyer attack in all naval history. The *Nicator* followed in her track. The *Moorsom* was close at hand. The *Petard* and *Turbulent*, by a quick turn, were probably even somewhat ahead. This brilliant attack commenced just as Beatty was hoisting his recall. The advance of the five British destroyers was disputed by the *Regensburg* and the four very powerful G-boats of Flotilla II, which had commenced firing about 4:38 (Fig. 32–L). As if this were not enough, the secondary batteries of Scouting Group I opened a heavy fire on the *Nestor* and *Nicator*. Through the gracefully rising shell fountains of this deadly drum fire, the two destroyers dashed at high speed, avoiding hits by what can only be termed a succession of miracles. By 4:48 Bingham had come in to 7,000 yards from his target. The *Regensburg*, *G101*, and *G102*, while still maintaining a heavy fire, for some most unaccountable reason had turned back. This opened the way for a further advance of the British boats. The two rear German destroyers of this group, the *G103* and *G104*, did not follow Heinrich, but on the initiative of their captains continued to the southward with the intention of making a torpedo attack. While there was now no opportunity for torpedo fire, they were well disposed to fire on the British destroyers. Having the heavy armament of four 4.1-inch center-line guns, this is the mission they should have taken for themselves.

Meanwhile, two German destroyers had been performing one of the bravest exploits of the battle. While the *V27* had her steam line cut at 4:34 (Fig. 32–C), the *V26* had turned back promptly to her assistance. A few minutes later the *S35* also turned back to save the crew of the *V29*, which at 4:35 had been hit by the *Petard's* torpedo (Fig. 32–E). Evidently, it was a part of the German doctrine that destroyers should save the crews of crippled destroyers, as well as those of larger ships. This had an important moral advantage, in that destroyers would push home their attacks with more resolution if they were assured of rescue when necessary by other destroyers. It also had the good material effect of saving a large number of skilled officers and men, an asset only less important than the ships themselves. On the other hand, it would be disadvantageous if during an attack this doctrine should serve as an excuse for boats to turn back and fail in the execution of their missions.

We believe that the German doctrine was an excellent one, if the work of rescue was distinctly secondary to the firing of guns and torpedoes at appropriate targets at proper ranges and if it were carried out after the attack was completed. In brief, the work of rescue should be performed during the retirement of the destroyers, not during their advance to the fight. While the facts in this case are not entirely certain, it would appear that this time the destroyers had left their stations prematurely for the purpose of rescue. It is probable that they could have been used more effectively by continuing their fight against the British destroyers, which fired their torpedoes with effect as late as 4:53 from favorable positions. In making this comment, we do not wish to reflect in the slightest upon the two destroyer captains concerned. They were undoubtedly carrying out their doctrine. That, it looks to us, was not properly defined.

The rescue work of the *V26* and *S35* was one of the finest exploits of this great battle, so replete with deeds of extraordinary heroism. The *V26*, skillfully handled by Lieutenant Commander Hans Köhler, came alongside the *V27* and rescued her entire crew, including two badly wounded men (Fig. 32–K). Then, at about 4:38 she sank the *V27* by gunfire, proceeded alongside the *V29* and took off part of the crew of that vessel (Fig. 32–v). The *S35*, Lieutenant Commander Ihm, rescued the remainder in an equally gallant manner at about 4:48 (Fig. 32–v). This rescue work was performed while under a heavy fire from the British destroyers, in particular from the *Obdurate*, *Morris*, *Nerissa*, and *Termagant*. The *Regensburg* and Flotilla II covered the *V26* and *S35* in fine style, scoring two 4.1-inch hits on the *Obdurate*, which had closed in to 3,000 yards (Fig. 32–o).

The sinking of the *V27*, though probably well justified, proved to be unfortunate. As things turned out, the boat was not threatened by superior forces and it might have been possible to have towed her home, though this would have taken another destroyer out of the battle. It was just at that time that Hipper was sighting the German main body. This information probably had not got to Köhler, busy as he was with his immediate duties. Had he learned it in time, it might well have altered his decision to sink the *V27* with his own guns. Incidentally, it would have been well for Hipper to have sent a general signal to all his forces by flag hoist as soon as he had sighted the main body. This would have been of great value to his cruiser and destroyer units and, under somewhat different conditions, might have saved the *V27*. It is of primary importance for a commander to broadcast to his forces vital information of this character.

Hipper, however, was busy enough. Already his secondary batteries were cracking out their salvos at the *Nestor* and *Nicator*. At 4:44 he ordered the main batteries to open on the 5th Battle Squadron (Fig. 31–T). It was 15 minutes since any of his ships had been hit. This brief recess doubtless had rested them for the new ordeals ahead. As the range to the British battleships was 19,000 yards, the German fire was ineffective. At 4:45, just after the Germans had commenced firing at him, Evan-Thomas, evidently believing that he had avoided the destroyer attack, came back two points toward Hipper, reforming column (Figs. 31–U and 32–T). It was about that time that the *Valiant* reported sighting two torpedoes, but this probably was a false alarm (Fig. 32–T). The 5th Battle Squadron opened a heavy fire on the German battle cruisers, also without effect. About 4:46 Hipper reformed column on course about south (167°). About one minute before Beatty had reported (Figs. 30–I, 31–W, and 32–U) by flags and radio that the German main body bore SE. (122°). At the same time, the *Lion* changed course to north (347°).

Goodenough, after having reported the German battleships at 4:38, stood toward them to get a better look. The *Dublin* and *Birmingham* fell in behind the *Southampton*. The *Nottingham*, after firing a torpedo at the German battle line (Figs. 31–P and

32–Q), did likewise. At 4:42 Scheer went divisions column left two points to NNW. (324°) (Fig. 31–R). Goodenough carefully watched their approach. Finally, at 4:45, when the range had decreased to 14,000 yards, he turned his squadron together to the westward at full speed (Fig. 31–v). At the same instant, Scheer ordered fire distribution from the right and one minute later, at 4:46, signaled "Open fire" (Fig. 31–x).

Beginning about 4:48 the *König* fired at the *Lion;* the *Grosser Kurfürst* at the *Princess Royal;* the *Markgraf* at the *Tiger;* the *Prinz Regent Luitpold* probably at the *New Zealand,* range about 21,000 yards (Fig. 31–x). This fire was entirely ineffective and the British battle cruisers received no damage. Beatty had turned away at just the right moment. He shares the credit for this skillful maneuver with Commodore Goodenough, who had given him such accurate and prompt information of the approaching enemy.

The *Kaiser, Friedrich der Grosse,* and the eight ships of Battle Squadron I opened fire on the 2d Light Cruiser Squadron at about 14,000 yards. However, the great number of splashes around their targets rendered spotting so difficult that all ships but the *Ostfriesland* and *Nassau* soon ceased firing. The light cruisers dodged the salvos by zigzagging with such remarkable success that not a single hit was made. An officer of the *Southampton* estimated that in all 50 to 60 heavy shells came within 100 yards of his ship during the next hour. If we allow for a certain exaggeration in this estimate, the escape of these little cruisers remains a veritable miracle. The Germans here missed an opportunity to swell the British losses. Just as this cannonade was commencing, the *Southampton's* radio was sending out a complete contact report, timed 4:46 (Figs. 31–y and 32–w). The commodore evidently thought this information was worth one or two light cruisers and was prepared to pay that price. In this case, as usual, fortune favored the bold.

At this time we must interject a brief statement as to the reactions of Jellicoe and Hood to the enemy information reports they received between 4:30 and 4:48 while Scheer was entering the fight.

Promply, at 4:30 Jellicoe received Goodenough's report (Fig 30–E) of a cruiser bearing SE. (122°). The position reported by the *Southampton* was about 9 miles too far to the eastward. At 4:38 both the *Southampton* and *Champion* reported the main body, which the British usually called the Battle Fleet, to Jellicoe. Though these cruisers actually were close together, the positions they reported differed by 25 miles, each being 12 or 13 miles in error. The *Southampton* (Fig. 30–G) reported the course of the enemy correctly as north (347°), but the *Champion* made a fantastic guess of ENE. (54°). Jellicoe dismissed the *Champion's* report and sent the stirring laconic signal to his Battle Fleet: "Enemy's battle fleet is coming north." At 4:46, as we have already seen, the *Southampton* sent in a complete amplifying report (Fig. 30–J). To show how such a signal should be written, it is quoted herewith:

Course of enemy's battle fleet, N., single line ahead. Composition of van *Kaiser* class. Bearing of center, E. Destroyers on both wings and ahead. Enemy's battle cruisers joining battle fleet from northward. My position Lat. 56°–29' N., Long. 6°–14' E.

Unfortunately, the position of the reporting ship was very much in error. In fact, the position reported corresponded with that of the German Battle Squadron I.

Jellicoe made no change of course as a result of these reports. When we note the positions of the reporting vessels (all much too far to the eastward) and the reported course of the Germans as north (347°), it will be seen that his present course was well selected to bring him squarely against the German main body. Hood apparently chose his course with the same end in view. Evidently, he did not conceive that his orders to support the Battle Cruiser Fleet required him to effect a direct junction with Beatty's battle cruisers. His mission could best be accomplished apparently by steering for the enemy rather than his own forces. We certainly do not complain of this well-judged decision. As will later be seen, it had far-reaching results, highly favorable to the British. That luck favored Hood does not detract from his glory.

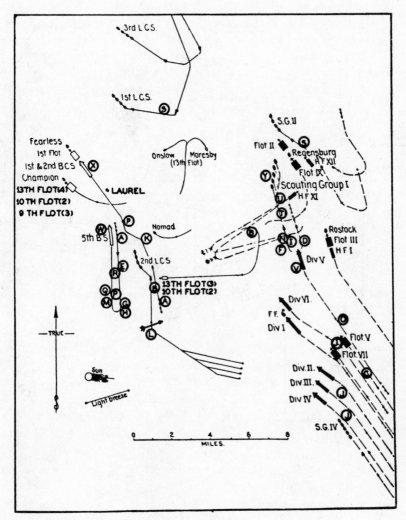

FIG. 33. 4:48-5:10 P.M.

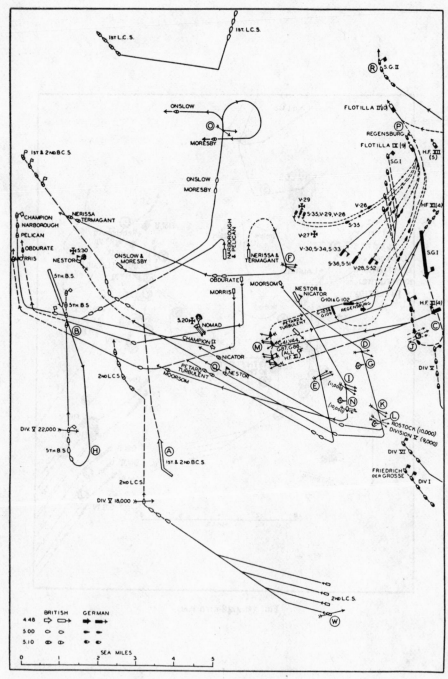

FIG. 34. Destroyer operations, 4:48–5:10 P.M.

The 2d Light Cruiser Squadron and the 1st and 2d Battle Cruiser Squadrons having escaped from the German main body, it remained to be seen whether the 5th Battle Squadron could be turned about in time. At first glance, it would seem that this did not involve a difficult problem. Evan-Thomas should have known, and probably did know, of the presence of the German main body, because the *Barham's* radio was still intact and three information reports had been sent by radio. It would certainly seem that her communication personnel would have been listening on at least one of the circuits used. Furthermore, at 4:48 Beatty hoisted the flag signal for a counter-march to starboard by the 5th Battle Squadron just as salvos began to fall about his own ships (Fig. 33–A). The use of such a specific signal as this was highly disadvantageous, but was in line with Beatty's previous methods of controlling the 5th Battle Squadron. Evan-Thomas should have been told to reverse course without prescribing the exact method to be used. In fact, when the reversal of course was actually made, it would have been better to have turned his ships about together rather than in succession, as required by Beatty's signal.

At 4:50 Evan-Thomas sighted the *Lion* steaming northward at high speed. At this time, he came under the fire of the *Kronprinz* and *Kaiserin* at about 22,000 yards (Figs. 33–C and 34–B). These two battleships apparently had not commenced firing on the battle cruisers and now found a more favorable mark. It was very fortunate for the 5th Battle Squadron that most of the German battleships had commenced firing on the British battle cruisers. At 4:51 Scouting Group I, which since 4:48 had been under the fire of the British battle cruisers (Fig. 33–A), commenced a counter-march toward the enemy (Fig. 33–D). At 4:53 the *Barham* passed the *Lion* and the fire of the 5th Battle Squadron was blanketed somewhat by their own battle cruisers (Fig. 33–E). Finally, Evan-Thomas commenced his counter-march when distant about 21,000 yards from the German main body, which he had not yet sighted (Figs. 33–G and 34–H). Evidently, the smoke made by the other British vessels had obscured the range in this direction, except for certain narrow lanes. Such visibility as existed seems to have favored the Germans. The time of Evan-Thomas' counter-march is variously stated, but 4:55 seems to be a good average of the different reports. At 4:56, just as the *Barham* was swinging around, she received her second hit of the day (Fig. 33–H). The shell did considerable damage. This was the first hit received by a capital ship for about 16 minutes.

Unmoved by his heavy losses, Beatty was continuing the fight in gallant style against the German battle cruisers. One of the officers of the 5th Battle Squadron wrote:

The battle cruisers were a splendid sight as we passed them, firing fast and furiously, in perfect station with the blank spaces of the *Queen Mary* and *Indefatigable* filled up, and seemed to be as full of fight as ever.

The only apparent damage to any of the four remaining ships was the *Lion's* "Q" turret, which was trained away from the enemy. Despite the fine appearance of the battle cruisers, the range evidently was too great to make any hits.

Just as the *Barham* was steadying on a northerly course about 4:58, Evan-Thomas for the first time sighted the German battleships; but now he was threatened by another danger. Some 10 minutes before, while Flotillas IX and II were in full retreat, four other German destroyers had commenced their advance to a torpedo attack. These boats were the *G41*, flag boat of Flotilla VI, and the *V44*, *G87*, and *G86* of Half Flotilla XI. The flotilla commander, Commander Max Schultz, had decided on his own responsibility to attack. Under the fire of the withdrawing British destroyers, he pushed in at full speed. At 4:58 he fired seven torpedoes from a position (Fig. 34–M) two points forward of the beam of the 5th Battle Squadron, distant from it about 11,000 yards. This could not be called a favorable position for torpedo fire at a target of only four ships that were steaming at 25 knots. On the other hand, had he pushed in closer, this would have forced the British battleships away from his own, which was most undesirable. From his firing position, there was a slight chance of getting a hit that would reduce the speed of one of the British ships. This might have justified the firing of a small number of torpedoes.

We have already mentioned Hipper's counter-march to the northward. Now, we must describe some of the conditions under which it was effected. On the *Lützow's* starboard beam, the *Nestor* and *Nicator* were coming in at a sharp angle at their highest speed. Though covered with a heavy fire from the 5.9-inch guns of the battle cruisers, they appeared, and in fact were, undamaged. A little farther away but also in an excellent position for torpedo fire were the *Petard, Turbulent,* and *Moorsom.* Ahead was seen Battle Squadron III engaging the 5th Battle Squadron. It was evidently time for Scouting Group I to reduce the speed of the retiring British battleships by gunfire. Hipper, therefore, not only counter-marched, but did so toward the British battleships and those dangerously close destroyers. It was the bold decision of a gallant leader.

Just as Hipper commenced his turn, Scheer signaled by flags to the entire fleet "to operate against the rear of the enemy." It is probable, however, that Hipper commenced his turn before this signal was reported to him. If it was in obedience to Scheer's signal, it was made with remarkable promptness, particularly as this signal was annulled at 4:53. In either event, Hipper deserves commendation.

At 4:50 Beatty had ordered his destroyers to close him and take station ahead (Fig. 33–B). Those that were close at hand obeyed the signal. Others in close contact with the enemy either failed to see the distant flags or very properly disregarded them, having good Nelsonian precedent for such procedure. Commander Bingham, in the *Nestor*, was now leading the most spirited destroyer attack of all history. He seems to have dashed in to the incredibly short range of 3,000 yards to fire his third torpedo (Fig. 34–D) just as *Lützow* was commencing to turn. It is probable that he did not allow for this radical maneuver by his target and that the *Nestor's* torpedo accordingly went far to the right. On the other hand, so far as we can determine, the

Petard reserved her fire until about 4:53, when the *Lützow* must have reached her northerly course. Then, she fired her two remaining torpedoes at a range of about 5,000 yards from a very favorable position (Fig. 34–E). Her captain, Lieutenant Commander E. C. O. Thompson, had made a daring and skillful attack. The *Turbulent*, which was following the *Petard*, probably also fired torpedoes at that time, but as she was later sunk we shall never know. The *Nerissa*, Lieutenant Commander M. G. B. Legge, also fired two torpedoes from what seems to have been a very good position (Fig. 34–F) about 6,000 yards from Scouting Group I. The *Termagant*, which was following closely in her wake, did not believe that the opportunity was suitable for torpedo fire. Possibly, the position was not so favorable as shown in Fig. 34. It should be remembered that the tracks and positions of destroyers are merely estimated. However, every effort has been made to have them represent accurately the accomplishments of the individual destroyers.

About 4:55 the *Lützow* reopened fire on the British battle cruisers at about 16,000 yards (Fig. 33–F). Just two minutes later the *Seydlitz* was hit forward by a torpedo after having completed her counter-march (Figs. 33–I and 34–J). Two other torpedoes crossed through the formation near her, one running on the surface. It is probable that these three torpedoes were fired by the *Petard* and *Turbulent*. Though considerable water entered the battle cruiser and caused a slight list, she was able to maintain her station in the formation throughout the rest of the action. Fortunately, the torpedo bulkhead held, permitting the continued use of all magazines.

After firing her third torpedo at Scouting Group I, the *Nestor*, followed by the *Nicator*, stood on with magnificent daring toward the oncoming German battleships. The *Moorsom*, ably commanded by Commander John C. Hodgson, followed them at some little distance. About 4:53 the *Nestor* received her first hit, a 4.1-inch shell apparently fired by the *Regensburg* (Fig. 34–G). A few minutes later, the *Rostock*, from her position ahead of the battle line, opened fire on the daring destroyers, while the secondary batteries of the *König, Grosser Kurfürst,* and *Markgraf* soon joined in. This did not by any means deter the gallant Bingham, who kept boldly on. Soon, the *Nicator,* about 4:57, fired a torpedo from a very favorable position about 10,000 yards sharp on the bow of Division V (Fig. 34–K). About one minute later, the *Nestor* was hit in the engine-room (Fig. 34–L), probably by the *Rostock*. Bingham turned the *Nestor* away sharply to the westward, and the *Nicator* followed. Neither boat fired their fourth torpedoes at this favorable opportunity. The *Nestor* was not hit again. The *Nicator* escaped without a single hit, which is little short of a miracle. This is attributed largely to her captain's system of chasing the German salvos, *i.e.,* turning towards the last one in the expectation that the enemy would apply the proper range correction to the next. An officer gives this vivid picture of the bridge: "Throughout the whole action, the captain was leaning coolly against the front of the bridge, smoking his pipe and giving his orders to the helmsman." Such was that splendid destroyer skipper, Lieutenant Jack E. A. Mocatta.

Meanwhile, the *Moorsom* had also been making a splendid attack on the German battleships. At 4:57 she fired two torpedoes (Fig. 34–I) and at 5:00 two more (Fig. 34–N) from favorable positions sharp on the bow of Division V. In return, the destroyer received a hit in her after fuel tanks, through which leaked most of her oil. None of the torpedoes fired at the German battleships reached its mark. The British doctrine of firing one or two torpedoes at a time was faulty. Torpedoes evidently have better chances of hitting or of influencing the course of the battle when fired together in large salvos. The German torpedo doctrine was superior to the British in this respect. The three British destroyers that had pressed home their attack against the German main body probably took some little pressure off Evan-Thomas at this critical time.

While these torpedoes were being fired at the German battleships, Scheer, undeterred by their menace, ordered his six divisions to head two points more toward the enemy. At 4:58,

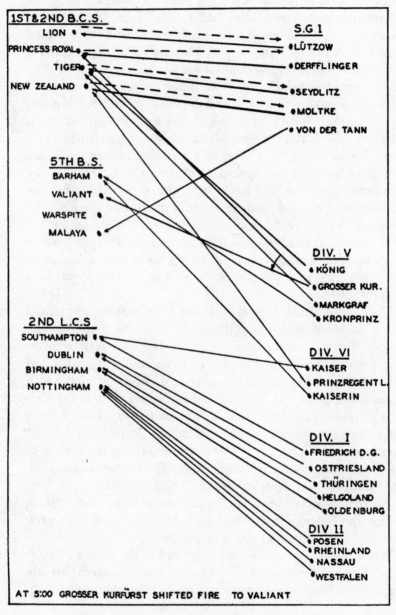

SKETCH VIII. Fire distribution at 4:58 P.M. Not to scale.

Photo from Ulrich Schreier

S.M.S. "FRANKFURT"

The light cruiser *Frankfurt* was the flagship of Rear Admiral Boedicker, Commander of Scouting Group II, at Jutland. The *Frankfurt* was hit and slightly damaged when leading a torpedo attack on Hood's battle cruisers.

R. Perkins, "Jane's Fighting Ships"

H.M.S. "SOUTHAMPTON"

The light cruiser *Southampton* was the flagship of Commodore Goodenough, Commander of the 2d Light Cruiser Squadron, which acted as advance scouts for Beatty's battle cruisers. The *Southampton* was the first British ship to sight the German Main Body. She kept continuous contact and rendered excellent scouting service prior to and during the Battle of Jutland. The *Southampton* came under the fire of German cruisers, received 18 hits, and was seriously damaged. During the battle, one of her torpedoes sank the light cruiser *Frauenlob.*

therefore, the divisions turned to NW. (302°) and went maximum speed (Fig. 33–J). Accurate salvos now began to fall about the *Barham* from the *Kronprinz* and *Kaiserin*. About 5:00 the *Grosser Kurfürst* shifted target from the *Princess Royal* to the *Valiant* (Fig. 33–O). The *König* shifted from the *Tiger* to the *Barham*, but as only her forward turret would bear on that target she also shifted to the *Valiant*. Only the *Markgraf* continued to fire on the *Tiger* and the *Prinz Regent Luitpold* on the *New Zealand*. The fire of these last two German battleships was very deliberate on account of the range and had little, if any, effect. It is unfortunate that these German ships did not shift fire to the 5th Battle Squadron. Although the distribution of fire in accordance with any system is difficult under conditions such as these, it is believed that the division commanders, and possibly even the commander in chief, should have made some effort to regulate it. The simple signal, "Fire distribution from the right," evidently was not sufficient to bring some order in the selection of targets. Sketch VIII shows the fire distribution at 4:58 P.M.

At 5:00 a 12-inch hit on the *Barham* caused heavy personnel losses (Fig. 33–M). This was probably the shell that put out of action both her main and auxiliary radio, but it is possible that some of this damage was caused by the hit received at 4:56. At 5:02 the *Barham* was again hit (Fig. 33–Q). This time the shell struck amidships. It was the third hit in about 6 minutes. The *Valiant*, though literally covered with shell splashes, miraculously escaped without a single hit.

The information concerning the *Warspite* is extremely vague. Alone of all this squadron, her official report is virtually useless to the historian. On the other hand, the statement of her executive officer in *The Fighting at Jutland* is a vivid and interesting personal account. However, it makes no pretense of being accurate as to time and evidently was not based on any record actually written down during the fight. Incidentally, it mentions about 22 major caliber hits as compared with the 13 officially admitted by the British Admiralty. It seems from German accounts that the *Warspite* was not under fire at this time, but an

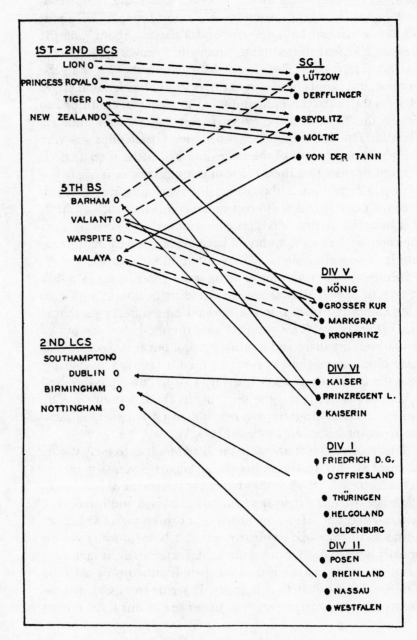

SKETCH IX. Fire distribution at 5:08 P.M. Not to scale.

officer of the *Malaya* says that a cloud of projectiles fell just astern of her. The *Malaya* was at this time under fire of only the *Von der Tann*, which had but two 11-inch guns left in action. The *Malaya's* captain turned her slightly to the northward before getting to the turning point of the ships ahead and thus increased the range at which the Germans later fired on her. The Germans, of course, did not fire at the turning point, as marked by a spot on the water, but fired at the actual ships. Of course, the idea of firing at a knuckle in a line is now recognized as futile, although it at one time gained some supporters from officers ignorant of the problems of controlling main battery gunfire.

At 5:00 Goodenough (Fig. 33–L) made an excellent information report. He said that the German main body bore east (77°), distant 10 to 11 miles, and was on course north (347°). Unfortunately, as will be related later, his own position as reported was considerably in error.

Meanwhile, at 4:57 Hipper had ordered Scouting Group I to distribute fire from the right, ship against ship. As the *Von der Tann* had no target in this distribution, she shifted target at 5:00, as above related, to the *Malaya* (Fig. 33–N). By this time, Hipper's fire had again become effective. The *Tiger* was hit on the superstructure (Fig. 33–K). Two shells hit the *Lion*, one of them wrecking the galley. (Fig. 33–P). Whereupon, at 5:01 P.M., Beatty turned away sharply to the northwestward, ordering the 5th Battle Squadron to "prolong the line by taking station astern."

The last signal was an unfortunate one. It was a tactical signal with a definite meaning that the 5th Battle Squadron should follow directly in the track of the battle cruisers. If Beatty had himself so narrowly missed coming under the effective fire of the German battleships, it should have been evident that the *Malaya*, 9,000 yards astern, would be exposed to great danger. Apparently, Evan-Thomas felt bound by this signal of his senior. He says that, after completing the turn to the northward, he "altered course a little farther to starboard to follow and support the battle cruisers." Beatty's squadrons needed no support, while Evan-Thomas was in a very dangerous situation. From 5:00 to

5:10 the 5th Battle Squadron steered 000°, while the German battleship divisions were steering on the average about 320°. Thus, the 5th Battle Squadron during this critical period was actually converging on the enemy by about 40°. In consequence, the range to the German battleships decreased from 21,000 to 19,000 yards from 5:00 to 5:10, despite the fact that the British were using from 2 to 4 knots excess speed. The course steered by Evan-Thomas at that time bade fair to cause the destruction of his splendid squadron. How much Beatty's signal contributed to that situation only Evan-Thomas is in a position to state. At any rate, the signal to "prolong the line by taking station astern" was most ill-advised. It might well have resulted in a great catastrophe.

It was 5:05 when the 5th Battle Squadron reopened fire (Fig. 33–R). The *Barham* and *Valiant* fired at the German battle cruisers at 18,000 yards, while the *Warspite* and *Malaya* engaged the leading battleships at about 20,000 yards (Sketch IX). The *Seydlitz* immediately came under a very effective fire, probably from the *Valiant*, although the latter claims she was firing at the second ship from the right, which would be the *Moltke*. It is possible that the *Von der Tann* might have been somewhat out of position at that time, due to trouble with her boilers and was not counted by the *Valiant*. At 5:06 the *Seydlitz* was hit forward (Fig. 33–T). Two minutes later she was hit again in the same part of the ship (Fig. 33–U). At 5:10 the right gun of her "B" turret was damaged by a third hit (Fig. 33–Y). This was splendid shooting for the 5th Battle Squadron. The *Warspite* and *Malaya* were also doing well against Division V. At 5:09 the *Warspite* landed a 15-inch shell against the *Grosser Kurfürst's* side armor, while a minute later the *Markgraf* received a similar hit from the *Malaya* (Fig. 33–v). As against these five hits Evan-Thomas had given, he received only one in return, the *Barham* being hit aft at 5:09 (Fig. 33–w). He was giving a wonderful gunnery performance.

Now, we must see what Scheer had been doing to take advantage of the great opportunity given him by the converging course of the 5th Battle Squadron. At 5:05 he ordered a 2-point turn to the right by divisions to NNW. (324°). Apparently, these signals were sent merely as a general guide for the main body. Probably, the signal for maximum speed implied that exact formation was no longer required. Behncke, pushing Division V to 23 knots, opened out a big gap between it and Division VI. Also, the division commanders were steering considerably different courses. In a pursuing action such as this, some irregularity of formation had no disadvantage and allowed each division commander to utilize the maximum capabilities of his ships.

For the reason above stated, the range to the 5th Battle Squadron was still decreasing. Already the *König, Grosser Kurfürst, Kaiserin,* and *Kronprinz* were firing at its ships, also the *Von der Tann,* probably only with a single turret. At 5:08 the *Kronprinz* shifted from the *Barham* to the *Malaya.* Two minutes later the *Kaiser,* having ceased firing on the 2d Light Cruiser Squadron, joined in the concentration on the battleships. At this critical moment, between 5:08 and 5:12, all the British battle cruisers ceased firing (Fig. 33–x). Beatty withdrew entirely from the fight and for about half an hour did not fire a shot. This left the 5th Battle Squadron to fight heavy odds. The fire distribution at 5:08 is shown in Sketch IX.

At this interesting moment, we must leave the heavy ships and return to our story of the light forces. Let us work down from the van to the rear. At 5:00 P.M. the 1st and 3d Light Cruiser Squadrons were at last approaching the scene of battle. They were headed down between the two battle cruiser columns, the 1st Light Cruiser Squadron being about 3 miles ahead of the 3d. The *Wiesbaden* having joined Scouting Group II, that group had turned into position ahead of Scouting Group I. It was followed by the *Regensburg* and the destroyer flotillas. At 5:05 Boedicker opened fire on the 1st Light Cruiser Squadron at about 12,000 yards (Fig. 33–s). It will be remembered that Alexander-Sinclair had told Napier at 4:30 that he thought by keeping together they could deal with Scouting Group II, 8 ships to 4. Here was the opportunity he had mentioned, for Napier was within easy supporting distance. However, Alexander-Sinclair turned directly away and ran at full speed from Scouting Group II, though not hit by a single shell. By 5:10 he had reached a safe range of 15,000 yards. The 3d Light Cruiser Squadron turned away without engaging. Thus, 8 British light cruisers declined action against 4 German ships.

It will be noted that Napier, the senior commander, took no steps to co-ordinate the movements of the two light cruiser squadrons in the van. The British tactical organization was singularly ineffective. Directly under Beatty were 2 battle cruiser squadrons, 1 battle squadron, 3 light cruiser squadrons, and 4 destroyer flotillas, as well as the *Engadine*. Thus, he had to deal directly with no less than eleven commanders spread over a wide area. There certainly should have been one commander of the light forces in the van and one in the rear to exert any kind of tactical control over such a large force. Not only were no such commanders formally appointed, but it seemed against the doctrine of the Fleet for the senior officer in any given part of the battlefield to assume command of the forces operating in it, when their co-ordination was necessary for effective action against the opposing enemy forces. This should be the unwritten law in any fleet.

The behavior of two British destroyers, the *Onslow* and *Moresby*, offered a sharp contrast to that of the light cruisers in the van. Since leaving the *Engadine*, they had been trying to overtake the 5th Battle Squadron. When Beatty was seen coming to the northward, they took station on his starboard bow and proceeded on a northerly course. This course decreased the range to the German forces rapidly. Soon the destroyers came under the fire of Scouting Group II and the secondary batteries of Scouting Group I. For some minutes they steamed gallantly through this hail of shell. Then, it became evident that they could not advance much closer from that position against such a powerful enemy. The *Onslow* reluctantly turned away, believing that the range was too great to fire a torpedo. The *Moresby* fired one in a fairly good position about 11,000 yards on the bow of Scouting Group I (Fig. 34–O). She says that it was aimed at the third German battleship. However, as this was distant 18,000 yards, it is probable that her point of aim was the *Seydlitz*, the third battle cruiser. Her torpedo was not sighted by any German ship. At 5:10 Hipper ordered Heinrich to concentrate his flotillas on the starboard bow of Scouting Group I (Fig. 34–P).

Farther south, all of the British destroyers were withdrawing except the *Nomad* and *Nestor*. The former was now stopped. Two 4.1-inch shells had exploded in the *Nestor's* engine-room. Fragments had cut her arteries, the lines through which her high-pressure steam coursed to her whirring turbines. Gradually, her throbbing boilers had bled to death. The *Nicator* was ordered to save herself. The *Petard's* offer of a tow was refused (Fig. 34–Q). Bingham feared that it would cause the loss of two ships instead of one. However, there was probably time for the crews of both the *Nomad* and *Nestor* to be rescued by other destroyers after their sea valves had been opened. Unfortunately, this was not the British doctrine. With Spartan heroism, they prepared to fight their ships to the end. There was always a chance that they might hit the oncoming battleships with their remaining torpedoes. Hats off to those brave destroyer sailors.

At the very rear of the British array, the 2d Light Cruiser Squadron was chasing the German salvos with such success as to avoid all hits. An officer who was conning the *Nottingham* during this interesting period tells us how this was done. He writes:

A salvo of four 11-inch shells would fall, say 200 yards over, all in a bunch as they invariably did, so that if one shell had hit us probably all would have hit. Then, the next salvo would fall only 100 yards over, and the next—well, obviously, something had to be done about it or the next salvo would fall on us; there were about 45 seconds to do it in. A little helm put over quickly and an alteration of about 20 degrees towards the last salvo, this the German would not notice and so would not allow for, and having seen his last shot fall over he would come down in his range 100 yards, and the next salvo would fall where we had been, but now about 50 or 100 yards short of us. Salvo after salvo we were able to dodge in this way.

It is interesting to note that the success of this scheme actually depended upon the efficiency of the German fire control, and also upon the incredibly small spread of their salvos in range.

By 5:10 all the ships except the *Ostfriesland* and *Nassau* had ceased firing on the light cruisers. Though firing at target practice conditions and at moderate range, neither of these ships had been able to make a single hit.

CHAPTER XIII

PURSUIT OF THE BATTLE CRUISER FLEET
5:10 P.M. TO 5:55 P.M.

LET US NOW return to the magnificent rear-guard action being fought by Rear Admiral Evan-Thomas. We have noted that between 5:08 and 5:12 the battle cruisers, under Beatty's personal leadership, had ceased firing and disappeared. This left the 4 British battleships to engage the 5 battle cruisers of Scouting Group I and the 7 battleships of Battle Squadron III. However, the odds were by no means as heavy as would appear from these figures. Let us see what fire the German ships were delivering.

When Beatty disappeared in the mists, Scouting Group I ceased firing on his battle cruisers. Hipper's vessels were pretty well exhausted after their long fight and the range to the 5th Battle Squadron was close to their maximum. There was no signal for them to shift target to the battleships. However, the *Lützow* at an unstated time commenced firing on the *Barham*. At 5:16 the *Derfflinger* commenced firing on the *Valiant* with high-explosive shell. At 5:25 the *Seydlitz* fired on the *Warspite*. The *Moltke* did not fire on the *Malaya* until 5:27. The *Von der Tann* had been firing on the same target with her only remaining turret since 5:00; but, as will soon be related, this turret at about 5:19 went out of action. Thus, it will be seen that the fire of the battle cruisers was not very effective.

Coming now to Battle Squadron III, we find that at about 5:10 the *König* and *Grosser Kurfürst* opened fire on the *Valiant*, but only 6 minutes later the latter German battleship had to cease firing on account of the long range. The *Kronprinz* fired on the *Malaya*. The *Markgraf* by some queer condition of visibility was able to see the *Tiger* and continued to fire on her until 5:25, using only her forward turret during the latter part of this shoot. The *Kaiser* fired on the *Malaya*. The *Prinz Regent*

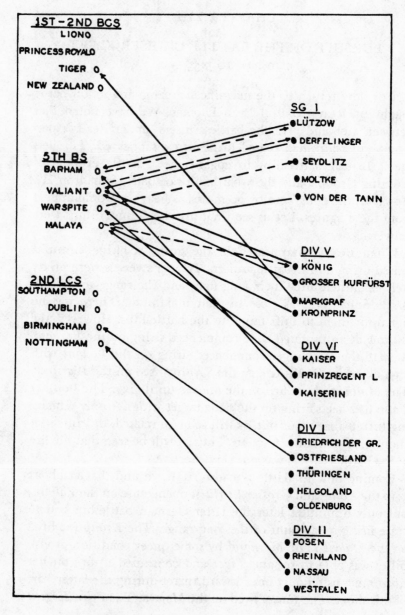

SKETCH X. Fire distribution at about 5:15 P.M. Not to scale.

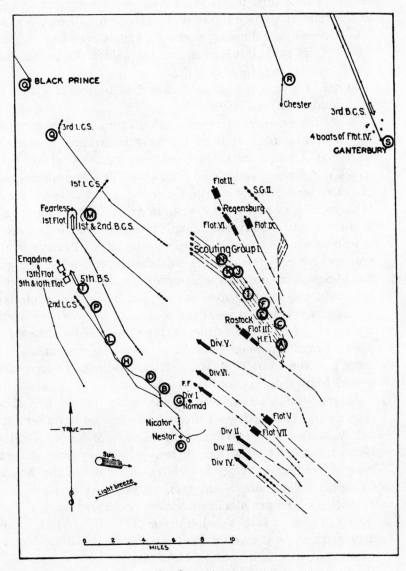

BLACK PRINCE

Chester

3rd B.C.S.

4 boats of Flot. IV.
CANTERBURY

3rd L.C.S.

1st L.C.S.

Flot. II.

S.G.II.

Regensburg

Fearless
1st Flot.
1st & 2nd B.C.S.

Flot.VI.

Flot. IX.

Scouting Group I

Engadine
13th Flot
9th & 10th Flot.
5th B.S.

2nd L.C.S

Rostock
Flot III.
H.F.I.

Div. V.

Div VI.

F.F
Div I
Nomad

Nicator

Nestor

Div II.

Flot V

Flot VII

Div. III.

Div. IV.

TRUE

Sun.

Light breeze

0   2   4   6   8   10
MILES

FIG. 35. 5:10-5:35 P.M.

Luitpold about 5:10 ceased firing on the *New Zealand.* Her new target is not stated, but it may have been the *Warspite,* as that vessel was not then under the fire of any other German ship and is believed to have received at least one hit about this time. The *Kaiserin* was shooting at the *Barham.* Groos says that the British ships stood out well against the golden sky to the westward, but the range was very great.

Sketch X shows the probable fire distribution at 5:16 P.M. It is notably without system.

With this general discussion as a background, we may relate the more important facts of this very interesting period. At 5:10 Evan-Thomas increased speed to 25 knots. At 5:11 a shell struck the *Barham* amidships (Fig. 35–B). It was probably one of a salvo fired by the *Kaiserin,* the rear ship of Battle Squadron III, which by a queer chance was now firing on the leading ship of the 5th Battle Squadron. Evan-Thomas immediately turned sharply away, heading just a little to the left of Beatty's battle cruisers. Nevertheless, despite this change of course, the 5th Battle Squadron during the 25-minute period commencing at 5:10 P.M. still converged about 20° on Battle Squadron III. This counter-balanced its slight advantage in speed, 25 knots against about 22. In consequence, the range between these opposing forces remained constant at about 19,000 yards. The range between Evan-Thomas and Hipper decreased during this period from about 17,500 to 16,000 yards.

At 5:14 the *Warspite* was hit, probably for the first time (Fig. 35–D). The shell went through the base of her after funnel. As against these two hits on the *Barham* and *Warspite,* the German battle cruisers suffered heavily, as they were at comparatively effective ranges for the 15-inch guns of the British battleships. Beginning about 5:11, as described by Groos, the *Seydlitz* received five hits in succession, probably from the *Warspite* and *Valiant* (Fig. 35–A). Turrets "C," "D," and "E" were damaged and Nos. 4 and 5 guns of the port broadside battery were destroyed. At 5:13 the *Lützow* was hit on the water line (Fig. 35–C), probably by the *Barham.* Nevertheless, Hipper turned toward the enemy to NNW. (324°). At 5:17 he signaled to reduce speed (Fig. 35–E).

During this time, the *Barham, Valiant,* and *Warspite* had been firing intermittently at the German battle cruisers, selecting as a target the ship that stood out best through the haze. The *Malaya* continued to fire at Division VI. A destroyer officer wrote:

It was a magnificent sight to watch these four splendid battleships firing their broadsides of 15-inch. There was something tremendously heartening about the look of them, and the very concussions of their broadsides was most inspiring.

At 5:19, just two minutes after Hipper had signaled to reduce speed, an order came from Scheer: "Pursue the enemy." As this signal was being received, the *Derfflinger* received another hit (Fig. 35–F). About one minute later, the *Von der Tann* ceased firing. Due to a material defect, the guns in her only undamaged turret had failed to return to battery. However, Captain Zenker very correctly kept his ship in the line in the hope of drawing some of the enemy's fire. At the same time, being rear ship, he could zigzag in order to reduce the chances of being hit. Incidentally, several of the British battleships veered out of column at times when the concentration against them was heaviest. This undoubtedly is a desirable maneuver under such conditions.

Meanwhile, at 5:15, Scheer had turned the battle line two points by divisions toward the enemy to NW. (302°). It seems that the *Barham* was no longer under a very effective fire. On the other hand, numerous well-bunched salvos fell about the other three ships. The *Malaya,* in particular, came under a heavy concentration. Six to nine salvos a minute were falling about her. At 5:20 she received her first hit (Fig. 35–H). The shell landed forward, below the water line abreast "B" turret. At that time breaks began to appear in the clouds low on the western horizon and the sun shone through them directly into the eyes of the German pointers.

It was about 5:21 when Admiral Evan-Thomas turned two points to the right "to support the battle cruisers." The latter, being entirely out of the fight, and having speed superior to that of any German ships, needed no support. On the other hand, the turn toward the enemy did endanger the 5th Battle Squadron. However, Evan-Thomas' motive was so splendid that we cannot criticize his gallant decision. On the contrary, we commend his resolute conduct. It had indeed something of the Nelsonian touch. Tactics is not always a matter of cold-blooded calculations of the probabilities and chances. Sometimes an instinct to fight regardless of consequences animates great leaders. If this change of course was to result in serious damage to the 5th Battle Squadron, it would also hurt very much the badly damaged German battle cruisers, which were now distant only about 17,000 yards.

At 5:23 Hipper signaled to increased speed, in accordance with Scheer's previous order to pursue (Fig. 35–J). At 5:25 the *Lützow* received two heavy hits which put her radio entirely out of action (Fig. 35–J). At that minute, the *Seydlitz*, after a rest of 15 minutes, opened fire on the *Warspite*. Simultaneously, Scheer ordered the entire Fleet to increase speed. At 5:26 Hipper with superb gallantry turned his ships (Fig. 35–K) two points more to the left against the powerful British battleships, steadying on NW. (302°). The next minute the *Moltke* opened fire on the *Malaya*.

These actions of the opposing forces brought on a very fierce battle. It was indeed fortunate for Evan-Thomas that he had the advantage of the visibility during that critical period. At that, his ships were heavily hit. Most of the German fire was concentrated on the *Malaya*, the rear ship. At 5:27 a shell landed on "X" turret (Fig. 35–L). Three minutes later two more hits (Fig. 35–P) caused terrible injuries to her secondary battery. Powder fires spread along the casemates, killing or burning most of the crews of the starboard 6-inch battery. Despite these casualties, British seamen thought of nothing but victory. One of their turret officers wrote:

They had no thought that we should come off worse than the enemy, but only wanted to know how many German ships were left requiring to be finished off. They were full of confidence that every shell was doing its bit, and many and varied were the benedictions that went with every round fired.

That the British were shooting well is proved by the fact that at 5:30 the *Lützow* was hit once and the *Derfflinger* twice (Fig. 35–N). At that time Scheer signaled for a change of course two points to the right for the battle line to NNW. (324°).

According to the British Admiralty, the *Warspite* was heavily hit at that time. It is probable that three hits were received. According to the statement of her executive officer, shells pierced her side armor, exploded in the captain's cabin, and hit "X" barbette. Realizing the grave danger of his position, Evan-Thomas at 5:30 signaled for "utmost speed." However, he was not yet out of danger, for at 5:35 the *Malaya* (Fig. 35–T), which had dropped behind her proper station, was hit forward. Two minutes later, at 5:37 (Fig. 37–D), two more shells pierced her hull below the water line. These were the last hits received at this time by the 5th Battle Squadron. Despite the fact that the range to Scouting Group I was only about 16,500 yards, the decreasing visibility prevented all effective fire. At that time, there was a complete lull in the fight between the capital ships.

As nearly as can be determined, the *Seydlitz* received 5 hits between 5:10 and 5:37; the *Derfflinger*, 3; and the *Lützow* 4; a total of 12 hits, all against the three leading battle cruisers. On the British side, the *Malaya* received 8 hits; the *Warspite*, 4; and the *Barham*, 1, a total of 13. The hits on the German ships were made by 15-inch shells and resisted by 12- and 11-inch armor. Those received by the British ships were 12- and 11-inch shells and resisted by 13-inch armor. From this comparison it will be seen that Evan-Thomas had rather the better of the fight, which is a great tribute to the efficiency of his squadron and his own skill as a leader.

Nevertheless, he had undoubtedly been favored with good fortune. The *Malaya* was the most seriously damaged of his ships. She had suffered much superficial injury and had 96 casualties. Under-water hits had given her a list to starboard of 4°. The *Warspite*, according to the Admiralty, "had been heavily hit," but had not been seriously damaged and had suffered only a few casualties. The *Valiant* had led a charmed life, escaping numerous salvos by only a few yards. The *Barham*, though hit 6 times, had not been seriously injured. The ships of the 5th Battle Squadron had demonstrated their great defensive strength. Also, they had done some fine shooting. In every respect they had proved themselves far superior to the British battle cruisers. However, it was lucky for Evan-Thomas that the *Warspite's* steering gear was not carried away or that some other particularly effective hit had not reduced the speed of one or more of his ships.

There was a remarkable opportunity for the British destroyers during this retirement. It would have been very simple for a few boats to have laid a smoke screen to conceal the 5th Battle Squadron from the German battleships, while still permitting it to engage the battle cruisers. The westerly breeze was perfect for this simple scheme. However, Beatty himself had discouraged this expedient by taking the 1st Flotilla, which had not been engaged and was still intact, to form an anti-submarine screen for his disengaged battle cruisers at 5:20. This flotilla could have been used to much greater advantage in supporting the 5th Battle Squadron, to which it had originally been attached. The 9th, 10th, and 13th Flotillas were now concentrating on the *Champion* after their attacks. Captain Farie could have used some of these destroyers to lay the screen, but the signal should preferably have come from Beatty or Evan-Thomas. Much as the British had spoken of the Germans using smoke screens and destroyers to cover a retirement, they do not seem to have contemplated using the same means to cover their retirement. This was the perfect opportunity for the use of a smoke screen. It would instantly have disengaged Evan-Thomas from the pursuing battleships and might have permitted him to damage the battle cruisers seriously. Had the Germans passed into the screen, the British destroyers would have enjoyed a heaven-sent opportunity for a determined close-range torpedo attack.

It will be noted that Beatty was entirely out of the fight for this critical period. Evan-Thomas had been told to prolong the line astern and then had been left to fight it out alone against four effective battle cruisers and four battleships. Had Beatty remained in the action, the forces engaged would have been about equal. The most charitable explanation of this amazing situation is that Beatty felt that his battle cruisers were no longer able to stand up against their German opponents, at least without a period of rest. They had been decisively defeated by an inferior force.

Hipper made a resolute attempt to damage the retiring enemy, though his ships were suffering heavily from the British great 15-inch shells. We believe that his splendid ships should be credited with most of the hits made on the 5th Battle Squadron during this period. The contrast between the leadership of Hipper and Beatty during this period is striking.

Meanwhile, the *Nestor* and *Nomad* have been lying helpless in the path of the German battle line. Larger and larger grow those great war-gray ships. Their stacks, upper works, turrets, and finally their hulls rise slowly out of the gray waters of the North Sea. The decreasing distance dissipates the mist that softens the southeasterly horizon. Now, their outlines are clear and distinct, their dark silhouettes grim and menacing. High-breasted waves rising over sharp bows and trailing clouds of gray-black smoke give evidence of their speed.

On the *Nestor's* low steel decks, officers and men make their last preparations. There stands Commander E. B. S. Bingham, as resolute in impending disaster as he has been gallant in dashing attack. With him is Lieutenant M. J. Bethell, high-spirited, calm, courageous. Both know that the end is inevitable, and very near. Only two things remain to be done. First, their one remaining torpedo must be accurately directed at the approaching enemy in a last effort to sell their lives as dearly as they may. Second, and perhaps more important, the *Nestor* must finish in style.

The *Nomad* lies closest to the approaching battleships. Golden-yellow gun flashes flicker from the upper works of the German ships. White shell fountains rise about the low, gray destroyer. A deluge of projectiles rip and tear her hull and decks, killing and wounding many with their jagged splinters. In this deadly barrage, Lieutenant Commander Paul Whitfield carefully aims and fires all his four torpedoes. Slowly his ship sinks beneath the waves. The crew takes to the water about 5:20 (Fig. 35–G).

It will now be the *Nestor's* turn. Young Bethell orders the cables to be laid out on deck, ready for a tow. He knows there will be none; but it is well to busy the men in some useful undertaking. For a time, this will distract the thoughts of the crew from the shell barrage that must soon burst over them. The German battleships know the menace of a destroyer's torpedoes. Even though their fate be certain, British seamen will never neglect to fire their last torpedoes with careful aim. Therefore, the destroyer must be sunk before their last torpedoes can be fired; or, at least, she must be forced to shoot them at such long range that they will have little chance of reaching their targets with appreciable chances of hitting. So, when the *Nestor* is still distant 10,000 yards, the 5.9-inch guns of Battle Squadron II begin their music. Gun flashes play along the sides of the great gray ships. Brownish smoke puffs wreathe their masts and stacks before they are blown clear by the gentle southwesterly breeze. Salvos land in rapid succession about the *Nestor*. For a time, her life seems charmed, but she has not the speed to dodge the salvos. As the range decreases, the German fire control becomes more accurate. The little ship is buried under the falling cascades of the shell fountains. Deadly fragments of shells bursting short on impact with the water whir over her decks or cut through her fragile sides. At last, she shakes and trembles under the impact of direct hits. Here and there a man is struck down by jagged splinters of flying steel. The last torpedo is fired with calm and deliberate aim. Water rushes through shell holes on the starboard quarter. The *Nestor* lists to starboard, then settles ominously by the stern. Bingham orders: "Abandon ship." The dinghy has been shot to pieces, but the motor boat is lowered and shoves off, heavily ballasted with men. Life rafts are loaded to their fullest capacity. The whaleboat lies alongside. A few men strive to plug with clothing the gaping holes in her side, but their fight is a losing one. The last men embark in that sinking boat. Bingham and Bethell alone remain on deck. "Now where shall we go?" asks Bingham. "To Heaven, I trust, Sir," answers Bethell. Then he sees a mortally wounded signalman. This poor fellow cannot be left, for such is not the tradition of the British Navy. Bethell runs toward the wounded man. A shell bursts over the young lieutenant. Among its clouds of smoke and gas the hero disappears, making such an exit from life's stage as any sailor might envy. Bingham can do no more. At his order, the whaleboat pulls away from the sinking *Nestor*. It does not float for long and soon its passengers are swimming in the icy water. Quickly, the motor boat comes to their assistance. Some of the swimmers are pulled aboard, others cling to the gunwales. The *Nestor's* bow now rises high in the air. Amid the crackling shell bursts, three last cheers ring out for the gallant ship. Then, as her stem points almost vertically into the sky, the *Nestor's* crew salutes her with "God save the King." To the tune of this inspiring requiem, with a rush of water and a hiss of steam, the little ship disappears. The *Nestor* has finished in style.

It was about 5:30 P.M. when the *Nestor* sank (Fig. 35-o). German destroyers of Flotilla VII rescued 80 officers and men from the *Nestor* and 72 from the *Nomad*. The *Nestor* and *Nomad* could have rendered very valuable service by sending in enemy information reports, giving the exact composition of the German main body if their radios were intact. However, it is probable that the damage to their engine-rooms put out of action their radio motor generators and it is not known whether they were equipped with storage batteries. The fact that six pre-dreadnaught battleships were with the German main body would have been of much interest to Jellicoe, as it meant that

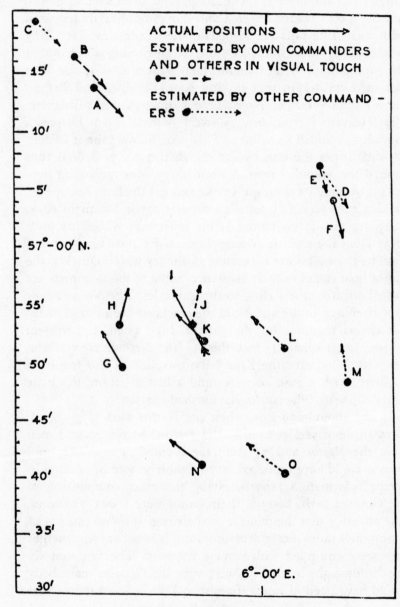

FIG. 36. Positions of flagships at 5:35 P.M.

16 knots was the maximum speed that the German battle line could maintain. That gave Jellicoe, with about 19 knots, a speed advantage of about 3 knots.

The German airships were now nearing the High Seas Fleet. At 5:10 the *L14* said that she was in square 091 Epsilon IV. This was 35 miles distant from the *Friedrich der Grosse* in the direction indicated by the arrow at z, Fig. 38. She reported being on course N. by E. (358°). At 5:30 the *L21* reported that she was in square 068 Gamma IV. This position was 60½ miles from the *Friedrich der Grosse* in the direction of the arrow at Y, Fig. 38. So far as known, no effort was made to inform the airships of the position of the High Seas Fleet or to direct them to scout the area ahead of it. It appears that here was an opportunity to utilize the airships to good advantage. It is not known whether the airships intercepted any of the German messages and attempted to search ahead of their own Fleet. In any event, none of the airships sighted any of the German or British forces that day.

Let us turn to Jellicoe and Hood and trace briefly their movements from 4:48 to 5:35 P.M. Those British forces were rapidly approaching the scene of action. At 4:51 Jellicoe sent an urgent and inspiring message to the Admiralty: "Fleet action is imminent." At 5:00 two important dispatches reached the commander in chief. The first was the excellent report of the *Southampton*, which gave not only the position of the sending ship (Fig. 38–A1) and the bearing of the enemy, but also for the first time the distance of the enemy. These data allowed the exact position of the German main body to be plotted (Fig. 38–A2). The plotted position was 7½ miles to the eastward of the correct position of the *Friedrich der Grosse* at 5:00 (Fig. 38). That error was of considerable importance. Also, it was aggravated by an error in the German course. Goodenough reported it to be north (347°), when for some time the Germans had been steering NNW. (324°). The error in estimating the course of an enemy almost 10 miles away was not excessive; but, unfortunately, just as the *Southampton's* aerials were radiating the message, Scheer turned

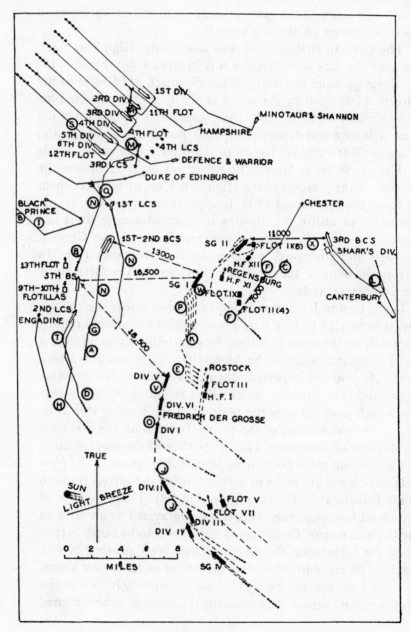

FIG. 37. 5:35–5:55 P.M.

two more points to the left to NW. (302°), thus introducing a 45° error in Goodenough's dispatch.

At 5:00, there also arrived the report of the Admiralty that fixed the position of the German main body at 4:09 (Fig. 30–D). That gave the course of the Germans as NW. (302°) and their speed as 15 knots. That report was of interest principally in indicating that the enemy was much farther to the westward than shown by the cruiser reports.

In order to keep Beatty informed of the movements of the Battle Fleet, Jellicoe at 5:13 reported the position, course, and speed of the latter. The position reported was Jellicoe's estimate of the *Iron Duke's* position at 5:00. As shown in Fig. 38, the *Iron Duke's* actual position was later determined to have been about 4 miles to the southeastward of the estimated position as reported by Jellicoe to Beatty (Fig. 38–B). Also, Jellicoe omitted to state that his reported position was as of 5:00 P.M. Therefore, Beatty could only assume that it was the *Iron Duke's* position as of 5:13, the time group of the dispatch. That made Jellicoe seem to Beatty to be 4.3 miles back on his course, i.e., farther to the northwestward than he actually was. As those two errors were cumulative, they introduced an error of about 8 miles in Jellicoe's position as estimated by Beatty. He thought that the Battle Fleet was that distance to the northwestward of what later proved to be its actual position. This, as will be seen, had unfortunate results later. While Jellicoe had a very incorrect estimate of Scheer's position, Beatty was equally in error as to Jellicoe's position. As Jellicoe would naturally head for Scheer and as Beatty would try to lead Scheer toward Jellicoe, these errors were not only unfortunate in themselves, but also had a curious interacting effect.

This was aggravated by a bad lapse in the tactical scouting of Beatty's light cruisers. In our study of this subject, we have noticed that information reports are received in bunches, with long intervals that try the patience of the officer in tactical command. This is very annoying when the enemy has previously been making frequent radical changes of course. On May 31, there was one of those blank intervals between 5:00 and 5:40

P.M. during the most critical part of the approach of the Battle Fleet. It seems almost incredible that this should have been a fact. It is true that the radio of both the *Lion* and *Barham* had been wrecked. However, there still remained three light cruiser divisions and two destroyer flotilla commanders in light cruiser flagships.

We have noted that Goodenough at 5:00 had reported that the German main body was on course north (347°). We have also related that Scheer soon afterwards changed course to NW. (302°). His battleships maintained substantially that course for the next 45 minutes. That fact must have been evident to Goodenough. As there had been such a decided change in the course of the enemy from what he had just reported, one would think that he would have sent a correction fairly promptly. Goodenough states that he was under a very heavy fire "from time to time" during that period, but that would hardly account for his failure to send an information report. Jellicoe would have been much helped by just a few words: "Course of main body NW." (302°).

The 1st Light Cruiser Squadron was in an excellent position for tactical scouting. Alexander-Sinclair might not have been able to see the German battleships, but could have easily kept in touch with the battle cruisers. However, he failed to go near enough to the enemy to maintain touch with even these vessels. At 5:27 Alexander-Sinclair says that he received a signal from Beatty to keep touch with the enemy battle cruisers. The mere fact that it was necessary to send such a signal to a light cruiser commander makes further comment unnecessary. In obedience to these orders (Fig. 35–M), Alexander-Sinclair turned to the northward and soon sighted Scouting Group I at an estimated distance of 16,000 yards. He estimated that the course was parallel to his own. He made no report of this contact. Instead, at 5:35 he submitted (to use his own word) that he had passed a submarine two hours before. Five minutes later he reported to Beatty that the enemy battle cruisers were "altering course to starboard." This was not logged as being received by the *Lion*.

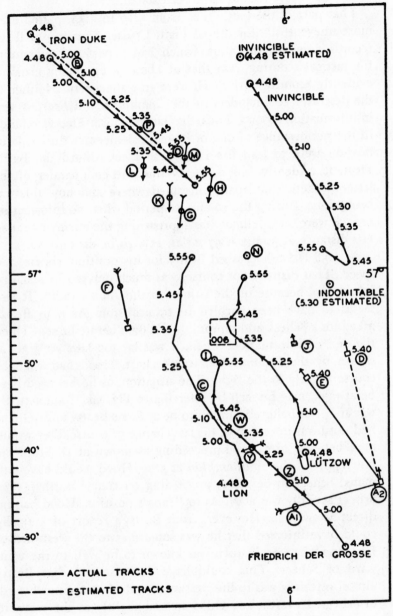

FIG. 38. Tracks of flagships, 4:48-5:55 P.M.

It obviously would be of little or no use to Jellicoe. A definite estimated course should have been stated.

That part of the battle, i.e., from 5:10 to 5:35, passed even more uneventfully for the 3d Light Cruiser Squadron. All the records show for this unit, which had a perfect opportunity for tactical scouting, was that at about 5:21 enemy cruisers, evidently Scouting Group II, were in sight astern. Neither of the destroyer commanders in the *Champion* and *Fearless* sent in information reports. Thus, the Battle Cruiser Fleet had failed in the performance of one of its most elementary duties. If its mission were to lead the High Seas Fleet toward the Battle Fleet, it evidently was necessary that the commander of the latter be kept continually informed where and how this was being done. During the 40-minute period when no information reports were sent, Jellicoe was approaching the enemy 25 miles. His distance at 5:00 was 57 miles; at 5:40 it was only 32.

At 4:56 Hood had asked Beatty for his position, course, and speed. That dispatch, of course, was much delayed in reaching its address because of the injury to the *Lion's* radio. It also seems to have been garbled in transmission. At 5:30 Beatty asked for a "check and repeat." It was 6:06 before he sent Hood the desired information. Then, it was far too late. At 5:30, as shown by the *Indomitable's* track chart, Hood had changed course slightly to the right. The situation, as he believed it to be at 5:35, may be seen by referring to Fig. 36. Hood actually was at *F*, but believed himself to be at *E*. As Beatty and Jellicoe had not been informed of his last change of course, they would have believed him to be proceeding as shown at *D*. From the last report of the *Southampton* at 5:00, Hood would have estimated Scheer to be at *M*, proceeding on course north (347°). Scheer actually was at *N*. As to Beatty's position, Hood had no direct knowledge. However, from Beatty's report of 4:45, he could have inferred that he was somewhat to the westward of Goodenough, who in turn was known to be well to the westward of Scheer. This could have demonstrated that Beatty almost certainly was to the westward, and of course northward, of Scheer. Nevertheless, Hood steered slightly to the eastward of Scheer's reported position. His motive in doing so can never be determined. When it is realized that Scheer actually was at N, far to the westward of that indicated from Goodenough, or M, it is easy to see how Hood made contact with the enemy so far to the eastward, with such far-reaching and very fortunate results.

At this time, we must interject a word concerning eager Commodore Tyrwhitt at Harwich. He had doubtless intercepted many of the messages of Jellicoe and Beatty. At 4:45 he could restrain his impatience no longer. He flashed a wire to the Admiralty: "Have you any instructions?" It was only five minutes later that Jellicoe reported that a fleet action was imminent. In the Harwich Force, there were immediately available 5 light cruisers, 2 destroyer leaders, and 16 destroyers. A force of such considerable strength might prove of great value. At 5:10, having received no reply, Tyrwhitt decided that it was time to go. "I am proceeding to sea," he told the Admiralty. Five minutes later, in reply to his first query, he was told: "Complete with fuel. You may have to relieve light cruisers and destroyers in Battle Cruiser Force later." When the Admiralty learned that the commodore was leaving Harwich, he was ordered "to return at once and await orders." Nelson, as you know, once put his telescope to his blind eye and said that he could not see the signal to withdraw from action. It was unfortunate that Tyrwhitt could not have pleaded deafness as well when such an astounding message was brought to him, as did Appius Claudius on an occasion he thought dishonorable to Rome.

It is a real pleasure to be able to turn from such proceedings to relate the entry of Hood's detachment into the action, for Hood was a dashing cruiser commander; and with him as a destroyer leader was the skillful and heroic Loftus Jones. Under such commanders as these, bold leadership and resolute fighting were certain.

At 5:30 Hood was steering about 157° at 25 knots. With his squadron of three old battle cruisers was a division of four fine destroyers. Ahead some 5 miles was the light cruiser *Canterbury,* while about 6 miles somewhat forward of his starboard beam was the *Chester*. Both these cruisers had just been commissioned and it is probable that their crews had not reached a high state of training. As we have seen, Hood's entire detachment was heading well to the eastward of both the reported and actual positions of the High Seas Fleet. As early as 5:30, the *Chester*, hearing gunfire to the southwestward, turned to investigate (Fig. 35–R). Two minutes later, the *Canterbury* reported to Hood that she could see flashes ahead (Fig. 35–s). That was an inaccurate report, as the flashes must have been nearer the starboard beam. Her report, if taken literally, would have given Hood an erroneous idea of the situation.

Soon there occurred the first of a long series of surprise contacts in low visibility. In those contacts, there was usually a great preponderance of force on one side or the other and victory rested almost invariably with the "heaviest armaments." This teaches the lesson that in reduced visibility concentration is of primary importance.

At 5:36 the *Chester*, which was steaming at full speed, sighted what was thought to be a cruiser with one or two destroyers somewhat on her port bow. The visibility was very poor at the time to the southwestward and it was difficult to make out the strange ships. One of the *Chester's* officers states that "they appeared to be not unlike our 1st Light Cruiser Squadron." What the *Chester* saw was Scouting Group II: the *Frankfurt*, *Pillau*, *Elbing*, and *Wiesbaden*. Those ships had a total of eighteen 5.9-inch guns on the broadside. The *Chester*, originally built for the Greek Navy, had a broadside of six 5.5-inch guns, a new weapon for the British Navy. The Germans quickly recognized the *Chester* as hostile and used the British recognition signal that the *B109* had broadcast to the Fleet. Boedicker was hopeful that by this stratagem he could lure this single enemy under the guns of his entire group. The *Chester* makes no mention of this use of a British signal by the Germans. As soon as the strange ships were sighted, she changed course to the northward to avoid possible torpedo fire. About 5:40, she challenged the strange vessels. Immediately, the Germans covered her with salvos, the range being about 7,000 yards (Fig. 37–F).

The *Chester* was able to get out one salvo, when the third or fourth German salvo came on board her. This destroyed all the fire control communications and caused heavy casualties to the guns' crews. It rendered any return fire ineffective. Several more salvos hit, causing very heavy casualties. Flotilla II, commanded by Captain Schuur in the *B98*, now entered the fight against the crippled *Chester*. The *Chester* turned away sharply to NE. (32°), with the German light cruisers in hot pursuit. Boedicker soon found that he had too heavy a concentration on one target; so the *Elbing* and *Wiesbaden* were directed to cease firing. The range was down to 5,600 yards and it seemed that the *Chester* must be doomed, but Captain R. N. Lawson commenced zig-zagging. He chased the German salvos as the 2d Light Cruiser Squadron had done so effectively, except that he threw the Germans out in deflection rather than in range. Thus, the *Chester* was able to escape without further damage. However, in a 19-minute battle, which ended only at 5:55, she was hit 17 times. Those hits put three guns out of action, rendered her fire ineffective by destroying her fire-control communications, and caused 77 casualties. However, the structural damage to the ship was surprisingly small and the engineer department was still able to make the full speed of 26½ knots. Light cruisers seem to have been able to withstand numerous small-caliber hits and to dodge the heavy-caliber salvos.

We now come to the only instance of effective fire of heavy guns against light cruisers that the entire battle could show; but in this case the light cruisers were surprised at very short range and hit before they could commence maneuvering. As Scouting Group II pursued the *Chester*, the latter was withdrawing to receive the support of the 3d Battle Cruiser Squadron. Thus, Boedicker was running into a surprise even greater than that he had just effected against the *Chester*. About 5:40 Hood had seen the gun flashes of the *Chester's* fight about 7 miles away on the starboard bow. Soon thereafter he altered course about nine points (101°) to the right (Fig. 37–L) to come to her assistance and to get into the fight. As the *Chester* continued on to the northward at her maximum speed, the 3d Battle Cruiser Squadron swung gradually to about 340° in succession. The *Canterbury* followed astern. The destroyer division was in column on the port quarter. Soon, the *Chester* was seen in the center of a heavy barrage of shells, heading across the *Invincible's* bow. The German gun flashes were seen and the battle cruisers pointed their turrets in their direction. Finally, at 5:55 the dim shapes of Scouting Group II emerged from the mists (Fig. 37–x). Hood hauled down the flag signal that ordered: "Open fire and engage the enemy." The range was only about 11,000 yards and the hostile forces were converging at a sharp angle. Boedicker had been ambushed. As the three battle cruisers loosed their first salvos, the gallant Loftus Jones in the *Shark* charged at full speed toward the foe.

While Boedicker was being so completely surprised from the eastward, he was being menaced from the northwestward also. About two minutes before Hood had sprung his deadly trap, the rumble of distant gunfire had been heard on the port bow of the *Frankfurt*. Salvos of heavy shells began to fall far short of the German cruisers. That fire was from the *Defence* and *Warrior*. In the former, was the gallant Sir Robert Arbuthnot, commanding the 1st Cruiser Squadron. Those two vessels had been proceeding as a scouting unit ahead of the 5th Battleship Division. The *Duke of Edinburgh* had been stationed about 4 miles to the southwestward of the *Defence* and the *Black Prince* about double that distance. We will soon tell how the latter ship made contact with the 3d Light Cruiser Squadron and sent in a misleading contact report at 5:42. At that time Arbuthnot had ordered his squadron to concentrate on the *Defence*. Apparently, the *Black Prince* was threatened by some salvos that fell over the 1st Battle Cruiser Squadron which, as will soon be described, had again become engaged. She turned back to the westward. It may well have been that she was hit and damaged at the time. The *Duke of Edinburgh* under some ineffective fire headed toward the *Defence* at full speed and was closing rapidly. Scouting Group II could be seen by Arbuthnot on the starboard hand distant about 16,000 yards. At 5:53 the *Defence* and *Warrior* opened fire, but Arbuthnot had been over-anxious. His 9.2-inch shells fell so short that fire ceased after three salvos. By chance, however, these seemingly useless shots may have served a useful purpose: To draw the attention of all in Scouting Group II away from the direction from which Hood, under cover of unfavorable visibility, was approaching.

Before describing the results of this engagement, so unfortunate for the Germans, we must return to the main battlefield. Hipper and Scheer, entirely unaware of the overwhelming force that was standing down upon them from the northward, were still pressing their pursuit of the Battle Cruiser Fleet. We have noted that at about 5:37 the fire of all the capital ships had become ineffective. After a few minutes the battle thunder commenced in a new direction. Beatty had re-entered the action. Let us see how.

It will be remembered that since 5:12 the British Battle Cruiser Squadrons had been enjoying a recess in the battle. As early as 5:25 Beatty had hoisted the flag signal: "Prepare to renew the action." At 5:35, as shown by the signal record, or slightly before, as shown by Beatty's track chart, he had altered course to NNE. (9°). What his motive was, other than to renew the action, has never been stated. The narrator is forced to guess that his purpose was to make contact with Jellicoe's cruiser screen.

In order to examine this interesting situation, let us clearly visualize the relative positions of the *Lion* and *Iron Duke* at 5:35 (Fig. 36). Beatty's estimated position at *J* was distant 30 miles from his estimated position for the *Iron Duke*, at *C*. Beatty says that he estimated the bearing of the *Iron Duke* to be N. 16° W. (331°), shown by the feathered arrow at *I*, which points directly toward *C*. Actually, the *Lion* was at *H*, distant only 20 miles from the *Iron Duke* at *A*. The bearing of the latter was about 355°, or 24° different from Beatty's estimate. These actual positions were determined long after the battle and need not concern us in estimating the situation from Beatty's viewpoint.

From direct observations at 5:12 and an estimate that the German courses would thereafter approximate his own, Beatty could determine quite accurately the positions of the *Lützow* and *Friedrich der Grosse* relative to the *Lion*. If we apply the *Lion's* error in navigation, Beatty's estimate would place the *Lützow* at L and the *Friedrich der Grosse* at O. The actual positions were at K and N, respectively. Based on Goodenough's report at 5:00, the *Friedrich der Grosse* would be at M by 5:35, but Beatty would not be inclined to use a subordinate's report when he had seen the German Scouting Forces as late as 5:12.

Beatty could have estimated that a course about NNW. (324°) would lead the Germans into Jellicoe's hands. If he continued to lead them in that direction, one of two things must happen. The Germans must either run directly into the British Battle Fleet or pass it in the decreasing visibility, and Jellicoe had a good chance whichever contingency came to pass. If the Germans ran directly into the Battle Fleet disposed about at right angles to their line of advance, the High Seas Fleet must have been completely surprised. It must have fought under the most disadvantageous conditions with the battleships strung out in a long column and the battle cruisers far ahead and completely out of support. The best for which Scheer could have hoped in those conditions was that his battleships might have escaped by a quick reversal of course while his battle cruisers were being destroyed. If the Germans passed the Battle Fleet, the Grand Fleet could have interposed in mass between them and their bases. With good handling, this meant the annihilation of the High Seas Fleet.

Instead of luring the Germans to the NNW. (324°) to create either of the favorable developments, Beatty changed course to NNE. (9°), or about 45° to the right. Possibly, he interpreted the Grand Fleet instructions to indicate a deployment to the eastward and was desirous of gaining distance in that direction so he could take up his appointed station in the van when the Battle Fleet deployed. Possibly, he hoped to effect a concentration with the 5th Battle Squadron against Scouting Group I and gain a tactical success by attacking it from ahead. Possibly, believing himself at J and Hood at D, he desired to close on Hood to get his support. In any event, his decision had far-reaching and exceedingly unfavorable effects. It prevented, as

we shall see in due time, either of the highly favorable developments that must have resulted had he continued to lead the
Germans to the NNW. (324°).

We will not trace the consequences of Beatty's radical change
of course. That movement placed his four ships directly across
the path of Scouting Group I which was coming on in line-of-
bearing formation. Consequently, as his foe appeared out of
the mist distant only 14,000 yards, Hipper was constrained to
swing sharply to the right into column at 5:39 (Fig. 37–E) on a
northerly course. He then changed course in succession to NE.
(32°). No sooner had Hipper commenced those maneuvers, than
Beatty opened fire, about 5:40 (Fig. 37–G). The *Lion* and *Princess Royal* fired on the *Lützow;* the *Tiger,* on the *Seydlitz;* and
the *New Zealand,* on the *Derfflinger.* Evan-Thomas also brought
the 5th Battle Squadron to NNE. (9°) and followed Beatty. The
Barham and *Valiant* fired on the battle cruisers, while the
Warspite and *Malaya* selected the *König* and *Grosser Kurfürst*
for their targets. As indicated by Hipper's order to the *Moltke,*
Scouting Group I fired intermittently on the 5th Battle Squadron. However, the setting sun was now in the eyes of the German
pointers and the visibility was rapidly decreasing. At 5:42 the
Derfflinger ceased firing and did not fire a shot until 6:16. This
shows the very unfavorable weather conditions for the Germans
during that period.

No hits were received by the British ships at that time. At
5:45 the *Lützow* was hit once. Two minutes later Hipper turned
toward the enemy two points to NNE. (9°) and an entirely ineffective fight continued (Fig. 37–K). At 5:44 Scheer had ordered
the main body to come to course north (347°) and for the leading ship, the *König,* to take the guide (Fig. 37–J). Rear Admiral
Behncke in the *König* headed still more to the right toward
Hipper on course about NNE. (9°). Since 5:43 all firing from
the German battle line had ceased. The visibility conditions
evidently favored the British, for at that time many salvos fell
about the *König.* She received her first hit of the battle at 5:48
(Fig. 37–O).

At 5:50 Hipper (Fig. 37–P) turned his battle cruisers to north

(347°). About the same time, Beatty also turned about two points toward the Germans. These changes of course soon brought the range between the opposing battle cruisers down to 13,000 yards. The British battle cruisers were firing very rapidly. Probably also, the *Barham* and *Valiant* were firing at Hipper at about 16,500 yards. The Germans could make no effective reply, as the low-lying sun shone directly in their eyes. We know that the *Derfflinger* was not firing at this critical time. The British had effected a powerful concentration, their gunnery being aided by the visibility conditions. In a few minutes, between 5:53 and 5:55, the *Lützow, Derfflinger,* and *Seydlitz* were hit (Fig. 37–w). Those hits inflicted serious injuries on the German ships. The hit on the *Derfflinger* penetrated her forward torpedo room. That was one of the danger spots of every capital ship of that era, because of the impracticability of subdividing that large space into small water-tight compartments. As that room filled with water, the ship's bow sank lower and lower. The *Seydlitz* was hit by several shells, and a fire started in her forecastle.

At this critical moment, the *Lützow* was no less than 7 miles ahead of the *König.* Therefore, Hipper was entirely beyond effective support should a surprise contact be made with other British forces in the rapidly decreasing visibility which now varied between 10,000 and 17,000 yards. Furthermore, Hipper's interval from the main body was constantly increasing. Hipper considered himself in danger of torpedo attack from the northwestward. In fact, the 1st Flotilla in company with the *Lion* was in an ideal position. Its advance could have been effectively supported by the 1st and 3d Light Cruiser Squadron. Beatty felt it necessary to retain his destroyer flotilla as an anti-submarine screen, a procedure used by no other capital ships on either side during the actual fighting. At 5:47 Beatty had ordered the "Light cruisers" (presumably the 1st and 3d Light Cruiser Squadron) to attack with torpedoes (Fig. 37–N). Neither squadron, however, made any effective effort to execute those orders. Alexander-Sinclair acknowledged their receipt at 5:50 but continued on a course diverging from the enemy until 5:54 "to get into position." Evidently, he never succeeded in doing so.

So we see that Hipper as well as Boedicker was in a situation actually dangerous and potentially critical. Just how critical he did not know, for the Battle Fleet was almost upon him. At 5:53 he formed column on course about NE. (32°) and at 5:55 he quickly swung the *Lützow* (Fig. 37–w) sharply to the right to course east (77°). This was a very timely and fortunate maneuver for Scouting Group I.

At this time we must return to Jellicoe in order to see what information he received during the interesting period from 5:35 to 5:55. We have noted that Goodenough reported the position of the German main body at 5:00, giving its course as north (347°). As no change in that course of the enemy had been reported by 5:35, Jellicoe could assume that there had been no radical change during that period. This would make *M*, Fig. 36, the probable position of the main body at 5:35. At that moment Jellicoe estimated the position of the *Iron Duke* at *B*, distant from the *Friedrich der Grosse* 30 miles.

It was time for Jellicoe to announce to the Fleet something regarding his intentions as to deployment. It is a difficult task to deploy a fleet that is closely grouped in one formation. It is a much more difficult task to effect a junction between two detachments of a large fleet and to deploy the united force virtually in one maneuver, all while the enemy is in close contact. To do so in an orderly manner, it is necessary that the commander in chief announce his intended deployment course some time in advance. In this case, upon deployment for battle, all the units of the Battle Cruiser Fleet would have to take assigned stations on one flank or the other of the battleship divisions. To do this without creating confusion, it would be necessary for them to make their plans in advance and probably make some movements toward their assigned positions before the actual order to deploy was given. It was essential that they be informed as to whether Jellicoe intended to deploy to the right or left.

What then might Jellicoe have told the Grand Fleet as to his intentions at 5:35? The course of the Battle Fleet was SE. by S. (134°). This seemed well selected to make contact with the German main body. Under the conditions, it was both the best and simplest procedure to make the initial deployment at right angles to the course. If the deployment should be to the left, the deployment course would be 44°; if to the right, 224°. In order to fight a decisive action, it obviously was desirable to deploy to the side which would point the Fleet nearest to the German bases. As Helgoland at that time bore 156° from the *Iron Duke,* it is evident that a deployment to the right, i.e., on course 224°, would be preferable. Therefore, it is suggested that Jellicoe should have sent the following enciphered general signal at 5:35: "I intend to deploy on course 224°." That would not commit Jellicoe to anything more than a deployment to the right and an action in the direction of Helgoland. At the time of his actual deployment signal, he could alter this deployment course to the southward as much as the situation would permit; or after deployment he could change the course of the Fleet to the left until he reached 156° or as much more as would cut the line of retreat of the Germans.

The announcement of such an intended deployment would certainly have avoided much of the confusion, which actually occurred. Also, it should be remembered that, with the double advantage of superiority of numbers and surprise, it was not necessary for Jellicoe to make a perfect deployment as regards the High Seas Fleet. His superiority in numbers would nullify any slight disadvantage he might be under at the time of deployment and the situation could quickly be remedied. Furthermore, there was every reason to believe that Jellicoe with some information, at least, of Scheer could make the contact under more favorable conditions than the latter, who was without the slightest knowledge of Jellicoe's position or any intimation that he was even at sea.

By 5:40 the German main body, if proceeding in accordance with Goodenough's last message on course north (347°), would have arrived at *D,* Fig. 38. However, it was at that time that

Goodenough got through another of his excellent information reports. It gave the *Southampton's* position (Figs. 37–H and 38–C) and said that the enemy's battle fleet (which we call the main body) had altered course to NNW. (324°). The position reported showed the *Southampton* had made good a course of 319° between 5:00 (Fig. 38–A1) and 5:40 (Fig. 38–C). This served to offer a confirmation that NNW. (324°) had been about the average course of the main body during that period. On that assumption, the *Friedrich der Grosse* would be at *E,* Fig. 38, or about 13 miles eastward of the *Southampton's* position at 5:40 (Fig. 38–C), as compared with a distance of 11 miles at 5:00. As these facts checked so well, we may take *E,* Fig. 38, as the position in which Jellicoe would believe Scheer to be at 5:40. That this was 10 miles distant from the actual position of the *Friedrich der Grosse* was due mostly to an unfortunate error in the *Southampton's* navigation, for which Goodenough cannot be held responsible. It emphasized the necessity for having the navigator of a flagship continue his navigational duties during action and not take over the duties of the officer of the deck.

While Jellicoe was digesting this information, a fantastic message came from the cruiser *Black Prince,* on the right wing of the cruiser screen. At 5:33 that vessel had made contact with the *Falmouth,* leading the 3d Light Cruiser Squadron, at a distance of 5 miles (Fig. 35–Q). Three minutes later, Napier signaled her (Fig. 37–B): "Battle cruisers engaged to SSW. (189°) of me." The careless failure to begin this sentence with the word "our" had far-reaching results. It is a typical example of inexcusable errors in transmitting information. The *Black Prince* assumed that the battle cruisers mentioned by Napier were German, not British. At 5:40 her captain informed Jellicoe that enemy battle cruisers were 5 miles south (167°) from her (Figs. 37–I and 38–F). As that position would make them about 22 miles from the probable position of the German main body (Fig. 38–E), it must have been most confusing for a time. Probably Jellicoe concluded that it was Beatty that the *Black Prince* was reporting, not Hipper. However, even that assumption must have been very disconcerting because, if the *Black Prince* were in her proper position, it would place Beatty about 7 miles more to the westward than he actually was (Fig. 38–F). While the *Black Prince* must eventually have realized her error, no correction was made.

At 5:45 Rear Admiral Arbuthnot in the *Defence* (Figs. 37–M and 38–G) reported "ships in action" bearing SSW. (189°) and steering NE. (32°). The position of the *Defence* as reported in that message was within 1 mile of her actual position. Her bearing gave a very accurate location of the British battle cruisers. It is unfortunate that Arbuthnot had been unable to identify them as such.

At 5:50 came in three other items of information. First, there was a long dispatch from Goodenough (Fig. 37–T). It stated that the German main body had altered course to north (347°), which was absolutely correct. Assuming that the *Friedrich der Grosse* had been steering that course since 5:40, when she apparently was at *E*, Fig. 38, her position at 5:50 would have been at *J*. The *Southampton's* own position as reported at *I* indicated that she had gone sharply to the northeastward, closing in the distance to the main body to 10 miles. That was of interest as indicating that the Battle Cruiser Fleet also was probably heading to the northeastward and closing the enemy. That was correct.

Goodenough unfortunately included a peculiar mistake in his otherwise excellent information report. He said that the German battle cruisers bore SW. from their battleships, while of course they actually bore to the northeastward. That mistake may have been merely a communication error, or possibly Battle Squadron II had been mistaken for the battle cruisers. While that information must have been puzzling to Jellicoe, from the viewpoint of deployment, it was not essential that he know the correct relative position of the German battle cruisers. He was after the battleships, and the battle cruisers could easily be brushed out of the way wherever they might appear.

The other two reports received at 5:50 gave further indications of Beatty's position. The *Calliope,* in which Commodore Le Mesurier flew his broad pennant, stated (Fig. 37–R) that she had observed what appeared to be gun flashes bearing SSW. (189°) That was exactly on the correct bearing of the *Lion*. The *Calliope's* actual position at 5:50 was at *H*, Fig. 38. Her navigational position, as estimated by Jellicoe at that time, would be at *M*. However, as the *Calliope* was in direct sight of the *Iron Duke* and as she saw the gun flashes, the positions of the *Iron Duke, Calliope*, and the gun flashes were all relative and errors in navigation did not enter into the situation. If the gun flashes could have been identified as made by the *Lion*, Jellicoe would have had an excellent idea of Beatty's position.

The third report was from the *Marlborough*. Vice Admiral Burney reported "gun flashes and heavy firing on the starboard bow" (Fig. 37–s and 38–k). It is unfortunate that he should have made such an indefinite report at 5:50 when five minutes before, according to his official report, the *Lion, Princess Royal, Tiger,* and *New Zealand* had been sighted heavily engaged with an enemy whose gun flashes could also be seen. The *Marlborough's* navigational position by Jellicoe's estimate would have been at *L*, Fig. 38, but as she was in plain sight from the *Iron Duke,* her relative position only was of importance to Jellicoe.

It is quite remarkable that practically all of Jellicoe's information at this critical time came from his own cruisers, or even battleships, which had to guess at the situation. The 1st and 3d Light Cruiser Squadrons were, or could have been, thoroughly familiar with the situation. They could at the very least have reported the position of their own forces to Jellicoe. Only one partial attempt was made to furnish that information. At 5:48 Napier in the *Falmouth* (Fig. 37–Q) reported to Arbuthnot: "Two heavy enemy ships bearing SSE. (145°), steering NE. (32°)." This obviously was a most indefinite report, but it had some value as indicating the position of the van of either Scouting Group I or Battle Squadron III. However, it was not addressed to Jellicoe, nor did Arbuthnot forward it to him. Figure 37 clearly shows how well situated Napier was from 5:50 to 5:55, to supply Jellicoe with accurate information of the Battle Cruiser Fleet and the forces it was engaging.

The three information reports received about 5:50 fixed

accurately the position of a force of heavy ships, almost certainly the battle cruisers or the 5th Battle Squadron. This permitted the *Black Prince's* inaccurate report of the same force to be discarded. Also, the *Southampton's* reports had fixed the position of the German main body (Fig. 38–J), inaccurately it is true. Therefore, this was the time, we respectfully submit, for Jellicoe to broadcast by every available means of communication: "Grand Fleet deploy on course SW. by W. (224°)."

Three points may be raised concerning this suggestion. We will discuss each in turn.

First, could such a deployment be effected while the force of capital ships to the SSW. was still not definitely identified? It was hardly conceivable, from the reports received, that the force could be the German Battle Fleet. Then, it must be either the Battle Cruiser Fleet or the scouting forces. In either case, a deployment to the right on course 224° would prove very favorable. If the forces should prove to be the Battle Cruiser Fleet, there was sufficient time, even by using visual signals, to make an orderly deployment of the entire Grand Fleet, with the battle cruisers and the 5th Battle Squadron in their assigned stations in the van. If, on the other hand, the unidentified force should prove to be the German battle cruisers, they would then be annihilated. Also, if they should be followed by the main body, that force could be engaged under very favorable conditions on an opposite course in such a way as to give Jellicoe every opportunity to cut their line of retirement by encircling their southern flank. Thus, the inability of Jellicoe definitely to determine the identity of the force should not have prevented him from ordering the deployment to the southwestward.

The second point is this: Should the deployment have been made while the position of the German main body had still not been determined definitely? Our answer to this question is that his first task was to deploy the Grand Fleet. The deployment of the six battleship divisions, of course, would be simple. However, the assembly of the cruisers and destroyers of the Battle Fleet in their proper battle stations on the flanks would be considerably more difficult. The gaining of their proper battle stations by the various units of the Battle Cruiser Fleet would in the decreasing visibility, be extremely difficult. Having on numerous occasions observed the deployment of a fleet much smaller than the Grand Fleet at Jutland from the conning tower of the flagship of the officer in tactical command, this writer can fully realize the difficulty of effecting an orderly deployment at Jutland. Once the deployment was commenced, Jellicoe would have moved a load from his shoulders and every sub-ordinate commander could have acted in accordance with his general ideas, instead of being left completely in the dark and forced to guess the manner in which Jellicoe would deploy. Once he had deployed his battle line, Jellicoe could have either moved it in any way desired against the main body of the High Seas Fleet, depending upon the information received, or changed course with the battle line in succession to about 150° towards Helgoland. The question might be asked: why not deploy on this course in the first place? The answer to this is twofold: (1) It would be a maneuver of some difficulty for the battle line and would require some time to execute; (2) it might result in a head-on collision with the German battle line. Therefore, the measures we have suggested would be rather the more conservative. However, a deployment on about 180° or 190° would have many arguments in its favor and would, in our opinion, have resulted most favorably for the British.

The third question is quite important: Would visibility conditions favor shooting to the eastward? In this question there was a great amount of chance. Jellicoe states that he had determined by observation that the visibility was best to the southward. This is demonstrated by the fact that in the firing at 6:35 the British had a decided advantage in visibility. On the other hand, it is just as conclusively demonstrated that at 5:55 the British had just as great an advantage in firing to the eastward. We know that the German fire was entirely ineffective to the westward against the British battle cruisers at the short range of 13,000 yards, while the British ships firing at 13,000 and 16,500 yards made four hits in two minutes. A most important consideration at the time was that the sun bore 280° and that

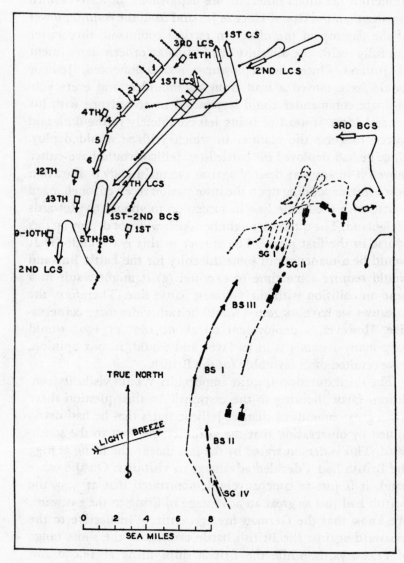

SKETCH XI. Figure 40 revised on assumption Jellicoe deployed
to course 224° at 5:55.

the Germans were shooting directly into its low slanting rays. Thus, the visibility conditions favored firing to the eastward. Therefore, we are confirmed in our belief that a deployment to the southwestward would have been proper at 5:55. We have endeavored to analyze the situation from the viewpoint of Jellicoe at that time and not from other information learned later. Jellicoe's difficulties at that time are fully realized and this suggestion is made primarily as a solution for those very difficulties. Sketch XI is our idea of what might have happened if a deployment signal on course 224° had been executed at 5:55. It is assumed that the units of the Battle Cruiser Fleet would not be able to execute the deployment until 6:00. Of course, it is possible that some unit commander would fail to get the signal and that his unit would be delayed thereby. That would not affect the general picture of the situation at 6:10 as presented by Sketch XI.

It is interesting to note that in Fig. 38 the *Iron Duke* according to Jellicoe's estimate, would be at *O,* while Beatty's estimate would put her at *P.* The *Lion* at 5:55, according to Beatty's estimate, was at *N.* Jellicoe's actual position and Beatty's actual position are indicated on the full black lines where marked 5:55.

CHAPTER XIV

DEPLOYMENT OF THE BATTLE FLEET
5:55 P.M. TO 6:20 P.M.

LET US NOW describe the last stages of the approach, with its fierce minor actions, beginning at 5:55. We will begin at the eastward fringes of the battle and work our way westward. It will be remembered that the 3d Battle Cruiser Squadron had opened a surprise fire on Scouting Group II at about 11,000 yards. One of the first salvos fired by the British battle cruisers landed squarely on the small cruiser *Wiesbaden* at 5:47. Great 12-inch shells penetrated her thin hull amidships and put out of action both main engines (Figs. 39–B and 40–B). As her life-giving steam slowly bled away, the mortally wounded cruiser quickly lost speed and soon came to a dead stop. Chief Stoker Zenne, her only survivor, tells vividly how the auxiliary machinery stopped and even the lights went out through large sections of the ill-fated ship. The unnatural silence chilled the high spirits of the gallant members of her crew condemned to stand to their posts in the interior of the ship with no definite knowledge of the disaster that had overtaken their ship. Nevertheless, there was no thought of surrender and all hands were resolved to fight to the finish.

It was not until 5:58 that Boedicker could make out the 3d Battle Cruiser Squadron on a sharply converging course at about 8,000 yards. It would seem that a sharp turn away together to the westward would have been in order; but only a few minutes before gun flashes had been seen in that direction. The *Defence* and *Warrior,* as previously related, had fired a few ranging salvos that fell short. In the background was seen a mass of destroyers and light cruisers in the area the British so appropriately call "Windy Corner."

Boedicker now had that famous "option of difficulties" of which Wolfe was wont to talk. He counter-marched the *Frank-*

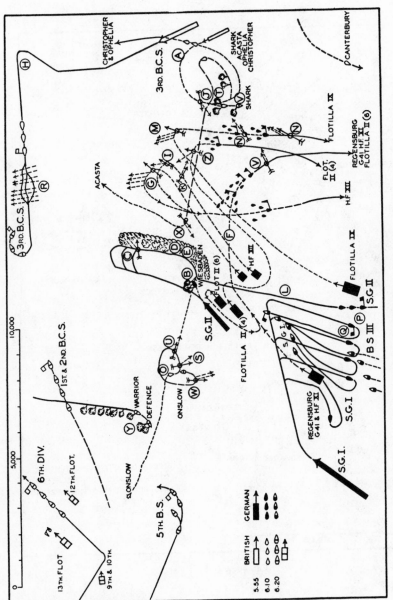

Fig. 39. Destroyer operations, 5:55-6:20 P.M.

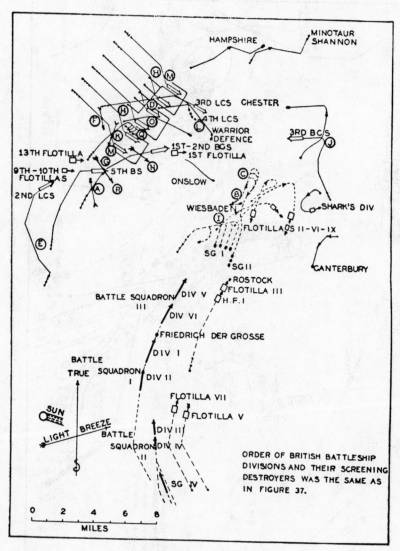

FIG. 40. 5:55-6:10 P.M.

furt to the right to the reverse course, apparently without signal (Figs. 39–C and 40–C). It seems from the German diagrams that the *Pillau* and *Elbing* went rather past the turning point of the flagship before following her around. During that turn toward the enemy, the *Pillau* was hit by a 12-inch shell in the forward fireroom. It exploded with terrific effect. Four boilers were put out of action and the ship's bridges were demolished. Fortunately, her steering gear could still be used and it was possible to make 24 knots, which allowed her to remain with Scouting Group II. Her presence, however, was doubtless somewhat of a mental hazard for Boedicker.

After completing the turn, an artificial screen of smoke, made by throwing over smoke boxes, soon concealed Scouting Group II from her overwhelming enemy. It was a perfect example of the use of smoke. The range, which at 6:00 had decreased to 7,000 yards, rapidly increased and no further hits were received. (Fig. 39–D). In fact, Boedicker had done well to escape annihilation. Flotilla II, *B98* flag boat, which had been proceeding with the light cruisers in two groups, turned back with them to the southward for a time.

To Hipper, proceeding on an easterly course, the situation looked more and more doubtful. His ships had been continuously engaged for over two hours. The *Lützow* already had received no less than 10 definitely located hits from heavy shells, the *Derfflinger* had been hit 7 times, and the *Seydlitz* had received 14 shell and 1 torpedo hit. The *Von der Tann's* entire main battery had been silenced. There had been no time to clean fires in the coal-burning boilers while running at full speed and the rear ships were having great difficulty in keeping station. The lack of readily accessible oil fields was proving a serious handicap to the Germans, as the British vessels used oil for fuel. On both sides Hipper could see flashes from guns penetrating the mist, with the dim shapes of destroyers and light cruisers in the background. The hostile battle cruisers were still firing at him, while the low slanting rays of the setting sun made impossible any effective German reply.

For these reasons Hipper came to a radical decision. At 5:58

he ordered his destroyers to attack. It appears that the signal was decidedly premature when no British capital ships, other than the 1st and 2d Battle Cruiser Squadrons, and possibly the 5th Battle Squadron, were in sight. The signal was addressed by Hipper to Scouting Group I by visual signal, apparently in the hope that some ship would forward it to Commodore Heinrich in the *Regensburg,* which incidentally was then only a short distance ahead of the *Lützow.* It is probable that the message did not reach the destroyer commanders in time to influence their action.

At 5:59 Hipper signaled for Scouting Group I to make a battle turn to starboard, to form column on the reverse course, and to reduce speed. It seems from Groos's chart that the execution of the battle turn was delayed for a few minutes, probably until about 6:02 (Fig. 40–I). It then was made in a manner somewhat different than ordered. Meanwhile, at 6:00 there came a startling visual signal (Fig. 39–E) from the *Frankfurt:* "Am under fire of enemy battleships." Simultaneously, that message went by radio to Scheer. It was followed by another (Fig. 39–L) at 6:06: "Enemy battleships are in 025."

Let us see for an instant what occasioned this fateful error on the part of Boedicker. Though he was distant only 7,000 yards from the 3d Battle Cruiser Squadron, it had been impossible to distinguish it as such through the veil cast by the North Sea mist and the smoke of stacks and guns. When one sees the well-known picture of the *Invincible* going into action, with a dense smoke screen issuing from her stacks, he can be more lenient with Boedicker's mistake. The latter thought he saw cruisers and either battle cruisers or battleships. The *Elbing* and *Pillau* believed that four British battleships were present. It may have been upon reports from those vessels that Boedicker based his positive reports. We will trace later the most unfortunate effects of this error.

After Scouting Group II had hidden itself behind its artificial smoke, a new development had taken place. At 6:04 Hood had changed course sharply left to about 266° (Figs. 39–H and 40–J). Possibly, it was his intention to pursue Scouting Group

II, which was now withdrawing to the southward. Possibly, he had heard gunfire to the westward and was endeavoring to make a closer junction with the Battle Fleet. However, it was evident that his principal idea was to join and support Beatty. His orders on that point had been clear. Hood must have felt that thus far, despite the great effect of his independent action, he had failed to comply with them. His leading idea, in our opinion, is clearly expressed in the laconic signal he sent to the *Falmouth* at 6:12: "Where is *Lion?*" Hood must have seen the German destroyers. He must also have realized that a change of course to the westward would expose his squadron to the hazard of torpedo hits. However, that danger did not deter him from coming as quickly as he could to the assistance of his commander and running into the thick of the fight. One could wish, however, that Hood had been given an entirely free hand. We believe that he could have accomplished much by remaining to the eastward of the Germans and acting independently in the position that the *Canterbury* later occupied for a time.

Boedicker was not the only one to mistake the identity of the 3d Battle Cruiser Squadron. He had been accompanied by Half Flotilla XII, under Lieutenant Commander Lahs. The latter, not yet having been engaged and, as Scheer writes, "recognizing the gravity of the situation," was eagerly pressing forward when, as he thought, numerous large battleships suddenly appeared on a northwesterly course. Lahs's motive in this interesting situation was probably to disengage Scouting Group II and at the same time attack what he believed to be the British Battle Fleet—the ardent ambition of every German destroyer officer.

Half Flotilla XII was in two groups. In the first were the *V69* (flag boat), *S50,* and *V46*. These were fine fast boats of 34 knots, mounting six torpedo tubes, of which five could be discharged on one broadside. They advanced to within about 7,500 yards of the battle cruisers and fired four torpedoes (Fig. 39–G). The time at which they fired and their firing position relative to their target are quite doubtful; but after a careful consideration of all factors and, in particular, the fact that the torpedoes arrived in the vicinity of the battle cruisers about 6:12, we conclude that they must have been fired about 6:04, just as Hood turned to the westward. The German accounts, though indefinite, seem to indicate that they were fired earlier, but we can hardly believe that the German destroyers would have fired their torpedoes from such an unfavorable position as existed before Hood's change of course.

In the second group of two destroyers, the *V45* fired one torpedo, possibly more, at the battle cruisers (Fig. 39–I). The *G37* fired one torpedo (Fig. 39–K) at the approaching British destroyers, led by Loftus Jones in the *Shark*.

As Half Flotilla XII withdrew from the attack, it passed through the approaching V-formations of Flotilla IX. This splendid organization, led by Commander Goehle, though it had suffered so heavily in the 4:30 destroyer battle, was still full of fight and eager to attack. Most of its boats were drawn into the mêlée with the British destroyers. Only the *V28, S52,* and *S35,* were able to fire torpedoes, presumably one each, at the battle cruisers at about 6,500 yards (Fig. 39–M). On the return from the attack, the *V28* fired another torpedo at about 4,500 yards at the British destroyers at 6:08 (Fig. 39–N). That torpedo probably was aimed at the *Acasta*. About the same time, the *S36* fired two torpedoes at two "light cruisers" at 8,500 yards. Those targets probably were the destroyers *Ophelia* and *Christopher* retiring. At any rate, the expenditure of torpedoes at two light cruisers at such a long range was a useless waste of valuable torpedoes.

Closely following Flotilla IX were four boats of Flotilla II, the *G101, G102, G103,* and *G104.* Those destroyers were very large, 1,660 tons, mounted four 4.1-inch guns and carried six torpedo tubes. As they advanced, they met considerable interference from the retiring destroyers and light cruisers. The Germans, it seems, were staging a "Windy Corner" act of their own. Only two of the boats actually sighted "a squadron of battleships." Of them, only the *G104* at 6:08 fired a single torpedo at about 7,500 yards (Fig. 39–z).

As the remaining six boats were commencing an advance to the northeastward, Commodore Heinrich in the *Regensburg* directed them to follow him. Accordingly, they took station in rear of the *G41* and Half Flotilla XI. Heinrich led the combined flotillas against the *Shark's* division and the *Canterbury*. The British cruiser turned to the southward and engaged the *Regensburg* at long range. As the *Canterbury* stood south, the brunt of the German blow fell on the *Shark's* division at about 6:04 (Fig. 39–F). Loftus Jones already had won a reputation for bold decision and capacity to take independent action. Among such a host of brave men, his gallantry and daring were outstanding. Leading his division in the *Shark*, he came under a heavy fire from the greatly superior German destroyers. At 6:05 he fired one of his two torpedoes at the *Regensburg* (Fig. 39–J). As the range rapidly decreased, a shell carried away the oil suction lines and the *Shark* soon came to a dead stop.

About 6:08 the *Canterbury* drew the fire of the *Regensburg* at 9,000 yards, but the *G41* and *B97* still made Shark their particular target. The *B98*, *B110*, and *B112*, and other boats of Flotilla II and Half Flotilla XI fired on the *Canterbury, Shark,* and *Acasta* in the confused mêlée. The British destroyers each carried three 4-inch guns on the center line. The *Ophelia* had four 21-inch center-line torpedo tubes, but the other three destroyers had only two tubes each. That was a serious handicap in an action against a large destroyer force, where shallow-running torpedoes would have been effective. At this juncture, let us leave this sharp engagement in which the overwhelming German superiority was at length making its weight felt against the heroic resistance of Loftus Jones.

It is interesting to note that at one of the critical moments of the action no less than three of the best German flotillas had allowed themselves to be drawn into engagements with small British detachments. The heavy blow in the air had first been caused by the erroneous belief that British battleships were present. The German commanders did not realize that they were firing at such a difficult target as three battle cruisers running at very high speeds. They thought that they recognized those ships as battleships and even believed they distinguished the *Agincourt* among them. That indicated to them that the three ships in sight must be followed by at least five more (to complete one battle squadron) or probably the entire enemy battle line. In such a situation, torpedo fire by the German destroyers in a large volume would have been highly desirable.

Most of the German destroyers were diverted from the 3d Battle Cruiser Squadron, against which they might with some luck accomplish something of moment, into a fruitless action with a few British destroyers. So well had Loftus Jones drawn the German torpedo boats toward his division that only nine torpedoes were fired from that powerful concentration of destroyers against the battle cruisers. The *Canterbury* also had her share in this diversion of the German flotillas. We shall see later how effective was the torpedo control of the destroyers and how narrowly Hood's squadron escaped several torpedo hits.

Only the *Von der Tann* seems to have fully executed Hipper's order of 5:59 to form column on the reverse course, *i.e.*, west (257°). The other vessels steadied on course about 195° in a line-of-bearing formation. Apparently, Hipper had decided to fall back upon his supporting battleships and the other three ships had followed his motions. Boedicker's reports of hostile battleships to the northeastward and the evident effect of their fire on the *Wiesbaden* demonstrated his danger from this direction. The concentration of so many German flotillas against the *Shark's* division and the *Canterbury* must have indicated that there were strong forces in that direction.

A single British destroyer to the northward now appeared as the leader of a new attack. This was the *Onslow*, Lieutenant Commander J. C. Tovey, a name well worth remembering. This enterprising and alert captain had kept on the *Lion's* engaged bow. Since his attempt to attack at 5:10, he had waited for his opportunity, as every destroyer captain should. Now, he saw the *Wiesbaden* lying close to the track of Beatty's column. Fearing that she might be able to fire her torpedoes at the battle cruisers, Tovey at 6:05 headed directly toward her.

Just as he saw the *Onslow* starting ahead, Hipper heard the rumble of heavy guns and saw their flashes in the misty background of the destroyer. Other forces were attacking the *Wiesbaden*. In fact, Arbuthnot at 6:00 had turned the *Defence* and *Warrior* directly at the crippled cruiser. The *Wiesbaden*, seeing their threatening approach, gallantly fired upon them with her broadside of four 5.9-inch guns. Her shooting was so effective as to send a shell against the *Warrior's* forward turret. It is probable that others also found their marks. Thus, at 6:05 the two British cruisers returned the fire with their powerful batteries of 9.2-inch guns. Their concentration was perfectly timed and their shooting good. Each ship straddled with her second salvo, scoring several hits (Fig. 40–L). At 6:08 the *Onslow* opened fire on the same target at 4,000 yards (Fig. 39–O). The heroic *Wiesbaden* commenced that dramatic and remarkable resistance that was unsurpassed even by those legendary exploits of Olaf Trygvesson, Regnier Klaaszoon, and Richard Grenville, and every other naval hero of whom I have heard.

Meanwhile, Scheer had been doing some deep thinking. He realized that his plan to enter the Skagerrak could no longer be carried out. He says:

But we were bound to take into consideration that the English Fleet, if at sea, which was obvious from the ships we had encountered, would offer battle the next day.

Therefore he was considering what steps should be taken to shake off the hostile light forces so that their expected night torpedo attacks could be avoided. These statements show vividly the enormous advantage now enjoyed by Jellicoe. While he was greatly concerned to know the exact bearing of the German battleships, his opponent thought only of engaging the British battleships "next day." That was one of the first favors fortune so lavishly bestowed upon the British commander in chief.

At 5:55 Scheer again increased speed to 17 knots. The two leading battle squadrons were now well closed up. Battle Squadron II, composed of pre-dreadnoughts, was still considerably in the rear; but, as these ships would be a liability rather than an asset in a fleet action, this was a good place for them. Behncke in the *König* gradually eased off to the right toward the northeastward. By 6:10 he was headed directly at the *Von der Tann*, which was then distant about 5,000 yards. Meanwhile, about 6:02 Scheer had received the report from Boedicker that he was under the fire of enemy battleships. Behncke evidently was steering in the exact direction in which these ships were reported. Still Scheer in no way altered his dispositions, evidently confident that the commander of Battle Squadron III would meet the situation when it arose.

During the period from 5:55 to 6:10, not a German battleship had fired a shot. The German commanders realized the danger of their extended and irregular fleet disposition and remedied it by commencing a close and orderly concentration, which would give them a great advantage when they encountered the confused and irregular disposition in which the Grand Fleet now found itself. However, in effecting this close concentration, Scouting Group II had virtually been expended and the best half of the destroyers had been prematurely drawn from their main attack mission into an engagement of secondary importance. Also, despite such severe loss of light cruisers, neither Scheer nor Hipper had even an approximately correct idea of the actual situation. What is worse, each had become fixed with the idea that the British battleships bore to the northeastward. That erroneous impression, based upon Boedicker's reports, colored all their estimates and influenced their decisions.

Now, if ever, was the time for the airships to show their value. Why were they not present to grasp this opportunity of a life time? Two of them, as previously related, were in the immediate vicinity. The continuous roar of gunfire must have been heard for many miles and scores of radio messages were filling the air, yet neither of the airships had reached the scene of battle, though there had been ample time for them to have done so. It is noted that Scheer sent no messages to the airships during this entire operation. It is believed that he should certainly have communicated directly with the *L14* and *L21* and directed

them to search ahead of him. As it was, the airships completely
failed the High Seas Fleet this eventful day.

We shall describe now the junction of the Battle Cruiser
Fleet with the Battle Fleet. It had many interesting features.
At 5:55 the *Lion* was 6 miles, bearing about 180°, from the
Marlborough. Their courses were almost at right angles. If both
were to continue on their present courses for 10 to 12 minutes,
there would be a collision of the formations they were leading.
It was evident that many subordinates in the Grand Fleet must
make important decisions quickly if hopeless confusion were
to be avoided. For the subordinates to arrive at correct decisions, some idea of the intended deployment of the Grand Fleet
was a primary essential.

At 5:55 Jellicoe asked the *Marlborough*: "What can you
see?" At 6:00 the reply (Fig. 40–F) was received: "Our battle
cruisers bearing SSW. (189°), steering east (77°), *Lion* leading
ship." About this time, Jellicoe at last saw the *Lion* for himself, distant 5 miles. This definitely fixed the identity of the
forces previously reported to the southward by many of his
vessels. At 6:00 Beatty was still 7,000 yards from the *Marlborough*. There was still time for a deployment to the southwestward with only a little initial confusion. It is true that the
exact bearing of the German battleships was not known, but
they could have been assumed to be well to the southward and
eastward, and heading on a northerly course. It was not essential for Jellicoe to have an exact bearing of them before he
deployed. The most important thing now in the prevailing low
visibility was to effect an orderly junction with the Battle
Cruiser Fleet and make an effective deployment of the combined
forces. He could still do this by a deployment to the southwestward. Possibly, Beatty might overlap the leading battleship division for a few minutes, but with his excess of speed
the battle cruisers would soon be clear.

After deployment, which would not at this late instant have
been quite as effective as shown in Sketch XI, both Beatty and
Evan-Thomas would have been in their proper stations ahead,

supported by half the light cruisers and over half the destroyers. In the rear would be Hood, with his three battle cruisers, all the heavy cruisers, half the light cruisers, and a strong destroyer force. All those forces would be disposed directly in the line of Scheer's advance, perfectly located for beginning an action on opposite courses. The only hope in that situation would have been for Scheer to have reversed course for an action in the direction of Horn Reefs. His van would then be composed of the very weak and slow Battle Squadron II, supported by the small and obsolete light cruisers and two flotillas of the oldest destroyers. The result would have been inevitable disaster for the High Seas Fleet.

Such was not to be. No deployment signal, not even one telling Jellicoe's intentions as to deployment, flew from the yardarms of the *Iron Duke*. The squadron commanders would have to guess the intentions of their commander in chief—let us hope correctly.

As early as 5:56 Beatty had sighted the *Marlborough* and her division (Fig. 40–A). Apparently, he assumed that Jellicoe would deploy to the eastward. If that should prove correct, it was Beatty's business to get past the British battleships with all speed, so at 6:00 he changed course to about 62° (Fig. 40–G) and soon afterwards to east (77°). As these changes of course toward Scouting Group I coincided with Hipper's abrupt turn away, they did not result in the close-range action that Beatty believed probable. The movement of Beatty across the front of the British battle line was extremely dangerous. A fleet having battle cruisers must get them to one flank of its battle line before the action with the opposing battle line commences. If not, the battle cruisers are liable to be annihilated by the enemy battleships, while they will interfere with the fire of their own. To pass from one side of the British battle line to the other, a distance of about 6 miles, would require 40 minutes under the most favorable conditions. If the British battle cruisers were fired on by the German battleships during that period, Beatty had the choice of being annihilated or of trying to withdraw through his own battle line, with the probability of collisions and the certainty of great confusion at a most critical moment. He was extremely fortunate in this instance to be able to avoid this option of difficulties, as will later be described in detail.

At 6:01 Jellicoe signaled Beatty: "Where is enemy's B.F.?" The next minute he turned his six battleship divisions simultaneously to south (167°) (Fig. 40–H). Excessive speed was no longer necessary, so he slowed the Battle Fleet to 18 knots which would allow the ships to close up to their stations prior to deployment, which was highly necessary. Many ships were far in rear of their positions. At 5:58 the 4th Light Cruiser Squadron had commenced to concentrate (Fig. 40–D). It might just as well have been assembled from the beginning. Concentration on the left ship cleared the area ahead of the fleet to some extent, but all the destroyers were still disposed in anti-submarine screens about the battleships.

At 6:05 there came from the *Marlborough* (Fig. 40–K) a signal that the 5th Battle Squadron bore SW. (212°). One minute later Jellicoe received from Beatty (Fig. 40–N) the laconic message: "Enemy B.C.'s bearing SE. (122°)." Though Beatty states in his official report that "at this time only 3 of the enemy battle cruisers were visible, closely followed by battleships of the *König* class," he entirely failed to mention the all-important battleships. This is the more remarkable in that Jellicoe had just inquired about them at 6:01. As a result, Jellicoe did not hear of the German battleships until eight minutes later. This fact is not stated as a direct criticism of Beatty, but rather as showing that his staff was not properly organized for sending enemy information reports. It is realized fully that a commander who is fighting an action cannot personally concentrate his attention on this function of detached forces. However, he can assign an officer to the duty of sending enemy information reports frequently, without the necessity in critical situations of referring these to the commander or even to the chief of staff. Such decentralization of staff duties is, in our opinion, necessary for the service of information and is exactly in line with the necessary decentralization of duties on board a large ship in action.

We must heartily commend the visual communication system of the Grand Fleet. We particularly like the laconic wording and the great rapidity with which the dispatches were sent from ship to ship. Radio communication was also very rapid and the errors were kept to a very small percentage. During nearly two years of war, the entire communication system had grown to be very efficient and it is doubtful that it can be equaled even today, despite many technical improvements.

Though Jellicoe about 6:06 had the entire picture, except for those elusive battleships that Beatty saw but did not report, the commander in chief evidently considered it necessary to get a bearing of them before deployment. In truth, in ordinary circumstances and in high visibility, this was most desirable. In this situation, it would seem that he might have assumed that Scheer was directly following Hipper. However, the report from Goodenough that the battle cruisers were to the southwestward of their battleships must have been very confusing. What he most urgently needed at 6:06 was a correction of the erroneous report from Goodenough or a new information report from him. Most unfortunately, at 5:55 the 2d Light Cruiser Squadron had turned directly away from the Germans at 26 knots. At 6:03 Goodenough, having opened the range to over 20,000 yards, again paralleled the Germans. Meanwhile, a message timed at 6:00 was going on the air. It said that Goodenough had lost sight of the German Battle Fleet (battleships or battle line would have been a better term), but was engaging their battle cruisers. This would seem to confirm the previous statement that the battle cruisers were to the southwestward of their battleships. While Goodenough reported a correct fact in stating that the German battleships had disappeared, the assertion was misleading. Their disappearance was due to the radical change of course of the 2d Light Cruiser Squadron away from them, while Jellicoe might infer that it must have been due to a radical change of course by the Germans. The very statement that Goodenough was engaging the battle cruisers was most curious, as he was distant from them about 20,000 yards and had only 6-inch guns. Possibly that was a mistake in coding.

It must have indicated to Jellicoe that Goodenough was very close to Hipper and that some most unusual situation had occurred, for only at such a time would light cruisers engage battle cruisers.

It must be frankly stated that Jellicoe was very poorly served by the light cruiser squadrons during this critical time. It would have been worth the deliberate sacrifice of several ships of this type to get reliable information. If the light cruiser commanders furnished no information just prior to deployment, can Jellicoe and Beatty escape the blame for their ineffectiveness, particularly as the British had practically invented this useful type and had led the world in its development? The commanders had served for a long time in the Grand Fleet under war conditions and should have received far more effective training. This is said with a full realization of the difficulties confronting the light cruiser commanders. Arbuthnot was playing the rôle of a light cruiser commander, but unfortunately was commanding an entirely different type. We confess to a desire to have had Tyrwhitt with his highly trained force show what light cruisers could have done at Jutland.

At 6:06 Jellicoe turned his battle line left to course SE. (122°). This was one point more to the left than his original course of SE. by S. (134°). As the line of bearing of division leaders was still NE. by E. (44°), this maneuver threw the flagships of the 1st and 2d Divisions one point forward of the *Iron Duke's* beam, while those of the 4th, 5th, and 6th were one point abaft her beam.

At 6:08 Jellicoe ordered destroyer disposition No. 1 (Fig. 40–o). That signal concentrated two of the three screening flotillas to the eastward and one to the westward of the battle line. It was the first indication of Jellicoe's intention to deploy with an initial northeasterly movement. In other words, he had decided to make his first movement of the battle line away from, rather than towards, Helgoland. It was that decision that lost Jellicoe the last opportunity to surprise the High Seas Fleet. Beatty had first tried to beat them back or drive them to the eastward, rather than to lure them on to the northwest into

Jellicoe's hands. Jellicoe was now arranging to make the first
general movement of the mass of his battleships away from the
enemy rather than towards them. Thus, he could neither surprise them nor immediately cut their line of retreat.

The signal to the destroyers was sent with flags. As some of
the destroyers probably repeated it, a number of other British
commanders could read the signal and thus probably received
valuable information as to the intentions of the commander
in chief. However, it would have been much more effective had
Jellicoe informed the entire Fleet of his intentions. This could
have been done by means of a flag signal, which in a few minutes
could have spread through the entire Fleet.

Though Jellicoe by his signal to the destroyers had indicated
his plan for deployment, he still insisted on having a bearing
of the German battleships before hoisting the actual deployment
signal. There was only one unit of the Fleet that could now
give him that information. This was the 5th Battle Squadron.
Those ships in the changing visibility had sighted the German
battleships through the mist at frequent intervals. In fact, the
Valiant had fired a torpedo at them at 6:00, while the *Malaya*
had done the same thing 5 minutes later. As the torpedoes had
to run 18,000 yards to reach their targets, it is evident that they
were wasted. At 6:06 the *Barham* had sighted the *Marlborough's*
division. Believing that unit was now leading the Fleet in a long
column, Evan-Thomas decided to gain his proper station ahead
of it. Accordingly, at 6:07 he changed course to east (77°),
which rapidly closed the range on the Germans. At 6:10 the
Barham (Fig. 40–R) signaled to Jellicoe: "Enemy's battle fleet
SSE. (145°)." The message was sent with flags and by radio.
Just as this signal was being started on its way, Jellicoe at 6:10
repeated his urgent message to Beatty: "Where is enemy's
B.F.?"

Meanwhile, Hipper had sighted Battle Squadron III coming
towards him. Having greatly closed his interval on it, Hipper
commenced at 6:10 a simultaneous turn of his battle cruisers
to starboard to course about 15°. A few of his ships seem to

have been firing on Beatty, for at 6:09 the *Lion* received a hit in the forecastle which caused a heavy fire.

By 6:10 most of the light forces of the Battle Fleet had commenced their deployment. The 2d Cruiser Squadron was far to the left and was assembling about 10 miles to the northeastward of the battleship divisions. The 4th Light Cruiser Squadron had assembled and was now proceeding ahead of the 2d Battle Squadron. Here also the 3d Light Cruiser Squadron was in position. The 4th and 11th Flotillas were steaming at full speed in an attempt to get clear of the battleships and assemble on the left battle flank. The *Defence, Warrior,* and *Duke of Edinburgh* of the 1st Cruiser Squadron were heading directly between the hostile fleets. The latter ship in particular was laying a dense screen of smoke from her stacks. The *Black Prince* apparently had disappeared to the westward, although some British reports placed her with Arbuthnot. The 12th Flotilla, in trying to take station to the westward of the battleships, ran at right angles into the 1st Flotilla and had to stop and back to avoid collision with the battle cruisers. The 1st Light Cruiser Squadron had got terribly mixed up with the battle line (Fig. 40–Q) without having made any effective effort to attack with torpedoes as directed. Perhaps, the attitude of Alexander-Sinclair can best be gained by the signal he sent at 6:02 to Napier: "I was told to keep in touch with the battle cruisers. It seems to be getting a bit thick this end. What had we better do?" No answer arrived to that amazing message.

Beatty's battle cruisers, steaming at high speeds, were pouring dense smoke-clouds into the area between the opposing fleets. Words can hardly describe the confusion caused by the junction of the two British fleets at "Windy Corner." "There was handling of ships," writes a British officer, "in that ten minutes of crossing the Battle Fleet's front such as had never been dreamt of by seamen before." That not a single collision occurred in that mêlée was due to the marvelous seamanship of the captains.

At 6:14 Jellicoe (Fig. 41–B) finally received news of the il-

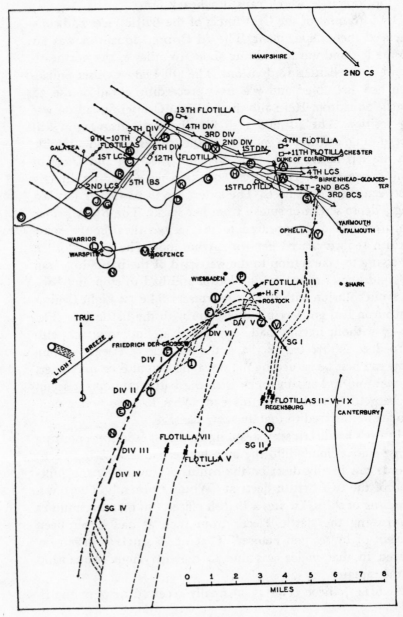

FIG. 41. 6:10-6:30 P.M.

lusive German battleships from two independent sources. Beatty reported that they bore SSW. (189°). At practically the same instant there arrived Evan-Thomas' message of 6:10, stating that they bore SSE. (145°). Jellicoe immediately at 6:15 executed his deployment signal by flags and radio (Fig. 41–c). His plan was rather complicated. The 1st Division, led by Vice Admiral Jerram in the *King George V*, was to change course one point to the left, steading on SE. by E. (112°). The other five divisions were to change course seven points to the left to NE. by E. (44°). That would form, in about 3 minutes, a long column of 20 ships heading 44°, while the 1st Division in the lead would extend the column toward 112° with four more ships. Then, as each ship of the long column came to the turning point, it would go six points to the right to follow the 1st Division. A glance at Fig. 41 will show clearly the method of deployment for the battleships.

This deployment had two important disadvantages. Although it was important to take the High Seas Fleet by surprise, the bulk of the Grand Fleet would for a considerable time be steaming away from, rather than towards, the enemy. Also, for a long time the 1st and 2d Battle Cruiser Squadrons would be directly in the line of fire of the British battleships and their smoke would greatly interfere with the fire of the latter ships. Still, if a deployment to the eastward were considered essential, it was about the best that could be done under the circumstances.

The British were to pay dearly for not bringing their battle line with its overwhelming strength quickly into action. Already Beatty, and to some extent Hood, had forced the Germans to concentrate. Jellicoe now allowed their concentrated forces to overwhelm isolated British units, exposed by the confusion of the deployment to defeat in detail. The British were indeed fortunate that the disasters soon to occur were not more numerous.

At 6:10 Hipper, as we have seen, had ordered Scouting Group I to turn together to starboard to the reverse course and then form column. The *Von der Tann*, being somewhat separated

from the other ships, turned to port instead of to starboard—
very commendable initiative on the part of Captain Zenker.
That closed him in to his proper distance. Behncke with fine
initiative headed the *König* at the *Lützow* on course about 57°.
By the time the battle cruisers had completed their turn, the
König was about 2,500 yards in rear of the *Von der Tann*. That
effective concentration was completed at 6:15, just as Jellicoe
was executing his deployment. At 6:14 Boedicker signaled to
Heinrich to send a destroyer to take the *Wiesbaden* in tow.
This is interesting as showing the authority of a senior officer
to issue orders to a junior not in the normal chain of command when it appeared essential. It is an entirely proper principle of command.

As the British deployment commenced at 6:15, the 5th Battle
Squadron and the 1st Cruiser Squadron came toward the Germans from opposite directions on sharply converging courses.
The fire of the well-concentrated High Seas Fleet fell ruthlessly
upon them. Let us trace the fortunes of those two units for
a time. Evan-Thomas in the *Barham* could see only the 6th
Division, led by the *Marlborough*. He thought that unit was
leading the battle line. To gain his appointed station ahead,
he had changed course sharply toward the Germans. It placed
him in a very dangerous position. About 6:15 the *Kaiserin*
opened fire in the uncertain visibility at about 12,000 yards.
(Fig. 41–E). At 6:18 Evan-Thomas, noting the British deployment toward the northeastward, decided to counter-march to
the left to follow the 6th Division. The *Barham* commenced
the movement and the *Valiant* followed in her track. The
Warspite started her turn too soon, possibly by design, and
was turning inside the *Valiant*. The *Malaya* was close aboard on
her port hand, evidently turning deliberately before her turn to
throw out the German fire, as she had done before. About 6:19
Captain Phillpotts of the *Warspite,* in order to clear the
Malaya, shifted his rudder temporarily from left to right. It
stuck with 20 degrees right rudder. It seems that this casualty
resulted from a hit aft by the *Kaiserin* (Fig. 41–L). The explosion of the 12-inch shell displaced a bulkhead and threw

R. Perkins, "Jane's Fighting Ships"

H.M.S. "IRON DUKE"

The battleship *Iron Duke* was the flagship of the Grand Fleet at Jutland. Flying the flag of the Commander in Chief, Admiral Jellicoe, this battleship led the Battle Fleet from Scapa Flow at 9:30 P.M., May 30, 1916, to rendezvous with units of the Grand Fleet from Cromarty and Rosyth.

Although in the entire action after the High Seas Fleet had come in contact with the British Battle Fleet, the *Iron Duke* received no casualties at Jutland.

S.M.S. "FRIEDRICH DER GROSSE"

The battleship *Friedrich der Grosse* flew the flag of Vice Admiral Scheer, Commander in Chief of the High Seas Fleet, at Jutland. It was this ship that sent out Scheer's famous order—*"Gefechtskehrtwendung nach Steuerbord."* During the night action, the *Friedrich der Grosse* and four other ships attacked the British armored cruiser *Black Prince* at point-blank range. After being under fire for four minutes, the latter sank with her entire crew.

the steering engine out of line. As the ship began to swing rapidly to the right, she narrowly escaped a disastrous collision with the *Valiant,* which probably would have caused the loss of both ships. The *Warspite* continued to turn rapidly toward the Germans, under a heavy fire. One of her officers writes:

So terrific was the noise of the bursting shell that no one in the conning tower could hear the Captain's orders, added to which the Navigator was temporarily blinded by our gun flashes, with the result that the Captain himself had to work the telegraphs and use the voice tubes, etc. He very soon arrived at the conclusion that the only way to prevent actually running right into the enemy's line was to continue the turn to starboard.

Shell after shell hit the ship. Time after time her side armor was pierced. Her upper works were literally wrecked, but no projectile found a vital spot. Two things saved the *Warspite.* One was the fact that her rapid turning at 25 knots threw out many German salvos. In fact, it made hitting merely a matter of chance. The other was the stalwart construction of that splendid class of ships, said by Jane's *Fighting Ships* to be the best battleships ever constructed for the Royal Navy.

It was about 6:15 when salvos began to fall about the 6th Division. About that time the *Prinz Regent Luitpold* commenced firing at what she thought was a ship of the *King George V* class. Possibly, it was the *Marlborough,* practically a duplicate in appearance. Also, it is probable that many salvos aimed at the 5th Battle Squadron fell about the 6th Division. In fact we know that the *Hercules* was straddled at 6:16 (Fig. 41–G). At 6:17 the *Marlborough* sighted Battle Squadron III and fired seven salvos at one ship in 4 minutes (Fig. 41–J). That firing probably was ineffective. The *Colossus* was narrowly missed by a salvo evidently aimed at the 5th Battle Squadron. However, the course of the 6th Division was divergent from the enemy and by 6:21 all the intermittent and ineffective firing ceased for the time.

We have seen already how Arbuthnot had headed in with the *Defence* and *Warrior,* probably to destroy the *Wiesbaden* before she could fire her torpedoes at the British battle line. So intent was the gallant admiral on hunting down that little cruiser that he had no eyes for anything else, British or German. At 6:15 he passed directly ahead of the *Lion,* which had to swing sharply to the left to avoid imminent collision (Fig. 41–D). Nor did Arbuthnot see the German battle cruisers directly ahead of him. On the other hand, the *Lützow* saw the two British cruisers approaching at high speed. At first it was thought that no hostile cruisers could be coming in so close, but at 6:16 Captain Harder opened fire at about 7,500 yards. The *Derfflinger,* which had not fired for so long a time, joined in. The *Grosser Kurfürst, Markgraf, Kronprinz,* and *Kaiser* did likewise (Fig. 41–F). Both main and secondary batteries were used. The latter laid down a fixed barrage through which Arbuthnot had to pass. Both the cruisers were the center of a veritable hurricane of salvos. At 6:20 the *Defence* (Figs. 39–Y and 41–M) blew up as a result of two successive hitting salvos from the *Lützow.* The magazine of her forward turret had exploded. Not a man of her brave crew survived the disaster.

The dramatic destruction of the *Defence* had a painful moral effect. It occurred in plain sight of nearly all the Grand Fleet and many eyewitnesses describe it vividly. An officer of the *Warspite* writes:

Then I saw a sight which I shall never forget. Just as we were getting abreast of her, when she was about 1,000 yards away, a large salvo fell around her; there was a small flash, and then her sides seemed to burst all ways; a terrific flame shot up and clouds of smoke; her masts and funnels seemed to part all ways, and she was gone. All you could see was a huge column of smoke, on the top of which was a black object, which looked like a gun. Thirty seconds elapsed, and then the smoke lifted, and for 5 seconds we saw her bottom, and then she slid down to the bottom of the sea. As far as I could see not a vestige of wreckage remained on the surface.

The *Warrior* had been following the *Defence* closely. She was hit repeatedly, but by good fortune her magazines held intact. She went off to the westward towards the 5th Battle Squadron.

Strangely enough, Captain Molteno says that at no time could he see more than three of the German ships firing at him and had not sufficient data upon which to send an enemy information report, which he states is "always the principal duty of a cruiser." All through the fight, he kept firing on the *Wiesbaden*, claiming to have finished her off.

While the Germans were overwhelming the *Defence* and *Warrior*, the British battleships, unable to fire at hostile ships of a similar type, concentrated a fierce fire upon the battered but heroic *Wiesbaden*. The 3d Light Cruiser Squadron also engaged that helpless cruiser. The *Falmouth* fired a torpedo at 5,000 yards, which apparently did not hit. The *Wiesbaden's* man-of-war flag still flew proudly and she made such resistance as was possible until every one of her guns was put out of action. Captain Reiss was killed, at what time is uncertain. Lieutenant Commander Berger continued the fight.

By about 6:17 Scouting Group I was in column formation in rear of the *Lützow*, which was heading for the *Wiesbaden* (Fig. 41-1). At the same time, Behncke turned Battle Squadron III simultaneously two points to the left so that the *König* also was heading for the disabled cruiser (Fig. 41-1). He was thus ready to give Hipper immediate support in case he should run into superior forces.

Let us now picture the situation as viewed by Scheer. As early as 6:02 he had heard that Scouting Group II was under the fire of enemy battleships. Again, at 6:10 a second message from Boedicker reported that the enemy battleships were in Square 025, while the *Wiesbaden* was unable to maneuver in Square 024. Scheer knew that the 5th Battle Squadron was to the north-westward. The new forces to the northeastward, if battleships, must be a squadron of at least eight ships and might well indicate the presence of the entire British Battle Fleet. The German battle line was now pointed directly at the reported position of the new force. This evidently was a highly unfavorable manner in which to approach what must logically be considered a greatly superior enemy force.

But Scheer was an unusual man. He was as cool as ice, and

just as unperturbed. His reactions were essentially direct and simple. Many writers in trying to attribute to him brilliant and far-reaching plans have misjudged Scheer and have deceived themselves. He was almost the exact counterpart of our General Grant. In a letter to the author, he makes the following interesting statement: "While the battle is progressing a leader cannot obtain a really clear picture, especially at long ranges. He acts and feels according to his impressions." We must imagine Scheer as he received Boedicker's reports. There was certain definite information, from which many facts could be inferred; but underlying it all was one simple impression that could hardly escape him. One thing he knew: Scouting Group II was in danger and the *Wiesbaden* was in need of immediate assistance. Upon seeing Behncke turn toward the enemy at 6:17, one minute later, as he says, "I turned with the fleet two points to port so as to draw nearer the group and to render assistance to the *Wiesbaden*."

Actually, Battle Squadron I did not carry out the signal literally as made. At the time, the *Friedrich der Grosse* was at a point where the long column bent about two points to the right. Instead of following in the wake of Battle Squadron III, the fleet flagship maintained its course which was about the same as that of Behncke's squadron after its simultaneous turn had been made. Battle Squadron I followed in the lead of the *Friedrich der Grosse*, which had the effect desired by Scheer. Battle Squadron II executed the signal exactly.

Despite the terrible propaganda that was directed against the German Navy during the war by its enemies, there was a spirit of loyal comradeship among its officers and sailors that is worthy of the highest praise. Despite the oft-repeated claim that the German officers, ashore and at sea, were only too willing to drive their men into useless slaughter, the plain facts of Jutland show a remarkable spirit of loyalty, cohesion, and self-sacrifice. Time and time again commanders and captains came to the assistance of their threatened comrades with magnificent courage. Perhaps, they even carried this desire to save their comrades too far and risked too much for a single ship or a few men; but they evidently had used this idea of standing together to build the morale of the High Seas Fleet and in this task they had succeeded to a very high degree.

After clearing the 1st Cruiser Squadron at 6:15 (Fig. 41–D), Beatty proceeded on a northeasterly course. The cruisers blanketed Beatty's fire and the *Lion* for a time lost touch entirely with the enemy. Some of the other battle cruisers fired occasional, ineffective salvos at Scouting Group I. A German salvo, probably aimed at the *Warrior,* landed on the *Princess Royal* about 6:19. Two shells found their marks, one of them completely wrecking "X" turret. The *Princess Royal* says that the hits were made at 6:22, but she was far out of line with the *Warrior* by that time.

While these actions were proceeding between 6:10 and 6:20, two little British destroyers were attacking Scouting Group I with torpedoes. They were the *Onslow* and *Acasta.* We left the *Onslow* attacking the crippled *Wiesbaden.* After having fired 58 rounds of 4-inch shell at the cruiser, Lieutenant Commander Tovey saw better game to the southward. In fact, the turn of Scouting Group I to the northeastward had brought the *Onslow* about 11,000 yards on its port bow in an excellent position from which to launch a torpedo attack. Tovey saw quickly that he had a heaven-sent opportunity for an attack against the enemy battle cruisers. He pushed in to 8,000 yards. Then, being in an excellent position, he turned the *Onslow* to bring the enemy on his starboard beam and gave the order to fire torpedoes. In those days, an officer on the bridge could not indicate by electrical gear the angle on which to set the torpedo tubes and then fire them himself from the bridge by merely making an electrical contact. There intervened an unfortunate delay in getting his torpedoes fired. By that time, the Germans were alive to the danger and the *Lützow* opened fire with her secondary battery. Just at the time the first of the *Onslow's* torpedoes left its tube, two 5.9-inch shells exploded in her foremost fireroom (Fig. 39–s). That was at 6:13 P.M.

As a result of those hits, clouds of steam enveloped the *Onslow's* torpedoes that had not been fired. Receiving an incorrect report that all had been discharged, Tovey turned back toward the *Wiesbaden*. Finding then that he had three torpedoes remaining, Tovey fired one deliberately at the cruiser at 3,500 yards (Fig. 39–U). It exploded abreast the *Wiesbaden's* bridge. The young, alert Sub-Lieutenant R. L. Moore, who had played a prominent part in all these events, called his captain's attention to a long line of German battleships that were following close to their battle cruisers. As the *Onslow* was only about 8,000 yards on their port bow, this was far too good a chance to be missed. So, about 6:18—much action is packed in such minutes— the remaining two torpedoes were sent on their way toward the battleships (Fig. 39–w). By that time three more shells had hit the *Onslow*. Her feed tank was punctured and her precious supply of fresh water quickly leaked into the bilges. The engines slowed down, but the gallant little ship slowly crept out of range of her numerous opponents. One of her torpedoes passed the *Kaiser* at 6:25, running on the surface. There is no record of the other. Despite the fact that she failed to win a well-deserved success, her record is one of the most effective and her example one of the most inspiring in this great sea fight. As will be told later, the *Onslow* was taken in tow by the *Defender* and after many hazards of the sea was brought safely into port.

We must relate now the story of the *Acasta* and in doing so tell of the gallant *Shark*. We left the four destroyers of Loftus Jones's command, supported by the *Canterbury* engaging a much superior German destroyer force, led by Commodore Heinrich in the *Regensburg*. The *Shark* had been seriously damaged. The *Acasta* had been hit twice and was endeavoring to assist her wounded comrade. The *Ophelia* and *Christopher* were both undamaged and had retired towards the 3d Battle Cruiser Squadron. The heroic defense of the *Shark* is one of the epics of naval history. Lying dead in the water, with little or no hope of escaping a seemingly inevitable destruction, she was fought to the end with steady British bulldog courage. When only one of her guns remained intact, it was manned by her few survivors: Midshipman T. Smith and two seamen, J. Howell and C. Hope. The captain, though slightly wounded in the leg, directed its fire. Torpedo Coxswain William Griffin stood by the captain to carry out his orders. An effort was made to load the spare torpedo in one of the tubes that had been fired, but a shell exploded its air flask.

It was about this time, 6:15, that the *Acasta* approached. Her captain, Lieutenant Commander J. O. Barron, asked if he could be of assistance. Jones replied in the picturesque language re-counted by one of his men: "Don't get sunk over us." As Barron reluctantly withdrew, the Germans pressed their attack to within 600 yards. About 6:18 the *G41* fired a torpedo which probably missed (Fig. 39–v). Shell after shell hit the little ship, but still she fought back with her single gun. Gradually, the German destroyers departed, evidently believing that the British destroyer must soon sink. Thus, Loftus Jones had a short inter-mission before the curtain would be raised for the final act of the *Shark's* tragedy.

After leaving the *Shark*, Barron saw the German battle cruis-ers returning. Again he advanced to the attack, though many hits had already retarded his progress. At 6:20, when about 5,000 yards from the *Lützow*, the *Acasta* fired a well-aimed torpedo (Fig. 39–x). The gallant destroyer was by this time covered with hits; one carried away her steering gear, another wrecked the engine-room. Fortunately, her steam was able to carry her out of the fight. She stopped directly in the path of the British battle line. There was no more she could do; so her crew gathered aft, her bow being way down in the water, and cheered each of the battleships as they passed. That inspiring incident must have raised the spirits of their eager crews to the highest pitch. The *Acasta* and Barron also had done well.

Meanwhile, Commodore Heinrich had assembled Flotillas II, VI, and IX, and withdrew rapidly to the southwestward in readiness for another attack. His withdrawal disengaged the *Canterbury*. About 6:17 she had received her only hit, a 4.1-inch shell that did not explode. She proceeded to the southward and about 6:20 engaged Scouting Group II at long range. The German cruisers, despite their superiority, did not press the fight.

In rear of the diversion created by the *Onslow* and *Acasta,* Beatty and Hood made their junction. No answer to Hood's query concerning the *Lion* came from the *Falmouth,* but Hood's attention was now concentrated on another matter that concerned his squadron very directly. About 6:13 a number of German torpedoes were seen approaching from the southward. The *Invincible* hoisted the signal to disregard her movements (Figs. 39–R and 41–A). She stopped and turned to starboard. Clouds of steam indicated that her safety valves were blowing off. Soon the *Indomitable* and *Inflexible* also saw torpedoes approaching. The *Indomitable* turned away to starboard at full speed, while the *Inflexible* turned to port toward the approaching tracks. Almost by a miracle, the torpedoes were avoided. In all the *Indomitable* saw 5 torpedoes and *Inflexible* 3. It is probable that the Germans fired 9 at this squadron. No less than 5 torpedoes were avoided by close margins, while a sixth passed directly under the *Inflexible.* The German torpedo control was excellent in this attack, but they were most unlucky. The element of luck looms large in everything that has to do with torpedoes. As this writer was a torpedo officer in 1912, he can vouch for the accuracy of this statement.

About 6:15 the *Invincible* started ahead again and steadied on her westerly course. The other two ships formed column on her. Hood proceeded at 20 knots. About 6:17 the *Lion* was seen dead ahead, a most fortunate rendezvous for Hood. He promptly counter-marched to starboard (Fig. 41–H). In inspiring style, he took station 3 miles ahead of the *Lion.* It was an excellent decision.

We have carried our story of all parts of the wide battlefield to 6:20.

CHAPTER XV

THE BATTLE LINES ENGAGE
6:20 P.M. TO 6:55 P.M.

THE 10-MINUTE period beginning at 6:20 had many interesting developments. During most of that time the Battle Fleet was not engaged. The rear divisions were heading away from the enemy. The van divisions, while converging, were still at ranges too great for effective fire under the existing visibility conditions. In addition, they were blanketed by the 1st and 2d Battle Cruiser Squadrons, the *Duke of Edinburgh,* and many destroyers that were endeavoring to gain their stations on the left battle flank. As those vessels were proceeding at their maximum speed, the dense smoke clouds from their stacks obscured the range. The actions that took place during the period resulted from close-range contacts between the closely concentrated High Seas Fleet and isolated British detachments.

The principal opportunity for a German success at that time resulted from the jamming of the *Warspite's* rudder. As the German battleships realized what a chance they had to sink a British battleship, many of them concentrated their fire on their crippled enemy. It will be remembered that the *Kaiserin* had been firing on this target for some minutes. At 6:20 the *Friedrich der Grosse* and soon afterward the *König, Helgoland, Ostfriesland,* and *Thüringen* joined in (Fig. 41–N). Their ranges varied between 10,000 and 15,000 yards. Both main and secondary batteries were used. At first glance, it would seem that a single ship, no matter how well constructed, could not live under the accurate fire of six battleships at such short ranges; but when the conditions under which the Germans were shooting are analyzed, it will be seen that their gunnery officers really had a very difficult problem of fire control. In the first place, with the target running in a wide circle at 25 knots, it was impossible to predict the range and deflection for future salvos, even if they had been correctly known at any given time.

It was impossible to determine the range and deflection because, with six ships firing on the same target from quite different directions, the salvos of a particular ship, could not be identified. Conditions were made even more difficult by the heavy clouds of smoke that covered the *Warspite*. Therefore, all that could be done was to deliver a great volume of fire into a given area in the hope that a percentage of shots would hit.

When it is considered that one of the German battleships fired no less than 20 salvos at the *Warspite,* it will be seen that mere luck would give some hits. The *Official Narrative* allows a total of 13 hits on the *Warspite* for the entire action. The account of the executive officer gives detailed descriptions of quite a few more. Accepting as final the 13 hits described in the Admiralty *Narrative* and allowing 4 to have occurred before 5:35, 9 were received during this period. In addition, there evidently were many more 5.9-inch hits. The conning tower, turrets, and machinery spaces were intact. The principal damage was done by several hits on the water line that let large quantities of water into the ship, which compelled a reduction of speed to about 16 knots. The unarmored parts of the ship were wrecked. It is remarkable that there were only 33 casualties. The executive officer writes:

Men everywhere were simply splendid and all very cheery. I confess that I myself found it mighty unpleasant and unnerving, although I had plenty to do, but for those who merely had to wait it must have been a thousand times worse. The noise was perfectly appalling, and you couldn't hear at all between decks, and the worst of it was one knew nothing.

After the *Defence* had blown up, the ships firing on her had shifted fire to the *Warrior* which had been following closely astern. That cruiser was riddled with at least fifteen heavy shell and six 5.9-inch projectiles. Hits below the water line flooded both engine-rooms, which had to be abandoned by their crews. The engine throttles were left open and the engines continued to turn even though partly submerged in water. They kept going long enough to bring the *Warrior* past the *Warspite* about 6:30 and out of the action. The *Warrior* suffered 100 casualties. Captain Molteno and his resolute crew now engaged in a long struggle to save their sinking ship. Next morning, as will be related, the *Warrior* sank after her crew had been rescued by the *Engadine*.

The *Duke of Edinburgh,* steering an erratic course, was also in the midst of salvos probably aimed at other ships, during that period. She escaped without a hit. She finally proceeded on the port bow of the *Lion*. Immense smoke clouds poured from her stacks, which interfered greatly with the fire of the British battleships. The *Black Prince,* the fourth vessel of the 1st Cruiser Squadron, possibly was under fire at this time and may have been seriously hit. However, nothing definite can be learned concerning the movements of this vessel except that, as first supposed, she was not sunk at this time.

The 2d Light Cruiser Squadron remained at the rear of the British battle line. At 6:20 Goodenough reported that the German battle line bore SSE. (145°) and was steering NE. (32°) (Fig. 41-O). The 1st Light Cruiser Squadron had been unable to get through the battle line to take its appointed position on the left battle flank. It was now proceeding along the unengaged side of the battle line after having lost much valuable time by several reversals of course. The *Galatea* fell out of the column due to an engineering casualty and the *Inconstant* was leading the squadron.

Having thus described conditions in the rear of the battle line, let us examine the interesting situation in the van. Hood, after completing his counter-march, turned several points toward the enemy to place himself directly in advance of the battle line on a southeasterly course. About 6:20 he opened fire on Scouting Group I from a position nearly ahead of it (Fig. 41-P). At 6:21 Beatty (Fig. 41-Q) increased speed to 26 knots and reopened fire on the German battle cruisers. The *Lion* and *Princess Royal* fired only intermittently, but the *Tiger* and *New Zealand* were able to get off 7 and 11 salvos, respectively. At 6:25 Beatty changed course to the southeastward in Hood's track. One minute later, Hood reduced speed to 20 knots, apparently to allow Beatty to overtake him. At 6:27 Beatty reported that the German battle line bore south (167°) and that the nearest ship was distant 7 miles (Fig. 41–w). It appears as if Beatty's report were based upon the German battle cruisers rather than upon their battleships.

Napier brought the 3d Light Cruiser Squadron into position on the engaged bow of the 3d Battle Cruiser Squadron. Unfortunately, the *Birkenhead* and *Gloucester* parted from him. Napier added the 6-inch batteries of the *Yarmouth* and *Falmouth* to the heavy concentration being brought against Scouting Group I. Each of the light cruisers fired a torpedo at the same target at 6:25 (Fig. 41–s). The *Falmouth* was hit by one 5.9-inch shell, probably from the *Derfflinger*, that cut the voice tubes to the foretop. A ricochet hit her aft. Though under the fire of several of the German battle cruisers and battleships, the light cruisers escaped practically undamaged. Napier had handled them boldly and skillfully. The *Ophelia* at 6:29 fired a torpedo at the German battle cruisers at about 8,000 yards.

Gradually, the British battleships were getting into the fight. At 6:24 the *Agincourt*, last ship in the battle line, finally got clear of Beatty's smoke and opened fire on a German battle cruiser with her large battery of fourteen 12-inch guns (Fig. 41–R). A minute later, the *Bellerophon* of the 4th Division did the same. However, it seems that the salvos of those ships were fired rather deliberately and with frequent intermissions. They were not effective. The British battle line was in considerable confusion. For that, Beatty was originally responsible. Evidently to avoid getting too close to the German battleships, he had been compelled to converge sharply on the leading battleship divisions since 6:15. Of course, that did not clear the range as quickly as a course that more nearly paralleled the deployment course. This will be seen from an examination of Fig. 41. Had he steered a direct course from his 6:15 position (Fig. 41–D) to his 6:30 position, it would obviously have been better calculated to clear the 1st Division than the circular course he actually took. However, he evidently felt that the direct course would expose him to a concentration by the German battleships, the effectiveness of which he had just witnessed in the case of the *Defence*. In order to allow the battle cruisers to clear the range, Jellicoe about 6:26 reduced the speed of his battleship divisions to 14 knots (Fig. 41–U). That sudden decrease of 4 knots for a single column of 24 ships naturally caused great confusion. All the rear ships were bunched up. Some slowed to 8 knots and others even had to stop to avoid collision. In addition, at 6:26 Jerram found it necessary to head about two points away from the enemy. That movement was made to clear Beatty. The smoke and mist prevented all but two of the battleships from finding a worthy target for their salvos. Most of them fired on the *Wiesbaden*, which answered her powerful enemies with a single gun. Let us turn now to the German side of the picture.

Beginning about 6:21 the *Lützow* and *Derfflinger* had come under a heavy fire. By 6:25 it had become quite effective. The fire from the 3d Battle Cruiser Squadron seems to have worried Hipper most. As the gun flashes had been right ahead, he had been compelled as early as 6:20 (Fig. 41–P) to begin a gradual turn to the southeastward to bring the hostile ships on his port beam. Behncke had conformed to that movement and at 6:30 he was closely following the *Von der Tann*.

While turning away, the leading German battle cruisers had suffered somewhat severely. At 6:25 Lieutenant von der Decker in the *Derfflinger's* after control recorded: "*Lützow* heavily hit forward. Ship on fire. Much smoke." Groos says: "From 6:26 on *Lützow* was struck time after time near the bow." The gunnery officer of the *Invincible* claims several hits. Admiral Hood called up to him: "Your firing is very good. Keep at it as quickly as you can. Every shot is telling." It is probable that as many as four hits landed on the *Lützow* between 6:26 and 6:29, while the *Derfflinger* received one hit at 6:26 (Fig. 41–V).

In reply to the British fire, the Germans could do little or nothing. The visibility to the northward was extremely unfavorable. All that could be seen was a ring of flashes. All that could be done by the van at that critical time was to land a chance 12-inch shell into the destroyer *Defender's* forward fireroom and even this failed to explode. The nose of an 11-inch armor-piercing shell penetrated into the *Attack's* wardroom, but served only to give her officers an interesting souvenir. The *Defender*, though badly crippled, took the completely disabled *Onslow* in tow. After their tragic blow in the air at 6:05, all the flotillas of the scouting groups had withdrawn in company with the *Regensburg* to the disengaged bow of Scouting Group I. However, the *Rostock* with Flotilla III and Half Flotilla I, a total of eleven boats, passed ahead of Division V and took station for attack. Scouting Group II for a time had shown some signs of getting back into the fight. At 6:23 Boedicker re-engaged the *Canterbury*. Three minutes later the *Frankfurt* received a 6-inch shell hit, but Boedicker made no effort to press the fight against the single cruiser. As soon as he saw the battle cruisers turn southward, he did the same. At 6:30 Scouting Group II was 4 miles south of Hipper, instead of in its proper station right ahead or on the engaged bow to meet the *Falmouth* and *Yarmouth*. That efficient German division took no further part in the day action, but kept maneuvering in a circle far out of the fight. If Boedicker was concerned for the injured *Pillau*, he should have directed her to proceed singly, while he returned to the battle with the *Frankfurt* and *Elbing*.

At 6:25 Scheer received a curious message from the commander of Flotilla V. It quoted statements of prisoners from the *Nomad* that 60 large ships were in the vicinity, including 20 new battleships and 6 battle cruisers. The prisoners apparently had told the yarn some time before, probably soon after they had been picked up, say at 5:35. It looks as if they had concocted some fantastically false information for the benefit of their captors. When Scheer received it at 6:25, this fairy tale by pure chance was very close to the truth.

At 6:29 Jellicoe hoisted a signal that gave the appearance of aggressive action: "Subdivisions separately alter course in succession to SSE., preserving their formation." That meant that all odd-numbered ships in the battle line would turn simultaneously to 145°, even-numbered ships following in their tracks (Fig. 41–x). The result would have been twelve columns of two ships each, all steaming on parallel courses. It would have resulted in decisive action. It is what Nelson would have ordered, together with his favorite signal, "Close action"; but it was not to be, for beneath this bold and fortunate signal we find in parentheses the single melancholy word, "Negatived."

It looks by this signal as though Jellicoe intended to gain contact with the enemy, whom by the way he had never definitely seen. Either Beatty's report of 6:27 or the actual sighting of the enemy by Jellicoe himself about 6:30 probably caused its cancellation. Therefore, it seems as if the motive for the projected change of course was to gain contact with the enemy rather than to push the action to a decision. It is true that there was one good argument against the execution of the signal at the time. The 5th and 6th Divisions were still headed to the northeastward, not having reached the deployment course. Their execution of the signal would place the battle line in a somewhat complicated formation. However, this would have had no really important consequences, as they could easily drop back to the line of bearing of the first four divisions if this were desired. In fact, this change of formation would probably have helped them to get into their proper stations more promptly, a problem which imposed serious difficulties in a long column of 24 ships.

At 6:30 a rapid change took place in the battle, for at last, 15 minutes after deployment, the British battleships in overwhelming strength came into action. By this time Beatty's battle cruisers were practically clear. The range to the enemy averaged only about 12,000 yards. Through the mist and smoke, the dim outlines of the German ships appeared. One by one the British battleships shifted their fire from the *Wiesbaden* to a more equal foe. At 6:30 the *Colossus, Hercules,* and *Iron Duke* opened fire. Others followed as soon as they could discover targets. There was no attempt at any systematic fire distribution, nor was a signal made to open fire. Each ship picked out the target that stood out best and commenced firing at it.

The confusion in the British battle line added another difficulty to the problems of the gunnery officers. Jellicoe's signal to reduce speed to 14 knots had been considerably delayed in transmission. As a result, some ships had kept on at 18 knots, while others had slowed to 14. Ships had to sheer out to avoid collision and overlapped each other for considerable periods.

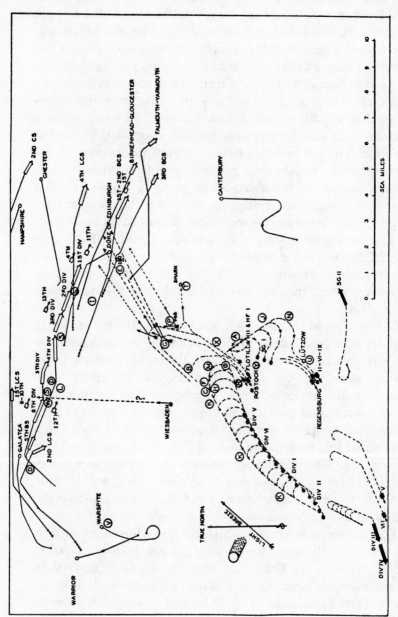

FIG. 42. 6:30-6:45 P.M.

Strangely enough, the *Iron Duke* seems to have been the worst offender, for she blanketed both the *Thunderer* and the *Conqueror* of the 2d Division. However, the former was able to get away three salvos between the *Iron Duke* and the *Royal Oak*. The *St. Vincent* could not avoid masking the fire of the *Neptune*, even by stopping. The *Marlborough* astern of the *St. Vincent* had to reduce speed to 8 knots. The changes of course and speed adversely affected the fire control of many ships at a critical time.

Nevertheless, the Germans fought under even greater disadvantages, for the British battleships were entirely invisible to them. All that was available as a target was the *Warspite*, and the effectiveness of their fire on that ship was rapidly decreasing. Due to their entire lack of knowledge of the position of the British battleships, the German battle line (Fig. 41) was less favorably disposed for battle than was the British. It was indeed fortunate for them that Hood had forced the head of their colume around to the southeastward before the British battleships could open fire with real effect. Had they still been on a northeasterly course at 6:30, their situation would indeed have been serious.

Probably, the concentration of the British fire on the German capital ships beginning at 6:30 can best be shown by means of a table:

Time	Firing ship	Range	Salvos	Hits claimed
6:30	*Iron Duke*	12,000	9	6
6:30	*Hercules*	16,000	7	0
6:30	*Colossus*	——	3	0
6:30	*Benbow*	——	1	0
6:30(?)	*Barham*	——	3	0
6:31	*Conqueror*	12,000	3	0
6:32	*Agincourt*	——	–	1
6:32	*Orion*	11,100	4	1
6:33	*Monarch*	12,000	3	0
6:33	*Thunderer*	——	3	4
6:35	*Benbow*	12,500	4	0
6:40	*Neptune*	11,000	2	0

Total hits 12

In addition, the three ships of the 3d Battle Cruiser Squadron were firing with excellent effect and the four ships of the 1st and 2d Battle Cruiser Squadrons might possibly have made a hit or two. Their firing was at about 10,000 yards.

The effects of this fire on the German capital ships was soon evident. At 6:30 the *König* was hit (Fig. 41–z). The next minute the *Derfflinger* was hit by one and possibly more heavy shells (Fig. 42–A). She probably was hit by 6-inch shells fired by the *Falmouth* and *Yarmouth*. One of her 6-inch guns was damaged. The *König* was hit again at 6:32 (Fig. 42–c) and at 6:34 (Fig. 42–F), while the *Markgraf* was hit once and probably twice at 6:35 (Fig. 42–H). Due to hot bearings, one of her three engines had to be stopped. About this time, the *Lützow* was hit about three times, bringing her total of hits to 20 (Fig. 42–J). Thus, no less than 12 hits had been received in five minutes.

Those hits had done serious damage. The *Lützow* had taken in a great quantity of water forward and was down so far by the head that it was difficult for her to maintain her speed. The *Derfflinger* had, as above stated, one 6-inch gun put out of action. The *König* had so many compartments flooded that she took a 4½-degree list. Her radio also was destroyed. Quite a few of the destructive hits had been scored by Hood's squadron. Standing on the *Invincible's* bridge, he had noted the excellent effect of the shooting of his battle cruisers.

We have remarked Hood's encouraging order to his gunnery officer to "keep at it as quickly as you can." Soon after he had said that, the *Invincible* momentarily came out into a lane of clear visibility losing the immunity from German fire that she had enjoyed up to that time. At 6:31 the *Lützow* and *Derfflinger* commenced firing at her. Though they had been shooting for nearly three hours and had received numerous hits, all their turrets and fire control gear were intact. They now proceeded to give a marvelous illustration of what the German ships could do when they could see their targets. The range was about 9,500 yards. Von Hase claims that the *Derfflinger* straddled with her first salvo. The *Lützow* did the same with her second. Several hits were observed. At 6:33 the third salvos of both German battle cruisers hit the *Invincible* amidships. A shell pierced "Q" turret, blew off its roof, and exploded the magazine. The ship broke in half and sank immediately. Her bow and stern still projected above the water. As her name could easily be read on the stern, it was a sad sight to the Grand Fleet as its units passed close aboard during the course of the action (Fig. 42–E). The Germans had gained their third great success. Von Hase claims the glory for the *Derfflinger*. Groos awards it to the *Lützow*. In any event, it was another proof of the value of German material and the efficiency of personnel that ships so battered as the *Lützow* and *Derfflinger* after two minutes of firing could sink the flagship of a fresh and undamaged force. It is probable that the *Invincible* was hit about six times.

The *Inflexible* now led the 3d Battle Cruiser Squadron. As the *Indomitable* passed the wreck of the *Invincible,* four men on a raft could be seen cheering her. Upon orders from Beatty, the four brave men and two others who were in the water were later rescued by the destroyer *Badger*. The gunnery officer, Commander H. E. Dannreuther, and two men from the foretop were among the survivors. An officer from the conning tower and a gunner from one of the turrets escaped by miracles the fate that met 1,025 brave officers and men. An officer of the *Badger* says:

The commander was really marvelously self-possessed. I can hardly understand to this day how a man, after going through what he had, could come on board us from the raft as cheerly as if he was simply joining a new ship in the ordinary course of events. He laughed at the armed guard, and assured us that he hadn't a scratch on his body, and that he had merely, as he put it, stepped into the water when the foretop came down.

Certainly in that battle the British and Germans, officers and men alike, entered into a noble rivalry of heroism and courage that did honor to the naval profession as well as to their countries. Every navy owes them a debt of gratitude and can draw an inspiration from their gallant deeds. Ian Hamilton, after witnessing the wounded *Inflexible* leaving the Dardanelles, wrote in his diary: "Ten thousand years of peace would fail to produce a spectacle of so great virtue." This vivid sentence we apply to the tragic drama of Jutland.

It was immediately after the destruction of the *Invincible*, or about 6:36, that Scheer made his famous *Gefechtskehrtwendung nach Steuerbord,* meaning a battle turn to starboard to the reverse course (Fig. 42–K). Three minutes later he ordered course west (257°). Boedicker's report that battleships were to the northeastward had given him an erroneous conception of the situation as it existed at 6:36. In fact, as we shall see, that error continued much longer to color all Scheer's ideas of the situation. Actually, except for the visibility, the tactical position of the High Seas Fleet was not particularly unfavorable. It is true that Battle Squadron II was far to the rear but in our opinion, that was just the right place for such inferior and obsolete vessels, which should have been left in port. Hipper had turned rather too far to the southward; but, everything considered, Scheer was nearly as well disposed at 6:36 as the British were. However, from the sketches in his book, it is evident that he placed the British to the eastward, rather than to the northward. He believed that they were enveloping both bows of his battle line. Under the circumstances, he considered it necessary to disengage the Fleet in order to resume the battle under more favorable conditions. To do so he ordered a battle turn to the rear.

Scheer did not disengage because of a feeling that he was in a critical position. In a letter to this writer, which has been partly quoted before, he said:

While the battle is progressing, a leader cannot obtain a really clear picture, especially at long ranges. He acts and feels according to his impressions. In looking at the diagrams that are made subsequently, it would seem as if we must have regarded our position as critical. In reality this was not the case. We were under the impression of the splendid effectiveness of our gunfire and of the fact that the entire battle line remained most conveniently arranged both while under fire and during the regrouping for the night march.

This statement applies to the second disengagement of the High Seas Fleet as well as the one now being considered.

By instructions the famous battle turn was to be executed by a ripple movement from the rear. However, as Squadron II was quite some distance away and was really not a part of the battle line, Captain Redlich immediately turned the *Westfalen,* rear ship of Squadron I, to course west (257°). He was followed by the entire squadron. The ships of Squadron III then followed. The *Markgraf,* with one engine out of commission, had difficulty in maintaining her station. The *König* did not get the signal to turn until 6:40, but as she meanwhile had gone to course south (167°) following the battle cruisers, the delay had no particular disadvantage. She received three more heavy hits during her withdrawal: at 6:36 (Fig. 42–M); at 6:38 (Fig. 42–O); and at 6:40 (Fig. 42–R).

Scouting Group I received the signal for the battle turn at 6:38. The *Von der Tann* turned to the eastward, while the others turned to the westward. Already at 6:37 the *Lützow* had left the formation (Fig. 42–N). Twenty heavy shells had caused serious injuries. She was down so far by the head that 15 knots was all that Captain Harder dared to steam for fear that his bulkheads would collapse.

The turn-away of the Germans had two interesting developments: one in the rear; the other in the van. Let us describe first the situation in the rear. There a great opportunity to destroy the *Warspite* was finally lost. That vessel was still circling. Although heavily hit, she fortunately had not been reduced in speed, although later it was necessary to slow considerably. The high speed had made her a difficult target to hit. At 6:26 the *König* ceased firing. At 6:35 the *Friedrich der Grosse* and *Helgoland* lost their target in smoke and mist. The *Thüringen* shifted target to the *Malaya.* The *Kaiserin* had ceased firing. That left only the *Ostfriesland* in action. However, the *Nassau* opened fire about 6:35, followed three minutes later by the *Oldenburg.* The fact that the German vessels were turning rapidly and the increase of range to 14,000 yards reduced the effectiveness of their fire on the *Warspite,* which was now able to straighten out on a northerly course. After completing their turn the *Nassau* and *Oldenburg* ceased firing. Finally, at 6:45 the *Ostfriesland* ended her long shoot. The *Warspite* could now take stock of her injuries sustained during two complete circles under the fire of a powerful concentration of battleships. As before stated, she had received about 9 heavy hits during that time, bringing her total to 13. Her heavy 13-inch armor and solid construction had stood the ship in good stead, but pressure on the engine-room bulkheads caused by water that had entered through shell holes on the water line made it advisable to hold her speed to 16 knots (Fig. 42–v).

Captain Phillpotts desired to regain his station with the 5th Battle Squadron. It was some time before the steering gear could be made ready and it then was necessary to steer from the steering engine aft. By that time the Battle Fleet was out of sight. Phillpotts reported that he could steam at 16 knots and asked for the position of the Battle Fleet. In reply Evan-Thomas properly directed him to proceed to Rosyth. At 8:30 course was set in that direction. As repairs were effected, speed was gradually increased to 19 knots.

The *Warrior* also came out of the action. At 6:55 she was joined by the *Engadine* (Fig. 43–K). As both the cruiser's engine-rooms were filled with water and steam, it was impossible to stop her engines. As she continued on at slow speed, the *Engadine* followed closely, ready to render assistance.

Now let us view the interesting situation in the van where the German destroyers had perhaps their best opportunity of the day. Slightly before 6:30 Commodore Michelsen in the *Rostock* had passed through the gap between the battle cruisers and battleships. She was closely followed by Flotilla III (7 boats) and Half Flotilla I (4 boats). Those destroyers had not been engaged thus far. They were all new boats, averaging about 1,050 tons, with speeds from 32 to 34.5 knots. All carried 6 torpedo tubes, of which 5 could be fired on one broadside. A glance at Fig. 41 will show that they were in a perfect position from which to launch a large-scale torpedo attack on the long column of 27 British battleships. One of the very best

opportunities of the day was in the hands of Commodore Michelsen. Let us see what use he made of it.

About 6:32 Michelsen ordered Flotilla III to concentrate for
attack (Fig. 42-B). The flotilla commander, Commander Hollmann, ordered each boat to fire 3 torpedoes while turning to starboard. That meant a salvo of 21 torpedoes. Hollmann advanced
to the northeastward at high speed and soon saw the dim outlines of capital ships about 7,000 yards away. They evidently
were the 1st and 2d Battle Cruiser Squadrons, which were about
3,000 yards nearer the destroyers than the van of the British
battle line. As the visibility was low and he had not yet been
taken under fire, Hollmann judged that he could make a much
closer attack. As he continued his advance, he received a most
remarkable signal from Commodore Michelsen who in the *Rostock* had remained well in the rear. The message timed, we
estimate, about 6:36 directed the destroyers not to attack.
That time is three minutes earlier than the communications
record, but fits better into the course of the action and with the
times at which the torpedoes crossed the line of the battle
cruiser formation.

It seems that Michelsen believed that the enemy would turn
away and that the torpedoes would be wasted. How he could
come to that conclusion when the *König* close at hand was
being hit time after time is difficult to see. Perhaps, the message was sent several minutes later, when the British fire slack-
ened, due to the German retirement. Even then, would it not
be natural to attribute the reduction of fire to the German
retirement, which he could see, rather than to a British retirement, at which he could only guess? In any event, we suggest
that more initiative should have been left to the flotilla commander. If Michelsen were not willing to run in close where he
could see the situation, which was perfectly proper, he should
have signaled Hollmann: "Act at discretion."

Commander Hollmann was placed in a very embarrassing
position by Michelsen's positive order. He could see the hostile
ships clearly. The British salvos were falling about his boats.
It must have seemed too good an opportunity to lose. Never-

theless, Hollmann obeyed his orders and commenced a retirement. The decision has two sides. (1) Suppose Hollmann argued as follows: Michelsen ordered me to concentrate for attack. Now, he directs me not to attack. However, he does not see the enemy capital ships as I do. I have, therefore, some vital information not available to my senior. Therefore, I am justified in disregarding his order. (2) Suppose Hollmann had taken the other side: Michelsen can see all the salvos falling about our battleships. He knows that the enemy is here in great strength. Why does he give such a positive order not to attack? Why does he not allow me to act at discretion? There must be some sudden change in the situation, perhaps orders from Scheer. My senior has some information not known to me. He must have some good reason for his action. I must obey. Thus, while we wish Hollmann had attacked, if only on a destroyer commander's instinct, we cannot blame him for acting as he did.

Although the order to attack had been canceled, the German destroyers fired about four torpedoes. Groos says the *G88* and *V73* each fired one torpedo, and we believe the *S32*, of Half Flotilla I, which Scheer's reports state accompanied Flotilla III, fired two more. The four torpedoes seem to have been fired between 6:34 and 6:38 (Fig. 42–G). They evidently were directed at the British battle cruisers, for about 6:40 the *Tiger* saw three torpedo tracks, while a fourth passed directly under the *Princess Royal*. It was unfortunate that the Germans did not aim their tubes at the van of the British battle line, which offered a much better target. Probably, they could not distinguish the battleships in the mist and the smoke made by the battle cruisers. A glance at Fig. 42 will show what a wonderful opportunity for torpedo fire was lost at that time.

It is possible that the torpedo which the *Marlborough* avoided at 6:45 (Fig. 42–w) was fired by Flotilla III, but it seems most unlikely that one should have been discharged at such a distant target, unless it was fired by accident, something that has happened at times even in peace-time exercises. It seems probable

that torpedo was fired by the *Wiesbaden* and we have so indicated in Fig. 42.

As the *V48*, *S54*, and *G42* were returning toward their fleet,
they sighted a destroyer to the eastward, which must have been
the *Shark*. On that badly crippled boat, only one 4-inch gun
was still in commission. Some of the survivors had manned it
to make a last desperate defense. Commander Loftus Jones,
slightly wounded, had left the wrecked bridge to control the
fire of that gun in person. Despite the powerful concentration
against him, Jones was able to land a shell squarely in the
V48's engine-room, which greatly reduced her speed. In fact,
it seems that the German destroyer was brought to a stop for
some time, but later was able to go ahead very slowly. It was
About 6:40 when the *V48* was injured (Fig. 42–P). The *S54*
now fired a torpedo at the *Shark* at a range of 4,000 yards. It hit
about 6:45 (Fig. 42–T.) . The *Shark* was hit about the same time
by numerous shells, one of which carried away the leg of the
gallant British captain. The ship gradually sank lower and
lower into the water and Jones gave the word for the ship to
be abandoned. About thirty men took to the water and clung
to the life lines around the edges of two rafts. Loftus Jones, already mortally wounded, soon died in the icy waters. About
7:00 the *Shark* sank. The rear of the battle line passed close to
the rafts, it is said by the British account within one mile, but
evidently they were not seen. Most of the men died quickly
from the cold, and at 10:00 P.M. when the Danish ship *Vidar*
arrived on the scene, she was able to save only six men. Loftus
Jones, who fought to the last with unsurpassed heroism, was
awarded the Victoria Cross by a grateful country. So long as
warships plow the seas will his story be told. Our salute goes
to a gallant captain and his brave crew.

Now we come to the saga of the *V48*. We know that ship
was fought to the finish with magnificent courage and resource.
Unfortunately, there were no survivors and we cannot single
out the individual exploits of any particular persons. Perhaps,
Lieutenant Commander Eckoldt and his crew that fought so

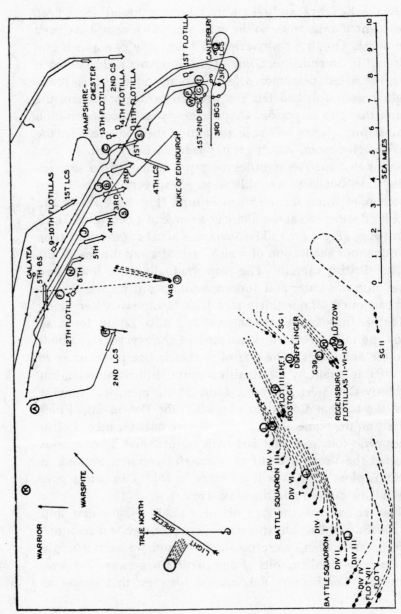

FIG. 43. 6:45–7:00 P.M.

well would wish their little ship to have all the honor. Soon after the *V48* had been crippled by the *Shark's* shell, she came under a heavy fire from the British battle line. The *G42* turned back to her assistance, but had to retire again under the devastating barrage. Seeing that his battle line was suffering severely, the captain of the destroyer, Lieutenant Commander von Arnim, laid a smoke screen that covered Battle Squadron III from the British fire. It was a splendid display of real initiative. It shows that even a little destroyer may play an important part in a fleet action.

While lying crippled, the *V48* seems to have fired two torpedoes, for only in that way can we account for two which are known to have been sighted by British ships, except the rather remote possibility of their having been fired by the *Wiesbaden*. It looks as if the first torpedo was fired about 6:40, for it passed the *Duke of Edinburgh* at 6:47 (Fig. 43–B). At 6:45 she fired a second torpedo, which probably was the one that hit the *Marlborough* at 6:54 (Fig. 43–F). The remainder of the saga of the *V48* will be related from time to time.

At 6:33 Jellicoe had increased the fleet speed to 17 knots. That was the second radical change he had made in seven minutes. Any officer who has had experience in a large fleet knows the confusion that large changes of speed will make in a column of 24 ships, particularly under battle conditions. Before the line could reach a proper degree of regularity, the great chance to damage the Germans had been lost. About 6:35 Beatty, having cleared the 1st Division, slowed to 15 knots. A minute later the battleships one by one lost sight of their targets and ceased firing. At that time, the *Marlborough* completed 9 rapid and effective salvos on the *König*, claiming 6, and actually getting, 4 hits. By 6:40 all was quiet in the battle line, except for a few salvos directed at the *Wiesbaden*. The six battle cruisers, however, could still see the *Lützow* and *König*. They directed a heavy fire at those ships. The *König* was hit at 6:41 (Fig. 42–R) and the *Lützow* received two hits at 6:45 (Fig. 42–U). It was during that part of the engagement that the four torpedoes passed through the 1st Battle Cruiser Squadron, as already described.

The mere fact that firing had ceased must have proved to Jellicoe that the enemy had withdrawn. Still he took no action until four minutes after his last ship had ceased firing. Then, at 6:44 he changed the fleet course to SE. (122°), one point to the right (Fig. 42–s). This obviously was entirely inadequate. There were no German destroyers in sight at the time, except the crippled *V48*. Certainly he should have turned toward the last position of the enemy, *i.e.*, to the southwestward, and should have proceeded until the situation developed. Meanwhile, his light cruisers should obviously have pressed in and relocated the enemy, supported as necessary by the battle cruisers. He had a big superiority in those types and now was the time to use it. He could well have afforded to expend a few light cruisers, if necessary, to get information of the enemy.

While Jellicoe was opening the range by proceeding on course SE. (122°), let us see what his light cruisers were doing to clear up the situation which, by the way, was still extremely foggy when Jellicoe wrote his book after the war. In the van, the *Canterbury, Falmouth,* and *Yarmouth* were admirably placed to gain information of the enemy. The *Canterbury* at 6:35 had been within 9,000 yards of Scouting Group I when the battle turn was made. She made no report whatever. Unfortunately, she chose that time to withdraw from her very advantageous advanced position to the disengaged bow of the battle cruisers. Her track chart shows Scouting Group I on an easterly course until 7:10. That demonstrates her utter ignorance of the movements of the enemy. In extenuation, it should be said that ship had newly joined the Fleet and probably was not ready for the opportunity that chance had thrust upon her.

The same excuse, however, does not hold good for Napier in the *Falmouth.* He also crossed the track of the 3d Battle Cruiser Squadron and took station slightly on its unengaged bow, though neither of his ships were damaged. At 6:40 Beatty asked for the bearing of the German battle cruisers, a query which probably gives the credit for the hits on the *Lützow* to the *In-*

domitable and *Inflexible*. Napier's reply is one of the strangest on record: "Last seen 1820. Altered course to W., engaged by 3d B.C.S." The time stated was largely in error. Napier states in his report that the turn of the Germans was after 6:30. The error in time probably caused Beatty to doubt the correct part of Napier's signal: That the Germans had turned to the westward. Napier's report said that the turn of the Germans away from him left him "without an enemy to engage." That was a curious reason for turning away himself. His manifest duty was to maintain contact with the enemy at all costs and report the movements of the enemy to Jellicoe.

In sharp distinction to this remarkable conduct of the British light cruisers in the van was the correct decision of Goodenough in the rear. The latter (Fig. 43–A) at 6:47 "turned in towards the German battle line partly to finish off a disabled battleship, but more to observe the enemy's rear more clearly, their course being in doubt." Here, the commodore expressed admirably the proper mission for the British light cruisers in this situation. Evidently, the "disabled battleship" was the *Wiesbaden,* but it was correct to finish her off, no matter what she might be.

The 4th Light Cruiser Squadron, though originally placed in advance of the battle line, had now got far on the disengaged bow of the *King George V,* the leading ship. At 6:43 Le Mesurier changed course abruptly 12 points to starboard to pass ahead of the battle line and to take station on its engaged bow. The decision was correct, but the method of execution left something to be desired, for he selected a collision course on the 1st Division. At 6:51 he shot close across Jerram's bow (Fig. 43–c), compelling the latter to alter course temporarily to starboard to avoid collision with the rear light cruisers. However, despite the narrowly avoided collision, we are glad to see that this squadron was really closing in upon the enemy on a southwesterly course.

Though Jellicoe received no timely information from his light cruisers, there was some information of the enemy's movements available even in the *Iron Duke,* for at 6:40 Jellicoe reports that the second battleship was seen "to turn 16 points to starboard." He says that from personal observation the Germans had received "heavy punishment and the second battleship was seen to turn out of the line badly on fire and settling by the stern." Why did he not, as we have already indicated, close the enemy?

We have seen that his fears of mines were more imaginary than real. Furthermore, had the Germans laid a field of floating mines where their battleships had been, the British could still have closed in 8,000 yards without danger. As to submarines, it must have been perfectly evident that it would be mere chance if any should be present. By the greatest stretch of the imagination, there could not be more than two or three. The Germans could use their submarines to advantage only by planting a trap and then luring the British into it. This obviously was not the case now, for it was the Germans who had been lured by Beatty. As to destroyers, the weak attack of Flotilla III was not even noticed by the British. The reason alleged for the cancellation of the 6:29 signal, i.e., that the British were in a curved line, no longer existed, nor was it a good reason at any time, for by 6:38 all six battleship divisions were in one long straight column. The battle cruisers were well grouped ahead. By 6:40 the British had had 25 minutes to make their deployment and even Jellicoe admits that at that time "our deployment was complete." Every reason pointed toward a decision to follow the enemy, but, as we have seen, Jellicoe contented himself with a 1-point turn to SE. (122°). On that course he proceeded for 11 precious minutes, making no effort to follow the enemy, who then was distant over 11 miles. Let us leave him proceeding with his mighty battle line of ships whose crews swarmed on deck to get some air and take a look around.

At 6:50 Beatty ordered the 3d Battle Cruiser Squadron to prolong the line astern. To facilitate the execution of that signal it was essential that the *Lion* should maintain her course and increase speed, while the *Inflexible* counter-marched. Just as the *Inflexible* started the maneuver to starboard at 6:55, the *Lion* commenced turning in a circle (Fig. 43–1). It has been stated that her gyro compass went out and that this was not realized until so late that a complete circle had to be made. It is also possible that the *Lion* was endeavoring to avoid the imaginary submarine that Beatty reported to Jellicoe at 5:54 (Fig. 43–G). At any rate, that costly maneuver used up 10 minutes of valuable time to no purpose. At 7:00 Beatty ordered the 1st Flotilla to form submarine screen No. 3 about the battle cruisers (Fig. 43–W). The *Christopher* and *Ophelia* had joined the 1st Flotilla. As the *Defender* had fallen out, the re-enforcement raised the strength of the 1st Flotilla to 10. Beatty's order tied down a powerful destroyer force to a defensive mission and prevented its use for torpedo attack.

The 3d Light Cruiser Squadron and the *Canterbury* followed Beatty's movements in circling and thus lost an excellent opportunity to gain distance ahead of Beatty for tactical scouting. There seems to have been more attention given to maintaining a given station on the battle cruisers than in performing a mission in the most effective manner. About 6:55 the two sections of the squadron rejoined. At 7:00 the *Canterbury* was about to take station as rear ship in the squadron, which would give it a strength of five ships for the remainder of the operation (Fig. 43–Q). It was not until about 7:05 that Beatty's six battle cruisers were properly redisposed on a southerly course with the two vessels of the 3d Battle Cruiser Squadron in the rear.

CHAPTER XVI

THE BATTLE LINES RE-ENGAGE
6:55 P.M. to 7:20 P.M.

At 6:55, when the two Fleets were about 11 miles apart, both commanders made radical maneuvers. At 6:50 Jellicoe had asked Burney if he could see any enemy battleships. Before Burney's laconic "No" could be returned, the commander in chief had made his decision. As scarcely a shot had been fired by any British battleship for the last 15 minutes, Jellicoe at last came to the rather obvious conclusion that "the range was apparently opening." At 6:55 he turned his battleship division flagships simultaneously to south (167°) (Fig. 43–J).

No sooner had that been executed than a series of alarming messages began to pour in. First came Beatty's incorrect radio dispatch timed at 6:45 that a submarine was in sight. The addition of a geographical position to the message when the *Lion* was in immediate contact with the British battle line could have no possible advantage and might, if used by Jellicoe, have created an erroneous impression, as it was certain to be much in error. Its inclusion in the dispatch probably delayed its transmission, but it probably was unfortunate that erroneous message was not delayed indefinitely.

At 6:57 the *Marlborough* reported being hit by a mine or torpedo. That was very disconcerting, as no German destroyers had been seen attacking. The inference was that the damage had been inflicted by either a submarine or a mine layer. It is true that little or no credence could be given to the latter possibility by any person familiar with the existing situation, because no German vessel, except a submarine, could have got into the position where the *Marlborough* was hit (Fig. 42–w). However, it fitted in exactly with Jellicoe's preconceived ideas that the Germans would use mines. The mine possibility was quickly eliminated by a message from the *Marlborough* at 6:58 that she had been hit by a torpedo. In fact, a quick survey of the damaged area had revealed the fragment of a torpedo. The *Marlborough* deserves great credit for her quick dispatch (Fig. 43–N).

At 7:00 Jerram (Fig. 43–S) sent the third alarming message to Jellicoe: "There is a submarine ahead of you." A minute later, the *Duke of Edinburgh* (Fig. 44–A) reported by flag signal that another submarine was two points on her port bow. The three incorrect reports, added to the one correct report of actual damage to the *Marlborough*, must have induced Jellicoe to say to himself: "This is just exactly what I expected."

We know now, of course, that no submarines were present. The torpedo that hit the *Marlborough* was probably fired by the *Wiesbaden* or *V48*, as has already been related. On board the battleship, it was thought the torpedo had been fired by a submarine, as witnesses thought they saw a periscope 1,000 yards on the starboard beam. Fortunately, that impression was not reported to Jellicoe. Flag officers and captains in battle would do well not to make alarming reports of submarines unless they are almost certainly correct. The torpedo hit caused considerable damage to the *Marlborough*, flooding several compartments and admitting a steady flow of water into the forward fireroom. However, the ship could still make turns for 17 knots and therefore remained in the battle line.

About 7:00 Jellicoe received an information report from Goodenough (Fig. 43–R). It stated that the German battle line bore SSW. (189°) from him and was steering ESE. (100°). At the same instant, a message from Beatty (Fig. 43–P) stated that the enemy was to westward. That report was timed at 5:55, but evidently was meant to be 6:55. The two reports fixed with fair accuracy the position of the German main body, for if the *Southampton* and *Lion* were not in direct sight of the *Iron Duke*, their approximate positions were known. Goodenough also gave the priceless information that the Germans were again heading to the eastward. That gave Jellicoe warning that another contact could soon be expected. His urgent task was now to place his battle line at right angles to the bearing of the enemy. For that he wanted precisely the bearing of the enemy and his distance from the fleet guide, the *Iron Duke*. Instead he received the bearing from a designated geographical position, which he knew was immensely in error. Also, the bearing he received was in error about two points, as Goodenough had evidently mistaken the German battle cruisers for their battleships. The distance was not stated, but might be assumed as the limit of visibility, about 12,000 yards. Therefore, if he could see the *Southampton*, Jellicoe would plot the position of their battle line at 7:00 as about in the position of Scouting Group I (Fig. 43), steering about 100°. As it happened, the British battle line was disposed almost exactly at right angles to the bearing of the enemy, as thus located. Thus, he could consider himself ready to meet the new advance of the enemy with crushing effect. Actually, as we shall see later, the errors of Goodenough in reporting the bearing and course of the enemy resulted in a much less favorable situation. No criticism of Goodenough is implied. It was easy to mistake the battle cruisers for the battleships and easier still to make a 2-point error in their course. Nor could he have been responsible for the faulty method of making information reports, at such a time as this, with reference to a position stated in terms of latitude and longitude rather than relative to the fleet guide.

While Jellicoe was now proceeding under conditions that must have looked so favorable, Scheer was returning to the attack. Except for a chance hit on the *Markgraf* at 6:52, the High Seas Fleet had entirely disengaged itself; but Scheer now decided to make another push at the enemy. Let us see what his information was and what his motives were. At 6:45 the *Moltke* (Fig. 42–Y) had reported that the British van bore E. by S. (88°). That was a rather inaccurate and indefinite report. The use of such terms as "van" in enemy information reports creates a vague impression. Actually, the only British ship that bore as much to the right as 88° was the *Canterbury*. It would be misleading to call a single light cruiser the van of the enemy formation. Actually, the British Battle Fleet at that time bore about NNE. (9°). The report probably served to confirm Scheer's impression, based on Boedicker's reports of the 3d Battle Cruiser Squadron, that the British were much more to the right than they actually were. That belief is shown by the sketches in Scheer's report and in his book.

Scheer tells us his motives in his official report, which probably was not prepared with a view to its publication. His motives were so simple that naval critics the world over seem unable to credit them. They endeavor to put brilliant schemes in the mind of a simple fighting seaman, who said he was guided largely by his impressions. In our opinion, Scheer's very simplicity has deceived his critics. He was a fighting admiral, no hot-headed, impetuous Nelson, but an icy, calm U. S. Grant. He believed, contrary to Jellicoe, that caution is often the most dangerous attitude. Boldness and surprise seemed to him a safer course than to run away. He was willing, contrary to Jellicoe, to leave something to chance. This is how he reasoned: If he tried to avoid action, the *Wiesbaden* and probably the *Lützow* would have to be abandoned. The British would have time to force another action upon him before dark and to cut his line of retreat. He writes:

There was only one way of avoiding this: to deal the enemy a second blow by again advancing regardless of consequences, and to bring all the destroyers to attack. This maneuver would necessarily have the effect of surprising the enemy, upsetting his plans for the rest of the day, and, if the attack was powerful enough, of facilitating our extricating ourselves for the night. In addition, this afforded us the opportunity of making a final effort to succour the hard-pressed *Wiesbaden,* or at least to rescue her crew.

In particular, critics have scoffed at this last idea. We do not. Scheer says in his report that he could clearly see the *Wiesbaden* defending herself bravely against overwhelming odds. In his book he says: "The fight of the *Wiesbaden* helped also to strengthen my resolve to make an effort to render assistance to her and at least save the crew." The story of Chief Stoker Zenne of the *Wiesbaden* tells over and over again how the few survivors constantly expected that they would receive assistance, at least from their destroyers. The wisdom of risking a fleet to save a single ship may be debated, but Scheer's motive in returning to the attack shows a loyalty and cohesion in the splendid High Seas Fleet that is most admirable. On a later occasion,

Scheer risked his battleships to save a single submarine. The knowledge that the commander in chief would stand by every ship in distress with his entire force certainly contributed to the unsurpassed morale of his officers and men. There are times when a magnificent will to fight "regardless of consequences," to use Scheer's words, is more effective than a cold-blooded decision based on pure reason.

It was at 6:55 that the signal for Scheer's second *Gefechtskehrtwendung* was executed (Fig. 43–L). The ships again commenced their turn to course east (77°). Battle Squadron II was handled independently of the two squadrons of first-line battleships. The *Regensburg*, with Flotillas II, VI, and IX, promptly turned eastward and hurried toward the head of the line. Heinrich, entirely on his own initiative, ordered the flotillas to attack. The orders to the destroyers were sent at 6:52 and 6:54, evidently as soon as the signal flags for the battle turn were hoisted. The signals were probably sent by a display of the checkered "Z" flag, which meant *"Torpedoboote Ran!"* ("Torpedo boats charge!"). We confess to a liking for those expressive, but untranslatable, expressions of the German signal book. Those orders by Heinrich were a magnificent example of Scheer's indoctrination and his subordinate's bold and intelligent decision. Both cannot be too highly praised.

The reaction of Commodore Michelsen, in our opinion, was far less correct. At 6:55 he ordered Half Flotillas I and XII to go to the assistance of the *Lützow* (Fig. 43–H). It will be noted that the latter unit belonged to Heinrich's command. In fact, he had just ordered Flotilla VI, of which it formed a part, to attack. In response to Michelsen's order, the *G37* and *V45* of Half Flotilla XII and the *G38* and *G40* of Half Flotilla I covered the *Lützow* with a smoke screen, while the *G39* of Half Flotilla I took Vice Admiral Hipper from the *Lützow* for transfer to another ship (Fig. 43–M).

The assignment of the *G38, G39,* and *G40* of Half Flotilla I to those duties was, we suggest, a grave error. None of these boats had been engaged nor fired a single torpedo. They were excellent and comparatively new boats. The *G37* and *V45* of Half Flotilla XII had been engaged only once and were undamaged. The former had fired only one torpedo and the latter either one or two. Their detail to the *Lützow* depleted Flotilla VI to seven boats, just as it was about to commence a decisive mass attack. The use of four good destroyers to guard a single ship that had no further offensive value, seriously reduced the fighting strength of the High Seas Fleet at a critical moment. The *S32*, which was just returning from an attack, could have covered the *Lützow*, as she proceeded at 15 knots, with a smoke screen and then might have taken Hipper on board. Some boats of Flotillas V or VII, which were of a very small type, might have been used for that purpose, or later some boats that were damaged or had fired all their torpedoes.

As the smoke screen laid by the destroyers drifted to the northeastward, it covered the four remaining battle cruisers. They were badly in need of a respite, brief though it might be. In addition to other damage, the *Derfflinger's* obsolete torpedo nets had been cut adrift by a shell and seemed about to foul one of her propellers. It was necessary to stop the ship for several minutes while the crews of "C" and "D" turrets cleared away the nets.

Hipper intended to hoist his flag on the *Seydlitz* and the *Lützow* informed that ship to that effect. While passing the *Derfflinger* in the *G39*, Hipper directed her captain to take command until his flag was again hoisted. The *Derfflinger* turned to the northward. The *Seydlitz*, *Moltke*, and *Von der Tann* followed. To me the vessels of Scouting Group I present a superb picture of naval warfare. Let me try to paint it for you.

The *Lützow* slowly steams off. Twenty great shells have mortally wounded the great ship. Her bows are deep in the water. Huge smoke clouds curl ominously from her fiercely burning forecastle. Her guns are silent. Her officers and crew, already more than decimated by bursting shells, must fight, as Paul Jones said, two more deadly enemies: fire and water.

In the *Derfflinger's* steel-clad conning tower stands a man worthy to succeed even stout-hearted Hipper. Already Captain Hartog has shown that he can give punishment, now he must prove that he can take it, for soon he must lead the famous "death ride" of the battle cruisers. The *Derfflinger* has not come scatheless through her many engagements. Already nine heavy shells have crashed into this stout, Tirpitz-built ship. Fortunately, they have not reduced her speed or put out of action any of her well-armored and crack-shooting turrets. Gunnery Officer Georg von Hase is ready for new encounters.

In the *Derfflinger's* wake comes the *Seydlitz*. Resolute Captain von Egidy has fought her this day in a manner worthy of the fast galloping hero of Rossbach whose name she bears. Not even that inspiring picture of the Prussian cavalry general throwing away his pipe as the signal for the irresistible onslaught of his cavalry squadrons could surpass the prolonged and desperate fighting of the battle cruiser named to commemorate his valor. Already fourteen heavy shells have done extensive damage to her hull and turrets, while a torpedo has torn a great hole in her under-water compartments.

The *Moltke's* four heavy hits have done much superficial, but no decisive, damage.

On the other hand, the *Von der Tann,* after her sensational success in blowing up the *Indefatigable,* has been wrecked by the explosions of three great 15-inch shells. These, together with gunnery failures, have put her entire main battery out of action. This, of course, is no reason why she should leave the line, for Captain Zenker can still offer his ship as a target for the enemy, thus drawing some of the fire off his comrades.

Let us now return to the conning tower of the *Friedrich der Grosse.* In our opinion, Scheer did well to return to the attack. His reasons for doing so we thoroughly approve, but his manner of carrying his decision into effect could, we suggest, have been improved. He had redeployed his Fleet on a course that led directly into the center of the British battle line. If at 6:45 the *Moltke* reported that the enemy's van bore 88°, a course for the German battle line of 77° would obviously lead against the center of the enemy. Scheer says that his "acknowledged purpose was to deal a blow at the center of the enemy's line." He says that his reversal of course "led to the intended result." Furthermore, Groos makes the remarkable statement that Scheer had determined on another attack with full strength directed against the middle of the enemy's formation in the full knowledge that this would expose him to the danger of the enemy "crossing the T" for the second time. In fact, all the German sketches made soon after the action showed their belief that the High Seas Fleet was in an even more dangerous situation than it actually was. Groos, in explanation of Scheer's headlong thrust, says that "the decision corresponded more to the intuition of the moment, and was so bold and keen, as well as against all the rules of the game, that only success could justify the maneuver." We cannot subscribe to the method Scheer employed.

How then could Scheer have re-engaged with better chances of success? It is difficult to say what he should have done, because we do not know exactly what information there was at his disposal. However, he did know that the enemy was generally to the eastward. Therefore, we suggest that he might to advantage have ordered a change of course in succession to about south (167°), or possibly SSE. (145°). He could have commenced the movement at 7:00 and his 16 battleships would all have been on the new course by 7:16. Scouting Groups I and II could have assembled ahead of the battle line. On the disengaged side of the scouting groups, the destroyers could have been assembled over an area wide enough to permit their attacks being pushed home without interference between flotillas.

That redeployment would have permitted all the battleships to get into the action under favorable conditions by 7:16, the time that Scheer turned away the second time. It would have avoided the necessity to endanger the heavily battered battle cruisers and would have permitted the light cruisers to regain their proper stations in the van. It would have given the destroyers their best opportunity to attack. It would have permitted the Germans to fight on a course toward their bases. Finally, the battle squadrons could have been disengaged at any time by a simple simultaneous 90-degree turn to the westward. The maneuver had two disadvantages. (1) There might have been some enfilade on the knuckle in the line, but that was far better than an enfilade of the entire line, as actually occurred. (2) It would not have brought the *Wiesbaden* inside the lines; but to draw the battle away from her to the southward was perhaps the best chance the Germans had to save that ship. On the other hand, the maneuver would have directly covered the withdrawal of the *Lützow*. In making this suggestion we have tried to place ourselves in Scheer's position and to advocate only such a maneuver as he might have made effective. Let us now return to the narrative of the battle.

It was about 7:03 when the *Iron Duke* passed the wreck of the *Invincible* (Fig. 44–B). The destroyer *Badger* was standing by, rescuing her few survivors. Jellicoe asked her: "Is wreck one of our own ships?" Soon the sad reply came in: "Yes, *Invincible*." A bad omen this must have seemed—the very name an irony. What a depressing sight for a commander in chief just reaching the critical point of his long career of service!

At 7:03 the *Marlborough* commenced maneuvering to avoid three torpedoes (Fig. 44–E). It is probable that these were fired by the *V48* about 6:45 (Fig. 43–O). It is possible that the *Wiesbaden* had fired them. At any rate, that cruiser was suspected of having fired the torpedoes, for the 5th and 6th Divisions now opened a terrific fire on her (Fig. 44–C). The third and fourth salvos of the *Marlborough* seemed literally to split her open and bring down her funnels. At that time the *Colossus* fired on a destroyer and claimed to have sunk her (Fig. 44–K). Her target evidently was the *V48*, but her claim seems to have been exaggerated. The German destroyer appears to have been steaming slowly to the southward. She probably was hit and further damaged by the British battleship. However, she evidently was able to fire her sixth torpedo, for at 7:08 one narrowly missed the *Agincourt* (Fig. 44–M). What a shame that we cannot have the intimate story of the *V48's* adventures during that period!

About 7:04 Scouting Group I was again taking its station ahead of the battle line. Battle Squadrons III and I were in single column on course east (77°). The *Markgraf* reported that her port engine was out of operation and that she was unable to maintain her station in formation (Fig. 44–L). However, she seems actually to have done so. The German battleships could easily maintain 15 knots with two of their three engines. The *Regensburg*, with Flotillas II, VI, and IX, was just south of Scouting Group I, again in readiness for attack. Half Flotilla V

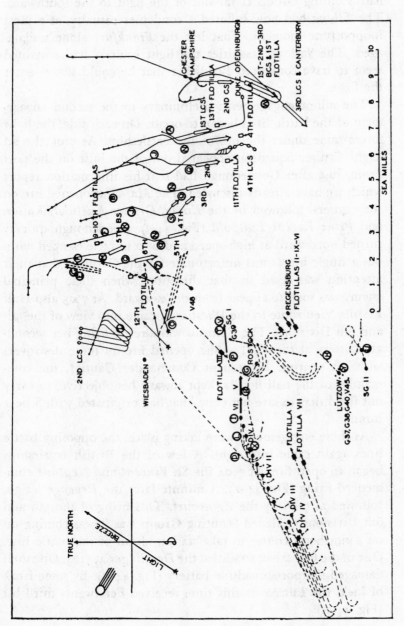

FIG. 44. 7:00-7:15 P.M.

of Flotilla III was steaming toward the *Wiesbaden*. Boedicker had Scouting Group II far out of the fight to the southward. The *Elbing* had now suffered a condenser casualty, at a most inopportune moment. That left the *Frankfurt* alone undamaged. The various casualties the light cruisers had sustained seem to have convinced Boedicker that he could not re-enter the fight.

The minor engagements preliminary to the second engagement of the battle lines began to occur. On each side, the light forces came under the fire of the battleships. At 7:05 the 2d Light Cruiser Squadron appeared out of the mist on the port beam, just after Goodenough had sent his information report which we have already discussed. The *Markgraf* opened fire on the cruisers, followed by the *König, Grosser Kurfürst, Kaiser,* and *Prinz Regent Luitpold* (Fig. 44–I). Goodenough quickly turned northward at high speed and by a miracle escaped without a single hit. It was unfortunate for the Germans that their attention was fixed in that direction, when their principal enemy was soon to appear from the eastward. At 7:05 also Half Flotilla V en route to the *Wiesbaden* came into view of the 5th and 6th Divisions. The *Colossus* was already firing her secondary battery at the *V48*, so she opened fire on those destroyers with "A" turret. Lieutenant Commander Gautier, the commander of the half flotilla, kept toward his objective, to carry out the orders to save her crew, that had originated with Scheer himself.

As these engagements were taking place, the opposing battle lines again came into sight. A few of the British battleships began to open fire. At 7:04 the *St. Vincent* and *Neptune* commenced firing (Fig. 44–F). A minute later the *Revenge* let go, followed at 7:06 by the *Agincourt*. This firing of the 5th and 6th Divisions enfiladed Scouting Group I as it was coming up on a northerly course to take station ahead of the battle line. One of the first salvos straddled the *Derfflinger* at 7:04. One shell damaged the port broadside battery (Fig. 44–G). By some freak of luck, the *Lützow* at this time received her twenty-third hit (Fig. 44–H).

Just as this firing was commencing, Jellicoe executed a some-what remarkable signal at 7:05. He turned all his 24 battleships simultaneously three points toward the enemy to SW. by S. (201°). This placed the battle line in a very intricate formation. It was already disposed in six parallel columns. The four ships of each division were now in a 3-point line of bearing. This would require two successive maneuvers to deploy into a single column of 24 ships. A simpler maneuver would have been for the division flagships to change course simultaneously, being followed in succession by the ships in their divisions.

As we have said before, what would have helped Jellicoe most at that time would have been a rotation of his front to the right. Unfortunately, all his available information indicated that he was properly disposed for the expected contact. Actually, his battle front was by no means at right angles to the bearing of the enemy and as a result his right-flank divisions made con-tact at close range, while those on the left flank were virtually out of the fight. This implies not the slightest criticism of Jelli-coe. He was poorly served by his light forces and it was not until 7:12 that the *Iron Duke* got a bearing of the enemy. Further-more, when two fleets make a right-angle contact in low visibil-ity, the resultant situation almost entirely depends upon chance. The writer has personally seen the great difficulty in handling a fleet under such conditions, when the situation was not nearly so unfavorable as that which confronted Jellicoe. In any case, even though Jellicoe's Fleet might have been better disposed, it was in a much more favorable position than that of Scheer.

It seemed that a fight to the finish now must take place, for the Fleets had come into contact at incredibly close ranges. The Germans were headed directly into the center of the Grand Fleet. They were in the most unfavorable and dangerous situa-tion imaginable. Jellicoe enjoyed the overwhelming advantages of position, visibility, and numbers, each in a very great degree. Scheer's bold plan was to be put to a terrible test.

At 7:09 Half Flotilla V came under fire from the *Bellerophon* and *Benbow*, and shortly afterward from the *Neptune, Canada,* and *Iron Duke.* Convinced that he could never reach the *Wies-*

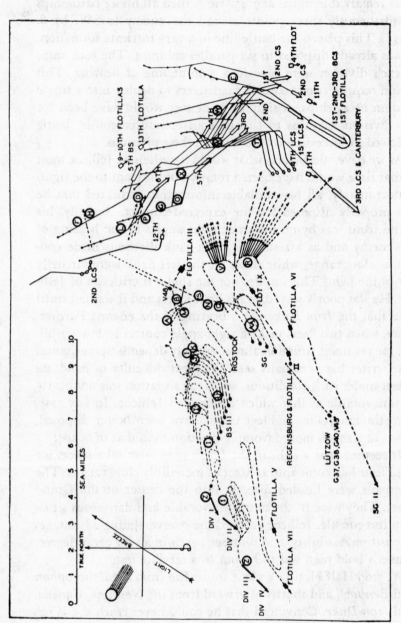

FIG. 45. 7:15-7:30 P.M.

baden under such a powerful concentration, Gautier turned back. About 7:10 the *V73* fired one torpedo at the 5th Battle Squadron and the *G88* fired three at the 5th Division (Fig. 44–O). Somewhat later, probably at about 7:17, three torpedoes were sighted by the *Neptune* (Fig. 45–D). She avoided them by maneuvering, at the cost, however, of being masked by the *St. Vincent*. At 7:18 the *Barham* avoided the fourth torpedo (Fig. 45–H). Half Flotilla V was in a very favorable position for torpedo fire and it is unfortunate that better advantage of it was not taken.

Meanwhile, at 7:09 Jellicoe (Fig. 44–N) had turned back his battleships simultaneously to south (167°). He had sighted the *Regensburg* and her flotillas coming up from the southwestward and perhaps Flotilla III to the westward. In his intricate formation, it would be difficult to avoid torpedoes. He rightly decided that he must get his battle line into division columns.

It was about 7:12 that the majority of the British battleships commenced firing (Fig. 44–Q). We can best show the volume and effect of their fire by a table:

Time	Ship	Range	Salvos	Hits claimed
7:04	Neptune	10,200	4	2
7:04	St. Vincent	10,000	20	Many straddles
7:05	Revenge	11,000	16	6
7:06	Agincourt	11,000	—	4
7:10	Ajax	19,000	1	0
7:12	Marlborough	10,500	14	5
7:12	Hercules	9,000	6	2
7:13	Iron Duke	15,400	4	1
7:14	Monarch	18,000	5	2 straddles
7:15	Colossus	9,000	5	4
7:15	Royal Oak	14,000	7	2
7:15	Orion	19,000	6	2 straddles
7:16	Centurion	17,500	—	0
7:17	King George V	——	6(?)	—
7:17	Temeraire	12,000	7	—
7:17	Bellerophon	11,000	6(?)	2 straddles
7:17	Benbow	——	7	1
7:20	Canada		4	2 straddles
7:20	Superb	11,000	4	2
7:20	Collingwood	8,000	2	—

Total hits   29

In addition to the vessels of the six battleship divisions above listed, the Battle Cruiser Squadrons and the 5th Battle Squadron fired for a few minutes beginning at 7:17, but data are lacking as to numbers of salvos fired and probable hits.

We will describe now the actual effects of the immense volume of fire on the High Seas Fleet and tell how the Germans escaped from a most hazardous and even critical situation. Since 7:04, as we have seen, Scouting Group I had been under a heavy fire. About 7:10 the *Derfflinger* steadied on course east (77°) and Captain Hartog increased speed (Fig. 44–P). The concentration of fire on the *Derfflinger* now increased. As the leading vessels of Battle Squadron III, on course about E. by S. (88°), emerged from the mist and smoke at 7:12, an enormous volume of fire was concentrated upon them. Close behind Squadron III came Squadron I. In order to allow the battle cruisers to take their station ahead, Behncke had been forced to slow down. That had resulted in his squadron piling up on his flagship. For a time some of the ships of Division VI even had to stop and back. The *König*, in order to bring her broadside to bear, had to change course to the southeastward. Two heavy shells crashed into her (Fig. 44–R).

When the British shells commenced falling about the leaders of the German battle line, they could see nothing of their enemies but a continuous ring of flickering gun flashes. No range-finder readings could be taken of the British battleships. It was impossible to find any point of aim. Obviously, no effective reply could be made to the deadly fire of the British at very moderate ranges. The situation, as Groos admits, was "the most unfavorable during the entire battle." Von Hase says: "We were in a regular death trap." It looked as if Scheer's attempt to surprise the enemy by acting "against all the rules of the game" would prove to be one of the most colossal errors of all naval history. His mistake had given Jellicoe the greatest opportunity for a victory of annihilation perhaps in all the long course of naval history. Could he win such a victory, it must have a decisive effect on the greatest war of history. It now remained to see whether Jellicoe could grasp this remarkable opportunity, or if he failed to do so, whether Scheer by a desperate maneuver could extricate his Fleet from such a critical situation.

First, let us see what steps Scheer took. His various orders were issued between 7:13 and 7:21. In those 8 minutes, he had to make decisions that might exert a decisive effect upon the entire war. He could see very little of the situation in the van and even less of the enemy's movements. Even after the war, his ideas of the existing situation were most inaccurate. No commander in chief of history could have been under such compressed tension as was Scheer during those few minutes when the fate of the world hung in the balance. We have only admiration for Scheer's unsurpassed resolution and clear-cut decisions in this most critical situation. Our observations and comments on the methods he employed imply not the slightest criticism. They are based on many years of detailed study and a knowledge that Scheer did not possess until long after the war. They are offered entirely for the purpose of drawing such tactical lessons as we may from this interesting situation. Their purpose is to serve as a guide for the future, not as a criticism for the past.

According to Groos, Scheer decided that he must extricate his battle line from this highly dangerous situation. To do so, Scouting Group I should attack without regard to losses, so that with their help, the mass attack of destroyers could be brought as close as possible to the enemy battle line, while, under the protection of this maneuver, the battle line could be turned to the reverse course and thus withdraw from the enemy envelopment.

In accordance with this plan, Scheer ordered Scouting Group I at 7:13: "*Gefechtswendung! Rein in den Feind! Ran!*" This meant for it to make a battle turn toward the enemy and to charge into him regardless of losses. At 7:14 or 7:15, however, Scheer ordered the battle cruisers to operate against the enemy's van. Some time between 7:16 and 7:18, probably the latter, he ordered the battle line to make a *Gefechtskehrtwendung* (battle turn to a reverse course) (Fig. 45–1). Only at that time did the destroyers advance beyond their battle cruisers, though Heinrich 20 minutes before had told them to attack. Scheer himself did not order the destroyers to attack until 7:21.

The first question is: How could the German battle cruisers really help the battle line to escape, except by offering themselves as targets for the British fire? How four terribly damaged battle cruisers could give appreciable support to a destroyer attack against 27 battleships is not clear. All they could do would be to draw the hostile fire on themselves rather than on their battleships. In this, we can see no possible object. If the British were certain to get some hits, it would be better for the Germans to take them on their battleships, which were practically undamaged, rather than on the badly damaged battle cruisers. Furthermore, the four remaining German battle cruisers were far more useful to them than an equal number of battleships. The fact that Scheer changed the order for Scouting Group I to attack regardless of consequences only one or two minutes later is a virtual admission that he had made a mistake. In our opinion, the order of 7:13 was a very serious mistake. It was wrong not only in this particular situation, but wrong in principle. However, we must again point out that errors at such a time as this were to be expected. No one can even imagine the strain under which Scheer acted during that period.

If Scheer thought the situation so desperate as to demand the virtual sacrifice of the battle cruisers at 7:13, why did he delay the signal for the turn of his battle line until about 7:18? Possibly the slowing of Battle Squadron III had thrown the van into such confusion that Scheer considered the battle turn impracticable until order was restored. Probably, the signal was delayed in transmission and was not executed until Scheer knew that it had been received by all ships of the battle line. Furthermore, it was highly important that all ships have a few minutes' warning in order to rectify their positions and to make their preparations to execute such a difficult and important signal. Everything considered, we believe that, if Scheer decided to reverse his course at 7:13, it was really very satisfactory to be able to execute the signal five minutes later. If the apparent delay was unfortunate, it was unavoidable and the inevitable result of Scheer's determination to attack the center of the British battle line in the way he had done.

It was likewise unfortunate that there were no destroyers immediately available for the purpose of covering the retirement of Scouting Group I and Battle Squadron III by means of a smoke screen. The *Rostock* was present; but Michelsen had sent Half Flotilla I to the *Lützow* and Half Flotilla V toward the *Wiesbaden*. The position of Half Flotilla VI is not stated, but it had probably followed Half Flotilla V in the direction of the *Wiesbaden*. Flotillas V and VII were far in the rear, where they could perform no useful functions. The Germans suffered heavily by the dispersion of their destroyers at this critical moment.

It is further noted that Scheer did not order the destroyers to attack until 7:21. Perhaps, he counted on their attacking without his orders. Perhaps, he even intercepted Heinrich's signal, and only sent his message to make sure that their attack would be pushed home.

It would seem that orders should have been issued at 7:13 in the following order of priority: (1) destroyers of the Scouting Forces to attack; (2) Scouting Group I to withdraw at full speed; (3) the battle line to reverse course; and (4) destroyers of the main body to cover the retirement of all capital ships, and in particular the battle cruisers, with smoke screens. All these measures should have been ordered as nearly simultaneously as possible by both radio and visual methods.

With these observations, let us now trace the execution of Scheer's withdrawal. At 7:13 the *Derfflinger* and *Seydlitz* were under a terrific concentration of fire. About 7:14 Scheer's signal came in to charge the enemy and to fight to the death. Hartog immediately repeated the signal and set the course SE. (122°). At 7:15 he signaled 23 knots (Fig. 44–T) and swung round to south (167°). The range to the 5th and 6th Divisions had decreased to 7,500 yards. Not even their stout armor can repulse 15-inch shells at this point-blank range. The death-ride has begun!

At 7:15 a 15-inch shell pierced the *Derfflinger's* "D" turret, coming through the roof (Fig. 44–V). It exploded among the busy gun crews. Its deadly, jagged fragments and splinters

mowed down the brave men who had fought so well under
Chief Gunner Arndt's effective leadership. Worst of all, two
powder charges were ignited. Terrible white-hot flames roared
through the turret and down the ammunition passages into the
handling-rooms. Fortunately, the magazine doors held tight and
repulsed the flames, thus saving the *Derfflinger* from the fate of
the three British battle cruisers. Of all that magnificent turret
crew of 75, only one was saved. Their deaths, if terrible, were
mercifully quick. We salute those brave sailors.

At 7:15 the High Seas Fleet received two other widely scattered hits. The *Helgoland*, way back in Squadron I, took one
(Fig. 44-x), while the *Lützow* received the other, bringing her
total to 24 (Fig. 44-y). The *Elbing* reported that a condenser
was leaking and that she could no longer run at high speed
(Fig. 44-u). Flotillas VI and IX near Scouting Group I were advancing to the attack.

As Scouting Group I turned in succession to a southerly
course, great projectiles struck its ships in rapid succession. At
7:16 the *Seydlitz* was hit aft by one and possibly two shells (Fig.
45-a). Between 7:16 and 7:22 the *Derfflinger* received about
three heavy hits, mostly from the *Colossus*. One of them was a
massive 15-inch shell that exploded under the bridge. Great
sheets of deck plating were hurled into the air. A roaring fire
played through the wierdly twisted mass of wreckage. The
6-inch gun crews tried to subdue the raging flames while two
other projectiles crashed through the stacks and exploded on the
water line, scattering a rain of steel through their ranks. At
7:19 the *Von der Tann* was hit on her after conning tower (Fig.
45-m). Splinters poured through the slits and killed all inside.
About 7:20 she avoided a torpedo (Fig. 45-s) fired by the *Revenge* at 7:15 (Fig. 44-z). Incidentally, at 7:16 the *Derfflinger*
had herself fired a torpedo (Fig. 45-b). This cannot be identified
in British accounts.

At 7:23 the *Derfflinger* was hit twice, bringing her total since
7:04 to 7 (Fig. 45-q). The first shell, 15 inches in caliber, penetrated the port quarter of "C" turret barbette and exploded
under the guns. No less than ten powder charges were ignited

in the turret and handling-rooms. Five men, badly burned, saved themselves through the opening left for throwing out the empty cartridge cases. The other 73 died at their posts. With his men stayed the brave turret commander, Lieutenant von Boltenstern. Again, the tight-fitting magazine doors prevented an explosion.

The second hit at the time was by a 12-inch shell that struck the curved surface of the conning tower. It rocked and vibrated under the terrific impact as though in an earthquake. Officers and men were hurled about like puppets. The navigator and several men were wounded by the sharp steel splinters that flew through the eye slits. Fortunately for the *Derfflinger,* the shell was repulsed by her stout armor and exploded outside. The greenish-yellow gases generated by the bursting charge filtered into the conning tower. The control party saved their lives by quickly donning their ever-ready gas masks, but that made their work more difficult.

By that time, two casualties compelled von Hase to assume direct and complete control over his main battery. All voice tubes and telephones leading to the foretop had been cut. The chief spotter, whose excellent observation of the fall of the *Derfflinger's* salvos had contributed so much to her successes, could no longer control the fire of his guns, so excellent Lieutenant von Stosch now remained a silent spectator of the remainder of the fight. The second casualty was the entry of gas into the range transmitting room in the bowels of the ship. That deprived von Hase of all the complicated fire-control equipment below and left him only a single telephone for communicating his battle orders, ranges, and deflections to the two remaining turrets. Still he had to do something and do that quickly; for, as he looked aft, a terrible picture met his eyes. "From both after turrets great flames were now spurting, mingled with clouds of yellow smoke, two ghastly pyres."

But what could four guns and their tired crews do when it was impossible even to see the enemy through the thickening mist and smoke?

I looked through my periscope toward the enemy. Their salvos were still bursting around us, but we could see nothing of the enemy, who were disposed in a great semi-circle round us. All we could see were the great reddish-gold flames spurting from their guns. The ship's hulls we saw but seldom. Without much hope of hurting the enemy, I ordered the two forward turrets to fire salvo after salvo. I could feel that the fire soothed the nerves of our men. If we had ceased firing at this time, the whole crew would have been overwhelmed by despair. But as long as we were firing, things could not be so bad.

The situation as pictured by von Hase was the same throughout the rest of the High Seas Fleet. The visibility conditions at that time were highly unfavorable to them, a fact admitted even by the British. That condition might have been due to the visibility itself, which was different in different directions. Possibly, it was better toward the setting sun than away from it. Most probably, it was due to the fact that the Germans were in the weather position, *i.e.*, toward the wind. Thus, all the smoke and gases from the stacks, guns, and fires drifted in front of their telescopes and range finders. On the other hand, the smoke from the British ships blew clear. Also, the Germans used coal to a greater extent than the British did and that made much more smoke, particularly when proceeding at high speed.

At 7:17 Hartog had received Scheer's signal to operate against the enemy's van. As that was exactly what he had been doing since 7:15, no further action on his part was required. At 7:20 Hartog changed course very gradually away from the enemy (Fig 45–N).

It was between 7:16 and 7:18 when Scheer executed his *Gefechtskehrtwendung*. By the *König's* log, that maneuver was timed at 7:16, but the signal log of the *Friedrich der Grosse* records it at 7:18. The latter time was probably correct. The maneuver (Fig 45–I) was particularly difficult because of the crowding of the ships of Battle Squadron III, the failure of the *Markgraf's* engines, and the number of hits received just as the maneuver was about to commence. Just at 7:18 the *Grosser Kurfürst* received four hits and the *König* one Figs. (45–J and K). The maneuver was further complicated by the fact that some ships waited, as required by the instructions, for the ships next astern to commence to turn, while others turned immediately because of the gravity of the situation.

Let us now see how the turn was made by the ships of Squadron III. The *Kaiserin*, the rear ship, was well out of position before the turn was even started. She had closed up rapidly on the *Prinz Regent Luitpold* when Behncke had slowed. Even though she had virtually stopped, it was necessary for her to sheer out to starboard. That made the turn particularly difficult for her. The *Kaiser*, leading Division VI, seems to have had no special difficulty. The *Kronprinz* was much hindered by the *Markgraf*, next ship ahead of her, commencing the turn immediately upon the execution of the signal. The *Kronprinz*, therefore, had to delay her turn until she could clear the *Markgraf*. She just avoided a number of salvos. The *Markgraf* was hindered in making the turn by the fact that her port engine was still out of action. Captain Seiferling believed that he must get clear of his division in order to avoid collision. Thus, instead of completing the turn with the proper amount of rudder, he steadied for a time on course SW. (212°). That, in turn, made it difficult for the *Grosser Kurfürst* which, as above related, had just received 4 hits in rapid succession (Fig. 45–J) at 7:18, as the maneuver began. While turning, the heavy concentration of fire continued and probably the *Grosser Kurfürst* received 3 more hits, bringing her total to 8, of which 3 had been on the water line forward. Through these shell holes water had entered in such great quantities that the entire forward part of the ship was now filled up to the main deck. Another hit had caused many of the port coal bunkers and double bottoms to fill with water, giving the ship a 4-degree list to port. In that critical condition, it was necessary to parallel the course of the *Markgraf* for a time before completing the turn.

As above related, the *König* had received a hit at 7:18, abaft "C" turret. Previous hits and counter-flooding had put the ship down by the head. There were 1,600 tons of water in the hull. Due to her radio having been destroyed the *König* did not receive the order to turn; but, as Behncke had already turned her to a southerly course to bring her battery to bear, it was easy for her to follow the other ships during the reversal of course. Captain Brüninghaus took station about 400 yards north of the formation and laid a smoke screen to cover it from the British fire. The southwesterly breeze blew the smoke toward the enemy and saved the *König* from further hits.

As Half Flotilla V returned from its attempt to save the crew of the *Wiesbaden*, it passed through the close formation of Battle Squadron III, probably adding to its difficulties. There is no mention of a smoke screen by these destroyers, though that would have been most effective in relieving the concentration on the battleships. The latter were for some time in a most critical situation, steaming slowly along in line of bearing formation. Fortunately, for a reason we shall soon see, the British fire had now decreased in both volume and effectiveness. This was about 7:20 P.M.

Having thus followed Battle Squadron III through its turn, let us observe how Scheer's signal was executed by Battle Squadron I. That unit seems to have been steaming at normal speed and at proper distances when the turn was commenced. Behncke's reduction of speed apparently had not yet reached Battle Squadron I. Vice Admiral Schmidt decided that in the existing critical situation he could not afford to wait for the ships at the rear to commence turning first and execute the maneuver as a ripple movement. If that method were used, it might well cause an interval of several minutes to elapse between the time of turning of the first (rear) ship and of the last (leading) ship. The fates of empires hung on minutes now and instructions had properly to go before the weight of cold hard facts. So Schmidt turned his flagship, the *Ostfriesland,* immediately upon the execution of the signal. In order to make room for the crowded ships ahead, Scheer directed Captain Fuchs of the *Friedrich der Grosse* to make the turn to port instead of to starboard. These two departures from the set methods helped the Fleet to escape from a critical situation. "Once again," says Groos, "it was due to the brilliant seamanship and training of the admirals and commanding officers that neither the turn of the fleet flagship to port was misunderstood nor collisions resulted." If the British light forces had shown marvelous seamanship at "Windy Corner," here the German battle line gave an even more remarkable performance. No praise is too high for the superb ship handling in this highly difficult and critical situation. Those long years of intensive peace-time training were now paying dividends.

At 7:22 Scheer signaled for course west (257°). The British fire was declining. However, at 7:25 a chance salvo landed about the *Kaiser* (Fig. 45–U). Fortunately, there was only one direct hit, which pierced the casemate armor. Fragments of shells that burst alongside wrecked the torpedo nets and riddled the living quarters. As the *Kaiser* received two hits in all, it is probable that the other landed about this time. At 7:27 Scheer ordered course SW. (212°) and increased speed to 17 knots. Battle Squadrons II and I took up the new course and formed column. However, Battle Squadron III continued on course west (257°) in line of bearing formation. Except for a narrowly averted collision between the *Kaiserin* and *Prinz Regent Luitpold*, this squadron, much assisted by the increase in speed to 17 knots, was quickly regaining its formation. It formed as follows: *Prinz Regent Luitpold, Kaiserin, Kaiser, Markgraf, Kronprinz, Grosser Kurfürst, König.* It will be noted that the *Prinz Regent Luitpold* and *Kaiserin* had changed places, also the *Markgraf* and *Kronprinz*. Battle Squadron III was now quite some distance from the *Friedrich der Grosse.*

We have noted that the *Derfflinger* received her two last hits at 7:23. Just at that time, Captain Hartog turned Scouting Group I away about two points together (Fig. 45–Q). About that time, his ship came behind the smoke of Flotillas VI and IX as they advanced to the attack. Beatty, however, was still able to bring some fire on the rest of the group. At 7:27 Scouting Group I turned away again to about 245° without signal (Fig. 45–AA). At that instant, the *Seydlitz* was hit twice. The right gun of her after turret was damaged and one 5.9-inch gun was put out of action. The *Markgraf* received the last hit of this phase of the action at 7:35, a 5.9-inch casemate being destroyed. That brought her total hits to 5 and the total received by all ships during this period to 28, agreeing with British claims. At last, the gallant battle cruisers of Scouting Group I and the battleships of Squadron III had gained a well-deserved security behind the clouds of smoke pouring from the stacks of Flotillas VI and IX, whose exploits we will soon recount.

To lay the background for the recital, we must first trace the movements of the Grand Fleet between 7:12 and 7:20 P.M. We have told how the majority of the battleships opened fire with considerable effect, beginning at 7:12. A glance at Fig. 44 will show the truly remarkable situation that existed. A fleet in action should have the line of bearing of its battle line at right angles to the bearing of the enemy. Scheer's line of bearing, on the contrary, was parallel to the bearing of the enemy. Thus, he was in the worst possible situation. The British formation, while not so bad as the German, was far from perfect. It made an angle of about 45 degrees with the bearing of the enemy. The danger of the situation to the British will be evident if we suppose that at 7:15 the Germans were to change course in succession to the northward. Then, a short run would have permitted them to enfilade the western flank of the British battle line, concentrating Battle Squadrons III and I on the 6th Division and the 5th Battle Squadron.

It was not until 7:12 that Jellicoe could determine the true bearing of the enemy by direct visual contact. That quickly determined him to rotate his battle front to the right to south (167°). He decided to form all six divisions on that course, using the 3d Division as the base unit for the maneuver. At 7:12 he ordered the 1st Battle Squadron to take station in rear of the 4th. About one minute later, Vice Admiral Sturdee, who was leading the 4th Division in the *Benbow*, turned eastward by subdivisions (Fig. 44–s) to avoid the threat of torpedoes fired by Half Flotilla V about 7:10 (Fig. 44–o). Sturdee then took station in rear of the 3d Division. That maneuver fitted in perfectly with Jellicoe's order for the 1st Battle Squadron to form astern of the 4th.

At 7:16 Jellicoe, in furtherance of his plan to rotate the battle front, directed the 2d Battle Squadron to take station ahead of the 4th. No immediate action by the 1st and 2d Battle Squadrons resulted from Jellicoe's signals of 7:12 and 7:16, except that at 7:18 the 6th Division changed course somewhat to port (Fig. 45–L). The 5th Division held its course though threatened by the torpedoes fired by Half Flotilla V. As that flotilla turned back from its mission to save the crew of the *Wiesbaden* under very heavy British fire, the *V73* had fired one torpedo and the *G88* three (Fig. 44–O). Three of the torpedoes were narrowly avoided by the *Neptune* of the 5th Division by maneuvering at 7:17 (Fig. 45–D). At the same time several salvos from the *Seydlitz* straddled the *Colossus* (Fig. 45–G). They caused two direct hits, while fragments from two other projectiles that burst short on contact with the water hailed over the ship. Those 11-inch hits did comparatively little damage, wounding only five men. No other hits were received by any British capital ships during the period. The fourth torpedo fired by Half Flotilla V was avoided by the *Barham* at 7:18 (Fig. 45–H). It passed just ahead. Half Flotilla V really had an excellent opportunity for torpedo fire. An attack mission at that time would have had a much more favorable effect on the course of the battle than the task of rescuing the crew of a totally crippled ship. It is unfortunate that Gautier did not change his mission when he saw the excellent opportunity that was presented. Destroyer commanders should always consider that torpedo fire at capital ships is their permanent mission and this should take absolute priority over all other missions assigned when really favorable opportunities for attack are presented. Senior commanders should indoctrinate their destroyers to this effect and give them full freedom of action. We commend heartily the captains of the *V73* and *G88* for firing torpedoes on their own initiative in this situation.

At 7:18 Jellicoe, evidently impatient at the lack of action by the 2d Battle Squadron in obeying his signal, ordered Jerram to "increase speed of engines" and to "proceed at utmost speed." Apparently, in order to allow Jerram to sheer in ahead of the *Iron Duke,* Jellicoe reduced the speed of the battle line to 15 knots at 7:20. Up to this time the British fire had gradually reached its maximum effectiveness. Ship after ship of the battle line had joined the fight. The 5th Battle Squadron had re-entered the fight at 7:17 (Fig. 45–F). The visibility had become very favorable for the 2d Battle Squadron on the eastern flank of the British line. Despite the fact that the unit was at a comparatively greater distance from the enemy than the 1st and 4th Battle Squadrons, it had begun to fire with effect at ranges from 16,000 to 18,000 yards. Beatty, realizing at last that he was far out of the fight, had increased speed to 22 knots (Fig. 44–w) at 7:12 to close to more decisive ranges. At 7:17 his ships commenced firing (Fig. 45–E). Thus, virtually all the 33 British capital ships present were in the fight. As we have seen, the Germans were unable to make any effective reply to this terrific concentration of fire. The crisis of the greatest sea battle of history had been reached!

CHAPTER XVII

THE GERMAN DESTROYERS ATTACK
7:20 P.M. TO 8:00 P.M.

JELLICOE's attention was now focused upon the German destroyers, which were advancing in a most menacing manner. What the British commander in chief had long expected was about to take place. Before we relate Jellicoe's reaction to this threat, we must tell how the Germans conducted their famous torpedo attack. Could a few little destroyers cover the retreat of the High Seas Fleet and prevent the pursuit which, if pushed relentlessly, must result in its virtual annihilation?

We have seen that Michelsen had ordered Flotilla III to proceed to the rescue of the *Wiesbaden's* crew, and that the flotilla commander had sent Half Flotilla V, consisting of the *V71*, *V73*, and *G88*, on that mission. There remained of this flotilla, therefore, only the *S53*, the flotilla flag boat, the *S54*, and the *G42*. Michelsen had ordered Half Flotilla I to proceed to the *Lützow*. His two remaining flotillas, V and VII, were still far in the rear. The reason for their absence from the van is not clear when we consider the desperate character of Scheer's deliberate thrust against the center of the British battle line and the degree to which he depended upon his destroyers for the accomplishment of his purpose.

This unfortunate disposition of the flotillas of the main body compelled Heinrich to make at least the first and most important attacks with the destroyer flotillas of the scouting forces. These, as we know, were Flotillas II, VI,, and IX. Flotilla II consisted of ten very large destroyers. Most of them had been in the one-sided engagement with the *Shark's* division and a few had participated at long range in the destroyer action of 4:30; but, as Groos says, "they still had all their torpedoes," except for a few fired at the British destroyers. It is a curious fact that there is on record no signal ordering Flotilla II to attack, though such signals were sent to Flotillas VI and IX. It is said that Captain Schuur endeavored to attack, but was prevented from doing so by a long series of difficulties. The excuses offered are not entirely convincing and the failure of the destroyers to attack was, to say the least, unfortunate, particularly as three boats of Flotilla VI remained with them.

Therefore, there remained for the first two waves of attack only Flotillas VI and IX, and even the full strength of these flotillas was not available. Flotilla VI had consisted originally of the flag boat, the *G41*, Half Flotilla XI of three boats, and Half Flotilla XII of five boats. Of the latter, however, the *V45* and *G37* had, by Michelsen's orders, joined the *Lützow*. The *V69*, *V46*, and *S50*, most unfortunately, remained with Flotilla II. There remained, therefore, only the *G41*, flag boat of Commander Max Schultz, the *V44*, flag boat of Lieutenant Commander Rümann, the *G86*, and the *G87*. These four boats had been in both the 5:00 P.M. and 6:00 P.M. attacks and had fired some of their torpedoes. Flotilla IX, having lost the *V27* and *V29* in the 4:30 attack, mustered now nine boats. These also had expended a part of their torpedoes.

As a third attacking wave, there was available Flotilla III. While that flotilla originally had consisted of seven boats, the *V48* had remained between the lines and the *G42* had not rejoined since the advance toward the *Wiesbaden*. The remaining five boats had taken part in heavy fighting and had fired some of their torpedoes.

It was 7:15 when Heinrich, in the *Regensburg*, led out Flotilla IX and Half Flotilla XI (of Flotilla VI) to attack. It was done entirely on his own initiative. He thought that the attack of his destroyers would be the only means of saving the van units of the Fleet from the heavy concentration of enemy fire. His decision, made 6 minutes in advance of Scheer's orders, will make Heinrich's name forever memorable as a destroyer commander. It contributed largely to saving the High Seas Fleet from very serious losses. As the *Regensburg* reached the *Derfflinger*, she turned back under a very heavy fire to bring up Flotilla II. That was the proper duty of the second leader of destroyers. He could have accomplished nothing by proceeding with the attacking waves of destroyers; he would serve now as a rallying point after the attack.

It was gallant Commander Max Schultz who led the German destroyer attack, in the *G41*, flag boat of Flotilla VI. After him in the usual German "V" formation came Half Flotilla XI: the *V44*, *G87*, and *G86*. Almost immediately, Schultz came under a heavy fire from the British battle line. It was 7:16 when the *Royal Oak* opened fire with her secondary battery broadside of seven 6-inch guns. Two minutes later, the *Agincourt* commenced a very accurate fire from ten 6-inch guns, the heaviest secondary battery in either fleet. The *Marlborough* joined at 7:19 at about 11,000 yards. One minute later the *Temeraire* followed at 9,000 yards, while about the same time the *Vanguard* fired with her main battery of 12-inch guns.

The handful of German destroyers advanced with magnificent gallantry through the terrific barrage. About 7:20 the first shell struck the *G41* forward; it killed two officers and two men on her bridge. Shortly afterward a heavy shell, probably from the *Vanguard*, exploded on the water close ahead of the *G86*. Her captain, Lieutenant Commander Grimm, and nine men were wounded. Considerable injuries were inflicted on the *G86* by the fragments of the shell, including damage to one torpedo. Many more of the British ships now joined in the barrage, so Schultz turned away. Lieutenant Wagner, torpedo officer of the *G41*, though mortally wounded, personally fired two torpedoes with his last remaining strength, a deed of heroism to be treasured by every member of the naval profession. Each of the other boats fired three torpedoes (Fig. 45–R). They seem to have been aimed at the van of the British battle line. The time of firing we calculate to have been between 7:22 and 7:24. The range to the nearest British battleships was about 7,500 yards.

After firing 11 torpedoes, the four destroyers withdrew under cover of a dense smoke screen. However, that did not seem to protect them from the 4th Light Cruiser Squadron, which fired on them heavily at 9,000 yards (Fig. 45–T). The *G41* and *G86* were forced to reduce speed below 25 knots because of their injuries.

Flotilla IX, nine boats strong, advanced under the cover of the smoke laid by Half Flotilla XI. About 7:23 Commander Goehle, in the *V28*, came through the screen. A heavy fire was immediately concentrated on his flotilla. The flag boat was hit near the bow. That shell made a large hole just above the water line. About 7:25 Goehle turned to the southward. Between 7:26 and 7:28 his flotilla fired 18 torpedoes, followed by 2 more about 7:30 (Fig. 45–v). These times are calculated principally from the times at which it is known that the torpedoes passed through the British line. The very heavy fire literally deluged the boats at a range of about 7,000 yards. Considerable loss was experienced and the formation of the flotilla was in consequence quite irregular. Thus, the *S51*, *S36*, and *V28* were able to fire only 1 torpedo each. The *V26* fired 2, while the *S52*, *V30*, *S34*, *S33* and *S35* fired 3 each. The 20 torpedoes were directed mostly at the 6th Division, although a few were pointed toward the 5th.

Gallant Flotilla IX paid in full for its splendid attack. The *S35* was hit by a heavy shell. She broke in two and sank almost immediately. Unfortunately, it was the *S35*, under brave Lieutenant Commander Ihm, that had rescued part of the crew of the *V29*. Every one of the brave men on board was lost. The *S51* received a hit that put one boiler and the steering engine out of commission. As the *V28*, due to her injuries, could make only 17 knots, Goehle, the flotilla commander, turned the command over to Commander Tillessen. The flotilla withdrew under cover of a heavy smoke screen without further injuries. To see with what resolution the torpedo attacks were delivered, it will be noted that out of 13 boats participating one had been sunk and four seriously damaged.

Let us now see what answer the Grand Fleet made to the well-executed attacks that sent 31 torpedoes toward their battle line. As stated before, the effectiveness of the British fire on the German capital ships reached its maximum about 7:20. From that time on its volume and effectiveness declined sharply. There were a number of reasons for this. (1) The German battle line turned away. This radical change of course increased the difficulties of the British fire-control parties; and, after the turn was completed, the range increased rapidly. (2) The German battle cruisers, beginning about 7:20, made several turns away together. (3) Smoke from the approaching destroyers and the *König*, blown before the southwesterly breeze, began to obscure the range. (4) The Battle Fleet was beginning to fire on the German destroyers.

There were to be added two additional reasons for the rapid decrease in the British fire. It will be remembered that Jellicoe at 7:12 had ordered the 1st Battle Squadron to take station astern of the 4th, while at 7:16 the 2d had been ordered to take station ahead. By 7:20 nothing had been done toward the execution of those orders, except that at 7:18 the 6th Division had made a slight change of course to the eastward. The commander of the 2d Battle Squadron, in the van, apparently felt that he could not change course until he had gained the necessary distance to the front. That Jellicoe realized his difficulty is shown by his signal at 7:18 for the 2d Battle Squadron to proceed at utmost speed; but, as long as the 4th Battle Squadron kept on at 17 knots, it was evident that it would take many minutes for Jerram, who was probably making 18 or 19 knots, to gain the necessary distance. Therefore, at 7:20 Jellicoe had decreased the speed to 15 knots to allow the battle line to remedy its confused and irregular formation. However, the remedy in this case was about as bad as the disease, as a change of speed in a battle line of 24 ships is almost certain to cause great difficulties in keeping proper stations.

Already the British commander in chief had been considering possible maneuvers to avoid the German torpedoes. The methods to be employed had been carefully analyzed in advance, as great weight had been given to the well-known efficiency of the German torpedo service. At 7:21 Jellicoe considered that the first wave of the German destroyers, Half Flotilla XI, had reached a menacing position for torpedo fire. While desiring to turn the entire battle line away from this menace, he felt that this would create a danger of collision between the 2d and 3d Divisions; so he ordered the 2d Battle Squadron to go ships left four points together. A minute later he ordered all battle squadrons and attached cruisers to go left two points by subdivisions. That created a most confused situation when considered in conjunction with previous signals. Here are a few questions that might be asked:

First, should the 2d Battle Squadron, having just turned ships left four points, now turn two points more by subdivisions? Did the previous order to take station ahead still hold?

Second, should the 1st Battle Squadron still obey the order to take station astern of the 4th?

The situation was not improved by a new signal at 7:25 for the entire Battle Fleet to go left two more points by subdivisions. In that confusing tactical situation, Jellicoe was well served by his division commanders. They brought the battle line into order despite his confusing and conflicting signals. In fact, it was only the 4th Battle Squadron, under his own personal command, that was maneuvered in accordance with the signals. Jerram, in the van, rightly guessed that, having turned four points away at 7:21, neither the 7:22 nor 7:25 signals applied to him, although his squadron was included in the address. Curiously enough, Jerram now signaled for the 2d Battle Squadron to go ships right four points, forming the 1st and 2d Divisions into column on course south (167°) (Fig. 45–w). At first glance this would appear to have been an example of splendid initiative on the part of Jerram and a desire to regain touch with the enemy, his squadrons never having been in any real danger from the torpedoes. Unfortunately, he states that the "*King George V* had to alter course to starboard to avert collision with light craft in the van." The "light craft" in question was the 2d Cruiser Squadron, which had been so late in reaching the scene of action. It now served the useful purpose of driving the British van toward the enemy, an evolution that was essential if the enemy were ever to be re-engaged before dark.

Let us describe the handling of the 1st Battle Squadron. When the 7:22 signal was executed, the 5th Division turned its subdivisions left about six points instead of the two ordered

(Fig. 45-0). Evidently, Rear Admiral Gaunt believed that he should get in rear of the 4th Battle Squadron as quickly as possible. Possibly, he saw that the brunt of the torpedo attack would fall upon the rear of the British line and thought it well to get clear by a maneuver much more radical than that ordered for the entire Fleet. He did not execute the 7:25 signal. Instead, at 7:27 he turned his subdivisions right and formed column in rear of the 3d Division (Fig. 45–x). By 7:22 the 6th Division had turned about two points away from the enemy, so Burney did not turn farther to the left. He did, however, divide his division into two subdivisions (Fig. 45–P). That apparently was merely an attempt to comply with orders, as it afforded no advantage whatever and, in fact, was a useless maneuver. Burney did not execute the 7:25 signal. However, two minutes later he followed the example of Gaunt and formed in single column in rear of the 4th Division. Evidently, both these admirals believed that the order to follow the 4th Battle Squadron still held good. Both, we believe, correctly interpreted Jellicoe's vaguely expressed wishes and handled their divisions with excellent judgment. Naturally, these various maneuvers greatly interfered with the fire control of the battleships and increased the range to the enemy. Effective fire on the Germans was impossible under such conditions, even if the Germans had not turned so sharply away from the Grand Fleet.

By his turn of the battle line away from the enemy, Jellicoe had used one of the standard methods of avoiding torpedo salvos or of minimizing their effect. Another method would have been to send out his own light cruisers and destroyers to repulse the attack. At 7:30 the 3d Light Cruiser Squadron was in an excellent position to perform this duty without in any way interfering with the fire of the capital ships. Beatty issued no order to Napier. Napier says: "Being ahead of our Battle Cruisers we kept that position." The 4th Light Cruiser Squadron was also well situated, but was in the line of fire of the battle cruisers. Le Mesurier was eager to act on his own initiative, but was hampered by conflicting signals from Jellicoe. At 7:22, just as the first turn away was being executed, Jellicoe had ordered the 4th Light Cruiser Squadron to "prepare to attack torpedo vessels of enemy. Proceed at your utmost speed." That was a very puzzling signal to receive, as Le Mesurier was already firing on the German destroyers. Why Jellicoe should have used the word "prepare" at such a time is rather difficult to conceive. One minute after that signal, that is, at 7:23, Jellicoe directed the 4th Light Cruiser Squadron not to get in the line of fire of the battle cruisers. Presumably, that instruction also would apply to the British battleships, but Le Mesurier evidently did not construe it that way, for at 7:25 he went ships right 90° toward the enemy (Fig. 45–T). That was an excellent move, as it allowed the light cruisers to pursue Half Flotilla XI as it withdrew, but it did throw them in the line of fire of the 1st Division. It actually had no disadvantage, as the turn away had made the fire of the leading battleships entirely ineffective at the time. At 7:26 Commodore Hawksley followed the example of Le Mesurier by ordering half of his 11th Flotilla to attack the German destroyers. That unit joined the 4th Light Cruiser Squadron and entered the fight at long range.

Jellicoe's turn away from the German destroyers has caused many interesting comments from naval critics. To offer a fair comment, we must place ourselves in Jellicoe's position. He had just received word that the *Marlborough* had been hit by a torpedo. Numerous reports of submarines had been coming in from all directions. Some ships had even been firing at imaginary periscopes. It is true that when the situation is analyzed, it can be shown that under the conditions of this action any important submarine operations were highly improbable. Nevertheless, many high commanders were fully convinced that large numbers of submarines were on the battlefield. Having passed the wreck of a great ship, Jellicoe had received the melancholy news that it was the *Invincible*. What more logical for him to assume than that she had fallen victim to one of the submarines? We cannot blame Jellicoe too much for turning away from the German destroyers. He was a cautious commander, who had convinced himself that he could control the naval situation without running any risks. To turn away from the evident menace was surely the safest course of action. He had told the Admiralty that he would play the game safe. It had agreed with his cautious attitude. It got from the Grand Fleet exactly the kind of a battle he had told the members they would get—to the last detail. If that was not what the situation demanded, the fault lies with the Admiralty, not with Jellicoe. If the Admiralty desired to carry on a Nelsonian plan of campaign, it should have relieved Jellicoe upon the receipt of his letter of October 30, 1914, and Sir Roger Keyes should have been appointed to the command.

Personally, we believe that the whole attitude of the British Navy had changed since the days of Drake, Hawke, Jervis, Nelson, and Cornwallis. Then it was young; now it had grown old. In the old days, England was a small country fighting for its place in the sun. Its policy was aggressive. Its statesmen, soldiers, and sailors were willing to take their chances. When they won, they doubled the stakes and gambled again. Now, the British Empire covered the globe. Its task was not to get more, but to hold what it had. Its national policy was defensive, rather than offensive. That affected its naval strategy and tactics and turned the British Navy to thoughts of defense, rather than of offense. That attitude was, we suggest, given a powerful impetus by the writings of Sir Julian Corbett. As historian of the old days, he praised to the skies the daring of Drake and Cornwallis, but then developed for modern times a system by which it was no longer necessary to defeat the enemy. All that was required was that he be kept from coming out too far. It was Nelson's idea to lure out the enemy and then annihilate him. In the World War, it was hoped that the enemy would stay just as close to home as possible. When he came out to a great distance, he was to be opposed by a greatly superior force which would maneuver against him and push him back "without leaving something to chance." If everything was just right for the Grand Fleet, it would try to damage the enemy to the extent that it could be done without running any risks. As will be shown later, that policy did not change after Jutland and actually became less aggressive.

Personally, we do not concur in the new system of British

strategy ushered in by the facile pen of Sir Julian Corbett; nor do we believe that such a cautious, even Fabian, attitude as was shown by the Grand Fleet in the field of tactics was warranted by the situation. We suggest that Jellicoe should have headed in division column directly for the area in which the Germans had fired their torpedoes. To present one's bows to the approaching torpedoes is one of the most certain methods of avoiding hits. In a line of division columns, the individual ships have every opportunity of maneuvering to avoid torpedoes when sighted closed aboard. As the German boats occupied a comparatively small area there was little chance that the torpedo salvos would make a criss-cross pattern, which is so dangerous to a battleship formation. The light cruisers and destroyers on the battle flanks should have been pushed well forward to engage the German destroyers.

By that procedure, it is probable that the British battleships would have received some torpedo hits. As we know the situation now, we do not believe it probable that over 2 of the 31 torpedoes fired would have hit. That, however, is arguing from hindsight. Let us try to reconstruct the situation as Jellicoe might have estimated it. He could tell that about 13 destroyers had attacked. To allow 4 torpedoes for each destroyer would be a most liberal estimate, as the Germans had a maximum of five torpedo tubes bearing on one broadside. That made a total of 52 torpedoes. One could count on at least 4 erratic runs out of 5 shots. For ships approaching bows on, or nearly so, 1 hit in 8 would be a very liberal percentage of hits. Take 6 hits, therefore, each of which might do about as much damage as the actual hit on the *Marlborough*. That torpedo, in fact, did an unusual amount of damage. Let us say that those 6 hits would cause three ships to fall out of the line and that one of the three ships would sink. Was this too much to pay for 15 minutes of fire on the German battleships that he knew were being heavily hit while engaged in a difficult maneuver?

Of course, there were other German destroyers and they would have attacked after a time; but the later decisions could have been based on the results of the first attack. At any time, if

Jellicoe saw that the cost of his pursuit was becoming too heavy; it was his option to haul off. However, there are two points that must be considered as very favorable to the British. (1) Every German ship whose speed was reduced was certain to be destroyed, while that was not the case for British ships. (2) The British had an overwhelming destroyer force available for night attacks, which must be very effective against even slightly damaged ships and the German second-line battleships, while the German destroyers would have expended all their torpedoes and would have become disorganized as a result of their day-time attacks. The British have become accustomed to talking about the failing light at 7:20. Actually, the sun set at 8:19 and, as we shall show, it was still light enough to fight at 9:00. Therefore, this illusion had better be forgotten. There were still 100 minutes of fighting time at 7:20 P.M.

There is one more question that it might be appropriate to raise at this time. The principal weapon that the Grand Fleet had to fear was the German destroyer force. Here was a time to find out whether that fear was real or imaginary. Here was a chance to substitute for theory some practical experience in countering those dreaded torpedo attacks. Would it not be worth, let us say, two battleships to find out what the Germans could do and to get some actual experience? The attack of 13 boats could not possibly endanger Jellicoe's naval supremacy. It was a perfect opportunity for an experiment, if nothing more. If the danger of the attacks should prove more imaginary than real, that was well worth knowing. If the attacks were really effective, that also was worth knowing. Two ships would be a cheap price for definitely removing that one large question mark from the problem of naval tactics.

These comments must be construed as applicable only to the Battle of Jutland and the situation of 1916. They by no means indicate that in a similar situation in a future war battleships should necessarily turn into a powerful destroyer formation. That is an entirely different question, to be judged on its merits in every particular case.

Meanwhile, Scheer at 7:21 had ordered all flotillas to attack

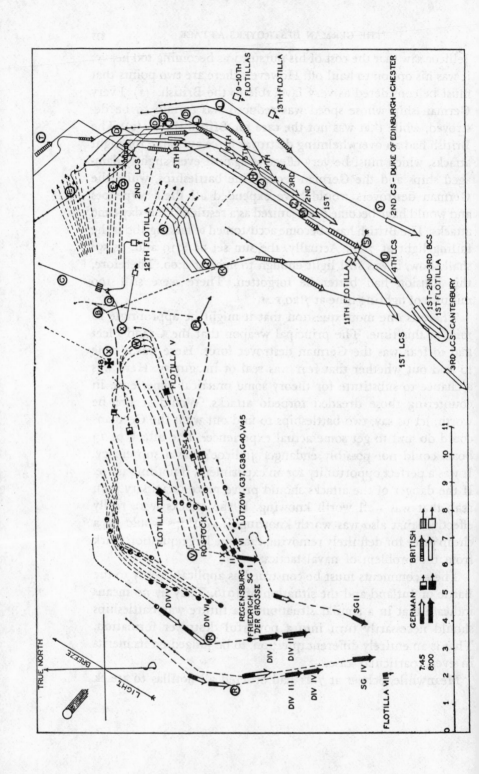

TRUE NORTH

BREEZE

LIGHT

7:45
8:00

GERMAN

BRITISH

FLOTILLA VIII

SG IV

DIV III
DIV IV

DIV I
DIV II

SG II

FRIEDRICH DER GROSSE SG I
REGENSBURG

DIV VI
DIV V

FLOTILLA III

ROSTOCK

LÜTZOW, G37, G38, G40, V45

SS54

FLOTILLA V

V48

1ST LCS

11TH FLOTILLA

12TH FLOTILLA

2ND LCS

5TH BS

9-10TH FLOTILLAS

13TH FLOTILLA

1ST
2ND
3RD
4TH
5TH

4TH LCS

1ST-2ND-3RD BCS

1ST-2ND-3RD BCS
1ST FLOTILLA
1ST-2ND-3RD FLOTILLA

3RD LCS-CANTERBURY

2ND CS - DUKE OF EDINBURGH-CHESTER

0 1 2 3 4 5 6 7 8 9 10 11

and Michelsen had repeated the order to them. Flotilla III had passed through Division V and was advancing as a third wave of attack, five boats strong. At 7:30 it passed through the smoke made by Half Flotilla XI and Flotilla IX. Flotilla V was also coming from the rear of the line. Flotilla II had given up the idea of attacking but, if Jellicoe had pressed his advance indefinitely, he must have eventually dealt with that flotilla. Before we relate the experiences of these later attacking waves, let us return to the Grand Fleet and see how its units avoided the 31 torpedoes that were approaching it.

As will be remembered, the 11 torpedoes fired by Half Flotilla XI seem to have been directed at the van of the British battle line. Just as they were fired, about 7:22 to 7:24, the leading battle squadron had turned away four points. That seems to have taken its ships beyond the range of the German torpedoes. In fact, they must have run 12,000 to 13,000 yards to have reached the 2d Battle Squadron. Eight of the 11 torpedoes fired by Half Flotilla XI were sighted by British vessels. Beginning about 7:30, 6 torpedoes passed through or ahead of the 4th Light Cruiser Squadron in the course of five minutes (Fig. 46–A). A seventh at 7:35 was sighted by the destroyer *Oak* as it passed at slow speed about 200 yards ahead of the *Iron Duke* (Fig. 46–G). About the same time the *Inflexible* sighted a torpedo passing about 150 yards astern (Fig. 46–H). It will be seen that those torpedoes did not greatly endanger any capital ship.

The torpedoes fired by Flotilla IX, 20 in all, seem to have been directed toward the rear of the battle line. The 5th and 6th Divisions were not only at the closest range, but when the torpedoes were fired they turned slightly towards them, rather than away, as did the 2d Battle Squadron in the van. No less than nine tracks were sighted by the 6th Division (Fig. 46–F), while the 5th Division saw three more (Fig 46–E). Fortunately, both these divisions were quite separated from the remainder of the battle line at that time and had ample room for individual ships to make radical maneuvers. Two other torpedoes fired by the boats of Flotilla IX were probably those sighted by the *Revenge* at 7:43 (Fig. 46–O). If this be the case, we can account for 14 of the 20 torpedoes fired. The remainder probably ran between the 6th Division and the 5th Battle Squadron.

We shall describe in some detail the methods used by the British battleships in dodging the German destroyers. The 5th and 6th Divisions were steering courses nearly at right angles to the tracks of the torpedoes and that made it necessary to maneuver radically to avoid being hit when the torpedo tracks were sighted. At 7:35 the *Colossus* (Fig. 46–E), leading the 5th Division, sighted a torpedo approaching and turned sharply to port to avoid it. At the same time, the *Collingwood* sighted a torpedo approaching from about 20° abaft the beam. The rudder was promptly put left and the ship had swung almost parallel to the track of the torpedo when it passed close under the stern. At the same time, another torpedo passed 30 yards ahead. The calm sea permitted the lookouts in the tops to see the torpedoes at a considerable distance, estimated in one case as 2½ miles. That advantage together with prompt maneuvering saved the 5th Division several hits.

The 6th Division was exposed to a much denser torpedo salvo and its ships in consequence had many narrow escapes. The *Marlborough,* already hit by 1 torpedo, sighted 3 more approaching from the starboard bow and beam at 7:33 (Fig. 46–F). An officer in the foretop says:

The tracks were quite clear to us aloft and could be picked out when nearly a mile away. At once we reported to the bridge, and they altered course to starboard, so that No. 1. track, the farthest off, passed ahead of us, but Nos. 2 and 3 were nearly on top of us before the ship commenced swinging. No. 2 passed so close to the stern that we lost sight of its track from the top, and we should certainly have been hit if the stern had not been swinging away under the influence of helm; and No. 3, which I saw break surface when about 500 yards on our beam, came straight for the ship, and its track came right up against our starboard quarter—it must have been running below its depth and went right under the ship.

As the *Marlborough* was sheering out to the right, the *Revenge* turned sharply to the left. One torpedo passed 10 yards ahead, while another went 20 yards astern. Lookouts in the

Hercules' tops also reported torpedo tracks approaching. She was able to turn about six points to the left before the torpedoes reached her. That placed the ship nearly parallel to the tracks. One torpedo came along the starboard side and passed 40 yards ahead. The second went under the stern, "very close." The *Agincourt* likewise turned about seven points to port according to information sent from the tops to the conning tower. One torpedo passed along the starboard side of the ship and another on the port. Thus, by promptly maneuvering and a good deal of luck, the 6th Division had avoided no less than 9 torpedoes. The handling of the ships according to information sent from the tops was remarkably effective, particularly in view of the fact that it was devised on the spur of the moment. It had not been recognized before that the tracks of German torpedoes would be so clearly visible. The fact that ships could be maneuvered with such effect to avoid approaching torpedoes was one of the principal lessons of Jutland. Incidentally, the 1st Battle Squadron, by being disposed at right angles to the approaching torpedoes, was exposed to more danger than if Jellicoe had headed for the area from which they had been fired.

Just as all the torpedoes were crossing the line, Jellicoe at 7:35 signaled (Fig. 46–D) for the leading ships of the battleship divisions to alter course to S. by W. (179°). That was followed one minute later by a signal to form the battle line into column (Fig. 46–J). At 7:40 the course of the Fleet (Fig. 46–L) was changed to SW. (212°). Three minutes later the *Revenge* in the 6th Division changed course to port to avoid two torpedoes, both of which passed astern (Fig. 46–O). They apparently had been fired by a boat of Flotilla IX during the retirement. The battle line was now entirely out of touch with the enemy, even the German battle cruisers were distant about 12 miles.

Beatty had ceased firing at 7:40 (Fig. 46–M). At that time, the *Inflexible* issued an erroneous report of a submarine on her starboard beam. While the High Seas Fleet had entirely passed out of sight of Jellicoe, Beatty was enjoying some rather good visibility, for at 7:45 (Fig. 46–S) he first lost sight of the German capital ships. In his report he says that at 7:32 the leading enemy battleship bore NW. by W. (291°). However, it was not until 7:45 that he sent a searchlight message to the 2d Cruiser Squadron asking that the bearing of the enemy be passed to the leading battleship division, together with the statement that the enemy was steering SW. (212°). That was an excellent report, but the delay of 13 minutes in starting it off was unfortunate. It was not received by Jellicoe until 7:59.

Although it certainly must have been evident by 7:45 that the Germans had completely disengaged their Fleet, it is noted that neither Beatty nor Jellicoe made any attempt to close them or to develop the situation. Beatty had the 1st and 3d Light Cruiser Squadrons immediately available for reconnaissance, but failed to use them for that important mission. Even the 4th Light Cruiser Squadron had commenced a retirement towards Beatty at 7:36. As that unit withdrew, a torpedo passed the *Constance* at 7:39 (Fig. 46–K). As we shall see later, it was probably fired by the *G88* of Flotilla III. We surely cannot blame Le Mesurier for his unfortunate retirement, for Jellicoe had consistently restricted his actions. At 7:32 he had warned the 4th Light Cruiser Squadron specifically: "Do not go too near enemy's Battle Fleet." Why was it necessary to send such a signal to the only light cruiser commander who at that time was showing some conception of his duties?

In his fear that some of his ships would come under enemy fire, Jellicoe at 7:40 specifically recalled the 11th Flotilla which was operating in the vicinity of the 4th Light Cruiser Squadron. Two minutes later he sent the anxious message: "Tell *Castor* to come back; destroyers recalled." It is indeed a curious fact that Jellicoe, who thought it so necessary for his battleships to avoid the German destroyers, was now so anxious that his light cruisers and destroyers should avoid the German battleships. His supercautious attitude is the more remarkable in that, since the loss of the *Invincible,* everything had been going his way. All the reports of submarines had resulted in nothing. Finally, he had avoided the principal destroyer attack of the day without receiving a single hit. However, instead of being encouraged by those most favorable developments, he seems to have even increased his passion for running no risks, for avoiding even the semblance of danger.

As will be remembered, Flotilla III had come out of the smoke about 7:30 P.M. That flotilla consisted only of the *S53*, *V71*, *V73*, and *G88*. The *S54* was coming at full speed to rejoin, but was about 600 yards in rear. The *G42* was still missing, as was also the *V48*. The first four boats sighted only British destroyers and light cruisers, the 12th and 11th Flotillas and the 4th Light Cruiser Squadron. A brief engagement with those light forces occurred about 7:33. The *G88* fired a torpedo at a unit of light cruisers or destroyers, probably the 4th Light Cruiser Squadron. The torpedo is believed to be the one that passed the *Constance* at 7:39 (Fig. 46–K). The flotilla then withdrew, suffering no losses. The fifth boat, the *S54*, proceeded somewhat closer to the enemy and sighted the British battle line. At 7:45 she fired a single torpedo at about 10,000 yards (Fig. 46–P).

About 7:30 Flotilla II, accompanied by the *Regensburg*, by a wide maneuver had finally gained a position from which it could have launched an attack to the southward of Flotilla III. However, Heinrich saw that the action had ceased and believed that no useful purpose could be served by another attack. So, he ordered Flotilla II to follow the *Regensburg* which then proceeded to the westward at high speed. Flotillas VI and IX rallied on Heinrich about 7:45. A powerful attack by Flotilla II might have had important results. If it had run into the 3d and 4th Light Cruiser Squadrons that were covering the British van at that time, it would probably have been driven back before reaching a favorable position for torpedo fire; but could it have come in astern of the light cruisers in the area from which the *S54* fired her single torpedo at 7:45 (Fig. 46–P), it is very possible that Jellicoe would have made a further turn away. This, as we shall see, would probably have prevented the action of 8:25 P.M. and would have avoided giving to Jellicoe the wonderful opportunity presented to the Battle Fleet at that time. However, the effect of a possible attack by Flotilla II at 7:45 is mere speculation. No criticism of Heinrich is intended.

Meanwhile, at 7:35 the *Faulknor*, the destroyer leader flag boat of the 12th Flotilla, had opened fire on an isolated German destroyer 5,000 yards on her starboard beam. Three minutes later the 1st Division of the flotilla, the *Obedient*, *Mindful*, *Marvel*, and *Onslaught*, joined in the firing (Fig. 46–c). Their target was seen to bear the letter "V" on her bow, but the numbers following had been obliterated by shells. It was evidently the *V48*, already heavily damaged and steaming slowly to the southwestward. Soon afterward the *Southampton* and *Dublin* opened fire on the same German destroyer and observed hits amidships. The *Obedient* asked permission to attack. At 7:43 Captain Stirling in the *Faulknor* granted that request and two minutes later the division moved out (Fig. 46–Q). As we read the story of Hannibal from the Roman historians, so we have reconstructed the saga of the *V48* from the British accounts. We allow an officer of H.M.S. *Obedient* to end our story:

She opened fire from her forecastle gun at us, but did not score a hit, and an early salvo from one of us carried away this gun, the bridge, and the foremast, whilst within a minute or so another salvo from the *Mindful* holed her along the water line abreast her foremost funnel. Very shortly afterward she turned over on her port side and sank.

It will be noted that gallant little ship, already greatly damaged, endeavored to fight off four fresh destroyers with a single gun. When that was destroyed and all means of resistance at an end, the *V48* went down with colors flying (Fig. 46–x). No attempt was made to rescue her crew and not a single man was saved. Hail to her unknown heroes! Sleep well, brave comrades!

Probably, the reason why no attempt could be made to save the few survivors of the *V48* was that salvos commenced to straddle the first division from German destroyers to the westward. They must have been Flotilla V which at 8:50 had emerged from the smoke screen on an easterly course. Commander Heinecke saw nothing but some destroyers in the distance, so he turned back at 8:52 (Fig. 46–w).

We now return to Scheer. The High Seas Fleet was retiring

on a southwesterly course when we left it about 7:40. During the retirement, Scheer's information of the enemy had been very inaccurate. At 7:42 he received a dispatch from Boedicker timed at 7:22 that the *Lützow* was under the heavy fire of strong enemy forces bearing NE. (32°). That information was quite accurate at the time it was sent; but, due to the rapidity with which the situation was changing, the most northerly battleships, the 5th Battle Squadron, bore about 70° when it was received. In giving consideration to enemy information reports, it is essential to remember the times at which they are sent and also very important that the sender use a time group corresponding to the situation he is reporting.

At 7:45 Scheer ordered course south (167°) for the High Seas Fleet (Fig. 46–R). Three minutes later he received a message from the commander of Flotilla IX, which bore the time group of 7:40, but Groos says that it was sent at 7:15. It said that the enemy force comprising more than 20 ships was steering on course ESE. (100°). That message, Groos says, was the first definite proof that Scheer had of the presence of the entire Grand Fleet. While the course of the enemy thus reported was approximately correct for about 7:25, while the British were turning away from the torpedo salvos, it was very incorrect for 7:40, when the message was timed. At that time, the British were steaming SW. (212°) rather than ESE. (100°). It was probably that message that caused the false impression in the *Friedrich der Grosse* "that the last blow at the enemy's center had caused the British to abandon the pursuit." It doubtless confirmed the correctness of Scheer's decision to proceed to the southward, a movement that would soon again involve the High Seas Fleet in another dangerous contact with the enemy. At 7:50 Scouting Group I (Fig. 46–v), which had been retiring on a westerly course, formed column on about 190° to close in gradually on the battleship divisions. Divisions VI and V continued to proceed in line of bearing on a southwesterly course to close in on the *Friedrich der Grosse*.

At 7:50 Captain Bauer, Leader of the Submarines, in the

light cruiser *Hamburg*, accompanying Scouting Group IV, sent
a dispatch to the light cruiser *Arcona* in Emden for all available
submarines to proceed to the northward, reporting their 5:00
A.M. positions.

We have seen that Beatty at 7:45 reported that the leading
German battleship bore NW. by W. (291°) (Fig. 46–s). It is likely
that only the *Lützow* was in sight at that time. At 7:47 he followed that report with his well-known signal: "Submit van of
battleships follow battle cruisers. We can then cut off whole of
enemy's Battle Fleet." At the same time, he changed course
about two points toward the enemy (Fig. 46–u). In a few
minutes, however, he resumed his old course, SW. (212°), and
continued at 18 knots. Actually, the British battleships were
following Beatty and he made no particular effort to cut off
the German Fleet or, for some time yet, even to regain contact
with it.

Before Jellicoe received Beatty's suggestion at 7:54, information had arrived from Goodenough (Fig. 46–t) that the Germans
at 7:15 had detached an unknown number of ships that were
steering NW. (302°). That probably referred to the temporary
movement of Battle Squadron III to the northwestward about
7:22. When received, its effect must have been most puzzling to
Jellicoe. He had just resumed the guide of the fleet at 7:52
and was ready for another advance toward the enemy, when the
bearing of the latter could be determined. As he was trying to
figure this out, a violent cannonade commenced in the van at
7:55. That, though it must have further puzzled the commander
in chief, was only the *Hampshire, Shannon,* and *Duke of Edinburgh* sinking an imaginary submarine (Fig. 46–y).

Fortunately, at 7:59 there arrived Beatty's message, probably
based on an observation of 7:32, as shown by par. 25 of his
report. It purported to give the bearing of the leading German
battleship at 7:45 (Fig. 46–s). That message, though it may
have referred to either the *Lützow* or *Derfflinger,* was substantially correct and quite definitely fixed for Jellicoe the position of the enemy. He immediately turned the battle line by

divisions to course west (257°). At 8:00 Beatty ordered the 3d
Light Cruiser Squadron to "sweep to the westward and locate
the head of the enemy's line before dark." At last it looked as
if the British leaders were trying for another fight. With the
Germans steering south (167°), it was evident that the two Fleets
would soon be in close contact.

CHAPTER XVIII

THE LAST DAYLIGHT ACTIONS
8:00 P.M. to 9:15 P.M.

AT 8:00 P.M. the British forces (Fig. 46) were well concentrated and disposed in a gradually curving formation about 16 miles long. In the van was the 3d Light Cruiser Squadron, re-enforced by the *Canterbury*. Then came the three battle cruiser squadrons in a single column. On their starboard quarter was the 1st Light Cruiser Squadron, astern the 4th Light Cruiser Squadron, and on their port quarter, the 2d Cruiser Squadron, re-enforced by the *Duke of Edinburgh* and *Chester*. Then, at a considerable interval, came the 24 battleships, all well disposed in a single column. In rear were the 5th Battle Squadron and the 2d Light Cruiser Squadron. All the destroyers had been recalled and were well formed in flotillas, available for any service.

The High Seas Fleet on the contrary was in a confused formation, heading generally to the southward. The three battle squadrons were proceeding separately, with Battle Squadron III quite a distance to the rear and Battle Squadron I overlapping Battle Squadron II. Scouting Group I was converging on Battle Squadron I in an attempt to take station ahead. Its four remaining, heavily damaged battle cruisers were in a very exposed and dangerous position in case of contact with British capital ships. It is believed that Scheer might well have ordered that group to take station in the rear or on the unengaged side of the battleships. The *Lützow* with four destroyers was nearest the enemy. She was proceeding to the westward at 15 knots to withdraw from her very exposed position. All the German destroyers, except Flotilla VII, were proceeding westward to regain touch. They were still considerably scattered as a result of their attacks. Due to serious injuries, a number of them were proceeding at

S.M.S. "POMMERN"

This battleship (pre-dreadnought), under the command of Captain Bölken, was in Division II of Squadron II of the German Battle Fleet, at Jutland. This ship suffered hits in an early evening brush with Beatty's battle cruisers and, in the early morning of June 1, was blown up with the loss of all hands by a torpedo attack of the British 12th Destroyer Flotilla.

R. Perkins, "Jane's Fighting Ships"

H.M.S. "DEFENCE"

The armored cruiser *Defence* was the flagship of Rear Admiral Arbuthnot, Commander of the 1st Cruiser Squadron. When the Battle Fleet was deploying, the *Defence* and the other cruisers of that squadron were in advance. The *Defence* came under the fire of Hipper's battle cruisers. As a result of two salvos from the *Lützow*, she blew up under the eyes of the deploying battleships and lost every officer and man on board.

reduced speeds. Nevertheless, at 8:00 Scheer issued the laconic order: "All flotillas attack."

As the Germans were thus unwittingly steaming in confused formation toward another inevitable contact with the enemy, the *Lützow* had signaled an important message to the *Seydlitz:* "Enemy bears SSE. (145°). Is drawing ahead of the *Lützow* to port. Six battle cruisers strong." That message was based upon an observation of 7:49, before the British had passed out of sight. It reflects great credit upon Captain Harder that, with all his other difficulties, he could find time to send that important message. The *Seydlitz* at 8:02 passed the message to Commodore Heinrich in the *Regensburg* (Fig. 47–A). At 8:05 Heinrich received the same message from Boedicker in the *Frankfurt*. However, neither of those commanders thought to pass that important information on to Scheer, who was quite close to the *Regensburg*. Heinrich did send it to Flotilla II. Therefore, the commander in chief remained under the impression that the British were not following him. It was even thought that their formation had been shattered. That false impression seems to have influenced Scheer in repeating at 8:12 the order for all flotillas to attack. He must have felt that the British were proceeding to the eastward and that it would be necessary for the destroyers to start promptly if they were to make their expected night attack.

Promptly at 8:00 Napier spread the 3d Light Cruiser Squadron, plus the *Canterbury,* on a north (347°) and south (167°) line at 1-mile distance on course west (257°) at 24 knots. At 8:09 he reported (Fig. 47–c) to Beatty: "Ships bearing N. by W. (335°)." They evidently were the German battle cruisers. One minute later Beatty signaled to his battle cruisers to open fire. However, as no enemy ships could be distinguished, no fire was opened. At 8:15 the *Princess Royal* reported a collision with what was thought to have been a German submarine. At 8:17, evidently to develop the situation (Fig. 47–I), Beatty headed west (257°). At the same instant, Napier made out the five old light cruisers of Scouting Group IV steering across his scouting

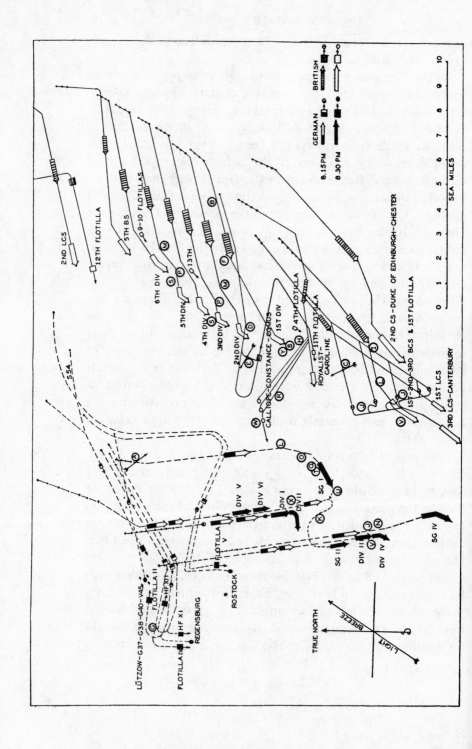

line at right angles. His flagship, the *Falmouth*, opened fire at 8:17 at 9,600 yards (Fig. 47–J).

As the *Falmouth* opened fire, Scouting Groups II and IV sighted for the first time the British light cruisers. Commodore von Reuter, commanding Scouting Group IV, could see the enemy but indistinctly. The *Stettin*, his flagship, and the *München* fired a few salvos with their 4.1-inch guns. He changed course slightly toward the enemy in the hope that the visibility would improve.

Boedicker sighted two of the British light cruisers. In rear of them, he saw the van of the battle cruiser column. He quickly made an information report at 8:19, just as the sun set below the horizon in the northwest (Fig. 47–K). In the right center of square 162 Gamma he placed two *Chatham* class light cruisers. In 008 were hostile battle cruisers steering SW. (212°). That gave quite an accurate picture of Beatty's forces, though the use of position squares when the forces were in such close contact were useless. The relative bearings and distances of the enemy forces from the fleet guide or other large ship would have been of better assistance to Scheer.

After making that report, Boedicker reversed his course and ran to the northwestward. The reason given for that radical maneuver was that he felt it necessary to get out of the line of fire of Scouting Group I and Battle Squadron I. A glance at Fig. 47 will show that Scouting Group II was entirely out of the line of fire of those units. Boedicker was slightly in the line of fire of Battle Squadron II, but that could easily have been cleared in a short time. It is true that the *Pillau* had been reduced to 24 knots, while the *Elbing* had said that she could not make high speed because of a condenser casualty. Still the batteries of his three ships were intact or virtually so and all still had sufficient speed to keep up with the Fleet. In our opinion, Boedicker should have remained in the van to support the weak and old light cruisers of Scouting Group IV against their more powerful opponents. Since 6:00 P.M. Scouting Group II had done virtually nothing.

As early as 8:18, the *Princess Royal* sighted the German battle cruisers about 60° on the starboard bow. The *Tiger* soon sighted the old battleships of Squadron II. At 8:20 a new action of great intensity commenced between those forces (Fig. 47–L). Before we describe that last action between heavy ships in the World War, we must turn for a time to another action that was being fought in the van of the Battle Fleet and that had great possibilities for the British.

At 8:05 the *Calliope*, flagship of the 4th Light Cruiser Squadron, had sighted smoke to the WNW. (279°). About 8:11 the *Castor* (Fig. 47–D) sighted destroyers to the northwestward (302°). Commodore Hawksley ordered 8 new destroyers of the 11th Flotilla to follow the *Castor* to attack them. Three minutes later he signaled to Jerram that German destroyers bore NW. (302°) (Fig. 47–E). At 8:15 he told Le Mesurier that there were 12 German destroyers. One minute later that officer, with the *Calliope, Constance,* and *Comus,* turned to support Hawksley (Fig. 47–H). The two other cruisers maintained their stations. At 8:18 Le Mesurier opened fire. His target was Flotilla V which was returning to the High Seas Fleet after its futile attack of 7:50.

It will be remembered that the *Iron Duke,* according to the signal record, had received Beatty's request that the van of the Battle Fleet should follow him at 7:54. The Admiralty *Narrative* says that Jellicoe did not actually receive that message until after 8:00. At any rate, it was 8:07 when Jerram (Fig. 47–B) received Jellicoe's action upon Beatty's suggestion: "2d B.S. follow our battle cruisers." At 8:15, Jerram turned the 1st Division (Fig. 47–F) somewhat to the left in the estimated direction of the battle cruisers. The latter were entirely out of sight 6 miles to the southwestward. Just as Jerram turned off, the *Marlborough* on the other flank of the battle line sighted another of those mysterious, ever-present, but imaginary, submarines. At 8:18 Jerram signaled to the 2d Battle Squadron: "Follow me." The 2d Division, however, held its westerly course for the present. At 8:20 Beatty's heavy gunfire could be heard and even his gun flashes could be seen. One minute later, therefore, Jellicoe paralleled Jerram by turning his divisions (Fig. 47–M) to WSW. (234°).

We must now see how Beatty was faring. Fortunately, the situation at the time of contact was favorable to him, when it might have been quite the contrary. Rather sharp on Beatty's starboard bow were the six old and thoroughly obsolete ships of Battle Squadron II. As those ships mounted only four 11-inch guns each, the entire six were a match for about two of the British battle cruisers. The German ships, furthermore, could not make out the British battle cruisers clearly enough to open fire. Beatty was nearly ahead of the four German battle cruisers. All the latter ships, except the *Moltke,* had been terribly battered. Furthermore, they also could scarcely see their enemies. By rare good chance, the British had been given another great opportunity, for the sun had just set directly behind the Germans. That fact gave the British an advantage in visibility.

Thus, the British had caught Scouting Group I in a most critical situation. The *Lion* and *Princess Royal* opened on the *Derfflinger;* the *Tiger* fired on one of the ships of Battle Squadron II; the *New Zealand* and the *Indomitable* selected the *Seydlitz* as their target; the *Inflexible* probably shot at the *Von der Tann.* Just as firing commenced at 8:20, Hartog eased away two points in succession (Fig. 47–L). A minute later Beatty did the same (Fig. 47–L). At 8:24 the *Seydlitz* was hit amidships (Fig. 47–O). About two minutes later the *Derfflinger's* "A" turret was placed temporarily out of action by a direct hit (Fig. 47–Q). Every main battery gun was now silent on that splendid ship. Then both Beatty and Hartog turned away about two points more and the range began to increase.

About that time, Battle Squadron II opened fire with its 11-inch guns. Scouting Group IV at 8:21 had reported four light cruisers. Only the *Stettin* and *München* were able to fire about eight salvos each with their little 4.1-inch guns against the 3d Light Cruiser Squadron's 6-inch batteries. The British light cruisers upon their first contact had assembled in column formation on a southwesterly course. By 8:23 they were able

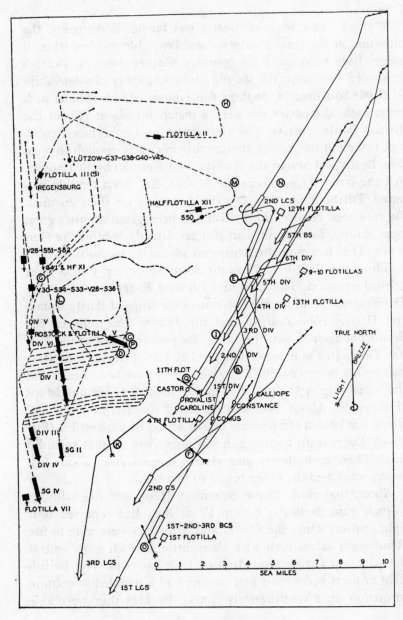

FIG. 48. 8:30-9:00 P.M.

to present a great superiority of fighting strength in the cruiser action. The *München* was hit twice in her upper works, four men being killed. At 8:30 von Reuter, seeing that he could do little against such a superior force in the unfavorable visibility, turned away sharply together to the westward (Fig. 48). Napier at 8:28 reported to both Jellicoe and Beatty that he was engaging enemy cruisers.

At 8:30 the *Seydlitz* was struck by heavy shells on "D" turret and the bridge (Fig. 47–T). The latter hit inflicted heavy casualties. Every man on the bridge was killed and a number of persons in the conning tower were killed or wounded. Hartog turned away sharply to the northwestward (Fig. 47–U). The British soon shifted fire against Battle Squadron II and a sharp action on parallel courses ensued (Fig. 47–V). Only the *Hannover, Schlesien,* and *Hessen* were able to fire with any effect. At 8:32 their 11-inch shells hit the *Lion* and *Princess Royal* (Fig. 48–B) and the *Indomitable's* funnel was pierced, probably by a secondary battery projectile. The low-power, 40-caliber 11-inch guns of the old battleships were compa..atively ineffective, even at the close range of 10,000 yards. The *Schleswig-Holstein* was hit by a heavy shell that damaged a 6-inch gun and caused twelve casualties (Fig. 48–C). The *Schlesien* was hit near the secondary control station and one man was killed. The *Pommern* sheered out of formation, apparently hit. At 8:35 Rear Admiral Mauve turned Battle Squadron II eight points away from the enemy by simultaneous movement and firing soon died out (Fig. 48–D). In that brief action the British had received only two heavy hits, against about seven for the Germans. Thus, Beatty had the satisfaction of ending his part in the battle with a decided, if minor, success.

It was very fortunate for Beatty that Scouting Group I was directly in the line of fire of Battle Squadron I during the action. The High Seas Fleet was very poorly disposed at the time. The terribly injured battle cruisers should by all means have been placed astern or preferably on the lee side of the battle line. Battle Squadron I which was undamaged should have been placed in the van, where it could have borne the brunt of the fighting. That squadron was now in reverse order. The *West-falen*, commanded by the able Captain Redlich, was leading. At first he attributed the firing in the van to Scouting Group II shooting at periscopes, particularly as torpedo tracks were believed to have been sighted by the *Westfalen* and *Rheinland*. However, in any event their own battle cruisers were in the line of fire and the enemy, whose shells were bursting close to the *Westfalen* and *Nassau*, could not be distinguished. Only the *Posen* was able to fire for a few minutes.

When Hartog turned to the northwestward at 8:30, Scouting Group I ran directly across the bows of Battle Squadron I. The *Westfalen* was forced to turn away about nine points to the westward. Thus, Beatty was saved a contact with the German battleships. By equally good fortune, the *Westfalen's* chance maneuver probably saved the German battleships a close-range contact with the British battle line. Let us see how this might have taken place.

During the action in the van, a very interesting contact had occurred between the 4th Light Cruiser Squadron and Battle Squadrons I and III. We have seen how Le Mesurier opened fire on Flotilla V about 8:18. At 8:24 the destroyers withdrew under cover of a smoke screen. Le Mesurier followed them at full speed, getting the *Constance* and *Comus* out on the starboard quarter of the *Calliope* so as to gain a clear field of fire. At 8:26 the German battle line came into sight at about 8,000 yards (Fig. 47–R). Two minutes later the Germans sighted two of the light cruisers and some of the destroyers of the 11th Flotilla. The *Prinz Regent Luitpold* fired one salvo from her main battery and the *Kaiser* two, while the *Markgraf* used her secondary battery (Fig. 47–X). At 8:30 the *Calliope* fired a torpedo at the close range of 6,500 yards (Fig. 47–W) and turned back. An officer of the *Calliope* writes:

Only our high speed and zigzagging saved us from annihilation. As it was, we seemed to be in the middle of splashes, and the noise of the bursting shell and flying fragments was absolutely deafening.

The *Calliope* was hit five times. She had two 4-inch gun

disabled, 10 men killed and 23 wounded. Le Mesurier had done very well in clearly developing an obscure situation.

We now come to the intensely interesting part of the contact. It will be remembered that at 8:21 the British battleship divisions had taken course WSW. (234°) (Fig. 47–M). As the Germans were steering south (167°), it will be seen that the two Fleets were converging at an angle of 67°. The Germans were entirely unaware of the presence of the British battle line, although an action could be heard in the van. The British battle line could see the *Calliope, Constance,* and *Comus* engaging hostile destroyers about 3 miles ahead, while a little on the port bow the thunder of Beatty's guns told that he was again at grips with the enemy. At 8:25 Jellicoe headed the battle line west (257°), two points toward the enemy. Jerram, leading the 1st Division, did not make that change of course. He kept on WSW. (234°), evidently considering that the order to follow the battle cruisers still held good. The 2d Division, however, did make the change of course, although it had been ordered by Jerram to follow him.

No sooner had the change of course to west (257°) been made when "B" turret of the *Iron Duke* sighted "nine heavy ships ahead." They undoubtedly belonged to Battle Squadrons I and III, distant about 18,000 yards. Though it was now six minutes after sunset, the fact that ships could be sighted at such a distance shows that there was still ample visibility for a fleet action of possibly 30 minutes' duration. This will be demonstrated conclusively later. Whether the sighting of the German battleships by "B" turret was reported to Jellicoe is not stated. However, when at 8:28 the 4th Light Cruiser Squadron was clearly seen to be under heavy gunfire, it must have been evident to all that contact had again been made with the High Seas Fleet. At 8:28, just when it seemed that a new action under favorable conditions was imminent, Jellicoe turned his divisions (Fig. 47–s) four points away to SW. (212°). That again formed the battle line in a single, though somewhat irregular, column.

While, with this last change of course, the two Fleets still converged at an angle of 45°, the fortunate incident already described now withdrew the Germans from their dangerous position. At 8:30 the 2d Battle Squadron was within 14,000 yards of the *Westfalen* and 11,000 yards of the *Von der Tann.* The *Monarch* and *King George V* both saw the flashes of the enemy guns on their starboard bows, but, just as it seemed that the 2d Battle Squadron might get into the fight, Scouting Group I turned away sharply from the British battle cruisers. That, as we have seen, forced Battle Squadrons I and III to swing to the westward and saved them from a decisive contact with the British battleships. Still, as that change of course was made in succession, there was a chance that the rear of the line might come under the British fire.

As the British battle line continued on its course of SW. (212°), the usual alarms continued. At 8:31 the *Benbow* sighted what was thought to be a torpedo passing from port to starboard, *i.e.,* from her disengaged side. Fortunately, she did not report that most alarming incident. At 8:33 the *Inconstant* of the 1st Light Cruiser Squadron, on the other hand, did report the imaginary submarine she saw. A rather fine signal came from the newly commissioned battleship *Royal Sovereign* at Scapa: "Permission to join your flag." A report from the *Warrior* said that she was in tow of the seaplane carrier *Engadine.*

By 8:35, when the action in the van ceased, the range between the opposing battle lines was only 12,000 yards. It was somewhat after 8:40 when the last German battleship, the *König,* reached the turning point to course west (257°). She was then distant only 10,000 yards from the center of the British battle line. It was at that time that the *Monarch* made the following very significant note "*Calliope* hit, 1,000 yards on starboard beam." Also, the *Comus,* replying to an inquiry from Jellicoe as to what she was firing at, significantly replied: "Enemy's B.F. bearing west." (Fig. 48–E). Just a little more aggressiveness on the part of Jellicoe would still have gained him a great success. All he needed to say was: "Course west (257°). Speed 19. The fight will be to the finish."

We must now see what the German destroyers were accomplishing. We have noted that Scheer had issued a general order for the flotillas to attack at 8:00. At 8:12 he repeated the order with the modifications that the attack would be at night and under the direction of Commodore Michelsen. That placed Heinrich in an embarrassing position because, in accordance with the order of 8:00, he already had issued orders to certain of his destroyers. Scheer's first order had been both premature and incomplete. About 8:00 Heinrich had concentrated Flotillas II, VI, and IX near the *Lützow* to the northeastward of the German battle line; but he found ready for attack only Flotilla II and the *V69, S50,* and *V46* of Half Flotilla XII. Those vessels had followed Flotilla II while Flotilla VI was attacking. The boats of Flotilla IX and Half Flotilla XI that had participated in the 7:25 attack had either expended all their torpedoes or had only one remaining, probably from a tube that would bear on only one broadside. Therefore, Heinrich divided the remaining eight boats of Flotilla IX into two groups. In the first were the *V28* and *S51,* both damaged by gunfire, and the *S52.* Those three boats under Commander Goehle were sent to Battle Squadron I. The five remaining boats, the *V30, S34, S33, V26,* and *S36,* were sent under command of Commander Tillessen to Commodore Michelsen who, with the *Rostock* and Flotilla V, was to the westward of Battle Squadron I. The *G41, V44, G87,* and *G86* of Flotilla VI were also sent to join the *Rostock.* Those two detachments may have been sent away in accordance with the order of 8:12, giving to Michelsen the charge of the night attacks. They joined up soon after dark. Figure 48 shows their positions as estimated for 9:00, just before dark.

Meanwhile, at 8:15 Heinrich had sent off Flotilla II, 10 fine large boats of the newest type, to search and attack in the sector ENE. to ESE. (54° to 100°). At the same time, Half Flotilla XII (3 boats) went in sector ESE. to SE. (100° to 122°). He evidently did not seriously credit the report of the *Lützow* that six battle cruisers bore SSE. (145°). Possibly, he believed that the British battleships were not following them or were doing so at a great interval. Also, he seems to have fallen far in rear of the Fleet while organizing the attack. His directions as to when the attacks were to commence were confusing and conflicting. Scheer's two orders for the attack contributed to the confusion. In addition, Heinrich had given Flotilla II permission to return to Kiel via the Skagerrak if the route via the German Bight (Helgoland Bight) was "not found advisable." From these facts, it is not surprising that the attack was a complete failure. What is more, they deprived the High Seas Fleet of its strongest flotilla.

There were two primary reasons for the failure of the destroyer attack: (1) It was started so early that the flotillas came in contact with the British long before dark. (2) It was directed so far to the northward that no contact was made with the British battle line. The only vessels sighted were the 2d Light Cruiser Squadron and the 12th Flotilla far in the rear. About 8:45 Flotilla II sighted those forces and withdrew without firing a shot (Fig. 48–H). Captain Schuur broadcast the information that he was being forced off to the northwestward by five light cruisers and numerous destroyers in square 020. That was received an hour later. Schuur by all means should have tried to turn the flanks of the British light forces or at the very least he should have maintained touch until dark, when he could easily pierce their formation; but he did neither, despite his very high speed of 32.5 to 36 knots.

At 8:52 the three boats of Half Flotilla XII came under the heavy fire of the 2d Light Cruiser Squadron at a range of 5,000 yards (Fig. 48–M). Lieutenant Commander Lahs made a determined effort to break through, but after a 20-minute fight he was driven off to the westward. The *S50* was hit by a 6-inch shell. One boiler and the generators were put out of action. As she could steam at only 25 knots, she left the half flotilla to rejoin the Fleet. Thus, the boats best capable of making night torpedo attacks were uselessly expended before the night began. Here the Germans lost one of their best opportunities to inflict damage on the Grand Fleet.

After Flotilla II and Half Flotilla XII had left for their attacks, the *S53*, *V71*, *V73*, *S54*, and *G88* of Flotilla III joined the *Regensburg* at 8:45. Heinrich proceeded with those boats southward to join the High Seas Fleet, the van of which was distant no less than 7 miles.

While those engagements were taking place at the rear of the line, there had been several interesting developments in the van. At 8:36 Scheer, still unaware of how closely he had missed a contact with the British battle line, had ordered a course of south (167°) for his Fleet. There was some delay in the execution of his order, and it is very fortunate that there was. The *West-falen,* leading Battle Squadron I, obeyed the order at 8:43 (Fig. 48–G), but it was not until 8:50 that Scouting Group IV and Battle Squadron II steered southward, also a most fortunate delay. Scouting Group I, for some curious reason, turned southeastward (Fig. 48–L) directly toward the British battle line. At 9:00 it swung sharply to the westward (Fig. 48–P) just in time to avoid running full into the British battleships, distant about 8,000 yards. This is another proof of our previous comment that Scouting Group I should have been ordered to the disengaged side of the battle line long ago.

The second turn of the High Seas Fleet to the southward again converged the opposing Fleets at a sharp angle. Again, it appeared that a contact was inevitable. Scheer seemed insisting on offering opportunity after opportunity to his opponent, who insisted on declining these favors.

Many reports arrived in the *Iron Duke.* At 8:45 Jerram reported that the British battle cruisers were not in sight. The next minute Jellicoe directed Beatty to indicate the bearing of the enemy. It is almost characteristic that he should ask for such information from a commander whose position was unknown to him and whose bearing would therefore be useless, while a few minutes before a light cruiser in plain sight had given a positive bearing of the German Battle Fleet, at which she was firing 6-inch guns. Incidentally, that message from Jellicoe was received in the *Lion* as coming from the *Galatea.*

At 8:46 there arrived a good report from Napier (Fig. 48–K). He said that an unknown number of battle cruisers bore north (347°) and were steering WSW. (234°). Unfortunately (as has been mentioned repeatedly), the British vessels used the dangerous practice of including navigational positions in their contact reports even after the Fleet had been concentrated. To make such a system of any value, it was necessary for the *Iron Duke* to have signaled a reference position for the guide after the Fleet had been assembled, say at 6:30. Then, the other ships within sight could have rectified their positions in accordance with the signaled position of the *Iron Duke*. That precaution had not been taken. In consequence, while Napier was actually about 11 miles ahead of the *Iron Duke*, the position appended to his report was 5 miles astern of that ship. Fortunately, that error was quite obvious and probably did not cause confusion. The best thing that Napier could have done under the circumstances was to estimate his own position relative to the *Iron Duke* and then report the position of the enemy with reference to that vessel. Admittedly, this was an inaccurate method, but at least it was something that Jellicoe could have understood.

Nevertheless, there were contact reports from ships nearer at hand. The *Caroline* and *Royalist* of the 4th Light Cruiser Squadron had taken a position about 2 miles on the starboard bow of the *King George V*. There they had been joined by the *Castor* and 8 destroyers (or possibly all) of the 11th Flotilla. At 8:45 (Fig. 48–I) the *Caroline* sighted 3 ships which she believed to be German pre-dreadnought battleships, but were actually the leading ships of Battle Squadron I. The leading ship challenged the *Caroline* by searchlight. Convinced that the strange battleships were hostile, the *Caroline* signaled the *Royalist*: "Attack with torpedoes." Both ships, however, seem to have kept their course and there were no immediate developments.

About 8:57 Jellicoe received a report from the 2d Light Cruiser Squadron (Fig. 48–N) timed 8:55 that it was engaging destroyers and that "enemy ships, number unknown," bore west (257°). Two minutes later, at 8:59, there came a long-delayed message that Beatty had sent at 8:40 (Fig. 48–F). It stated that hostile battle cruisers and pre-dreadnought battleships bore 313°, were distant 10 to 11 miles, and were steering

SW. (212°). Beatty added that his own course was SW. (212°) and speed 17 knots, the same as those of the Battle Fleet. Though it was evident that a contact with the High Seas Fleet was again imminent, it was already 40 minutes after sundown and Jellicoe had decided against a night action; so at 9:01 he ordered the Battle Fleet to swing away to south (167°) by divisions (Fig. 50–D). Thus, he had turned away simultaneously with Scouting Group I from a contact that if aggressively pressed would probably have meant the destruction of the German battle cruisers. Beatty, accompanied by the 1st and 3d Light Cruiser Squadrons, did not obey that order, as it was not addressed to him. The 2d Cruiser Squadron, however, being directly under Jellicoe's orders, turned to south (167°). The system of command in the Grand Fleet after the forces commanded by Jellicoe and Beatty effected a junction was very indefinite. This applied particularly to the units of the Battle Cruiser Fleet. Had Beatty taken command of all the forces in the van and Evan-Thomas of those in the rear, the Fleet could have been handled much more effectively. Apparently, the commanders of the six cruiser squadrons and the seven destroyer flotillas acted entirely on their own, except when they came directly under the eyes of Jellicoe. In only a few cases did their commanders take any positive action; they generally followed along watching the battle. It is noteworthy that Jellicoe never issued an order of any kind, except to report the bearing of the enemy, to Beatty. While this in many respects was admirable, it is believed that general instructions should have been issued from time to time or that Beatty should have been informed at least of the plans or intentions of the commander in chief.

At 9:00 Beatty replied to the message that he thought had come from the *Galatea* (Figs. 48–0 and 50–B). He reported that the bearing of the enemy was N. by W. (335°). That very accurate report was intercepted by the *Iron Duke* at 9:04. At the same time, he informed Jellicoe of his navigational position and said that he was on course SW. (212°) at 17 knots. The bearing of the enemy was given at N. by W. (335°) and his course as WSW. (234°). The actual position of the *Lion* and bearing

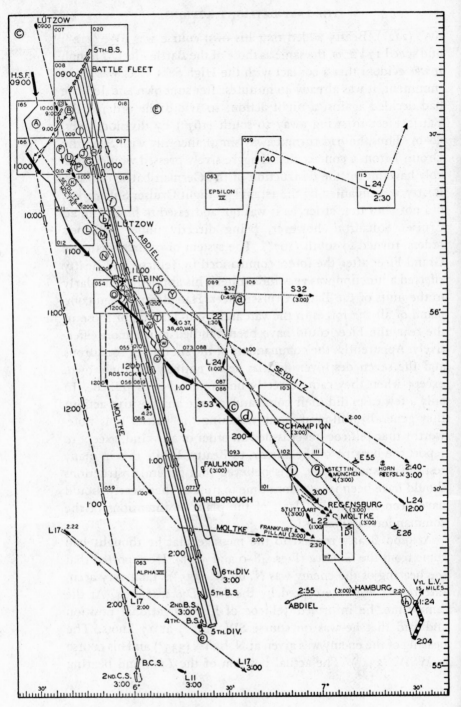

FIG. 49. 9:00 P.M., May 31, to 3:00 A.M., June 1.

of the enemy are shown at Fig. 48–O and Fig. 50–B. The reported navigational position of the *Lion* and bearing of the enemy are shown at Fig. 49–B. The difference between the reported and actual positions of the *Lion* was 4½ miles. The *Iron Duke* did not receive the long message addressed to Jellicoe until 9:41, 37 minutes after the shorter message to the *Galatea* had been intercepted. The arrangements made by the fleet flagship for intercepting messages were highly commendable. It is very important that the fleet flagship guard the greatest possible number of circuits, and in particular those used by ships and aircraft in close contact with the enemy.

Meanwhile, the last daylight contact had occurred. The *Caroline*, *Royalist*, *Castor*, and 8 destroyers had finally reached a position 8,000 yards from the *Westfalen*. As she was the leader of a column of 16 battleships, it will be seen that British vessels, by mere chance, had reached a highly favorable position for torpedo fire. At 9:05 the *Caroline* again hoisted the signal to attack with torpedoes. She fired two and the *Royalist* one (Figs. 49–D and 50–G). The 11th Flotilla which was in close company turned away and did not attack (Fig. 50–F).

Vice Admiral Jerram had sighted the ships of Battle Squadron I as early as 9:00 (Fig. 50–C); but he was convinced that the dimly outlined ships were the British battle cruisers. In that belief, he was supported by the navigator of his flagship, who had recently been on duty in the Battle Cruiser Fleet. At 9:05 Jerram was so sure of the identity of the strange ships that he reported to Jellicoe British battle cruisers bearing WNW. (279°) and steering SW. (212°) (Fig. 50–H). When the *Caroline's* signal to attack was reported to him, he immediately flashed a message to her: "Negative attack; those ships are our battle cruisers." The *Caroline* replied: "Those are evidently enemy ships." To this Jerram replied: "If you are quite sure, attack."

The British did not have to wait long for that question to be settled definitely. About 9:01, as previously stated, Scouting Group I had turned away sharply to the westward (Fig. 50–E). It was either to avoid a threatened torpedo attack or to take station at the rear of their battle line. Since 9:00 the *Westfalen*

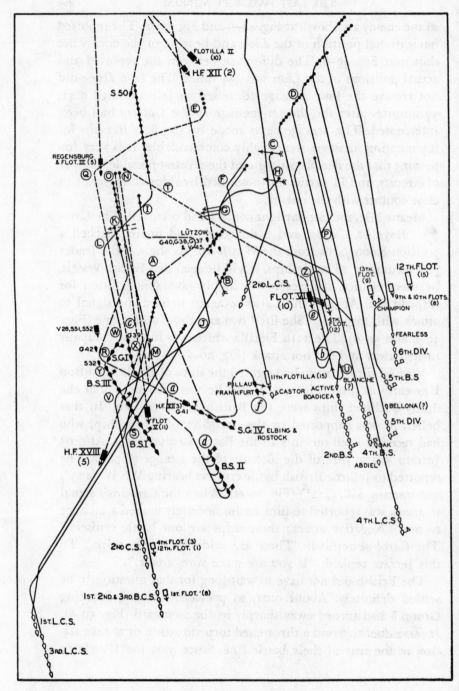

FIG. 50. 9:00-10:00 P.M.

and *Nassau* had seen strange vessels on their port beam. However, it was at first thought that they might be Scouting Group IV; but, when the *Westfalen's* challenge went unanswered and many destroyers, supported by two light cruisers, were clearly made out at 9:08, the *Westfalen* and *Nassau* opened fire for about three minutes (Fig. 50–I).

The 2d Battle Squadron heard that heavy firing and as late as 9:11 the German battleships were still in sight. However, Jerram made no effort to determine the cause of the shooting, but continued on his course of south (167°). As the two Fleets were now diverging sharply, the German battle line disappeared into the mist and darkness. Another great opportunity, or rather several opportunities, had been lost. About 9:15 one torpedo passed ahead of the *Nassau*, while a second went under the ship abreast her forward turret (Fig. 50–K). Probably, the torpedo's wake met the ship at this point, while the torpedo itself passed just ahead. About this time, 9:15, one of the German ships fired a star shell. It was seen by all the British ships immediately present, and they now could be certain that the strange ships were hostile, as the British were not furnished with such projectiles.

We must here discuss several remarkable points: (1) Why did the 11th Flotilla turn away without firing torpedoes. (2) Why did not Jerram open fire with his main battery guns? (3) Why did Jellicoe turn so prematurely to the south? These three most unfortunate decisions combined to lose Jellicoe one of his last opportunities for a decisive success.

As an answer to the first question we have the remarkable statement of Commodore Hawksley who in the *Castor* was leading the 11th Flotilla. The 8 boats of that flotilla in company carried 32 torpedoes. The remaining 7 boats must have been close at hand. Of course, Hawksley could not see all the line of 16 German ships. Instead, he thought he saw "a line of battle cruisers," presumably 4 or 5 ships. Thus, he did not realize what a wonderful torpedo target had been presented to him through no effort of his own. He intercepted the message from Jerram to the *Caroline*, stating that the strange ships were British battle cruisers. However, when those "battle cruisers" opened fire on the *Caroline* and *Royalist*, it was quite evident that they were enemy ships.

Now let Hawksley tell the story in his own words:

I turned the flotilla away from the battle cruisers and expected the fleet to open fire on them. The leading battle cruiser then fired a star shell, which appeared to justify the opinion that they were enemy ships; but as the fleet still held their fire, it was not dark enough to make an attack unsupported by fire from the fleet. The battle cruisers turned off to starboard and were lost sight of.

That attitude showed a singular lack of aggressiveness for a destroyer commander. The destroyer is largely a weapon of opportunity. A remarkable opportunity had been thrust into Hawksley's hands, an opportunity that every true destroyer captain hopes will some day be given to him. Hawksley refused it and justified his refusal by purely formal and conventional arguments which were not applicable to the situation. There is every reason to believe that he could have made an effective torpedo attack if he had followed the lead of the *Caroline* and *Royalist*. If two light cruisers could fire torpedoes at 8,000 yards without receiving a single hit, certainly destroyers could have done the same at much less range without receiving appreciable loss. Hawksley turned away without even making a try and before a single shot was fired at him. If he felt that it was still too light for a close attack, he had to wait only 10 minutes and come in slowly under cover of darkness. The torpedoing of several German battleships at that time, with possible reduction of speed, might have had incalculable results. Hawksley's opportunity to achieve greatness had slipped from him.

Jerram evidently made an honest mistake in not opening fire. He had good authority to support him in his belief that the strange ships were British battle cruisers. Moreover, the change of course of the Battle Fleet at 9:01 might have seemed to indicate that Jellicoe did not desire to bring on an action at that time. However, there was a lack of initiative and aggressiveness on his part. If in doubt as to the identity of the strange ships, why did he waste time in conversing with the *Caroline* when he might have sent some destroyers toward them. Such action would have given him the answer in a few minutes in a way that could not have been misunderstood. However, his lack of initiative and aggressiveness was the usual attitude of most of the commanders in the Grand Fleet. For that attitude, Jellicoe himself must bear the responsibility. It resulted directly and inevitably from his deliberate policy of "not leaving anything to chance." That Jellicoe recognized this inertness in his subordinate commanders is shown by his comments after the battle. He writes:

The principal changes that were made in the Battle Orders was in the direction of laying still further emphasis on the discretionary power which was vested in the Flag Officers commanding squadrons. . . .

But how could subordinates act with decision and daring when the whole policy of the commander in chief was not to leave anything to chance?

There is another point that must be made. The sun had set in the northwest or directly in rear of the German forces as viewed by the British. That gave the latter immense advantages in visibility both for main battery gunfire and for torpedo attacks. That is demonstrated by the facts that the Germans never saw Jerram and that they failed to hit two light cruisers at 8,000 yards.

We now come to Jellicoe's change of course to south (167°) at 9:01. It was the result of his decision to avoid a night action. He said:

I rejected at once, the idea of a night action between the heavy ships, as leading to possible disaster, owing, first, to the presence of torpedo craft in such large numbers, and secondly, to the impossibility of distinguishing between our own and enemy vessels.

It is very true that those difficulties might lead to "possible disaster," but what might be "possible disaster" to Jellicoe might well be "probable disaster" to Scheer. Except for the *Marlborough* and *Warspite*, the hulls of every British capital ship were intact and they were able to steam at full speed. In the High Seas Fleet, quite a number of vessels had shell holes through their hulls, while the *Lützow, Derfflinger,* and *Seydlitz* had been severely damaged in all parts of their structure. Their secondary batteries and searchlights were generally inoperative and many of their communication facilities had been destroyed. It cannot be claimed that the British were ignorant of the German losses, for Jellicoe's report devotes seven pages to the proof of destruction of German ships. In fact, it is well known that the British believed that the German losses had been much greater than they actually were. Furthermore, the High Seas Fleet was encumbered by six slow and very vulnerable pre-dreadnought battleships.

Another point of interest is the fact that the British destroyers were practically intact and had fired only a very few torpedoes. On the other hand, it was known that the German destroyers had made frequent attacks and had fired many torpedoes, only one of which had hit a capital ship. Furthermore, the British had an overwhelming superiority in light cruisers which could assist their own destroyers and help to beat off the German destroyers. Both the 2d and 4th Light Cruiser Squadrons had demonstrated their value in that respect only recently.

Let us continue with Jellicoe's line of reasoning. He wrote:

The result of a night action under modern conditions must always be very largely a matter of pure chance. I was loath to forego the advantage of position which would have resulted from an easterly or westerly course, and I therefore decided to steer to the southward, where I should be in a position to renew the engagement at daylight, and should also be favorably placed to intercept the enemy should he make for his base by steering for Helgoland or toward the Ems and thence along the North German coast.

The first argument that a night engagement would be pure chance was merely a repetition of Jellicoe's favorite argument that he could leave nothing to chance. Certainly, there would have been chance in a night action, more than in a day action; but we believe that in this specific case Jellicoe had made an over-statement in expressing the opinion that a night action "must always be very largely a matter of pure chance." When we consider Jellicoe's enormous superiority in every respect, we must state our confident belief that the chances were greatly in Jellicoe's favor.

The argument about steering an easterly or westerly course is perfectly futile. If he had continued on his present course, 212°, he would have quickly brought on a night action or have driven the Germans far to the westward. In that case, it would be easy for him to interpose between the Germans and their bases in the morning, particularly in view of his 3-knot superiority in speed over the German pre-dreadnoughts.

In his book, Jellicoe supports the arguments given in his report by claiming that his searchlights were poor and stating that only a few of the secondary batteries of his ships had directors. Many of the German ships had their searchlights wrecked by shell fire and they did not have directors even for their main batteries. His continual thought was of what the Germans could do to him rather than what he could do to the Germans.

Whether or not it was correct for Jellicoe to have avoided a night action in order to re-engage with certainty at dawn is largely a matter of opinion, with much to be said on both sides. A bold commander would have endeavored to annihilate the High Seas Fleet. That is undoubtedly what Paul Jones, Perry, and Farragut would have done. It is what Nelson did at Aboukir Bay. A cautious commander would have put off the fateful decision, just as Jellicoe did. All that could condone Jellicoe's decision not to fight at night was his positively stated intention to engage the next morning. Unfortunately, it will be shown that when morning came he had found another plausible reason why he could not fight. In fact, our analysis of the conditions existing throughout and after the battle, discloses that Jellicoe had excellent opportunities to take action that would have resulted in a decisive success at 5:55, 6:30, 7:15, 8:40, 9:00 P.M., and 2:00 A.M. In every one of the situations, he found a different set of reasons why it was better to refuse the present opportunity thrust into his hands in order to wait for a better one. Thus, one after the other, he refused six highly favorable opportunities to fight to a decision. He had the fatal defect of not being able to leave something to chance. He who will not risk cannot win!

Irrespective of the correctness of Jellicoe's decision to steer south (167°), the execution of that plan was premature by at least 15 minutes. The sun had set at 8:19 but twilight lasts long in those northern latitudes at the beginning of June. It was late enough for main battery gunfire at medium ranges until 9:15 or possibly later. In proof of this we have in addition to the foregoing statements concerning contacts at that time, the fact that Jellicoe displayed a flag signal to his Fleet at 9:17, while Beatty made a flag signal at 9:30. Even 5 minutes of concentrated fire from the 2d Battle Squadron at 8,000 yards would have had very important effects.

It is well to point out at this time that south (167°) could be only a temporary course if Jellicoe desired to re-engage. It would place the Grand Fleet in a position between the entrances to the three German swept channels, but would not block any of them. To determine this, compare the positions of the Battle Fleet in Figs. 58 and 59 with the locations of the German channels shown in Sketch I. The chances were very strong that Scheer would use one of the two channels that led past Horn Reefs, as such a route would be the shortest and most direct to the protection of the German mine fields and to the German bases. It would, therefore, have been a wise decision to have headed directly for Horn Reefs at about 15 knots. If the Germans intended to use that route, this would be demonstrated by numerous contacts by midnight. If no contacts were made by midnight or 1:00 A.M. at the latest, it would be quite evident that the Germans did not intend to go via Horn Reefs. Then, there would still be time to intercept them off Terschelling by proceeding at full speed. That plan would have been improved by having the 1st and 3d Light Cruiser Squadrons and the 1st Flotilla cover the Terschelling route by conducting a night search between the present position of the Germans and Terschelling Island.

That Jellicoe realized perfectly the situation he would create by steering south (167°) is shown by the statement in his book that he intended to steer for Horn Reefs at daylight. However, he does not seem to have realized that if he waited that long there were excellent chances that the Germans would get past him.

CHAPTER XIX

THE EVENING ENCOUNTERS

9:15 P.M. TO 11:00 P.M.

At 9:12 Commodore Goodenough reported that he had driven enemy destroyers to the westward. Instead of giving his estimated position relative to the fleet guide or the rear battleship division, he expressed it in latitude and longitude (Fig. 49–E). The position unfortunately was about 15 miles too far to the southeastward. If taken literally, his message meant that he was driving the German destroyers directly into the British battle squadrons. It is probable, however, that Jellicoe realized that his navigational position was much in error.

At 9:17 Jellicoe ordered the three battle squadrons to form in three parallel columns, eight ships each, at 1-mile intervals. That order evidently was designed to make his formation more compact and easier to handle. This, of course, was an important advantage. However, in case of attack by German destroyers, the close formation had its disadvantages. It gave the flank squadrons no room in which to maneuver away from an attack without running into the other squadrons. Also, torpedoes fired at the flank squadrons would run through the other two, thus in many cases tripling their chances of hitting. Even in case of a chance contact with the German battleships, we believe that full intervals would have been more advantageous. It would have permitted an earlier deployment of the squadrons, would have prevented "overs" from falling into the squadrons away from the enemy and would have gained more maneuvering room. When we describe the British destroyer attacks on the head of the German battle line, try to imagine what would have happened had Scheer used a formation similar to Jellicoe's.

Each of the British squadrons formed column in its own way and at its own time. The 4th Battle Squadron, which Jellicoe led in the *Iron Duke*, executed the order promptly at 9:25 (Fig.

50–P). At 9:45 the 2d Battle Squadron formed single column
(Fig. 50–b) and then sheered in to close the interval from the
fleet guide. The 6th Division was already 2 or 3 miles behind
its proper station due to the fact that the *Marlborough* had
been unable to make the fleet speed of 17 knots. While making
turns for that speed, her injury reduced her actual speed through
the water to 16 knots or less. The 5th and 6th Divisions closed
in gradually to reduce their interval from the fleet guide. At
9:45 Jellicoe issued a reference position of the *Iron Duke* (Fig.
49–G). Her actual position (Fig. 49–H) was about 2 miles to the
northeastward. The issue of a reference position at that time was
of not much value, because so few units were in actual visual
touch with the fleet guide. The position should have been
issued before darkness set in. It is realized that there might not
have been time about 9:00 P.M. From personal experience, it is
realized how difficult it is to find an opportunity for such a
general message to the fleet. An officer handling a fleet must
always keep in mind the communication situation. It does no
good to make a decision that cannot be transmitted to the fleet.

If Jellicoe had such a high opinion of the dangers of an attack
on his battleships by the German destroyers, it is most surprising
that he did not use his strong destroyer flotillas for an attack
on the German battle line. Jellicoe says:

The Grand Fleet battle orders contained a great deal in the way
of discussion and instructions on the subject of torpedo attack in
a fleet action. The duties of light cruisers and destroyers in this
connection were dealt with at considerable length, and stress was
laid on the supreme importance both of making early torpedo attacks on the enemy's line and of immediately countering such attacks. . . .

Scant attention seems to have been paid to those instructions
during the fleet action, to which evidently they principally referred. There was now an unparalleled opportunity for an
attack at dusk and just after dark, *i.e.,* between 9:15 and 9:30.
There was every probability that such attacks if pushed home
would inflict heavy losses on the German capital ships. The
German dispositions might even have been disrupted had

Jellicoe told his flotillas to attack to the finish. However, the British commander in chief had entirely different ideas, for at 9:27 he ordered the flotillas to take station 5 miles astern of his own battle line.

Jellicoe states that there were three reasons for this order to his destroyers: (1) They would be in an excellent position to attack the High Seas Fleet if it proceeded to the southward toward its bases. (2) They would screen the battleships against the attacks of German destroyers. (3) They would be at such a distance from his battleships as would render unlikely any contacts between them during darkness.

These reasons will bear some analysis. As regards the first, it is of interest to see that Jellicoe selected a course for his battleships with the deliberate purpose of avoiding contact with the German battleships. Nevertheless, he says that his destroyers, while only 5 miles in rear of the battleships, were "in an excellent position for attacking the enemy's Fleet." These two statements obviously contradict each other. The fact that the British destroyers made contact with the German battleships beginning at 11:30 was the result of pure chance. Any officer cognizant of the problems of night search and attack by destroyers will freely admit that it is a case of extraordinary luck for a destroyer force to proceed on a short 4-mile front generally away from a closely arrayed force of enemy battleships and then make contact with those battleships over two hours after dark. For destroyers to have any reasonable chance of making contact with hostile battleships during the night, it is necessary to proceed *toward* the hostile force *immediately* after dark on a *broad* front. If contact is not made almost immediately, the chances of success decline very rapidly with the passage of time. Therefore, we can say with certainty that Jellicoe's order to his destroyers was not effectively designed for an attack against the German battleships.

A glance at the relative positions of the Fleets at 9:35 will show that a German destroyer attack was to be expected from the west rather than the north. While Jellicoe could not know the dispositions of the enemy as well as we can now, he must certainly have known that the enemy was to the westward. If the British destroyers were designed to screen the British battle-ships, they should have been disposed to the westward rather than to the northward.

In only one respect was Jellicoe's disposition of his destroyers well designed to accomplish its stated objects. It did prevent the British destroyers from making contact with their battle-ships during the night. Unfortunately, due to causes which we shall describe, they likewise failed to make contact far into the next day when their presence was much desired.

To sum up, it is our opinion that Jellicoe missed a remarkable opportunity by not ordering his destroyers to attack. There was every chance that would have gained for the British the follow-ing advantages: (1) A number of torpedo hits would have been made on German capital ships, reducing their speeds in some cases. (2) The High Seas Fleet would have been forced to the westward, probably in considerable confusion, thus preventing it from reaching the protection of the mine fields by daylight. (3) Positive information would have been learned as to the posi-tion of the High Seas Fleet early in the evening and further information would have been received from time to time. (4) Such attacks by the larger and heavier-gunned British de-stroyers would have forestalled German destroyer attacks and disorganized the German destroyer force.

It will be remembered that the plans for an earlier operation provided for the laying of mines south of Horn Reefs in the hope of ambushing the German forces. Jellicoe now judged that such a mine field might be effective against the High Seas Fleet as it returned to port; so at 9:32 he ordered the *Abdiel* to lay the mines as previously planned. That order was not received by the *Abdiel* until 10:05. She proceeded at 10:15 (Figs. 49–f and 51–G). It was an excellent idea.

Beatty was still proceeding on course SW. (212°) at 9:16 when he received a dispatch from Jellicoe, sent at 9:10, that the course of the Fleet was south (167°). The 2d Cruiser Squadron had headed south (167°) about 9:03. Ten minutes later Heath, see-ing that Beatty was keeping on to the southwestward, headed toward him (Fig. 50–J). Both Beatty and Heath in the gathering darkness narrowly escaped collision with superior forces. Battle Squadron II had continued on course south (167°) and the *Westfalen* had headed back to that course at 9:15 (Fig. 50–L). At 9:25 Scouting Group I also headed south (167°) to take station in rear of Battle Squadron III (Fig. 50–Q). Thus, both the British units were headed directly across the path of the oncoming High Seas Fleet. It was very fortunate that contact was avoided, for at 9:25 the 2d Cruiser Squadron was less than 6,000 yards from Battle Squadron II. In fact, Rear Admiral Dalwigk in the *Hannover* had sighted the British armored cruisers as early as 9:20 (Fig. 50–M). At 9:30 he reported four hostile ships in sight ahead in square 166. (See Fig. 49 for all position squares mentioned until 3:00 A.M.)

Beatty changed course to south (167°) at 9:30 according to the signal record and at 9:24 according to his report (Fig. 50–S). Because of the "gathering darkness" and for other reasons he did not close the Battle Fleet. That was a good decision, as a contact between two large friendly forces after dark is highly dangerous. About 9:35 Heath followed the battle cruisers to course south (167°) at an interval of 1 mile (Fig. 50–V). Beatty reported his position at 9:35 (Fig. 49–F) and showed that he was using the fleet course and speed. We now have the curious spectacle of this long column of 12 British ships steaming directly ahead of the High Seas Fleet on the same course, as if it were a vanguard for the Germans. With Beatty were the 8 remaining destroyers of the 1st Flotilla. With Heath were the 4 destroyers that had accompanied his ships on their screening stations: the *Midge*, *Hardy*, *Owl*, and *Mischief*. The 1st and 3d Light Cruiser Squadrons were on the starboard bow of the battle cruisers.

Scheer had resolved to steer for Horn Reefs and to maintain his course regardless of consequences. It was evident to him that he must utilize the five short hours of darkness to reach his swept channel that led past Horn Reefs. It was essential that he keep to this course at the highest possible speed. He must have reached that decision about 9:06, for at that time he notified Captain Strasser by radio: "Early air reconnaissance near Horn

Reefs very essential." That was an exceedingly dangerous message to send, because, if the British could decipher it, his intentions would be revealed. Groos says that the British intercepted and deciphered the dispatch, but we have found no reference to it in the British accounts.

Scheer evidently was not pleased to see Captain Redlich in the *Westfalen* turn sharply away at 9:08 to avoid torpedoes fired by the *Caroline* and *Royalist*, for two minutes later he issued his orders for the night: "Course of main body SSE. ¼ E. (142°). *Durchhalten*. Speed 16. Battle cruisers in rear of battle line." *Durchhalten* was one of the picturesque, but untranslatable, German orders. It meant very emphatically that the course was to be maintained without deviation. However, we shall note a number of instances when Captain Redlich very properly deviated from the established course.

At 9:15 came some bad news from the *König*. Behncke reported that the *Lützow* had disappeared astern, steering on course south (167°) at slow speed in square 007. Scheer could do nothing to help her. The *Lützow*, favored by darkness and low visibility, must make her "night ride" to Horn Reefs as best she might. The four destroyers that were still accompanying her could at least save her crew.

Scheer's order for course 142° at 9:10 apparently did not reach the *Westfalen*, for that ship continued on course 167° until about 9:40. Then, instead of changing course to the left, he went to the right to about 221° to clear Battle Squadron II (Fig. 50-w). At 9:29 Scheer had repeated the instructions for Battle Squadron II and Scouting Group I to take station astern. He directed Scouting Group II to take station ahead, with Scouting Group IV to starboard. As it happened, not a single one of those orders was executed, so confused had become the situation in the High Seas Fleet. In fact, even the German official account is quite confused, the text sometimes conflicts with the sketches and both text and sketches at times conflict with the signal record. We must make such order as possible out of this chaos; but first let us emphasize the great difficulty of a large fleet making extensive changes in its dispositions after dark. That should be done before dark. We believe that the orders at 9:10 and 9:29 could have been issued much more advantageously an hour earlier.

Rear Admiral Mauve had received the order for Battle Squadron II to take station at the rear of the battle line at 9:25, just as he saw the 2d Cruiser Squadron ahead. He believed that it would be undesirable to turn to the rear until he had cleared up the situation; but finally, about 9:58 by Groos's chart 33, the six ships of Battle Squadron II turned together to the reverse course (Fig. 50–d). That such a difficult maneuver was executed without lights on a very dark night speaks volumes for Mauve and his well-trained captains. We know no one who would like to try that maneuver even under peace-time conditions.

At 9:20, when Rear Admiral Dalwigk in the *Hannover* had sighted the 2d Cruiser Squadron, he had ordered Commodore von Reuter to resume station ahead. The latter turned the *Stettin* to the southeastward to obey that order (Fig. 50–R). About 9:45 (Fig. 50–a) Scouting Group IV passed astern of Battle Squadron II and continued to the southeastward until about 10:00. Then, von Reuter took up the fleet course. The *Elbing* of Scouting Group II, having been slowed down by condenser trouble, took station in rear of the column. Behind her fell in the *Rostock*, *G41*, and Half Flotilla XI.

Von Reuter, though far to the southeastward of the battle line, believed that he was in his proper position on its starboard side. Probably, he assumed that the *Westfalen* had been steering her course of 142° since 9:10 as ordered by Scheer, while she had been steering 167° and 221°. It was not von Reuter's fault that he was out of position. His case is a good illustration of what happens when a fleet disposition is changed during darkness.

Scouting Group II, now consisting only of the *Frankfurt* and *Pillau*, at 9:40 headed to the eastward. Therefore, that group took station far to the eastward instead of ahead of the battle line. In fact, Boedicker was even east of von Reuter. He probably also assumed that the *Westfalen* was steering the fleet course.

We must now take up the complicated story of the German flotillas. We left Flotilla II and the *V69*, *S50*, and *V46* of Half Flotilla XII being driven back to the westward by the 2d Light Cruiser Squadron about 9:00. The *S50* had been damaged in this fight and was trying to relocate the German forces. The *Regensburg* was steaming to the southward after the Fleet with the *S53*, *V71*, *V73*, *S54*, and *G88* of Flotilla III. With the *Lützow* far in the rear were the *G37* and *V45* of Half Flotilla XII and the *G38* and *G40* of Half Flotilla I. Proceeding southward to join Battle Squadron I were the *V28*, *S51*, and *S52* of Flotilla IX. En route to the *Rostock* were the *V30*, *S34*, *S33*, *V26*, and *S36* of Flotilla IX and the *G41*, flag boat of Flotilla VI, with the *V44*, *G86*, and *G87* of Half Flotilla XI. Flotilla V was with the *Rostock* and Flotilla VII was either with or approaching her. The *G42* of Flotilla III and the *S32* of Half Flotilla I were proceeding to join the battle line. The *G39* with Hipper on board was accompanying the battle cruisers.

It will be remembered that Scheer at 8:12 P.M. had ordered night attacks under the direction of the First Leader of Destroyers, Commodore Michelsen. We have seen that produced some confusion because the Second Leader of Destroyers, Commodore Heinrich, had already ordered Flotilla II and Half Flotilla XII to attack. That situation was very well cleared up by a message Heinrich sent at 8:26 to Michelsen, stating just how the two units had been directed to attack. Michelsen, in turn, at 8:31 directed Heinrich to order the dispositions for the boats under his orders. Meanwhile Heinrich, as we have seen, had sent all his remaining destroyers of the Scouting Forces to Battle Squadron I and the *Rostock*. As those boats either had been damaged or had expended practically all their torpedoes, it did not interfere with the effectiveness of the German night attacks. We have noted, while the *Regensburg* was proceeding southward, she encountered five destroyers of Flotilla III. Heinrich had directed those boats to keep with him. Thus, it will be noted that Heinrich had some of Michelsen's destroyers, while Michelsen had some of Heinrich's.

In Heinrich's attack order of 8:30 to Flotilla II and Half

Flotilla XII, there had been a provision that the "initial point" for 8:30 would be sent to them later. At 9:00 Heinrich informed those destroyer units that at 9:00 the rear ship of the battle line was in the lower part of square 165 on course south (167°). Evidently, he intended that, by working back from that position with the reverse course, the initial point for 8:30 could be determined. That message must have been the basis for the dispatch the Admiralty sent Jellicoe at 9:58: "At 9:00 P.M. rear ship of enemy B.F. in Lat. 56°–33′ N., Long. 5°–30′ E., on southerly course." That position (Figs. 49–A and 50–A) was exactly in the lower part of square 165. That leads to the conclusion, confirmed by later events, that the British had the German position chart. It is not probable that position was fixed by direction finders. Of course, these instruments might have fixed the position of the *Regensburg* and assumed that she was the last vessel of the battle line. However, that would have meant a 16-mile error for the direction finders, for the *Regensburg's* actual position (Fig. 49–C) was about 16 miles north of the position reported to Jellicoe. Actually, Heinrich made a very large error in reporting the position of the *König* in lower 165, for, as shown by Figs. 49 and 50, she was about 9.5 miles north of that position. That error, strangely enough, was transmitted to Jellicoe. It must have been very confusing to him, as it placed the German battle line much farther to the southward than it actually was, and than other information indicated. That may have induced Jellicoe to discredit other information furnished him by the Admiralty. Incidentally, the Admiralty had done another splendid piece of intelligence work and could not be blamed for Heinrich's error in navigation. Here, in fact, was an instance of entirely unintended radio deception. If the Germans had known that the British had broken their codes and ciphers, they had endless possibilities in using radio deception.

At 9:02 Michelsen ordered Flotillas V and VII to attack. The sectors assigned were to the southward of those assigned by Heinrich for the units that had already advanced to the attack. Flotilla VII was to search from SE. to S. by E. (122° to 157°), while Flotilla V was assigned the sector from S. by E. to SSW. (157° to

189°). Square 165 was designated as the origin of the search. It was one square too far to the south. Michelsen's orders were evidently intercepted by the British shore stations. It was probably the basis for the Admiralty's message timed 9:05 and sent at 9:55: "Three destroyer flotillas have been ordered to attack you during the night." That message may have been based upon a combination of the messages of Michelsen and Heinrich.

There was considerable confusion in the execution of Michelsen's attack order. In the first place, he had not been able to reach the van of the battle line, the position from which he had intended to launch the attack. Flotillas V and VII were old and small destroyers. They had been steaming at high speeds for many hours. Their fires were dirty and their firemen exhausted. In consequence 17 knots were all they could make. Even when steaming at 15 knots, their presence was disclosed by smoke and sparks from their stacks. In consequence, when the attack was ordered at 9:02, the *Rostock* and the flotillas were close on the starboard beam of the *König*, the rear battleship. That made it necessary for the destroyers to proceed through their battle line in the growing darkness, if they were to advance promptly in their assigned sectors. Such procedure not only involved the danger of collision with the battleships, but also introduced the possibility of the destroyers being mistaken for enemy vessels. There was also a fear that Flotillas V and VII might make contact with the destroyers that had already been ordered to attack. Even more probable was contact with the German light cruisers of Scouting Groups II and IV. Therefore, severe, perhaps insuperable, handicaps were imposed on Flotillas V and VII even before their attack actually commenced about 9:25 (Fig. 50–N and 0).

Commander von Koch, Commander of Flotilla VII, had planned to divide his 9 boats into a number of groups, so as to cover the entire sector assigned. However, in view of the many difficulties confronting the flotilla, he decided that would involve too many complications; so he retained it in one formation. It was already 9:30 when he passed astern of Battle Squadron III (Fig. 50–T) and commenced his advance at 17 knots. At

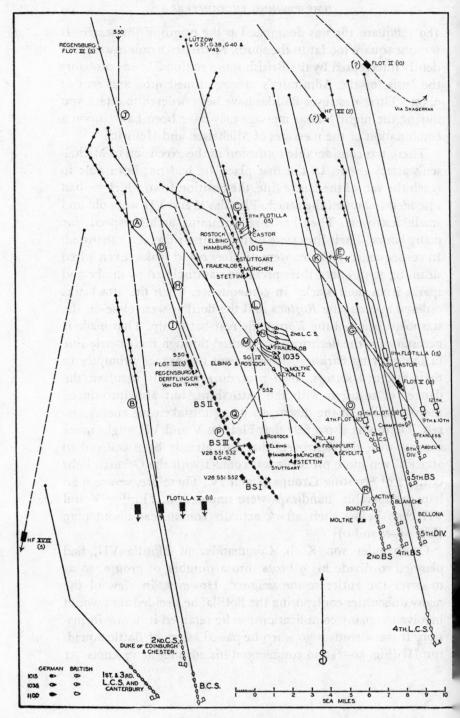

FIG. 51. 10:00-11:00 P.M.

that time a friendly battleship mistook the flotilla for hostile destroyers and opened fire at 2,000 yards. Before the boats could disappear in the failing light a salvo had fallen within 50 yards of the *S23*. To avoid the fire of his own ships, von Koch changed course to the left to SE. (122°). That course was the extreme left limit of his 3-point sector and deflected his advance northward away from the British battle line. It was, to say the least, most unfortunate.

Meanwhile, Commander Heinecke had led Flotilla V, 11 boats in all, on course S. ½ W. (173°). His flotilla was much delayed in gaining a position ahead of the battle line and did not deploy into groups for search and attack until 11:00 P.M. It will be noted that no German destroyers proceeded in the sector between SE. (122°) and S. ½ W. (173°), four and a half points in width. Unfortunately, that was the sector in which the British battleships probably would have been located.

After dispatching Flotillas V and VII to the attack at 9:02, Michelsen in the *Rostock* proceeded at high speed toward the van of the Fleet. By 9:30 he was close to the *Hannover*, which only 10 minutes before had sighted the 2d Cruiser Squadron. Michelsen was now joined by the 5 boats of Flotilla IX that Heinrich had sent on. They were the *V30*, *S33*, *S34* of Half Flotilla XVIII and the *V26* and *S36* of Half Flotilla XVII. At 9:40 Michelsen directed that unit to attack the enemy just reported by Dalwigk (Fig. 50-x). Evidently, he realized that his orders were too indefinite, for 15 minutes later he assigned the sector between SW. and SSW. (212° to 189°) to Half Flotilla XVIII, apparently that title included all 5 boats. They probably proceeded as one body under command of Commander Tillessen, Commander of Half Flotilla XVIII, in the *V30*. As Groos says, "the success of this attack was problematical from the start." The comparatively slow speed of the German destroyers did not permit contact with the 2d Cruiser Squadron which had disappeared into the darkness. Furthermore, the change of course of the cruisers to the south (167°) at 9:35, to follow Beatty, lost to Tillessen all hope of contact, as he was steering a divergent course. Furthermore, the destroyers probably did not average more than one torpedo per boat, a fact of which Michelsen probably was ignorant, as he had not witnessed the operations of Flotilla IX. Finally, those boats had participated in three most determined attacks and their personnel must have been tired to the point of exhaustion.

The long column of German battleships proved difficult to handle during the very dark night. It was impossible to maneuver such a force. All that could be done was to prescribe a fleet course and hope that it could be followed with some degree of accuracy. Even such a simple method of control proved difficult for Scheer in the ninth ship, to exercise. We have seen that he had prescribed 142° as the fleet course, while the *Westfalen* at 9:35 had gone about 221° to clear Battle Squadron II. By 9:43 that had been accomplished and Redlich turned back to about 147° (Fig. 50–Y). At 9:45, according to the signal record, Scheer ordered course SSE. ¾ E. (137°) for the main body. Groos in his text indicates that Scheer merely repeated the order for course SSE. ¼ E. (142°). At 10:02 the *Westfalen* turned left to about 130° in accordance with Groos's chart 31 (Fig. 51–A); but at 10:08 she sheered right to about 157° (Fig. 51–D). The reasons for steering these various courses when a different one had been prescribed by Scheer are not stated.

There are much conflicting data concerning the time at which Vice Admiral Hipper shifted his flag from the *G39* to the *Moltke*. However, the signal record presents three distinct signals establishing the fact that the transfer took place about 9:55 (Fig. 50–C). Immediately upon boarding the battle cruiser, Hipper set out at 20 knots to resume station ahead of the battle line. Apparently, the *Moltke* had not received either of Scheer's signals that directed the battle cruisers to take station in the rear. Hipper's movement resulted in the disruption of Scouting Group I as an organized unit and created much confusion. Also, it led the badly injured battle cruisers into many hazardous situations. The *Derfflinger* and *Von der Tann* could steam at only 18 knots. Consequently, they fell far in rear of the *Moltke* and *Seydlitz*. When the *Derfflinger* and *Von der Tann* were abreast of the fleet flagship, Scheer ordered them to take station in the rear.

Having reached a position near the rear of Battle Squadron III, Rear Admiral Mauve counter-marched Battle Squadron II in the darkness and took station in natural order after the *König*. That was a fine maneuver (Fig. 51–H). At 10:25, five minutes after Mauve had taken station, the *Von der Tann* and *Derfflinger* dropped into position in rear of Battle Squadron II (Fig. 51–I). Finally, the *Regensburg* with her five boats of Flotilla III took station in rear of the *Derfflinger*. At 10:27 Heinrich was joined by the *S50* which had been damaged in the action with the 2d Light Cruiser Squadron (Fig. 51–J). At last, the German battle line had been formed. Jellicoe had given the Germans a much needed respite. It was indeed fortunate for the latter that during such a critical period Jellicoe had failed to take the offensive against their battle line either with battleships or destroyers.

Already contacts between the light forces had begun. On the German side, Scouting Groups II and IV, as we have seen, had taken station far to the eastward of their battle line. Flotilla VII was proceeding on course SE. (122°). On the British side, the *Castor*, 11th Flotilla, and 2d Light Cruiser Squadron were to the northwestward of their battle line, while the 4th Flotilla was directly in rear of its right flank. The prelude to the heavy fighting of the night consisted of four brief engagements between those opposing light forces. The actions increased in intensity from the bloodless clash at 9:50 to a desperately fought engagement at 11:20.

At 9:50 Flotilla VII, 9 small destroyers, made contact with the 10 large destroyers and 2 leaders of the 4th Flotilla. As in many cases during that eventful night, the data concerning that brief contact are quite conflicting. The *Garland's* report timed at 9:02 evidently should have been 10:02 as recognition signal lights would hardly have been displayed as early as 9:02 P.M. The 4th Flotilla had been ahead of the 2d Battle Squadron at 9:27 when the order had been given for all flotillas to take station 5 miles in rear of the battle squadrons. Course was reversed about 9:30 and the flotilla headed north (347°) between the battleship columns (Fig. 50–U). About 10:50 the flotilla reversed course to the southward. While turning, the fourth boat in the column, the *Garland,* sighted 4 German destroyers (Fig. 50–Z). The *S24* sighted the British destroyers at the same instant, but believed that they might be Flotilla II; so she showed the colored lights of the German recognition signals. As no reply to that challenge was made, the *S24, S16, S18,* and *S15* each fired one torpedo (Figs. 49–1 and 50–e), 9:58. The *Garland* immediately opened fire and turned away, reporting by radio to the flotilla commander: "German destroyers steaming SE. (122°)." The *Garland* saw two torpedoes and the *Fortune* one. The latter fired a single shot along its reverse track. Flotilla VII turned to the southward for a search in that direction; but as the Grand Fleet was making 17 knots, the same as the German destroyers, no further developments resulted. At 10:02 the *S24* reported a contact with hostile destroyers in square 054. That square was about 28 miles to the southward of the actual place of contact.

At 9:58 the *Frankfurt* and *Pillau* sighted the *Castor* and the 11th Flotilla, the boats of which were mistaken for cruisers. The German light cruisers each fired a torpedo at a range of about 1,000 yards and turned away sharply to the northwestward (Fig. 50–f). Boedicker reported 5 enemy cruisers on course ENE. (54°) in square 017. That was one square too far to the eastward, as the contact occurred in square 010. The *Castor* apparently did not sight Scouting Group II during that brief contact.

At 10:05, however, the *Castor* sighted ships on the starboard bow (Fig. 51–C). After a few minutes, the German ships challenged, using a part of the correct British recognition signal. At 10:12 two ships turned their searchlights full on the *Castor* and opened fire at 1,100 yards (Figs. 49–K and 51–F). They were the *Hamburg* and *Elbing,* in the rear of the long column headed by Scouting Group IV. From her dispatch timed at 10:21, the *Rostock* also seems to have been engaged.

The well-directed German shell fire scored again and again on the British light cruiser, making a total of 9 or 10 hits. In a few minutes, bursting shell killed 13 and wounded 23 of her complement. The material damage was comparatively slight. However, the three shells struck the bridge and put all signal gear and radio instruments temporarily out of action. That prevented Hawksley from issuing orders to the 11th Flotilla, 15 large destroyers, at a critical moment. The destroyers, put on their own, failed signally to take advantage of a most fortunate opportunity to injure the enemy. It was the old story of inertness and lack of initiative. Only the *Magic* and *Marne* fired torpedoes at targets distant only 1,000 yards, which were displaying searchlights as perfect points of aim. The excuses that they were blinded by the *Castor's* gunfire and thought that she was fighting friendly ships only serve to make their failure more glaring. Hawksley's admission that "a good opportunity of firing torpedoes was lost," we consider most restrained. The *Castor* fired the third torpedo from the British forces. The *Hamburg* was hit twice by shells that wounded three men. One British torpedo was sighted coming directly for the *Elbing*. Every effort to avoid it failed and the torpedo passed directly under the ship. Evidently, its depth mechanism had been set for deep-draft battleships. When all classes of hostile ships may be encountered at close ranges during darkness, at least some torpedoes should be set for an 8-foot depth.

It was not until 10:50 that Hawksley was able to report via the *Kempenfelt* that he had been engaged with enemy cruisers. The action, however, had been noted in the battle line. The *Benbow* states at 10:12: "Firing commenced on starboard beam" (Fig. 51–E). The *Rostock* at 10:21 reported having been engaged with enemy light cruisers and destroyers on a southerly course in square 012. That square was one too far to the southward.

At 10:19 the *Elbing* reported to the High Seas Fleet that the British recognition signal after 10:00 P.M. was *U*. At 10:33 the *Frankfurt* corrected that message with a broadcast dispatch that the recognition signal was *UA* instead of *U*.

Hawksley did not renew the action or search to the westward to determine what was behind the German light cruisers. It is true that his signal gear had been destroyed and he could not have assumed for the present the actual leadership of the destroyers, but he could have called alongside the leading destroyer and given orders for the senior destroyer commander to take charge and search to the southwestward. That might have well won a brilliant success, for he was distant only 4 miles from the German battle line and had available 15 fine destroyers. It was another case of inert leadership for which Jellicoe must be charged with the primary responsibility. To order destroyers to take station 5 miles in rear of the battleships without assigning any mission, without telling them the direction of the enemy, or without adding even a sentence to guide their conduct paralyzed that powerful force to a great degree during all the night. His stated object of giving the destroyers opportunities to attack German battleships was not at all understood by the flotilla commanders. Only one, Captain Stirling, after making contact with the enemy, deliberately attacked his battle line. On the present occasion, Hawksley states that he continued on course south (167°), "my object being to be within reach of the fleet at daybreak." To operate a fine flotilla with such a perfectly futile mission as that was evidently the natural result of Jellicoe's passive leadership and Fabian tactics. That splendid flotilla made no further contact with the enemy. The rest of the night was a perfect blank. Must not Hawksley have seen the prolonged engagements that occurred later? Why did he not follow the old rule of marching to the sound of the guns, which applies perfectly to night destroyer operations? Finally, he failed to make contact with the British battleships at dawn. Need we say more?

At 10:05 the *Princess Royal* indulged in some target practice, firing for 15 minutes on cruisers on the starboard beam (Fig. 51–B). They could only have been vessels of the 1st or 3d Light Cruiser Squadrons, which were somewhat forward of the beam. Fortunately, her fire was ineffective. Such mistakes are always liable to occur, but it is rather remarkable that the firing should have continued for so long.

About 10:30 there were some minor contacts between the rear boats of the 4th Flotilla and German destroyers. Evidently, the latter must have been boats of Flotilla VII which had been following along to the southward at 17 knots. At 10:27 the *Contest* reported to the *Tipperary* that she had fired one round at three destroyers astern that were steering SE. (122°). Three minutes later, the *Garland* reported to the *Castor* that she had fired at destroyers astern (Fig. 51–K). The battleship *Canada* evidently intercepted the first signal, for at 10:30 she signaled the *Iron Duke*: "*Contest* to Captain D. Urgent. German T. B. D. steering NE." As the message of the *Contest* was sent by flashing light, the incident shows how closely the Fleets were in contact and how narrowly the German destroyers missed their objective. Had their flotilla commander searched the entire sector assigned to him and not proceeded merely along its northern limit, the location of the British battleships would have been highly probable.

About 10:30 the 2d Light Cruiser Squadron came into contact with Scouting Group IV (Fig. 51–I). The hostile columns were converging at a slight angle. On each side there was doubt as to whether the strange vessels were friend or foe. This doubt was emphasized by the fact that the two Fleets were steaming on nearly parallel courses. Usually, the course of a strange unit encountered during darkness is one of the best means of determining whether it be friend or foe. At that critical moment of contact, two large vessels steaming at high speed appeared on the starboard beam of the *Stettin* which carried the pennant of Commodore von Reuter. They were the *Moltke* and *Seydlitz* endeavoring at 22 knots to take station ahead of the German battle line (Fig. 51–M). To avoid collision, the *Stettin* had to slow down. As the formation bunched up, the three next ships, the *München*, *Frauenlob*, and *Stuttgart*, sheered out to port. The *Hamburg* and *Elbing* which had recently engaged the *Castor* were also forced out of column. The *Rostock*, the seventh ship, seems to have been somewhat astern.

The *Stettin* challenged the strange cruisers on the port hand with colored lights about 10:35. Both columns burst into fire at the point-blank range of 800 yards (Figs. 49–L and 51–N). The two leading British vessels, the *Southampton* and *Dublin*, turned on searchlights, as did most, if not all, the German vessels. The *Southampton* and *Dublin* were deluged with the effective fire of the four leading German cruisers. The upper decks of the *Southampton* were wrecked and the guns' crews virtually annihilated. Powder fires burned fiercely as high as the mastheads. In a few minutes, there were 35 killed and 41 wounded, a total of 76, according to the official report, or 89 or 90 according to two officers on board. She was hit 18 times in all, but the 4.1-inch shells did little damage to the structure of the ship.

The torpedo lieutenant of *Southampton* performed a memorable exploit. Let him tell us of it:

On the bridge the full glare of the searchlights of the leading enemy ship was on us, and we could see nothing, but I had already received enough impression of the general direction of advance of the enemy for the purpose of torpedo fire, so I passed down an order to the torpedo flat and waited impatiently for a reply. When it came through (the report "ready") I fired at a group of hostile searchlights, which were the only things visible.

As we shall soon see, that torpedo did more damage than all the 18 hits received by the *Southampton*.

This statement, however, might well require some modification, had not luck favored the little British cruiser, for powder charges caught fire amidships where the ammunition hoist led down into the magazine. The fire spread down the hoist into the ship. Two great white flames roared fiercely as high as the foretop. An explosion seemed inevitable, but the cruiser seemed to have been better designed than the three great battle cruisers that had been lost, for the flames were unable to gain entry into the magazine and finally died out. Fortune had favored the brave!

The *Dublin* was hit 13 times by the fourth and fifth German ships. However, the damage inflicted by their 4.1-inch shells was comparatively slight. The greatest injury was caused by a shell that hit the chart house and destroyed all the charts. Lieutenant Perry Strickland, the navigator, and 2 men were killed, while 24 men were wounded. The *Nottingham* and *Birmingham* did not turn on their searchlights. They directed their fire at the German searchlights through the smoke clouds of the ships ahead. They came under little German fire and were not hit during the action. During the fight, all the British ships had turned away rather sharply from the enemy.

The Germans had rather the better of the gun battle, though most of their ships were hit. The *Stettin* was about to fire a torpedo, when two hits destroyed a searchlight and pierced a steam line. Clouds of steam obscured the view and prevented the torpedo from being fired. The unfortunate bunching of the other ships prevented all from firing their torpedoes, except the *München*. That ship was hit twice by 6-inch shells. The *Hamburg* also was hit twice. One shell struck the bridge, killed the executive officer and 10 men, while others were wounded. The *Elbing* was hit by a single shell that wrecked her radio station and caused 18 casualties.

It was the gallant little *Frauenlob* that suffered heaviest. The *Southampton's* torpedo hit her in the auxiliary machinery space. The ship listed far to port. Lights and ammunition hoists failed. Hits aft set the ship afire. Groos says with pride:

But nothing shook the heroic determination of her crew. Standing in water up to their waists, the crew of No. 4 gun, under Boatswain's Mate Schmidt, continued to fire. Then flames and floods made an end to the struggle. The cruiser capsized, and with three hurras for Kaiser and Empire, the captain, 11 officers, and 308 men gave their lives for their country.

Thus, with true Germanic courage, the little *Frauenlob* passes from our story, leaving another glorious page in naval history. As will be told later, 5 men of her crew were saved after many hours in the water.

The *Stuttgart* avoided the *Frauenlob* only by sheering sharply to the right. She lost the Scouting Group and joined Battle Squadron I. The *Hamburg* also became separated from the formation when the *Moltke* sheered across her bow. She proceeded independently for the rest of the night. The *Elbing* and *Rostock* were able to maintain contact with the *Stettin* and *München*, thus giving von Reuter four ships. During the confusion, the *Seydlitz* lost touch with the *Moltke* and both vessels proceeded independently ahead of the Fleet.

After the fight, Goodenough assembled his squadron and proceeded after the Battle Fleet on course about 140°. Due to an injury to his radio, it was not until 11:38 that his report of the action, sent via the *Nottingham*, reached Jellicoe. This hard-fought action, as admitted by the Admiralty *Narrative*, was clearly seen by the entire Grand Fleet. Most of the vessels believed that German destroyers were in action. The *Active*, which was in rear of the 2d Battle Squadron, reports having seen light cruisers in action only 1 mile distant. The *Boadicea* and *Thunderer* clearly saw the fight. The *Boadicea* believed that several German cruisers were engaging a single British ship, evidently the *Southampton*. The *Thunderer* believed that British destroyers had attacked a strange cruiser.

After proceeding for some distance with the 2d Light Cruiser Squadron, the *Dublin* about 11:10 lost the ship ahead (Fig. 52–A). She endeavored to proceed to the southward, but the loss of all her charts and an injury to her compass prevented her from regaining contact until the next day. Also, about 11:10 the remainder of the squadron made contact with the 5th Battle Squadron (Fig. 52–A). The *Southampton* and *Nottingham* sheered off to the right and followed the Fleet on a southerly course. The *Birmingham* had to turn sharply to the left to avoid collision. She took station on the starboard quarter of the *Malaya* and maintained that station during the night.

If we might offer a comment on the light cruiser action, it would be to emphasize the fact that the torpedo is a much more deadly weapon under such conditions than the gun. It is remarkable that each side fired only one torpedo. The old German cruisers were fitted with only two submerged tubes, one on each side. The British ships had the same armament. As it took several minutes to reload a submerged tube, it is doubtful whether any ship could have fired more than one, or at most two, torpedoes. Light cruisers of today have powerful batteries of above-water tubes which should be very effective in such night encounters.

About 10:40 the *Moltke* came in contact with the *Thunderer,* rear ship of the 2d Battle Squadron, and the attached light cruiser *Boadicea* which was following her (Figs. 49–M and 51–O). The *Moltke* challenged with colored lights. The *Boadicea* distinctly made out a "large cruiser." She reported to the *Thunderer* that enemy ships were on the starboard beam. The *Thunderer* saw a German challenge repeated three times. "Fire was not opened," her captain reports, "as it was considered inadvisable to show up battle fleet unless obvious attack was intended." That, it is true, was a good reason for withholding fire, but how could the *Thunderer* know that obvious attack was not intended. Suppose the *Moltke* had been the leader of a German battle squadron, which was highly probable. Then, the Germans might have got in their first salvo. At such close range, that might have been quite enough to finish the *Thunderer.* In the situation, as it existed, the *Thunderer* could probably have badly damaged the *Moltke* by opening fire. That, in turn, might have brought German destroyers against the British battle squadrons. The choice of decisions as to whether the *Thunderer* should or should not have opened fire is therefore quite evenly balanced.

Meanwhile, the *Marlborough's* torpedo hit had created a most dangerous situation for the 6th Division. Her speed had so decreased that by 10:00 P.M. she was 4 miles behind her proper station in rear of the 5th Division. The 5th Battle Squadron had originally taken station in rear of the 6th Division. At 10:05, however, Evan-Thomas found that he had got well ahead of the *Marlborough,* so he counter-marched to starboard. At 10:07, having rejoined the division, he counter-marched to port. At 10:12 the *Barham* ranged up abreast the *Marlborough.* As she was seen to be steaming quite slowly, Evan-Thomas went ahead at 18 knots to overtake the British battle line. It is most fortunate that he did not remain in rear of the 6th Division, for Burney fell farther and farther to the rear and finally lost contact entirely with his battle line. He did not report this very dangerous situation to Jellicoe, nor did he send on the three good ships of his division to join the battle line. As will be seen, he narrowly escaped disaster through contact with the German battle line.

At 10:41 the Admiralty, according to its *Narrative,* reported to Jellicoe: "German Battle Fleet ordered home at 9:14 P.M. Battle cruisers in rear, course SSE. ¾ E., speed 16 knots." That was one of the most remarkable feats of naval intelligence recorded by history. The course was that given in Scheer's signal of 9:45. The speed had been obtained from his message of 9:14. Both were absolutely correct and were invaluable information to Jellicoe. It will be noted that both course and speed are stated as absolute facts by the Admiralty. The statement that the High Seas Fleet had been ordered home showed that the information had been obtained from German radio messages. Neither in his report nor in his book did Jellicoe even mention that important message. It is true that a course and speed under some conditions would be information of momentary value only; but here was a message sent just as darkness set in. It was a very specific course, not used for maneuvering purposes, but evidently to gain a navigational position; and the course led to the vicinity of Horn Reefs. Thus, this course disclosed Scheer's intentions for the night march of his Fleet. His plans were given into the hands of his enemy!

At 10:50 the *Iron Duke* received Hawksley's dispatch stating that he had been engaged with German cruisers. As the commodore had said that he was proceeding south (167°) at 17 knots, he must be proceeding in quite close company with the battle squadrons. As the action had taken place an hour and a quarter after the Grand Fleet had gone south, it was valuable evidence that the High Seas Fleet was not making a detour to the westward to return home via Terschelling. On the contrary, it was a precise confirmation of the Admiralty's dispatch and clearly indicated that the High Seas Fleet was returning via Horn Reefs lightship. It would be most remarkable for the German cruisers to take that route, while the battleships proceeded via Terschelling. Nevertheless, Jellicoe failed to change the course of the Grand Fleet toward Horn Reefs. Furthermore, he failed to pass on to the Fleet, and particularly to the cruisers and destroyers, the reported course and speed of the High Seas Fleet, as forwarded to him by the Admiralty. The very least he could have done was to order the 4th Light Cruiser Squadron, which was immediately available ahead of the Battle Fleet, to cover the approaches to Horn Reefs and to gain positive information of the High Seas Fleet if it were proceeding in that direction. He might also have warned all light cruisers and destroyers making contacts with German capital ships to report such contacts immediately.

We shall now look at that interesting situation from the viewpoint of Scheer. At 10:12 a dispatch from the *G40* was received by Michelsen in the *Rostock*. It stated that at 9:30 the four destroyers that evidently were escorting the *Lützow* were in square 018 center, course SSW. (189°), speed 13 knots. Though the dispatch was broadcast to the Fleet, Scheer does not appear to have received it at that time, for at 10:15 he ordered the *G42* to send a group of destroyers to locate the *Lützow*. He said that she had been lost to sight in square 008 on course south (167°), steaming at slow speed, information that had come from the *König* an hour before. The German accounts do not state what action was taken by the *G42* on that order. The *G42* was attached to Flotilla III, but had not rejoined her flotilla since about 7:00 P.M. She was not a flag boat of a flotilla or half flotilla and had no boats under her orders. In the circumstances, all she could do was to proceed to the *Lützow* herself or inform Michelsen of her orders. Apparently, Scheer did not realize that there were already four boats with the *Lützow*.

At 10:32 Scheer set the course of the High Seas Fleet SE. by S. (134°). The *Westfalen* obeyed the order at 10:45 (Fig. 51–P).

At 10:36 Michelsen ordered all flotillas to concentrate by 3:00 A.M. in the vicinity of Horn Reefs, otherwise to return via the Skagerrak. As before stated, it was very dangerous to mention Horn Reefs in a radio message. Apparently, the British were unable to decipher that important information. We consider the permission for the destroyers to return via the Skagerrak to have been a grave error. No destroyers should have been permitted to return via the Skagerrak, except those badly damaged or carry-

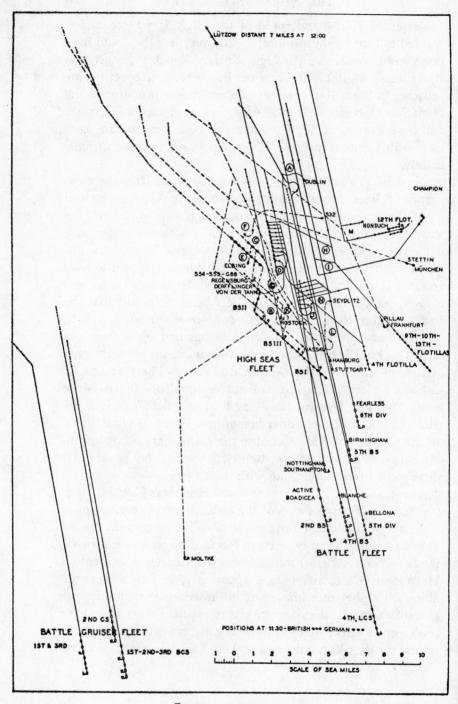

FIG. 52. 11:00-12:00 P.M.

ing the crews of large ships that had sunk. It was of the utmost importance to have all the flotillas with the Fleet at daylight next morning, when a decisive engagement should have been expected.

At 10:38 an interesting dispatch came to Scheer from the *Rostock*. It said that at 10:21 she had fired on enemy light cruisers and destroyers on a southerly course in square 012. This, as we have seen, referred to the action with the *Castor* and the 11th Flotilla. Square 012 was one too far to the southward. As it happened the German battle line was just entering that square when the message was received. Therefore, it indicated that British light forces were directly in the path of the Fleet. However, even that alarming information did not deter the calm and resolute commander in chief from holding his course toward Horn Reefs. Here we see Scheer at his very best, prepared to cut his way through the enemy regardless of consequences.

A message arrived from Flotilla VII at 10:45. It stated that at 10:02 in square 054 the flotilla had made contact with enemy destroyers going southward at high speed. A minute later there arrived the delayed report from the *Frankfurt* that at 10:02 she had been in action with enemy light cruisers. It referred to the torpedo fire of Scouting Group II against the *Castor* and the 11th Flotilla. At 10:53 the *Lützow* reported that at 10:32 she was still in square 007, on course S. by W. (179°). She was now making only 11 knots. She asked where the enemy was expected. Scheer, apparently not realizing that she was accompanied by four destroyers, ordered the *S52, S51,* and *V28,* which were close to his flagship, to proceed to the *Lützow's* assistance. Only the *S52* executed that order and steamed to the northeastward (Fig. 51–Q). The other two destroyers had been damaged and reduced in speed.

At 10:55 the *Moltke* made a second contact with 2d Battle Squadron (Figs. 49–N and 51–R). She does not appear to have been sighted by the enemy. Unfortunately, the British ships disappeared before her torpedo tubes could be brought to bear. Also, the destruction of her radio equipment prevented the *Moltke* from reporting the presence of the hostile battleships.

Not only would this have been most useful to Scheer, but it might well have permitted Flotilla V, which was now advancing, to have made contact with the British battle squadrons. At 11:20 the *Moltke* made a third contact with the 2d Battle Squadron (Figs. 49–0 and 52–B). After escaping from that contact, she set her course to the southward. She was unable to report this third contact until 1:04 A.M. Then, a dispatch from the *G39* which still accompanied her gave the important information, too late to be of value to the German destroyers. Incidentally, the *G39*, which had six torpedoes still remaining, had quite an opportunity for an individual attack during those contacts if he actually sighted the enemy.

CHAPTER XX

ENCOUNTERS WITH THE 4TH FLOTILLA
11:00 P.M., May 31, TO 12:30 A.M., June 1

UP TO 11:00 Scheer had received numerous reports of British cruisers and destroyers, but no information had come in concerning their battleships since 7:30. Even that information had been most indefinite. He had not the slightest reason to believe that the British Battle Fleet was so close at hand. It was, therefore, impracticable to launch any offensive thrust against it or to estimate with any degree of certainty, a course for the High Seas Fleet that would avoid the far superior British forces. However, to reach Horn Reefs, it evidently would be necessary to risk engagements with the British light forces. Nobody, of course, could have guessed that practically all of the enemy destroyers were closely concentrated across the direct route of the High Seas Fleet to Horn Reefs. As his battleships had not yet come in contact with the hostile destroyers and as the British light forces were reported on southerly courses, it was evident that an organized night destroyer attack was not to be feared. It would be a matter of pure chance where contacts were made. To go straight through the enemy at maximum speed would tend to minimize the attacks. Maneuvering or detours by his Fleet would delay his progress to his destination and permit more night destroyer attacks, while permitting the British Battle Fleet to interpose before daylight. Finally, Scheer was confident of his ability to beat off the hostile destroyers with his well-trained secondary batteries. In that respect, he was fortunate in having in the van the squadron which had received no damage during the day action. To fight his way through to Horn Reefs was, in our opinion, the only way he could save his Fleet from an enemy determined to fight to the finish and regardless of losses.

At 11:02 Scheer set the course of the High Seas Fleet another quarter point to the left. He sent the message direct to the *West-*

falen: "Course SE. ¾ S. (131°) to Horn Reefs lightship." At the same time, he broadcast the position of the Fleet at 11:00 P.M. as in square 012 and repeated the course that he had just set. It appears that the *Westfalen* steered a bit to the right of the signaled course, but that may be explained by the changing variation. The course of the *Westfalen* led 12.5 miles outside of Horn Reefs lightship.

The course of the High Seas Fleet was now converging sharply with that of the Grand Fleet. As the Germans were proceeding 1 knot slower then the British, the combination of courses and speeds sent the High Seas Fleet slowly across the rear of the Grand Fleet. As the British flotillas were disposed 5 miles in rear of the British battleships, the relative movement of the High Seas Fleet brought it in contact with all the various flotillas in turn, except 11th Flotilla. Had the rival commanders in chief spent a month together planning how to arrange for the German battle line to run through the British destroyers so as to give the latter their best chance to attack, no more favorable plan could have been found than the one Providence provided on the night of May 31. It seemed that, as Jellicoe and his subordinates rejected opportunity after opportunity, fortune finally offered them even better ones that could not be entirely refused or evaded, despite their many attempts to do so. Certainly in all naval history there were never such opportunities literally forced upon commanders and captains as upon that eventful night. Think of being able time after time to fire torpedoes at point-blank range at the head of a single column of 24 capital ships, almost entirely unprotected by destroyer and cruiser screens!

It might be added that night destroyer attacks for many years before 1916 were one of the favorite operations of the United States Navy. Our destroyers, under the able and inspired leadership of Captain W. S. Sims, had developed great proficiency in those attacks. As an ensign about 1912, this writer distinctly remembers performing the duties of an assistant torpedo umpire in U.S.S. *Michigan.* It was my task to determine the torpedo hits made by a destroyer division on that ship, while steaming as one of a battleship division on a dark night. The attack was conducted in a most impressive and effective manner. If the 4th Flotilla had been American destroyers on the night of May 31, I am certain that there would have been disaster to either the Germans or ourselves, probably to both!

The British destroyers had originally been deployed in five groups from east to west. At 10:15 the groups were composed as follows: the *Castor* and 11th Flotilla (15 destroyers); the 4th Flotilla (12 destroyers); the *Champion* and 13th Flotilla (9 destroyers); 9th and 10th Flotillas (5 destroyers); and 12th Flotilla (15 destroyers). That gave the formidable total of 2 light cruisers and 56 destroyers. Included among the latter, were 4 large destroyers which the British called flotilla leaders. All the destroyers burned oil and were able to make full speed on short notice and to maintain it for long periods. They were large seaworthy boats, undamaged by the day action. All but a very few had their full quota of torpedoes intact. The *Moorsom,* whose oil supply had been reduced by hits in her fuel tanks, had commenced her return to port and is not included in the above tabulation. Proceeding with the destroyers was the armored cruiser *Black Prince* which has been mentioned as being on the starboard quarter of the *Marlborough* during the first watch.

After the *Castor's* serious injuries in the 10:15 action, Hawksley had led his flotilla to the eastward to break off the action. Thereafter, the flotilla had continued to the southward. Its exact position has not been stated, but at 11:26 the commander of the 4th Flotilla informed the *Garland*: "11th Flotilla is on our starboard beam." That, as will be shown later, was incorrect. It seems that the *Castor* had gone farther to the eastward, for at 12:04 she exchanged a flashing light signal with the commander of the 12th Flotilla. At any rate, as gun flashes were seen through the entire night, the flotilla could easily have attacked the High Seas Fleet had Hawksley so desired. As we have seen, he felt that his object should be to join the Battle Fleet at dawn. However, it was not until 6 hours later, at 8:40 A.M., that he was able to make contact, all need for his force then having ended.

Shortly before 11:30, the 4th Flotilla sighted strange vessels to starboard. The flotilla was disposed in a long single column.

First came the First Half Flotilla, consisting of the *Tipperary* (bearing the flotilla pennant of Captain C. J. Wintour), *Spitfire*, *Sparrowhawk, Garland,* and *Contest*. Next came the Second Half Flotilla: the *Broke* (Commander W. L. Allen), *Achates, Ambuscade, Ardent, Fortune, Porpoise,* and *Unity*. All those destroyers carried four torpedoes in their tubes ready for instant firing, a total of 48. Each boat carried an additional spare torpedo. The course of the flotilla was south (167°) and its speed 18 knots.

The vessels sighted were the *Westfalen, Nassau, Rheinland,* and *Posen*. All had six 5.9-inch guns on each broadside for the primary purpose of repelling destroyer attacks. They led the long single column of 24 capital ships in close order. On the port beam of the leading battleship division were the light cruisers *Rostock, Stuttgart, Elbing,* and *Hamburg* and the destroyer *S32* of Half Flotilla I. A considerable distance on the port bow were the *Stettin* and *München* of Scouting Group IV. The *Frankfurt* and *Pillau* of Scouting Group II were about 4 miles on the port beam of the *Westfalen*. Speed was 16 knots and course about 133°. The opposing forces were therefore converging at about 34°, or three points. Their dispositions are shown in Figs. 52 and 53.

There existed great doubt in the British destroyer column as to the identity of the strange vessels. That was the case on the bridge of the *Tipperary*. Captain Wintour as late as 11:26 thought he had made contact with the 11th Flotilla, as shown by his signal to the *Garland:* "11th Destroyer Flotilla is on our starboard beam." That message may have been in reply to an unrecorded message from the *Garland* reporting the strange vessels, as that vessel's report notes the sighting of German cruisers at 11:25.

By 11:30 the range from the *Tipperary* to the strange ships had decreased to about 1,000 yards (Figs. 52–c and 49–r). At last, Wintour flashed the recognition signal. The *Westfalen* overwhelmed the little ship with a hurricane of fire from her 5.9-inch guns. The *Nassau* and *Rheinland* quickly entered the fight with both 5.9-inch common shell and 3.5-inch shrapnel.

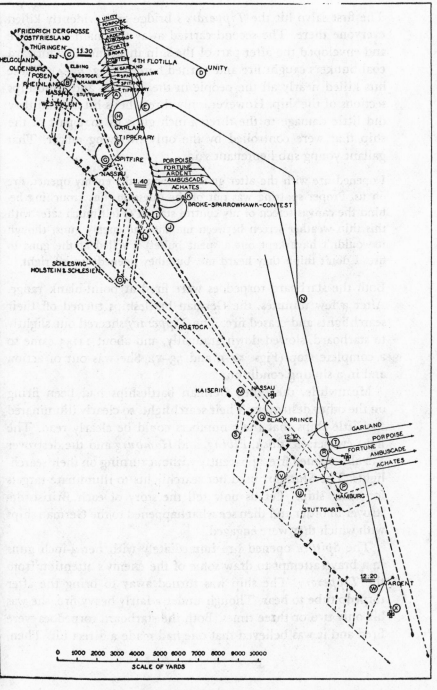

FIG. 53. Attacks of the 4th Flotilla. 11:30 P.M.-12:20 A.M.

The first salvo hit the *Tipperary's* bridge and evidently killed everyone there. The second carried away the main steam line and enveloped the after part of the ship in steam. The forward coal bunkers caught fire and burned fiercely (Fig. 53–A). Those hits killed nearly all the people in the forward and amidships sections of the ship. However, only three shells hit aft and they did little damage to the three 4-inch guns in that part of the ship that were controlled by the only surviving officer. That gallant young sub-lieutenant said:

I opened fire with the after guns as soon as the enemy opened fire on us. Proper spotting was out of the question, but crouching behind the canvas screen of my control station (I felt much safer with this thin weather screen between me and the enemy guns, though it wouldn't have kept out a spent bullet) I yelled at the guns to fire. I don't think they heard me, but they opened fire all right.

Both the starboard torpedoes were fired at point-blank range. After a few minutes, the German battleships turned off their searchlights and ceased fire. The *Tipperary* sheered out slightly to starboard, slowed down gradually, and about 11:35 came to a complete stop (Figs. 52–D and 53–F). She was out of action and in a sinking condition.

Meanwhile, the other German battleships had been firing on the other destroyers. Their searchlights so clearly illuminated the little ships that their numbers could be clearly read. The light cruisers *Rostock, Elbing,* and *Hamburg* and the destroyer *S32* also opened fire, apparently without turning on their searchlights. The *Stuttgart* used her searchlights to illuminate targets for other ships. Let us now tell the story of each British destroyer in order and then see what happened to the German ships with which they were engaged.

The *Spitfire* opened fire immediately with her 4-inch guns in a brave attempt to draw some of the enemy's attention from the *Tipperary*. The ship was turned away to bring the after torpedo tube to bear. Though under a fairly heavy fire, she was hit only two or three times. Both the starboard torpedoes were fired and it was believed that one had made a direct hit. Then,

Lieutenant Commander Trelawny turned away to reload his spare torpedo. At that instant a salvo hit the ship. "You seemed," said an officer on another ship, "to disappear with a salvo hitting you amidships, one great sheet of flame." The torpedo davit was wrecked and most of the torpedo crews were wounded.

The *Sparrowhawk* fired one torpedo at the third German ship and turned away, apparently without having been hit or even detected by the enemy. Such good fortune was not to continue throughout the night for this little ship.

The *Garland* fired a torpedo at a 3-funneled cruiser and also opened an effective fire from her guns. Lieutenant Commander Goff, after some quick maneuvering to avoid collision with other destroyers, bravely headed back toward the *Tipperary* to render such assistance as might be possible.

The *Contest* fired one torpedo at a 3-funneled cruiser, the one mentioned so prominently in all the destroyer reports, and hauled away to the eastward.

The *Broke*, leading the Second Half Flotilla, was not discovered. She fired a single torpedo from her starboard after tube and turned to the southeastward.

The *Achates, Ambuscade, Ardent, Fortune, Porpoise,* and *Unity* turned away without attacking with torpedoes. Those boats thus lost a marvelous opportunity for effective torpedo fire. The lack of an attack mission, which should have been assigned by the commander in chief, is very evident. The equal lack of initiative on the part of the captains shows a marked deficiency in their training and indoctrination. The *Unity* fired with her guns at two vessels she thought to be German destroyers.

Meanwhile, immediately upon opening fire, the *Westfalen, Nassau,* and *Rheinland* had turned away together sharply to W. by S. (246°), still maintaining a heavy fire. Vice Admiral Schmidt turned the remaining five vessels of Battle Squadron I together to the same course. The *Westfalen's* fire was particularly rapid and accurate. In five minutes she fired ninety-two 5.9-inch shell and forty-five 3.5-inch shrapnel.

Curiously enough, none of the German ships were hit by the

8 torpedoes fired at such point-blank range. On the other hand the British gunfire was quite effective. The *Westfalen* was hit once and her captain and 7 men were wounded. Two hits wrecked searchlights on the *Nassau* and killed one officer and 10 men. The *Rheinland* lost 10 killed and 20 wounded as a result of two hits. The effect of destroyer gunfire against battleships at night was an interesting, if unexpected, lesson of Jutland. However, it should be realized that at night a battleship's secondary battery control stations and searchlights, as well as the ship control party on the bridge, are entirely exposed to fire and the ships themselves are disclosed by their searchlights. It is evident that all the ships' control parties, except possibly the officer conning the ship, should have the protection of the conning tower when night action of any kind is expected. To steer from the unprotected bridge is merely to invite loss of control over the ship with the imminent danger of collision.

The German cruisers were in a dangerous position between their own battleships and the British destroyers. If they maintained their stations there was a probability that they would be torpedoed, while if they turned away there was danger of collision with their battle line. Possibly, their safest course would have been to turn full speed into the destroyers. The *Rostock* turned away about the same time as the *Nassau* and *Rheinland*, of which ships she was abeam, and thus avoided collision. The *Elbing* was farther back abeam the *Posen*. That ship does not appear to have turned away until after the *Rheinland;* so, when the *Elbing* turned away, she found that the *Posen* was still coming on. She went across the bows of the battleship. The latter tried to ease the force of the collision, but could not avoid it entirely. Her ram cut into the *Elbing's* starboard quarter (Figs. 52–E and 53–B). The shock was very slight, but both the cruiser's engine-rooms quickly flooded and she took a list of 18°. The badly damaged cruiser drifted to starboard of the German battle line, unable to steam or to fight. Thus, the British indirectly had more than counter-balanced the loss of the destroyer leader *Tipperary*. British accounts indicate that the *Rostock* was torpedoed at that time, but Groos states that she was hit later in a manner that will soon be described. The *S32* was hit during the engagement and badly damaged by two shells (Figs. 52–F and 53–C). She headed at reduced speed for Lyngvig on the Danish coast. About 11:35 the *Westfalen* ceased firing and resumed the fleet course. The other battleships followed her motions. Such was the first contact between the 4th Flotilla and the High Seas Fleet. The losses were quite in favor of the British, but the latter had lost a marvelous opportunity for a decisive success. The 4th Flotilla resisted bravely, but it did not attack!

We must now trace the movements of the scattered British destroyers. After disengaging herself, the *Spitfire* had headed east for a few minutes, then she went back to south. Trelawny estimated that his spare torpedo would have been loaded in a starboard tube by that time; so he turned back at 27 knots to fire it at a ship that had a searchlight playing on the *Tipperary*. He did not know that the torpedo could not be loaded. The *Spitfire* fired a few rounds at the German searchlight, then she sighted two large ships crossing her bow from starboard to port. They were thought to be cruisers, but actually they were the *Westfalen* and *Nassau* resuming their southeasterly course. It was now about 11:35 P.M.

The *Nassau* saw a destroyer close aboard on her port bow. She put her rudder left and tried to ram at full speed. The two ships crashed together, port bow to port bow (Figs. 52–G and 53–G). The result was most remarkable. The *Spitfire's* bow tore a hole 12 feet in diameter in the *Nassau's* port bow. She carried away as a trophy 20 feet of the battleship's side plating. One of the latter's 5.9-inch guns was torn from its supports. One of the *Spitfire's* officers wrote:

You can imagine how the 1/8-inch plates of a destroyer would feel such a blow. I can recollect a fearful crash, then being hurled across the deck, and feeling the *Spitfire* rolling over to starboard as no sea ever made her roll. As we bumped, the enemy opened fire with their foc'sle guns, though luckily they could not depress them to hit us, but the blast of the guns literally cleared everything before it. Our foremast came tumbling down, our for'ard searchlight found its way from its platform above the fore-bridge down to the deck, and the foremost funnel was blown back till it rested neatly between the two foremost ventilator cowls, like the hinging funnel of a penny river steamboat.

Fortunately, the ship received only two actual hits from the German guns. They passed through the bridge screens. One of them grazed the captain's head and blew him off the bridge to the upper deck, 24 feet away. His escape without serious hurt was quite as remarkable as that of his ship. The *Spitfire* was lucky to get clear with 25 casualties and 60 feet of her forecastle stove in.

Soon after the *Spitfire* had escaped that danger and her survivors were trying to find out how much of a ship they had left, they were threatened with a second collision. A large ship steaming at high speed, with huge clouds of smoke rising from a fire between her decks virtually grazed the destroyer's stern. Some believe that was the *Black Prince*. Trelawny thought her to be the *Moltke*, but that vessel was then quite distant from the German battle line, having made three earlier contacts with the British battle squadrons. We believe that the strange ship most probably was the *Seydlitz* (Fig. 52–G).

As the *Sparrowhawk* turned away from the Germans, she lost sight of the *Spitfire* ahead of her. Seeing the *Broke* on a southerly course, she took station astern of her about 11:34 (Fig. 53–E).

The *Garland,* after turning away for a short distance, came back to the assistance of the *Tipperary* which was burning furiously. As she approached the *Tipperary* about 11:35, two German cruisers, probably the *Hamburg* and *Stuttgart,* suddenly appeared and opened fire (Fig. 53–H). The *Garland* was forced away to the eastward. The *Tipperary,* despite her fearful injuries and enormous losses, did not sink immediately. However, the raging fires prevented all access to the forward part of the ship and exploded the ready ammunition on deck from time to time. Fortunately, the forward magazine did not explode. The few remaining officers and men busied themselves in throwing over such heavy weights as they could reach and in preparing two Carley rafts in which to abandon ship when the time came. There was little that could be done for the numerous badly wounded men. The heroism of those poor fellows was beyond all power of words to describe. The ancient classic heroes never surpassed the calm patience with which the simple British seamen awaited certain and terrible death.

The *Contest's* movements are quite indefinite. All that is known is that she still kept with the flotilla. We will assume that she took station in rear of the *Sparrowhawk* (Fig. 53–E), but she may have fallen in farther down the line or even at the rear.

The *Broke,* after turning to the southeastward, went back to the southward, the *Sparrowhawk* and *Contest* falling in astern. The *Achates, Ambuscade, Ardent, Fortune,* and *Porpoise* followed the *Contest,* thus reforming a column of eight destroyers. They should not be considered as in exact formation. In fact, the probability is that they were spaced at most irregular distances and did not always follow exactly in the wake of the ship ahead. About 11:33 the *Unity* lost the formation (Fig. 53–D) and about 3 minutes later joined the 9th Flotilla, which was next to the eastward (Fig. 52–H). As the *Broke* turned back to a southerly course, she passed the *Tipperary* about 1,000 yards distant to starboard. Commander Allen intended to renew the attack on the German ships. About 11:40 the *Broke* again came into contact with the *Rostock,* which was now about 1,000 yards on the port beam of the *Westfalen* (Figs. 49–S, 52–J, and 53–I). Both vessels challenged at the same time. The *Rostock* covered the *Broke* with an accurate fire, while soon afterward the *Westfalen* and *Rheinland,* the second ship in column since the *Nassau's* collision with the *Spitfire,* fired on the *Sparrowhawk.* Battle Squadron I turned away together promptly to avoid torpedoes.

Commander Allen of the *Broke* ordered his second starboard torpedo to be fired. He called for full speed and 20 degrees left rudder. When one engine-room telegraph had been moved and the helmsman had 15 degrees on the rudder, a salvo struck the ship. It completely wrecked the lower bridge and did much damage in the forward firerooms (Fig. 53–J). The rudder was jammed. The torpedo was not fired. The German salvos continued about the ship until a total of about 7 hits had been received. They caused extremely heavy casualties. When the ship neared an easterly course, Allen who was conning from the upper bridge ordered her steadied. He now learned for the first time how completely the lower bridge had been wrecked. Then, he saw another destroyer close ahead and called down to back the engines but all the personnel below were killed or wounded and the telegraphs were destroyed. Nothing could be done to avoid the collision.

The *Sparrowhawk* had turned away with the *Broke*. Orders were given to fire her remaining starboard torpedo, but it is not stated that it was actually fired. Believing that the *Broke* had steadied on course east, Lieutenant Commander Hopkins tried to parallel her. When he realized that the *Broke* was continuing her turn, it was too late to do anything. The *Broke* hit the *Sparrowhawk* squarely at right angles just forward of the bridge. The terrific impact of two vessels, each making almost 28 knots, can hardly be imagined. The *Broke's* stem cut halfway through the ship, but in doing so her own forecastle was wrecked. Four of the *Sparrowhawk's* people were thrown over on the forecastle of the other ship and six of *Broke's* men were knocked overboard and lost. Fortunately, the change of course of the German ships soon took them out of range. Their searchlights went out and their salvos ceased. That saved the two crippled destroyers from instant destruction. They hung together, rolling and crunching into each other.

The destroyer following the *Sparrowhawk* was probably the *Contest*. It was likely at that time that the latter fired her torpedo at a "large 3-funneled ship," evidently the *Rostock*. Soon afterward the *Contest* rammed the *Sparrowhawk* at full speed (Fig. 53–K). The latter's stern was cut away for 5 feet and her rudder wedged left. The *Contest's* bow was bent over at right angles, but she still was able to proceed at 20 knots, throwing a fountain of water high into the air.

The *Achates* narrowly escaped a collision with the *Broke* and kept on in the hope of joining the First Half Flotilla, which

R. Perkins, "Jane's Fighting Ships"

H.M.S. "SHARK"

The destroyer *Shark*, whose Captain was Commander Loftus Jones, was a unit of the 4th Destroyer Flotilla. This ship was one of four destroyers acting as scouts and anti-destroyer screen for the 3d Battle Cruiser Squadron under Rear Admiral Hood.

In breaking up the attack of the German Destroyer Flotilla II on Hood's battle cruisers, the *Shark's* engines were made useless by a shell hit. An hour later she was abandoned, as she sank, by about 30 survivors of her crew, all of whom died during three hours in the icy water, except 6 who were picked up by the Danish ship *Vidar*.

S.M.S. "B98"

The *B98*, flag boat of Flotilla II, flew the flag of Captain Schuur, Chief of Flotilla, and was attached to Scouting Group II. She was prominent in the Battle of Jutland, particularly in the early engagement with H.M.S. *Shark*. In fact, two destroyers of Flotilla II, *B109* and *B110*, were the vessels to sight the scouts of the Grand Fleet and thus bring on the Battle of Jutland.

Commander R. B. C. Hutchinson thought would be ahead. Soon afterward, he made out cruisers between his ship and the German battle line. In the belief that they were friendly, he canceled the order to fire torpedoes. Thus, he lost an excellent opportunity to damage the enemy. How British cruisers could be so close to German battleships without coming under their point-blank fire is difficult to see. It is doubtless true that officers will decide according to their impressions at such times as this, and we must make allowance for the uncertainty of all this night fighting with the strain it imposed upon the captains who knew nothing of the enemy at any time during the night. "I respectfully submit," writes Hutchinson with much justification, "that in future the maximum amount of information may be given to destroyers as to the disposition of our own forces."

The *Ambuscade* fired two torpedoes and turned away to the eastward, following the *Achates*. At 11:42 she reported by radio to her flotilla commander in the *Tipperary:* "Have fired two torpedoes and heard one explosion." Brave Wintour would never read that optimistic message. The *Ardent, Fortune,* and *Porpoise* followed the *Ambuscade* in her retirement, apparently without being heavily engaged or firing torpedoes. By all means, they should have pushed in for an attack, thus showing the initiative that is the primary characteristic of every efficient destroyer captain. In such chance encounters as these, no orders can be issued by seniors. There must be in the heart of each captain the fervent will to attack. As Admiral Sims said before the World War: "The destroyer is a projectile, the captain its fuse!"

We have seen that only three or four torpedoes were fired during this second contact of the 4th Flotilla. It was probably the best chance the flotilla had. The first time there might have been some excuse for uncertainty and surprise, but the second time all eight destroyers should have been prepared to attack to the finish. However, even the very small volume of torpedo fire had some effect. A torpedo hit the *Rostock* as she was trying to pass between the *Westfalen* and *Rheinland* to clear the line of fire of the latter (Figs. 52–K and 53–L). She was also hit by two shells,

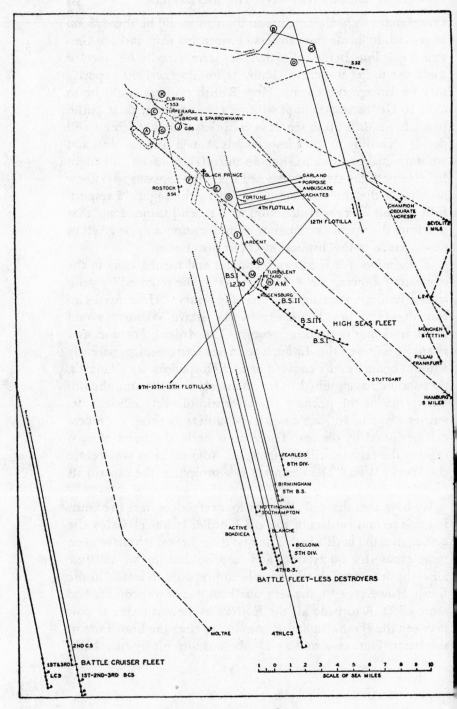

FIG. 54. 12:00-1:00 A.M., June 1.

probably fired by the *Broke*. The torpedo which was running on the surface hit abreast No. 4 fireroom. It was an unlucky spot for the Germans. Steam lines were cut, the lighting circuits were damaged, and the steering engine failed. Only the fact that the battleships turned away sharply saved the *Rostock* from collision. Finally, two firerooms were flooded and the main engines stopped. With 930 tons of water in the ship, she listed 5° to port. In this seriously damaged condition, the *Rostock* proceeded slowly after the Fleet, being compelled to stop frequently. The German light cruisers seem to have had little defensive strength against torpedo hits. The 4th Flotilla had gained a second advantage over the Germans, but again a marvelous opportunity had been lost.

In order to avoid collision with the *Rostock* as she lay in the path of the battle line, the *Schlesien* and *Schleswig-Holstein* sheered out of column at 12:05 A.M. (Figs. 53–O and 54–A) and took station in rear of the battle cruisers at the rear of the line.

After contact had been broken about 11:45, the *Westfalen* returned promptly to the fleet course towards Horn Reefs. There was a brief lull in the fighting. Commander Hutchinson in the *Achates* assembled the *Ambuscade, Ardent, Fortune,* and *Porpoise* in that order. About midnight, the *Garland* took station in rear of the *Porpoise* (Fig. 53–N). That gave him a strong force of six destroyers, most of which still had all their torpedoes. Hutchinson again returned to course south (167°). Let him stand by for the inevitable contact and the third opportunity for the 4th Flotilla. Meanwhile, why should he not inform Jellicoe of the German battleships?

In Fig. 52 it will be noted that almost directly ahead of the *Westfalen,* distant 4 miles, was the British 6th Division. The same distance on the starboard bow was the 5th Battle Squadron. Both those British units were in a singularly dangerous situation. Had not the *Westfalen* lost about 10 minutes, 2.5 miles along the fleet course, due to turns away from the British destroyers, the opposing battleships would almost certainly have been in contact. What would have resulted is difficult to guess.

It is very possible that seven British battleships could have held their own against the van of the German battle line and possibly the British destroyers would then have attacked! On the other hand, as Jellicoe feared, the Germans might have been greatly superior in night fighting efficiency and the action would probably have ended before Jellicoe could make up his mind to intervene with his poorly disposed battle squadrons. Who knows? But it is interesting to see that the very possibility Jellicoe was trying to avoid failed to happen by the narrowest lucky chance.

At midnight Captain Redlich had a very awkward situation to handle, but did it well. He sighted two light cruisers to port. He took care to challenge and they proved to be the *Stuttgart* and *Hamburg* (Fig. 53–M). The *Westfalen* had to sheer out momentarily to avoid collision. That was a piece of calm, steady judgment when it would have been easy to have sunk two of his own ships.

At 12:10 the *Westfalen* sighted a destroyer close aboard on the port hand. She challenged. There was no answer; so, for the third time, Redlich turned on his searchlights, opened fire, and turned away about 90°. The *Rheinland, Posen, Oldenburg,* and *Helgoland* joined in the fight, which became one of the fiercest of the night (Figs. 49–V and 54–D). The brunt seems to have fallen on the rear of the destroyer column. The *Westfalen* was about abreast the *Fortune.* The *Achates* reports only being chased to the eastward by enemy cruisers, probably the *Hamburg* and *Stuttgart* (Fig. 53–P). She was not hit nor did she fire a torpedo, though the opportunity was one of the best during the entire night. Her position was well up on the *Westfalen's* bow, ideal for torpedo fire, whether the Germans continued on in column or turned away in a line of bearing formation.

The *Ambuscade* which was not in quite such a good position fired a well-directed torpedo and turned away without being hit. The *Ardent* at first turned toward the enemy and fired a torpedo from a favorable position; then she turned off to the eastward under the fire of the *Rheinland.* The *Fortune* was the first destroyer discovered by the Germans and came under a very heavy concentration of fire. The *Westfalen's* first salvo wrecked her bridge and shot down her foremast (Fig. 53–R). Hit again and again, she burst into flames which illuminated her clearly to the enemy. Right gallantly did she fight back at her gigantic opponents, directing her fire at the *Oldenburg*. Possibly, she also fired torpedoes. Lieutenant Commander F. G. Terry fought his ship to the finish with magnificent heroism. Before the *Fortune* sank, about a dozen of her crew were able to embark on two rafts.

The *Porpoise* also came under a heavy fire. Commander Colville turned her away quickly to avoid hitting the *Fortune*. He failed to fire torpedoes from a most favorable position. A shell hit his ship in the after fireroom, putting two boilers out of action (Fig. 53–T). Another shell hit the bridge and carried away the steering gear. The ship fortunately was screened by the smoke and steam issuing in great clouds from the *Fortune*. She was able to escape without more hits, but took no further part in the action.

The *Garland*, while turning away, fired a torpedo at an estimated range of 800 yards. She was not hit.

This attack seems to have been the only one in which the 4th Flotilla sent torpedoes through the German battle line. The *Rheinland* avoided the *Ardent's* torpedo by only 50 yards (Fig. 53–U). The *Posen* saw the tracks of two others, probably fired by the *Ambuscade* and *Garland*, but was able to avoid them by maneuvering (Fig. 53–V). The *Oldenburg* was hit by a 4-inch shell which killed or wounded 7 officers and 15 men. The helmsman fell, severely wounded. Captain Höpfner, although himself wounded, took the wheel and steadied the ship on her course. That one hit, probably made by the *Fortune*, shows the effectiveness of destroyer gunfire when directed against the bridge of a battleship in a close-range night encounter. In the third contact with the 4th Flotilla, the Germans had won a fine success. The skill of their battleships in repulsing night torpedo attacks was of a very high order.

While the van of the High Seas Fleet was engaging the destroyers, the center was winning an easy success. The *Thüringen*, sixth ship in the column, was the first ship that did not fire on the destroyers. While her lookouts were straining their eyes to pick up more destroyers, they saw a large ship on the port beam. Her four stacks indicated that it could not be a German vessel. Nevertheless, a challenge was made to make sure. The *Nassau*, which was still out of the column on the port beam of the *Friedrich der Grosse*, also was watching the strange ship. When the vessel, which we now know to have been the large armored cruiser *Black Prince*, failed to answer the recognition signal and quickly turned away, the Germans threw their searchlights on her. They quickly saw that their target was a British cruiser (Figs. 49–v, 53–q, and 54–e). The *Thüringen* opened fire with main and secondary batteries. At the range of about 1,000 yards scarcely a shot missed. The *Ostfriesland*, *Nassau*, and *Friedrich der Grosse* joined in the unequal fight. The cruiser, now burning like a gigantic funeral pyre, lay directly in the path of the *Nassau*. To avoid collision, the latter turned toward the German line. For a time, collision with the *Kaiserin* seemed inevitable. The *Nassau* backed full speed. The *Kaiserin* sheered out to starboard. Only the quickest action had avoided a disaster (Figs. 53–s and 54–f). After being under fire for only about 4 minutes, the *Black Prince* blew up. None of her crew was saved. The *Nassau* took station behind the *Hessen* as the last ship in the battle line.

No sooner had the *Black Prince* been destroyed at 12:15 A.M. than there was another burst of fire from the van. Lieutenant Commander Arthur Marsden had brought the *Ardent* back again to a southerly course in the hope of regaining contact with some of the 4th Flotilla. Soon he saw smoke. Believing it to be British destroyers, he closed in. Soon he saw large ships. "It was too late to get away," says Marsden, "so I attacked immediately and fired a torpedo from a favorable position at the leader." What he had found was the van of the German battle line. At 12:20 fire opened (Fig. 53–w). The *Westfalen* with her first salvo carried away the *Ardent's* bridge. The Germans, as usual quickly turned away. In about 4½ minutes twenty-two 5.9-inch and eighteen 3.5-inch rounds were fired. The *Ardent* was completely wrecked (Fig. 54–1). Searchlights were extinguished and the *Westfalen* resumed the fleet course.

The heroism of the *Ardent's* crew in the terrific fight was magnificent. Her brave captain writes:

Our three guns that had been barking away like good 'uns ceased firing one by one. I looked out on to the forecastle and saw and heard the captain of the forecastle exhorting the only remaining man of his gun's crew to "Give them one more," but that "one more" was never fired, and I saw later both of these brave souls stretched out dead.

After the firing ceased, Marsden made what efforts he could to save the few remaining men. The leading signalman said to him: "Well, the old *Ardent* done her bit all right, sir." "Several of my best men," says the captain, "came up and tried to console me, and all were delighted that we had at length been in action and done our share."

About 12:30 another German ship hit the *Ardent* with five more salvos and she sank quickly (Figs. 53–x and 54–L). Her few survivors took to the icy waters. Marsden says:

I spoke to many men and saw most of them die one by one. Not a man of them showed any fear of death, and there was not a murmur, complaint, or cry for help from a single soul. Their joy was, and they talked about it to the end, that they and the *Ardent* had "done their bit," as they put it.

We would like to add a word of tribute to those men, but words fail us. Next morning, the destroyer leader *Marksman* rescued Marsden and one other survivor.

It was about 12:10 when the rear of the German battle line reached the *Tipperary*. She was still burning fiercely. At the rear of the line were the *Regensburg* with five destroyers of Flotilla III. At 12:12 Commodore Heinrich sent the *S53, S54*, and *G88* to investigate the burning ship (Fig. 54–c). Soon afterward the flag boat, the *S53*, received an order from the *Rostock* for a destroyer to stand by her. The *S54* was designated for the duty. She reached the *Rostock* about 12:15 (Fig. 54–G) and soon afterward took her in tow. The *S53* next rescued 9 British sailors from a raft alongside the *Tipperary*. After inquiring for the name of the crippled destroyer, the *S53* left without firing a shot, thus giving the few remaining men of her crew a chance for their lives. Then a strange cruiser was sighted. When she failed to answer the challenge, the *S53* prepared to fire a torpedo into her, but before it could be done a flashing light spoke the following urgent message: "Here *Elbing*. Am disabled. Please come alongside." Before the request could be complied with, a roving searchlight illuminated a large 4-funneled flotilla leader. That was the *Broke* which lay virtually helpless with 83 officers and men killed and wounded.

As the *S53* and *G88* opened fire, the *Broke* answered it with her port after gun which alone could be manned. Two shells hit the *Broke* amidships without doing much damage. Then, both German destroyers fired torpedoes and turned away. One torpedo passed directly under the British destroyer without hitting. Possibly, it was set for a deep-draft target or was fired at so close a range that the initial dive carried it under the target. The reason why the *S53* and *G88* felt it necessary to turn away before finishing off a helpless antagonist was that the *Elbing* evidently was urgently in need of assistance. Thus, the Germans lost an opportunity to increase the British losses by 1,704 tons.

While proceeding towards the *Elbing*, the *G88* encountered a British destroyer and attempted to sink her with bombs. While she was thus engaged, it is said that five destroyers appeared and drove her off. Thus, the *G88* lost contact with both the *Elbing* and the *S53* (Fig. 54-J). If the *G88* actually went alongside a deserted destroyer and exploded bombs, it could only have been the *Fortune*. However, it is possible that the *G88* only approached a destroyer for the purpose of sinking it with bombs. If so, the destroyer probably was the *Sparrowhawk*. An officer of that ship describes the approach of a German destroyer to within 100 yards. The after gun was manned by the officers and prepared for a last resistance. It was resolved to let the German destroyer commence the fight. After a few tense minutes, she disappeared without firing a shot. About 12:20 the *S53* joined the crippled *Elbing* (Fig. 54–K).

It will be remembered that the *S52* was proceeding to the *Lützow* in accordance with Scheer's order. At 12:15 she had a surprise encounter with the *Castor* and 11th Flotilla. Though the *Castor* opened fire at point-blank range, the *S52* escaped without a hit. She headed for the Jutland coast. At 12:30 she reported having made contact with British destroyers in square 016 on course south (167°). That square was one to the northward of the one in which the *Lützow* was then located. It will be noted that practically every German ship making a contact during the night reported it direct to Scheer. That was in sharp contrast to the British system. Not a single destroyer of the 4th Flotilla had reported the important information in their possession to Jellicoe. In their voluminous correspondence, both official and unofficial, the task is not even mentioned.

It might well be asked what the destroyers of the other British flotillas were doing while the 4th Flotilla was having its four encounters with the High Seas Fleet. It is well known that most, if not all, the destroyers in rear of the Battle Fleet saw the actions clearly. It will be noted that the van of the High Seas Fleet had moved entirely across the rear of the British formation by 12:30. It had passed through the original stations of every flotilla with Jellicoe. It is one of the most remarkable instances of luck in history. What use did the British destroyers make of the astounding opportunity thrust upon them?

We have already commented upon the failure of the 11th Flotilla to attack, despite the fact that an officer of the *Marne* said that he could see gun flashes all night long and also the burning *Tipperary*. Nothing further need be said.

When the first action of the 4th Flotilla commenced at 11:30 P.M., the 13th Flotilla, led by Captain Farie in the *Champion*, was immediately to the eastward. A little farther away were the 9th and 10th Flotillas, led by Commander Goldsmith in the *Lydiard*. In the 13th Flotilla were 9 boats and in the 9th and 10th together 5. Thus, a formidable force of 1 light cruiser and 14 destroyers was immediately available to support the 4th

Flotilla and make torpedo attacks under the most favorable conditions against a single column of 24 capital ships, an opportunity of which a destroyer captain dreams, scarcely daring to express it in words.

The reaction of Captain Farie to the situation was simply astounding. When the Germans opened fire on the 4th Flotilla, some of the wild shots and erratic salvos fell near the 13th Flotilla. The *Nerissa* reports that salvos fell between her and the *Moresby* and that searchlights were seen abaft the starboard beam. As those destroyers were respectively the third and fourth vessels in column, the 13th Flotilla was therefore somewhat ahead of the battleship column. With its vastly superior speed, the 13th Flotilla could easily gain a position directly ahead of the German column and attack on both bows. That probably would have had decisive results.

However, such aggressive action was farthest from Farie's thoughts. Here is what he says:

About 11:30 P.M. heavy firing was opened on our starboard beam, apparently at some of the destroyers between the Thirteenth Flotilla and the enemy. I hauled out to the eastward as I was unable to attack with any of our own flotilla, our own forces being between me and the enemy. I then resumed course south; firing was observed at intervals during the night on our starboard beam.

Here is the action of a flotilla commander placed in rear of the battle squadrons for the purpose, as Jellicoe says, of attacking the enemy. Stirling took his 12th Flotilla to attack the enemy. Wintour's captains in the 4th Flotilla fought to the end when they encountered the enemy. Farie withdrew from the scene of action before a single shell had hit one of his 10 vessels.

This was not the worst. Let the British *Narrative* describe how Farie hauled out, as he says, to the eastward: "The *Champion*, leading the 13th, thereupon altered course to the eastward, and increased to high speed without signal, and of her flotilla only the *Obdurate* and *Moresby* managed to maintain touch." It was at 11:37 that the *Champion* changed course to east (77°) (Fig. 52–1). Not content with that, Farie about 11:52 changed course to about 37°. At 12:05 he finally resumed course south

(167°). He had put a distance of 11 miles between himself and the Germans. His rapid withdrawal had other unfavorable effects that will be told later.

The 9th and 10th Flotillas, which were close beyond the 13th, also clearly witnessed the 11:30 action and some shells fell near them. Commander Goldsmith says: "Fire was opened on us by a line of large ships which we took to be our own." The *Landrail* also thought the ships firing were friendly. The *Liberty* distinctly made out four heavy ships at a distance of about 4,000 yards. "Searchlights were trained on the flotilla and heavy firing continued." At 11:40 the *Champion* was seen to disappear to the eastward and the *Lydiard* altered course four points away from the enemy to southeast (122°). At that time a curious incident occurred and Goldsmith unknowingly received two fresh accessions of strength. The *Unity*, having lost contact with the 4th Flotilla, took station in rear of the *Laurel*, the rear ship of the 9th and 10th Flotillas (Fig. 52–H). The *Nerissa*, in turning to follow the *Moresby* after the *Obdurate* and *Champion*, took station astern of the *Unity*. Thus, 1 boat of the 4th and 7 of the 13th Flotilla were added to Goldsmith's column of 5, a fact of which he remained in entire ignorance. By 12:15 the *Lydiard* had gained a distance of 5 miles to the eastward of the *Westfalen*, meanwhile witnessing in the distance the various attacks of the 4th Flotilla and the destruction of the *Black Prince*.

By that time, it certainly must have been demonstrated to Goldsmith that the large ships he had seen were the German battleships. Could it be possible that five distinct actions over the course of 50 minutes could all be British ships fighting each other? Therefore, when at 12:10 the *Lydiard* changed course to 225°, directly across the line of advance of the enemy, it must have been accepted by his captains that they were at last to make a massed attack upon the German battleships. But no! Goldsmith's only idea was "to get on the other side of the big ships, who still spasmodically opened fire toward us." Was this the way British flotilla commanders took advantage of heaven-sent opportunities? However, if Goldsmith would not attack, Chance, Luck, Providence, or whatever one may prefer to call it, took command of the 9th, 10th, and 13th Flotillas and led his boats to the attack. How a force of British destroyers made a perfect attack, all but the firing of torpedoes which Providence could not do, entirely against the will and without the knowledge of their commander we shall soon relate.

Just to the eastward of the 9th and 10th Flotillas at 11:30 P.M. was the 12th Flotilla. It was composed of 15 of the newest boats. What is far more, the flotilla had a real commander, Captain A. J. B. Stirling. Men on these ships clearly saw the action of the 4th Flotilla at 11:30, but the flotilla remained on its course until 11:45, when the *Champion* and some destroyers were sighted dead ahead, steaming to the eastward at high speed. Had Stirling known that the light cruiser was being followed by only two destroyers, he probably could have passed astern of them by holding his course or altering a little to the starboard. But naturally he supposed that the *Champion* was followed by about 10 destroyers. To avoid collision and confusion, he changed course sharply to east (77°) to parallel the *Champion*. Speed was reduced to 15 knots to allow her to pass ahead. Just as the *Faulknor,* flag boat of his 12th Flotilla, had changed course, two strange cruisers suddenly appeared on the starboard side of the rear of the column of destroyers. They opened fire. The vessels which were converging sharply on the destroyer column were the *Frankfurt* and *Pillau* (52–M). The *Menace* and *Nonsuch* had to maneuver with full rudder to avoid collision. The latter, turning to the eastward at 33 knots, lost touch with the flotilla. Before she had time to fire a torpedo, the cruisers had disappeared into the darkness.

At 11:50, a few minutes after turning away to the eastward, Stirling signaled to Hawksley with flashing light: "1st B.S. is south five miles. Am I to follow you or steer south after fleet?" It would seem that Stirling had mistaken the *Champion* for the *Castor* in sending that message. While probably the message was sent by a flashing light that could be seen through only a small arc, the inclusion of the first sentence was dangerous, as it might have been intercepted by a German ship with unfortunate results.

At 12:00 the *Champion* was seen to be converging on the *Faulknor* and Stirling was forced to change course to the northeastward. At 12:05 the *Champion* resumed course south (167°). At the same instant, Stirling signaled course ESE. (100°) and passed astern of the *Champion* (Fig. 54–B). According to the *Narrative*, it was not until 12:15 that the change of course was executed. At that time, Stirling received a reply from Hawksley: "Keep in touch with fleet." Stirling reports that at 12:15 he resumed course south (167°), at 17 knots. The *Narrative* times that at 12:20. Our figures follow the official report of Captain Stirling and the official signal record, not the *Narrative*.

At 12:16 the *Faulknor* noted that two hostile cruisers ahead opened fire and that the flotilla spread to avoid them. Groos's chart 36 places the *Stettin* and *München* nearest the 12th Flotilla at 12:16. Therefore, we have assumed that those vessels made the contact (Fig. 54–H). However, the strange vessels may have been the *Frankfurt* and *Pillau* or even the *Champion* and her two destroyers.

The forcing of the 12th Flotilla away from the High Seas Fleet at that time by the *Champion* was highly disadvantageous to the British. In fact, we consider that it was the most unfortunate result of Captain Farie's rapid withdrawal from contact with the enemy, for Stirling was one commander who was really intent upon attacking and who did not need an order to do so. Had he deliberately, as we believe he would, attacked the German battle line from its port bow and ahead with the full strength of his efficient flotilla and repeated the attacks from midnight until his flotilla was expended, such action probably would have had decisive results. When we see what he accomplished with a part of his flotilla after day was breaking, it is quite probable that such a resolute commander could have crippled several first-line battleships and have driven Scheer to the westward by his determined attacks. The Grand Fleet, by Farie's conduct on that occasion, lost an excellent chance for an important, and perhaps decisive, success. Farie, in avoiding the fight, prevented from fighting the one British flotilla commander who was intent on so doing.

We must now place ourselves on the bridge of the *Friedrich der Grosse* and see what information Scheer had been receiving during the eventful hour that ended at 12:30 A.M. Scheer witnessed the various attacks of the 4th Flotilla and was able to see the effectiveness of the fire of his battleships. However, information soon arrived of damage to his own ships. At 11:52 a report from the *S32* stated that she was disabled in square 070, one too far to the southward. The squares are clearly shown in Fig. 49. Three minutes later there arrived a very sad message from the *G40* timed at 11:05: "*Lützow* can proceed only at slow speed. Navigational aids lacking. Position in square 016. Course south (167°). Battery reduced to one-third strength." The navigational position did not check with previous information. It indicated a run of 13 miles in the 35 minutes that had elapsed since 10:30, when the *G40* had reported her in the center of square 018. Actually, the *Lützow* was in the northern part of square 011.

Soon after that report, Scheer received part of a message from the *Frankfurt,* the remainder being obliterated by British interference. It reported a force of four British armored cruisers on course SSE. (145°) in square 093 without stating the time. That square was about 26 miles directly ahead of the *Westfalen.* Some grave error had evidently occurred. Possibly, the square reported should have been 073. The German accounts do not explain Boedicker's report. It is possible that he had mistaken the 12th Flotilla for larger vessels. Also, he may have made contact with the 6th Division, as the *Seydlitz* did at that time.

Strangely enough, at 12:08 a similar message was received from that battle cruiser, except that the course of the enemy was reported as south (167°). It seems that the *Seydlitz* had sighted three or four ships at 11:45, distant about 1,600 yards (Figs. 49–T and 52–L). The German ship was in no condition for further fighting of any kind, so she flashed the British recognition signal and turned northward. It was probably the 6th Division with which she had made contact. The light cruiser *Fearless* had taken station in rear of this battleship division.

Shortly after midnight, she says that a German battleship was seen to pass down the starboard side on a northerly course.

As she was not engaged by the ships ahead, no action was taken, it being too late to fire a torpedo when she could be identified. Her course led directly toward the destroyers astern.

Admiral Burney thus reports that incident:

About midnight, smoke was observed ahead of *Marlborough,* which crossed from starboard to port and back again from port to starboard, and then came down to the starboard side. It appeared to be a large ship and was challenged by *Revenge,* who was answered by two letters, though they were not the correct ones. She then disappeared. *Revenge* says that the order to open fire was actually given, but was later counter-manded.

Again, the British had lost a priceless opportunity. It is true that Burney can give some good reasons for failing to open fire. It would be unwise to expose the position of his division to the enemy, as it was separated from the Battle Fleet. Also, the *Marlborough* was damaged, but here was the practical certainty of sinking a German capital ship, which also was separated from her battle line and probably also was disabled. Jellicoe's defensive attitude had certainly penetrated throughout his entire Fleet. Never was a fleet better indoctrinated with the ideas of its commander in chief.

After going northward for a few minutes, the *Seydlitz* ran into three British destroyers about midnight (Fig. 52–N). They were probably the *Broke, Sparrowhawk,* and *Contest.* The battle cruiser sheered off to the eastward. At 12:12 the *Seydlitz* resumed her course for Horn Reefs at 21 knots. She observed frequent firing to the westward, but made no further contacts. The reports of Admiral Boedicker and the *Seydlitz* failed to reach the German destroyers. That was unfortunate, as the position given would have indicated a good direction for their searches.

At 12:09 news of another casualty arrived. A radio message from the *König* said: "*Rostock* disabled." Shortly afterward

came a message direct from Commodore Michelsen. He reported
having been hit by a torpedo in square 055. He made the very
optimistic estimate that he could still proceed at 17 knots. Information now arrived that at 11:55 the *L22* had ascended for
scouting on course N. by W. (236°). At 12:10 the *G9* of Flotilla
V reported hostile cruisers in square 069 on course south (167°).
Soon afterward, she added the fact that they had disappeared
to the southward. The position reported was about 8 miles
south of the van of the battle line. It fact, it was the exact square
in which the Battle Fleet was then located. At 12:18 Flotilla
II reported that it was returning to port via the Skagerrak.

To show how this came to pass, we must now tell the story
of the futile night search of the exhausted German flotillas. They
had been assigned search and attack sectors as follows:

ENE. to ESE.—Flotilla II (10 boats)
ESE. to SE.—Half Flotilla XII (2 boats)
SE. to S. by E.—Flotilla VII (9 boats)
S. by E. to SSW.—Flotilla V (11 boats)
SSW. to SW.—Flotilla IX or Half Flotilla XVIII (5 boats)

It will be remembered that Flotilla II and Half Flotilla XII
had been repulsed by the 2d Light Cruiser Squadron about 9:00
P.M. Of the latter unit, the *S50*, being damaged, had rejoined
the *Regensburg,* while the *V69* and *V46* had rejoined Flotilla II.
After dark, the flotillas had again commenced search in their
assigned sectors. Of course, it was futile. If they had failed to
locate the British battleships in their first attempt, it was of
no use to advance again into the same area, particularly as their
objective must have moved a long distance in the meantime.
Flotilla II went far to the rear of the British forces and sighted
nothing. Then, its commander took advantage of the authority
given by Heinrich and Michelsen to return via the Skagerrak.
That, in our opinion, was the least excusable of all the errors
made by the German commanders. It cannot be said too emphatically that a powerful force of 10 very large destroyers, with
nearly 60 torpedoes, had nothing to fear from any force it might
encounter during the night. Its very high speed suited it per-

fectly for night search and attack. Also, it could easily have re-joined the Fleet in the early morning hours off Horn Reefs. Had Jellicoe forced action on the High Seas Fleet at that time, the absence of Flotilla II would have been very severely felt. For that mistake, we cannot find, or even imagine, the slightest excuse. Unfortunately, this criticism must bear upon Michelsen, Heinrich, and Schuur, the three highest destroyer commanders. The *V69* and *V46* had observed at a great distance the action between Scouting Group IV and the 2d Light Cruiser Squadron about 10:30 P.M. The destroyers did not contact any enemy forces.

We have already told how Flotilla VII made a number of contacts with the 4th Flotilla. After disengaging his flotilla from the British units, Commander von Koch had turned to SSE. ½ E. (140°). At 11:55 he detached Half Flotilla XIV and sent it on course SE. by E. (112°) at 16 knots to search his sector more effectively. From midnight on a number of actions between German ships and British destroyers were witnessed. Von Koch properly decided not to intervene in those fights.

It has been noted that Flotilla V was much impeded in its advance by having to pass several times through the German battle line. It was not until 11:00 P.M. that Commander Heinecke divided his 11 boats into four groups for a search in the general direction of S. ½ W. (173°). As 18 knots was the maximum speed at which the boats could run smokeless and as their course was diverging about 6° from the course of the Battle Fleet, it was evident that they had little, if any, chance of making contact with the British battleships. Errors in navigaion and in signals added to their difficulties. Also, the order that they must rejoin the Fleet at 2:00 A.M. off Horn Reefs cut short their search. Therefore, as early as 11:30 the two western groups of Flotilla V, consisting of the *V2*, *V4*, *V6*, *G9*, and *G10*, turned back to course SE. (122°) to avoid getting too far from their rendezvous. The 6 easternmost boats must have been rather close on the starboard beam of the *Westfalen*, for at 11:35 a torpedo, evidently fired by the 4th Flotilla, passed under the *G11*. At

12:04 A.M. the *G9* and *G10* sighted a light cruiser on the port bow and soon afterward reported it to Scheer. It might have been the *Rostock, Hamburg,* or *Stuttgart.* On the other hand, it might have been one of the British light cruisers that were then in company with the British Battle Fleet. It is too bad that the destroyers did not definitely establish the identity of the vessel sighted by means of recognition signals. At 12:20 A.M. the *G9* and *G10* were fired on by their own battleships. At 12:40 they sighted Flotilla IX. That unit of 5 boats, under Commander Tillessen, had been searching on course SW. by S. (201°), but at midnight had changed course for Horn Reefs. Thus, all the German flotillas, through a series of unfortunate incidents, had entirely missed their objectives, the British battle squadrons.

Despite the numerous conflicts between the destroyers of the 4th Flotilla and the German battleships, no definite information of the High Seas Fleet had reached Jellicoe. It seems simply incredible that no destroyer had reported the presence of the German battleships. The nearest to such a report was the radio dispatch from the *Ambuscade* to the *Tipperary* timed at 11:42: "Have fired two torpedoes and heard one explosion." That message was picked up by the *Indomitable* and signaled to Beatty. Apparently, it did not reach Jellicoe.

However, the continuous firing in the rear of the Battle Fleet was seen by many, if not all, of the battleships. The vessels of the 6th Division describe it most accurately. It was particularly distinct to the 5th Battle Squadron. The *Malaya,* the rear ship, clearly

observed what appeared to be an attack by our destroyers on some enemy big ships steering the same way as ours, two of which used searchlights. . . . The leading ship of the enemy, which was seen by the flash of the explosion, had two masts, two funnels, and a conspicuous crane (apparently the *Westfalen* class.)

A turret officer of the *Malaya* describes his "very vivid impression" of this action and says that German shells fired at British destroyers fell around his ship. The *Valiant* also gives a very detailed and accurate description of the action, but believed the German ships were cruisers. The *Birmingham*, which was on the starboard quarter of the *Malaya*, saw the action clearly. She "observed two or more large enemy ships switch on their searchlights and open fire on some of our destroyers." She believed the ships to be battle cruisers. She sent an excellent report to both Jellicoe and Beatty: "Urgent. Priority. Battle cruisers, unknown number, probably hostile, in sight NE. (32°) course S. (167°)."Unfortunately, the *Birmingham* added a navigational position (Fig. 49–P), which was exactly 25 miles to the northward of her actual position (Fig. 49–Q).

One would think that message, inaccurate though it was, would have roused Jellicoe to action. Nothing could have been simpler than to ask the *Birmingham* to verify her position, or to state it with reference to the battle squadrons. Also, he could have sent broadcast messages to his flotilla commanders, inquiring as to whether they had encountered German capital ships. However, even had Jellicoe known the position of the High Seas Fleet, there is no reason to believe that he would have acted differently than he actually did. He has stated most emphatically that he would not fight at night. Therefore, he would not have closed the enemy until 2:30 A.M. When that time came, as we shall soon see, he discovered another reason why he could not fight by day. Did it ever occur to the British commander in chief that there might also be some reason why the German admiral, with only half the strength of the British force, might also not be inclined to fight?

CHAPTER XXI

THE 12TH FLOTILLA ATTACKS
12:30 A.M. TO END OF BATTLE

WE HAVE mentioned the *Lydiard's* change of course to the south-westward at 12:10 A.M. Goldsmith's movement was calculated to bring him to the westward of the German battle line without a contact. If he had in his column only the 5 destroyers of the 9th and 10th Flotillas, Goldsmith would have accomplished his purpose, futile though it was; but, unknown to him, his column had been increased to 13 boats by accessions from the 4th and 13th Flotillas. Therefore, the rear of his column came in contact with the German battle line in a perfect position for a torpedo attack from both bows (Fig. 49–x). The last four destroyers were the *Narborough, Pelican, Petard,* and *Turbulent* (Fig. 54–M). At 12:30 A.M. they found themselves passing at right angles directly across the line of advance of the *Westfalen.* On that ship's starboard bow were the *Narborough* and *Pelican,* while on the port bow were the *Petard* and *Turbulent.* The *Petard* says that when the *Westfalen* turned on her colored vertical string of recognition lights (two red over one white) she was not distant over 500 yards. She then recognized a division of German battleships.

The *Westfalen* acted promptly and decisively in that critical situation. She turned a searchlight on the *Pelican,* but before fire had opened swung it to the *Petard.* That ship, as fortune would have it, alone of all the 13 British destroyers, had fired all her torpedoes. Therefore, she increased to full speed and turned slightly to port to avoid a collision. She crossed about 200 yards ahead of the *Westfalen,* but did not take advantage of the opportunity to fire at the latter's bridge. If it be urged that the change of bearing was too rapid for training the 4-inch guns, it can be replied that did not prevent the 5.9-inch guns of the

Westfalen from following their target; for, as soon as the starboard battery of the battleship could bear, she let go several salvos, hitting the *Petard* with 6 out of 19 shots. Fortunately, they, though causing 15 casualties, did the *Petard* no important damage. So she was able to continue her escape at high speed. In considering the encounter, it will be interesting to guess what might have happened if both the *Petard* and *Westfalen* had been equipped with 50-caliber machine guns.

The *Turbulent*, when she was first discovered, was well on the *Westfalen's* port bow, in a perfect position for torpedo fire. In fact, the torpedoes could not have missed. It is not known whether she had any torpedoes in her starboard tubes, as she had been in the 4:30 P.M. attack. If so, they evidently were not fired before the *Westfalen's* port battery opened fire with deadly effect. The Germans saw their first salvo destroy the *Turbulent's* after gun with all its crew. The destroyer, in order to escape being rammed, turned left and took a course parallel to the *Westfalen.* The latter turned one point to starboard to keep her port battery bearing. In a few minutes, after the expenditure of 34 rounds of 5.9-inch and 3.5-inch shells, the *Turbulent's* boilers exploded and she sank with all hands. That was about 12:32 A.M. (Fig. 54–N).

Meanwhile, what advantage were the *Narborough* and *Pelican* taking of their unique opportunity to attack? It may be remembered that they had failed to attack in the 4:30 P.M. engagement, alleging the most remarkable excuse that friendly boats were in the way. Unfortunately for the two boats, there can be no similar excuse on this occasion and their conduct proved to be even more highly questionable than before. The *Pelican* makes the astounding statement that the "position was unfavorable for attack." On the contrary, it required only a very simple turn to the right to make it perfect, particularly as the *Pelican* had so quickly evaded the German searchlights. The *Narborough* says that she was distant about 1,000 yards when the first contact was made. Her report describes accurately the damage to the *Petard* and the sinking of the *Turbulent*. It is said that the hostile "vessel was immediately lost sight of owing to heavy smoke." Actually, the smoke was a perfect aid to assist the *Narborough* in maintaining contact with the hostile forces and a valuable screen under which she might approach to fire torpedoes. The inertness of the *Pelican* and *Narborough* is inexcusable.

The *Nicator*, next ahead of the *Narborough*, clearly saw the entire attack, but her captain, who had done so splendidly in the 4:30 P.M. action, did nothing. An officer of the ship describes how he saw "three or four big ships, obviously Germans, silhouetted for a moment." The *Nicator* had only one torpedo remaining at 5:00 P.M., but probably had now loaded her spare torpedo, giving a total of two. None of the other destroyers present makes any reference to the action. Commander Goldsmith did not discover that there were vessels of other flotillas present until 6:00 A.M. The whole episode is a glaring example of ineffective leadership and inertness.

"The most fatal heresy in war," writes General Ian Hamilton, "and, with us, the most rank, is the heresy that battles can be won without heavy loss, I don't care whether it is in men or ships."

The High Seas Fleet proceeded on its course. It had dispersed, crippled, or sunk the vessels of the brave 4th Flotilla. The 11th, 13th, 9th, and 10th Flotillas had not even disputed its progress. Only the 12th Flotilla and the *Champion, Obdurate,* and *Moresby* of the 13th, having been driven to the eastward, were still converging on the High Seas Fleet. It was doubtful whether those flotillas could make contact before daylight. At the cost of serious damage to two light cruisers, the German battleships had forced a passage through the very center of the British destroyer mass, sinking 5 and seriously damaging 5 more. It was a brilliant feat of arms on the part of the Germans. High credit should go to the captains leading the battle line and particularly to Captain Redlich of the *Westfalen,* who had proved fully worthy of the high responsibility thrust upon him.

Behind the two Fleets was a mass of crippled vessels, which

were endeavoring to save themselves as best they might. We shall recount briefly the story of those vessels while the opposing Fleets proceed for an hour and a half without any important event. On the British side, the following vessels had been put out of action in the daylight actions: the *Warspite, Marlborough, Warrior, Onslow, Defender, Acasta,* and *Moorsom.* Night battle had added to the list the *Southampton, Dublin, Broke, Sparrowhawk, Contest, Porpoise, Tipperary,* and *Spitfire.*

At 8:30 the *Warspite* had set her course westward for Rosyth at 16 knots, the maximum speed at which it was then believed she could proceed. The *Marlborough* had been steaming at 15.8 knots ever since her torpedo hit at 6:54 P.M. The condition of the forward fireroom bulkhead was becoming more and more serious and further reduction in speed was becoming imminent. Already she was 6 miles in rear of the 5th Division. At 8:00 P.M. the *Warrior,* completely helpless, with both engines out of action, directed the *Engadine* to take her in tow. At 8:40 that was accomplished in an estimated position in Lat. 57°-10'; Long. 5°-42'. The *Engadine* went ahead at 10 knots, which gave an estimated speed of 8.2 knots for the first hour. As the sea began to increase before the northwesterly wind, speed gradually was decreased to about 6 knots through the water. There was still hope that the *Warrior* could be saved.

Since 7:15 P.M. the *Defender* had been towing the *Onslow* at 12 knots. At 1:00 A.M. the rising sea parted the towline and the two destroyers proceeded slowly in company toward the estimated direction of Aberdeen. The *Acasta* lay on the battlefield in a crippled condition. To the southwestward, she could see a burning ship, the *Wiesbaden.* The *Southampton* was following in the rear of the Battle Fleet. The *Dublin* was endeavoring to do the same; but, her compass having been affected by gunfire, she seems to have remained some distance in the rear. The *Tipperary* remained helpless and was gradually settling in the water. The fires still prevented access to the forward part of the ship. The crew was preparing to abandon ship on two small Carley rafts. The *Sparrowhawk* was unable to steam or steer, but was in no danger of sinking. Efforts to cut loose her jammed rudder were unavailing. The *Broke,* with enormous casualties but in fairly good material condition, was proceeding northward at slow speed. Her radio had been destroyed. The *Contest,* with speed reduced to 20 knots, had steamed to the northeastward. The *Porpoise* had partly repaired her injuries and was steaming homeward at slow speed. The *Spitfire,* though terribly damaged, was doing the same.

On the German side, the *Wiesbaden, Lützow, Elbing, Rostock,* and *S32* were out of action. The *Wiesbaden* was still floating, but a careful inspection of the ship indicated that she would not float much longer. Her few survivors had built a few small rafts to use when the ship sank. She was seen by the *Acasta* as late as 2:00 A.M. Soon afterward she sank. Her men died one after another. Only one, Chief Stoker Zenne, was rescued by the small steamer *Willi* after having been 38 hours in the rough and icy sea. The courage of this resolute seaman in sustaining the mental and physical tortures of such an experience is almost incredible.

The situation of the *Lützow* was rapidly growing desperate. At midnight her position, as reported by the *G40,* was some 26 miles in rear of the German battle line. Incidentally, square 010 in which the *Lützow* was reported at midnight was northwest of square 016 in which she had been reported at 11:05 P.M., though her course had been to the southeastward during that period. Speed had been reduced to 7 knots. The water was rising rapidly. It finally had reached the dynamos and only the auxiliary lighting circuits were available. The forward turret was awash and water was entering the forward firerooms. The end was evidently near.

The *Elbing* was practically helpless and unable to steam. The *S53* was standing by. The *Rostock* was in better condition; but, unfortunately, the torpedo hit had salted most of her boiler feed water and she was forced to stop. The *S54* took her in tow and proceeded at 10 knots. The *S32,* while proceeding slowly toward the Danish coast, sighted a British light cruiser at 12:45

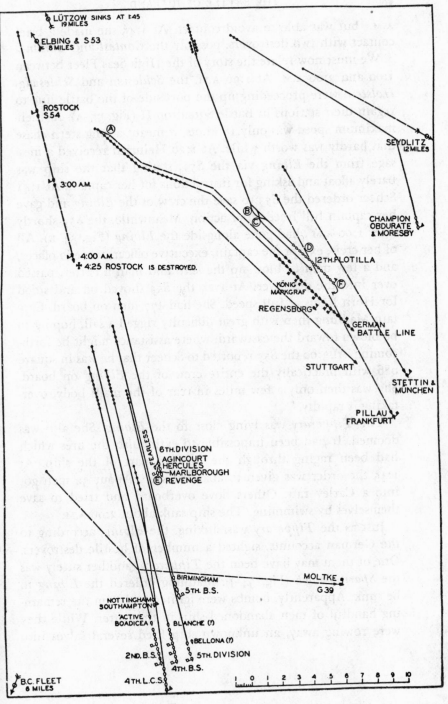

LÜTZOW SINKS AT 1:45
19 MILES

ELBING & S 53
8 MILES

ROSTOCK
S 54

Ⓐ

3:00 A.M.

4:00 A.M.
✝ 4:25 ROSTOCK IS DESTROYED.

Ⓑ
Ⓒ

KÖNIG
MARKGRAF

REGENSBURG

STUTTGART

SEYDLITZ
12 MILES

CHAMPION
OBDURATE
& MORESBY

Ⓓ

12TH.FLOTILLA

Ⓕ

GERMAN
BATTLE LINE

STETTIN &
MÜNCHEN

PILLAU
FRANKFURT

FEARLESS

6TH.DIVISION
AGINCOURT
HERCULES
MARLBOROUGH
Ⓔ REVENGE

NOTTINGHAM
SOUTHAMPTON
ACTIVE
BOADICEA
BLANCHE (?)

BELLONA (?)

2ND. B.S.
4TH. B.S.
5TH. DIVISION

B.C. FLEET
8 MILES

4TH. L.C.S.

BIRMINGHAM
5TH. B.S.

MOLTKE
G 39

1 0 1 2 3 4 5 6 7 8 9 10

FIG. 55. 1:00-2:00 A.M.

A.M., but was able to avoid contact. At 1:45 she made a brief contact with two destroyers, possibly the *Contest* and *Garland*.

We must now relate the story of the High Seas Fleet between 1:00 and 2:00 A.M. At 1:00 A.M. the *Schlesien* and *Schleswig-Holstein* were proceeding up the port side of the battle line to regain their stations in Battle Squadron II (Fig. 55–A). As their maximum speed was only 18 knots, it meant a long stern chase that hardly was worth while. At 1:20 Heinrich received a message from the *Elbing* via the *S53*, stating that the ship was barely afloat and asking for instructions for her captain. At 1:41 Scheer ordered the *S53* to save the crew of the *Elbing* and gave her captain full freedom of action. Meanwhile, the *S53* shortly after 1:00 A.M., had gone alongside the *Elbing* (Fig. 54–K). All of her crew, except the captain, executive officer, torpedo officer, and a few men to blow up the ship and man a cutter, passed over into the destroyer. At 1:25 the *S53* shoved off and stood for Horn Reefs at full speed. She had 477 men on board. Captain Madlung then with great difficulty rigged a sail, hoping to be blown toward the eastward, where assistance might be forthcoming. At 3:00 the *S53* reported to Scheer that he was in square 086 with practically the entire crew of the *Elbing* on board. She was then only a few miles in rear of the main body, overtaking it rapidly.

The *Tipperary* was lying close to the *Elbing*. She also was doomed. It had been impossible to extinguish the fires which had been raging through the forward part of the ship. At 1:45 the order was given to abandon ship. About 32 men got into a Carley raft. Others dove overboard and tried to save themselves by swimming. The ship sank about 2:00 A.M.

Just as the *Tipperary* was sinking, the *Elbing*, according to the German accounts, sighted a number of hostile destroyers. One of them may have been the *Tipperary;* another surely was the *Sparrowhawk* (Fig. 54–J). Madlung ordered the *Elbing* to be sunk. Apparently, bombs were ignited and then the remaining handful of men abandoned ship in the cutter. While they were rowing away, an unknown ship fired several salvos into the sinking *Elbing*. A few minutes later, the cutter came upon some of the crew of *Tipperary* swimming in the icy water. The surgeon was rescued but, unfortunately, there was no room in the small boat for more. Madlung burned blue lights in the hope of attracting the attention of some British ship to the drowning men. About 7:00 A.M. the cutter met the Dutch fishing steamer *Kjmuiden 125*, which took the *Elbing's* men to Holland. Madlung had done well in most distressing circumstances.

Meanwhile, the *Sparrowhawk* had distinctly sighted the *Elbing*, which she reported as a 3-funneled cruiser of the *Mainz* class. The after gun was manned for a fight to the finish; but, suddenly and providentially, to the great relief of the destroyer's brave complement, the strange ship was seen to be settling by the bow. Soon she disappeared beneath the sea.

The crowded raft on which the *Tipperary's* men were embarked floated about 1 foot under the icy water. One after another, most of the poor fellows froze to death. To keep up their spirits, they sang "It's a Long Way to Tipperary." The remnant of the gallant band, about 18 in number, finally was rescued by the *Sparrowhawk*. The display of resolute courage in facing the torture of a slow and terrible death was worthy of the finest naval traditions.

At last, at 1:27 A.M. came the important information of the *Moltke's* contacts. A dispatch from the *G39* timed at 1:04 stated that at 12:30 the battle cruiser had been in square 059 on course south (167°) at 24 knots. Hipper's message added that he had been forced off his course by four hostile battleships and would seek to rejoin the Fleet at dawn. That was the first report of British battleships Scheer had received for many hours. Unfortunately, the report told principally of the *Moltke* and only incidentally of the British battleships. Had Scheer been given the time and place of the contact with them and their course, all of which were known to the *Moltke*, he could have estimated rather closely the position of the Grand Fleet. As it was, Scheer might have reasoned from the fact that the *Moltke* had been forced to south (167°) to avoid the enemy, that the latter's course was either south or somewhat east of south, an indication that British battleships were in close proximity but probably were steering a somewhat divergent course. At any rate, regardless of what inference he may or may not have drawn from Hipper's unsatisfactory contact report, Scheer held to his course, determined to fight his way through at any price. Incidentally, the *Moltke* at 1:00 A.M. had gained a position about 6 miles on the starboard bow of the *Iron Duke* (Fig. 55). She now headed sharply to the eastward and about 1:25 A.M. passed very closely ahead of the Battle Fleet, a very narrow and lucky escape. By 2:00 she was about 12 miles on the *Iron Duke's* port beam and well clear of danger.

At 1:29 Heinrich detached the last two destroyers with him, the *V71* and *V73*, to proceed to the *Rostock*. A minute later, the *Nassau* told Scheer that she had taken station in rear of Battle Squadron II. At 1:31 a message was intercepted from the *L22* reporting several lights in square o68. The center of that square was about 8 miles on the starboard quarter of the main body. However, Groos's chart 35 places the actual position of the *L22* at 1:30 in the upper right corner of square o88, no less than 20 miles northwest of the reported position. Evidently, there was a large error in the *L22's* navigation which, of course, was to be expected.

At 1:35 there came a report from the *L24*, giving her position at 1:03 in square o87 on course NE. by N. (20°). That agreed with the actual position of the ship on Groos's chart 35. At the time of her report, she was 6 miles on the *Westfalen's* port beam and close to the *Seydlitz* and several light cruisers. That ship had nothing to report.

Ever since 1:00 A.M. the condition of the *Lützow* gradually had become more serious. To relieve pressure on the forward bulkheads, an attempt was made to run her stern first, but the draft of the bow increased to 17 meters (about 18.6 feet) and the propellers came out of water. Calculations showed that there were about 8,000 tons of water in the ship. As she might capsize any minute, gallant Captain Harder ordered the crew to abandon ship. At 1:20 fires were hauled and the crew mustered on the quarter-deck in due order. The *G37, G38, G40,* and *V45* went alongside. "Thereupon the crew," says Groos, "after giving three hurras for His Majesty the Kaiser and the *Lützow,* left the ship in perfect order and quiet, wounded first." At 1:45 the water was up to the bridge. Harder ordered the *G38* to fire two torpedoes into the giant battle cruiser and she disappeared beneath the waves. The four destroyers got under way in company. The *G40* carried 260 men; the *G38,* 66; the *G37,* 500; and the *V45,* 215. The overcrowded boats prepared to fight their way through to Horn Reefs against any opposition (Fig. 55).

At 1:46 the *Regensburg* ordered all flotillas to assemble near the van of Battle Squadron I. About that time Flotillas IX and V rejoined the Fleet and by 2:00 the *V2, V4,* and *V6* were on the port beam of the *Westfalen.* The light cruisers *Stuttgart, München, Stettin, Frankfurt,* and *Pillau* were a few miles ahead and on the starboard bow.

Meanwhile, the 12th Flotilla on course south was again nearing the German battle line (Fig. 55–B). It was disposed in two half flotillas. The first was led by Captain Stirling in the flotilla leader *Faulknor.* On his starboard quarter was the 1st Division, composed of the *Obedient, Mindful, Marvel,* and *Onslaught.* The 2d Division, the *Maenad, Narwhal, Nessus,* and *Noble* were on the *Faulknor's* port quarter, abreast the 1st Division. In rear of those divisions was the *Marksman,* leading the 2d Half Flotilla, composed of the *Opal, Menace, Munster,* and *Mary Rose.*

At 1:43 the *Obedient,* Commander Campbell, called to the *Faulknor* by megaphone, "Enemy SW." At 1:45 the *Faulknor* also sighted "strange ships on starboard bow steering SE." They were soon made out to be the *Kaiser* class battleships in the first streaks of dawn. Stirling paralleled the enemy and increased speed to 25 knots (Fig. 55–B). He ordered the 1st Division to attack. The order was obeyed instantly. According to British accounts, the Germans turned away and disappeared in the early light. Thereupon, Stirling canceled the attack and the division rejoined him.

The German story is different. At that time, the German destroyers, as above stated, were rejoining their battle line. Only a few minutes previously recognition signals had been exchanged with the boats of Flotillas V and IX. Therefore, when the *König* at 1:47 sighted destroyers on the port hand, the presumption was that they were the boats of other flotillas making their junction as ordered. However, the *König* opened fire and the strange boats disappeared at full speed. No mention is made of a turn away by the German ships, though it is possible that the *König* and other ships adjacent might have done so for a few minutes.

It seems that Commander Campbell lost a real opportunity on that occasion. He certainly could not have made a very definite or aggressive attack. The *König* was the last first-line battleship in column. After her came the second-line battleships *Deutschland, Pommern,* and *Hannover.* Next came the *Nassau* of Battle Squadron I. The second-line battleship *Hessen* followed her, while the *Schlesien* and *Schleswig-Holstein* were on the port beam trying to regain position. In rear of the *Hessen* came the damaged battle cruisers *Von der Tann* and *Derfflinger.* Thus, beginning with the *König*, there were within striking distance 9 capital ships, all of which either had received severe damage or were second-line ships of small defensive strength. They constituted ideal torpedo targets. At the time, Stirling had 9 boats well concentrated for attack, and presumably the other 5 would have followed him in. Their torpedoes undoubtedly would have been highly effective and might even have been decisive.

However, the attack was not to be made. Misled by the *Obedient's* report that the Germans had disappeared, Stirling decided to parallel the enemy, gain distance ahead, turn to a reverse course, and then attack. That complicated plan was not signaled and immediately resulted in such confusion that even the British Admiralty cannot account for the activities of half the boats that composed the flotilla during that period.

The *Faulknor's* increase of speed without signal naturally resulted in a stringing out of the destroyer column and undoubtedly was the primary cause of so many of the rear destroyers losing the rest of the flotilla. In particular, it was disastrous for the *Mindful*, second ship in the 1st Division. She had only two boilers in use and consequently had to leave station (Fig. 55–c). She fell far to the rear of her division.

After the *Faulknor* increased speed to 25 knots, Stirling ordered the 1st Division to take position astern. Presumably, the 2d Division fell back astern of the 1st, as the *Maenad* mentions training her two double tubes to starboard. Incidentally, that torpedo armament was highly favorable for attack. As the tubes of the new destroyers were on the center line, all could be trained either to starboard or port, thus permitting a salvo of four torpedoes to be fired instantaneously. That arrangement, however, was not without some disadvantage, for, as will be seen later, the time taken to train the tubes from one broadside to the other made it necessary for the captain to know some time in advance which broadside would bear on the enemy.

At 1:52, while running at high speed to the southeast, Stirling sent an important message to his radio room. It read, "To C-in-C. Urgent. Priority. Enemy's battleships in sight. My position ten miles astern of 1st Battle Squadron" (Fig. 55–D). That was an excellent contact report. In particular, we like the idea of giving position relative to the battle line, rather than a navigational fix. However, instead of 10 miles in rear of the battle line, the contact actually occurred 26 miles on the port quarter. To one who has had no experience in war or tactical exercises, such an error must seem excessive, but in the haste and stress of action and in the small chart house of a destroyer, such mistakes are easily possible. Stirling, in charge of a destroyer attack of vital importance, could not give his personal attention to sending a contact report. That duty must have been turned over to a junior officer, who probably was directed to make haste in order to get the message on the air before the *Faulknor* came under the close-range fire that might be expected to destroy her radio equipment as well as the ship.

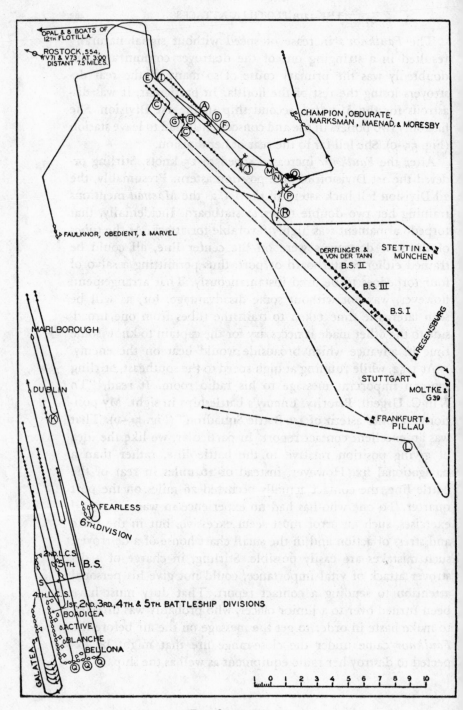

FIG. 56. 2:00-3:00 A.M.

That message and others that followed are some of the mysteries of Jutland. Stirling states that it was sent twice on power. The Signal Record in the Jutland Papers says: "This signal was incompletely logged in *Faulknor's* log, and there are no records of it having been received in *Iron Duke*." That statement fails to fix the responsibility for the grave error in communications. It does not state specifically whether any other British ships received the message. As notes concerning the other two messages from the *Faulknor* cover the point explicitly, it may be inferred that message was received by other British ships but was not received by the *Iron Duke* either directly or through another ship. At any rate, that important information evidently did not reach Jellicoe. As will be shown later, that failure in communications, although interesting to note, had no actual influence on the course of the battle.

At 2:00 Stirling counter-marched to starboard. He was followed by the *Obedient, Marvel,* and *Onslaught* (Figs. 55-F and 56-A). The latter boat states that she turned to port rather than starboard, but that seems unlikely. Almost immediately, the German battleships were sighted. In the early morning light there loomed up four vessels of the *Kaiser* class. Actually, Stirling saw Division V, led by the *Markgraf, Kronprinz, Grosser Kurfürst,* and *König.* The *Markgraf* flashed the recognition signal, but, even when no answer came, there remained much doubt on her bridge as to whether she was encountering friend or foe. It was now fairly light, which made it difficult to distinguish lights in the mist and drizzling rain. The *Kronprinz* also did not recognize the destroyers as hostile. The *Grosser Kurfürst,* however, opened fire on three destroyers about 2:03 and commenced turning six points away from the enemy (Fig. 56-C). The *König* and *Deutschland* also turned away and fired at the destroyers through the smoke of the ships ahead, which was being blown toward the enemy by the rising southwest wind.

The delay of the Germans in opening fire was highly favorable to the British. About 2:02, the *Faulknor* had fired one tor-

pedo at the *Kronprinz* (Fig. 56–B). At 2:03, a few seconds before
the Germans fired, the second torpedo left its tube, aimed at the
Grosser Kurfürst. The destroyers were steaming at 25 knots on
an opposite course. The range was fairly long, about 1,800 yards,
and was increasing as the Germans turned away. Also the German ships were turning rapidly. It was too light for searchlights
and the targets were mere dim shapes in the mist and rain. Sight
lenses were covered with moisture. As a result, the leading three
destroyers escaped without a hit, although entire salvos landed
within 50 yards of them. Gallantly, they fired their 4-inch guns
against the German battleships, but that fire was equally ineffective.

At 2:05 the *Obedient* fired her first torpedo at the *König* at a
range of about 2,000 yards. Between 2:05 and 2:08 the *Marvel*
fired 4 torpedoes in succession. From about 2:07 to 2:10 the
Onslaught fired 4 torpedoes, 2 set for high-speed, short-range
shots and 2 for slow-speed, long-range shots. At 2:10 the *Obedient* fired her second torpedo at Battle Squadron II. Thus, four
destroyers succeeded in firing 12 torpedoes at moderate ranges
without sustaining a hit.

It was about 2:09 when the *Faulknor* reached the *Schlesien*
and *Schleswig-Holstein*, which were about 500 yards on the port
beam of the rear ships of the German battle line. Those vessels
opened a rapid fire on the destroyers. Stirling took them for
cruisers and believed they were advancing against him. He
turned away to N. by E. (358°) and increased to full speed (Fig.
56–E). As the *Faulknor* disappeared in the mist, the German
fire shifted to the boats astern.

The *Onslaught* was hit on the bridge about 2:12 by one or
more shells of the third salvo from the *Schleswig-Holstein*. The
bridge was completely wrecked. Lieutenant Commander A. G.
Onslow, who had handled his ship so gallantly and effectively,
was mortally wounded. The executive officer was killed. There
were 5 other casualties.

During the attack Stirling sent two radio messages. At 2:07
he broadcasted: "Urgent. Am attacking." It was not received by

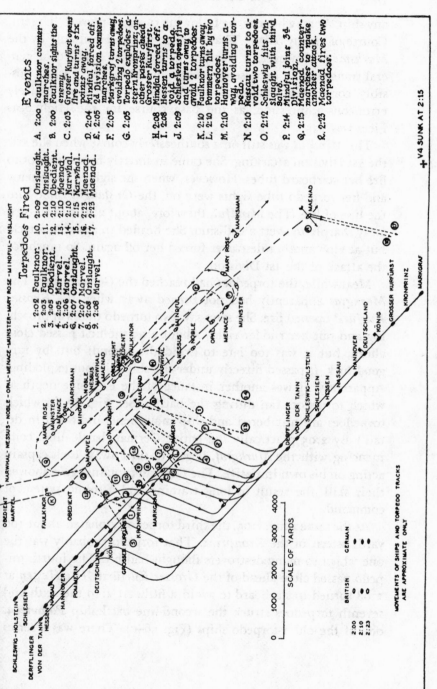

Events

A. 2:00   Faulknor countermarches.
B. 2:00   Faulknor sights the enemy.
C. 2:03   Grosser Kurfürst opens fire and turns six points away.
D. 2:04   Mindful forced off.
E. 2:05   2d Division countermarches.
F. 2:05   Markgraf turns away, avoiding 2 torpedoes.
G. 2:05   Torpedo explodes astern Kronprinz; another passes ahead Grosser Kurfürst.
H. 2:08   Mindful forced off.
I. 2:08   Hessen turns to avoid a torpedo.
J. 2:09   Schlesien opens fire and turns away to avoid 2 torpedoes.
K. 2:10   Faulknor turns away.
L. 2:10   Pommern hit by two torpedoes.
M. 2:10   Hannover turns away, avoiding a torpedo.
N. 2:10   Nassau turns to avoid two torpedoes.
O. 2:12   Schleswig hits Onslaught with third salvo.
P. 2:14   Mindful joins 34 Division.
Q. 2:15   Maenad countermarches to make another attack.
R. 2:23   Maenad fires two torpedoes.

Torpedoes Fired

1. 2:02   Faulknor.
2. 2:03   Faulknor.
3. 2:05   Obedient.
4. 2:05   Marvel.
5. 2:06   Marvel.
6. 2:07   Onslaught.
7. 2:07   Marvel.
8. 2:08   Onslaught.
9. 2:08   Maenad.
10. 2:09   Onslaught.
11. 2:10   Onslaught.
12. 2:10   Obedient.
13. 2:10   Maenad.
14. 2:10   Narwhal.
15. 2:15   Narwhal.
16. 2:23   Maenad.
17. 2:23   Maenad.

✝ V4 SUNK AT 2:15

OBEDIENT · NARWHAL · NESSUS · NOBLE · OPAL · MENACE · MUNSTER · MARY ROSE · MINDFUL · ONSLAUGHT
MARVEL   FAULKNOR

SCHLESWIG-HOLSTEIN · SCHLESIEN
DERFFLINGER
VON DER TANN
HESSEN NASSAU
HANNOVER
POMMERN

SCALE OF YARDS

0   1000   2000   3000   4000

MOVEMENTS OF SHIPS AND TORPEDO TRACKS ARE APPROXIMATE ONLY

BRITISH   ● ● ●
GERMAN   ● ● ●

2:00
2:10
2:23

FIG. 57. Attack of 12th Flotilla.

any ship. At 2:12 he sent the following twice on power: "Urgent. Course of enemy SSW." That message was received only by the *Marksman*. However, it was just as well that it failed of general transmission, because the course of SSW. (189°), while possibly correct for the time, would have created an entirely erroneous impression, as the base course for the High Seas Fleet was 135°.

The *Mindful* was still on a southeasterly course when she saw the 1st Division attacking. She came in smartly in an attempt to fire her starboard tubes. However, when she sighted the enemy and her torpedo tube sights were on, the *Onslaught* came into the line of fire. The *Mindful*, therefore, about 2:04 had to turn away sharply to avert a collision. She headed in again to attack, but at 2:08 another destroyer forced her off again. So much for the attack of the 1st Division.

Meanwhile, the torpedoes had reached the German line. The *Markgraf* apparently had not turned away when the *Grosser Kurfürst* opened fire. She soon saw two torpedo tracks approaching and put her rudder right. About 2:05 the first passed close ahead, but it was too late to avoid the second; but, by rare good luck, it passed directly under the ship without exploding. Apparently, it was another instance of the excessive depth at which torpedoes ran during the battle. (See Fig. 57, in which torpedoes are numbered and ship movements indicated in detail.) By 2:05 practically the entire German battle line, commencing with the *Markgraf*, began to turn away, each captain acting on his own initiative. The German captains again showed their skill, the result of long training and a sound system of command.

At the same time, 2:05, the third torpedo detonated about 100 yards astern of the *Kronprinz*. That torpedo probably was the one which so many destroyers thought had hit. The fourth torpedo passed close ahead of the *Grosser Kurfürst*. The *Hessen* at 2:08 turned to starboard to avoid a fifth. At 2:10 the sixth and seventh torpedoes struck the second-line battleship *Pommern*, one of the old 1-torpedo ships (Fig. 56–c). There was a series of explosions. Flames leaped as high as the mastheads. The ship broke in two and capsized. Not a soul was saved. Thus in less than a minute there perished 844 officers and men. Here was the result of taking to sea with the Fleet inferior ships that could not withstand even a single torpedo hit. Had those torpedoes hit a first-line battleship, the chances are strong that she could have maintained the fleet speed of 16 knots.

The *Hannover* turned slightly to starboard to avoid the wreck of the *Pommern*. As she did so about 2:10, the eighth torpedo passed close under her stern. She continued to swing through eight points (90°) away from the enemy. Sighting destroyers to port, the *Nassau* also turned eight points away. The ninth and tenth torpedoes passed ahead and astern of her. The *Schlesien*, which was out of the column on the port quarter of the *Nassau*, opened fire on the *Onslaught* and turned away to avoid the eleventh and twelfth British torpedoes. The *Schleswig-Holstein* kept on her course and opened fire on the *Onslaught*. As above stated, her third salvo, fired at 1,000 yards, struck the *Onslaught's* bridge. That was about 2:12.

The *Maenad* had trained her torpedo tubes to starboard in the expectation that Captain Stirling would attack on a south-easterly course. When the *Faulknor* turned unexpectedly to starboard, the *Maenad* did not follow the 1st Division around, but held on until her torpedo tubes were trained to port. Then, about 2:05 the *Maenad* counter-marched, followed by the *Narwhal*. About 2:10 the *Maenad* sighted the German battleships and fired one torpedo (No. 13) at a range of about 4,000 yards. By that time, the turn away of the Germans had greatly opened the range. The *Maenad* had closed up quite well on the *Onslaught* and came under a heavy fire. The *Onslaught* was seen to be hit and to turn away from the enemy. The *Maenad* followed her, the *Narwhal* fired two torpedoes (Nos. 14 and 15), the second about 2:15. The *Maenad* then reversed course to starboard (Fig. 56–I), trained tubes on that side, and closed in until she again sighted the German battle line. She fired two torpedoes (Nos. 16 and 17) about 2:23 at 4,000 yards (Fig. 56–J).

During that attack, the *Maenad* was under a heavy fire to which she replied with her after 4-inch gun, claiming several hits.

The *Narwhal* did not follow the *Maenad* as she turned to the southeast, but kept on to the northward. However, the falling out of the *Mindful*, *Onslaught*, and *Maenad* caused such a long gap in the column that the *Narwhal* never was able to gain contact with the 1st Division, which now consisted only of the *Obedient* and *Marvel*. Those two boats alone remained in contact with the *Faulknor* (Fig. 56).

None of the five torpedoes fired by the *Maenad* and *Narwhal* were sighted by the Germans, who had returned to their base course. The *Maenad* claims to have scored a torpedo hit on a German battleship, but it cannot be substantiated and remains another of the mysteries of Jutland. Possibly, the explosion of the *Pommern* was seen and the times were confused.

The *Nessus* and *Noble*, which originally followed the *Narwhal*, did not fire torpedoes and there is no information whatever concerning their movements, except what is shown on Diagram 45 in the Admiralty *Narrative*. It would seem that they followed the *Narwhal* throughout the attack. Probably, by the time they reached a firing position, the Germans had turned away so far as to be out of sight except for the flashes of their guns. Also, it is possible that the heavy German fire induced them to keep on the *Narwhal's* starboard quarter. The *Nessus* was hit by a shell which put one boiler out of action and caused 15 casualties.

At 2:15 a mysterious incident occurred at the van of the German line. The *V2*, *V4*, and *V6* of Flotilla V were about 200 yards on the port beam of the *Westfalen* and *Rheinland*, steaming to take station ahead. A sudden explosion blew off the bow of the *V4*, killing 17 and wounding 2. The *V2* and *V6* rescued the survivors in the heavy sea. At first glance it would seem that this damage might have been caused by a wild torpedo fired by the 12th Flotilla, but Groos states positively that was not the case. Since the British attack was directed at the rear of the German line, it seems improbable that torpedoes could have reached its van.

The flotilla leader *Marksman* seems to have kept on to the southeast until she sighted the destroyer leader *Champion* at 2:20. The four boats of the division did not attack and nothing is known of their movements, except what is shown by Diagram 45 in the Admiralty *Narrative*. They probably left the *Marksman* and followed the *Nessus* and *Noble* to the northwestward. By the time they reached the point of contact, the Germans doubtless had disappeared to the westward due to their 8-point change of course. The *Mindful* took station in their rear.

Thus, seven boats of the flotilla had failed to fire torpedoes. As they must have clearly seen the explosion of the *Pommern*, their failure to attack would seem to indicate an inexcusable lack of initiative. Many of the British captains lacked that spirit of aggressive initiative that must always be the prime characteristic of destroyer captains and of cavalry officers in war ashore. Thus, the attack of the 12th Flotilla, while well delivered by the leading boats, failed to win the decisive success which seemed probable. Knowing the enemy's course, we might wish, for the prestige of all destroyer officers, that Stirling had gained a position ahead of the German line so that it could be attacked from both sides. However, that probably was too much to expect under the difficult circumstances. We realize fully, as the result of four years' experience in destroyer commands, the difficulties inseparable from all night destroyer operations. It will be noted that our only criticism of the British destroyers during this eventful night is that on many occasions they did not attack enemy ships in plain sight and at close range. We have only admiration for Stirling's aggressiveness and skill in the attack. Unfortunately, half of his captains did not follow the lead he so boldly gave them.

The *Champion*, *Obdurate*, and *Moresby*, all under Captain Farie, had been steaming on course SE. (122°) until 1:45. Then, course was changed to south (167°). At 2:15, evidently hearing the attack of 12th Flotilla, the *Champion* headed west (257°) (Fig. 56). At 2:20 the *Marksman* sighted the *Champion*. Her log reports an engagement with two cruisers and four destroyers. At that time, Farie signaled the *Marksman* by flashing light,

"Where are enemy's ships?" The *Marksman* replied, "Suspicious ships south." At 2:25 the *Champion* changed course to south (167°). At the same time, Farie asked the *Marksman*, "Where is our battle fleet?" The *Marksman* replied, "Bearing south." That, it will be noted, was the same bearing on which she had just reported suspicious ships. Now, as Corbett says, "ships were clearly seen to the southward." At 2:30 the *Marksman* signaled the *Champion:* "What are ships bearing south?" Farie replied, "Germans, I think." While that exchange of signals was taking place, he turned away from them to about 125° (Fig. 56–M). The *Marksman* now took station in rear of the *Moresby* and the *Maenad* fell into column in rear of the *Marksman*, having just completed her attack. At 2:34 the *Moresby* sighted four *Deutschland* class ships bearing west, distant 4,000 yards (Fig. 56–N). "I considered action imperative," says Lieutenant Commander Roger Alison, "hoisted compass west, hauled out to port, firing an A.S. torpedo at 2:37." Evidently, after sheering out to port, Alison turned with left rudder around the rear of the column and fired one starboard tube (Fig. 56–P). Unfortunately, the ship rolled heavily to port when the sights of the forward tube bore on the enemy, and it was not fired. That implies an accuracy in aiming which was certainly not necessary when firing at four ships. Only the *Schleswig-Holstein* sighted the British destroyers, but they disappeared before fire could be opened. At 2:42 the *Von der Tann* avoided the *Moresby's* torpedo by maneuvering. We very much admire Alison's spirit in that attack. It offered a sharp contrast to the ineffective leadership of Captain Farie, who at 2:34, as the *Moresby* was attacking, turned sharply to east (77°), directly away from the Germans, whose identity he well knew (Fig. 56–O). That was the third time he failed to attack and deliberately headed away from the enemy. If he did not feel it practicable to attack with his light cruiser flagship, he could have directed the four destroyers present to attack. Though it was now daylight, the very low visibility was favorable for torpedo attacks, as the *Moresby* had definitely proved.

After the actions above described, the *Faulknor*, *Obedient*, and *Marvel* passed astern of the High Seas Fleet and steered to the southward at 2:20. Five minutes later, an enemy vessel was sighted. Apparently, it was a cruiser standing toward them. Stirling altered course to west (257°). At 2:30 the strange vessel was lost to sight and the *Faulknor* went back to south (167°). The *Narwhal* led the six boats which did not attack around the rear of the German line to the southwestward. That group was joined about 2:14 by the *Mindful*. The crippled *Onslaught*, steering from aft, took station in rear of the *Mindful*. The commanding officer of the *Opal* took charge of the group of nine boats. At 2:45 the *Champion*, with the *Obdurate*, *Moresby*, *Marksman*, and *Maenad*, turned to the northwestward (Fig. 56). Captain Farie was endeavoring to execute Jellicoe's order of 2:12 for all detached units to rejoin his flag.

Let us now turn to the flagship of the Grand Fleet and trace the important developments during that decisive period. At 1:48, just as Stirling was making his contact with the German battle line, the Admiralty informed Jellicoe that apparently enemy submarines were coming out of German ports and that a damaged enemy ship, probably the *Lützow*, had been in Lat. 56°–26′, Long. 5°–41′ at midnight. That position was in the center of square 010, in which the *G40* had reported the *Lützow* at that time. It is probable that the British had deciphered her report and that they had the German position chart. Actually, the *Lützow* at that time was at least 6 and probably 9 miles farther to the southward than reported by either the *G40* or the Admiralty. Jellicoe, according to Corbett, did not receive that important dispatch of 1:48 until 2:40. This would seem an excessive delay.

By 2:00 the *Talisman* and her four submarines were in Lat. 54°–30′, Long. 4°–00′. At 2:07 the Admiralty directed the *Talisman* to send two of her submarines to Lister Deep, *i.e.*, west of the Island of List. They were to remain on station two days and to attack damaged ships.

Meanwhile, the *Marlborough's* condition was becoming more

and more serious. Already, she had dropped about 12 miles behind her station. The Admiralty *Narrative* states that Jellicoe
was unaware of the fact that four of his battleships had lost touch.
At 1:56 it was reported that the *Marlborough's* forward fireroom
bulkhead no longer would stand the constantly increasing pressure; so she hauled out to starboard and slowed to 12 knots. The
Revenge continued on at 17 knots. Burney immediately informed Jellicoe of the incident. The loss of four battleships at
that time was a most unfortunate one. Undoubtedly, it weighed
heavily in Jellicoe's estimate of the situation at 2:00, for at that
time Jellicoe had a last opportunity for a decisive success. He
could still arrive at the entrance to the swept channel off Horn
Reefs simultaneously with Scheer, were he to turn immediately
to east (77°).

We remember Jellicoe's statement, as expressed in his book,
that when at 9:00 he had turned south, it had been his intention
at dawn to head for Horn Reefs. At 2:00 dawn had arrived and
the time had come to carry out his intention; but he now decided that would be impracticable until his destroyers had been
assembled. His book is very clear and explicit on that point.

The difficulties experienced in collecting the Fleet (particularly the
destroyers), due to the above causes, rendered it undesirable for the
Battle Fleet to close the Horn Reef at daylight, as had been my
intention when deciding to steer to the southward during the night.
It was obviously necessary to concentrate the Battle Fleet and the destroyers before renewing action.

Therefore, the discussion concerning the failure of Jellicoe
to receive Stirling's three messages is interesting only from a
communication viewpoint, for Jellicoe clearly shows that, regardless of what information he received of the Germans, he had
no intention of proceeding toward Horn Reefs.

It is clear that at 2:12 his decision had been made, for at
that time he informed all commanders that he would alter
course to north at 2:30. All detached forces were ordered to "con-
form and close." The *Iron Duke's* predicted position for 2:30
was Lat. 55°–07', Long. 6°–21'.

That was the first order given by Jellicoe to concentrate the

Fleet. As concentration of the Fleet was necessary, in his opinion, before renewing the action and carrying out his intention to steer toward Horn Reefs, it is remarkable that he had not long previously issued orders for the Grand Fleet to concentrate at dawn. It will be noted that the Germans had little trouble in concentrating their forces, although their cruisers and destroyers were at least as widely scattered as those of the British. The German destroyers, however, had been ordered well in advance to concentrate at 3:00, while no such instructions had been issued to the British flotillas. The German system of command through the first and second leaders of destroyers was vastly more effective than the British system of placing their flotillas directly under Jellicoe and Beatty, for in practice Hawksley's command proved to be only nominal.

It was not until 2:39 that the *King George V* commenced the turn to the northward (Fig. 56–Q). Jellicoe feared that in the mist and drizzle he suddenly might encounter the German Battle Fleet. He decided, therefore, to form his battleships in a single column of 20 vessels so as to be ready for a surprise contact before his destroyers and cruisers could be assembled. He believed he would have to accept the risk of submarine attack, which in the poor visibility was very slight. At 2:33 the *Benbow* reports that the *Iron Duke* opened fire, probably at a suspected submarine. At 2:44 the 5th Battle Squadron commenced a counter-march to starboard to take station ahead of the battle line. At 2:50 the *King George V* hoisted the fleet guide. At 2:55 the *Birmingham* rejoined the 2d Light Cruiser Squadron. Jellicoe had now in company 23 battleships and 13 light cruisers: 5 of the 4th Light Cruiser Squadron, 3 of the 2d Light Cruiser Squadron, the *Galatea* of the 1st Light Cruiser Squadron, and the 4 attached vessels. One destroyer, the *Oak*, was present. Meanwhile, at 2:30 the *Marlborough* which now was proceeding singly counter-marched to course north (347°) (Fig. 56–K). About 2:55 the 6th Division, which the *Fearless* had rejoined, also counter-marched to north (347°) (Fig. 56). That division at 3:00 was about 7 miles from the battle line and about 11 miles in rear of the *Marlborough*.

At 2:30 Beatty had turned northward in conformity with Jellicoe's order. A garbled message from the *Birmingham* had led him to believe that the Germans were to the westward. At 11:30 that cruiser had reported battle cruisers on course south. As received by Beatty, the course of the enemy was WSW. He had intended to ask permission to sweep to the southwest at daylight, but he abandoned that plan upon receipt of Jellicoe's message timed at 2:12. With Beatty were 6 battle cruisers, 4 cruisers, 8 light cruisers, and 12 destroyers. (The *Chester*, which at 2:30 was ordered to proceed to the Humber, is excluded from the total.)

We have placed the *Galatea* with the Battle Fleet, although there are conflicting data regarding her movements. Commodore Alexander-Sinclair reports: "At 2:35 A.M. on 1st June, on the Battle Cruisers being sighted, *Galatea*, who was then able to steam 24 knots, rejoined the First Light Cruiser Squadron." That time evidently was in error, for immediately before that statement Alexander-Sinclair says that he remained "at the head of the Battle Fleet" for the night, and at 2:58 Goodenough, who was with the Battle Fleet, signaled him: "Do you know where battle cruisers are?" Alexander-Sinclair replied by searchlight, "No, have not seen them since yesterday evening."

At 2:52 Beatty ordered the course changed to NNE. (9°). At the same time, he reported to Heath that the estimated bearing of the Battle Fleet was 038°, distant 16 miles. Actually, at that time, the *Iron Duke* bore 50°, distant 13 miles. Thus, his estimate was very close.

At 2:54 Jellicoe received word from the *Abdiel* that the mine field had been laid in accordance with orders. Here was one hope that further injuries might be inflicted upon the enemy. It will be remembered that the *Abdiel* had proceeded on that duty at 10:15 at 31 knots on course SSE. (145°). The course actually made good was about 142°. At 12:30 Horn Reefs light vessel was sighted bearing E. by S. (88°). At 1:24 the *Abdiel* arrived in the assigned position 15 miles, 215° from Vyl light vessel. Speed was reduced to 15 knots and a mine field of 80 mines, 10 to the mile, was laid. Course for the first 40 mines was 158° and for the second 40, 201°. At 2:04 the field was completed and course set north (347°) at 30 knots. Although the Germans did not enter the *Abdiel's* field, it was an excellent illustration of the proper use for mine-laying cruisers or destroyers after a fleet action.

At 2:52 the Admiralty finally directed the 5th Light Cruiser Squadron and 9th and 10th Flotillas under Commodore Tyrwhitt to join Jellicoe "to replace squadrons or flotillas short of fuel." The commodore was ordered to proceed toward Lat. 55°–30', Long. 6°–00' until he received orders from the commander in chief. He was furnished with the positions of the British submarines in the approaches to the German bases. Tyrwhitt received his orders at 3:09. At 3:50 he sailed with 5 light cruisers, 2 flotilla leaders, and 16 destroyers. Not until 3:20 did the Admiralty inform Jellicoe of Tyrwhitt's orders. We have already commented upon the incomprehensible attitude of the Admiralty concerning the Harwich Force and nothing further would need to be said concerning that subject were it not for Corbett's attempt to justify the delay of the Admiralty. He claims that it had no ill effects, as the Harwich Force could not in any event have arrived in time to be of use. That, of course, is argument after the event, in its worst form. It was 315 miles from Harwich to Horn Reefs light vessel. Had Tyrwhitt, at the first report of contacts, say at 3:00 P.M., left Harwich at 25 knots to take a position of readiness, and had he been ordered at 5:00 to continue on to join Jellicoe at the same speed, he could have been within 15 miles of Horn Reefs light vessel at 3:00 A.M., June 1. From the fact that at 3:00 Beatty's destroyers had been at sea for 29 hours at speeds from 17 to 30 knots, and certainly averaging well over 20 knots, it is evident that Tyrwhitt's destroyers easily could have run 12 hours at 25 knots with sufficient fuel remaining for quite extensive operations. In any event, his destroyers certainly could have covered the approaches to Terschelling Channel. Had the Germans been delayed in returning via Horn Reefs as was highly probable in the case of aggressive action by the Grand Fleet or had the High Seas Fleet been forced

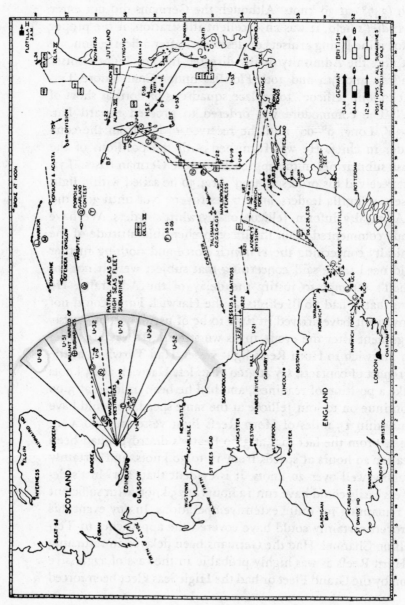

FIG. 58. 3:00 A.M. to noon, June 1.

to return via Terschelling, a re-enforcement of 23 fine cruisers and destroyers would have been most effective.

Let us now return to the High Seas Fleet. At 1:55 a report arrived from the *L24* timed at 1:40 that she had been fired on by several vessels in square 069 Epsilon IV. No ships report even sighting an airship at that time, much less firing on one. Doubtless, the *L24* had witnessed an action between ships, which she thought were firing on her. The square reported was 45 miles north of the fleet flagship and was evidently greatly in error. That was only the first of a series of perfectly fantastic reports from the *L24*.

At 2:01 the commander of Flotilla III in the *S53* reported that he had practically all the crew of the *Elbing* on board and was in square 086.

At 2:09 Scheer received a report from the *L17* timed at 2:00 that she was in square 063 Epsilon IV steering NW. by N. Evidently, that position was incorrect, for the German charts estimate that she was in square 063 Alpha VII, which if correct places her within a few miles of Beatty's forces at the time of her report.

The *Regensburg* ordered all boats of Flotillas V and VII having torpedoes to take station ahead of the battleship column ready for "new attacks." Other boats were ordered to join the *Regensburg*, which also proceeded to take position ahead of the *Westfalen*.

At 2:30 Scheer gave a reference position to the High Seas Fleet. The main body was placed in the right center of square 101. Course was given as SE. by S., speed 16 knots. At 3:29 the Admiralty furnished Jellicoe with that exact information. The position was given as Lat. 55°–33′, Long. 6°–50′. That was on the eastern edge of square 101.

At 3:47 Scheer received a garbled message from the *L24*, reporting "further enemy light forces" in square 115. Three minutes later, there came a message from Boedicker, giving the 2:30 position of the *Frankfurt* and *Pillau* as square 111. That was about 12 miles northwest of their correct position and placed

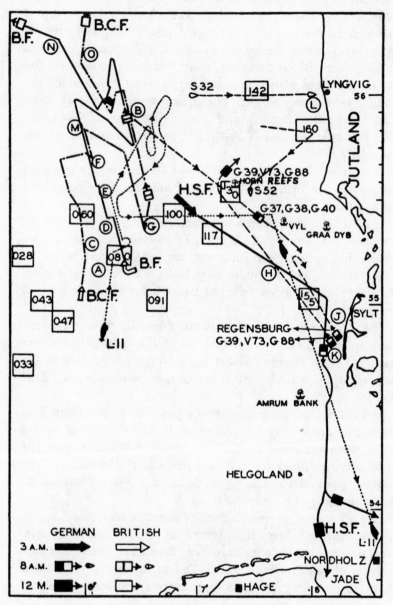

FIG. 59. 3:00 A.M. to noon, June 1.

them on the port hand of the Fleet, while actually they were to starboard. Their course and speed were the same as those of the battle line.

At 2:55 Hipper reported through the *G39* the condition of Scouting Group I. The *Seydlitz* was reported badly damaged; the *Moltke* had 1,000 tons of water in her fuel; the *Derfflinger* and *Von der Tann* had only two guns ready for action. Evidently, Scheer could count no longer upon his battle cruisers. In fact, their very severe damages now made them far more of a liability than an asset. The *Moltke's* position at 2:30 was given in square 117 left.

At 2:20, just as it was fairly light, the four German destroyers that were carrying home the *Lützow's* crew sighted the *Contest* and *Garland*. Lieutenant Commander Beitzer decided to engage them with shallow torpedo shots. However, as the opposing boats passed rapidly on opposite courses, only the *V45* fired one torpedo at 3,300 yards. There was ineffective gunfire for a few minutes at ranges as low as 1,300 yards (Fig. 59–B).

At 2:40 the *Seydlitz*, with both gyro compasses out of commission and greatly down by the head, ran squarely on Horn Reefs, where she stuck fast for three hours. When at 5:40 she was pulled off, the big battle cruiser limped slowly homewards and by able seamanship was brought to the mouth of the Jade where she was hurled on the beach. As will appear, however, the difference in time of replacement between having such a ship sink and having her preserved even in a semi-wrecked condition was nearly three years.

At 4:25 the *Rostock* under tow was sighted and engaged by the *Dublin*, sustaining such damage that she had to be sunk by her crew, which was taken aboard the *S54*, *V71*, and *V73* (Fig. 59–F).

The most important incident marking the return of the High Seas Fleet was the misfortune to the *Ostfriesland* some 20 miles northwest of List. About 5:20 she struck a mine (Fig. 59–H), which both the British and Germans believe was one laid early in the month. Although seriously injured, the battleship made port.

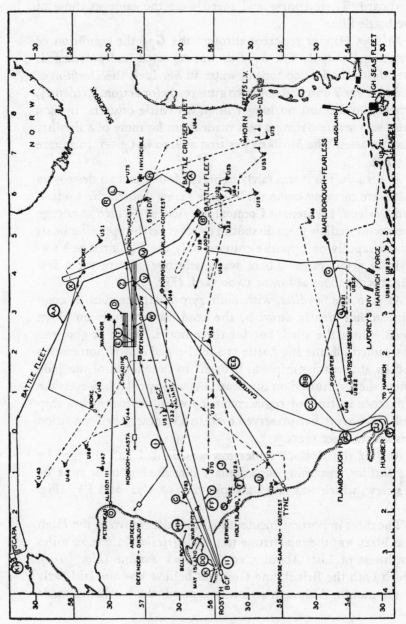

Fig. 60. Noon, June 1, to noon, June 2.

Shortly after noon the German ships were not only once more behind the barrier of the defensive mine fields but also beneath the shelter of the coast artillery.

The British were on the way back to their own bases.

At 2:21 Burney shifted his flag as second in command from the *Marlborough* to the *Fearless,* his temporary flagship, and at 3:15 from the latter to the *Revenge,* and the crippled *Marlborough* headed for the Tyne under escort of the *Fearless.* Not only the *Revenge* but also the remaining two ships of that division (the *Hercules* and *Agincourt*) were unable to rejoin the rest of the northward-bound Battle Fleet.

So far as concerns the Grand Fleet, the rest was anti-climax. At 4:40 Jellicoe informed Beatty that the Germans had withdrawn to their bases, upon receipt of which message Beatty proceeded towards the commander in chief and effected the junction within half an hour. The two forces of capital ships then separately swept areas to the south and southeast, scanning the horizons for the enemy silhouettes which the British were reasonably certain no longer were to be found on the North Sea. At noon Jellicoe was in Lat. 56°–20′, Long. 5°–26′ E. He had advised the Admiralty at 11:08 that the only further assistance he desired of Tyrwhitt was in re-enforcing the *Marlborough's* escort. Four of the Harwich destroyers were assigned to that duty. Inasmuch as a torpedo had barely missed the *Marlborough* at 11:00 A.M. and as she was having a very difficult voyage, it was with relief that she picked up the screening destroyers at 2:30 P.M. The *Marlborough* made the Humber, not the Tyne, the following morning.

That message of 11:08 releasing the Harwich force was the final acknowledgment by Jellicoe that, for better or for worse, the Battle of Jutland had slipped from the reach of his decisions into the unalterable molds of history. As the Admiralty *Narrative* laconically states, "It only remained to return to harbour." Jellicoe set the course for home about the time that Scheer heard the splash of the *Friedrich der Grosse's* anchor in Wilhelmshaven Roads.

The following morning at almost the same hour, 7:00 A.M.,

the Scapa and Rosyth forces steamed into their familiar road-steads, with grim vacancies marking the absence of the *Queen Mary*, *Indefatigable*, *Invincible*, and the other comrades left behind. The units not seriously enough damaged to be docked or otherwise laid up for major repairs were reported ready for sea on 4 hours' steaming notice, at 9:45 that same night, June 2.

(Figure 58 shows movements of the various forces from 3:00 A.M. to noon, June 1, and Fig. 60 shows movements from noon, June 1, to noon, June 2.)

CHAPTER XXII

THE EFFECTS OF JUTLAND

IT WOULD be futile for us to attempt to discuss that oft-debated question: who won the battle? In land warfare it usually is possible to say that one army or the other won a tactical victory because it held the battlefield. Even then, a tactical victory often has been without any strategic significance. In other words, it has had no effect upon the campaign in progress or upon the war as a whole. In naval warfare it means nothing to hold the battlefield. What we really want to know are the effects of the battle upon the naval campaign in its entirety and upon the ultimate consummation of the pending hostilities. It will be appropriate, therefore, for us to discuss:

(1) The material and personnel losses.

(2) The effects of the battle upon the plans and conduct of the opposing commanders in chief.

(3) The effect of the battle upon the morale of the respective belligerents.

The direct losses fall under three headings: (1) ships sunk; (2) ships damaged; and (3) personnel killed and wounded.

In war a ship sunk is definitely deleted from the assets of a navy. The replacement of a large vessel involves a delay of at least three years and an immense expenditure of money, material, and labor, which must be diverted from other war activities. On the other hand, ships that are badly damaged can be repaired in a maximum of a few months. The *Derfflinger* was ready for sea in four and a half months; the *Seydlitz*, in three and a half. All the other vessels that were damaged at Jutland were repaired within two and a half months. Even the most extensive repairs are very cheap in the money, labor, and material required in comparison to the cost of a similar new ship. For these reasons, the relative tonnage of ships sunk in a naval battle is far more significant than the relative damage inflicted on ships that remain afloat and in the possession of their flag.

The following tabulation shows the relative tonnage of British and German ships sunk:

FIRST-LINE SHIPS

British		German	
Queen Mary	26,350	Lützow	26,700
Indefatigable	18,800	Wiesbaden	5,600
Invincible	17,250	Elbing	4,400
Tipperary	1,430	Rostock	4,900
Turbulent	1,100	V27	960
Fortune	965	V29	960
Ardent	935	S35	956
Shark	935	V48	1,170
Sparrowhawk	935		
Nestor	890		
Nomad	890		

SECOND-LINE SHIPS

Defence	14,600	V4	687
Warrior	13,550		
Black Prince	13,350		

THIRD-LINE SHIPS

		Pommern	13,200
		Frauenlob	2,700
Total	111,980	**Total**	62,233

In order to enable the reader to arrive at a fairer appraisal of the ships sunk, we have divided them into three categories, based upon all-around operating value. Some explanation may be in order as to why certain German vessels have been classed as "second-line" or "third-line." The pre-dreadnaught battleship *Pommern* certainly was useless for all fleet operations, although possibly she might have been of some value in the Baltic. When British pre-dreadnought battleships were lost from time to time throughout the war, the effect upon the naval situation was deemed insignificant.

The three British armored cruisers, *Defence, Warrior,* and *Black Prince*, were of little real value in a fleet action. They were, however, of some use as a screen for the Fleet during the approach to action. Furthermore, their type was suitable for escorting transports and merchant vessels and for operating against disguised raiding cruisers.

The German light cruiser *Frauenlob* was of a very small and obsolete type with a speed of only 21.5 knots. She was even too slow for inclusion among the old cruisers of Scouting Group IV. The destroyer *V4* was a small ship of only 687 tons and of little value for operations with the Fleet, as shown in the foregoing account of the night operations.

The question might be raised as to why the *Invincible* and *Indefatigable* are not regarded as "second-line." The latter was a valuable ship and comparable in effectiveness to *Von der Tann*. The *Invincible* was a much earlier and smaller type; in fact, she was the pioneer of the battle cruiser type for which Fisher took such credit. While somewhat inferior to the *Von der Tann*, she was worthy of a place in the battle cruiser line and played a prominent part in the battle by disabling the *Wiesbaden* and by delivering a rush of effective hits on the *Lützow*. The *Invincible* was one of the ships that had destroyed Von Spee's squadron at the Falkland Islands. Thus, we consider that she was still a "first-line" ship.

It will be noted that the losses sustained by the opposing Fleets in ships sunk were in almost the same ratio as the strength of the opposing Fleets, about 8 to 5. Therefore, the ships sunk did not in any way affect the relative strength of the opposing forces, taken as a whole. However, they did reduce considerably the British superiority in battle cruisers; in fact, upon completion of the new *Hindenburg*, the Germans with 5 ships against 7 seriously would threaten British supremacy in that important type.

Let us now consider the ships damaged, remembering that this was of far less importance than the permanent losses caused by ships sunk. Of the capital ships, the *Oldenburg*, *Nassau*, *Rheinland*, and *Westfalen* received a total of five 4-inch hits and are not entered in the table, as their material damage was insignificant. Many British ships received 5.9-inch hits. It will be appropriate to consider the damaged units under three categories, as follows:

VESSELS SERIOUSLY DAMAGED

British		German	
Warspite	13 hits	Seydlitz	21 hits
Marlborough	torpedo hit	Derfflinger	17 hits
		Ostfriesland	mine hit

VESSELS MODERATELY DAMAGED

Lion	12 hits	König	10 hits
Princess Royal	9 hits	Grosser Kurfürst	8 hits
Tiger	16 hits	Markgraf	5 hits
Barham	6 hits	Von der Tann	4 hits
Malaya	8 hits	Moltke	4 hits

VESSELS SLIGHTLY DAMAGED

Colossus	2 hits	Kaiser	2 hits
New Zealand	1 hit	Helgoland	1 hit

In general, it may be concluded from this tabulation that the German capital ships, excluding ships sunk, received slightly heavier damage than the British. The *Seydlitz* and *Derfflinger* received greater injuries than any British ships, though the injuries to the *Warspite* also were extensive. Counting a torpedo or mine hit as equivalent to 5 gun hits, the British received 72 hits to 83 for the Germans on capital ships that did not sink.

The damage inflicted on light cruisers was considerably in favor of the Germans, the British receiving 66 hits and the Germans 15 hits, including one from a 12-inch shell.

SERIOUSLY DAMAGED

British		German	
Chester	17 hits	Pillau	1 heavy hit
Southampton	18 hits		
Dublin	13 hits		
Castor	10 hits		

SLIGHTLY DAMAGED

Canterbury	1 hit	Frankfurt	3 hits
Falmouth	1 hit	Stettin	2 hits
Galatea	1 hit	München	5 hits
Calliope	5 hits	Hamburg	4 hits

The damage inflicted on destroyers was greatly in favor of the Germans:

British		German	
Acasta	3 hits (out of action)	S50	1 hit
Defender	1 heavy hit (out of action)	B98	1 hit
Moorsom	1 hit	G40	1 hit
Onslaught	1 hit (out of action)	S32	3 hits (out of action)
Broke	9 hits and collision (out of action)	S51	1 hit
Onslow	5 hits (out of action)	G41	1 hit
Marne	1 hit	V28	1 hit
Petard	6 hits		
Porpoise	2 hits		
Spitfire	8 hits and collision (out of action)		
Contest	collision (out of action)		

The British had seven destroyers out of action to one for the Germans.

As to damage inflicted on vessels that did not sink, the Germans had the disadvantage in capital ships and the British in light forces. That, of course, was unfavorable to the Germans. Furthermore, as the British were greatly superior to the Germans in dockyard facilities, it meant that they could repair an equal amount of damage much quicker than could the Germans. Therefore, the Germans had to postpone future operations until August and were then without the services of two of their battle cruisers, while all British damage was made good much earlier.

With respect to personnel losses, the Germans had a great advantage, their total casualties being 2921 against 6945 for the British. This disparity is accounted for by the greater ship losses of the British and by the fact that they saved only a handful of men from their vessels that were sunk, except in the cases of the *Warrior* and *Sparrowhawk*. On the other hand, the Germans by rescuing almost the entire crews of the *Lützow*, *Elbing*, and *Rostock* had over 2,000 shipless officers and men available to replace casualties, including 434 wounded in the surviving vessels, and to use for other purposes. In Rear Admiral Hood the British undoubtedly lost one of their best officers.

Everything considered, we believe that the material and personnel losses were about in proportion to the relative strengths of the two Fleets before the battle. Therefore, in this respect there was no advantage to either side.

Let us now determine, if we can, what effects the battle had on the plans of the commanders in chief and the future course of the naval campaign in the North Sea. As regards the plans of Scheer, it is evident that the operations could not be resumed until many of his vessels were repaired. This caused a delay of two and one-half months in the prosecution of the campaign.

However, at the end of this interlude, Scheer was determined to continue the campaign as before. He spoke of "the success obtained" but officially did not claim a victory. He was perfectly content with both personnel and material. He wrote to the Emperor:

The battle has proved that in building up our Fleet, and in the development of the individual types of our ships, we have been guided by correct strategical and tactical views, and that we should, therefore, continue along the same lines.

He was more convinced than ever that the capital ship "is and remains the foundation of sea power."

Scheer was also convinced, as he had believed previously, that he could not engage in a finish fight with the enemy. He admitted that the destroyer attacks were "finally successful in enabling us to break away completely from the enemy." He was very careful not to predict results.

Should the future operations take a favorable course, it may be possible for us to inflict appreciable damage on the enemy; but there can be no doubt that even the most favorable issue of a battle on the high seas will not compel England to make peace in this war. The disadvantages of our geographical position compared with that of the Island Empire, and her great material superiority, can not be compensated for by our Fleet. . . .

That, in our opinion, was an absolutely correct estimate of the situation. It was true, in every particular, before as well as after the battle. Under the circumstances, the High Seas Fleet had done as well as reasonably could have been expected. By running immense risks, Scheer had ended up just where he had begun, as far as the relative strength of the two Fleets was concerned. Jellicoe, on the other hand, had maintained his relative strength, without assuming any major risks.

One reason why Scheer stated his opinion so positively was that, in a paragraph following the passage quoted above, he strongly advocated the resumption of unrestricted submarine warfare as the only means of attaining "a victorious conclusion of the war within measurable time." In this, also, Scheer was to a great degree correct. Such a campaign offered a better prospect of success than did any of the alternatives open to Germany. Whether a victory would result was by no means certain, but everything in war is uncertain. As Scheer had been striving by every means to gain the Kaiser's permission for submarine warfare, his expression reflected no change in his views or in his plans. As far as we can determine, the battle had no effect on Scheer's strategic handling of the High Seas Fleet other than to cause an interlude in his active operations until August.

An examination of Jellicoe's statements indicates that as a result of the Fleet's experiences on May 31, he intended to operate in the future with even more caution than he had exercised prior to and during the battle.

Let us analyze the moral consequences of the action. In this respect, Jutland necessarily affected not only the opposing Fleets, but all the embattled armies and the public opinion of the entire world. The month of June was utilized by Jellicoe to repair his damaged ships and to make certain alterations that the battle had proved to be necessary. No fleet cruises were conducted during the month. During the first week in July, the repairs were completed on nearly all the damaged ships. During July the Fleet put to sea only once, for an exercise in the vicinity of the Shetland Islands far north of Scapa. On the night of July 24, the *Warspite* and *Valiant* collided in Scapa Flow and had to be docked to repair their injuries. On July 29 the *Chester* and *Marlborough* rejoined the Fleet. It will be noted that all of

Jellicoe's offensive measures to draw out the Germans ceased after Jutland.

In Germany, on the other hand, the carefully and temperately worded report of Scheer definitely proved that the High Seas Fleet had made a very creditable performance. At that time, the armies of the Central Powers had been suffering very severely from the numerous offensives of the Allies. On June 4, Brusiloff launched a Russian attack in Galicia to relieve the hard-pressed Italians in the Trentino. The transfer of the assault troops for use against Italy had so weakened the Austrians' Galician front that it gave way before the Russians almost without resistance. Brusiloff, besides making huge gains of prisoners and territory, achieved his prime purpose of halting the enemy's drive against Italy. The Austrians ceased their attack in the Trentino to rush re-enforcements to Galicia. In turn, the Italians counter-attacked and regained much of the ground they had lost. As Brusiloff continued his successes, the Germans were compelled to take over much of the Galician Front. It was most difficult to find reserves for that purpose. Falkenhayn was still attacking at Verdun and by June 24 his brave troops had reached their high-water mark against the memorable French resistance. The artillery preparation for the Somme offensive commenced that same day. On July 1, the British and French attacked. The remorseless campaign of attrition was on. However, the name of "Verdun" by this time had become a symbol whose importance completely eclipsed the relative unimportance of the position from a strictly physical standpoint. Failure to win that single town meant that the final moral effects of the entire battle would be against the Germans. All through July and into August, the Somme and Galician battles continued.

On August 1, the Italians captured Gorizia, another symbolic stronghold, from the Austrians. Rumania was on the verge of entering the war.

Is it any wonder that the news of Jutland was heartening to the Germans? Previously, the Fleet had remained safely in port while the Army was being decimated time after time. The Navy had proved now that it too could do something when the opportunity was presented. It had shown that it could fight. It could relate tales of heroism of its own officers and men. At least the Fleet had met the overwhelmingly stronger enemy face to face and had come home after inflicting on him heavier losses than it had sustained. Jutland was the one bright spot for Germany during that tensely anxious period from June to November and it shone with the greater brilliance because of that dark background.

The authoritative accounts are unanimous in declaring that the effect of the battle upon the morale of the High Seas Fleet itself was excellent. The report of the Austrian naval attaché, not meant for publication, is particularly convincing in that respect.

Allegations that Jutland contributed to the later mutinies in the High Seas Fleet do not seem to be substantiated by the facts. Likewise, the charge that the battle precipitated the declaration of submarine warfare and thus, through American intervention, brought about Germany's downfall, is not, in our opinion, a sound interpretation. More will be said later on these points.

In the Grand Fleet, the action had certain unfortunate moral effects. The spectacle of four large British ships blowing up must have had a sobering influence upon the hundreds of officers and men who beheld one or more of those dramatic and horrible disasters. The effect of the heavy losses is disclosed in the messages of Jellicoe and Beatty. The formation of a "Beatty school" and a "Jellicoe school" was highly unfortunate. Resentment on the part of officers in the Fleet against the press was strong. However, the deep-seated British courage and determination were not affected, and there is every indication that another fight would have been as fiercely, if not as gayly, fought by them as was Jutland.

In one respect, Jutland benefited the British Navy. The overconfidence of certain elements was rudely shattered. That caused many improvements to be made in both material and training.

In various unofficial statements, it has been suggested that the reason that Jellicoe did not push the fight more aggressively was that, if he had attempted to wipe out the Germans, the losses that almost certainly would have been suffered by the Grand Fleet would have transferred the supremacy of the sea to a neutral power, presumably the United States. At the time of Jutland, the British had 42 first-line capital ships against 23 for the Germans, assigned to the respective commanders. It is a generally accepted probability that, if two such fleets fight each other to a finish, the superiority of one accumulates like compound interest. In fact, many experts claim that the relative strengths were really not 42 to 23, but the squares of those numbers, 1764 to 529, or more than 3 to 1. This we think is rather too great a ratio but certainly, to have destroyed 23 German ships, the loss of 14 British ships would seem to be a conservative estimate of the probable price. Such an outcome would have reduced the British strength to 28 capital ships.

On May 31, 1916, the United States had only 12 first-line capital ships, about 45 destroyers, mostly of a small type, no effective cruisers, and a few small submarines. It is, therefore, difficult to perceive even a remote chance that a finish fight against the High Seas Fleet would have entailed a surrender of naval supremacy to the United States. On the contrary, it is strongly believed that a "Trafalgar" on May 31, 1916, would have re-established British naval supremacy for a long time to come. Such ascendency depends as much upon moral as upon material factors and, in our own humble opinion for what it may be worth, the British lost that imponderable and invaluable moral ascendency at Jutland. Jellicoe forgot what Napoleon had said: "The moral is to the physical as three to one." Calculations of cold tonnage are by no means all that count in naval warfare. Never again would American or Japanese sailors be overawed by the powerful, even overwhelming, force of British naval tradition. The sequel was that in 1922 Great Britain conceded parity to the United States, *having already scrapped for reasons of economy many of the ships she had saved at Jutland by Fabian tactics.*

But would not a "Trafalgar" at Jutland have had other more immediate and even more important results? Without hazarding too precise a guess as to the effect of the annihilation of the High Seas Fleet upon the post-Jutland U-boat campaign (more fully analyzed below), the course of Russian internal affairs and military activity, the operations and commerce of the Baltic, and the struggle on the Western Front, it hardly will be disputed that the eventual allied victory would have been hastened with a saving of countless lives.

When there is examined the entire interlocking complexities of the military operations, who can say whether or not a German annihilation at Jutland comparable, say, to the Russian at Tsushima, would not have been followed by the collapse of the Central Powers in the critical summer of 1916?

There arises the question: How should the British Admiralty have reacted publicly after the battle? It undoubtedly was a most difficult dilemma for Lord Balfour and the British government. In our opinion, they had just two courses to follow. They had to choose between the retention of the Nelsonian tradition for the British Navy or its acknowledged replacement by the Corbett-Jellicoe doctrine of negative warfare. In the latter case, the Admiralty should have stated, in substance: Jellicoe will be given our full support. We must educate the people to understand that naval warfare has changed. There can never be another decisive battle and, furthermore, we don't care if there isn't. We don't have to fight. Our task now is to build up an overwhelming force that will deter the enemy from venturing out too far in any move hostile to Britain. Time will tell. We shall win in the end, but it may take two, three, or four years more. So be patient. The Grand Fleet is on watch and the British Isles will not be harmed.

If the spirit of old was to prevail, the Admiralty should have admitted that it had supported Jellicoe's plan of Fabian tactics but now realized that a great opportunity had been lost to annihilate the enemy. The attitude then should have been: We frankly admit our mistake. There can still be a Nelson, a Hawke, a Drake, or at least a Cornwallis or Collingwood. We are reverting to our tradition. We believe, as did Henry Whyte, after the first day's fight with the Spanish Armada, that the offensive must be Britannia's rôle in warfare. We are going to make a right-about-face. Lord Balfour, First Lord, and Admiral Sir Henry Jackson, First Sea Lord, have resigned. We propose to replace Jellicoe, because he is out of step with the Nelsonian tradition, and Beatty, because he lacks tactical skill. There will be a general shake-up throughout the Fleet. In confidence, we are going to give important consideration to officers who have shown the aggressiveness, initiative, and technical proficiency necessary for the proper exercise of commands in a fleet henceforth to be dominated by the doctrine of Nelson. Furthermore, we are going to repair every defect of material and remedy every deficiency of training. We are going to learn how to make night destroyer attacks and the battle cruisers are going to have some intensive target practice. All we beg is that Scheer and Hipper will give us another chance at them, ship for ship if they insist, anywhere in the North Sea.

There was the choice: to fight or not to fight. Ours, in the place of the Admiralty, would have been to fight. Theirs was not to fight. That decision fastened upon the British Navy an incubus of which it will not rid itself for many a year. Every British commander with an instinctive willingness to assume risks, which is the very foundation of naval and military greatness, will be confronted with a formidable library purporting to prove by every form of skillful plea and clever argument that Jellicoe won the World War without "leaving anything to chance."

It may be appropriate to make a few observations as to the conduct of the principal British and German commanders, summarizing scattered comments noted on previous pages. These appraisals are based on the tactical ability displayed at Jutland.

We consider Hipper to have given by far the best performance in the battle. His skill and resolute spirit stamp him as one of the greatest leaders in naval history. His only mistake was his movement of the battle cruisers to the van during the evening, and that probably was due to the failure to receive Scheer's orders and to a praiseworthy, if ill-judged, desire to regain what he considered his proper station.

Next, we confess to an admiration for Heinrich and two of his flotilla commanders, Max Schultz and Goehle. The battle squadron commanders, Behncke, Schmidt, and Mauve, all did well, but had little opportunity for independent action. Scheer's remarkable resolution and particularly his night movements have our full commendation, but his numerous tactical mistakes during the latter part of the day action prevent his being called a skillful tactician. None of the German commanders could be called "poor."

On the British side, we consider that Evan-Thomas displayed the most effective tactical leadership. This view is based upon his remarkable performance during his pursuit by the High Seas Fleet. Next we rank Hood who might have earned first place had he lived longer. His brief half hour's work was highly brilliant. Among the light force commanders, we like the work of Goodenough, Le Mesurier, and Stirling. Credit has been given in the foregoing narrative to many splendid destroyer captains and nothing more need be said here about the excellence of those individuals, nor the valiant spirit of the crews they commanded.

Jellicoe, in our opinion, conducted his Fleet ably in accordance with an inherently erroneous conception of naval warfare. Beatty committed numerous errors prior to 6:00 P.M. and did not show tactical skill. Despite spirited and aggressive leadership, we think him distinctly inferior as a technician to both Jellicoe and Scheer. Several British commanders could be classed as poor.

As between Jellicoe and Scheer, we believe in general that Jellicoe executed a poor conception of war excellently, while Scheer executed an excellent conception of war poorly. Jellicoe had skill, but as the Spartan said, "Skill that can not fight is useless." Scheer had personality and could fight, but was deficient in skill. Jellicoe was a McClellan; Scheer, a Blücher without his

Gneisenau. It would be most interesting to know what, if any-thing, Captains Adolph von Trotha and von Levetzow contrib-uted to the formulation of Scheer's decisions between 6:45 and 7:30 P.M.

It might be asked: Which Fleet, everything considered, showed the greater efficiency at Jutland? It is difficult to judge. The only time when there was a fight upon even terms was at the beginning of the battle cruiser action. There can be no question but that the German battle cruisers proved themselves greatly superior to the British battle cruisers. In the engagement between 5:00 and 5:40, we are inclined to believe that the 5th Battle Squadron slightly outfought the Germans in a situation where the forces actually engaged were about equal in strength. In the fleet action, the relative gunnery efficiency is impossible to determine. The maneuvering of the German battle line was superb and the attacks of Flotillas VI and IX excellent. The dodging of torpedoes by the British battle line showed remark-able skill. The night gunnery of the Germans was excellent, and the operations of the British destroyers, except those of the 12th Flotilla, were generally unsatisfactory. The damage control in the German ships was remarkably efficient. In general, we be-lieve that, ship for ship, the High Seas Fleet was somewhat more efficient than the Grand Fleet but by no margin that came close to counter-balancing the great British superiority in numbers. Scheer might have been able to fight with even chances of suc-cess a British fleet superior by 6 to 5, but certainly not one superior by 8 to 5.

CHAPTER XXIII

THE REST OF THE WAR

WE HAVE SEEN that the situation in mid-August was most critical for the Central Powers. It must have required considerable courage for Scheer to return to his bold campaign of offensive operations, but as he had been unable to convince Bethmann-Hollweg that unrestricted submarine warfare should be resumed, it was necessary for the High Seas Fleet to do what it could.

On the evening of August 18 at 10:00 P.M., Scheer sailed to carry out his daring Sunderland plan. Hipper, with two battle cruisers and three battleships, was to proceed in advance of the Fleet to bombard that point on the English coast. With his main body of 15 battleships, Scheer was to follow in support. In the North Sea were 24 German submarines. The previous operations had shown that British departures from their bases usually were made under cover of darkness. Therefore, the submarines were disposed far out in the North Sea so that they could make contact with the British during the daylight hours. Eight German airships were out, 4 to the north and 4 to the south of the German line of advance. They would inform Scheer of isolated detachments on which he might fall and warn him of the approach of superior forces before which he must withdraw. The plan was excellent. Its successful execution depended, however, upon the degree of accuracy of the reports from the airships.

Even before he left port, Scheer relinquished the advantages of the initiative and of surprise. Sending radio messages while still in his own waters, he permitted the British to conclude, as early as the forenoon of the eighteenth, that the High Seas Fleet was assembling for a sortie into the North Sea. Thus, just as Scheer was leaving his bases, the British were doing the same. Jellicoe had been on sick leave in southern Scotland, but there was even time to rush him out to sea in the light cruiser *Royalist*.

The British plans had changed considerably since Jutland. Beatty was not to operate independently as before, but directly under Jellicoe's command. The Battle Fleet and Battle Cruiser Fleet were to rendezvous at daybreak of the nineteenth 100 miles east of Rosyth. The entire force, as a single tactical organization, would then turn southward at 17 knots. Beatty would be from 20 to 30 miles in the van, but connected to the Battle Fleet by linking cruisers, so that he and Jellicoe could exchange messages by visual signals. The 5th Battle Squadron remained under direct control of the commander in chief. He had a total of 38 capital ships.

That plan was in accordance with what Jellicoe misconstrued to be the lesson of Jutland. Actually, it was a strictly defensive arrangement which lost him one of his best chances of success. Scheer had adopted the very daring plan of sending on ahead under Hipper 2 battle cruisers and 3 battleships, which probably could not make over 22 or even 21 knots. The British could have used in advance 6 battle cruisers and 5 splendid battleships with a speed of 25 knots. Contact between such unequal forces would have given Beatty the opportunity to gain revenge for his defeat at Jutland.

On that occasion, Tyrwhitt was coming up with all his force in scouting formation from the southward. The newly formed 4th Flotilla, consisting of 1 light cruiser and 9 destroyers, based on the Humber, was also at sea. Something effective must have been said to the Admiralty about the exclusion of the Harwich Force from the Battle of Jutland.

Jellicoe had adopted another excellent measure. The 11th Flotilla at Blyth maintained two submarines constantly on watch off Horn Reefs, while the Harwich submarines watched continuously the Terschelling channels. The boats were now for the first time fitted with long-range radio equipment.

The operation that resulted from those dispositions was of great interest, but cannot be described in detail. Both fleets quickly encountered the hostile submarines. Even before dawn, the High Seas Fleet ran squarely into the *E–23*, Lieutenant Commander Turner. The first two torpedo shots missed, but the third hit the *Westfalen*, last ship of the battle line. She turned back to port escorted by destroyers. The *E–23* surfaced and reported the passage of the High Seas Fleet. Jellicoe now had positive information.

The previous evening he had received at first-hand a warning of what he might expect from the German submarines. At 7:55 P.M., while the commander in chief was about to transfer from the *Royalist* to the *Iron Duke*, a torpedo missed one of the screening destroyers.

At 5:55 the next morning the light cruiser *Nottingham*, ahead of the battle cruisers, was hit by two torpedoes fired by the *U–52*, Lieutenant Commander Walther. The *Dublin* kept turning about the damaged vessel to keep the submarine down, but Walther got in a third hit at 6:26. The *Nottingham* sank at 7:10, just as two destroyers arrived to save her crew.

Scheer continued to make frequent use of his radio, and from 5:30 on his movements were traced by the British radio direction finders. At 9:30 his position was fixed about 100 miles from Sunderland and his course was determined. Jellicoe meanwhile was advancing toward the Germans at full speed, while Tyrwhitt was coming up from the southward. By 10:00 all elements of the British forces had been located by German airships, but, as usual, their messages left Scheer entirely in the dark as to the enemy movements and dispositions. By 12:15 Hipper and Beatty were only 30 miles apart and advancing towards a contact due within half an hour. At that momentous time, the *L13* committed the worst airship blunder of the entire war. She reported that a force of battleships, cruisers, and destroyers, 30 vessels in all, was coming up from the southward. That, of course, was the Harwich Force, which contained nothing larger than a light cruiser. Scheer immediately changed his plans and headed for Tyrwhitt. The latter, not having made his expected contact with the Germans, had turned back. Thus, Scheer missed Tyrwhitt and Jellicoe missed Scheer.

In time both commanders in chief realized the situation.

Scheer could do nothing but retreat, hoping that he had led Jellicoe into his submarine trap. Jellicoe could only retreat, ordering Tyrwhitt to proceed off Terschelling, "so that," in Jellicoe's vague wording, "he might be ready to deliver a night attack on the enemy's Fleet with the Harwich Force." It is unknown whether Jellicoe mentioned a night attack to Tyrwhitt.

As the Grand Fleet was withdrawing, the *Falmouth* was hit by two torpedoes fired at 4:52 by the *U–66*. In proceeding to port, the former was hit by two more torpedoes and ultimately sank. There were no fewer than 22 submarines reported by the Grand Fleet during the operation.

At 5:00 Tyrwhitt made contact with the High Seas Fleet and followed for a night attack. Both commanders now made strange decisions. Although Scheer could have driven off the British with his superior forces, he declined to do so, but instead accepted the risk of a destroyer attack. It seems a questionable decision, as Scheer might have gained a success over Tyrwhitt or at least have given the German crews the satisfaction of having driven off the enemy.

Tyrwhitt did not attack. Jellicoe says in cryptic words: "The conditions for night attack proved to be unfavorable, and at 7:30 P.M. the commodore reported that he had abandoned the pursuit." Gibson and Harper, highly favorable to Jellicoe, say:

After dark, he was recalled by a wireless message from Jellicoe, which ordered him to return to his base, since the Grand Fleet was too far away to give him support in the event of action.

Neither version is creditable to the British. To be in plain sight of 20 capital ships at dark is a wonderful opportunity for any destroyer commander. Any situation, except possibly a full moon, would be favorable for a night attack. On the other hand, destroyers making a night attack do not need or desire any support from their capital ships, as that would expose those ships to the attacks of the enemy's destroyers. That the British deliberately refused the opportunity for a night attack and that Scheer was perfectly willing to risk it disproved the claim that the British had gained a moral ascendency over the Germans as a result of Jutland. The British forces on August 19 were certainly handled with even more caution than on May 31.

Incidentally, if Scheer turned away from Jellicoe at 12:15 P.M. because of a knowledge of Jellicoe's dispositions, his action was highly commendable, as he had nothing to gain from engaging in enemy waters a force double his own in strength.

That German sortie resulted in imposing on the Grand Fleet even greater restrictions than had fettered it at Jutland. Jellicoe wrote in his book:

The experience of August 19th showed that light cruisers, proceeding at even the highest speed unscreened by destroyers, ran considerable danger from enemy submarines. The enemy's submarine commanders were no doubt increasing in efficiency, and risks, which we could afford to run earlier in the War, were now unjustifiable. Representations were made to the Admiralty to the effect that it was considered that in the future light cruisers should be screened by at least one destroyer per ship; the number of destroyers available for the Grand Fleet did not at the time admit of this, but as the total complement of 100 (the number intended to be allotted to the Fleet) was reached, destroyers could be assigned to most of the light cruisers in the advanced line, provided many were not absent from the Fleet carrying out extraneous services.

The ease with which the enemy could lay a submarine trap for the Fleet had been demonstrated on the 19th of August; what had constantly puzzled me was that this had not been done very frequently at an earlier stage in the War. Since, however, it had been attempted and with some success, there seemed to be every reason to expect a repetition of the operation, and it was clear that it was unwise to take the Fleet *far into southern waters* unless an adequate destroyer force was present to act as a submarine screen for all ships. If the circumstances were exceptional and the need very pressing, it would be necessary to accept the risk. There was general agreement on this point between the flag officers of the Fleet and the Admiralty. (The italics are ours.)

Evidently the area covered during August 19 was considered to be "far into southern waters." Jellicoe practically did not venture south of Scapa with the Battle Fleet during the remainder of his command.

From the German viewpoint, the Sunderland operation finally demonstrated these points:

(1) That the airships upon which Scheer had placed such great reliance not only were useless but positively dangerous, due to their highly inaccurate reports.

(2) That the German submarines were unable to torpedo British capital ships.

(3) That this was the third successive cruise on which a German capital ship had been mined or torpedoed.

The results did not hold out much prospect for future operations. On the other hand, the German submarines were getting much better and the Germans no longer need fear night destroyer attacks.

Their situation ashore did not improve. The sanguinary Battle of the Somme continued. The Brusiloff offensive still was eating its way into Galicia, ever drawing more German re-enforcements from the west. On August 27, Rumania declared war. The next day Germany acknowledged the danger of the situation by calling Hindenburg and Ludendorff to the chief command. On September 7, the allied forces in Salonika launched the offensive that took Monastir.

Hindenburg called off the Verdun attacks, stiffened the Somme defense, and held the Rumanians fairly well in check. The Germans strove to gather a few reserves for an offensive against Rumania. Scheer planned another sortie for September, but the weather proved unsuitable for airship scouting, in which he still had faith, and the operation was canceled. He had been trying to get Bethmann-Hollweg to declare for unrestricted submarine warfare. Failing in that, on October 7 Scheer finally consented to resume submarine warfare under prize regulations. In that month, he again moved the Fleet into the center of the North Sea and made a thrust against the trade route between England and Norway. There were no contacts with the enemy.

The resumption of the submarine campaign met with striking success. The German submarines had both increased in numbers and improved in efficiency. In October and November the shipping losses rose rapidly. Whereas in the third quarter of

1916, 592,039 gross tons of shipping of allied and neutral nations was destroyed, in the fourth quarter the figure was almost doubled, 1,159,343.

That had effects on both the British and Germans. It impressed the former with the dangers of submarine warfare, and raised the hopes of the latter in that new method of attack while all looked gloomy on the land fronts.

On November 1, Jellicoe had a conference at the Admiralty and made a suggestion radically inconsistent with his former doctrine. He proposed to detach a destroyer flotilla from the Fleet for anti-submarine operations. As that would leave the 4th Battle Squadron without a destroyer screen, he expressed the opinion that the High Seas Fleet probably would avoid another fleet action but that it "could be engaged with every prospect of success," without those 8 British battleships. That was the first indication that the British were to assume far greater risks due to the German submarine offensive than even a Nelson could have incurred at Jutland.

Scheer continued to advance his arguments for unrestricted submarine warfare. Early in November, a German submarine ran aground on the Jutland coast. Scheer sent Battle Squadron III to its assistance. The British submarine *J–1*, Commander Lawrence, on patrol off Horn Reefs, sighted four battleships. He fired four torpedoes at a range of 4,000 yards beyond a strong destroyer screen. Two hits were made, one on the *Kronprinz* and one on the *Grosser Kurfürst*. It was very interesting as showing an increasing efficiency on the part of the British submarine captains. They had solved the problem of hitting battleships, strongly screened by destroyers, by firing a large torpedo salvo at moderate range. It was another proof to Scheer, if he needed it, that in his campaign against the Grand Fleet British submarines almost certainly would take a heavier toll than would the U-boats. It was occasioned by two facts: (1) The British submarines had been trained exclusively in operations against men-of-war, while the U-boats operated mostly against merchant vessels. (2) The geographical situation which forced Scheer to proceed through narrow channels on entering or leaving port greatly favored the British. This, therefore, was a final demonstration that the offensive operations against the Grand Fleet not only involved great risk, but were not profitable.

Scheer's attitude already had undergone a definite change. The Fleet was now merely the hilt of Germany's naval sword, the U-boats were the blade. That Scheer realized this is obvious from his communications to the Kaiser.

On November 22, Scheer attended a conference at Pless at which the Kaiser, Hindenburg, and Ludendorff were present. The offensive against Rumania at last was getting started and promised success, but evidently would expend the last German reserves. It was admitted that the German Army no longer could attack. In fact, it was so doubtful that it could maintain even a defense, that a large-scale strategic withdrawal to positions easier to hold was planned for the Western Front.

The prospects for success of a diplomatic "peace offensive" did not look good, but Bethmann-Hollweg urged that political form of attack. It was consented to; at least, it could do no harm and might have favorable naval and political effects. It would be launched at a favorable time during the Rumanian campaign so that it could not be considered a sign of weakness.

The only real offensive power the Germans still possessed lay in her submarines. It was decided to resort to them should the political attack fail to gain its objectives. Unfortunately, the Germans did not realize that an impending revolution in Russia was about to alter the entire international situation and make the submarine warfare, with its political consequences, unnecessary. As in the Seven Years' War, the defection of Russia would have saved Hindenburg just as it had Frederick.

Jellicoe now sensed more than ever that the German submarines were to take the leading rôle in the naval war. On November 28, after a final fleet cruise for battle exercises "in northern waters," he hauled down his flag to assume his new duties as First Sea Lord of the Admiralty, and Admiral Beatty took command of the Grand Fleet.

On December 5, the Germans captured Bucharest. On the twelfth, their peace note was published. On the twenty-sixth, the Allies rejected the proposals of the Central Powers. On January 9, after a conference at Pless, the Kaiser approved the proposal for unrestricted submarine warfare to begin February 1. Thereupon, the United States broke diplomatic relations with Germany and placed armed guards on American merchant vessels. A declaration of war was inevitable.

In Admiral Gleaves's work, *A History of the Transport Service,* he writes: "When the United States entered the war, German U-boats were sinking merchant ships at the alarming rate of 800,000 tons a month."

To illustrate the effect of those depredations upon allied morale and material, Admiral Gleaves quotes the following utterance of Admiral Beresford in July, 1917:

At the present rate of losses—British, Allied, and Neutral, average from 1st of February to 14th of July (say about six months)—I make out that British, Allies and Neutrals are losing ships at the rate of about seven million tons a year. I also make out that if the allied shipbuilding firms of the world put forward their full strength as at present, they could not produce more than four million tons of new shipping, in other words about one-half. I am also distressed at the fact that it appears to me to be impossible to provide enough ships to bring the American Army over in hundreds of thousands to France, and after they are brought over, to supply the enormous amount of shipping which will be required to keep them full up with munition, food and equipment.

The importance of the losses is admitted by numerous other authorities. Let us cite only two. Jellicoe says:

The danger which confronted the British peoples was never so great in any previous period as it was during the year 1917 when the submarine menace was at its height.

Telling of the critical situation on the Western Front at a conference on July 13, Ludendorff said:

The dangers could only have been diminished by the unrestricted submarine campaign. If it had not begun, no one could say whether we would now be holding firm on the Western Front.

By declining to run reasonable risks at Jutland, the British

Navy was confronted later by a threat incomparably more serious than that of the High Seas Fleet at that earlier time. In fact, we believe that it will be admitted that for Jellicoe to have charged directly into the the Germans at Jutland with every ship he had would have involved a danger far less than there existed in April, 1917, from the German submarines.

It may be asked how the annihilation of the High Seas Fleet at Jutland would have reduced the effectiveness of the German submarine campaign. We suggest the following evident effects of such a German defeat:

(1) A terrific moral blow to the German Navy and its remaining personnel.

(2) The submarine service would not have been able to draw practically all its picked personnel from the High Seas Fleet. The very highest caliber personnel was essential for effective submarine operations. At the time of Jutland, there were only 30 submarines attached to the High Seas Fleet's flotillas and 14 in the Flanders U-Flotilla. Thus, except possibly for crews of a few boats making final trials after construction, there was trained personnel available only for 44 submarines that could be used against England.

(3) British naval control of the Baltic would have prevented iron ore and other materials essential for the construction of submarines from being imported from Sweden.

(4) Shipyards on the Baltic coast building submarines might have been subjected to bombardment or naval air attacks.

(5) The passage of submarines from and to the German bases would have been made both difficult and dangerous by immense mine fields laid in Helgoland Bight.

(6) A great part of the light forces of the Grand Fleet could have been used for anti-submarine operations.

(7) The British shipyards could have been used to construct anti-submarine craft and merchant vessels instead of building ships for the Grand Fleet.

(8) There would have been no need for commencing the construction of four great battle cruisers of the *Hood* class.

(9) German submarines probably would have been employed for coastal defense in the Baltic, thus depleting the number available for offensive operations.

(10) Finally, we strongly suspect that, with all the many advantages of British control of the Baltic and the great military pressure of the Allies, the war would not have lasted long enough for an effective submarine campaign.

In March, 1917, the Russian revolution broke out. We suggest that a decisive victory at Jutland, resulting in British control of the Baltic, probably would have prevented or delayed that uprising. The supply of Brusiloff's Army with unlimited British munitions via the Baltic, the cutting of the German sea communications to their forces in Courland via Libau that Ludendorff said was of the "utmost importance," together with actual or threatened attacks against the German Baltic coast, well might have changed entirely the situation on the Eastern Front to Russian advantage or even have ended the war before the revolution broke out. Even after the revolution, the Russian government, with direct assistance from the Allies, might have been kept longer in the war.

The submarine campaign had one bad effect upon the German Navy. It confined the High Seas Fleet to playing a secondary rôle. Its material efficiency decreased because priority in labor and material had to be given to the submarines. Its best officers and men went into the submarine service. Gunnery and tactical efficiency suffered by ships remaining in port. Worst of all, its morale was sapped by inactivity, poor food, radical intrigues, loss of the best personnel, and other factors. At that stage, the High Seas Fleet served just three useful purposes:

(1) It secured the control of the Baltic.
(2) It controlled a small area in the North Sea off Helgoland.
(3) It was a threat to the Grand Fleet.

It was able to maintain the command of the Baltic until the very end of the war. In fact, in October, 1917, about half of the Fleet, including its best vessels, co-operated effectively with the

Army in the capture of Oesel Island in the Gulf of Riga. One motive for that joint operation was to give the men some active service after the August mutinies. All ships gave excellent performances and it seemed that the effects of the mutiny had been eradicated. In 1918, the Navy co-operated in an expedition to Finland.

In the North Sea, the presence of the High Seas Fleet prevented any important British operations in German waters. A cruiser action in April, 1917, showed that the British were still disposed to avoid running any risks in the pursuit of a very much smaller and somewhat slower German force. Commodore Reuter handled the German force brilliantly in that interesting operation. The fact that the North Sea mine barrage was laid in the northern part of the North Sea and not in the approaches to the German bases shows how effective the defense of the High Seas Fleet was considered; but it was as a potential offensive threat that the High Seas Fleet played its chief part.

Beatty's reports show that in disagreement with the opinion of Jellicoe, he expected the Germans to come out again. He spoke about having to fight 27 German battleships with 29 British and refusing to count upon ship for ship superiority. Repington, who visited Beatty aboard his flagship, quotes the Admiral as saying that "while the defeat of the Hun would alter nothing materially, a German victory would have immense consequences." All Beatty's talk is most remarkable, but at least it shows that he did not consider the threat of the German Fleet disposed of by Jutland. There is every reason to believe that memories of Jutland caused the British to take useless precautions up to the end of the war. The British still maintained large military forces in England to repulse a German landing.

While the High Seas Fleet did not conduct any important operations in the North Sea during 1917, German destroyers conducted raids in the Dover Straits while German light cruisers and destroyers destroyed two Norwegian convoys with heavy losses to their escorts. Although the submarine campaign was being beaten, the High Seas Fleet was again becoming a menace.

That situation induced Beatty early in 1918, with the approval of the Admiralty, to reduce the doctrine of the Grand Fleet almost to the defensive attitude of 1914, when Jellicoe had withdrawn to Irish waters, and in 1918 the Grand Fleet had no fewer than 46 first-line capital ships, including five United States battleships, with more of the latter available in reserve.

On April 23, Scheer conducted what Henry Newbolt, the British official historian, calls "perhaps the boldest operation undertaken by the German Naval Staff since the war began." It was the blow that Beatty most feared—an attack on the Norwegian convoy then escorted by British battleships. Unfortunately for Scheer, he had erroneous information as to the date of sailing of the convoy and his powerful and secret blow was dealt in the air. An unfortunate engineering casualty to the *Moltke* made it necessary to tow her all the way home from the Norwegian coast. Beatty headed for the Skagerrak, not for Horn Reefs, in an attempt to cut off the enemy, although he should have realized that a victory at such a critical time was most essential for his country. The High Seas Fleet returned to port without contact. If that were possible, the operation increased the defensive attitude of the Grand Fleet.

The crisis of the war occurred, as is universally admitted, on June 15-18, 1918. The terrible defeat of August 8, the breach of the Hindenburg Line, the collapse of Bulgaria, and then of Austria were successive blows that turned the tide against Germany and broke the will of the German High Command. There was disorganization throughout the German Army and the population. The Fleet did not escape contamination. When Scheer ordered a last sortie, there occurred a mutiny which flamed into open revolution. Resisted feebly by the naval leaders, it spread throughout the country. Germany signed the Armistice in admission of defeat.

Disgraceful as was the breakdown of the Fleet, it occurred only after all had been lost. Poor food that could not be improved, radical intrigues that might have been put down, decisive military defeat, war weariness, and the inactive rôle of the Fleet were causes of the mutiny that had nothing more than an accelerating effect upon the already inevitable end.

The inactivity of the Fleet was not caused by anything that had occurred since Scheer had assumed the command. Since January, 1916, the only alternatives were comparative inactivity in pursuing the objectives we have just described, an invitation for a decisive defeat in battle or in a gradual campaign of attrition. Jutland had demonstrated Germany's inability to defeat the Grand Fleet in a stand-up battle and Scheer was fortunate to receive that proof without losing a single ship from British mines and torpedoes and while making such a favorable impression on his enemy that the powerful threat of offensive operations by the High Seas Fleet worried the British until the very end of the war.

In conclusion, we believe that in 1914 the highly efficient High Seas Fleet might have offered battle to the numerically superior British Grand Fleet with an even chance of winning a tactical success. That, however, despite the consequences in morale, probably would not have had a decisive effect upon the strategic situation. By 1916, when the clash occurred at Jutland, the time for a finish fight had passed.

APPENDIX I

OPPOSING FORCES AT JUTLAND

GRAND FLEET (*British*)

BATTLE FLEET

Admiral Sir J. R. Jellicoe, Commander in Chief
Vice Admiral Sir C. E. Madden, Chief of Staff

Iron Duke (F.) (Capt. F. C. Dreyer)

Attached ships: destroyer *Oak*, flotilla leader *Abdiel* (fitted as a mine layer), light cruiser *Active* (Capt. P. Withers).

4TH BATTLE SQUADRON
Benbow (F.)

Vice Admiral Sir D. Sturdee, Commander of Squadron

Attached: light cruiser *Blanche* (Capt. J. M. Casement).

4th Division (Vice Admiral Sir D. Sturdee)

Benbow (F.) (Capt. H. W. Parker)
Bellerophon (Capt. E. F. Bruen)
Temeraire (Capt. E. V. Underhill)
Vanguard (Capt. J. D. Dick)

3d Division (Rear Admiral A. L. Duff)

Superb (F.) (Capt. E. Hyde-Parker)
Royal Oak (Capt. C. Maclachlan)
Canada (Capt. W. C. M. Nicholson)

1ST BATTLE SQUADRON
Marlborough (F.)

Vice Admiral Sir Cecil Burney, Second in Command, Grand Fleet
Captain E. P. F. G. Grant, Chief of Staff

Attached: light cruiser *Bellona* (Capt. A. B. S. Dutton).

6th Division (Vice Admiral Sir Cecil Burney)

Marlborough (F.) (Capt. G. P. Ross)
Revenge (Capt. E. B. Kiddle)
Hercules (Capt. L. Clinton-Baker)
Agincourt (Capt. H. M. Doughty)

5th Division (Rear Admiral E. F. A. Gaunt)

Colossus (F.) (Capt. A. D. P. R. Pound)
Collingwood (Capt. J. C. Ley)
Neptune (Capt. V. H. G. Bernard)
St. Vincent (Capt. W. W. Fisher)

2D BATTLE SQUADRON
King George V (F.)

Vice Admiral Sir T. H. M. Jerram, Commander of Squadron
Attached: light cruiser *Boadicea* (Capt. L. C. S. Woollcombe).

1st Division (Vice Admiral Sir T. H. M. Jerram)

King George V (F.) (Capt. F. L. Field)
Ajax (Capt. G. H. Baird)
Centurion (Capt. M. Culme-Seymour)
Erin (Capt. The Hon. V. A. Stanley)

2d Division (Rear Admiral A. C. Leveson)

Orion (F.) (Capt. O. Backhouse)
Monarch (Capt. G. H. Borrett)
Conqueror (Capt. H. H. D. Tothill)
Thunderer (Capt. J. A. Fergusson)

3D BATTLE CRUISER SQUADRON

Rear Admiral The Hon. H. L. A. Hood, Commander of Squadron
Invincible (F.) (Capt. A. L. Cay)

Indomitable (Capt. F. W. Kennedy)   Inflexible (Capt. E. H. F. Heaton-Ellis)

Attached: light cruisers Chester (Capt. R. N. Lawson) and Canterbury (Capt. P. M. R. Royds)

1ST CRUISER SQUADRON

Rear Admiral Sir Robert Arbuthnot, Commander of Squadron

Defence (F.) (Capt. S. V. Ellis)   Warrior (Capt. V. B. Molteno)
Duke of Edinburgh (Capt. H. Blackett) Black Prince (Capt. T. P. Bonham)

2D CRUISER SQUADRON

Rear Admiral H. L. Heath, Commander of Squadron

Minotaur (F.) (Capt. A. C. S. H. D'Aeth)   Hampshire (Capt. H. J. Savill)
Cochrane (Capt. E. La T. Leatham)   Shannon (Capt. J. S. Dumaresq)

4TH LIGHT CRUISER SQUADRON

Commodore C. E. Le Mesurier, Commander of Squadron

Calliope (F.) (Commodore C. E. Le Mesurier)

Constance (Capt. C. S. Townsend)   Comus (Capt. A. G. Hotham)
Caroline (Capt. H. R. Crooke)   Royalist (Capt. The Hon. H. Meade)

DESTROYER FLOTILLAS

12TH FLOTILLA

Flotilla leaders Faulknor (Capt. A. J. B. Stirling) and Marksman (Comdr. N. A. Sulivan)

Obedient, Maenad, Opal, Mary Rose, Marvel, Menace, Nessus, Narwhal, Mindful, Onslaught, Munster, Nonsuch, Noble, Mischief

11TH FLOTILLA

Light cruiser Castor (Commodore J. R. P. Hawksley) and flotilla leader Kempenfelt (Comdr. H. E. Sulivan)

Ossory, Mystic, Moon, Morning Star, Magic, Mounsey, Mandate, Marne, Minion, Manners, Michael, Mons, Martial, Milbrook

4TH FLOTILLA

Flotilla leaders *Tipperary* (Capt. C. J. Wintour) and *Broke* (Comdr. W. L. Allen)
Achates, Porpoise, Spitfire, Unity, Garland, Ambuscade, Ardent, Fortune, Sparrowhawk, Contest, Shark, Acasta, Christopher, Owl, Hardy, Midge, Ophelia

BATTLE CRUISER FLEET

Vice Admiral Sir David Beatty, Commander in Chief
Captain R. W. Bentinck, Chief of Staff
Lion (F.) (Capt. A. E. M. Chatfield)

1st Battle Cruiser Squadron (Rear Admiral O. de B. Brock)

2d Battle Cruiser Squadron (Rear Admiral W. C. Pakenham)

Princess Royal (F.) (Capt. W. H. Cowan)
Queen Mary (Capt. C. I. Prowse)
Tiger (Capt. H. B. Pelly)

New Zealand (F.) (Capt. J. F. E. Green)
Indefatigable (Capt. C. F. Sowerby)

5TH BATTLE SQUADRON

Rear Admiral H. Evan-Thomas, Commander of Squadron

Barham (F.) (Capt. A. W. Craig)
Warspite (Capt. E. M. Phillpotts)

Valiant (Capt. M. Woollcombe)
Malaya (Capt. The Hon. A. D. E. H. Boyle)

1ST LIGHT CRUISER SQUADRON

Galatea (F.) (Commodore E. S. Alexander-Sinclair)
Inconstant (Capt. B. S. Thesiger)

Phaeton (Capt. J. E. Cameron)
Cordelia (Capt. T. P. H. Beamish)

2D LIGHT CRUISER SQUADRON

Southampton (F.) (Commodore W. E. Goodenough)
Nottingham (Capt. C. B. Miller)

Birmingham (Capt. A. A. M. Duff)
Dublin (Capt. A. C. Scott)

3D LIGHT CRUISER SQUADRON

Rear Admiral T. D. W. Napier, Commander of Squadron

Falmouth (F.) (Capt. J. D. Edwards)
Birkenhead (Capt. E. Reeves)

Yarmouth (Capt. T. D. Pratt)
Gloucester (Capt. W. F. Blunt)

DESTROYER FLOTILLA

1ST FLOTILLA

Light cruiser *Fearless* (Capt. C. D. Roper)
Acheron, Ariel, Attack, Hydra, Badger, Goshawk, Defender, Lizard, Lapwing

13TH FLOTILLA
Light cruiser *Champion* (Capt. J. U. Farie)

Nestor, Nomad, Narborough, Obdurate, Petard, Pelican, Nerissa, Onslow, Moresby, Nicator

PART OF 9TH FLOTILLA
Lydiard, Liberty, Landrail, Laurel

PART OF 10TH FLOTILLA
Moorsom, Morris, Turbulent, Termagant

SEAPLANE CARRIER
Engadine (Lieut. Comdr. C. G. Robinson)

HIGH SEAS FLEET (*German*)

BATTLE FLEET

Vice Admiral Reinhard Scheer, Chief of the Fleet
Captain Adolph von Trotha, Chief of Staff
Friedrich der Grosse (F.) (Capt. T. Fuchs)

SQUADRON III
König (F.)

Rear Admiral Behncke, Chief of Squadron
Captain von Gagern, Staff Officer

Division V (Rear Admiral Behncke)

König (F.) (Capt. Brüninghaus)
Grosser Kurfürst (Capt. E. Goette)
Markgraf (Capt. Seiferling)
Kronprinz (Capt. C. Feldt)

Division VI (Rear Admiral Nordmann)

Kaiser (F.) (Capt. F. von Kayserling)
Prinz Regent Luitpold (Capt. K. Heuser)
Kaiserin (Capt. Sievers)

SQUADRON I
Ostfriesland (F.)

Vice Admiral Ehrhard Schmidt, Chief of Squadron
Captain W. Wegener, Staff Officer

Division I (Vice Admiral Schmidt)

Ostfriesland (F.) (Capt. von Natzmer)
Thüringen (Capt. H. Küsel)
Helgoland (Capt. von Kameke)
Oldenburg (Capt. Höpfner)

Division II (Rear Admiral Engelhardt)

Posen (F.) (Capt. Lange)
Rheinland (Capt. Rohardt)
Nassau (Capt. H. Klappenbach)
Westfalen (Capt. Redlich)

Deutschland (F.)

Rear Admiral Mauve, Chief of Squadron
Captain Kahlert, Staff Officer

Division III (Rear Admiral Mauve)	Division IV (Rear Admiral F. von Dalwigk zu Lichtenfels)
Deutschland (F.) (Capt. H. Meurer)	*Hannover* (F.) (Capt. W. Heine)
Pommern (Capt. Bölken)	*Schleswig-Holstein* (Capt. Barrentrapp)
Schlesien (Capt. F. Behncke)	*Hessen* (Capt. R. Bartels)

TORPEDO-BOAT FLOTILLAS

Commodore Michelsen, First Leader
Rostock (F.) (Capt. O. Feldmann)

Flotilla I (Lieut. Comdr. C. Albrecht, Chief of Flotilla)
Half Flotilla I (Lieut. Comdr. C. Albrecht)

G39 (F.), *G40, G38, S32*

Flotilla III (Commander Hollmann, Chief of Flotilla)

S53 (F.)

Half Flotilla V (Lieut. Comdr. Gautier)	Half Flotilla VI (Lieut. Comdr. Karlowa)
V71 (F.), *V73, G88*	*S54* (F.), *V48, G42*

Flotilla V (Commander Heinecke, Chief of Flotilla)

G11 (F.)

Half Flotilla IX (Lieut Comdr. Hoefer)	Half Flotilla X (Lieut. Comdr. F. Klein)
V2 (F.), *V4, V6, V1, V3*	*G8* (F.), *G7, V5, G9, G10*

Flotilla VII (Commander von Koch, Chief of Flotilla)

S24 (F.)

Half Flotilla XIII (Lieut. Comdr. G. von Zitzewitz)	Half Flotilla XIV (Comdr. H. Cordes)
S15 (F.), *S17, S20, S16, S18*	*S19* (F.), *S23, V189*

SCOUTING FORCES

Vice Admiral Hipper, Chief of Scouting Forces
Captain E. Raeder, Staff Officer

SCOUTING GROUP I

Vice Admiral Hipper, Chief of Scouting Forces
Captain E. Raeder, Staff Officer

Lützow (F.) (Captain Harder)

Derfflinger (Captain Hartog)   *Moltke* (Captain von Karpf)
Seydlitz (Captain M. von Egidy)   *Von der Tann* (Captain Zenker)

SCOUTING GROUP II

Rear Admiral Boedicker, Leader of Group
Commander Stapenhorst, Staff Officer

Frankfurt (F.), (Capt. T. von Trotha)   *Elbing* (Capt. Madlung)
Pillau (Capt. Mommsen)   *Wiesbaden* (Capt. Reiss)

SCOUTING GROUP IV

Commodore von Reuter, Leader of Group
Captain H. Weber, Staff Officer

Stettin (F.) (Capt. F. Rebensburg)

München (Capt. O. Böcker)   *Stuttgart* (Capt. Hagedorn)
Frauenlob (Capt. G. Hoffmann)   ¹*Hamburg* (Capt. von Gaudecker)

TORPEDO-BOAT FLOTILLAS

Commodore Heinrich, Second Leader
Regensburg (F.) (Capt. Heuberer)

Flotilla II (Capt. Schuur, Chief of Flotilla)
B98 (F.)

Half Flotilla III (Commander Boest)   Half Flotilla IV (Commander A. Dithmar)

G101 (F.), *G102*, *B112*, *B97*   *B109* (F.), *B110*, *B111*, *G103*, *G104*

Flotilla VI (Commander Max Schultz, Chief of Flotilla)
G41 (F.)

Half Flotilla XI (Lieut. Comdr. Rümann)   Half Flotilla XII (Lieut. Comdr. Lahs)

V44 (F.), *G87*, *G86*   *V69* (F.), *V45*, *V46*, *S50*, *G37*

Flotilla IX (Commander Goehle, Chief of Flotilla)
V28 (F.).

Half Flotilla XVII (Lieut. Comdr. Ehrhardt)   Half Flotilla XVIII Comdr. W Tillessen)

V27 (F.), *V26*, *S36*, *S51*, *S52*   *V30* (F.), *S34*, *S33*, *V29*, *S35*

¹ Flagship of Captain Bauer, Leader of Submarines, but attached to Scouting Group IV for tactical purposes.

APPENDIX II

CHARACTERISTICS OF CAPITAL SHIPS AT JUTLAND

BRITISH

	Speed	Main Battery			Armor	
		No.	Size	Caliber	Side	Deck
King George V	21.5	10	13″.5	45	12″	
Ajax	21.5	10	13″.5	45	12″	
Centurion	21.5	10	13″.5	45	12″	
Erin	21	10	13″.5	45	12″	
Orion	21	10	13″.5	45	12″	
Monarch	21	10	13″.5	45	12″	
Conqueror	21	10	13″.5	45	12″	
Thunderer	21	10	13″.5	45	12″	
Iron Duke	21	10	13″.5	45	12″	
Royal Oak	23	8	15″	42	13″	
Superb	20.75	10	12″	45	11″	
Canada	22.75	10	14″	45	9″	
Benbow	21	10	13″.5	45	12″	
Bellerophon	20.75	10	12″	45	11″	
Temeraire	20.75	10	12″	45	11″	
Vanguard	21	10	12″	50	9″.75	
Colossus	21	10	12″	50	10″	2″.75
Collingwood	21	10	12″	50	9″.75	
Neptune	21	10	12″	50	10″	2″.75
St. Vincent	21	10	12″	50	9″.75	
Marlborough	21	10	13″.5	45	12″	
Revenge	23	8	15″	42	13″	
Hercules	21	10	12″	50	10″	2″.75
Agincourt	22	14	12″	50	9″	
Lion	28	8	13″.5	45	9″	
Princess Royal	28	8	13″.5	45	9″	
Queen Mary	29	8	13″.5	45	9″	
Tiger	29	8	13″.5	45	9″	
New Zealand	25	8	12″	50	6″	
Indefatigable	25	8	12″	50	6″	
Invincible	25	8	12″	50	6″	
Inflexible	25	8	12″	45	6″	
Indomitable	25	8	12″	45	6″	
Barham	25	8	15″	42	13″	
Valiant	25	8	15″	42	13″	
Warspite	25	8	15″	42	13″	
Malaya	25	8	15″	42	13″	

GERMAN

	Speed	Main Battery			Armor	
		No.	Size	Caliber	Side	Deck
König	20.5	10	12"	45	14"	3"
Grosser Kurfürst	20.5	10	12"	45	14"	3"
Kronprinz	20.5	10	12"	45	14"	3"
Markgraf	20.5	10	12"	45	14"	3"
Kaiser	20	10	12"	50	14"	
Kaiserin	20	10	12"	50	14"	
Prinz Regent Luitpold	20	10	12"	50	14"	
Friedrich der Grosse	20	10	12"	50	14"	
Ostfriesland	20.5	12	12"	50	11".5	3"
Thüringen	20.5	12	12"	50	11".5	3"
Helgoland	20.5	12	12"	50	11".5	3"
Oldenburg	20.5	12	12"	50	11".5	3"
Posen	19.5	12	11"	45	11".5	
Rheinland	19.5	12	11"	45	11".5	
Nassau	19.5	12	11"	45	11".5	
Westfalen	19.5	12	11"	45	11".5	
Deutschland	18	4	11"	40	9".75	3"
Hessen	18	4	11"	40	9".75	3"
Pommern	18	4	11"	40	9".75	3"
Hannover	18	4	11"	40	9".75	3"
Schlesien	18	4	11"	40	9".75	3"
Schleswig-Holstein	18	4	11"	40	9".75	3"
Lützow	26.5	8	12"	50	12"	3"
Derfflinger	26.5	8	12"	50	12"	3"
Seydlitz	26.5	10	11"	50	11"	3"
Moltke	25	10	11"	50	11"	3"
Von der Tann	25	8	11"	45	9"	

APPENDIX III

CASUALTIES AT JUTLAND

BRITISH

Ship	Officers			Men		
	Killed	Wounded	Prisoners of War	Killed	Wounded	Prisoners of War
Marlborough	–	–	–	2	–	–
Colossus	–	–	–	–	5	–
Barham	4	1	–	22	36	–
Valiant	–	–	–	–	1	–
Warspite	1	3	–	13	13	–
Malaya	2	–	–	61	33	–
Lion	6	1	–	93	43	–
Princess Royal	–	1	–	22	77	–
Queen Mary (sunk)	57	2	1	1,209	5	1
Tiger	2	–	–	22	37	–
Indefatigable (sunk)	57	–	–	960	–	2
Invincible (sunk)	61	–	–	965	–	–
Southampton	–	1	–	35	40	–
Dublin	1	–	–	2	24	–
Chester	2	3	–	33	39	–
Defence (sunk)	54	–	–	849	–	–
Warrior (sunk)	1	2	–	70	25	–
Black Prince (sunk)	37	–	–	820	–	–
Calliope	–	2	–	10	7	–
Defender	–	–	–	1	2	–
Tipperary (sunk)	11	–	–	174	2	8
Broke	1	3	–	46	33	–
Porpoise	–	–	–	2	2	–
Spitfire	–	3	–	6	16	–
Ardent (sunk)	4	1	–	74	1	–
Fortune (sunk)	4	–	–	63	1	–
Sparrowhawk (sunk)	–	–	–	6	–	–
Shark (sunk)	7	–	–	79	2	–
Acasta	1	–	–	5	1	–
Moorsom	–	–	–	–	1	–
Turbulent (sunk)	5	–	–	85	–	13
Castor	–	1	–	13	22	–
Nessus	2	–	–	5	7	–
Onslaught	3	–	–	2	2	–
Nestor (sunk)	2	–	5	4	–	75
Nomad (sunk)	1	–	4	7	–	68
Petard	2	1	–	7	5	–
Onslow	–	–	–	2	3	–
Total	328	25	10	5,769	485	167

GERMAN

Ship	Officers		Men	
	Killed	Wounded	Killed	Wounded
Ostfriesland	–	–	1	10
Oldenburg	4	3	4	11
Rheinland	–	1	10	19
Nassau	2	2	10	13
Westfalen	–	1	2	7
Pommern (sunk)	71	–	769	–
Schlesien	–	1	1	–
Schleswig-Holstein	–	–	3	8
König	1	1	44	26
Grosser Kurfürst	3	1	12	10
Markgraf	–	1	11	12
Kaiser	–	–	–	1
Seydlitz	5	4	93	46
Moltke	–	–	17	22
Derfflinger	1	2	153	24
Von der Tann	1	3	11	32
Lützow (sunk)	5	5	106	49
Pillau	–	–	4	23
Frankfurt	1	1	2	20
Wiesbaden (sunk)	27	–	543	–
Elbing (sunk)	–	1	4	9
Rostock (sunk)	1	–	13	6
Stettin	–	1	9	26
München	1	4	7	15
Hamburg	1	4	13	21
Frauenlob (sunk)	17	–	325	–
S32	–	–	3	1
G40	–	–	1	1
B98	–	1	2	10
V48 (sunk)	6	–	84	–
V4 (sunk)	1	–	17	4
Flotilla VI	–	3	3	13
Flotilla IX	12	–	108	15
Total	160	40	2,385	454

BIBLIOGRAPHY

THE FOLLOWING list of books and selected readings confines itself to the Battle of Jutland and does not embrace material deal-
ing with the naval engagements and activities of the World War
in general. For the convenience of those who desire to read further on this interesting subject, this list has been made as complete as possible. Commander Frost had, of course, the opportunity to refer to many of the publications listed, but much of
his information for his study of the Battle of Jutland came from
personal letters and interviews with participants in this great
naval battle.

Alexander, Major Arthur Charles Bridgeman, *Jutland: A Plea for
a Naval General Staff*, London: Rees, 1923.

A. L. B., *Un Direttore del Tiro Alla Battaglia della Jutland*, Rivista
Marittima, anno 53, p. 5, Rome: 1920.

Amet, Jacques Marie Albert, *Le Jutland, Bataille Navale du Mai 31,
1916*, Paris: La Renaissance du Livre, 1923.

Anon., *Die Schlacht am Skagerrak! Der Ruhmestag der Deutschen
Flotte*, Berlin: Ullstein, 1916.

Applin, Arthur, *Admiral Jellicoe*, London: Pearson, 1915.

Aston, George, *The New Light on Jutland*, Nineteenth Century and
After, vol. 85, p. 671, London: 1919.

Bacon, Sir Reginald Hugh Spencer, Admiral, R.N., *The Dover Patrol: 1915-1917*. London: Hutchinson, 1919, and New York:
Doran, 1919.

Bacon, Sir Reginald Hugh Spencer, Admiral, R.N., *The Jutland
Scandal*, London: Hutchinson, 1925.

Baily's Magazine of Sports and Pastimes, *Earl Beatty, Admiral of
the Fleet*, vol. 113, p. 1, London: 1920.

Bashford, H. H. (See Hurd, Archibald).

Bellairs, Carlyon Wilfroy, Commander, R.N., *The Battle of Jutland*,
Quarterly Review, vol. 226, p. 283, London: 1916.

Bellairs, Carlyon Wilfroy, Commander, R.N., *The Battle of Jutland;
the Sowing and the Reaping*, London: Hodder & Stoughton,
1920.

Bernotti, Romeo, *Movimenti nella Battaglia dello Jutland*, Rivista Marittima, anno 54, p. 317, Rome: 1921.

Bertin, E., *La Guerre Navale en 1916 et la Bataille du Jutland*, année 45, sem. 1, p. 65, Paris: 1917.

Bingham, the Hon. Edward Barry Stewart, Commander, R.N., *Falklands, Jutland and the Bight*. (Introduction by Beatty), London: Murray, 1919.

Bischoff, Ernst, *Die Bedeutung des Skagerraktages*, Deutsche Rundschau, vol. 199, p. 323, Berlin: June 4, 1924.

Boyle, William Henry Dudley, Vice Admiral, R.N., *Gallant Deeds: Being a Record of the Circumstances under which the Victoria Cross, Conspicuous Gallantry, or Albert Medal were won by Petty Officers, Non-Commissioned Officers and Men during the Years of War, 1914-1919*, Portsmouth: Gieves, 1919.

British Admiralty, *Narrative of the Battle of Jutland*, London: H. M. Stationery Office, 1924.

British Admiralty, *Reproduction of the Record of the Battle of Jutland; prepared by Captain J. E. T. Harper and others in 1919-1920*, London: H. M. Stationery Office, 1927.

Brownrigg, Sir Douglas Egremont Robert, Rear Admiral, R.N., *Indiscretions of the Naval Censor*, London: Cassell, 1920, and New York: Doran, 1920.

Brownson, Howard G., Lieutenant Commander, U.S.N.R., *The Technical Aspects of Jutland*, U. S. Naval Institute PROCEEDINGS, vol. 60, p. 1249, Annapolis: 1934.

Buchan, John, *The Battle of Jutland*, London: Nelson, 1916.

Busch, Fritz Otto, *Die Schlacht am Skagerrak*, Leipzig: Schneider, 1933.

Busch, Fritz Otto, *Skagerrak (31 Mai-1 Juni, 1916), Persönliche Erinnerungen. Türmer*, Mai, 1934, p. 113, Berlin: 1934.

Butt, F. D., Lieutenant Commander, R.N., *Jutland: the Main Features* (Preface by Rear Admiral J. E. T. Harper), London: Charterhouse, 1924.

Bywater, Hector C., *Gunnery at Jutland*, Baltimore *Sun*, July 30, 1925 (letter of July 20) reprinted in U. S. Naval Institute PROCEEDINGS, vol. 51, p. 1780, Annapolis: 1925.

Bywater, Hector C., *Gunnery at Jutland*, Baltimore *Sun*, Sept. 19, 1926 (cable of Sept. 18) reprinted in U. S. Naval Institute PROCEEDINGS, vol. 52, p. 2328, Annapolis: 1926.

Bywater, Hector C., and Ferraby, H. C., *Strange Intelligence*, London: Constable, 1934.

Bywater, Hector C., *Their Secret Purposes*, London: Constable, 1932.

Bywater, Hector C., *Weapons of Jutland*, Nineteenth Century and After, vol. 87, p. 757, New York: 1920.

Campbell, Gordon, Vice Admiral, R. N., *Sailormen All*, London: Hodder & Stoughton, 1933.

Chack, P., *Les Sous-Marins Allimands pendant la Bataille du Jutland*, Revue Maritime, 1922, p. 618, Paris: 1922.

Chatterton, E. Keble, *Danger Zone*, Boston: Little, Brown, 1934.

Churchill, the Rt. Hon. Winston Leonard Spencer (First Lord of the Admiralty), *The World Crisis, 1914-1918*, London: Butterworth, 1927-31, and New York: Scribner's, 1923-31.

Cleary, F. J., *The Faith of Fighting Men; the Story of H. M. Destroyer "Shark" in the Action off Jutland Bank, May 31, 1916*, Outlook, vol. 137, p. 236, New York; June 11, 1924.

Copplestone, Bennet, *The Battle of the Giants*, Cornhill Magazine, vol. 44, p. 23, London: 1918.

Copplestone, Bennet, *The Secret of the Navy; What It Is and What We Owe to It*, London: Murray, 1918. American edition entitled *The Silent Watchers; England's Navy during the Great War, What It Is and What We Owe to It*, New York: Dutton, 1918. (Includes *"The Battle of the Giants"*.)

Corbett, Sir Julian Stafford, and Newbolt, Henry, *History of the Great War Based on Official Documents: Naval Operations*, New York: Longmans Green, 1920-31.

Corbino, Epicarmo, *La Battaglia dello Jutland Vista da un Economista*, Milan: Giuffrè, 1933.

Cornhill Magazine, *Ten Years After: The Battle of Jutland; or Little Fisher Bank*, vol. 60, p. 749, London: June, 1926.

Custance, Sir Reginald Neville, Admiral, R.N., *War at Sea: Modern Theory and Ancient Practise*, Edinburgh and London: Blackwood, 1919.

Degony, *La Bataille Navale du Mai 31*, Revue de Deux Mondes, période 6, tome 34, p. 79, Paris: 1916.

Delage, Edmond François Louis, *Le Drame du Jutland*, Revue de Paris, 1928, tome 6, p. 529, and Grasset, Paris: 1929.

Delage, Edmond François Louis, *Qui a Vaincu au Jutland?* Les Annales Politiques et Litteraires, vol. 92, p. 268, Paris: March 15, 1929.

Dewar, A. C., Captain, R.N. (See Eardley-Wilmot).

Dixon, William Macneile, *The British Navy at War*, London: Heinemann, 1917, and Boston: Houghton Mifflin, 1917.

Dorling, Taprell, Captain, R.N., *Endless Story: An Account of the Work of the Destroyers, Flotilla-Leaders, Torpedo-Boats and Patrol Boats in the Great War*, London: Hodder & Stoughton, 1932.

Eardley-Wilmot, Sir Sydney Morrow, Rear Admiral, R.N., *Our Navy for a Thousand Years; a Concise Account of all the Principal Operations in Which the British Navy has been Engaged from the Reign of King Alfred to the Present Time*. Revised and with additional chapters on "The Navy in the Great War" by Captain A. C. Dewar, London: Sampson Low, Marston, 1932.

Evans, F. P., *The True Cause of Our Impotence at Jutland*, Blackwood's Magazine, vol. 221, p. 427, London: 1927.

Fawcett, H. W., and Hooper, G. W. W. (Editors), *The Fighting at Jutland. The Personal Experiences of Forty-five Officers and Men of the British Fleet*, London: Hutchinson, (circ.) 1920.

Ferraley, H. C. (See under Bywater, Hector C.).

Ferrand, C., *Quelques Réflexions au Sujet des Mémoires de l'Amiral Jellicoe: le Début des Hostilités*, Revue de Paris, vol. 29, pt. 5, p. 419, Paris: Sept. 15, 1922.

Fiennes, Gerard, *Sea Power and Freedom*, Introduction by Rear Admiral Bradley A. Fiske, U.S.N., New York: Putnam's 1918.

Fisher, Admiral of the Fleet John Arbuthnot Baron, *Memories and Records*, London: Hodder & Stoughton, 1919, and New York: Doran, 1920.

Fleet Surgeon, *Jutland*, Cornhill Magazine, vol. 42, p. 385, London: 1917.

Fortnightly Review, *The Battle of Jutland*, New Series, vol. 100, p. 282, London: 1916.

Freeman, Lewis R., *Jellicoe Justified? The Battle of Jutland from the German Point of View*, Illustrated London Magazine, vol. 42, p. 179, London: 1919.

Freiwald, Ludwig, *Die Verratene Flotte: aus den Letzten Tagen der Deutschen Kriegsmarine*, Munich: Lehmann, 1931. Translated into English by Martin Moore, London: Constable, 1932.

Frost, Holloway Halstead, Lieutenant Commander, U.S.N., *A Description of the Battle of Jutland*, U. S. Naval Institute Pro-

CEEDINGS, vol. 45, p. 1829, Annapolis: 1919. (See letters from Scheer, Hipper, and Hase to Frost re this account, in U. S. Naval Institute PROCEEDINGS, vol. 47, p. 1083.)

Frost, Holloway Halstead, Lieutenant Commander, U.S.N., *The Results and Effects of the Battle of Jutland*, U. S. Naval Institute PROCEEDINGS, Vol. 47, p. 1325, Annapolis: 1921.

Frost, Holloway Halstead, Lieutenant Commander, U.S.N., and Hazard, G. J., *Jutland*, 5th U. S. Naval War College edition, Washington: Government Printing Office, 1927.

Frost, Holloway Halstead, Lieutenant Commander, U.S.N. (See also Green, Fitzhugh.)

Frothingham, Thomas Goddard, Captain, U.S.R., *The Naval History of the World War*, Cambridge: Harvard Press, 1924-1926.

Frothingham, Thomas Goddard, Captain, U.S.R., *The Test of Fact Against Fiction in the Battle of Jutland*, U. S. Naval Institute PROCEEDINGS, vol. 54, p. 169, Annapolis: 1928.

Germains, V. W., *A German Expert Narrative of the Battle of Jutland*, Fortnightly Review, vol. 108, p. 818, London: 1920.

Gibson, Langhorne, and Harper, John Ernest Troyte, Vice Admiral, R.N., *The Riddle of Jutland: An Authentic History*. Introduction by Sir Archibald Hurd, New York: Coward-McCann, 1934.

Gibson, Langhorne (See Schubert, Paul).

Gibson, R. H., *Three Years of Naval Warfare*, London: Heinemann, 1918.

Gill, Charles Clifford, Commander, U.S.N., *What Happened at Jutland: the Tactics of the Battle*, New York: Doran, 1921.

Giron, August Emil Otto, *Sjöslaget utanför Skagerrak den Maj 31 och Juni 1, 1916*, Stockholm: Marinlitteratur-föreningen, 1917.

Green, Fitzhugh, and Frost, Holloway Halstead, Lieutenant Commander, U.S.N., *Some Famous Sea Fights*, New York: Century, 1927.

Groos, O., Captain, German Navy, *Zur Skagerrakschlacht*, Marine-Rundschau (translation in Chicago *Tribune*, 1921), Berlin: 1921.

Guihéneuc, Olivier François Henri, *La Bataille du Jutland*, Revue de Paris, Année 23, tome 6, p. 41, Paris: 1916.

Guihéneuc, Olivier François Henri, *La Bataille Navale du Jutland, Mai 31, 1916*, Paris: Perrin, 1917.

Hale, John Richard, *Famous Sea Fights from Salamis to Jutland*, London: Methuen, 1931.

Halewyn, Jacques Alphonse Léon Marie d', *La Bataille Décisive; l'Événement—la Fixation—la Bataille Navale*, Soc. d' Éditions Geographiques, Maritimes et Coloniales, Paris: 1923.

Hannay, David, *The Battle of Jutland*, Edinburgh Review, vol. 233, p. 29, Edinburgh: 1921.

Harper, John Ernest Troyte, Vice Admiral, R.N., *The Lessons of Jutland*, Journal of the Royal United Service Institution, vol. 72, p. 243, London: 1927.

Harper, John Ernest Troyte, Vice Admiral, R.N., *The Truth About Jutland*, London: Murray, 1927.

Harper, John Ernest Troyte, Vice Admiral, R.N. (See also British Admiralty and Gibson, Langhorne).

Hart, Thomas C., Captain, U.S.N., *What Might Have Happened at Jutland*, U. S. Naval Institute PROCEEDINGS, vol. 51, p. 1143, Annapolis: 1925.

Hase, Georg Oskar Immanuel von, Commander, German Navy, *Der Deutsche Sieg vor dem Skagerrak am Mai 31, 1916; unter Benutzung des Amtlichen Quellenwerkes* (Foreword by Vice Admiral Adolph von Trotha). Leipzig: Koehler, 1926.

Hase, Georg Oskar Immanuel von, Commander, German Navy, *Kiel and Jutland* (Translated by Arthur Chambers and F. A. Holt from German). London: Skeffington, 1921.

Hase, Georg Oskar Immanuel von, Commander, German Navy, *Skagerrak; die Grösste Seeschlacht der Weltgeschichte*, Leipzig: Koehler, 1932.

Hazard, G. J. (See Frost, Holloway Halstead).

Heiberg, Carl Vilhelm Theodor, *Nordsoslaget den Maj 31, 1916; Beskrivelse af Slaget paa Grundlag af de Officielle Engelske tyske Beretninger*, Copenhagen: Lehmann, 1918.

Hersfeld, E. von, *Die Seeschlacht von dem Skagerrak*, Velhagen & Klasings, Monatschefte, vol. 30, bd. 3, July, Berlin: July, 1916.

Hervier, Paul-Louis, *Silhouettes Anglais: L'Amiral Jellicoe*, Nouvelle Revue, series 4, tome 22, p. 131, Paris: 1916.

Hervier, Paul-Louis, *Silhouettes Anglais: L'Amiral Beatty*, Nouvelle Revue, series 4, tome 24, p. 203, Paris: 1916.

Hinds, A. W., Captain, U.S.N., *Practical Lessons for the American Navy from the Battle of Jutland*, U. S. Naval Institute PROCEEDINGS, vol. 47, p. 1877, Annapolis: 1921.

Hooper, G. W. W. (See Fawcett, H. W.).

Hornby, William St. John Sumner, Captain, R.N., *The Battle of Jutland* (Foreword by Admiral Sir Cyprian Bridge), Retold from Viscount Jellicoe's Book, *The Grand Fleet.* London: St. Catherine Press, 1919.

Hunt, Livingston, *The Battle of Jutland, without Diagrams,* Harvard Graduate's Magazine, vol. 36, p. 495, Boston: 1928.

Hunter, Francis T., *Beatty, Jellicoe, Sims and Rodman,* New York: 1919.

Hurd, Sir Archibald Spicer, *The Admiralty, the Fleet, and the Battle of Jutland, May 31, 1916,* Fortnightly Review, vol. 101, p. 933, London: 1917.

Hurd, Sir Archibald Spicer, *The British Fleet in the Great War,* London: Constable, 1919.

Hurd, Sir Archibald Spicer, *The Truth About the Battle of Jutland,* Fortnightly Review, vol. 105, p. 523, London: 1919.

Hurd, Sir Archibald Spicer, and Bashford, H. H., *Sons of Admiralty: A Short History of the Naval War, 1914-1918,* London: Constable, 1919. American edition entitled *The Heroic Record of the British Navy: A Short History of the Naval War, 1914-1918.* Garden City: Doubleday Page, 1919.

Jane's All the World's Fighting Ships, Annual.

Jellicoe, Viscount John Rushworth, Admiral, R.N., *The Grand Fleet, 1914-1916; its Creation, Development and Work,* London: Cassell, 1919, and New York: Doran, 1919.

Jellicoe, Viscount John Rushworth, Admiral, R.N., *The Crisis of the Naval War,* London: Cassell, 1920, and New York: Doran, 1921.

Jouan, *Les Attaques de Torpilleurs à la Bataille du Jutland,* Revue Maritime, N. S., 1927, vol. 1, pp. 438 and 612, Paris: 1927.

Kalau von Hofe, Kurt Karl Friedrich, *Die Seeschlacht vor dem Skagerrak am Mai 31, 1916,* Berlin: Verlag Kameradschaft, 1917.

Kenworthy, the Hon. Joseph Montague, Lieutenant Commander, R.N., *The Real Navy,* London: Hutchinson, 1932.

Kenworthy, the Hon. Joseph Montague, Lieutenant Commander, R.N., *Sailors, Statesmen—and Others; an Autobiography,* London: Rich & Cowan, 1933 .

Kerr, Mark, Admiral, R.N., *The Navy in My Time,* London: Rich & Cowan, 1933.

Keyes, Sir Roger, Admiral of the Fleet, R.N., *Scapa Flow to the Dover Straits,* New York: Dutton, 1935.

Kipling, Rudyard, *Sea Warfare* (Destroyers at Jutland), London: Macmillan, 1916.

Kitchin, Frederick Harcourt (See under pseudonym Copplestone, Bennet).

Knox, Dudley W., Captain, U.S.N., *The Battle of Jutland*, Baltimore *Sun*, Jan. 10, 1925, reprinted in U. S. Naval Institute PROCEEDINGS, vol. 51, p. 501, Annapolis: 1925.

Krug, P., *De Ondergang van het Duitsche Admiraalschip "Lützow" na den Zwaren Zeestrijd bij Skagerrak*, s'Gravenhage: Van Stockum, 1917.

Kühlwetter, Friedrich von, *Skagerrak; der Ruhmestag der Deutschen Flotte*, Revised and enlarged by H. O. Philipp (Foreword by Rear Admiral Magnus von Levetzow), Berlin: Ullstein, 1933.

Laughton, L. G. Carr, *H. M. S. "Marlborough,"* Portsmouth: Gale & Polden, 1922.

Lehmann, E. A., *Zeppelins Save the Germans at Jutland* (Translated by H. Mingos), World Today, vol. 51, p. 186, Jan., 1928.

Leighton, John, *The Historical Perspective of Jutland*, Journal of the Royal United Service Institution, vol. 69, p: 73, London: Feb., 1924.

Leslie, Shane, *Jutland; A Fragment of Epic* (A poem with a preface by Commander Augustus Agar), London: Benn, 1930.

Lewis, Charles Lee, Associate Professor, U. S. Naval Academy, *Famous Old-World Sea Fighters* (Chapter on David Beatty), Boston: Lothrop Lee & Stoddard, 1929.

Leyland, John, *The Great Battle in the North Sea*, Nineteenth Century and After, vol. 80, p. 429, London: 1916.

Leyland, John (editor), *Souvenir of the Great Naval Battle, and Roll of Honour*, London: United Newspapers, Ltd., 1916.

Lorenz, Helmut, *The Sunken Fleet* (Translated by Samuel H. Cross, from German), Boston: Little Brown, 1930.

Luckner, Graf Felix Nikolaus Alexander Georg von, *Die Seeschlacht*, Grenzboten, Jahrg. 79, vol. 3, p. 351, and vol. 4, p. 28, Berlin: 1920.

Lützow, Friedrich, Commander, German Navy, *Unterseebootskrieg und Hungerblockade*, Berlin: Meyer, 1921.

MacNaughton, R. E., *Admiral Jellicoe: A Personal Reminiscence*, Canadian Magazine, vol. 45, p. 104, Toronto: 1915.

McAdie, A., *Phoenix at Skagerrak*, Harvard Graduates' Magazine, vol. 35, p. 33, Boston: Sept., 1926.

Mantey, Eberhard von, Vice Admiral, German Navy, *Unsere Kriegmarine vom Grossen Kurfürsten bis zur Gegenwart*, Berlin: "Offene Worte," 1934.

Mantey, Eberhard von, Vice Admiral, German Navy (editor), *Unsere Marine im Weltkrieg, 1914-1918*, Berlin: Vaterländischer Verlag, 1927.

Mille, Mateo, *Jutlandia, O La Gran Batalla Nutil*, Madrid: Dédalo, 1933.

Musser, Neil B., Lieutenant (C.C.), U.S.N., *Lessons of Jutland Affecting Design of Turret Armor*, U. S. Naval Institute PROCEEDINGS, vol. 51, p. 563, Annapolis: 1925.

Naval Annual, *The Jutland Controversy; An Historical Appreciation*, 1924, p. 90, London: 1924.

Newbolt, Henry (See Corbett, Sir Julian).

Novitzki, Victor, *Morskoi Boi Maya 18 u Beregov Yutlandii*, Petrograd: Ministry of the Navy, 1916.

O'Neill, Herbert Charles, *A History of the War*, London: Jack, 1920.

Parratt, Geoffrey, *The Royal Navy, the Sure Shield of the Empire*, London: Sheldon, 1930.

Parseval, Henri Louis Pie de, Capitaine de Frégate, *La Bataille Navale du Jutland (Mai 31, 1916)*, Paris: Payot, 1919.

Paschen, Günther, Commander, German Navy, *S. M. S. "Lützow" at Jutland*, Journal of the Royal United Service Institution (Translated from *Marine-Rundschau*), vol. 72, p. 32, London: 1927.

Pastfield, Rev. John Lawrence Robinson, *New Light on Jutland*, London: Heinemann, 1933.

Persius, Lothar, *Der Seekrieg*, Charlottenburg: Weltbühne, 1919.

Philipp, O., *Englands Flotte im Kampfe mit der Deutschen Flotte im Weltkriege 1914-1916 bis nach der Schlacht vor dem Skagerrak*, Leipzig: Hillmann, 1920.

Philipp, O. (See also Kühlwetter, Friedrich von.)

Pini, W., *La Battaglia dello Jutland*. Rivista Marittima, anno 59, Sept., p. 385; Oct., p. 5; Dec., p. 741; anno 60, Jan., p. 5; Feb.-Mar., p. 299; April, p. 23; May, p. 365; Rome: 1926-27.

Poidloüe, Alfred Marie, *La Bataille Navale du Skagerrak*, Paris: Éditions et Librairie, 1919.

Pollen, Arthur Joseph Hungerford, *The British Navy in Battle*. New York: Doubleday Page, 1919.

Pollen, Arthur Joseph Hungerford, *The Navy in Battle*, London: Chatte & Windus, 1919.

Pollen, Arthur Joseph Hungerford, *Who Lost Jutland?* Saturday Review, vol. 143, p. 894 and discussion, 143-935, June 18, 1927. London: June 11, 1927.

Puleston, Wm. D., Captain, U.S.N., *High Command in the World War*, New York: Scribner's, 1934.

Rawson, Geoffrey, *Earl Beatty, Admiral of the Fleet*, London: Jarrolds, 1930.

Revista Americana, *O Combate Naval da Jutlandia*, anno 8, Junho, p. 40, Rio de Janeiro: 1919.

Revista General de Marina, *La Batalla de Jutlandia*, tome 86, p. 473, Madrid: 1920.

Revue Maritime, *La Bataille du Jutland*, Documents Anglais et Allemands, N. S., 1921, p. 56, Paris: 1921.

Richard, E., *Le Jutland et les Principes—Essai Philosophique*, Revue Maritime, N. S., 1921, May, p. 577, Paris: 1921.

Richard, E., *Réflexions sur la Bataille du Jutland*, Revue Maritime, N. S., 1920, sem. 2, pp. 1 and 192, Paris: 1920.

Richmond, Sir Herbert William, *Sea Power in the Modern World*, London: Bell, 1934, and New York: Reynal & Hitchcock, 1934.

Rivista Marittima, *La Battaglia dello Jutland*, anno 49, trimestre 3, p. 43, Rome: 1916.

Russell, Sir Herbert, *Comments on the Admiralty Narrative*, London: The Naval and Military Record, August 6, 1924, reprinted in U. S. Naval Institute PROCEEDINGS, vol. 50, p. 1930, Annapolis: 1924.

Russell, Sir Herbert, *The Battle of Jutland*, The Naval and Military Record Feb. 10, 1926, reprinted in U. S. Naval Institute PROCEEDINGS, vol. 52, p. 747, Annapolis: 1926.

Salza, Silvio, *Tattica e Materiale di Artiglieria Navale alla Battaglia dello Jutland*. Rivista Marittima, anno 50, p. 330, Rome: 1917.

Sato, Ichiro (Japanese Naval Officer), *Naval Annual* 1921-22, p. 77, London: 1922.

Sauvaire, Jourdan, *Les Enseignements de la Bataille du Jutland en ce qui Concerne le Matériel Naval*, La Nature, vol. 51, p. 289, Paris: May 12, 1923.

Scheer, Reinhard Admiral, German Navy, *The Battle of Jutland*, In "These Eventful Years," vol. 1, p. 354, London: 1924.

Scheer, Reinhard Admiral, German Navy, *Germany's High Sea Fleet in the World War,* New York: Peter Smith, 1934.

Scheer, Reinhard Admiral, German Navy, *Vom Segelschiff zum U-boote,* Leipzig: Quelle & Meyer, 1925.

Scheibe, Albert, Commander, German Navy, *Die Seeschlacht vor dem Skagerrak am Mai 31-Juni 1, 1916; auf Grund Amtlieben Materials,* Berlin: Mittler, 1916.

Scheibe, Albert, Commander, German Navy, *The Jutland Battle,* Journal of the Royal United Service Institution, vol. 62, p. 31, London: 1917.

Schoultz, G. von, Commodore, Russian Navy, *With the British Battle Fleet: War Recollections of a Russian Naval Officer,* 1920.

Schubart, Hartwig, *Zur Seeschlacht am Skagerrak,* Grenzboten, Jahrg. 75, bd. 2, p. 343, Berlin: 1920.

Schubert, Paul, and Gibson, Langhorne, *Death of a Fleet; 1917-1919,* New York: Coward-McCann, 1932.

Schwarte, Max, *Der Grosse Krieg, 1914-1918,* vol. 4, Der Seekrieg (etc.), Leipzig: Barth, 1922.

Scott, Sir Percy Moreton, Admiral, R.N., *Fifty Years in the Royal Navy,* London: Murray, 1919, and New York: Doran, 1919.

"Searchlight," *Lessons from Jutland,* National Review, vol. 73, p. 277, London: 1919.

Sérieyx, Commandant, *Exposé de la Bataille du Jutland,* Revue Scien., vol. 68, p. 232, Paris: Apr. 26, 1930.

Sims, William Sowden (with Burton J. Hendrick), Rear Admiral, U.S.N., *The Victory at Sea,* London: Murray, 1920, and New York: Doubleday Page, 1920.

Skagerrak-Jahrbuch, *Deutsche Gedanken zum Skagerraktage,* 1927, p. 58, Lübeck: 1927.

Spiegel von und zu Peckelsheim, Edgar Freiherr, *Meere, Inseln, Menschen,* Berlin: Scherl, 1934.

Spiegel von und zu Peckelsheim, Hermann Paul Richard Freiherr, *Oberheizer Zenne; der letzte Mann der "Wiesbaden,"* Berlin: Scherl, 1917.

Stoss, Alfred, *Welthistorische Richtlinien als Wegweiser für Preussen-Deutschlands Zukunft, mit einem Anhang: Die Bedeutung der Seeschlacht vor dem Skagerrak,* Berlin: Deutschnationale Schriftenvertriebstelle, 1921.

Sydenham of Combe, Lord, *The Battle of Jutland,* English Review, vol. 38, p. 193, London: Feb., 1924.

Sydenham of Combe, Lord, *The Battle of Jutland*, English Review, vol. 46, p. 40, London: Jan., 1928.

Tirpitz, Grand Admiral von, *My Memoirs*, New York: Dodd Mead, 1919.

Touchard, Albert, *La Bataille du Jutland vue de l' "Iron-Duke,"* Revue Hebdomadaire, année 31, tome 5, p. 399, Paris: 1922.

Trotha, Adolph Lebrecht von, Vice Admiral, German Navy, *Admiral Scheer, der Sieger vom Skagerrak*, Lübeck: Coleman, 1933.

Two Who Took Part in It, *The Jutland Battle*, London: Burrup, Mathieson & Sprague, 1916.

Variot, Jean, *La Bataille du Jutland vue die "Derfflinger,"* Revue Hebdomadaire, année 31, p. 131, Paris: 1922.

Waldeyer-Hartz, Hugo von, *Admiral von Hipper*, London: Rich & Cowan, 1933.

Wallace, Major Claude, *From Jungle to Jutland*, London: Nisbet, 1932.

Wallace, Major Claude, *Premonition in War; A Story of Jutland*, National Review, vol. 71, p. 437, London: 1918.

Welch, Philip P., Lieutenant, U.S.N., *Tsushima and Jutland*, U. S. Naval Institute PROCEEDINGS, vol. 56, p. 591, Annapolis: 1930.

Wheeler, Harold Felix Baker, *The Life of Sir John Jellicoe*, London: Aldine, 1914.

Wilson, Herbert Wrigley, *Battleships in Action*, London: Sampson Low, Marston, 1926 and Boston: Little Brown, (circa) 1927.

Winkelhagen, Juan, *Das Raetsel vom Skagerrak; eine Quellenanalyse*, Leipzig: Weicher, 1925.

Wyllie, William Lionel, *More Sea Fights of the Great War, including the Battle of Jutland*, London: Cassell, 1919.

Young, Filson, *With Beatty in the North Sea*, Boston: Little Brown, 1921.

INDEX

Abdiel (HMS), 91
  Mine field laid by, 81, 86, 101, 417, 496
Acasta (HMS), 294, 313
  Hit by torpedo boats, 314
  Out of action, 315, 475
Achates (HMS), 444
Achilles (HMS), 115
Active (HMS), 434
Admiralty, British
  Action resulting from Yarmouth raid, 77
  Courses open to, after Jutland, 515
  Criticized, 134, 375-77
  Problems (1915), 13
  Question of Fleet distribution, 78, 93
  Reports to Jellicoe "German Fleet ordered home," 436
Adventure (HMS), 131
Agincourt (HMS), 296, 320
  Avoids torpedo, 348
  Fires on torpedo boats, 369
Airships, German, 50
  Scouting operations, 33, 45, 52-53, 55, 63, 141, 519
  Plan for Skagerrak operation, 121
  Raid on Tondern hangars by British, 36, 42, 81, 86
Ajax (HMS), 353
Alexander-Sinclair, Commo. E. S., 82, 149
  Criticized, 164, 179, 197, 218, 250, 268, 278, 305
Alison, Lieut. Comdr. R. V., 492
Allen, Comdr. W. L., 444, 451
Allied Expeditionary Forces
  Evacuate Gallipoli, 25
  Gallipoli campaign, 21
  Repulsed at Gallipoli, 23
Allied Powers
  Bulgaria declares war on, 24
  Capture Trebizond, 28
  Defeated at Dardanelles, 21
  Greek neutrality violated, 24
  Land in Salonika, 24
  Plans (1916), 26
  Plans for Somme offensive, 29
  War plans, 1
Ambuscade (HMS), 444
  Collision with *Garland* and *Ardent*, 47
Angora (HMS), 55
Antwerp, German attack on, 5

Arabic (SS): Sunk, 23
Arabis (sloop): Sunk, 32
Arbuthnot, Rear Admiral Sir Robert, 274, 282, 297, 309
  Criticized, 310
Arcona (SMS), 123-24
  Orders submarines to the northward, 386
  U-32's contact reported to *Friedrich der Grosse*, 136
Ardent (HMS), 444
  Collision with *Garland* and *Ambuscade*, 47
  Sunk by *Westfalen*, 458
Ariadne (SMS), 70
Armored Cruiser Squadron, 1st
  Attacks Scouting Group II, 274
Arndt, Chief Gunner: Praised, 358
Arnim, Lieut. Comdr. von.: Praised, 335
Attack (HMS): Hit by Scouting Group I, 321
Attentive (HMS), 131
Audacious (HMS): Sunk by mine, 12
Australia (HMS), 14, 115
  Collision with *New Zealand*, 47
Austria
  Army position Dec., 1914, 5
  Army war plans, 1
  Defeat in Serbia, 2
  Navy war plans, 1
  Plan (1916), 26
  Serbian campaign, 2
  Trentino campaign, 28, 106, 512

B98 (SMS), 273, 291
B109 (SMS), 149, 154, 156, 191
  Search *N. J. Fjord*, 146, 151
  Sights scouts of Grand Fleet, 151
  Signal, British recognition, "PL", 154, 272
B110 (SMS), 149
  Search *N. J. Fjord*, 146, 151
  Sights scouts of Grand Fleet, 151
B111 (SMS), 151
Bacon, Rear Admiral R. H. S., 42, 49, 117
Badger (HMS): Rescues 6 survivors of *Invincible*, 327, 348
Bagdad
  British movement against, 14
  Townshend defeated, 25

NAVIES AND MEN

An Arno Press Collection

Bragadin, Marc' Antonio. **The Italian Navy in World War II.** 1957

Bunker, John Gorley. **Liberty Ships.** 1972

Cagle, Malcolm W., and Frank A. Manson. **The Sea War in Korea.** 1957

Chatterton, E. Keble. **Q-Ships and Their Story.** 1972

Cocchia, Aldo. **The Hunters and the Hunted.** 1958

Cohen, Philip M. **Bathymetric Navigation and Charting.** 1970

Frost, Holloway H. **The Battle of Jutland.** 1964

Gray, J.A.C. **Amerika Samoa.** 1960

Johnson, Robert Erwin. **Rear Admiral John Rodgers.** 1967

Johnson, Robert Erwin. **Thence Round Cape Horn.** 1963

Keeler, William Frederick. **Aboard the USS Florida: 1863-65.** 1968

Lewis, Charles Lee. **Admiral De Grasse and American Independence.** 1945

Lewis, Charles Lee. **David Glasgow Farragut: Admiral in the Making.** 1941

Lewis, Charles Lee. **David Glasgow Farragut: Our First Admiral.** 1943

Lewis, Charles Lee. **Matthew Fontaine Maury.** 1927

McKee, Christopher. **Edward Preble.** 1972

Milligan, John D. **Gunboats Down the Mississippi.** 1965

Morris, Richard Knowles. **John P. Holland.** 1966

Paullin, Charles Oscar. **Commodore John Rodgers.** 1967

Raeder, Erich. **My Life.** 1960

Ransom, M.A., with Eloise Katherine Engle. **Sea of the Bear.** 1964.

Sloan, Edward William, III. **Benjamin Franklin Isherwood, Naval Engineer.** 1965

Swann, Leonard Alexander, Jr. **John Roach, Maritime Entrepreneur.** 1965

Thomas, Walter "R." **From a Small Naval Observatory.** 1972

Willoughby, Malcolm F. **The U.S. Coast Guard in World War II.** 1957